HISTORY OF BOSTON COLLEGE

History of Boston College
From the Beginnings to 1990

Charles F. Donovan, S.J.

David R. Dunigan, S.J.

Paul A. FitzGerald, S.J.

THE UNIVERSITY PRESS OF BOSTON COLLEGE
Chestnut Hill, Massachusetts

This book was designed by Mark T. Fowler
of Concord, Massachusetts. The text typeface
is Sabon, with Goudy Old Style and Optima used for special
matter. Coghill Composition Company of Richmond,
Virginia, was the typesetter. The dust jacket
and the four-color insert were printed by New
England Book Components of Hingham, Massachusetts.
The text printer and binder was Hamilton Printing
Company of Rensselaer, New York.

Library of Congress Catalog Card No. 90-070471

ISBN 0-9625934-0-0

Printed in the United States of America.

*To Saint Ignatius of Loyola, 1491–1556, in
the 450th year of the Society he founded.*

Preface

In 1947 Father David Dunigan published *A History of Boston College*. It was a well-researched volume that, regrettably, has been out of print for thirty years. When Father Paul FitzGerald, university archivist, and I agreed to cooperate in writing an updated account, we felt that there was no need to rewrite the history from the beginning through World War II. We did not decide then whether the Dunigan text should be edited, abridged, or kept intact; rather, we proceeded to write the history of the postwar period. Father FitzGerald's untimely death in 1987 left to me, with the advice of my editor, the decision about Father Dunigan's text. In brief, parts of it have been abridged and some connections with later text have been added. Also, extensive research at the Boston College Archives in Burns Library yielded a large amount of illustrative material which has been added to his part of the history.

Joint authorship with Father FitzGerald was both congenial and reassuring. A historian by profession, he had just published an elegant piece of research on higher education, *The Governance of Jesuit Colleges in the United States, 1920–1970,* which gave him a broad perspective on the recent history of Boston College. Our text was well advanced when Father FitzGerald died. Unfortunately he did not share in its completion and final editing.

Writing an account of recent and current events presents both hazards and limitations. When American historian William Prescott, famed for such books as *Ferdinand and Isabella* and *Philip II of Spain,* was asked shortly after the conclusion of the Mexican War why he did not undertake a biography of General Winfield Scott, he answered, "I had rather not meddle with heroes who have not been underground two centuries at least." And in 1936 when Boston's beloved historian Samuel Eliot Morison reached the twentieth century in his history of Harvard, he wrote: "It will be best to consider the rest of this book as a personal impression, subject to correction in fact, and to revision as perspective lengthens."

Happily many of the heroes and heroines of the latter part of this history still bestride the Boston College campus, and none is long departed. So it was with a lively awareness of Prescott's and Morison's reservations that Father FitzGerald and I—both participants in the events we undertook to record—wrote our history, hoping that most factual matters reported are correct, but realizing that judgments and evaluations offered are necessarily tentative.

ACKNOWLEDGMENTS

On behalf of the co-authors I thank, first, Father Joseph Duffy, secretary of the university, who assumed responsibility for guiding this history from manuscript to book form. Not the least of his contributions was to gain for the publication project the wise counsel of a veteran publisher, John T. Harney ('56). Eugene Bailey has been a meticulous and perceptive editor. The magnitude of his contribution only the author knows.

My secretary, Rose DeMaio, was a cheerful assistant in the research prior to writing and typist of all of Father FitzGerald's and my manuscripts as well as revisions of the entire history from Father McElroy to Father Monan. I am indebted to the Boston College Archives, especially to assistant archivist Aimee Felker for her provision of many of the images that enrich the text. Gary Gilbert, university photographer, provided re-productions of most of those images.

Chestnut Hill, Massachusetts   Charles F. Donovan, S.J.

About the Authors

Charles F. Donovan, S.J. (Boston College Class of 1933), was founding dean of the School of Education. From 1961 to 1968 he served as academic vice president, then became senior vice president and dean of faculties. Since 1979 he has been university historian. In addition to co-authoring this formal history of Boston College, he has written a series of essays, "Occasional Papers in the History of Boston College."

David R. Dunigan, S.J., was chairman of the Education Department at Boston College from 1939 to 1948. In 1947 he published *A History of Boston College*, which has been substantially incorporated into the new *History of Boston College: From the Beginnings to 1990*. From 1950 to his death in 1961 Father Dunigan was director of counseling and professor of education at the College of the Holy Cross.

Paul A. FitzGerald, S.J., was dean of the Graduate School of Arts and Sciences and a member of the History Department from 1956 to 1961. After several assignments elsewhere and some further years with the History Department, he became secretary of the university. He was university archivist at the time of his death in 1987.

Contents

CHAPTER 10

Growing Is Done Slowly   97

CHAPTER 11

Conflict and Adjustments   105

CHAPTER 12

Brave Vision   113

CHAPTER 13

The Towers on the Heights   125

CHAPTER 14

The Pre-World-War I Era   135

CHAPTER 31

"The Strike" and Other Protests   357

CHAPTER 32

Academic and Social Innovations   369

CHAPTER 33

An Overview of the Joyce Era   388

CHAPTER 37

Progress in Athletics   472

CHAPTER 38

A Mature University   488

CHAPTER 39

Pointing to the Twenty-First Century   517

Epilogue 541

The Evolution of
Father Gasson's Dream:
An Aerial Photographic Essay 543

Appendices

Index 565

HISTORY OF BOSTON COLLEGE

CHAPTER 1

Background for a Catholic College in Boston

An adequate understanding of the movement to provide Catholic educational facilities in Boston during the mid-nineteenth century requires some recognition of the attitudes toward Catholicism which prevailed at the time. In exploring the origin and early development of Boston College, it is important to keep in mind that this institution was planned and established by a religious group which, until a score of years before, held an insignificant position in the social life of the United States. Almost overnight, this group became a numerically powerful body which the longer-established elements in the population regarded as a threat to their institutions and traditions. It must be remembered, too, that the increase in the number of Catholics in the late eighteen-forties was composed largely of people relegated to one of the lower rungs of the social scale by persecution and famine in their native land, which had deprived them of means, education, and even health. Lastly, it should be recalled that constant intolerance and discrimination were exercised against these immigrants in their new home because they professed the "Roman" religion—a faith little understood and much feared on the American seaboard.

In the light of these conditions, it is not a matter of wonder why a Catholic college was not founded in Boston sooner, or why it was not founded as a university at once. On the contrary, it is amazing that it could be founded as soon as it was, and that, under the circumstances, it could ever survive to prosper as it has done.

Catholics in the Early Days

In the English colonies, Catholics never constituted a factor to be reckoned with. During the decade before the Revolution, in a total population of more than 2 million inhabitants,[1] only some 20,000, or less than 1 percent, were Catholics,[2] and these were settled principally in Maryland and Pennsylvania. At this period, Catholics were denied domicile in Boston and, if discovered there, were subject to many legal penalties. This condition endured until the adoption of the state constitution of Massachusetts in 1780. This act removed many restrictions from Catholics, but an oath with an explicitly anti-Catholic clause was still required of all officeholders until Massachusetts amended its state constitution in 1822.[3] In the meantime, the Catholic population was not growing in proportion with that of the rest of the country. As late as 1830, Catholics represented only about 2 percent of the nation's people.[4]

Immigration, however, which had increased sporadically during the late 1830s due to political and economic change in Germany, Scotland, and Ireland, became a deluge after the European famines of 1845–1847, and a large proportion of the incoming refugees were Catholic. Although Great Britain and the Continent felt the effects of a severe food shortage at this time, Ireland—unfortunately a single-crop country—suffered widespread starvation and utter destitution as a result of the potato blight which deprived it of food. Hundreds of thousands of Irish despaired that their country would ever survive this calamity and thought only of flight.[5] Within the next 20 years, some 2.5 million Irish abandoned their native land.[6] During part of this period, the decade from 1846 to 1856, almost 130,000 Irish entered Boston alone.[7] Since, as has been said, almost all of these newcomers were Catholics, one can understand the effect of this influx upon the religious sensibilities of Protestant Boston. Where before the existence of a few Catholics in the city could be ignored or met with calm disdain, now their presence in legion seemed to constitute a threat to everything the old-line "natives" held in esteem.

It was true that this new element in the population could not be assimilated easily. It retained its own group consciousness; it did not share in or sympathize with the English-flavored culture of which Boston was so proud; it was desperately poor; and it had been deprived by persecution of education and the leisure which is needed for finesse, and so could not erect a social structure even remotely comparable in dignity with that of the natives. Thus the Irish—or Catholics, since the terms had come to be synonymous—were destined to become the laboring class, the domestic class, and to await—with more or less resignation—the day when the situation would be rectified by the forces of nature which seemed to enjoy marvelous properties in this "land of promise."

The need for Boston's new immigrants to have their own Catholic schools was accentuated during the threescore years prior to the opening of Boston

College by the growing success of Horace Mann's drive to remove denominational religion from the Massachusetts schools. Mann did not intend, as Lord points out, to secularize education,[8] much less to paganize it, but the ultimate outcome—unforeseen and undesired—was to remove all but the most diluted religious influences from the public schools. What little remained was, of course, Protestant; the Catholic position, when not ignored, was ridiculed and misrepresented in the common textbooks.

The mounting tension between what was often a Catholic majority in public school classrooms and a dominant Protestant minority culminated in 1859 in a series of incidents known as the Eliot School Controversy.[9] This disturbance centered about the severe corporal punishment inflicted by a teacher upon a Catholic pupil of the Eliot School in Boston because of the child's refusal, upon instruction from his parents, to recite the Protestant version of the Commandments. The case was carried into the courts where, in disregard of the evidence, it was settled in favor of the teacher. The dispute gained national notoriety, and the injustices which the case involved forced the Catholics of Boston to conclude that the immediate establishment of an adequate school system of their own was imperative. Meanwhile, there was ever present a need for an adequate supply of educated leaders, both in the clergy and in the laity, and to supply this, Bishop John Fitzpatrick was seeking means to establish in Boston a low-tuition college for day scholars. He little dreamed that the fulfillment of this desire was finally at hand in the person of a dynamic Jesuit priest, Father John McElroy. The future founder of Boston College was born in Brookeborough, near Enniskillen, County Fermanagh, Province of Ulster, Northern Ireland, on May 14, 1782. During his long life span, roughly coinciding with the establishment and development of the United States and with the re-establishment and expansion of the Society of Jesus, he lived several careers.[10]

At the time of his birth the penal laws which prohibited Irish schoolmasters from teaching Catholics had not yet been completely removed in practice, hence the formal schooling he received was only of the most rudimentary sort. After leaving school he was employed on his father's farm until he reached the age of 21, when he embarked on a flax ship, *Serpent,* which sailed from Londonderry on June 25, 1803, and arrived in Baltimore August 26 after a voyage of 62 days. He lived in that city about a year with a younger brother who kept a drugstore, then moved to Georgetown where he worked as a clerk in a dry-goods store. It was during this period that he discovered his vocation for the religious state. He sought the advice of his spiritual director, Bishop Leonard Neale, then coadjutor to Archbishop Carroll and president of Georgetown College. Bishop Neale encouraged the young man, and undoubtedly counseled patience, for the bishop was aware that the suppressed Society of Jesus was on the verge of being re-established in the United States and would soon be in a position to accept candidates.

Mr. McElroy Becomes a Jesuit

Still surviving at that time in America were a small number of former Jesuits, among whom were Archbishop Carroll and Bishop Neale. Encouraged by the informal re-establishment of the order in England, they petitioned that a similar favor be granted to the priests on the American mission. This request was granted by the Jesuit General in 1804. During the following year, six of the missionary priests working in this country elected to re-enter the Society, and Father Robert Molyneaux was appointed superior. On October 10, 1806, nine novices destined to study for the priesthood and two lay-brother novices were received by the order and began their period of probation at Georgetown College. One of these scholastic novices was Benedict J. Fenwick, afterward bishop of Boston; one of the lay-brother novices was John McElroy.

Some ten months previously, on January 14, McElroy had entered the employment of Georgetown College as a bookkeeper and buyer; now in his new status, his duties remained much the same. Many years later he wrote:

> I entered the Society as lay-brother, employed as clerk, procurator, treasurer, assistant cook, gardener, prefect, teacher of writing, arithmetic, etc. In these duties was I occupied during the two years of Novitiate, often making my meditation the best I could in going to market, etc.[11]

He remained at Georgetown as a lay brother for nine years. During the war with Great Britain, he witnessed the burning of Washington from the college windows. In 1815 Father Grassi, the Superior of the Mission, took the extraordinary step of applying to the Jesuit General, Father Brzozowski, for permission to have Brother McElroy change his "grade" to that of scholastic and start studying for the priesthood. The permission was granted, and on July 31, 1815, John McElroy, at the age of 33, commenced the study of Latin grammar and other preparatory subjects under the tutorage of Father Grassi. He still carried out his miscellany of duties. "I was promised time to study, it is true, but as yet it has not arrived. . . ."[12] On April 5, 1816, he received tonsure and minor orders from Archbishop Neale, and on May 28, 30, and 31, 1817, after an interval of only 22 months from the inception of his studies, he was raised to major orders and the priesthood.[13] His ordination was the last episcopal act performed by his friend and guide, Archbishop Neale; a little over two weeks later it became the new priest's melancholy duty to prepare the aged prelate for death.

In the thirty years between his ordination and his eventual historic assignment in Boston, Father McElroy had a career that made him an imposing figure in the Church of the nineteenth century: as pastor and builder in Virginia and Washington, D.C.; as preacher and director of retreats; as theologian at the Fourth Provincial Council of Baltimore; and

Rev. John McElroy, S.J. (1782–1877), founder of Boston College.

as chaplain named by President Polk to serve the American forces in the Mexican War. In May 1847 he returned from Mexico and was sent to Philadelphia to investigate the possibility of opening a Jesuit college there; but circumstances were not auspicious for a college there at that time, so in October he left for Boston. Here, unknown to him, the great work of his life awaited him.

ENDNOTES

1. In 1775, for the purpose of taxation, Congress assumed the population to be 2,389,300.
2. John Gilmary Shea, *The Catholic Church in Colonial Days* (New York, J. G. Shea, 1886), p. 449.
3. See Arthur J. Riley, *Catholicism in New England in 1788* (Washington, D.C.: Catholic University of America, 1936), Chapter VII.
4. Based on figures drawn from "United States of America: Population," *Encyclopedia Brittanica*, 14th ed., 22:732; and Peter Guilday, "Roman Catholic Church," *ibid.*, 19:421.
5. Marcus Lee Hansen, *The Atlantic Migration, 1607–1860* (Cambridge: Harvard University Press, 1940), p. 249.
6. Oscar Handlin, *Boston's Immigrants, 1790–1865* (Cambridge: Harvard University Press, 1941), p. 52.
7. *Ibid.*, p. 229.
8. Robert H. Lord, John E. Sexton, and Edward T. Harrington, *History of the Archdiocese of Boston* (New York: Sheed and Ward, 1944), 2:311–312.
9. Bernadine Wiget, S.J., "The Eliot School Case" (contemporary MS. account, with newspaper clippings, 3 vols.), Maryland Provincial S.J. Archives, Georgetown University Library. Good brief account in Lord, Sexton, and Harrington, *History of the Archdiocese*, 2:585–601.
10. This summary of Father McElroy's life is based upon letters of Father McElroy concerning his early life in the Society of Jesus, *Woodstock Letters*, 44:9–14, 1915. Father McElroy's diary is preserved in the Maryland Provincial S.J. Archives, Georgetown University.
11. John McElroy, S.J., to Charles Stonestreet, S.J., July 21, 1857; Maryland Provincial S.J. Archives, Georgetown University Library. Published in *Woodstock Letters*, 44:9–10, 1915.
12. *Ibid.*
13. "Liber Continens Nomen, etc., Promotorum ad Ordines Majores, etc., 1633–1852," MSS. book No. 350B, Maryland Provincial S.J. Archives, Georgetown University Library.

CHAPTER 2

The Struggle for Land

Father McElroy's transfer to Boston in 1847 was not directly connected with the prospect of a Catholic college there, although the hope for such an institution had been entertained by him for several years. He appears to have made the first overture for a college in Boston to Bishop Fenwick in private conversation during August of 1842. Father McElroy had come to Boston on that occasion to give the diocesan retreat for the clergy, and he lived at the bishop's house. As a personal friend and former fellow novice with Bishop Fenwick, he was invited to accompany the bishop on his visits about the city for several days before the retreat actually began on August 12. This intimacy at least justifies one in supposing a benevolent reception for the idea of a college if Father McElroy actually proposed it. The only evidence that this topic was mentioned at this time is found in Father McElroy's casual assertion made several years later.[1] No record of such a conversation is found in Bishop Fenwick's diary which covers the period, nor in the letter which the bishop wrote to the Jesuit Provincial thanking him for Father McElroy's services.[2]

The Issue Revisited

Whether or not the matter was discussed then, it was mentioned very explicitly less than three months later in a letter which Father McElroy wrote to extend his felicitations to the bishop on the New Year. After offering his seasonal wishes and referring to various diocesan topics of

7

interest at the moment, he entered at some length upon the question of a college in Boston. An extended excerpt from the letter is given in a note at the end of the chapter which shows the boldness of McElroy in proposing a college to the bishop, as well as his complete confidence in the success of his proposal. The background was that the bishop planned to move his cathedral from its location on Franklin Street to a larger structure to be built elsewhere. McElroy urged that the old cathedral and adjoining property be given to the Jesuits, who could run a parish and start a college.[3]

The bishop evidently reacted favorably to McElroy's suggestion, and news of his interest in such an undertaking was conveyed in due course to Rome. A year after the above letter was written, the Jesuit General, Father John Roothaan, wrote to the rector of Holy Cross College in Worcester:

> You are well enough aware how cordially I approve, to what an extent I am ready to support the Most Reverend Bishop's [Fenwick's] design of setting up a college in the city itself of Boston; my advice to you has ever been that all your concern should center on a college such as this.[4]

In 1845 Father Roothaan wrote in a similar vein to the Jesuit Provincial of the Maryland Province:

> You are not unaware that it would be gratifying to us were you to establish a college in the city of Boston. Accordingly, after examining and deliberating on the details with your consultors, act *in nomine Domini*.

In reply, the Provincial, Father Verhaegen, wrote some months later:

> I visited the Bishop of Boston. He is seriously thinking of opening a college in his episcopal city, but so far has put nothing into effect. It is necessary, so he says, to proceed slowly, and this in order that the institution which he is planning may be worthy of our holy religion and of the Society.

In April of 1846 Father Roothaan was seeking further information on the subject:

> The Bishop of Charlestown [Charleston] has written to me about setting up a college in his episcopal city. But what about the college in Boston? I doubt whether the resources of the Province [of Maryland] will permit you to begin both at almost the same time.

In the meantime, the bishop was evidently making preparations to act along the lines suggested by Father McElroy in the letter mentioned above, because in July of that year (1846) Father Verhaegen reported to Rome that Bishop Fenwick was expecting to acquire a new site for his cathedral, in which event he would convey the existing cathedral and its site to the Jesuits:

> But if we have to wait until the new cathedral is built, even if we suppose it started this year, two entire years may pass. I think the Bishop follows too strictly the axiom, *festina lente*.

John Bernard Fitzpatrick, third bishop of Boston, was a friend and staunch supporter of Father McElroy in establishing a Jesuit college in Boston.

The Jesuits Come to Boston

On August 11, 1846, Bishop Fenwick died, and John B. Fitzpatrick, who had been consecrated coadjutor bishop of Boston two years earlier, succeeded to the sole responsibility of the office. A little over a year after taking office, Bishop Fitzpatrick decided to solve the bothersome problem of an insurgent congregation in Saint Mary's Church in Boston's North End by offering the church to the Jesuit Fathers.[5] The Jesuit authorities accepted, and when, as has been seen, they found an experienced pastor available for the position in the person of Father McElroy after his Mexican War chaplaincy, he was sent to Boston, where the bishop installed him as pastor with two Jesuit assistants on October 31, 1847.[6] This was, as the bishop himself said,

> . . . only the beginning of what I intend to do for the Society. The college is the main object of my concern; but I must wait for means. In the interim, your fathers living here will become known to the citizens, win their sympathy, while the bad disposition of the men who have opposed this and other of my plans will disappear.[7]

In a letter written in September of the following year (1848), Father McElroy mentions the bishop's intention to give the old cathedral and its land to the Jesuits upon completion of the new edifice, but that this prospect was still remote. The letter manifests a more immediate interest of Father McElroy's in some sort of elementary school, where the fundamentals of language could be taught and some instruction given in religion.[8] In his diary, Father McElroy records the solution he arrived at in regard to the school:

> In a short time, I discovered the great want of schools, and more church accommodations for the faithful. In February 1849 the former was in part provided for, by the opening of a school for female children under the Sisters of Charity in a house belonging to the church in Stillman Street, now in Lancaster Street, under the Sisters of Notre Dame. Finding that a surplus remained after defraying the expenses of the change and Church, I resolved to put it aside with the intention of purchasing in time, a site for a College & Church, if practicable, on the same lot.[9]

Bishop Fitzpatrick wrote a no-longer-extant letter on February 5, 1850, in which the prelate expressed satisfaction with the work the Society of Jesus was carrying on at Holy Cross College and in Boston.[10] From the tone of Father Roothaan's answer of May 8, 1850, the bishop had apparently made known the hope he entertained of one day seeing a Jesuit college established in that city.

> It is with genuine satisfaction that I learned from your letter, Monseigneur, of your desire to establish a day-school in your episcopal city when Providence shall have furnished you the means. I shall always be ready to support your zeal for the success of this enterprise as far as circumstances will make it possible for me to do so.[11]

However, when Father McElroy expressed hope that in the course of another year he would be able to open a school for boys, on the same plan as the one he had employed at Frederick, to accommodate some 300 boys, the General, "hitherto so sympathetic toward the project of a Jesuit school in Boston, seemed now to become skeptical as to its feasibility."[12] He inquired of the Maryland Provincial, Father Brocard, in January of 1851, "Is it true that a school in Boston for day-students is under consideration? New burdens when old ones weigh you down!"[13]

Purchase of the Jail Land

At this time the City of Boston announced the intention of offering at public auction on December 3, 1851, a portion of land compromising 31 building lots on which the city jail had stood.[14] The land was bounded by Leverett and Causeway streets on two sides; by property fronting on Lowell Street, on a third; and by other property fronting on Leverett, Wall, and Lowell streets, on the fourth. The sale of the land was subject to certain conditions, one of which was to the effect that the buildings erected upon this property could be dwellings or stores only.[15] On November 25, 1851, the city conveyed the entire tract to a Colonel Josiah L. C. Amee except for a strip of land dividing the lot in two, which the city retained and paved as an extension to Wall Street. On the side of this Wall Street extension farthest from Leverett Street, Colonel Amee built 10 dwelling houses, but when he found that he had difficulty selling them, he gave up his original plan of building others on the remaining land and instead offered it for sale.[16]

Father McElroy had been looking about for land suitable for a larger church and a college, as has been seen, almost from the moment he came to St. Mary's. According to his diary, he had noticed that the jail land had been offered for sale, and he had even gone as far as to engage a broker to offer "for an unidentified client" $70,000 for the entire lot. When the city authorities decided to open an extension to Wall Street through the lot, Father McElroy felt that the remaining land would be too small for his purpose and consequently withdrew from the market. His search to find a suitable site elsewhere, however, was in vain, so that when Colonel Amee expressed a desire to sell part of the jail land early in the year 1853, he turned his attention once more to this tract as a last resort.[17]

On investigation he discovered that in addition to the restriction limiting the buildings erected on the land to dwellings and stores, another condition obliged the buyer to erect 10 brick buildings facing the new (Wall) street. Colonel Amee, perceiving that these conditions were making it impossible for him to sell the land, petitioned the city council for a release or modification of the restrictions so far as they affected the vacant lots facing Wall Street, and the committee on public lands, acting under a vote of the city council, on March 9, 1853, modified the restrictions on the Wall Street lots so that the prohibition only ran against "buildings to be used for manufacturing or mechanical purposes, stables, gasometers, bowling alleys, etc."[18] Colonel Amee obtained a duly certified copy of the vote modifying the restrictions and reopened negotiations with Father McElroy. But all the difficulties were by no means removed. Father McElroy pointed out that the Wall Street lots by themselves were not deep enough for a church site unless he could also buy the adjoining lots which faced on Leverett Street and have them likewise freed from restrictions. Colonel Amee was willing to sell the additional land. He felt, with good reason, that the city authorities would agree to remove the restrictions on the Leverett Street lots, as they had done so readily on the adjoining land.

Father McElroy meanwhile had the title examined by the foremost real estate attorney in Boston at the time, N. I. Bowditch. The latter's opinion was that because Father McElroy proposed to build a church upon the premises and because the city had already modified the restrictions on the Wall Street lots, there would not be the slightest difficulty in securing the necessary modification on the remainder of the land. He believed that it was a mere matter of formality and that Father McElroy was perfectly safe in paying the purchase money. So, on advice of his counsel, Father McElroy paid the consideration and took the title from Colonel Amee on March 23, 1853.[19] The down payment was $13,000, and Father McElroy became responsible to the city for the balance of the purchase money, $46,480.59. Father McElroy was understandably pleased with this acquisition, since it included the buildings on the property, one of which, a granite, four-story structure originally built as a courthouse, cost the city $50,000 when new.[20]

Intolerance Forces a Withdrawal

When it became known that the jail land had been sold to a Catholic priest and that he proposed to build upon it a new Catholic church, a group of bigoted persons immediately agitated to have the committee on public lands first enforce the restriction limiting the use of the land to the erection of dwellings or stores and, second, put back in force the recently rescinded condition that the purchaser erect 10 brick dwelling houses on the Wall Street lots or forfeit the land. Their bigotry prevailed and the committee, exceeding its legal power, notified Colonel Amee and Father McElroy within a day of the purchase that the restrictions were once more in force; the order rescinding them, it was claimed, had been obtained by Colonel Amee through false representation.

After taking legal advice on the matter, Father McElroy disregarded this notification and directed his attention to the task of obtaining permission to erect a building other than a dwelling or store on the lot. The bishop joined Father McElroy in his efforts and caused the petitions to be made jointly by himself and Father McElroy—but without avail. Mr. Bowditch presented the petitioners' views before the mayor and joint committee on public lands at a hearing in the Common Council room on April 19, 1853; despite a most cogent and moving plea, their efforts proved fruitless.[21]

A petition signed by one Nathaniel Hammond and 924 others opposing the lifting of the restrictions had been presented to the committee, but on May 19, 1853, a counterpetition signed by 25 of the most prominent Protestant gentlemen in Boston was sent to the committee, urging that permission be given for the church to be built.[22] Included in the group were Edward Everett, former governor of Massachusetts and former president of Harvard; Rufus Choate, Harvard professor and undisputed social leader in Boston; William Prescott, the historian; James Collins Warren, dean of Harvard medical school; and Amos A. Lawrence, the prominent merchant who a few years after the jail land controversy purchased farm property in Chestnut Hill that decades later would become the new Boston College campus. But even the great influence of such men was disregarded; the mayor and aldermen agreed to allow the construction of the church, but the council would not concur.[23]

In March of 1856 the bishop and Father McElroy judged that the prospects of a favorable reception of their petition had brightened with the election of Alexander H. Rice as mayor and with a new council in session in which the Know-Nothings were in the minority. A copy of the petition which they submitted is found in Father McElroy's diary:

> To the Honble, the Mayor, Aldermen & Common Council of the City of Boston:
>
> The undersigned present themselves before your Honble body, to renew their petition made on former occasions, for the removal of certain restrictions, on four lots of land, fronting on Leverett Street, to enable them to erect an edifice for the purpose of Divine Worship. The subject of this petition has been discussed sufficiently to preclude the necessity of entering into details. The undersigned rest their hopes on the impartiality of the present councils, and of their sense of justice irrespective of any sinister bias. Three years have now elapsed since the purchase of the lands in question. This was done in good faith, not doubting for a moment, that the same authority which took the restrictions off ten lots would with more reason take the same off four lots, especially as it was for a church to accommodate hundreds who are deprived of the means of sanctifying the Lord's Day.
>
> The undersigned would also respectfully submit that independent of the annual installments already paid ($20,658.04) to the City Treasurer, taxes and interest have also been paid to the amount of 7995.77 for all of which no consideration has as yet been received from the land which remains unproductive in both a spiritual and temporal point of view. With this simple statement of facts, we place ourselves confidentially before your respective boards, that this our petition may be granted to enable us to commence this season, the erection of the contemplated church and your petitioners as they are bound will ever pray &c.
>
> Signed
>
> John B. Fitzpatrick, Bsp. of Boston
> John McElroy[24]

The petition was read in the board of common council and referred to the land committee, composed of members from both boards. After being debated there for a considerable time, a majority of the committee finally voted to remove the restrictions. The council itself deferred action on it for several weeks, until finally, on November 20, 1856, it was defeated by a vote of 25 to 15, with some eight not voting.[25]

Father McElroy took the defeat philosophically; he saw that although Catholic petitioners had not been granted what they had asked, the opposition was diminishing, and that many, including an increasing number of non-Catholics, were perceiving that Catholics were being deprived of fair and equitable treatment in a spirit of bigotry. Several members of the council charged the opposition openly with this bigotry, and others undertook to defend Catholic doctrines that were mentioned in their discussions. All of this permitted the venerable priest to reflect that the Church, by and large, had really won an important victory in this matter by securing the sympathy and interest of a large number of fair-minded citizens.[26]

On December 8, 1856, the annual city elections were held, and with respect to the issue of the jail land, almost all of Father McElroy's bitterest opponents were defeated. Now there were but six Know-Nothings on the council for the ensuing year, which encouraged the bishop and Father McElroy to renew their endeavors to have the restrictions removed by a new petition dated January 21, 1857.[27]

Weeks passed into months, and still no definite action was taken on the petition. On March 23 Bishop Fitzpatrick noted in his diary that the attitude of the City Council and Board of Aldermen gave little hope for the success of the petition to have the restrictions removed from the jail land. He concluded it would be best to sell that property and look elsewhere. He and Father McElroy found a promising site in the western part of the city at the corner of Spring and Milton streets.[28]

Father McElroy evidently investigated this property and found it available, because three days later he, together with the bishop and the Jesuit Provincial, who had recently arrived in Boston on his annual visitation, decided that it would be advisable to place the new church and college in the southern part of the city (the "South End") rather than in the western section. The bishop thereupon authorized the Jesuits, in the person of Father Stonestreet, the Provincial, to purchase land for that purpose.[29]

> My next step [wrote Father McElroy] was to ascertain the best means of disposing of the Jail lands. I applied to a professional gentleman, my counsel on former occasions, who had expressed at one time his wish to purchase the lands; he now declined but tendered his services very kindly, to dispose of it to the City, as he thought it would be rather difficult to effect so large a sale to private individuals. To this I gave my consent. . . .[30]

The city authorities were much relieved to have the matter ended at last, since "it puzzled interested politicians and made them uncertain in their calculations upon the Catholic vote in the municipal elections."[31] The first offer to the city was made in the last week of March, and on April 10 the matter was referred by concurrence of the aldermen and common council to the land committee. In contrast with their lethargic performances in the past, these various bodies acted upon the business with dispatch, and on the Saturday in Easter week, April 18, 1857, completed the purchase.[32] The sum which they paid immediately and which Father McElroy banked immediately, with no little satisfaction,[33] amounted to $64,771.80, which represented all the money he had advanced upon the land, with interest simple and compound upon the installments, and an advance of about $4500 which, with the income from the buildings upon the estate from the time of its purchase, amounted to a gain of about $9000.[34]

A Site in the New South End

Reflecting upon the sale of the jail land, Bishop Fitzpatrick was of the opinion that:

> . . . all things considered, it is no doubt better that the petition of the Bp. and Fr. McElroy has been so obstinately refused by the city authorities. The funds have accumulated by interest in the mean [time] and increased by the advance which the city pays. A college in the south part of the city will be easily accessible to a far greater number of Catholic children or youths. Not only the population of the city proper in the main part will be better accommodated, but South Boston, Roxbury and some other adjoining towns may enjoy all the advantages. This would not be the case had the college been placed in Leverett Street.[35]

This evidently represents a changed point of view, because only a few weeks before, Father McElroy referred to the bishop as merely "reconciled" to the prospect of the college being located in the South End.[36] But there were some, clerical and lay, who did not become reconciled to the thought of the change. Among the priests who would have preferred to have the college remain in the North End at all costs was Father Bernadine Wiget, S.J., assistant to Father McElroy in St. Mary's. It is not clear from his letters just how he planned to solve the impasse created by a hostile city government, but he vigorously resented the movement away from Leverett Street.[37] In support of his view, he cited the Irish of that section of the city, who, he claimed, were much incensed at news of the change. Father McElroy was conscious of this evidently ill-informed opposition, but prudently decided to say nothing and disregard it, in the hope that time would demonstrate the wisdom of his acts.[38]

The sale of the jail land was completed on Saturday; on Monday morning, April 20, Father McElroy was back again before the land commissioners seeking to buy a plot of land on Harrison Avenue, between Concord and Newton streets, which appears to have been brought to his attention by the well-disposed mayor of the city, Alexander H. Rice.[39] The lot contained 115,000 square feet and embraced an entire city block.

As soon as the proposal was made, new opposition sprang up. Some few of the council took alarm and spread the word to the newspapers. The excitement centered on the fact that the Catholics were going to take over an entire square of land in the center of the city,[40] with the result that the land commissioners voted during the last week in April to reject Father McElroy's offer.[41] He, however, shrewdly realizing that it was his effort to purchase the *entire* block that constituted the "audacious attempt on the part of ecclesiastical authorities . . . to acquire undue and colossal power," shifted his ground and renewed his petition, this time asking for only a section of the land.[42] The chief objection being thus removed, he was assured privately that permission for purchase would ultimately be given.

Days and weeks passed in the now familiar pattern of postponements, delays, and promises. The sought-for solution was always just around the corner; it would be settled "the next week end." On May 27 Father McElroy admitted to the Provincial how tried he was. "Since the 18th of April, the day I disposed of the Jail Land, until this day, I have been in continual communication with the Mayor, Councils & Land Commissioners and as yet nothing is concluded. . . ."[43]

He faced the situation with the patience of a saint and, at the same time, with the astuteness of a bank executive. When, with the approach of June, he began to have doubts that the Harrison Avenue negotiations would ever be terminated favorably, he began preparations for an alternative purchase. The prospect, as he outlined it in his diary, was:

> . . . a large building lately erected for a lying-in hospital by an association of Gentln. It cost, including the land (40,000 square feet), $64,000—they ask 60,000$ and the Broker employed to purchase it, thinks it can be had for much less. I have authorized him to give 50,000$—the only difficulty about it is that the title was given by the City, stipulating that an hospital of the above character be erected on it—to remove this restriction, can be done only by the City Councils—it is feared, that this will not be done, unless they are informed for what purpose the building is to be used, and if this be made known it is feared we cannot purchase it . . .[44]

The trustees accepted his offer of $50,000 under his condition that they secure the removal of the restriction by the city authorities. The petition was entered on June 8, 1857, and shortly after this was rejected.[45] Father McElroy wrote:

> July 17. Again the enemy has triumphed in defeating the above project—the Citizens . . . took the alarm that Fr. McElroy was about to erect a Church for the Irish; that he would have a large number of families of this class in the neighborhood; that he was also about to build a Jesuit College; that nothing else would satisfy these Jesuits than the Conversion of all the Bostonians &c., &c. From such fear, petitions were sent in to the Aldermen, against such buildings, three or four newspapers came out in the same strain the past week.
>
> Finding the opposition a formidable one, and a renewal of the Jail Lands, I concluded to abandon the project, of the Hospital & land, and fall back on the first site I had selected, fronting on Harrison Avenue.[46]

*   *   *

But victory was near. Father McElroy's efforts of four and a half years to secure property for a church and the future Boston College came to an end on the morning of July 22, 1857, when the land committee of the City of Boston finally agreed to sell him the tract he sought on Harrison Avenue.[47] The first stage of the struggle was over.

ENDNOTES

1. McElroy to Beckx, September 27, 1854. General Archives of the Society of Jesus in Rome, 9-XIX-4. Quoted by Gilbert J. Garraghan, S.J., "Origins of Boston

College, 1842–1869," *Thought*, 17:640–642. Hereafter the letters JGA in a reference will indicate that the material is preserved in these General Archives of the Society of Jesus in Rome.

2. Dzierozynski ad Roothaan, September 6, 1842, JGA. The letter of Bishop Fenwick given in a Latin version in this place was translated into English by Garraghan, "Origins," pp. 629–630.

3. McElroy to Fenwick, January 7, 1843, Diocesan Archives, Boston, Old Letters, "A," No. 16. It is cited in part here:

    "You must turn your attention to your [new] Cathedral. You can, and must erect it. Leave the Holy Cross [Cathedral] where it is, with the vacant lot adjoining for a College of *ours,* who would also attend the Church. This would be laying a solid & permanent basis for Catholicity, not only in the City, but through the Diocese. The education of boys in Christian Piety, together with the usual Classical studies, would be of infinite advantage . . . for your episcopal seminary, as also for our Society.

    "A few members will suffice for a College of day scholars which may easily be supplied, but for boarders, a large number is necessary, and then of peculiar qualifications, for government, etc. With four scholastics & one Brother we [i.e., at Frederick, Maryland] carry on our school, over a hundred boys, with the same course as in Geo. Town as far as Rhetorick—and the same teachers might as well have double the number. What an advantage to your Catholic youth in the City to be thus trained up—what edification to the faithful & credit to Religion. Excuse, my dear Bishop, the unauthorized effusions of one well known to you, who hopes he has nothing at heart but the well being of your important charge. In every respect they are crude ideas which may be improved, I am sure, and perhaps, something in time, with God's blessing, might grow out of them. I see nothing difficult in the project—when I commenced our little College, I had not a dollar in hand, it is now a reputable establishment without a cent of debt—the Sisters have begun in the same way—out of debt—The Church the same and on it is paid about 30,000$ having a debt of about 8000$ and all this in Frederick, where we have but about 1500 Caths. No doubt in my mind, but your Cathedral and a splendid one, can be erected, in a few years and a College also, for the accommodation of 300 boys."

4. This and the four succeeding quotations are found in Gilbert J. Garraghan, S.J., "Origins," p. 632.

5. Fitzpatrick, Memoranda of the Diocese of Boston (manuscript), Vol. III, p. 289, under date October 24, 1847, Diocesan Archives, Boston. Cf. also, Leahy, "Archdiocese of Boston," in Byrne (editor), *History of the Catholic Church in the New England States*, 1:127; and Robert H. Lord, John E. Sexton, and Edward T. Harrington, *History of the Archdiocese of Boston* (New York: Sheed and Ward, 1944), 2:474–475.

6. Fitzpatrick, "Memoranda," III, 289.

7. Quoted by Garraghan, "Origins," 636.

8. McElroy to Roothaan, September 4, 1848, JGA. (Garraghan, "Origins," 637).

9. McElroy, Diary, "A Brief History of the preparatory steps towards the erection of a college for our Society: and Collegiate Church in Boston," pp. 1 and 2 (in Vol. 4 of the MS. Diary).

10. Garraghan, "Origins," p. 637.

11. Roothaan to Fitzpatrick, May 8, 1850. Original in Diocesan Archives, Boston (Old Letters, "A," No. 49). The translation from the French is Garraghan's "Origins," pp. 737–738.

12. Garraghan, "Origins," p. 638. Father McElroy's letter: McElroy to Roothaan, August 7, 1850, JGA.

13. Roothaan to Brocard, January 8, 1851, JGA.
14. "A Plan of 31 lots of the Old Jail Land to be Sold at Public Auction," a plan and advertisement issued by the Committee on Public Lands, City of Boston, and dated: "Boston, 1851." Preserved in the Maryland Provincial S.J. Archives, Georgetown University Library.
15. *Ibid.*
16. William B. F. Whal, "Close of St. Mary's Jubilee, North End, Boston," *The Pilot* (October 16, 1897), Vol. 60, No. 41, pp. 1 and 5; same in *Woodstock Letters,* 27 (1898):92–93.
17. McElroy, Diary, "A Brief History of the Preparatory Steps, etc." MS. Vol. 4, pp. 1–3.
18. Whal, "Close of St. Mary's Jubilee," Vol. 60, No. 41, pp. 1 and 5.
19. *Ibid.*
20. McElroy, Diary, pp. 3–4.
21. N. I. Bowditch, *An Argument for a Catholic Church on the Jail-Lands* (a pamphlet, Boston: John Wilson and Son, 1853).
22. *The Pilot,* May 28, 1853.
23. McElroy, Diary, p. 5.
24. *Ibid.*, pp. 6–7.
25. *Ibid.*, p. 10; "Memoranda," November 20, 1856.
26. McElroy, Diary, p. 11.
27. *Ibid.*, p. 12.
28. Fitzpatrick, "Memoranda," March 23, 1857.
29. *Ibid.*, March 25 and 26, 1857.
30. McElroy, Diary, Part IV, p. 14.
31. Fitzpatrick, "Memoranda," April 20, 1857.
32. McElroy, Diary, Part IV, p. 14.
33. McElroy to Stonestreet, April 19, 1857, Maryland Provincial S.J. Archives, Georgetown University Library.
34. McElroy, Diary, Part IV, p. 15; Fitzpatrick, "Memoranda," April 20, 1857.
35. Fitzpatrick, "Memoranda," April 20, 1857.
36. McElroy to Stonestreet, May 7, 1857, Maryland Provincial S.J. Archives, Georgetown University Library.
37. Wiget to Stonestreet, May 7, 1857; also Wiget to Stonestreet, May 27, 1857, Maryland Provincial S.J. Archives, Georgetown University Library.
38. McElroy to Stonestreet, May 2, 1857, Maryland Provincial S.J. Archives, Georgetown University Library.
39. McElroy, Diary, Vol. 4, pp. 15–16. Mr. Rice's aid is claimed by Garraghan, "Origins," basing his assertion on a letter, McElroy to Beckx, February 1, 1859, JGA.
40. McElroy, Diary, Vol. 4, pp. 15 and 16.
41. Fitzpatrick, "Memoranda," May 3, 1857.
42. McElroy, Diary, Part IV, p. 16.
43. McElroy to Stonestreet, May 27, 1857, Maryland Provincial S.J. Archives, Georgetown University Library.
44. McElroy, Diary, Vol. 4, p. 16.
45. *Ibid.* There appears to be some confusion regarding the dates given by Father McElroy during this period; the most probable arrangement seems to be: July 17, rejection of the hospital petition; July 22, agreement to sell Father McElroy the Harrison Avenue land.
46. *Ibid.*, p. 19.
47. *Ibid.*, p. 20.

CHAPTER 3

Walls and a Roof

Harrison Avenue was laid out in 1844 while the South End of Boston was still a narrow neck of land surrounded by flats and the waters of the bay. In 1853 the work of widening the neck was begun by filling in the marshy lands on either side of it, and three years later a street railroad system was inaugurated, with the first line running from the Old Granary Burying Ground on Tremont Street to Roxbury. Overnight the South End became the desirable residential section of the city, and extensive building operations began.[1]

In his diary, Father McElroy recognized the advantage of this section for his new college, because "a better class of houses will be and are erected in the vicinity" and "the horse rail roads now introduced into various parts of the City, will afford easy access for Students from all parts of the city and vicinity."[2]

The lot which he had purchased from the city comprised 65,100 square feet of land, with 250 feet of frontage on Harrison Avenue; 270 feet on Concord Street, and 250 feet on the new, unnamed (James) street, "running with the cemetery wall, and thence by a dividing line to Harrison Avenue 250 feet."[3] The cemetery is evidently the one which Towle afterward remembered being removed by the authorities to make room for the college playground in 1866.[4] The price the city charged, since the land was to be Church property, was 50 cents a foot—a reduction of 25 cents a foot on the residential rate.

An architect, Patrick C. Keely, of Brooklyn, New York, was engaged at once, and plans were begun for the church. At the same time a Mr. Wissiben was chosen as architect for the college building.[5] On August 17, 1857, the first installment of the purchase price was paid to the city authorities in the amount of $3,750, leaving $28,000 to be paid in nine annual payments of $3,200, with interest at 6 percent.[6]

In September Father McElroy spent four weeks in New York with the architects going over plans and drawings for the church and college. The college, he decided, was to be housed in two separate buildings, each 90 feet by 60 feet, which would be connected by a small building 40 feet by 23 feet and three stories in height. Although the architect at first envisioned the church as a brick edifice with a stone facade, it was decided to take advantage of an offer from a New Hampshire contractor who owned his own quarries to build the entire church of white granite and, from the same stone, to build the basement of the college and the steps and platforms of both buildings. The stonework was to cost $62,000 complete. The contract with Mr. Andrews of Nashua, New Hampshire, was signed November 25, and contracts were placed with Messrs. Morrell and Wigglesworth of Newburyport for the carpentry work connected with the roofing, window frames, joists, and a first floor of plank for $18,000.[7]

On November 24, 1857, Father McElroy wrote in his diary:

> This week I make application to the board of land commissioners to sell me twenty feet more of land, fronting on Harrison Avenue and extending back to the new street; this would give us 270 feet front on three streets, the fourth boundary would be a little short of this—in this way, our lots would be nearly square. I hope to get it at the same price, 50 cents a foot.[8]

The new land, since it was to be used by the college exclusively, was to be taxed in the same manner as a private residence. Exception from taxation was not granted to the college until it was incorporated in 1863.[9]

Father McElroy attributed the courteous treatment which he had received of late from the city officials to the "pacific course" he had pursued in the jail land episode. For this favor he thanked God, who gave him patience to remain silent "amidst their opposition, contrary to the importunities of my friends, who advised a contrary course."[10]

Work Begins

On April 7, 1858, ground was broken on the site of the new church by Bishop Fitzpatrick, who took the first spadeful, followed by Father McElroy, who with his spade cut out "the sign of the Holy Cross, with the words In Nomine Patris, etc."[11] Stonecutters and carpenters had been on the location some time before this preparing blocks and window frames, so that when the work actually began it proceeded rapidly.

At seven o'clock on the morning of April 27, 1858, a small group

Boston College and the Church of the Immaculate Conception, completed in 1860, photographed some time before 1875 by Oliver Wendell Holmes.

comprising Bishop Fitzpatrick, Very Reverend John Williams, V.G., Reverend James A. Healy, chancellor, Reverend John Rodden, and Fathers Wiget, Janalik, and McElroy of the Society of Jesus gathered at the site of the church without publicity of any kind and unattended by any gathering of people to lay the cornerstone of the church.[12] This ceremony must also be considered as the laying of the cornerstone of Boston College, because both buildings were built simultaneously as one project and, as far as can be ascertained, no thought was given to a separate cornerstone laying for the college.

Through the month of May, despite heavy rains which repeatedly filled the excavations and made the use of steam pumps necessary, the work on the cellar walls of the college progressed surprisingly well. The concrete-filled trenches supported a first course of large granite blocks, and on top of this, three feet of rough masonry was leveled to receive granite basement walls 11 feet in height.

Father McElroy stated in June that about forty stonecutters were at work in a long range of sheds erected for them, and there was "a blacksmith's shop with four fires."[13] In July he reported that "the first floor of the College buildings is being laid, and the granite basement of the same commenced. 130 men are now daily employed on the premises—all bids fair to have the buildings enclosed before the severe winter."[14] In September the granite basement of the college was nearly finished and all the brick partition walls in the basement erected. In addition to this, the principal floors of the first story were laid and the brick commenced over them. Later that month, Father McElroy rejoiced that the walls of the college were completed to a stage where "the bricks are now carried up by steam power to the upper stories. . . ."[15]

New Expenses

The masons finished their task in October, and the carpenters commenced the laborious work of setting the roof. This carpentry work went on through November, December, and January, although all work on the church had to be suspended for the winter in mid-November. Father McElroy reflected with some heaviness of spirit that the brick partitions in the basement and throughout the building had added an unforeseen $11,855 to the original estimate, raising the masonry contract for the whole project to $76,855.[16]

At this time he applied to the superintendent of public lands in the city for the purchase of a strip 30 feet wide adjoining the north side of the college property, running from Harrison Avenue to James Street. On March 8, 1859, the city land committee acceded to his proposal and sold him the land (7350 square feet in addition to his previous purchase) for the old price of 50 cents a square foot, although the market price for the land when used for residential purposes had now risen to one dollar a square foot. Again Father McElroy took pleasure in calculating the saving which this reduction made possible. The sum, $3,075, Father McElroy considered as reparation by the city authorities for the annoyance other city officials had caused him in the past.[17]

Contracts which he let out in April for work in the interior of the college building were as follows: carpentry, $11,800; plastering, $2,820; plumbing, $1,775; and gas fitting, $488. In June an additional contract had to be made for steamfitters to lay pipes in the college before the flooring and walls were completed. Steam heating at the time was such an expensive proposition that Father McElroy pondered on it long before deciding to have it installed. Finally, he was persuaded that it was best "both as to security from fire, less expensive in the consumption of coal, free from dust, (and giving) an agreeable summer-like heat."[18]

In presenting an informal account of his stewardship up to this point in his diary, Father McElroy points out the various expenses which had unavoidably arisen and which had been unforeseen in the original contracts. The main burden of blame for his unpaid debts, however, he places on the failure of the Jesuits at St. Mary's to make the annual contributions he expected. When he started the buildings in the South End, he had on hand $80,000 he had collected for that purpose in a period of six years at St.

Mary's. He felt the Provincials had expected continued support from St. Mary's. His diary reported:

> Now if St. Mary's had united with me the past two years, as I expected, ten thousand dollars a year could have been raised to aid in these buildings. This was one of the greatest disappointments I met since I undertook to erect a College and Church for our Society. Fiat voluntas Dei.[19]

On October 1, 1859, Father McElroy, accompanied by one Father (Steinbacker), left St. Mary's rectory in the North End where he had been living and took up residence in the college building, despite the great inconvenience which must have been experienced by them during that winter through lack of proper heating equipment. However, greater trouble than a cold room soon arose in the form of difficulties in finding money to meet current expenses. Father McElroy's attempt to raise money by a mortgage on the college and church in January of 1860 proved fruitless when the conditions attached to the loan were found to be altogether unsatisfactory. A temporary expedient in this crisis was arranged by a bank which discounted notes for Father McElroy. But this he saw as a troublesome and uncertain solution, so he renewed his efforts to obtain a permanent loan.

Through the summer of 1860 two new and unforeseen outlays added to his financial burden. The first of these was for an iron fence set on granite piers to enclose practically all the property. This fence was required—for reasons no longer known—by the City of Boston, and represented an expense of $600 for the foundation work and $3.75 a foot for the railing, including gates and painting. The Harrison Avenue frontage alone cost about $2,000, according to Father McElroy's official estimate.[20]

Second, the fear of a possible explosion of the steam boilers caused Father McElroy to have them placed in a separate small building behind the church. It was found on trial that the church chimney was not large enough for the new boilers, and a new smokestack had to be built. The housing for the boilers cost $300, and the chimney cost $470.[21]

In the beginning of the month of September 1860, Father McElroy wrote that he had succeeded in arranging for the loan he desired.[22] A savings bank in Lowell, Massachusetts, loaned him $80,000, for which he gave a mortgage on the church and college. How this sum was disbursed is stated in the diary as follows:

> $29,320.51 was paid to the City of Boston. The balance refunded Mr. Carney what he had advanced for me, brokerage, commission, etc., leaving me a balance of $4901.49. . . . Besides this funded debt of eighty thousand I have two notes due in two banks of $10,000 each; these will have to be renewed once or twice and the interest paid. In two years I hope we can pay one or both from the revenue of the church collections, etc., other floating debts to be paid in the same manner. Thus there will remain charged on the church the interest of $80,000, say, four thousand eight hundred dollars

annually; this I think can be easily done and eight or ten thousand beside paid on the debt, with the assistance of St. Mary's paying $3,000 yearly.[23]

Friends and Finance

Andrew Carney, a friend of the Jesuit Fathers of long standing, helped the situation at this time by taking upon himself the cost of laying the sidewalks in front of the church and college. In the meantime, work had commenced on grading and sodding the grounds about the church and college. In September 1860 a drive to pay off the church debt was organized by Father McElroy, who asked 25 cents a month from persons willing to aid. Some eighty collectors turned in $400 from this source the first month. In December Father Barrister of St. Mary's in the North End loaned Father McElroy $4000. This helped ease the financial strain of the moment, and further assistance was received from two concerts held in the church prior to its formal opening, which apparently netted in the vicinity of $500 each. At the time of the opening of the church, the auction of pews, pew rent, concerts, and a one-dollar offering at the door on opening day realized another $3000.[24] After the church was dedicated on March 10, 1861, a small steady revenue was realized from collections and offerings, but church and college could not yet be regarded as financially secure.

In March of 1861 Father McElroy recorded that he was able to make a

Andrew Carney, generous friend of Father McElroy and benefactor of Boston College.

further purchase of land from the city at his previous price of 50 cents a foot. The latest purchase was 13,657 square feet adjoining the property he already owned. Since the market price of this land had now risen to $1.25 a foot, he estimated his "savings" on the whole transaction as amounting to $15,152.[25]

In his diary, Father McElroy writes of a special indebtedness:

> . . . there is one whose name I will not mention who has on all occasions aided me by his prudent counsel, and also by advancing means in every emergency that I called upon him, and when I applied to others it was without his knowledge—for he told me never to be embarrassed as long as he had means to relieve me. Still I felt a delicacy to call on him so often and tried to procure means elsewhere. Had it not been for this Gentn. I would not have been able to continue the work on the church but must have postponed it for an indefinite period. Our Lord, I hope, will reward him abundantly for his zeal and devotedness to His own House. He is one of the largest benefactors to the buildings.[26]

In March of 1862 Andrew Carney, the benefactor referred to above, instructed Father McElroy to have contractors come at his expense and remove the old brick wall on the former boundary of the college property, and to grade and fence the recently acquired strip so that it would form one parcel with the rest of the property. This work was commenced in April and completed in May at a cost of about $2300.[27] On this occasion trees, chiefly linden, were planted about the church and college, twelve on each side of the principal walk between the two buildings and some at the base of the terrace on Harrison Avenue. These were provided by members of the congregation who paid for the purchase and planting of individual trees at two dollars each as personal memorials.[28] Of interest in this connection is a photograph in the Georgetown University archives taken about 1880, showing the front of the church and some of these trees still standing. On the reverse of the picture is penciled in a contemporary hand: "Various members of the congregation donated the trees around the church, and the names of the donors clung to the trees. The two trees in front of the church were called Mr. and Mrs. Andrew Carney. That on the corner or side wall was Mrs. McEvoy. I do not remember the rest of the names."

*   *   *

The college buildings were completed by 1860, but, since the province did not at that time have Jesuits available to staff a new school, the buildings were used during the trying Civil War years of 1860–1863 as a seminary for Jesuits in training for the priesthood. Two men who would become legendary figures in Boston College history were assigned to the seminary: Father John Bapst and Father Robert Fulton. Fulton, who would later be the first dean and serve twice as president of the college, was a professor of theology in the seminary. John Bapst, who would be the college's first president, had the office of rector of the seminary.

ENDNOTES

1. Cf. *Illustrated Boston,* 2nd ed. (New York: American Publishing and Engraving Co., c. 1889), pp. 54–55.
2. McElroy, Diary, Vol. 2, pp. 13 and 15.
3. *Ibid.,* p. 16.
4. Henry C. Towle, "The Pioneer Days at Boston College," *The Stylus* (June 1897), 332–333.
5. James S. Sullivan, *A Graphic, Historical and Pictorial Account of the Catholic Church of New England, Archdiocese of Boston* (Boston: Illustrated Publishing Co., 1895), p. 204.
6. McElroy, Diary.
7. *Ibid.*
8. *Ibid.,* Vol. 2, p. 24.
9. *Ibid.,* last page.
10. *Ibid.,* p. 25.
11. *Ibid.,* p. 26.
12. *Ibid.,* p. 27.
13. *Ibid.,* p. 28.
14. *Ibid.,* p. 29.
15. *Ibid.,* p. 30.
16. *Ibid.,* p. 31. Also McElroy to Villiger, March 14, 1859, Maryland Provincial S.J. Archives, Georgetown University Library.
17. McElroy, Diary, p. 32.
18. *Ibid.,* p. 34.
19. *Ibid.,* pp. 36–37.
20. *Ibid.,* pp. 29 and 41.
21. *Ibid.,* pp. 41 and 46.
22. *Ibid.,* pp. 42–43.
23. *Ibid.*
24. *Ibid.,* 44 et ff., and 56.
25. *Ibid.,* p. 52.
26. The benefactor mentioned in this passage is identified in another place (Vol. 2, p. 60) as Andrew Carney. This excerpt from Vol. 2, pp. 53–55.
27. McElroy, Diary, Vol. 2, p. 56.
28. *Ibid.,* p. 60.

CHAPTER 4

The College Is Chartered

In the spring of 1863, although the Jesuit seminary still occupied the College buildings and although Jesuit authorities knew they could not muster a staff to open for classes in the fall, financial and legal reasons prompted incorporation. One financial reason for the early incorporation was to facilitate the arrangement of loans, which, it was found, would be extended to a corporation (the College in this instance) when they would be refused to an individual—even a priest. In May of 1863 Father McElroy was elected president of Boston College. This election, although perfectly legal, was for some reason never listed in the ordinary accounts of the presidents of Boston College, and in August 1863, three months after Father McElroy's investiture, Father Bapst was elected "first" president without any mention of the other election.[1]

Another financial reason for incorporating the College as soon as possible was to free it from the taxes (amounting at the time to some $700 a year) from which chartered educational institutions were exempt but which had been collected on the Harrison Avenue property (except the church) at a residential rate since the buildings had been built.[2]

The legal considerations which urged prompt incorporation centered about the title to the properties, which had been held until then in the name of Father McElroy. All the land and buildings on Harrison Avenue, as well as St. Mary's Church and residence in the North End of Boston, were legally the private property of Father McElroy,[3] and his sudden death—which was a distinct possibility for a man approaching his eighty-first birthday—would precipitate embarrassing complications. When it had been definitely decided to give up the scholasticate at Boston, nothing longer prevented the Fathers from seeking the advantages which incorporation would bring.

A Petition to the Legislature

Father McElroy had evidently been instructed by the Provincial in January of 1863 to commence the legal formalities connected with a petition for incorporation, because Father Paresce (the Provincial) inquired on February 20 what the prospects were for obtaining the charter.[4] On March 4 Father McElroy optimistically replied, "Our petition for the charter of our College was presented in the Legislature yesterday; there will be, I presume, very little opposition in the Legislature."[5] Less than three weeks later he was able to report:

> Our Bill for Chartering the College had its first reading in the Senate on Saturday last, and was ordered to be engrossed. On Tuesday last I was requested by letter to appear before the Committee on Education; I went with Fr. Welch, and told the C. what we wanted; I took with me Genl. Cushing who was very useful in suggesting and removing conditions I did not want &c. The Comme., about ten members, were extremely polite, even *kind,* and voted unanimously that a bill should be drafted in accordance with our understanding, &c., Genl. C. drew up the bill immediately before leaving the State House, I had it copied and the next day left it myself with the Chairman in the Senate Chamber. There is no doubt, I think, of its passage; when passed I shall send you a copy of it.
>
> In one section we are allowed to possess property not *exceeding* $30,000 annual income!!! This is generous. Another, to confer all the Degrees that are given in any college of the State; this includes Divinity, Medicine, M.A., and A.B.—so far it is all we could wish.[6]

To this announcement, the Provincial responded:

> I offer you my congratulations upon . . . the passage of the act for chartering Boston College. Please to get two authenticated copies of the Charter, one for yourself, the other to be kept in the archives of the Province. If however an authenticated copy should be too expensive, any copy of it, made by one of the scholastics will answer my purposes. As soon as the act will be signed by the Governor, it will be well to take measures at once for the transfer to the corporation of the property which you hold in your name, including St. Mary's Church. . . . You may draft some *by-laws* for the regulation of the corporation which I will examine when I come to Boston.[7]

An examination of the charter shows that although the act passed the House of Representatives and the State Senate of Massachusetts on March

31 and was approved by Governor John A. Andrews on April 1, an authenticated copy of the act was not obtained until May 28. On June 9 the following advertisement appeared in the *Boston Courier:*

> Notice is hereby given that the first meeting of the Proprietors of the charter, entitled "An Act to Incorporate the Trustees of the Boston College," will be holden on the sixth day of July next, at four o'clock in the afternoon, at the College Building, on Harrison Avenue, in the City of Boston, for the purpose of considering whether they will accept the act of incorporation granted to them by the Legislature, of electing officers, making by-laws, and otherwise organizing the Corporation, and transacting such business as may be requisite.

> Boston, June 19th, 1863.   John McElroy.
>   Edward H. Welch.
>   John Bapst.
>   James Clark.
>   Charles H. Stonestreet.
>   Persons named in the
>   Act of Incorporation.[8]

Meeting to Organize

According to the minutes of the meeting held on July 6, Fathers McElroy, Welch, and Bapst were present, and only two items of business were acted upon: the election of a secretary (Father Welch) and the voting to accept the act of incorporation. The second meeting of the Board of Trustees took place on July 10, at which the bylaws were adopted and:

> It was voted unanimously to elect the proper officers for the college for three years, which election resulted in the choice of the following: (Rev. J. McElroy having declined) Rev. J. Bapst was elected President, Rev. John McElroy, Vice-President; Rev. Robert Brady, Treasurer; Rev. E. H. Welch, Secretary. The following directors were also elected for three years: Rev. John Bapst, Rev. John McElroy, Rev. Robert Brady, Rev. E. H. Welch, and Rev. John Emig.
>   It was also voted to request Rev. John McElroy to convey all the property now vested in his name in the City of Boston, viz: the Church of the Immaculate Conception and Boston College in due legal form, also the Church and Parochial residence on Endicott Street also vested in the same Rev. John McElroy.[9]

Nine days later Father McElroy could write:

> On last Thursday [July] (16th) was finally concluded the conveyance of all property in my name, Boston College, Ch. of Im: Concep: St. Mary's Ch: and residence, to the Trustees of Boston College. Deo Gratias! I am indeed now a poor man, as a religious ought to be. The Deed is made out on

COMMONWEALTH OF MASSACHUSETTS.

In the year One Thousand Eight Hundred and Sixty-three.
AN ACT to incorporate the Trustees of Boston College.

Be it enacted by the Senate and House of Representatives in General Court assembled, and by the authority of the same, as follows: Section 1. F John McElroy, Edward H. Welch, John Bapst, James Clark and Charles H. Stonestreet, their associates and successors, are hereby constituted a body corporate by the name of the Trustees of the Boston College, in Boston, and they and their successors and such as shall be duly elected members of such corporation, shall be and remain a body corporate by that name forever: and for the orderly conducting the business of said corporation, the said trustees shall have power and authority, from time to time, as occasion may require, to elect a President, Vice President, Secretary, Treasurer and such other officers of said corporation as may be found necessary, and to declare the duties and tenures of their respective offices, and also to remove any Trustee from the same corporation, when in their judgment he shall be rendered incapable, by age or otherwise, of discharging the duties of his office, or shall neglect or refuse to perform the same, and also from time to time to elect new members of the said corporation: provided nevertheless that the number of members shall never be greater than ten. Section 2. The said corporation shall have full power and authority to determine at what times and places their meetings shall be holden and the manner of notifying the trustees to convene at such meetings, and also from time to time to elect a president of said college, and such professors, tutors, instructors and other officers of the said college as they shall judge most for the interest thereof, and to determine the Duties, salaries, emoluments, responsibilities and tenures of their several offices: and the said corporation are further empowered to purchase or erect and keep in repair, such houses and other buildings as they shall judge necessary for the said college; and also to make and ordain, as occasion may require, reasonable rules, orders and by-laws not repugnant to the constitution and laws of this Commonwealth, with reasonable penalties for the good government of the said college, and for the regulation of their own body; and also, to determine and regulate the course of instruction in said college, and to confer such degrees as are usually conferred by colleges in this Commonwealth, except medical degrees: provided nevertheless that no corporate business shall be transacted at any meeting unless one half at least of all the trustees are present. Section 3. Said corporation may have a common seal, which they may alter or renew at their pleasure, and all deeds sealed with the seal of said corporation, and signed by their order, shall when made in their corporate name, be considered in law as the deeds of said corporation: and said corporation may sue and be sued in all actions, real, personal or mixed, and may prosecute the same to final judgment and execution by the name of the Trustees of Boston College; and said corporation shall be capable of taking and holding in fee simple or any less estate by gift, grant, bequest, devise or otherwise, and lands, tenements or other estate, real or personal: provided, that the clear annual income of the same shall not exceed thirty thousand dollars. Section 4. The clear rents and profits of all the estate, real and personal, of which the said corporation shall be seized and possessed, shall be appropriated to the endowments of said college in such manner as shall most effectually promote virtue and piety and learning in such of the languages and of the liberal and useful arts and sciences, as shall be recommended from time to time by the said corporation, they conforming to the will of any donor or donors in the application of any estate which may be given, devised or bequeathed for any particular object connected with the college. Section 5. No student in said college shall be refused admission to or denied any of the privileges, honors or degrees of said college on account of the religious opinions he may entertain. Section 6. The legislature of this Commonwealth may grant any further powers to, or alter, limit, annul, or restrain any of the powers vested by this act in the said corporation, as shall be found necessary to promote the best interests of the said college and more especially may appoint overseers or visitors of the said college, with all necessary powers for the better aid, preservation and government thereof. Section 7. The granting of this charter shall never be considered as any pledge on the part of the Commonwealth that pecuniary aid shall hereafter be granted to the college.

House of Representatives, March 31, 1863
Paper to be enacted, Alex. H. Bullock, Speaker.
In Senate, Mar. 31, 1863,
Paper to be enacted, J. E. Field, President

April 1st 1863
    Approved,

        John A. Andrew.

Secretary's Department, Boston,
May 28,th 1863.

        I hereby certify the foregoing to be a true copy
        of the original Act.

Oliver Warner
    Secretary of the
    Commonwealth.

The legislature has twice approved amendments to the charter. In 1907 the name of the corporation was changed to the Trustees of Boston College (instead of *the* Boston College), authorization was given to grant medical degrees, and the corporation was authorized to hold additional real and personal estate. In 1971 the original limitation of 10 members of the Board of Trustees was removed.

parchment, handsomely executed, and left at the Register's Office to be placed on Record; the stamps cost $294.60.

Father Bapst was elected by the Trustees, as Prest., of the College, myself Vice Prest., Father Brady Treasurer & Fr. Welch Secy. pro forma, that the requirements of the Charter and By Laws might be complied with.

I would take leave to suggest your Revce. to continue to supply Fr. Bapst with what may be necessary to support the house until the College is opened for boys; the Revenue of the Church this year will not meet all the demands upon it, on acct., of the completion of the basement &c., &c., &c.,—you will perhaps find it convenient to leave one or more scholastics to study Moral &c., which can be easily done. . . .[10]

The latter suggestion must not be construed as a desire to reopen the College as a scholasticate. It was evidently Father McElroy's intention to solicit financial assistance from the Province in return for the board and room to be given some of the young Jesuits making certain parts of their course of studies in private or in preparation for examination. The idea was apparently not acted upon, for the Province catalog carried no names of such students until 1882, when a scholastic was listed as studying theology privately.[11]

The First President

When he came to Boston, Father Bapst was something of a national hero because of a harsh experience he had as a missionary in Maine. Born at La Roche, Canton of Fribourg in Switzerland on December 7, 1816,[12] he attended the Jesuit College at Fribourg. Upon completion of his course he entered the Society of Jesus on September 30, 1835. Shortly after his ordination on December 13, 1846, the Jesuits were expelled from Switzerland. Father Bapst, in company with a number of his fellow exiles, came to the United States, where he was assigned to missionary work among the Indians at Old Town, Maine.

To the difficulties which centered in a natural distaste for this type of work was added Father Bapst's inability to speak English or the Penobscot tongue. He overcame these handicaps gradually, however, and when the mission was moved to Eastport, Maine, in 1850, Father Bapst was appointed superior. In this new situation, his "parochial" responsibilities extended not only to the Indians but to large numbers of Irish and Canadian settlers in the section, and this led him to seek a more central base for the mission. Bangor was decided on in 1852, and from this town Father Bapst and his three assistants served as much as they could of the state of Maine.

Know-nothingism was rampant at the period, and the Jesuits' presence and ministry to their fellow Catholics was resented by many bigoted non-Catholics. At Ellsworth, a small town some 30 miles southeast of Bangor,

Rev. John Bapst, S.J., first president of Boston College.

Father Bapst was threatened with physical violence if he continued attending the local Catholics, but he disregarded the warning and went about his religious duties there as usual. On one of these visits (Saturday evening, October 14, 1854), he was seized by a mob, ridden on a rail to a distant point, stripped of his clothes, tarred and feathered, and some effort was even made to burn him alive. Exhausted and almost maimed by the inhuman treatment, he was left to return to his quarters as well as he could. When he arrived there, he was attended by friends, but many months passed before he recovered his health completely. The respectable citizens of the state, Protestant and Catholic, were shocked at this outrage, but their efforts to bring the guilty persons to justice proved fruitless. The deed had one happy result, however, for, like the blood of martyrs, it brought the faith to the respectful and sympathetic attention of many and undoubtedly contributed to the spread of Catholicism, not only in Maine, but throughout the nation.

In September 1859 the Jesuits withdrew from Maine, and Father Bapst was assigned to Holy Cross College in Worcester as spiritual father, where he remained until he was appointed rector of the new scholasticate at Boston the following July 2.

Empty Halls

To the new president, the College buildings, emptied of their scholastic inhabitants, took on a deserted look. On August 31 Father Bapst wrote, "Today the personal [sic] of the house will be reduced to its simplest expressing [sic]; there will be left here four priests, including Father Major [the minister], and five Brothers only."[13] And in another letter he wistfully complained of "feeling lost in the house."[14]

In the Catalogue of the Province of Maryland, *ineunte anno* 1864, the title *Seminarium Bostoniense* was replaced by *Residentia;* Father Bapst's rank was changed from rector to the lower rank of superior (to accommodate the rank of the house), and with him were left only Fathers Welch, McElroy, Fulton, and Power acting as assistant priests in the work connected with the Immaculate Conception Church. Father McElroy, weighed down by the infirmities of age, had been permitted to turn over his account books and the care of the financial management of the church and College to Father Bapst early in August,[15] and on November 10, he left Boston for good.[16] Of this period, Father Fulton later wrote, "We had a hard time. All the Scholastics going, Father McElroy, the Italians [i.e., the Italian priests who had been on the seminary faculty]; it was thought the people would desert us—it did not so result!"[17]

In addition to numerous tasks of the ministry, a serious worry occupied the attention of the superior and his assistants and served to keep their minds off the emptiness of the house. Both church and College rested under an overwhelming debt, which Father Fulton claimed was $156,666 in

John A. Andrews, the governor of the Commonwealth of Massachusetts who signed the Boston College charter.

November of 1863.[18] Devitt described the state of mind of the Jesuit community as "consternation" when the members discovered that the debt was over $150,000. According to the same authority, some of the more excitable members had even proposed giving the entire establishment—church and College—over to the bishop.[19]

The Problem of Funds

Father Bapst had written to the Provincial that after a careful examination of the accounts, he felt that in the ordinary course of events there would be an enormous deficit incurred during the coming year.[20] Whereupon he decided that waiting for something to happen would never save the situation, and he set out to *make* something happen. After Mass on Sunday, November 22, 1863,[21] Father Bapst called a meeting in the basement of the church of the prominent men in the congregation and made a clear exposition of the state of affairs. He also proposed a plan to raise the amount of $5000, which he felt was immediately needed. Among the men present was Andrew Carney, the wealthy clothing merchant of Boston, who had made numerous gifts to Catholic charities in the city and who had founded Carney Hospital in Boston some five months before.[22] He had been a loyal and generous friend to Boston College and the church of the Immaculate Conception since they had been first begun; he had given Father McElroy sums of money and had loaned him other large sums on convenient terms,[23] so he knew rather well the financial status of the church and the College. He at once saw that the $5000 for which Father Bapst had asked would barely meet the interest on outstanding loans and the most necessary expenses and that the position of the Fathers would not be permanently bettered by it. While the meeting was still in progress, Carney handed Father Bapst a card on which was written:

> I propose to pay to the Church of the Immaculate Conception the sum of $20,000, if the congregation will raise the same amount within six months.[24]

Father Bapst reported:

> The proposition was received with a tremendous applause; & to show they were in earnest $4,000 were subscribed on the spot by 64 men only, the meeting being very small. Now the impetus is given, the excitement is produced; it is in our power to have $40,000 within six months if the movement is skillfully directed. The cry is: we shall not lose the chance given by A. Carney!! If we are successful, the church is forever free from embarrassments and from any danger of falling into other hands. . . . Fr. Williams [the Vicar-general of the diocese of Boston during the prolonged absence of Bishop Fitzpatrick] sometime ago gave me permission to collect in any church in the city & in the country where I would be permitted by the pastors to do so.[25]

The First Fair

The $7000 mark was reached by the end of the first week,[26] and a group was organized to wait at the door of the church on Sundays to solicit further subscriptions.[27] Joseph A. Laforme of Boston, who was chairman of the committee of six[28] which nobly cooperated with Father Bapst in his great task, wrote:

> . . . in the course of a few weeks, Fr. Bapst, with the assistance of a few members of the congregation, succeeded in obtaining subscriptions to the amount of ten thousand dollars. Meanwhile it was found that other means must be resorted to for the purpose of obtaining the sum required under the proposition of Mr. Carney, and it was decided to hold a fair in the Music Hall of Boston.[29]

This decision was evidently reached early in January, because on January 26, Father Bapst wrote to the Provincial discussing a possible date. He favored some time in April, because as he explained:

> It is in the evening that money comes in; if the evenings are short, all is spoiled. The day to begin it will probably be appointed after tomorrow, and as soon as it is decided, I shall inform your Reverence.
> . . . We will announce the fair in the church and in the papers next week. The fair will be in aid to Boston College. That will make the object common to all the churches & even to the protestants, the college being chartered.[30]

In the same letter, Father Bapst asks the Provincial for information regarding the possibility of opening the College for externs the following September. He felt that some definite word regarding the opening would prove a valuable "sales point" in conducting the fair.

On February 8 he wrote again to advise the Provincial that the dates for the fair were from the fourth to the sixteenth of April.[31] According to Laforme, the fair opened on April 5,[32] but an unfortunate event occurred to dampen the spirit of all the workers: Andrew Carney died suddenly at half-past ten on Sunday evening, April 4. "He had a new attack," wrote Father Bapst, "of apoplexy, although the Dr. called it congestion of the lungs."[33] Arrangements were made to bury him from the Immaculate Conception Church at ten o'clock Wednesday morning, April 7, and he was laid to rest in the Carney Hospital, South Boston, which he had founded.[34]

In spite of this handicap, the fair proved to be, in Laforme's words, "up to that time . . . the most successful church fair ever held in Boston."[35] While the fair was still in progress, Father Bapst voiced some misgivings:

> The fair is the most splendid thing that ever was done here in that line; & yet it will not reach $20,000. The weather yesterday & today is far from being favorable, & other causes too long to be explained work strongly against it. It will probably realize $15,000 clear. We have one consolation; nothing has been wanted of what human ingenuity can do, in the part of the committee, of the ladies, & of the Pastors, to make it a grand fair. We resign ourselves to the will of Divine Providence for the result.[36]

Rev. Edward Holker Welch, S.J., one of the five Jesuit incorporators of Boston College.

Laforme, however, estimated that the fair realized $27,000. The same authority stated that some $25,000 worth of securities were bequeathed to the Immaculate Conception Church and the College by Andrew Carney. "Thus," observed Laforme, "within a few months from the beginning of his pastorship, Fr. Bapst had collected sixty-two thousand dollars towards the liquidation of the debt."[37]

*   *   *

In the spring of 1864 it was 17 years since Father McElroy had arrived in Boston with plans for a college. It was seven years since he purchased the property in the South End. It was five years since the church and the College buildings were completed. It was one year since the College's charter had been granted. At long last the dream was about to become reality.

ENDNOTES

1. The statement of Father McElroy's election is based on two letters of Very Reverend Angelo M. Paresce, S.J., Provincial of Maryland Province of the Society, to Father McElroy, dated April 10 and April 19, 1863; and on letters of Father McElroy to Father Paresce, dated April 16 and April 21, 1863. These letters are preserved in the Maryland Provincial S.J. Archives, Georgetown University Library.
2. McElroy, Diary, Vol. 1, MS. p. 68, under date December 1863. Maryland Provincial S.J. Archives, Georgetown University Library.
3. *Ibid.*
4. Paresce to McElroy, February 20, 1863, Maryland Provincial S.J. Archives, Georgetown University Library.
5. McElroy to Paresce, March 4, 1863, Maryland Provincial S.J. Archives, Georgetown University Library.
6. McElroy to Paresce, March 23, 1863, Maryland Provincial S.J. Archives, Georgetown University Library.
7. Paresce to McElroy, April 6, 1863, Maryland Provincial S.J. Archives, Georgetown University Library.
8. Transcribed from "Records of the Trustees of Boston College," manuscript volume of the minutes of the trustees' meetings, p. 1, BCA. *Note:* Devitt, in his short account of the history of Boston College printed in *Woodstock Letters,* was evidently led by this *Courier* advertisement into the error of dating the first meeting of the trustees as June 19—the date of the advertisement. The correct date obviously is July 6 (Devitt, "The History of the Maryland–New York Province; XVI, Boston College," *Woodstock Letters,* 64:403, 1935).
9. Records of the Trustees of Boston College, under date of July 10, 1863.
10. McElroy to Paresce, July 19, 1863, Maryland Provincial S.J. Archives, Georgetown University Library.
11. Catalogus Provinciae Marylandiae-Neo-Eboracensis, ineunte anno 1882, under "Boston College."
12. This synopsis of Father Bapst's life is based on the Catalogus Provinciae Marylandiae for the pertinent years and on the full account of Father Bapst's life, with transcripts of many of his letters, published in *Woodstock Letters,* 16:324–325 (1887); 17:218–229, 361–372 (1888); 18:83–93, 129–142, 304–319 (1889); 20:61–68; 241–249, 406–418 (1891).

13. Bapst to Paresce, August 31, 1863, Maryland Provincial S.J. Archives, Georgetown University Library.
14. Bapst to Paresce, August 28, 1863, Maryland Provincial S.J. Archives, Georgetown University Library.
15. McElroy to Paresce, August 4, 1863, Maryland Provincial S.J. Archives, Georgetown University Library.
16. McElroy to Paresce, November 25, 1863, Maryland Provincial S.J. Archives, Georgetown University Library.
17. Fulton, Diary, under date 1863.
18. *Ibid.*
19. Devitt, manuscript notes on history of Boston College, pp. 9–10, preserved in Georgetown University Archives.
20. Bapst to Paresce, December 1, 1863. Maryland Provincial S.J. Archives, Georgetown University Library.
21. Date fixed by McElroy reference to the incident as occurring two Sundays after he had just left Boston; since he left Boston on the tenth, this meeting must have taken place on the twenty-second. Cf. McElroy, Diary, November 1863, p. 67.
22. *The Pilot* (April 16, 1864).
23. See Chapter 3 for Father McElroy's indebtedness to and his estimation of Mr. Carney.
24. For an account of this entire incident in detail, cf. letter of Father Bapst to Father Paresce, December 1, 1863, Maryland Provincial S.J. Archives, Georgetown University Library.
25. *Ibid.*
26. McElroy, Diary, November 1863, p. 67.
27. Fulton, Diary, under date 1863.
28. "The names of those who formed this committee were: Hon. Hugh O'Brien, Joseph A. Laforme, Francis McLaughlin, William S. Pelletier, Patrick Powers, and Hugh Carey." From McAvoy, manuscript for "Father Bapst, a Sketch," p. 90 (omitted in published form); preserved in Woodstock College Archives, Georgetown University Library.
29. A. J. McAvoy, S.J. "Father Bapst; a Sketch," *Woodstock Letters,* 18 (1889):317.
30. Bapst to Paresce, January 26, 1864, Maryland Provincial S.J. Archives, Georgetown University Library.
31. Bapst to Paresce, February 8, 1864, Maryland Provincial S.J. Archives, Georgetown University Library.
32. McAvoy, *Father Bapst,* 18 (1889):317.
33. Bapst to Paresce, April 5, 1864, Maryland Provincial S.J. Archives, Georgetown University Library.
34. *Ibid.*
35. McAvoy, *Father Bapst,* 18 (1989):317.
36. Bapst to Paresce, April 12, 1864, Maryland Provincial S.J. Archives, Georgetown University Library.
37. McAvoy, *Father Bapst,* 18 (1889):317.

CHAPTER 5

Twenty-Two Pioneers

Simultaneously with these efforts to secure financial support, plans were being made to open the College in September of 1864 to lay students. As early as the previous November, Father McElroy had mentioned the opening as already decided on by the Provincial.[1] And on February 22, 1864, the Provincial, Father Paresce, reported to the Jesuit General in Rome:

> Next September it will be necessary to open a school for lay students in Boston. I have already put off the affair for three years, notwithstanding complaints from the public. It cannot be delayed any longer in justice to the persons who have contributed liberally to the building of the college in the hope of having their children educated by Ours or on grounds of prudence as our honor and reputation would be compromised thereby. I have, therefore, with my provincial consultors, come to the conclusion to open the college next September, beginning with two elementary classes of grammar, and then, each year, as the students advance in Latin and Greek, adding a class so as to build up step by step a complete college. I will shortly send your Paternity a *terna* [list of three nominees] for the Rector or Vice-Rector of this new college as you will think best.[2]

This prospect of opening the College within a few months was held out as an inducement to liberality at the fair,[3] and, as we have seen, it had its effect.

In August the Boston papers carried the definite announcement that the College would open its doors for the youth of the city:

BOSTON COLLEGE

The Benefactors and Friends of this Institution are respectfully informed that it will be opened September next. For further particulars, please apply at the College, Harrison Avenue.[4]

In *The Pilot* for August 27, 1864, the following advertisement appeared and was reprinted without change every week for the entire year, 1864–1865:

A.M.D.G.

ON THE FIRST MONDAY OF SEPTEMBER THE FATHERS OF THE SOCIETY OF JESUS will open, for the reception of Scholars the lower classes of Collegiate Instruction, the building adjoining THE CHURCH OF THE IMMACULATE CONCEPTION, Harrison Avenue, between Concord and Newton Streets. It is their intention to add a higher class each successive year, until the course of studies is complete.

The course of studies as in other Catholic Colleges, will last seven years, and embrace the English, Latin, and Greek languages, Arithmetic, Mathematics, Logic, Metaphysics, Ethics, Natural Philosophy and Chemistry, with the usual accessories.

The chief aim of the College is to educate the pupils in the principles & practice of the Catholic Faith; but the profession of that Religion will not be a necessary condition for admission.

It will be required of the Candidate for admission that he should be able to read & write, that he should understand the primary principles of Grammar and Arithmetic, and be of reputable character.

The Instructors have been selected from those who have already taught in other Colleges with success.

Terms: $30 for each session of about five months, to be paid in advance.

Should any student leave school in the course of a session, no deduction of price will be made in his favor, except in the case of expulsion.[5]

The above advertisement constitutes, as far as is known, the only prospectus issued by the College that year. It evoked the following editorial comment in *The Pilot,* after a paragraph calling attention to the opening:

Felix Faustumque sit!

Let us look at some of the advantages to be anticipated from this event. We need not argue the necessity of combining religious training with secular instruction. That point is decided. . . . But with what security shall we not confide our children to the Jesuit Fathers!

From the experience of a like Institution in a neighboring city, we anticipate that Boston College will be a fruitful seminary whence will issue in crowds youthful Levites to replenish the ranks of the secular clergy and the various religious orders.

But we need not only priests, but thoroughly educated lawyers, doctors, merchants—men of every profession. When our lads shall have thus been educated in common, we may expect that they will be welded together by common recollections, sympathies and life long friendships. They will be the better able to support each other in good, and advance the interests of the whole Catholic body.

Nor will it be an insignificant benefit that a larger number of priests will be resident among us, who will assist our clergy, at present so much overtaxed in the duties of the confessional and in instructing the people and will add by their very number to the splendor of religious ceremonies.

We invoke, therefore, for the nascent college, the zealous patronage of those who are interested in the advancement of religion and learning.[6]

The College Is Opened

Father Robert Fulton, who had been assisting in the work of the church, was assigned by the Provincial as the first prefect of studies for the new college. Father Fulton was born in Alexandria, Virginia, June 28, 1826.[7] His forebears on his father's side were Irish Presbyterians; on his mother's side they were Catholic O'Briens from County Clare. Robert served for four years as a page in the United States Senate, where he heard the orations of Webster, Clay, and Calhoun. Hoping to win an appointment to West Point, he enrolled in Georgetown College for preparatory studies, and while there felt the call to be a Jesuit. He became a novice in the Society of Jesus on August 31, 1843. As a scholastic (seminarian) he taught at Georgetown, Holy Cross, and several other Jesuit institutions. He was ordained a priest on July 25, 1857.[8]

The teachers designated to aid him in Boston were two scholastics, Mr. Peter P. Fitzpatrick, S.J., with five years' classroom experience, and Mr. James Doonan, S.J., with four years' experience, who were appointed to teach second and third grammar, respectively.[9] All was in readiness on Monday morning, September 5, 1864, when the College officially opened its doors,[10] but the expected rush of students never materialized:

> Father Fulton was dismayed to find that instead of an army of students that he had expected to see thronging through the gates of the new college . . . there were only 22 boys whose parents were eager to bestow upon them the advantages of a Jesuit education. This, however, was not due to any unfriend-liness; but, in those days, the Catholics of Boston were mostly poor, and were not overanxious to pay for what could be had for nothing in the schools and academies of the city. Moreover, they shared in the common superstition that nothing superior to the education of the public schools of New England had as yet been discovered.[11]

Of the number that did come, Father Fulton dourly observed in his diary, "Many came gratuitously, and only one or two had talent."[12] Yet a reporter

Rev. Robert Fulton, S.J., first dean and twice president of Boston College. For over 18 years, between 1864 and 1891, he shaped the academic standards and style of the College.

for *The Pilot* who visited the school after it had been in operation a few weeks saw a brighter picture:

> Father Bapst has the gratification of seeing at length the College which he has labored so hard to complete in progress. We visited the Institution last week, and were pleased to see the advancement already made. Classes have been organized, and the various members are becoming familiarized with the daily routine. Second Humanities is the highest department this year, and from it the other classes descend in order to Rudiments, where the little beginner is introduced with proud anxiety to the mysterious pages of the Viri Romae, and views the long highway of classics. . . . Thirty-two students comprise their total number at present but the good Fathers expect this little body will be augmented before long. Catholics & our fellow-citizens of other denominations should take the opportunity afforded to giving their children a classical education. The Jesuit Fathers are world-renowned instructors of youth, and many of our most intellectual men have owed their successes to the early training of the Society.[13]

Applicants continued to appear singly throughout the fall months, and by January 1 an additional 24 students were entered on the College register.[14] And 16 more had signed up before the close of classes in June. Unfortunately, about 25 percent of this number did not persevere after entering, so a notation in Father Fulton's handwriting in the College register, evidently written in June 1865, states: "Closed the First Year with Forty-eight (48) students. Sixty-two entered."[15]

Daniel M. C. McAvoy, the first student to register when the College opened in September 1864.

The time order for this first year is also found in this register, written in Father Fulton's hand:

8:30 a.m.	*Mass*
9–10:45	*Latin*
10:45–11:00	*Recess*
11:00	*Greek*
12:00	*Recess*
12:30	*Mathematics*
1:30	*French*
2:30	*End of classes*

(On Saturdays classes terminated at 1:30 p.m.)

A weekly report was read on Mondays at 11:45, evidently to each class by its own teacher, with a formal reading of marks before the whole school on the first day of every month.

Some of the textbooks used in the class of second rudiments in the opening year are preserved in the Boston College Library. The Latin composition book is Andrews,[16] written somewhat on the lines of the Bradley-Arnold Latin exercise text which was known to generations of English schoolboys. There does not appear to be very much gradation in the exercises, and little or no effort was made to emphasize the more important points or to minimize or exclude the less important ones. It would unquestionably be a difficult book for eighth-grade or first-year high school pupils and would make heavy demands on the teacher's skill. An examination of it raises one's esteem for the early scholars who used it. Judging by the inscription written by the owner on the flyleaf, the text was also used through third humanities (equivalent to third-year high).

The Initial Exhibition

As the termination of the first school year approached, Fathers Bapst and Fulton found themselves confronted with many problems, foremost among which was the task of arranging a creditable "exhibition," as the commencement exercises were then called. In May Father Bapst wrote the Provincial in tones reflecting his desperation at the difficulties which surrounded him:

> Fr. Fulton has just been with me in reference to the Exhibition to be given at the Commencement. It is necessary that it should be something creditable, as it is the only efficient recommendation we can offer to the public, in favor of our schools. There is hardly a secular priest who will say a good word on our behalf, but great many will be disposed to say a bad word against us; & yet

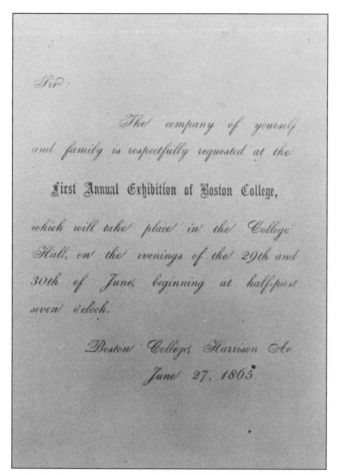

Sir:

The company of yourself
and family is respectfully requested at the

First Annual Exhibition of Boston College,

which will take place in the College
Hall, on the evenings of the 29th and
30th of June, beginning at half-past
seven o'clock.

Boston College, Harrison Av.
June 27, 1865.

*Invitation to the "exhibition" of
student accomplishments at the end
of Boston College's first academic
year, 1864–1865.*

the parents are generally influenced by their pastors as to what college they should send their boys. Therefore a great deal depends on that first exhibition at Boston College; by it we shall be judged.

This year, instead of diminishing the debt, we have added to it; & as the Bishop is going to begin his buildings at once & will not stop raising money for four or five years (a great damper on all fairs and collections for our church), our prospects for collecting money are very slim. The only way left us, is to increase the number of our Scholars, which cannot be done except by making the college popular and attractive. And besides strong studies & a good government, I don't see anything calculated to popularize our schools but some brilliant exhibition, & for the present nothing else seems available but a drama such as I have proposed. If it cannot be permitted now, it can never be permitted. In the present circumstances, I hope your Rev'ce will oppose no objection to it. We are discouraged enough already, it would be dangerous to increase our discouragement, although certainly we shall submit to your decision, no matter what the consequences may be.[17]

Such an appeal could hardly be refused, and so, when the following invitation was sent out in June, it was to attend a two-part exhibition as Father Fulton had wished:

Sir:

The company of yourself and family is respectfully requested at the FIRST ANNUAL EXHIBITION OF BOSTON COLLEGE which will take place in the College Hall, on the evenings of the 29th and 30th of June, beginning at half-past seven o'clock.

Boston College, Harrison Av.
June 27, 1865[18]

EXAMINATION AND EXHIBITION

OF

BOSTON COLLEGE,

THURSDAY, JUNE 29, 1865.

MUSIC.

EXAMINATION.

The matter assigned for the various classes, is as follows:

For the third class of Humanities, Nepos, Phædrus, Græca Minora, Latin and Greek Grammars.

For the first division of Rudiments, Viri Romæ, Latin and Greek Grammars.

For the second division of Rudiments, Geography, Latin Grammar.

For the third division of Rudiments, Geography, Spelling.

MUSIC.

DECLAMATION.

THE SCHOOL-BOY, ... Thos. J. Ford.
CORIOLANUS, ... Francis Norris.
HILDEBRAND, ... Vincent Laforme.
MUSIC, ... Geo. W. Lennon.
DUTIES OF PATRIOTISM, . . Frank McAvoy.

MUSIC.

Program of the first day of the exhibition at the end of the school year in 1865. The tests for the participants were of a somewhat elementary nature because few were of college age.

The exhibition consisted in a public examination of the pupils on the first day and a sacred drama, "Joseph and His Brethren," on the second. A reporter from *The Pilot* commented that the unostentatious opening of the College the preceding autumn had not prepared the public for the impressive manner in which the institution closed its first school year. According to this account, Father Fulton opened his remarks on the evening of the exhibition with an apology for the exercises which were to be presented. He enumerated the handicaps under which the school operated, among which were the small number of students and the fact that these boys were enrolled in the very lowest grades. Because of these considerations, he asked the audience's indulgence in judging the quality of the exhibition. But *The Pilot* critic recorded that the ensuing exercises were so excellently done that the audience considered the prefatory apology unnecessary.

On the second night, in addition to the play, there were selections by the Germania Band and the College choir and the award of premiums, with the venerable Father McElroy, as guest of the evening, presenting the silver crosses and books to the successful students. In passing, it might be noted that the list of prizes that night must have proved encouraging even to the lowliest pupil, since a count of the awards reveals that 64 were distributed among a student body of 48! In the summarizing judgment of the newspaperman, these first commencement exercises had "proved [the College's] claims on the patronage of a discriminating public."[19]

Father Bapst sent copies of the program to the Provincial on July 7, with the report that "our Examination and Exhibition . . . were certainly a success."[20] He continued:

> How many boys will we have next September, time will tell. [sic.] We ought to have at least one hundred paying boys, & then all will be right. But I have been so often deceived in my prophecies, that I prefer to wait until the schools open again to tell how many boys we shall have.
>
> Our Professors have well merited of Boston College. They have more than fulfilled their duties, they have done [a] great many works of supererogation, & they have been successful in all. But above all my thanks & gratitude are due to the Prefect of Schools, who has taken the great interest in them & made extraordinary exertions to put the college on such a footing as to insure its successful working. Without him Boston College would not get along. He is the man for Boston College.[21]

*   *   *

Thus the first year ended successfully despite very limited resources and a very limited response from the Catholics of Boston. The new school figured so little in the Catholic life of the city that not a single mention of the institution occurred in the pages of the quasi-diocesan paper from the reports on October 1 of its opening until the notice of its closing for the term in the July 8 issue. Three teachers and 48 pupils! But it was a beginning with credit, and the stouthearted little staff could now draw deep breaths of satisfaction and relief and look forward with renewed courage to the first Monday in September.

ENDNOTES

1. McElroy to Beckx, November 30, 1863, quoted in Gilbert J. Garraghan, S.J., "Origins of Boston College, 1842–1869," *Thought*, 17:651, December 1942. In this letter Father McElroy expressed the optimistic opinion that the College would "add considerable to the revenue of the house."

2. Paresce to Beckx, February 22, 1864, Jesuit General Archives in Rome, Maryland, 10-1-2, translated from the Latin and quoted by Garraghan, "Origins," p. 653.

3. Fulton, Diary, under date 1864.

4. Advertisement appearing in the *Boston Evening Transcript,* August 18, 1864, p. 1; and in *The Pilot* (August 20, 1864), p. 5.

5. *The Pilot* (August 27, 1864). *The Pilot* is preserved in the library of St. John's Seminary, Brighton. The *Transcript* mentioned above is preserved in the Boston College Library.

6. *The Pilot* (August 27, 1864).

7. This brief sketch of Father Fulton's life is based upon the autobiography contained in the first pages of his diary, a manuscript volume preserved in the Georgetown University Archives, Washington, D.C.

8. *Ibid.*

9. Catalogus Provinciae Marylandiae, S.J., ineunte anno 1865.

10. A valedictory delivered by Stephen J. Hart, June 28, 1877, transcribed in Callanan, "Reminiscences," *The Stylus,* 13 (March 1899):167.

11. Devitt, "History of the Maryland–New York Province," *Woodstock Letters,* 64:405 (1935).

12. Fulton, Diary, under date 1864.

13. *The Pilot* (October 1, 1864).

14. Register of Students, MS., BCA.

15. *Ibid.*

16. E. A. Andrews, *Latin Exercises; Adapted to Andrews and Stoddard's Latin Grammar,* 20th ed., revised and corrected (Boston: Crocker and Brewster, 1860).

17. Bapst to Paresce, May 10, 1865, Maryland Provincial S.J. Archives, Georgetown University Library.

18. The invitation is preserved in the Georgetown University Archives, Washington, D.C.

19. *The Pilot* (July 8, 1865).

20. Bapst to Paresce, July 7, 1865, Maryland Provincial S.J. Archives, Georgetown University Library.

21. *Ibid.*

CHAPTER 6

Consolidating a Gain

During the summer of 1865, the College issued a "Circular to the Parents and Guardians of Youth in Boston and the Vicinity"[1] which presented the advantages of attendance at a Jesuit school. It drew attention to the interest instructors had in the spiritual welfare of their charges and dwelt on the value of a classical course. Yet, lest anyone think that Latin, Greek, and religion were the only subjects offered at the new institution, the circular indicated the time which had been devoted to other subjects during the scholastic year just ended. Mathematics, penmanship, music, and coordinated courses in geography and history extending over several years were mentioned. The study of English was described as of primary importance:

> . . . Lessons in English Grammar were frequent, compositions ordinarily exacted every week. [Moreover] two hours a week were given to French under the direction of Mr. De Frondat, whose merit as a teacher the Directors hold in high estimation. By a weekly and minute report, parents were kept apprised of the conduct and progress of the pupils.
>
> In September next, as was promised, a more advanced class in Latin, Greek, English, French, and Mathematics, and a class of book-keeping will be added to the course. . . . The Sciences will be taught in the graduating class.[2]

Toward the close of this circular the offer was made to sell scholarships in perpetuity at $1000 each. The proposition was not developed beyond the statement of the fact, which the writer sought to bring to the attention of "parishes, religious societies, or wealthy individuals, [who] may be desirous of educating, in this manner, candidates for the priesthood: or parents [who] may find it for their interest to provide thus for the instruction of a numerous family of children."[3]

The Pilot for September 9, 1865, described the plan as follows:

> On sending a son to college, instead of paying the regular pension each session, the parent will pay the above sum once for all. The son having been educated, another may succeed, or the scholarship may be sold forever, or for a term of years. If retained, it may descend to the heirs of the original purchaser, subject to conditions he may prescribe.[4]

Continuing in an editorial vein, the paper remarked:

> Parishes, or parish priests, have regarded it almost as a duty to contribute to the education of candidates for the ministry. It will be evident that according to the plan we are discussing, they would be able, at much less cost, to make permanent provision for the education of their own youth who aspire to Holy Orders.[5]

The editor goes on to urge generosity on the part of the wealthy, but as far as can be determined, the offer met with very little response. *The Pilot* two weeks later reported a Joseph Sinnott as "the first to exhibit his generosity and zeal for Catholic education in founding a scholarship, to which he has nominated Henry Towle, a lad who has distinguished himself

Boston College Hall, the auditorium of the original college building.

in the Dwight School."[6] Twenty-two years later, the College treasurer's books showed that only six paid scholarships had been established up to that time; one by a Mrs. Kramer; one by the above-mentioned Mr. Sinnott of Philadelphia; three by Mrs. Anna H. Ward, of 2 Washington Place, New York; and one by a Father Orr.[7]

A Growing Student Body

There was, however, a marked increase in the regular student registration on the opening day, September 4. Father Bapst found time at eleven o'clock that morning, in the midst of the excitement, to pen a short and enthusiastic "bulletin" to the Provincial:

> We have entered thus far the names of 70 students, which is considered a success; three only of our old pupils having failed to make their appearance. The teachers & Fr. Fulton are in good spirits.[8]

The Pilot reported that the College had reopened with the number of pupils nearly doubled.[9] Any effort to estimate the total enrollment for that year is frustrated by the system of registration in force at the time, which showed only the *new* pupils enrolled. Thus, it is clear that at the end of the first term 48 *new* boys had enrolled, and by June the number had risen to 59.[10] But what the *total* enrollment was, one can only guess, working with this number of new students and Father Bapst's remark quoted above, that all but three of last year's pupils had returned (viz., 45 had returned). This figure of 104 should certainly be corrected for numerous withdrawals, yet how many withdrawals there were can no longer be ascertained. Since this is the only year for which this information is not available, an estimate could be made based on the regularity of increment observed in the other years. Thus:[11]

1864	1865	1866	1867	1868	1869	1870
48	?	81	100	114	130	140

The average gain for the latter five years is approximately 15 pupils a year; subtracting this number from the 81 (in 1866), we would have an estimated enrollment for 1865 of 66. As deflating and as contradictory as this figure seems, it receives at least some support from an ambiguous statement penciled under the final entry for this year in the College register: "Closed with upwards of sixty."[12]

The teaching staff, in anticipation of an enlarged student body, had meanwhile been increased to eight. This included four scholastics who were full-time teachers (Messrs. Peter P. Fitzpatrick, S.J., Michael Byrnes, S.J., James Doonan, S.J., and William Carroll, S.J.), all of whom taught Latin, Greek, English, and arithmetic; one priest (Fr. John Sumner, S.J., the College treasurer), who taught a part-time course in bookkeeping; and

The College gymnasium of the 19th century.

two part-time lay teachers, Mr. De Frondat, for French, and Dr. Willcox, for music; and the prefect of studies, Father Fulton, S.J.[13]

Boston College Life in the 1860s

A glimpse into the school life of that second year of Boston College is permitted us in the recollections of Dr. Henry Towle, mentioned above as holder of the first scholarship granted at the College:

> In 1865 I entered Boston College as a pupil. It was the second year of its existence as a school. . . . Fifty scholars, ranging in years from twenty-six to eleven made up the entire membership. . . . Most of us were in the Second and Third Rudiments, under Mr. Doonan, and a few in Third Humanities, under Mr. Fitzpatrick. . . . The first pupils were of all shades of industry and idleness. In that crowd of fifty there were men and boys of varying degrees of scholarship. Some of the elder came for reformation of character; some were belated aspirants for Holy Orders, who had acquired a vocation late in life; and with these were mingled boys just removed from the lowest grammar classes. . . . So thorough was the weeding of pupils of 1865, that only two of our number reached the class of Rhetoric in 1871, where our college course terminated.
>
> It was in '66 that the true school life which characterized Boston College began. We had a large influx of boys from St. Mary's school and from other sections of the city, and the classes assumed definite shape and form. . . . Having no traditions we soon adopted those of our teachers, and our College heroes were old graduates of Georgetown and Loyola. I wonder whether we sympathized with the dead Confederacy so much, merely because so many of our scholastics came from Maryland and that vicinity. We had an impression that "Maryland, my Maryland," was written by a Georgetown boy, and

therefore infinitely preferred its sentiments to those of "Marching Through Georgia." As far as I can recall the aims and ideals of the boys around me, we wished to be like some southern worthy, whose wit and mirth we read in some old college class book, or to learn from some teacher who was his fellow student in youth.[14]

Once the new year began, the school settled into a smooth and efficient routine. Father Bapst wrote in October that, with the exception of financial affairs, "The college is going on pretty well. Fr. Fulton wishes me to say that the teachers are very docile with him and give satisfaction."[15] The poor state of the school's financial condition was due, in part at least, to the withdrawal of the annual contribution hitherto made by St. Mary's Church in the North End. Father Bapst protested this loss repeatedly and vigorously. In February he had outlined his position to the Provincial:

> I saw Fr. Brady [the Superior at St. Mary's], in relation to the $3,000 [which had been given annually for the support of the college]; although he has just realized $8,000 by his last fair, which closed last week, yet he does not seem to be inclined to do much more for Boston College. Until our schools bring in some revenues, above the expenses, it will be impossible for us to get along without the $3,000. The Bishop insists that St. Mary's was given to the Society for the sole purpose of enabling us to build a College, & that all the revenues should go to that object. A congregation of 20,000 souls ought to be able to yield at least a surplus of $3,000, with proper management, without interfering at all with its own requirements. I hope your Rev'ce will see to it.[16]

The precursor of Bapst and O'Neill.

Another Fair

Evidently no action was taken, since eight months later he reported that he would need another fair or some other extraordinary means of raising funds.[17] The idea of a second fair as a solution to the College's financial difficulties was acted on the following spring, and in May *The Pilot* carried the preliminary announcement:

GRAND FAIR

For Boston College and the Church of the Immaculate Conception

A Free Scholarship in perpetuity in Boston College is offered to every Table that returns one thousand dollars. Churches, Societies, and others, willing to take the responsibility of a Table, thereby securing to themselves and successors for all time, the great privilege of educating, free from all expense, some deserving Catholic boy, are requested to make immediate application to Father Bapst.

The fair commences in October next. Full particulars at an early day.[18]

Toward the close of June, the date of the opening and the place of the fair were published as October 15 in the famous Boston Music Hall.

Meanwhile, the academic officers of the College had inaugurated a custom which was destined to live for many decades: the awarding of monthly certificates (or, as they were then called, "tickets") for proficiency in studies. The first publication of these awards appeared in *The Pilot* for May 12, 1866,[19] and thereafter this monthly listing in the "public press" became one of the great inducements to academic effort.[20]

On the evenings of July 2 and 3, 1866, the second annual examination and exhibition (commencement) were held in the College hall. The program on the first evening consisted of examinations of the second and third classes of humanities, the first and second divisions of rudiments; declamation; and music by the Germania Band. The declamation exercises were two: "Peace," recited by John Lane, and a satire written by Theobald Murphy and delivered by John McLaughlin and Terence Quinn, which was described by a reviewer for *The Pilot* as "full of point and fun."[21] The ceremonies of the second night were featured by a sacred drama entitled "Sedecias," with George W. Lennon in the title role, H. R. O'Donnell as Nebuchodonosor, and Daniel McAvoy (the college's proto-student) as Jeremias.[22] In the awarding of premiums which followed, 87 medals and "accesserunt" distinctions were announced and the 20 other pupils were named for "honorable mention." *The Pilot* representative commented:

The exhibition during the two evenings has added not a little to the good reputation of the College. The College at this present time has about seventy-five pupils, and is in a flourishing and progressive condition.[23]

When the College opened for the fall term, an extension of its facilities was made to provide in a rudimentary way for adult education. A library

The students' gaslit recreation room.

of 1000 books was established in the basement of the adjoining Immaculate Conception Church, and the room was equipped to serve as a *quasi* club for the Catholic young men of the city.[24] The membership fee was one dollar a year. In the course of time, lectures were given before the group and various activities sponsored by it, all of which prepared the ground for the later founding of the Young Men's Catholic Association by Father Fulton.

But the main concern of all associated with the College at this time was the second fair. This great event was opened to the public on Monday evening, October 15, 1866, at the Boston Music Hall, and continued daily thereafter from eleven in the morning until ten at night for three weeks.[25] The management had promised that this fair would be the most attractive and successful ever held in the city,[26] and if one can believe the enthusiastic notices which the affair received in the newspapers, it really lived up to its advance publicity. *The Pilot* pronounced it "a great success . . . elegant decorations . . . this one surpasses them all."[27]

When Gilmore's Band, one of the most popular musical organizations in the United States during the sixties, and the other features of the fair kept drawing crowds to the Music Hall without any appreciable falling off in attendance for the full length of the original engagement, it was decided to continue the fair for an additional week at the College hall after the closing of the Music Hall on November 23.[28] This was evidently done with satisfactory results, because Father Fulton records in his diary that the net proceeds rose to $30,728 and that his own table brought in some $4,600,[29] all of which constituted a new record for Catholic fairs.

On November 28 a complimentary dinner for the fair committee was given in the College,[30] and it was perhaps on that occasion that the founding of 18 scholarships in honor of those table sponsors who realized sums over

$1,000 at the fair was announced. The ledger in which the names of these patrons were recorded in the treasurer's office contains the following annotation evidently written at the time:

> Though the Patrons of the Fair Scholarships have a right to appoint to the places, Fr. Fulton, who directed the appointment of scholarships to them, for services rendered at the Fair, desired that the President of the College should see that they were given judiciously, i.e., to such as are brilliant, etc.[31]

In Father Fulton's opinion, "the free scholarships instituted after the Fair gave the first impulse and first ability to the College."[32]

*   *   *

Father Bapst and Father Fulton, president and prefect, constituted a remarkably able administration for the infant college. Fortunately they remained a team for the duration of Father Bapst's presidency.

ENDNOTES

1. Woodstock College Archives, Georgetown University Library.
2. *Ibid.*
3. *Ibid.*
4. *The Pilot* (September 9, 1865).
5. *Ibid.*
6. *Ibid.* (September 23, 1865).
7. BCA.
8. Bapst to Paresce, September 4, 1865, Maryland Provincial S.J. Archives, Georgetown University Library.
9. *The Pilot* (September 23, 1865).
10. Manuscript volume: "Register of Students," BCA.
11. Based upon a chart giving a summary of statistics concerning Boston College drawn up for the Provincial, apparently about 1882, Maryland Provincial S.J. Archives, Georgetown University Library.
12. Manuscript volume: "Register of Students," BCA.
13. *Catalogus Provinciae Marylandiae S.J., ineunte anno 1886, s.v.* "Collegium Bostoniense Inchoatum," and *The Pilot* (October 7, 1865).
14. Henry C. Towle, "The Pioneer Days at Boston College," *The Stylus*, 11 (June 1897):332–338.
15. Bapst to Paresce, October 11, 1865, Maryland Provincial S.J. Archives, Georgetown University Library.
16. Bapst to Paresce, February 8, 1865, Maryland Provincial S.J. Archives, Georgetown University Library.
17. Bapst to Paresce, October 11, 1865, Maryland Provincial S.J. Archives, Georgetown University Library.
18. *The Pilot* (May 26 and June 2, 1866).
19. *Ibid.* (May 12, 1866).
20. Cf. "Catalogue of the Officers and Students of Boston College for the Academic Year 1868–9" (first catalogue issued), p. 10: ". . . those who . . . are marked above a fixed number (usually about ninety or ninety-five), are rewarded with tickets, and the award is published in the Boston *Pilot*."
21. *The Pilot* (July 14, 1866).

22. *Ibid.* Other parts in the play were: T. G. Devenny as Elmero; T. J. Ford as Josias; J. Kenneely as Manassas; J. Baron as Rapsaris; A. Maher as Araxhes; John Eichorn and Joseph Finotti as youngest sons of Sedecias.
23. *Ibid.*
24. *Ibid.* (October 13, 1866).
25. *Ibid.*
26. *Ibid.* (October 20, 1866).
27. *Ibid.* (October 27, 1866); cf. also issue of November 3, 1866.
28. From a manuscript diary of the Immaculate Conception Church Sunday School, preserved in the Maryland Provincial S.J. Archives, Georgetown University Library.
29. Manuscript diary of Fr. Robert Fulton, S.J., under date "1866," preserved in Georgetown University Archives.
30. Immaculate Conception Sunday School Diary.
31. "Boston College Students' Accounts . . . 1879–1887."
32. Fulton, Diary, under date "1886."

CHAPTER 7

The Letter of the Law

In the summer of 1869 the first *Catalogue of the Officers and Students of Boston College* appeared, with a report on the academic year 1868–1869.[1] In this publication the tuition is announced as $30 a semester, payable in advance. The catalog states, however, that "provision is made for the instruction of indigent, but meritorious candidates, who should present their claims for admission before the commencement of the session."

The requirements for admission were "a good moral character, and a knowledge of the fundamental principles of Arithmetic and Grammar." In stating that the academic year contained two sessions, beginning on the first Monday in September and on the first Monday in February respectively, the catalog added, "but students are not precluded from entering at any time during the year."

Rules and Regulations

The hours of attendance were from half-past eight in the morning until half-past two in the afternoon, "with recesses at convenient intervals." Classes on Saturdays terminated at one o'clock. One hour a day was devoted to arithmetic and two hours a week to modern language, with the balance of the day given to Latin, Greek, and English.

In contrast to Holy Cross College, the charter of which made it an exclusively Catholic college, Boston College had an act of incorporation which provided that "no student in said college shall be refused admission to, or denied any of the privileges, honors or degrees of said college on account of the religious opinions he may entertain." This passage was quoted in the catalog with the comment, "Students that are not Catholics will not be required to participate in any exercise distinctively Catholic; nor will any undue influence be used to induce a change of religious belief."[2] However, Catholic students were required:

> ... to hear Mass every day, unless distance of residence should furnish reason for exemption; to recite the daily catechetical lesson; to attend the weekly lecture on the doctrines of the Church, and the annual retreat; to present themselves to their confessor every month; and, if they have never received the Sacraments of Penance, Confirmation or Holy Eucharist, to prepare for their reception.[3]

The educational background of new students varied so much that special arrangements frequently had to be made to accommodate them. On admission, the student was examined to determine the classes to which he should be assigned, and he was told that the rate of subsequent progress depended upon his own ability and diligence. The catalog warned that a pupil's general deficiency in preparation might cause him to be detained more than one year with the lowest class, and that a pupil's weakness in a specific subject might result in his pursuing that study in a lower grade than his regular classes.[4] The method of marking employed at that period was explained in the catalog:

> At the end of each recitation, its quality is recorded. Six is the highest number of marks given for a written exercise; four, for a translation or analysis; two, for any other exercise, and the same number for punctuality and good-conduct; the number being diminished by one for every fault. A copy of this record ... is furnished the parents every week.
>
>   At the end of each session an examination is held for all that was studied during the session. A separate examiner is assigned to each class. The examination is conducted in writing and lasts for about two weeks.[5]

At the annual exhibitions, according to this announcement, distinctions of three degrees were conferred. In addition, annual prizes were instituted of $50 in gold for the best English composition, $25 in gold for excellence in reading, and the same amount for excellence in declamation.

The detention period after school for minor infractions of rules, known to generations of Jesuit school pupils as "jug," was a regular institution at Boston College at this time. The catalog stated:

> For faults of ordinary occurrence—such as tardy arrival, failure in recitations, or minor instances of misconduct—a task, consisting of lines from some classical author, is committed to memory during the hour after the close of school.[6]

The advantages of the College library are briefly mentioned. It appears that a "trifling expense" was connected with the use of books by the pupils; this, in a very elementary way, corresponded to the "library fee" charged by most modern colleges.

Expansion in other directions was indicated summarily: "The liberality of a friend has already furnished a collection of minerals. A gymnasium has been begun, and an ample cabinet of philosophical instruments will be in readiness for the graduating class."[7]

Among the "activities" listed in the back of the catalog one finds first place accorded to the Sodality of the Immaculate Conception. Forty-one pupils were named as attending the sodality meetings, at which the Office of the Blessed Mother was recited in Latin and exhortations were delivered.

The Society of St. Cecilia, which boasted 39 members, supplied the music at the daily Mass and gave "its aid, when needed, at celebrations, either of the College, or the Church of the Immaculate Conception."

There were 22 members of "The Debating Society of Boston College," who exercised themselves in dramatic reading, declamation, and extempo-

The first page of the first cata-
log issued by Boston College.

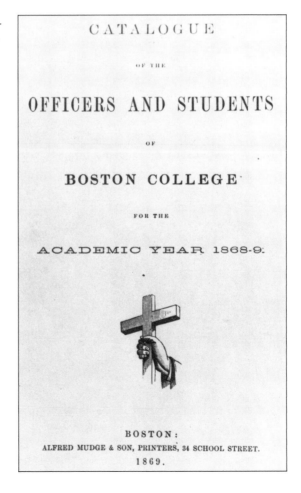

CATALOGUE

OF THE

OFFICERS AND STUDENTS

OF

BOSTON COLLEGE

FOR THE

ACADEMIC YEAR 1868-9.

BOSTON:
ALFRED MUDGE & SON, PRINTERS, 34 SCHOOL STREET.
1869.

raneous debate. Father Fulton was founder, director, and president of this organization, which today is proud to bear his name.

The catalog then listed the officers and teachers on the staff and gave a directory of the pupils and the classes to which they belonged. An official record of the Fifth Annual Exhibition, which was held on June 30, 1869, was given in full, together with a program for "Richard III," the closing play of that year. The last item in the catalog was a reproduction of a sample report card.

This very creditable catalog appears to be the exclusive work of Father Fulton. One gathers this from the remark which Father Fulton made in his diary to the effect that neither Father Bapst nor anyone else was permitted by the Provincial to have a voice in what pertained directly to the academic side of the school.[8] Father Fulton set high standards for the infant school and would not hear of the granting of the bachelor's degree until a certain maturity had been established. This was attested to by a Jesuit who taught under Fulton's leadership as dean. Father John Buckley wrote:

> About this time, in the year 1869, the question of a graduating class was mooted. Father Fulton would not hear of it, giving as his reason that the body was too weak yet to sustain the head. There could be no thought of such a thing until all the lower classes were strong and numerous enough to secure an unbroken succession. Eight more years [were to pass] by before the college attained her majority.[9]

It was not until 1877, when Fulton was president, that the College produced its first graduates.

The Appointment of a Successor

Because Father Fulton was so intimately a part of Boston College, one can understand the surprise felt by many that he was not selected as rector when Father Bapst announced his retirement from that office to become Superior of the New York–Canada Mission in August of 1869. Even Father Bapst was surprised, and on the night before he left for New York (that is, August 23), he wrote to the General of the Society in Rome to report that he himself, who could be presumed best acquainted with the situation in Boston, had not been consulted on the question of a successor. If he had been, he wrote, he would have suggested Father Fulton, to whom in a large measure the success of the College up to that time had been due.[10] He wrote:

> Boston College, despite serious obstacles in the way, seems now to enjoy a success beyond all expectations and to hold out great hopes for the future. Moreover, our church, as all admit, has dissipated many prejudices among non-Catholics, raised the religious spirit to a higher level and already brought not a few into the bosom of the Church. To whom are these things due? In great measure to Father Fulton. None of Ours is gifted with talents of a

REV. ROBERT W. BRADY, S.J.
Second President

Father Brady was born on October 6, 1825, in Hancock, Maryland. He attended St. John's College in Frederick City, Maryland, at a time when Father John McElroy headed it. He entered the Society of Jesus on August 31, 1844, and, before ordination, taught at Holy Cross College. After ordination he was assigned to St. Mary's Church in the North End of Boston and became superior there. In February 1867 he was named president of Holy Cross College, where he remained until he was appointed president of Boston College on August 27, 1869.[11]

---

higher order. None enjoys so much authority among the leading citizens of the town. Our most outstanding friends desire to have him for rector of Boston College, and, in truth, all things considered, he appears to be the worthiest, the fittest for the post.[12]

From this it should not be concluded that the priest selected to be second president of Boston College, Father Robert Wasson Brady, S.J., was not eminently suited to the position. He was a man of outstanding ability and winning personality,[13] who already had broad executive experience and who was destined to fill very high positions in the government of the Society of Jesus.

Father Bapst Leaves Boston College

During Father Bapst's farewell address to the congregation of the Immaculate Conception Church on Sunday, August 15, 1869, he took occasion to review his long connection with the church and the College.[14] The church, he recalled, was burdened with a debt of $156,000 when he assumed the duties of pastor some six years before, but he was able gradually to reduce this to $58,000. He thanked the congregation and friends of the College for making this possible and expressed the hope that their efforts would continue to be as effective as they had hitherto been, because a debt of

$18,000 had to be met during the coming year. He then announced that an offer of a gift had been made to reduce this debt by $10,000 on the condition that the congregation raise a like amount. The offer was made by the family of one of his fellow Jesuits, Father Edward Holker Welch, who was an assistant parish priest at the Immaculate Conception Church. Father Welch was a Harvard graduate and a scion of a wealthy Boston family; he had been converted to the Catholic faith with his classmate and dearest friend, Joseph Coolidge Shaw, who also became a priest and Jesuit.[15] The social prominence of the donor and the nature of the appeal for the balance, which *The Pilot* urged "as the last call he [Father Bapst] shall ever make on their generosity,"[16] sufficed to interest Catholic Boston in the cause.

The Pilot, two weeks later, made public a proposal to raise the money before Christmas by popular subscription and to present the check to Father Bapst, together with a testimonial letter and a list of the donors, on Christmas, so that he might have the honor and consolation of personally paying off the debt.[17] This tribute was to take the place of a parting gift, which Father Bapst had steadfastly refused. Upon Father Fulton fell the onerous duties of treasurer and promoter of the drive, and he undertook them with a zest which showed the great affection in which he held his former rector. In his diary, Father Fulton recorded that he was able to collect upwards of $11,000.[18]

Father Bapst's gratitude for this heart-touching "Christmas present" was expressed in the letter to the president and trustees of Boston College which accompanied the check for $20,000. After formally remitting the

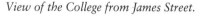

View of the College from James Street.

money and offering his thanks to Fathers Welch and Fulton and to all who had assisted, he observed that the sum would:

> ... enable you to meet the two notes which become due this year. Moreover, the enormous debt, which six years ago threatened the very existence of Boston College, is now reduced to thirty-eight thousand dollars; which leaves before you prospects so bright as to exceed all expectations.

He closed by saying that he was particularly consoled to find the names of many non-Catholics on the list of contributors, and expressed himself as deeply pleased that the act which terminated his long and happy association with the congregation of the Immaculate Conception should be connected with the reduction of the church debt.[19]

The opening of school for the term which saw Father Brady as president brought 59 new students to the college on Harrison Avenue, making a total of 130.[20]

The College as Beginners Knew It

Some impressions of Boston College as it appeared in 1869[21] are preserved in the "Reminiscences" of Patrick H. Callanan, who wrote:

> I remember well the old college building, with its brick-paved court-yard, its wooden fences to shut out all view of the church on the one side, and the greensward towards Newton Street on the other. I remember the high brick wall and the stone steps, and the iron gate that shut us *in* or *out,* as the case might be, from Concord Street. We old fellows remember the gymnasium, consisting of two upright posts with a crosspiece between, from which hung one pair of swinging rings and a trapeze. In addition to the swinging rings and trapeze, we had a set of parallel bars, and these three contrivances constituted the whole college gymnasium. ... It is a pity that no photographs of the original college buildings were ever taken or preserved. ... on the morning ... I entered college I was escorted ... to Father Fulton's door, to be assigned to ... classes. I came direct from New York State and from a very small town, where I had no chance for schooling, and I now confess that I did not know a verb from a noun. Well, Father Fulton took our names and put some questions to us, ... and after telling me that I was to go into some kind of a grade that was not yet established, as I did not know anything, we marched back through the old instruction hall, connecting both old college buildings, and we were finally landed in a room on the extreme northeast corner. I was distinctly told that I could not begin to study Latin that year, and perhaps not for two years, for which I was not sorry.[22]

It is interesting to learn from the official College register for September 13, 1869, that the Callanan boy was placed in the lowest form, second rudiments and second arithmetic, where he, at 15, would share benches with lads of 10 and 11.[23] And it is more interesting still to find that this boy from then on took almost every prize for which he was eligible and led in all extracurricular activities, despite his initial handicap. In afterlife he became the first Boston College graduate to be named a pastor in any diocese.[24]

*   *   *

Time was running out, meanwhile, on Father Brady's brief term in office. It seems probable, as Devitt thought,[25] that the appointment was, in its original concept, temporary—a view supported by an enumeration of the subsequent posts held by Father Brady. In any case, he left Boston College on August 2, 1870, and returned to St. Mary's Church, Boston, where, as superior, he built an impressive edifice and rectory. In 1877 he was appointed Provincial of the Maryland Province of the Society of Jesus and in 1886 selected for the high honor of representing his province at an important Jesuit conference in Rome.[26] He was succeeded in the presidency of Boston College by a man who was destined to hold that office for a total of some twelve years.

ENDNOTES

1. "Catalogue of the Officers and Students of Boston College for the Academic Year 1868–9" (Boston: Alfred Mudge and Son, 1869), 22 pp. The excerpts which follow in the text were taken *passim* from this publication.
2. *Ibid.*, p. 4.
3. *Ibid.*
4. *Ibid.*
5. *Ibid.*, p. 10.
6. *Ibid.*, p. 11.
7. *Ibid.*
8. Fulton, Diary, under date 1869.
9. J. Buckley, S.J., "Father Robert Fulton; a Sketch," *Woodstock Letters,* 25(1896):96–108.
10. Fulton, Diary, under date 1869.
11. J. Morgan, S.J., "Father Robert Wasson Brady, S.J.; a Sketch," *Woodstock Letters,* 20(1891):250–255.
12. Bapst to Beckx, August 23, 1869, Jesuit General Archives in Rome, Maryland, 10(?)-I-48, translated from the Latin and quoted by Garraghan, "Origins of Boston College," *Thought,* 17(1942):655.
13. Callanan, "Reminiscences," *The Stylus,* 12(1898):78, describing Father Brady as "much beloved" by the students.
14. *The Pilot* (August 28, 1869).
15. *Woodstock Letters,* 26(1897):446.
16. *The Pilot* (August 28, 1869).
17. *Ibid.* (September 11, 1869).
18. Fulton, Diary, under date 1869. At one meeting alone (November 17, 1869), $3,200 was subscribed (Sunday School Diary, Maryland Provincial S.J. Archives, s.v. "Boston," Georgetown University Library).
19. The letter dated New York, January 4, 1870, was published in *The Pilot* (January 22, 1870).

20. Statistical chart on faculty and students at Boston College prepared for the Provincial in 1885, Maryland Provincial S.J. Archives, Georgetown University Library.

21. Callanan gives the date of his entrance into the College as October 1870, but an examination of the official "College Register" shows that he entered September 13, 1869.

22. Patrick H. Callanan, "Reminiscences," *The Stylus,* 12(1898):9–10; 19–21.

23. Official College Register, under date 1869. BCA.

24. Callanan, *op. cit.,* p. 1.

25. Devitt, "The History of the Province, XVI, Boston College," *Woodstock Letters,* 64(1935):406.

26. Morgan, *op. cit.,* pp. 254–255.

CHAPTER 8

Prefect to President

During the summer of 1870, Father Fulton visited St. Louis. After his return, on August 2, he was notified of his appointment as vice rector and president of Boston College.[1] The title "vice rector," the same as that held by both Father Bapst and Father Brady, was employed instead of "rector" because the College was still technically "in the process of formation." The heading "Collegium Bostoniense Inchoatum" occurred in the official Jesuit catalog until the following year (1871–1872), when, for the first time, the simple title "Collegium Bostoniense" was employed and Father Fulton was listed as "rector."[2]

The elevation of Father Fulton to this post of distinction did not occasion any direct mention in the Catholic press, although a few weeks later an editorial urging support of the College took cognizance of the change. The editor of *The Pilot* wrote:

> The proximate opening of schools prompts us to say something of the institution which will soon be the only Catholic college in our diocese.[3]
> . . . That the College has done well is proved by the excellence of the public exhibitions, by the high places its students have gained on going to other institutions, and by the constant—though too slow—increase of numbers.
> . . . It is lawful to be taught by the enemy. Only see what exertions all the sects expend upon their institutions of learning. Let us imitate them, and aid in making our College a famous establishment.[4]

Father Fulton's part in making "our college a famous establishment" was an enormous amount of prosaic hard work. Four days after his appointment to the presidency, he wrote to a Jesuit official, in connection with a plea for additional help, an outline of his own duties:

> Father Fulton's duties during the coming year: All the ordinary duties of Rector, Procurator and Prefect of Schools; to supply for sick teachers and for Father Tuffer until he comes; to teach Rudiments till a teacher is provided. Besides confessions, sick-calls, and ordinary work of the congregation—to preach once a week in the lower chapel and to say that Mass; to preach at 10 once a month upstairs; once a week for the boys; once a week for each of two sodalities; and the Sunday School, & manage all, and the library, which takes much time; besides extraordinary preaching in the month of May, Lent, funeral sermons, & other business not to be enumerated. That is, more than the work which Fathers Brady & Fulton did last year. . . .[5]

A duty not mentioned above, but which took much of his time, was that of securing money to meet the debts of the College. When he became president the debt was $35,000, which he reduced by $11,000 his first year and by $10,000 in 1871.[6] He refers facetiously to his ability in this direction in a letter to the Province Procurator, written in May 1871, "I think you people who brag so much about being business men, must confess I have done well; for every copper has been of my own procuring, in 9 months, with extensive improvements going on."[7] The "extensive improvements" he explains elsewhere as "finishing the house and buying furniture for house and college."[8]

During Father Fulton's first term in office as president (August 2, 1870 to January 11, 1880), many innovations were introduced which directly or indirectly helped the young institution to assume a position of influence in the Catholic life of the city. Two of these deserve mention in some detail: the introduction of the Foster Cadets and the enlargement of the buildings and opening of the new College hall.

With Fife and Drum

The idea of having military drill at Boston College was evidently entertained by the authorities at least as early as Father Brady's administration (1869–1870), because in the catalog of that year the following notice appeared:

> The State authorities having granted a supply of arms, a drill master will be appointed, and due notice will be given as to the style of the uniform, and the time by which it must be procured.[9]

But it was not until October 1870 that the formation of a military company was announced by Father Fulton. Instrumental in bringing about the introduction of this training was Major General John Gray Foster, U.S.A.,

A Foster Cadet. Note the B.C. on the cap.

a popular hero of the Mexican and Civil wars who had recently been converted to Catholicism and at the time was engaged in engineering work in Boston.[10] In honor of this distinguished soldier, the group in the process of formation was called "The Foster Cadets."

The project was taken up enthusiastically by the students under the direction of the military instructor, Sergeant Louis E. Duval, a regular in the United States Army stationed at Fort Warren in Boston Harbor.[11]

> In the beginning all of the boys seemed to be enthusiastic at the innovation. We had no gymnasium, no playground, no foot-ball team, no opportunity, in fact, for anything in the line of athletics except an occasional base-ball game.[12]

Drill was compulsory for all except those who could produce a request for exemption signed by a physician. As time went by, the boys began to discover that drill was both an exacting and an exhausting exercise.[13] After considerable discussion among the students, a simple and inexpensive Civil War style uniform was settled upon, and the school catalog of 1870–1871 announced that "henceforth it will be of obligation to procure the College uniform."[14] Father Fulton immediately found serious trouble in enforcing the rule, and it soon became known that a number of the boys in the higher classes refused to comply.

The reasons were understandable. First of all, the students were almost without exception from families that were not financially well off; in addition to this, there were no philosophy classes in prospect; consequently, they would have to terminate their course or transfer to another college at the end of the school year (in rhetoric). This latter situation was a bitter disappointment to many who had thought—with or without encouragement from the College authorities—that when sufficient numbers finally arrived in the class of rhetoric, philosophy would be added to the course the following year in order that they might obtain their degrees from Boston College.[15]

When an issue was made of uniforms, large numbers simply dropped out of school. September 1871 presented a school opening that was a sad spectacle. The entire rhetoric and poetry classes failed to come back to the College; with them went almost all the members of the class of first humanities. The movement away from Boston College in the lower classes was described as "a regular stampede."[16]

Nonetheless, Father Fulton persevered in his determination to have a uniformed military company. The last hour of the school session on Tuesdays and Fridays was devoted, as usual, to drill, but this season saw a new drillmaster. The new faculty director of the military program, Mr. John J. Murphy, S.J., to whom the future growth and excellence of the Foster Cadets was due, arranged to have one of the most famous drillmasters in the United States, Captain George Mullins of the Montgomery Light Guard (Company "I," 9th Regiment), take charge of the Boston College cadets. This rekindled the enthusiasm of the student body, and the boys' interest was further heightened by the receipt of a full supply of guns, belts, knapsacks, and bayonet scabbards which had been sent down from Springfield through the kind offices of the governor of the commonwealth.[17]

The young lads who were forced by circumstances to take over the various official posts in the organization did their part so well and the rank and file became so skillful in the role of soldiers that they were emboldened to challenge the champion school of the City of Boston to a prize drill in the old Boston Theater. The challenge was refused by the school committee, but the interest of the city in these Catholic cadets had been aroused, and the boys' own self-confidence had been established. The result was a well-attended and brilliantly executed prize drill between two companies forming the Foster Cadets battalion. This took place in the College hall on June 15, 1872, before a board of judges consisting of General P. R. Guiney and Colonel B. F. Finan.[18]

For several years the streets in the vicinity of the College echoed to the music of fife and drum as the cadets marched here and there through the section, and on March 17, 1875, the Foster Cadets had a place of honor among some 900 parish cadets marching in the St. Patrick's Day parade. In the year 1876 Patrick H. Callanan, a student, was appointed drillmaster—a position which he held until his graduation in 1877. In the meantime, other interests occupied the attention of Father Fulton, with the result that he allowed the military program to receive less and less emphasis, until it was finally discontinued.[19]

A Program of Enlargement

During the period which witnessed the peace jubilee in the summer of 1872, the great Boston fire the following November, and the huge loss of life in the wreck of the *Atlantic* in the spring of 1873, the routine events at Boston College rarely made the newspapers. Nevertheless, the institution was growing slowly and sturdily, and the need was already felt for more room. As early as the summer of 1873, a proposal was voiced to extend the buildings and provide better facilities for the higher studies.[20] The following year the annual exhibition had to be canceled and the distribution of premiums made privately, because the program of alterations—already under way—prevented the use of the hall.[21]

The College authorities were able to announce in September that "the improvements of Boston College have advanced so prosperously that there will be no impediment to the opening of school at the usual time."[22] And when the registration opened that fall, 150 boys reported, a gain of 25 over the year before, as if to demonstrate the need for the expansion.[23] A writer on *The Pilot* estimated that "when the great building on St. [sic] James Street is finished, twice the number can be accommodated."[24]

The spectacular part of the alterations consisted in moving the rear building (the college proper) back to the sidewalk on James Street. To the delight of onlookers in the neighborhood, the large brick structure was shored up, placed on rollers, then painstakingly propelled backward by microscopic degrees, as a legion of workmen twisted a legion of jacks a quarter of a turn at a time to the beat of a drum.[25] Since the lower chapel in the church occupied only one-half the length of that building at the time, the balance of the area was employed for classrooms during the moving of the building.

In February 1875 the task was completed, and an addition on the church end of the building was ready for the painters. Commenting on the alterations, *The Pilot* noted that in addition to two assembly halls, Father Fulton had made provision for a gymnasium in the basement of the College and for two rooms nearby as quarters for a society which he had long intended to form. This club would provide worthy leisure-time occupation and recreation for the young Catholic workingmen of the city, who would not ordinarily come under the influence of the College.[26] As will be seen shortly, the organization known as the "Young Men's Catholic Association" was to be initiated within a few months.

The official opening of the renovated building took place on March 30, 1875, and the new College hall—reconstructed and enlarged to become "one of the most commodious as well as the most tasteful in the city"[27]— was inaugurated with a presentation of the play "Richelieu" on the same date.

Administrative Matters

A printed handbill containing the following "Rules for the Students of Boston College" was issued about this time:

> The College door will be opened by the Prefect at 8 A.M. On entering the Students will repair immediately to the cloakroom, where they will leave their books, overcoats, etc. in the charge of the Janitor; thence directly to the gymnasium where they are to remain til time for Mass.
>
> After Mass, each Teacher will accompany his class from the gymnasium to the classroom, and if any teacher should delay, his class is to await his coming in the gymnasium.
>
> The places for recreation are the gymnasium and the court formed by the three College buildings. All the rest of the premises will be "out of bounds," except when the Prefect gives permission to walk by the Church. Members of the Debating Society may be allowed by the Prefect to recreate in their own room, where no other Students shall be admitted.
>
> Playing ball, snow-balling, pitching, and all games which would endanger the windows, are altogether forbidden.
>
> No boisterous conduct is allowed in the corridors or classrooms at any time. Even in the gymnasium and during recreation, the behavior should be decorous.
>
> Robert Fulton, President
Boston College, Feb. 1, 1875[28]

The school was now completing its tenth year and was well organized. In his diary, Father Fulton looked back on these years and reflected how difficult they had been, but he had the consolation of being able to write:

> I count 40 of my boys who have entered the Novitiate preparatory to entrance into the Jesuit Order, become priests or gone to theological seminaries. Every year the number of scholars has increased a little. I have at this moment 158.[29]

The administrative work of the teachers had been lightened by the discontinuance of the weekly report card in 1872,[30] and now plans were under way to broaden the scope of the College's work by the introduction of an English major course in addition to the classics course already established. This movement was at the insistence of the archbishop, but it did not reach fruition until September 1878.[31]

A project dear to Father Fulton, though peripheral to Boston College, was the organization he established for Catholic young men of Boston for purposes of culture, religious development, and sociability. It was named the Young Men's Catholic Association. The College was generous to it over the years in giving it space and equipment. In time it took on the role of adult education, and for some years before its demise at about the time of the First World War, it had become an influential center of preparation for civil service examinations. For nearly half a century, Father Fulton's YMCA, always associated in the public's mind with Boston College, was a lively force in the Catholic life of Boston.

First Graduates

In 1876 Father Fulton considered the College finally ready for a senior class. The scholastic year 1876–1877 was the first to offer the final year of philosophy and, consequently, direct preparation for a degree. To the newly created professorship of logic, metaphysics, and ethics listed in the catalog of that year was appointed one whose name was familiar as being

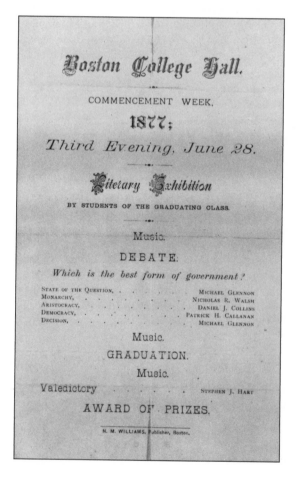

One of the programs for the first graduation, in 1877.

on the original staff which opened the college: Peter Paul Fitzpatrick, S.J., returning now as a priest to the scene of his labors as a scholastic.[32]

By June of 1877, nine young men were ready for graduation: John F. Broderick, Patrick H. Callanan, Daniel J. Collins, John M. Donovan, John W. Galligan, Michael Glennon, Stephen J. Hart, William G. McDonald, and William J. Millerick. Of this group, Hart, the valedictorian of his class, died within a few months of graduation. McDonald and Glennon became physicians, and all the rest became priests of the Archdiocese of Boston. On the occasion of the exhibition of the year before, Archbishop Williams commenced a custom of having the archbishop present the premiums. Commencement day, June 28, 1877, was to have still another distinction: the presence of the governor of the Commonwealth of Massachusetts, Alexander H. Rice, whose friendly interest in Boston College dated back to Father McElroy's purchase of the Harrison Avenue land in 1857.

Commencement week began auspiciously on June 26 with an exhibition in science by students of the graduating class, culminating in a demonstration of "the transmission of speech and music by Bell's telephone."[33] The audience on this evening was disappointing in size, but the performance of the boys elicited from one distinguished guest, Father Robert Brady, S.J., Provincial of the Jesuits and former president of Boston College, the comment that they were "better than any he had seen" in his visits to the various Jesuit colleges on the Atlantic coast.[34] On the following night, a much larger audience witnessed a Latin Play, "Philedonus," and acclaimed it "a prodigious success."[35] Father Fulton's dry commentary was: "The boys were quite intelligible—no mistake in prosody."[36]

Next morning, Father Fulton set out for Worcester to attend the Holy Cross exhibition and to meet Governor Rice with whom he arranged final details for that evening in Boston. With the governor's assurance that he would definitely be present for the graduation ceremonies, Father Fulton hurried back to Boston to make sure that everything was in readiness for the great occasion. He found the stage and hall beautifully decorated with plants, festoons of flowers, and alabaster vases filled with roses.

As the guests began to arrive, he was pleased to observe that at least one third of the priests of the diocese were present. The hall filled rapidly and the governor arrived toward the close of the "Literary Exhibition" which preceded the graduation ceremonies. His Excellency made a speech, which was followed by a formal reading of the College charter, then the valedictory,[37] and finally the awarding of degrees and awards. That night Father Fulton could write in his private journal after a description of the first graduation, "Three glorious days!"[38]

The Boy from Lowell

Toward the close of Father Fulton's first term of office, he was visited one day by a delicate-looking lad from Lowell who wished to enter Boston

College as a transfer student from St. Charles' College in Maryland. The lad's ambition was to enter poetry, second from the highest class in the college at the time and approximating what is now freshman year. Father Fulton brought the newcomer into an inner room where, in the boy's words, he:

> . . . took down some Latin books from a shelf—Ovid, Virgil, and Cicero. One after the other he handed them to me. He asked me to open anywhere and read. I did so from each of them and then translated and then construed.
>
> He asked me various questions, not to embarrass me, but to try my intelligence, I think, more than my memory. . . . we came to Greek. I read some Anabasis and some Homer. . . . After that, more as a conversation than critically, he took me over a fairly large field of history, and physics. . . .
>
> After a full forty minutes of this, he stood up and putting on his biretta turned to me and said, "I will show you to the class-room. The school is in session and I will present you to your professor." I followed him through the long corridors, and presently he halted before one of the doors marked with the name of the class.
>
> He knocked and instantly entered. I followed. At the desk was a chubby-faced little man with glasses, who impressed me at once as learned and gentle. He was my new professor—Father Boursaud.
>
> The large room was filled with a splendid lot of young fellows, who all rose as the Rector entered. "I have come to bring you a new student," he said. ". . . What is your name again?" he said to me. I told him. "William, let me introduce you to the class of Poetry, and boys," he continued, looking over the room, "if you don't work hard he will take all the honors."[39]

That day was February 3, 1879, and William Henry O'Connell, a future archbishop and cardinal, was to equal and better the prophecy Father Fulton made concerning him.

A glimpse of the class routine at the time is given in one of William O'Connell's letters, written in 1880, during his last year at the College:

> I am happy to tell you that I am going on with my study of philosophy at Boston College with considerable success. The professor is Father Russo. It seems that he and Father Mazzella, now in Rome, were both great admirers and students of Aquinas, and now that Leo XIII has commanded that the principles of Saint Thomas must be the text in all colleges, Father Russo has become something of a celebrity here. . . .
>
> Certainly Father Russo is a stern teacher. He never speaks a word to a soul except as he speaks to all in class. He sits at the rostrum looking like some great medieval scholar—great black eyes, a lean sallow face, and a look which turns you into stone if you don't happen to know your lesson.
>
> The lectures are in Latin. We follow him well enough, but when we are asked to recite, it is funny if it were not so tragic. As until now we have read plenty of Latin and spoken none, it is a fearful thing to hear the way cases and tenses are jumbled. But he is very patient about it. He never, never deigns to smile, but somehow I catch in his great liquid eyes a look of amusement which he strives hard to conceal.

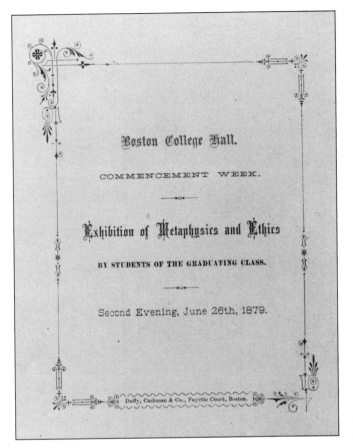

Boston College Hall.

COMMENCEMENT WEEK.

Exhibition of Metaphysics and Ethics

BY STUDENTS OF THE GRADUATING CLASS.

Second Evening, June 26th, 1879.

Duffy, Cashman & Co., Fayette Court, Boston.

A display of seniors' philosophical prowess was part of the commencement week exercises.

... I wish he would give us a short talk every day in English on the general bearing of the matter in hand, and then go on in Latin. I can see that the Latin terminology is more exact, but as yet it does not reach me intimately enough. After all, we are only beginning.[40]

The following June, William O'Connell closed a brilliant college career by receiving from the hands of Governor Long the first gold medal in philosophy, the first silver medal in physics, and the second medal in chemistry. That summer he was selected by Archbishop Williams to study for the priesthood in Rome.[41]

Father Fulton Leaves Office

Father Fulton's term in office should, according to Jesuit custom, have been three years in duration, renewable for an additional three years at the discretion of the General of the Order in Rome. The fact that the year 1879 saw him still in office was at once very extraordinary and very complimentary. According to entries in his diary,[42] Father Fulton himself had petitioned his superiors in this country and in Rome on several occasions to be relieved of his duties, but without results. The school year 1879–1880 opened with the largest enrollment in the school's history, 248,[43] a consideration which Father Fulton found gratifying. But the uncertainty with which he was obliged to regard the coming year because he was "overdue" in office diminished his enthusiasm considerably. The fall of 1879 witnessed more appeals directed to the Provincial from his pen, but the only reply he received was that the Provincial could not afford to move him just then; when a change could be made, he (Father Fulton) would receive a few weeks advance notice. With this he had to be content, and he carried on until Friday afternoon, January 9, 1880, when he received a letter from the Provincial announcing that he was being succeeded by Father Jeremiah O'Connor, S.J., an assistant parish priest connected with the Immaculate Conception Church. The change would be effective in two days time (January 11), and for the present (here Father Fulton must have gasped) Father Fulton would remain at Boston College as prefect of schools and "general assistant" to Father O'Connor. His astonishment at this directive may be understood when one reflects that the Jesuit custom, almost invariably, has always been to transfer an individual when his superiorship is terminated to another house of the Society. The wisdom and charity of such a practice is obvious, but if it needed demonstration, it would be found abundantly in this case. As it happened, Father Fulton liked and admired Father O'Connor very much, and he was able to write frankly, "I think Fr. O'Connor is doing first rate . . ."[44] and ". . . he has made a splendid beginning. . . ."[45] Nonetheless, he was soon obliged to confess that it was hard to see his pet projects abandoned and his decisions reversed.

Recognition of Achievement

On May 13, 1880, Father Fulton was relieved of his duties at Boston and assigned to St. Lawrence's Church (now St. Ignatius Loyola) in New York City. Before he left, several banquets and gatherings of the citizens of Boston gave testimony of the high regard in which he was held by Catholics and non-Catholics alike. The Young Men's Catholic Association tendered him a reception in the College hall on February 5, 1880, in anticipation of his impending change, at which John Boyle O'Reilly read an original poem dedicated as a farewell to Father Fulton entitled, "The Empty Niche." Governor John D. Long, Mayor Frederick O. Prince, and other distinguished speakers added their tributes.[46] On this occasion the Young Men's Catholic Association presented $500 to Boston College with which to found the Fulton Medal,[47] and a bust of Father Fulton by Martin Millmore was exhibited.

John Boyle O'Reilly, a close personal friend of Father Fulton, wrote editorially in *The Pilot*:

> The removal of the Rev. Robert Fulton, S.J., President of Boston College, and Rector of the Immaculate Conception Church, creates no common feeling of sorrow among Boston Catholics. Father Fulton has grown to be a

The first Boston College catalog appeared for the 1868–1869 academic year. The title page carried an emblem representing the apostolic mission of the Church and of the Society of Jesus: a hand presenting a cross. It was a generic emblem, not a seal of the College.

The 1882–1883 catalog had an early version of a Boston College seal: the traditional badge of the Society of Jesus encircled with the name of the College and the date of founding. The letters IHS surmounted by a cross, with three nails below and surrounded by flames, is a familiar shield of the Society of Jesus. This seal was used for 32 years.

In 1914 (the first year at Chestnut Hill) a more distinctive seal appeared. The arms of old Boston, England (St. Botolph's Town) contained three crowns. Two similar crowns adorn the new shield, but the third is replaced by the badge of the Society of Jesus. Below is the "trimount" (from Tremont, the early name of Boston), which is also on the arms of the archdiocese. On an open book in the center are the Greek words αἰὲν ἀριστεύειν (ever to excel). This seal appeared in each annual catalog until 1934.

The seal in the 1934 catalog (still used) was identical with that since 1914 except for the addition at the base of the shield of a scroll with the words Religioni et Bonis Artibus. Bonis Artibus has been interpreted by some to mean fine arts, but that is a poor translation and a too narrow statement of the University's mission. Others interpret Bonis Artibus as liberal arts because that was the original curriculum of the College. Still others, among them Father Francis Sweeney, argue suasively from the basic meaning of the Latin word bonis and from the commission of the University's charter to promote virtue, piety, and learning that Bonis Artibus means those studies and activities that promote the good (ethical) life.

feature of Boston Catholicity. His name and his person were everywhere respected and beloved. The remarkable influence he possessed, as a spiritual guide and as a friend, is rarely equalled. Under his wise and temperate direction, Boston College has grown into splendid promise, and the influence of his Order has become respected throughout the city and state. He is necessarily a large figure, socially and intellectually. It seems strange that such a man should ever be removed from a position so well controlled. But the system of his great Order is greater than the personality of its members. . . . Wherever he may go, Father Fulton carries with him the love and respect of Boston; and whatever may be his future, we say that he has built himself into our wall, we shall claim our share of his honors; and in his own heart we believe he must ever feel that he belongs particularly to Boston.[48]

*   *   *

During his 10 years as president, Father Fulton continued to function as prefect of studies (dean), an office he held for 16 years. Thus he was the most influential figure in shaping the academic character of the early College. Fortunately he was to return as president in the next decade, the only Jesuit to hold that office twice.

ENDNOTES

1. (His visit to St. Louis:) Fulton, Diary, under date 1870. (His appointment was vice rector:) *Catalogus Provinciae Marylandiae, S.J., ineunte anno 1871.*
2. *Catalogus Provinciae Marylandiae, S.J., ineunte anno 1871;* and *ibid., ineunte anno 1872.*
3. ". . . soon the only Catholic college in the diocese" referred to the creation of the new diocese of Springfield (Mass.), effected by a decree dated June 7, 1870, which removed Worcester and consequently Holy Cross College from the jurisdiction of the bishop of Boston. Cf. Sadlier's *Catholic Almanac,* 1871.
4. *The Pilot* (August 27, 1870).
5. Fulton to Lancaster (August 6, 1870), Maryland Provincial S.J. Archives, under "Boston," Georgetown University Library.
6. Fulton, Diary, under date 1870 and 1871.
7. Fulton to Lancaster, May 8, 1871, Maryland Provincial S.J. Archives, under "Boston," Georgetown University Library.
8. Fulton, Diary, under date 1870–71.
9. *Catalogue of the Officers and Students of Boston College for the Academic Year 1869–70,* p. 11.
10. Cf. articles on Foster by William A. Robinson in *The Dictionary of American Biography,* 6:549–550; and by Thomas F. Meehan in *The Catholic Encyclopedia,* 6:155–156.
11. Callanan, "Reminiscences," *The Stylus* 11(October 1897):387.
12. *Ibid.*
13. *Ibid.,* p. 389.
14. *Catalogue . . . of Boston College,* 1870–1871, p. 10.
15. This feeling of resentment is noticeable in several of the letters published in the Callanan reminiscences—e.g., Pazolt, Pfau, etc.
16. Callanan, "Reminiscences," *The Stylus,* 11(1897):520.
17. *Boston Daily Globe* (May 17, 1872); Callanan, "Reminiscences." p. 522.

18. Another exhibition drill was held on June 25, 1873, in the College hall before Generals Burrill and Guiney and Major Murphy of the Ninth Regiment, who acted as judges. Cf. Callanan, "Reminiscences," *The Stylus,* 12(1898):274.

19. Callanan, "Reminiscences," 12 (1898):278–279.

20. "Catholic Education in Boston," *The Pilot* (August 30, 1873).

21. *Ibid.* (June 27, 1874).

22. *Ibid.* (September 5, 1874).

23. *Ibid.* (September 19, 1874).

24. *Ibid.* (November 14, 1874).

25. *Calendar,* Immaculate Conception Church, February 1943, p. 17.

26. *The Pilot* (February 13, 1875).

27. *Ibid.* (April 10, 1875).

28. Handbill in the Callanan collection, BCA. Some rules omitted.

29. Fulton, Diary, under date 1875.

30. Noted in a fragmentary "Diary of the College" (1866–1885), Maryland Provincial S.J. Archives, under "Boston," Georgetown University Library.

31. *Catalogue . . . of Boston College . . . 1877–78,* p. 3.

32. *Catalogue 1876–77,* p. 12.

33. *Ibid.,* p. 27.

34. Fulton, Diary, under date June 26, 1877. Georgetown University Archives.

35. *Ibid.,* June 27, 1877.

36. *Ibid.*

37. This first valedictory address is transcribed completely in Callanan, "Reminiscences," *The Stylus,* 13(March 1899):166–171.

38. Fulton, Diary, under date June 28, 1877.

39. Letter of W. H. O'Connell to "Carl," dated Boston, March 3, 1879, from *The Letters of His Eminence William Cardinal O'Connell, Archbishop of Boston* (Cambridge: The Riverside Press, 1915), Vol. 1, pp. 34–35.

40. O'Connell, *Letters,* Vol. 1, pp. 37–40. Letter to "Oliver," dated Lowell, Mass., November 20, 1880.

41. Cf. letter of W. H. O'Connell to "Henry," dated Lowell, Mass., August 15, 1881, in O'Connell, *Letters,* pp. 41–46.

42. The material which follows was drawn from the manuscript "Diary of Father Fulton," *passim,* 1879–1880.

43. "Faculty and Students at Boston College," a manuscript chart of statistics evidently compiled in 1885. Maryland Provincial S.J. Archives, under "Boston," Georgetown University Library.

44. Fulton, Diary, March 22, 1880.

45. *Ibid.,* March 25, 1880.

46. Joseph H. Farren, "The Young Men's Catholic Association of Boston," *The Pilot* (March 8, 1930), in which the entire poem is printed.

47. Fulton, Diary, February 5, 1880.

48. *The Pilot* (January 24, 1880).

CHAPTER 9

The College in the 1880s

Father O'Connor's term in the presidency of Boston College passed smoothly, efficiently, and almost uneventfully. It was not a period of growth in the number of students, which remained just under 250, but two institutions very prominent now in the students' life trace their origins to Father O'Connor's regime: *The Stylus* and the Athletic Association.

The Stylus

The Boston College magazine, *The Stylus,* was founded in January 1883 in response to a student petition,[1] chiefly by members of the class of 1884. Father Thomas J. Stack, S.J., was the first faculty moderator of the paper.[2] The format of the magazine during its first decade differed considerably from that adopted later. The original page size was 10 by 12 inches, and there were about twelve pages to an issue, exclusive of the tan coated paper cover. The reading matter was presented in two columns to a page, and evidently financial considerations prevented the use of any illustrations. The usual offerings in fiction and poetry occupied the first five pages, followed by editorials, news items ("Domi" column), exchanges, alumni, and notices concerning the various school societies. Advertising, generally in the form of "business cards," occupied the final three pages.

REV. JEREMIAH O'CONNOR, S.J.
Fourth President

Father O'Connor was born in Dublin, Ireland, on April 10, 1841, and was brought to America as a young boy. He attended public grammar and high schools in Philadelphia and was a student at St. Joseph's College in the same city. He entered the Society of Jesus on July 30, 1860. Ordained in 1874, he was assigned to Boston College as a teacher of rhetoric in 1876. Two years later he took up parochial duties at the College's Church of the Immaculate Conception and became a distinguished pulpit figure. In his autobiography, George Santayana recalled his visits to the Jesuit church and commented on Father O'Connor's pulpit eloquence. As mentioned in the previous chapter, Father O'Connor assumed the presidency in 1880.

The first number of the new magazine was distinguished by the appearance of a "christening song" written especially for *The Stylus* by Father Abram J. Ryan, the priest-poet of the South. Incidentally, in what is now the O'Neill room of Bapst Library, Father Ryan is commemorated in a stained glass window along with such other American poets as Bryant, Whittier, and Longfellow.

Less than two years after its inception, *The Stylus* could boast of a circulation of 600 copies,[3] which appears remarkably good in view of the fact that the student enrollment for that year was only 263. Nevertheless, the editor, erroneously estimating the alumni and former students at 1500 in number, felt that these friends could easily double that circulation if they would.[4]

As it was, the paper enjoyed popularity with the students, and was termed by the professional press "unquestionably one of the best college papers published."[5] Moreover, it succeeded, through the ability of its managing editors, in establishing itself on a firm financial footing. When the alterations on the building in which it had offices were begun in the spring of 1889, however, *The Stylus* found itself without quarters, and it was forced temporarily to suspend publication. For over four and a half years, nothing was done to restore it, until in December 1893 the class of 1894, under the faculty directorship of Father Timothy Brosnahan, S.J., finally brought it once more into being.[6] Since that time, although it has come on thin days more than once, it has never suffered another interruption in publication.

First page of the first issue of The Stylus.

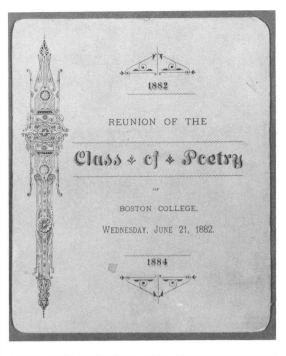

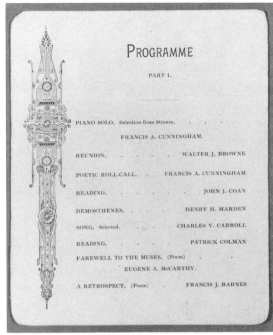

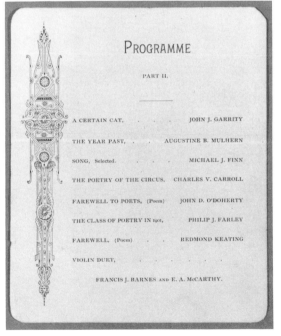

The "reunion" announced on the cover of the program is not a get-together of graduates. It was an academic exhibition by undergraduates, in this case the equivalent of freshmen with two years to go before graduating in the class of 1884.

Athletics Come of Age

The second institution established during Father O'Connor's presidency was the Athletic Association.[7] Until this time, athletics had not enjoyed any official notice, nor were teams organized in any sport except on a game-to-game basis.[8] This situation was explained by the lack of facilities in the early days of the College, by the fact that Boston College was for day scholars, and—until the mid-1870s—by the fact that the upper academic years of college, from which the boys old enough for intercollegiate competition would be drawn, had not been established. In his "Reminiscences," Father Callanan recounts some of the attempts at forming baseball teams in the period from 1870 to 1877.[9] The problem of a playing field was solved at various times by the "fair grounds" (a field opposite the buildings on Harrison Avenue) and by various fields in the suburbs at "picnic distance" from the College. But there was never an organized effort to train teams and to provide facilities for games until shortly after the opening of school in the fall of 1883. *The Stylus* reported:

> The enthusiasm of some of the students on the subject of athletics has at last found practical expression in the formation of the Boston College Athletic Club. Towards the end of October, a committee consisting of Messrs. T. W. Coakley, '84, J. P. McGuigan and T. J. Hurley, '85, and one or two others, waited upon the President, and obtained his sanction to the organization of an athletic club. The first step being thus successful, the same committee called a meeting of those interested in the question; and, after the usual and necessary preliminaries, the association was formed. The membership is already very large; and the energy shown at the meetings thus far, augurs well for the future. So that, with proper management on the part of the officers, we think great things may now be expected.[10]

Mr. D. Leo Brand, S.J., was appointed the first faculty moderator, and at the "semiannual meeting" of the association, evidently held sometime in February 1884, officers were elected.[11] In announcing the formation of the Athletic Association, the catalog for 1883–1884 stated, "Its object is to encourage the practice of manly sports, and to promote by these the *esprit de corps* of the College Students, who are its members."[12] The first contests played under the auspices of the new association were baseball games, which were reported by *The Stylus:*

> The baseball team has been reinforced by many efficient players. Under Manager Hopwood, it is prepared to do some good work in the field. Already it has defeated the South Boston Athletic Club 14–3, the Roxbury's 15–5, the Adams Academy nine 21–12, and though defeated by the Lynns, it owes its defeat not to the superior playing of its adversaries, but to the superior friendship of the Umpire to that nine. Our greatest victory has been the defeat of the X.Q.Z. Club of Lowell, by a score of 8 to 0. This club is one of the strongest in the state, and the vanquisher of the Lynns.[13]

"The First Annual Spring Games," a field day of track events, was also scheduled by the association for late in May 1884.[14]

Father Boursaud

Father O'Connor's term in office came to a close on July 31, 1884. He was succeeded by a former professor of poetry and rhetoric at the College, the Reverend Edward Victor Boursaud, S.J. When classes reconvened in Sep-

REV. EDWARD V. BOURSAUD, S.J.
Fifth President

Father Boursaud was born in New York of French parents on September 1, 1840. During his youth his family returned to France, and there he received part of his education. On his return to America he attended Mount Saint Mary's College, Emmetsburg, Maryland, from which he graduated in 1863. He entered the Society of Jesus on August 14, 1863. After ordination he was sent to Boston College for two years as a teacher of poetry and rhetoric. He served in Rome as secretary to the assistant from England on the Jesuit General's staff for four years, and then was recalled to Boston to become president of Boston College on July 31, 1884.[15]

tember, the new president was greeted warmly by the students. The man they saw before them was a mild-mannered, kindly scholar, an accomplished linguist, and one who, although only 44 years old at the time, had already been entrusted with a post of great confidence in the government of the Society of Jesus.

One of the first tasks he set for himself on assuming office was to remodel the basement of the Immaculate Conception Church, much used by the students of the College as the chapel. The area was deepened three feet, lengthened, and completely redecorated with most pleasing results.[16]

He was remembered by those who knew him in Boston as devoted to the poor and to workers. A strike of streetcar employees occurred during his term as president of Boston College, and Father Boursaud manifested his sympathy with the cause of labor by avoiding the streetcars and riding in the strikers' barges.[17] He was extremely popular with the students,[18] but his influence beyond the College walls was not as wide as that of Father Fulton.[19]

During the years of Father Boursaud's administration, attendance rose slowly but steadily. The year before he took office there were 250 students registered; two years later he had brought the number to 297, an increase just under 19 percent.[20]

In the catalog issued at the end of Father Boursaud's first year as president, mention is made for the first time of the master of arts degree and of the conditions under which it was to be granted: "For the . . . degree of A.M., it will be required that the applicant shall have continued his studies in College for one year, or studied, or practiced a learned profession for two years."[21] The degree was not, however, conferred on anyone by Father Boursaud, and later was granted only seven times in the history of the College prior to 1913.[22]

The Alumni Organize

In the meantime, a need was felt among the alumni for an organization to bring their numbers together. An editorial writer in *The Stylus* as early as March of 1884 had written:

> We feel that if these Alumni would organize, it would materially aid us by making the college more widely known and esteemed, and by infusing a lively and kindlier interest among the older students for us of the present. It would also be the means of bringing about those pleasant annual reunions which do so much to cement friendships begun in early life, and reflect lustre upon the college which was their other home. Such a step, we believe, would not be at this moment premature, and certainly is not impracticable.[23]

The appeal brought some response, but due to the unwillingness of any individual to come forward at this time as organizer, the project was postponed indefinitely.[24] Doctor Eugene A. McCarthy ('84) recalled that when he and some other graduates at a later period approached Father Boursaud to obtain his approval of an alumni association, they found the rector rather skeptical that enough alumni would be interested in organizing such a body to make it worthwhile. Young McCarthy and his friends withdrew undiscouraged and proceeded to sound out alumni opinion by mail. When, some months later, indisputable proof of the graduates' willingness to support such a venture was gathered, it was brought to Father Boursaud, and he at once gave the undertaking his approval.[25]

There were only 136 living alumni of Boston College,[26] but a large number of these met in the spring of 1886 and agreed to form an association. It was arranged to have the first reunion and banquet at Young's Hotel on June 28, 1886. The success of this initial gathering encouraged the new organization to make the function an annual affair.[27] The first president of the alumni association was Edward A. McLaughlin, and the first "first vice president" was the Reverend Thomas I. Coghlan ('78).[28]

Changes of Command

On August 5, 1887, Father Boursaud terminated his period in office and was succeeded in the presidency of Boston College by the Reverend Thomas

REV. THOMAS H. STACK, S.J.
Sixth President

Father Stack was born on July 3, 1845, near Union, Virginia (now West Virginia). He attended the Virginia Military Institute at Lexington, but his classes were interrupted by the outbreak of the Civil War. He enlisted in the army of the Confederacy and served for four years. After the war he attended Georgetown College and on September 1, 1868, he entered the Society of Jesus. He was ordained in 1881. He taught physics at Holy Cross and Georgetown and during three separate assignments at Boston College.

H. Stack, S.J., remembered as the founder of *The Stylus* and, at this time, a popular professor of physics and chemistry.

The news of his appointment as president of the College in the summer of 1887 was greeted with joy by the students who knew him, but their pleasure was short-lived. Father Stack was stricken with a fatal fever on August 22, only 17 days after his appointment, and on August 30 he died.[29]

Because of the suddenness of this loss, there was not time before the beginning of school to go through the lengthy formalities usually connected with the selection of a new president; therefore, a vice rector was appointed to carry on temporarily the administration of the College. Father Nicholas Russo, S.J., a professor of philosophy at the College of whom mention has been made previously, thus became vice rector and seventh president of Boston College.[30]

The Return of Father Fulton

Father Russo's term of office was brief and uneventful. On July 4, 1888, less than a year after taking over the presidency, he was relieved by Father Fulton, who returned after an interim spent in filling positions of great trust in the government of the Society of Jesus. Since leaving Boston, Father

REV. NICHOLAS RUSSO, S.J.
Seventh President

Father Russo was born on April 24, 1845, at Ascoli in Italy. His father, a physician, envisioned a medical career for his son, but young Nicholas hoped to become a Jesuit. Fearing his parents would block his plans, in August 1862 he ran away from home and in France applied for admission to the Society of Jesus. The Fathers of the Society could not receive him under these conditions, but parental consent was finally obtained and he became a Jesuit novice. His early Jesuit studies were made in France, but in 1875 he was sent to the United States for theological training. Ordained in 1877, he became a teacher of philosophy at Boston College. He was the first faculty member to publish a book; three scholarly works on philosophy and religion were published during the years 1885 to 1890.[31]

Fulton had been successively rector of St. Lawrence's Church (now St. Ignatius Loyola Church) in New York, rector of Gonzaga College in Washington, D.C., and then Provincial of the New York–Maryland Province of the Society of Jesus. While in this latter post, he was summoned to Europe to participate in a general congregation of his order, and in 1886 he was sent by the Jesuit General to Ireland as Visitor (Inspector General) to the Irish Province of the Society.[32]

For several years prior to Father Fulton's second sojourn in Boston, the question of adequate room for the growing College had been much discussed. There were two considerations which now urged immediate action upon Father Fulton. First was the insistent demand of the archbishop of Boston that an independent "high school" be formed to take the place of part of the seven-year European plan which was then in force, in order to cope with the rising popularity of the public high schools and to provide a terminal course for those students who did not wish to continue beyond the first four years. The second reason, also put forward by the archbishop, was the need for a well-designed and independent four-year commercial course.[33]

Neither of the suggested changes was entirely new to the College. The four years of high school, or a close equivalent, had been offered under another name for years; the fact, however, that they were not administrationally distinct from the college years was now considered a disadvantage. A commercial course of a kind had been offered previously, but it had been an insignificant branch of the regular school—perhaps considered a refuge for the less capable in the standard arts course. The numbers following the commercial subjects certainly were never very large. The reasons given to the archbishop for not acceding to his request at once centered on lack of classroom and office space.[34]

To these arguments for a new building, which were drawn from the needs of the school itself, may be added another extrinsic reason very close to the heart of Father Fulton: the pressing need for enlarged quarters for the Young Men's Catholic Association.

In the light of all these considerations, therefore, Father Fulton placed the enlargement of the school building first on his agenda upon taking office. Fortunately for this cause, he had a large number of friends who were willing to undertake the management of a drive to obtain funds; in

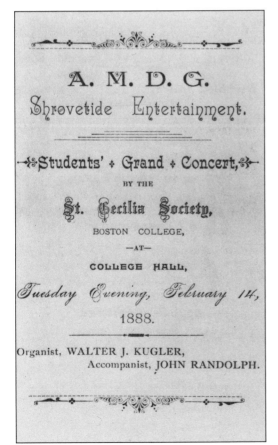

Music had a prominent role in student life.

addition to this, he made appeals to the congregation of the Immaculate Conception Church and enlisted the enthusiastic aid of the Young Men's Catholic Association. When ordinary means threatened to be inadequate, he had resort, against the advice of some, to a "fair," to bring the amount up to the desired $125,000.[35]

Further Expansion

The fund-raising was successful, and work began on the James Street building in the spring of 1889.[36] The plan was to extend the building in the direction of Newton Street at one end and in the direction of Concord Street at the other. Roughly, this would increase the frontage on James Street from about 150 feet to some 250 feet.

The work was held up considerably by strikes among the workmen in May 1889, and the alterations were consequently not completed until the spring of the following year.[37] In addition to the changes made in the main school building, the opportunity was taken to enlarge the connecting passageway from the priests' house on Harrison Avenue to the College building on James Street. This part was enlarged to twice its width[38] to provide additional living quarters for the faculty, more library room, and a faculty dining room.

Not everyone was enthusiastic in appraising these alterations. Father Devitt, who succeeded Father Fulton in the presidency of the College, wrote:

> The result [of the alterations] in the connecting building at least, was a combination of structural mistakes: dark corridors; extravagantly large and inconvenient dwelling-rooms; a library in separate sections; and a dining hall in the cellar.[39]

According to Father Devitt, the basic cause of all these defects was the decision to place the designing and construction of the new additions in the hands of one of the lay brothers of the community rather than in the care of a professional architect.[40]

Academic Separation of the Secondary School and the College

The enlarged building facilities, however, were but one contribution which Father Fulton made to a growing Boston College during his second term in office. Another change, no less important, was the introduction of an English "high school," which has already been mentioned in passing and which was begun in September 1889 at the request of the archbishop. This is the first mention of the term "high school" used officially in connection with this institution, and in the beginning it was employed exclusively to designate the four-year English or commercial course, as distinct from the seven-year classical course which led to the A.B. degree.

The English course Archbishop Williams had requested was begun in September 1879.[41] This was a four-year course at high school level, emphasizing English, bookkeeping, and various branches of mathematics. Father Fulton backed the new course, but one may conclude that the school administration was somewhat ill at ease in placing the English course in the catalog next to the favored classical program, since every catalog from 1879 to 1900 made the point that the English course was the archbishop's idea. The 1879 catalog spoke of the "earnest solicitation" of the archbishop for the course, and the next 20 annual catalogs said the new course was established at the "special instance" of the archbishop. The high hopes of the archbishop, who spoke of a possible enrollment of over 600 in the English course[42] were never realized. The highest enrollment in the course was 31 in 1891[43] and five years later the course had become a branch of the preparatory division.[44]

In the meantime, the terminology describing the classes of the classical course had gone through an evolution. Until the publication of the 1894–1895 catalog, the description of courses and textbooks was simply headed, "Course of Studies in the Classical Department." In 1894–1895 a division was made in listing the classes for the coming year (1895–1896) and the following were termed "Preparatory Classes": rudiments (second division and first division), third class of grammar, and second class of grammar.[45]

Another step in the direction of separating the secondary school and the college classes was taken in the catalog for 1896–1897, when the phrase "preparatory school" was used in describing the lower classes for the school year 1897–1898.[46] In September 1898 the distinction between the College and the preparatory school was further emphasized by the introduction of separate entrances to the building for the two divisions.[47] In this connection, it must be noted that both classical and English classes were embraced in the category of "preparatory school." This point is important in answering the question: "When was Boston College High School begun?" As may now be seen, some distinctions are necessary in making a reply to that question.

If by "high school" is meant the early classes in the course, then the high school existed from September 1864 on. If the question is intended to ask when the term "high school" was first used in connection with the lower classes at Boston College, another distinction must be made: The term "high school" was used off and on in a vague sense in connection with the English course from September 1889 on; in the strict sense of indicating all the preparatory classes, classical and English, it was not employed until 1903.[48]

Father Fulton's Farewell

In the meantime, the task of gathering the money necessary for the new building operations and the worries and criticism attending the construction itself were taking their toll on the already fragile health of Father

Fulton. He had the gratification of witnessing a marked increase of students entering the College in September 1890, which brought the enrollment to a new high of 315.[49] He mapped out plans for the current year and set them in motion, but found the severe rheumatic complaint from which he suffered growing worse as time went on. Samples of his handwriting during this period give eloquent testimony of the heroic efforts he was obliged to make even to write the briefest note. Despite this handicap, he had composed and preached the eulogy at the funeral of John Boyle O'Reilly in August[50] and had been celebrant at a Solemn Mass of Requiem for the poet attended by all the students of the College in the latter part of September.[51]

On the evening of October 15, 1890, a date which marked the fifteenth anniversary of the founding of the Young Men's Catholic Association of Boston College, the new wing of the building to be devoted to the association was formally opened. Archbishop Williams, former Mayor P. A. Collins, and Father Fulton were the speakers on the occasion.[52] This function, which was the crowning of his long labors in behalf of that organization, was to be the last he ever attended in Boston. The following morning he left the city for Hot Springs, Arkansas, in quest of his health.[53]

When no improvement in Father Fulton's condition was evident by mid-winter, the Provincial decided to appoint a vice rector to assume management of the College. He chose for the post a professor of philosophy at Holy Cross College in Worcester, Father Edward J. Devitt, S.J. This priest recorded in his diary under date of January 8, 1891, that the Provincial (Father Campbell), while making his yearly visitation at Holy Cross, had spoken to him of going to Boston as vice rector. He respectfully protested against the idea, but on the following day he learned that his objections had been overruled and that he was to go to Boston that very afternoon. The appointment came as a complete surprise to his fellow Jesuits, "no one having any inkling of it either at Worcester or Boston."[54]

It is a commentary on the College's position and influence in the eyes of non-Catholic Boston that the change of presidents received no mention at all in the columns of the *Boston Daily Advertiser* and merited only 41 words at the bottom of page 6 in the *Boston Evening Transcript* three days after the appointment.[55] Father Devitt's temporary status of vice rector was changed to that of full rector and president of the College by the Jesuit General, Father Anderledy, on September 3, 1891.[56]

*　　*　　*

Not only because of his long service as leader of Boston College, but because of his personality and intellectual force, Father Fulton was the most influential Jesuit in Boston cultural circles in the 19th century. His passing from the Boston scene definitely marked the end of an era.

ENDNOTES

1. *The Boston Globe* (?) (April 1895). Clipping in Georgetown University Archives (Lamson Collection).

2. *The Stylus*, 6(October 1887):11.

3. *Ibid.*, 3(November 1884):6.

4. *Ibid.* Actually, there were about 125 living alumni at the time. Cf. *Boston College Catalogue*, 1884–1885.

5. *The Pilot* (February 16, 1884).

6. *The Boston Globe* (?) (April 1895). Clipping in Georgetown University Archives (Lamson Collection).

7. A history of athletics at Boston College written by Nathaniel J. Hasenfus of the class of 1922 was published by the author in 1943.

8. Cf. *The Stylus*, 2(September 1883):5. Letter referring to Holy Cross game, spring 1883.

9. Callanan, "Reminiscences," *The Stylus*, 13(March 1899):155–157; and Henry C. Towle, "Pioneer Days," *The Stylus*, 11(June 1897):333.

10. *The Stylus*, 2(December 1883):18.

11. *Ibid.*, 2(March 1884):43; and *Boston College Catalogue* for 1883–1884, p. 30.

12. *Boston College Catalogue* for 1883–1884, p. 30.

13. *The Stylus*, 2(May 1884):53.

14. *Ibid.*, 2(May 1884):55.

15. *The Messenger* (New York), 37(May 1902):577–579; and *Woodstock Letters*, 31(1902):277.

16. *The Stylus*, 4(December 1885):14–15.

17. *The Pilot* (?) (c. March 18, 1902); clipping in Georgetown University Archives, Lamson Collection.

18. *Ibid.*

19. Devitt, "History of the Province; XVI. Boston College," *Woodstock Letters*, 64(1935):409.

20. "Number of Students in Our Colleges in the United States and Canada," *Woodstock Letters*, 13(1884):425; and 15(1886):352.

21. *Catalogue of Boston College* for 1884–1885, p. 6.

22. According to the Boston College *Alumni Directory* for June 1924, the following seven persons received the M.A. degree prior to 1913: 1877, Edward A. McLaughlin; 1878, James Herrmann; 1879, John F. Cummins; 1890, Michael A. Carroll; 1892, Henry V. Cunningham; 1904, Manuel de Moreira; and 1910, William F. Kenney.

23. *The Stylus* 2(March 1884):37.

24. *Ibid.*, 2(May 1884):56.

25. From a verbal statement of Doctor McCarthy to Father John W. Ryan, S.J., July 9, 1944.

26. *The Boston College Catalogue, 1885–1886*, Appendix.

27. *The Stylus*, 4(July 1886):75.

28. *The Boston Daily Globe* (June 29, 1886).

29. Halloran, *op. cit.*, pp. 1–3; *Woodstock Letters*, 16(1887):317–319; *Catalogus Provinciae Marylandiae S.J.*, *passim*; *Catalogus Provinciae Marylandiae–Neo Eboracensis*, 1881, et ff., *passim*.

30. Anon., "Father Nicholas Russo," *Woodstock Letters*, 31(1902):281–285.

31. Father Russo's works were:

    (1) *Summa Philosophica juxta Scholasticorum Principia, complectens Logicam et Metaphysicam* (Bostoniae: Apud Thomas B. Noonan et Socium, 1885).

    (2) *The True Religion and Its Dogmas* (Boston: Thomas B. Noonan & Co., 1886).

    (3) *De Philosophia Morale Praelectiones* (Neo-Eborace: Benziger Fratres, 1890).

32. *Catalogus Provinciae Marylandiae–Neo Eboracensis, passim*. Also, "Father Robert Fulton; a Sketch," *Woodstock Letters* 25, (1896):109–110.

33. "Historia Collegii Bostoniensis, pro anno 1889." Manuscript report in Latin written for the Jesuit General and Provincial, Maryland Provincial S.J. Archives, under "Litterae Annuae—Collegium Bostoniense." Georgetown University Library.

34. *Ibid.*

35. *Ibid.* and *Woodstock Letters,* 18(1889):114.

36. Anon., "Boston College, Its History and Influence," *Donahoe's Magazine,* 29(January 1893):68.

37. *Ibid.*

38. *Woodstock Letters,* 18(1889):256.

39. Edward I. Devitt, S.J., "History of the Maryland–New York Province; XVI. Boston College," *Woodstock Letters,* 64(1935):410.

40. Devitt, "History of the Maryland–New York Province . . . ," manuscript, with material omitted in the published version, Georgetown University Archives. MS., p. 21.

41. E.g., *The Boston College Catalogue, 1881–82,* pp. 3 and 12.

42. *The Pilot* (October 25, 1890).

43. English enrollment, Catalogue, 1891–1892, pp. 15–24.

44. Catalogue, 1896–1897.

45. *Ibid.,* 1894–1895, pp. 21–25.

46. *Ibid.,* 1896–1897, p. 31.

47. *The Stylus,* 12(1898):441.

48. First official use of the term "high school" in describing the entire preparatory division occurred in the *Catalogue,* 1903–1904, p. 34, in a statement outlining admission requirements in the college department. Up to that time, the phrase "preparatory school" had been used.

49. "Number of Students in our Colleges in the United States and Canada, October 1, 1890," *Woodstock Letters,* 19(1890):441.

50. *The Pilot* (August 16, 1890).

51. *Ibid.* (September 27, 1890).

52. *Ibid.* (October 25, 1890).

53. *Ibid.*

54. Manuscript Diary of Fr. Edward I. Devitt, S.J., preserved at Georgetown University Archives.

55. *Boston Evening Transcript* (January 12, 1891).

56. Anderledy to Devitt, September 3, 1891, Georgetown University Archives, Devitt papers.

CHAPTER 10

Growing Is Done Slowly

Father Devitt is remembered as the nineteenth century president who made the library his special priority. Up to that time, since the library was the least urgent demand made on a very limited budget, it had suffered from neglect. How this book collection was begun and the changes of fortune visited upon it are described in a short history of the library written by Father Devitt himself for the 1893–1894 issue of the College catalog.[1] In this history, he explains that financial conditions at the inception of the College did not permit the establishment of an adequate library. The first gift of books was made over a decade before the College opened by the Reverend Joseph Coolidge Shaw, S.J., who after his conversion went abroad and, with the money supplied by a well-to-do father, bought many volumes in Paris and Rome.

A second patron of the library was Colonel Daniel S. Lamson of Weston, Massachusetts, who gave more than a third of his own personal library to Boston College and in 1865 transferred to the trustees a proprietor's share of the Boston Athenaeum, which he had inherited from his father.[2]

A priest of the Boston Archdiocese, Father Manasses P. Dougherty, left a collection strong in Irish history and biography to the College. In 1882 the library acquired the books of the recently deceased Robert Morris, Esq., which aided immeasurably in the departments of English and American

REV. EDWARD IGNATIUS DEVITT, S.J.
Ninth President

Father Devitt was born in St. John, New Brunswick, on November 26, 1840. His family moved to Boston and settled in the North End, where he attended public schools. He graduated from Boston English High School and attended Holy Cross College for two years. On July 28, 1859, he entered the Society of Jesus. He taught at Gonzaga College in Washington, D.C. during the Civil War and walked with a group of Gonzaga students in Lincoln's funeral procession. After ordination he taught philosophy at Woodstock College and at Holy Cross before assuming the presidency at Boston College in 1891.

literature. Other donations were made, and accessions by purchase—on a modest scale—were finally authorized.

> In 1875 a secular priest, the Reverend Stanislas Buteux, bequeathed his collection of 5000 volumes to Boston College. The gift assumed a new value when one learned that the donor was an invalid through much of his life and in straitened financial circumstances, and that he had gathered this library with discrimination and at great personal sacrifice with the intention of presenting it one day to the Jesuit Fathers. Thanks to Father Buteux, the College library was enriched with full lines on slavery, the Civil War, and education, as well as with long files of periodical literature.

Until 1876 the library had rather restricted quarters in the small connecting building, but when this section was enlarged by Father Fulton that year, provision was made for adequate housing of the books on hand at the time. In the years that immediately followed, Father Russo (who acted as librarian) and Father Francis Barnum (later a missionary in Alaska) did much to make the library's holdings available by instituting an accurate card index.

When the alterations of the years 1889–1890 took place, the library, strangely enough, was forgotten, and the collection had to be divided and housed in various rooms. On becoming rector, Father Devitt succeeded in enlarging the number of books by some 25 percent, and he did what he could to provide accessible space for them. In May 1894 the College was in possession of 28,319 volumes "arranged in 137 cases, distributed over three rooms."[3]

Among other improvements made during Father Devitt's term in office was the enlargement of the science department, an improvement that was found worthy of mention in the *Woodstock Letters.*[4]

In 1890 the debating society, under Mr. A. J. Mullen, S.J., as moderator, took the name, "The Fulton Debating Society." An orchestra was organized among the students by Father Buckley during the school year 1890–1891, and a dramatic society, which called itself the "Boston College Athenaeum," was organized the same year under Mullen to take over the thespian chores until then performed by members of the debating society.[5] A natural history club called the "Agassiz Association" was formed in October of 1892 under the direction of Father Fullerton. *The Stylus,* which had suspended publication in 1889, resumed publication as a monthly with the December 1893 issue, under the faculty directorship of Father Timothy Brosnahan.[6]

Father Brosnahan Takes Charge

On July 16, 1894, Father Timothy Brosnahan succeeded Father Devitt as president of Boston College. During his four years in office he won the reputation of being an energetic, thorough, and progressive executive. His concomitant duties as prefect of studies required him to attend to the marks of the boys, to be present at the class "specimens," to counsel individuals and follow their school careers, and to maintain general direction over the extracurricular activities of the students. According to one who knew him, he applied himself rather "strenuously" to these tasks, but the results were welcomed by pupils and teachers alike.[7]

A singular contribution of Father Brosnahan was the extended exposition of the Jesuit philosophy of education that he introduced into the College catalog. The statement was so forceful that it was embodied in whole or in part in the catalogs of a number of other Jesuit colleges from coast to coast, and it appeared annually in the Boston College catalog until the early 1950s. It remains an important document in the history of Jesuit higher education.

Father Brosnahan was no narrow traditionalist. He introduced a course in physiological psychology, which was taught by a medical doctor who was a Boston College alumnus. He offered geology as an elective and added 90 hours of laboratory work to the chemistry course. Besides being an outstanding educator, Father Brosnahan was also a skilled manager. Dur-

REV. TIMOTHY BROSNAHAN, S.J.
Tenth President

Father Brosnahan was born in Alexandria, Virginia, January 8, 1856.[8] His early education was in private and parochial schools, and he attended the preparatory school of Gonzaga College in Washington, D.C. He entered the Society of Jesus on August 21, 1872. During his training he taught at Boston College for four years. After ordination in 1887 he taught at Woodstock College, and in 1892 he returned to Boston College as a professor of philosophy. Two years later he became president of the College.

ing his term, enrollment rose to 450. Finances were in good order, and in his last year he was able to make arrangements for the purchase of a large piece of property on both sides of Massachusetts Avenue not far from the College.[9]

Following his rectorship at Boston College, Father Brosnahan was a professor and later a prefect of studies at Woodstock College until 1909. In that year he was sent as professor of ethics to Loyola College, Baltimore, where he remained until his death on June 4, 1915.

Gentlemen of the Opposition

In looking back from the vantage point of the present, it is difficult to understand the excitement which attended the announcement in 1894 that Boston College would meet Georgetown in the first intercollegiate debate ever held between Jesuit institutions. But excitement there was, and the respective presidents negotiated for months on such details as the choice of judges and the necessary permissions that would have to be procured from the Provincial.[10] Father Brosnahan wrote to Father Richards, the rector of Georgetown:

> I asked that three boys be allowed to come and promised that they should be given quarters at the College & consequently all appearance of undue liberty

to be taken away. They are to come direct from Georgetown to Boston and to return in like manner. This is important, because if anything should happen . . . to give grounds for complaint, the scheme would end with its beginning.[11]

The much-heralded event took place—after two postponements—on May 1, 1895. Among the distinguished guests in a capacity audience in Boston College Hall that night were Bishop Brady, Vicar-General Byrne, Father Devitt (the former rector of Boston College), who had accompanied the debaters from Georgetown, and Father Richards, the president of Georgetown, who had come from an engagement in Buffalo for the occasion. It is recorded that the Boston debaters, Michael J. Scanlan ('95), Michael J. Splaine ('97), and John J. Kirby ('95), brought credit to their alma mater by their able defense of "The Equity of the Income Tax Law as Passed by the Last Congress," but in a close decision, decided finally by the vote of the chairman, they lost to the young men from the shores of the Potomac.[12] The philosophic Bostonians found consolation in the thought "that victory still remained in the Society [of Jesus]."[13]

Other innovations at this period took the form of improving and extending the school plant. On May 6, 1895, the Board of Trustees authorized Father Brosnahan to buy a small brick apartment house on 39 Newton Street, and the following March authorized the purchase of the adjoining building, No. 41.[14] This acquisition permitted the authorities to transfer the quarters of the Young Men's Catholic Association from the College building to 41 Newton Street, thus obtaining imperatively needed classroom space. The vacated YMCA wing of the building was occupied by the College for the opening of school in September 1898,[15] but the association did not have a formal dedication of their new quarters until January 24, 1899.[16]

The Sports Field Mirage

In June of 1898 the trustees had authorized another long-desired acquisition, grounds for an athletic field.[17] This land, purchased from the Oakes A. Ames Estate, consisted of some 402,000 square feet situated on both sides of Massachusetts Avenue beyond the then New England Railroad tracks. It had a frontage of about 500 feet on Massachusetts Avenue and ran back to Norfolk Avenue on one side, a distance of about 850 feet, with a mean width of 425 feet. It had about the same frontage on the other side of the avenue, with a depth of about 200 feet. On the easterly side of the property there was a row of tenement houses fronting on Willow Street.[18] This site, now occupied in large part by the Boston Edison Company's plant and employees' club, enjoyed the advantage of being within easy walking distance of the College. Moreover, there were rumors that the city would drain the adjacent marshes and put through a boulevard connecting Boston proper with South Boston and Dorchester.[19] Because of these

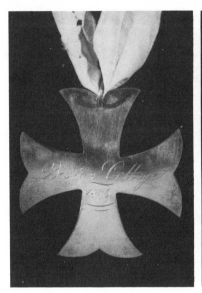

projected improvements, it was regarded as probable that some of the departments of the College would be moved to this new site.[20]

The announcement that the immediate purpose of the acquisition was to provide a large athletic field for the students was greeted with enthusiasm. *The Stylus* exulted, "There is nothing that brings greater joy to all than the final crowning of the efforts for an athletic field."[21] The students were given to understand that by the following spring, a portion of the land would have been cleared, enclosed, and laid out for baseball and track. There was even thought given to opening the field with a joint meet of some kind.[22] But these hopes were doomed to disappointment. Time went on, and nothing was done with the land, either by way of building on it for the school or of preparing it for athletics. In June 1900 the then president, Father Mullan, reported to the Alumni Association that it would cost $15,000 to prepare the new athletic field for use, and that this sum was not forthcoming.[23]

No competitive games ever were played on the tract, but some use was made of it as a practice field in the years that followed. The purchase, nevertheless, reflects credit on Father Brosnahan, despite the fact that the original plans for the land were never carried out, for—as he had surmised—the land gained so much in value (though for a reason different from that which he had foreseen) that one might say its original intention was achieved when the proceeds from its sale, which took place in 1912–1914, helped to finance the first part of the new Boston College.[24]

*   *   *

Toward the close of Father Brosnahan's period in office, he instituted some far-reaching changes which were destined to be brought to comple-

In the 19th century, inscribed sterling silver medals were awarded for excellence in each academic discipline. In 1876 Stephen J. Hart was medalist in rhetoric. Twenty years later John C. Sweeney, for excellence in analytical chemistry, received a medal depicting a laboratory flask over a flame.

tion by his successor. The College had gone through periods of alteration in 1876 and 1899 under Father Fulton, and was now, for the third time, to undergo extensive physical modification. One of these changes, the transfer of the Young Men's Catholic Association to 41 East Newton Street, has already been mentioned. Other adjustments affected the school itself, particularly with respect to the physical separation of college and high school studies.

From the College's inception in 1864, there was no separation of it from the preparatory classes. But in the Brosnahan years there were separate entries for the two student bodies and their classes were held in separate wings. With the moving of the Young Men's Catholic Association, their former gymnasium was upgraded and given to the College students, leaving the original gymnasium to the preparatory division. Thus a firm distinction between the College and the high school was established.[25]

ENDNOTES

1. Authorship of this article appears indicated by a passage in Father Devitt's manuscript history of the College, omitted in the printed version. He wrote, "It is characteristic of the Rector of that time [e.g., Father Devitt himself] that there appeared in the College Catalogue of 1893–94 a monograph of the college history. . . ." (the manuscript version of the history of Boston College is preserved in the Georgetown University Archives, Washington, D.C.).
2. Share No. 393 was first purchased by John Lamson in 1845 and bequeathed to Daniel Sanderson Lamson in 1859, who made a gift of the share to Boston College in 1865. This transaction is noted under the number of the share in an appendix to *The Influence and History of the Boston Athenaeum from 1807 to 1907* (Boston: The Boston Athenaeum, 1907).
3. *The Boston College Catalogue*, 1893–1894, pp. 18–21.

4. "Varia: Boston College," *Woodstock Letters,* 20(1891):295.
5. *The Boston College Catalogue* for the years 1890–1891; 1891–1892; 1893–1894.
6. *Ibid.,* 1893–1894, p. 73.
7. "Father Timothy Brosnahan," *Woodstock Letters,* 45(1916):105.
8. *Ibid.,* p. 99–117. The following account is based on this source.
9. *Ibid.,* p. 106.
10. Brosnahan to Richards, October 12, 1894, Georgetown University Archives.
11. *Ibid.*
12. "Boston College—The Intercollegiate Debate," *Woodstock Letters,* 24(1895):32–323.
13. *Ibid.,* p. 323.
14. "Records of the Trustees of Boston College," under dates May 6, 1895, and March 26, 1896. Manuscript volume in the Archives of Boston College.
15. *The Stylus,* 12(1898):440–441.
16. Farren, "The Young Men's Catholic Association," *The Pilot* (March 8, 1930).
17. "Records of the Trustees of Boston College," under date June 25, 1898.
18. *The Pilot* (July 9, 1898).
19. "Father Timothy Brosnahan," *Woodstock Letters,* 45(1916):106–107.
20. *The Pilot* (July 9, 1898).
21. *The Stylus,* 12(1898):453.
22. *Ibid.*
23. *The Boston Globe* (June 29, 1900).
24. "Father Timothy Brosnahan," *Woodstock Letters,* 45(1916):106–107.
25. *The Pilot,* September 1898.

CHAPTER 11

Conflict and Adjustments

On June 30, 1898, the Reverend W. G. Read Mullan, S.J., succeeded Father Brosnahan as president of Boston College. Father Mullan is remembered as a poised, soft-spoken man whose unaffected pleasure in being among students made him one of the most personally popular executives the College had known up to that time.

A Program for Improvement

Father Mullan was a courageous leader interested in improving Catholic education, and to that end he spoke his mind in unmistakable terms. At a meeting of representatives of Catholic colleges in the United States in Chicago less than a year after his inauguration, he delivered a paper on "The Drift Toward Non-Catholic Colleges and Universities" in which he pleaded vigorously for a modification of the then current Catholic boarding-school life and discipline, "so as to make both many times more attractive to young men."[1] He urged the separation of an institution's college department from the preparatory department, both in place and in administration, although not necessarily in the type of studies or the methods of instruction. He held that Catholic colleges:

> . . . should make some of the present courses of study optional, and enlarge and strengthen courses in History, History of Philosophy, Philosophy of

REV. W. G. READ MULLAN, S.J.
Eleventh President

Father Mullan was born in Baltimore on January 28, 1860. He entered the Society of Jesus on February 8, 1877, and was ordained after 14 years of classical and theological training and teaching experience at several Jesuit colleges. His promise of future leadership was acknowledged by his appointment shortly after ordination as dean at Fordham College. He was serving as a professor of rhetoric at Holy Cross College when he was called to the presidency of Boston College.

History, Political Economy, Constitutional History, advanced courses in English and the other modern literatures. They should raise, in many cases, the value of the A.B. degree, by stricter requirements for entrance and graduation, by a more thorough grading of classes, and by more masterly instruction.[2]

For the improvement of his own college, he carried out with enthusiasm the program of changes begun by Father Brosnahan. At the opening of classes in the fall of 1898, he effected the establishment of three completely distinct departments within the institution: the college proper, consisting of four regular classes leading to the degree of A.B.; the academic department, consisting of three classes preparatory for the college course; and the English department, consisting of graded classes in which English, modern languages, and the sciences were studied. In addition there was also a class for young students not old enough or well enough prepared to enter the academic department.[3]

In May 1899 he announced to the Catholics of Boston the plans he had for a better college, while admitting candidly the limitations under which the institution labored at the time.[4] He pointed out the advantages of developing the English department into a full-fledged English high school and of making the academic department a separate Latin high school. If endowments could be secured, he said, it was his ambition to establish professorships to which men of eminence outside the clergy could be elected—an accomplishment which, under existing conditions, was impossible at Boston College, since—apart from a few scholarships—no funds were available for professors' salaries.

Another point which deserved the attention of Boston Catholics was the lack of adequate room in the College. Growth, he informed them, was no longer possible within the existing building; classroom space for more than the present 460 students simply did not exist. He added a promise that if circumstances permitted, no tuition would be asked: "At the present time [he claimed], no student, however poor, is refused admission because he is unable to pay tuition, and of the four hundred young men registered in the college, scarcely more than half do so."[5]

A Question of Accrediting

Because Father Mullan constantly and sincerely endeavored to insure high scholastic standards, his indignation was understandable when Harvard University withdrew the name of Boston College from the list of institutions whose graduates would be admitted as regular students to the Harvard Law School. The new president of Boston College became engaged in a controversy with Charles W. Eliot, at that time approaching his thirtieth year as president of Harvard. The occasion was the decision of the Harvard Law

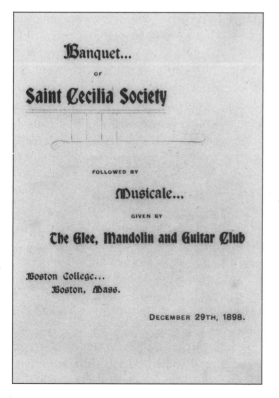

Voices and strings after dinner.

School in 1896 to admit only students with a bachelor's degree from an approved college. In drawing up the first list of approved colleges, the Harvard authorities included only one Jesuit college, Georgetown, where-upon representatives of Boston College and Holy Cross pointed out that their curricula were the same as that of Georgetown. On a revised list, these two colleges did appear, but when subsequently St. John's College, Ford-ham, made a similar claim, instead of granting the petition, the Harvard faculty committee reconsidered its former action and not only did not grant the Fordham request but on March 11, 1898, dropped Boston College and Holy Cross from the list.[6]

There followed a somewhat heated exchange of letters between Father Mullan and President Eliot in which the Harvard president made some rather disparaging generalizations about Jesuit colleges and Father Mullan repeatedly, but futilely, pressed Dr. Eliot to give the evidence that underlay his generalizations.[7]

Thus the dispute stood by the summer of 1900; but another incident had occurred in the meantime which had the effect of arousing partisan feeling still more. In an article in the *Atlantic Monthly* for October 1899 proposing the adoption of the elective system by the nation's high schools, President Eliot turned his guns on Jesuit education. Eliot, of course, had shocked the collegiate world a quarter of a century earlier by introducing the elective system at Harvard and had spent considerable energy defending it against the criticism of some of the most distinguished scholars and educators in the country. So, in attacking the fixed Jesuit curriculum in the waning hours of the nineteenth century, Eliot was firing one more defiant salvo at his critics of many years.

In his *Atlantic* article Eliot ridiculed two examples of prescribed curric-ula: that found in Moslem countries, where the Koran dictated a uniform education for all; and the curriculum of Jesuit colleges. That both examples were ecclesiastical, said Eliot, was significant, because only direct revelation from on high could justify a uniform curriculum.[8] Such public aspersion from a person of President Eliot's stature in a respected national journal called, the Jesuits felt, for a public response. The man chosen to speak for all the Jesuit colleges was a man of sharp mind and elegant pen, Father Timothy Brosnahan, recently retired as president of Boston College.

Brosnahan's rejoinder to the Eliot article was submitted to the *Atlantic Monthly,* but was rejected on the grounds that the magazine did not encourage controversy—even though an article by Professor Andrew West of Princeton University attacking Eliot's educational principles appeared in the *Atlantic* a month later.[9] (The editor of the *Atlantic,* Bliss Perry, himself a distinguished man of letters, years later acknowledged that his rejection of the Brosnahan article was a mistake.[10])

Father Brosnahan had his article published in the *Sacred Heart Review.* Because this publication hardly reached the audience that had read Eliot's remarks, the reply to Eliot was also printed in pamphlet form and distributed to educators and editors in all parts of the country.[11] It was well received. The editor of the *Bookman,* Professor T. H. Peck of Columbia University, praised it as containing "so much dialectical skill, so much crisp and convincing argument, and so much educational good sense."[12] And, indeed, one of Boston College's vice presidents was visited in the late 1960s by a senior who had taken a student-style "sabbatical" after his junior year to sample academic offerings elsewhere and who had sat in on a writing course at Harvard where the class was studying Brosnahan's reply to Eliot as a model of rhetorical excellence!

Father Brosnahan might have taken wry satisfaction had he lived to read in the history of Harvard written by Samuel Eliot Morison (who was awarded an honorary degree at Boston College in 1960) this judgment: "It is a hard saying, but Mr. Eliot, more than any other man, is responsible for the greatest educational crime of the century against American youth—depriving him of his classical heritage."[13]

The cause of the original disagreement between administrators at Boston College and Harvard—namely, the Law School's privileged list—appeared in the Harvard University catalog each year until the 1905–1906 issue when, in place of the list, applicants for admission were advised to make inquiries concerning the status of their particular college to the secretary of the law faculty.[14]

Experimentation and Adjustment

Meanwhile, by the year 1902 a program of unification of studies had been successfully put into practice by the colleges of the Jesuit province of Maryland after some three years of experimentation and adjustment. The authorities at Boston College reported to the Provincial at the close of that year that their part in the change had been carried out satisfactorily.[15]

As early as 1900 Father Mullan had announced that more rigorous entrance requirements were in force and that the preparatory school would thereafter comprise a full four-year course which, among other results, would render more time available for modern languages, mathematics, and history.[16] A history program providing for two lectures a week on the Reformation during freshman year and on the Middle Ages during sophomore was instituted. To strengthen the distinctively Catholic features of the curriculum, in addition to the ordinary catechism recitations, four distinct sets of weekly lectures on Christian doctrine were laid out for the various student levels. Written examinations at the end of the school year on the matter covered by the lectures were required of those following the courses, with special cash prizes offered for the most proficient.[17]

Among the laymen engaged at this time for a series of special lectures were Herbert S. Carruth, who lectured on the constitutional history of the United States; Doctor James Field Spalding, on modern English literature; and Manuel de Moreira, on French literature. The latter also conducted a

French academy among the more advanced French students in the College and directed the annual French play.

On July 30, 1903, Father Mullan was succeeded in office by the Reverend William F. Gannon, S.J., who continued without interruption the program of improvements begun by his predecessor. At the first high school graduation during his term in office, Father Gannon inaugurated the presentation of diplomas to the high school graduates.[18] In the same year (1904) he contributed to the increasing dignity of the annual commencement by securing an orator of national importance, the Honorable W. Bourke Cockran, to deliver the principal address.[19]

In a speech to the Alumni Association at that organization's banquet on June 23, 1904, he voiced his hope that athletics might be built up at the College, and he reviewed with satisfaction the success of the preparatory school sports during the past year.[20] The baseball nine had been reestablished, he reported, but the students training for the various teams were confronted by serious difficulties which apparently would hinder indefinitely the development of strong teams in the major sports. One may presume that he had in mind the lack of a gymnasium and a suitable playing field as prime requisites for an athletic program.

In May of 1905 a writer from *The Stylus* reported that the rector was persevering in his efforts to provide physical training for the students through athletics. Efforts were made to have the athletic field ready for baseball that spring, and the rector even encouraged by his presence the various intramural teams that had been organized. At the time, intercollegiate competition in baseball was impractical because of existing handicaps, but, *The Stylus* reported, "Our various class teams afford no end of interest and exercise to all the students. Witness the fields on Massachusetts Avenue on almost every afternoon and say not that true college athletics are dead at the college."[21]

*　　*　　*

Although in 1900 Boston College had had the largest college department and the largest high school department of any Jesuit institution in the

The Boston College Debating Society was started in 1868. It took the name of Fulton in 1890.

REV. WILLIAM F. GANNON, S.J.
Twelfth President

Father Gannon was born on March 31, 1859, and entered the Society of Jesus on August 5, 1876. His academic preparation for ordination was interrupted by six years of teaching mathematics and French at Holy Cross College and Fordham College. He was ordained in June 1891. Later he taught French at Holy Cross and St. Francis Xavier College in New York, and he served as assistant dean of discipline at Georgetown and as dean at St. Peter's College in New Jersey. During the years before his elevation to the presidency, Father Gannon became a well-known preacher and member of the Jesuit Mission Band.

United States,[22] both branches began to experience a discouraging falling off in attendance during the first years of the new century. The official figures for the entire student body beginning with the year 1898 were: 477, 475, 412, 370, 375, 350, 335 (the low point, in 1904), 350, and 457.[23] No reason was ever discovered for this fluctuation.

In 1905 St. Thomas Aquinas College in Cambridge, Massachusetts, closed its doors, and some of the students who were attending the two-year course there transferred to Boston College.[24] The increment at James Street was not large, but it did constitute part of a definite trend toward recovery which became noticeable by 1906. The movement upward was made permanent shortly afterward when the College received an impetus, the effects of which have been felt up to the present day. That impetus was the elevation to the presidency on January 6, 1907, of Father Thomas I. Gasson, S.J.

ENDNOTES

1. *The Pilot* (April 22, 1899).
2. *Ibid.*
3. *Ibid.* (August 20, 1898).
4. *Ibid.* (May 13, 1899).
5. *Ibid.*

6. Letter of Doctor Eliot to Rev. John F. Lehy, S.J., president of Holy Cross College, October 24, 1898. Copy preserved in Maryland Provincial S.J. Archives, Georgetown University Library. This letter is evidently substantially the same as the one which Father Mullan mentions as having received from President Eliot under the same date, cf. Father Mullan's covering letter for the published correspondence, *The Boston Globe* (June 25, 1900).

7. *The Boston Globe* (June 25, 1900).

8. Charles W. Eliot, "Recent Changes in Secondary Education," *The Atlantic Monthly,* 84(October 1899):443.

9. The Editors to Rev. Timothy Brosnahan, December 9, 1899, *Woodstock Letters,* 45(1916):109.

10. Bliss Perry, *And Gladly Teach* (Boston: Houghton Mifflin Co., 1935), pp. 170–171.

11. *Sacred Heart Review,* January 13, 1900. The pamphlet: *President Eliot and Jesuit Colleges,* by Timothy Brosnahan, S.J. (no publisher; no date), 36 pp.

12. *The Bookman* (New York), 11:111–112, April 1900. Cf. also *Woodstock Letters,* 29(1900):143.

13. Samuel Eliot Morison, *Three Centuries of Harvard* (Cambridge: Harvard University Press, 1936), pp. 389–390.

14. *The Harvard University Catalogue* for 1904–1905, under law school admission regulations.

15. "Historia Domus, 1899–1902," official triennial report to the Provincial from Boston College. Manuscript preserved in the Maryland Provincial S.J. Archives, Georgetown University Library.

16. *The Boston Globe* (June 29, 1900).

17. Anonymous letter entitled "Boston College and Church of the Immaculate Conception," dated June 29, 1903, in *Woodstock Letters,* 32(1903):112–113.

18. *The Stylus,* 17(June 1904):113.

19. *Ibid.*

20. *Ibid.,* 17(July 1904):205.

21. *The Stylus,* 18(May 1905):20.

22. *The Boston Globe* (June 29, 1900); *Woodstock Letters,* 29(1900):354.

23. Official figures from supplement entitled: "Students in Our Colleges in the United States and Canada," occurring each year in *Woodstock Letters,* 1898 to 1906.

24. *Seventy-Five Years: St. Mary's of the Annunciation, 1867–1942* (Cambridge, Mass., n.n., 1942), pp. 19 and 23. St. Thomas Aquinas College had developed from the high school of St. Mary of the Annunciation parish in 1881.

CHAPTER 12

Brave Vision

Thomas Ignatius Gasson was born September 23, 1859, at Seven Oaks, a small town in Kent, England, 25 miles southeast of London.[1] His father came from a French Huguenot family and his mother was descended from an old Kent family by the name of Curtis, several of whose members had held the rectorship of the parish church of St. Nicholas at Seven Oaks. Thomas did preparatory studies in St. Stephen's School in London. At age 11 he was placed under the tutelage of the Reverend Allen Edwards, a clergyman of the Church of England. Two years later in 1872 he left England for the United States.

Thomas' plans to settle with an older brother in Philadelphia did not come to pass. As he set about to support himself, he was befriended by two Catholic women, Catherine Doyle and Anne McGarvey, who in time arranged for his instruction in the Catholic faith. He was received into the Church in October 1874 in the Chapel of The Holy Family, now the Jesuit Church of the Gesu in Philadelphia. He joined the Society of Jesus on November 17, 1875. During his preparation for ordination he taught at Loyola College, Baltimore, and St. Francis Xavier College, New York City, before being sent for his theological studies to the University of Innsbruck in Austria.

On July 26, 1891, Father Gasson was ordained to the priesthood by the Prince-Bishop of Brixen in the University Church in Innsbruck. He re-

Rev. Thomas Ignatius Gasson, S.J., the "second founder."

mained at the university for an additional year of theology and performed the duties of chaplain in one of the charitable institutions of the city.

His first appointment upon his return to the United States in the summer of 1892 was to teach poetry for two years to juniors at Frederick, Maryland, before devoting a year to the required study of ascetical theology at the same institution. In August 1895 he was assigned to Boston College to teach the junior class, and two years later was made professor of ethics and economics, continuing to teach these subjects until his appointment as president of the College on January 6, 1907.

A New Site Is Considered

On March 13, a little over two months after his inauguration, Father Gasson suggested to the Jesuit Provincial that the College purchase the "magnificent site on Commonwealth Avenue towards Brighton."[2] One of the earliest references to this location had been made seven years before on July 21, 1900, in a letter from Henry Witmore, of the realty firm of Meredith and Grew in Boston, to Father W. G. Read Mullan, S.J., then president of the College.[3] Among the parcels of land which he described to Father Mullan was the following:

> . . . known as the old Lawrence farm, and I think [it] may safely be called one of the very finest pieces of land in the vicinity of Boston. It lies to the west of Chestnut Hill Reservoir, bordered on the east by the Park around the reservoir, and commands a superb view across the water over Brighton and Brookline toward Boston. . . . It . . . seems almost intended by nature for the site of a large institution. It divides naturally into three parts. In the centre is a nearly level plateau . . . ; buildings placed thereon would command the magnificent view before referred to, and themselves would be the central objects in the charming landscape to the west of the reservoir. South of this plateau, between it and Beacon Street, is a nearly level field . . . admirably suited to an athletic field. North of the plateau . . . is a tract . . . sloping from the higher land toward the Avenue and Reservoir Park.

It is interesting to note that the two other parcels of land proposed in this letter as alternative sites for Boston College have since been occupied by Catholic institutions: Mount Alvernia Academy on Waban Hill and St. Elizabeth's Hospital on the old Nevins estate at Washington, Cambridge, and Warren streets in Brighton.

Whether or not Father Mullan was already aware of the availability of the Lawrence land is not known, nor is there any record of his reaction to this offer. No further mention of it is found until 1907, when, with all authorities in agreement that the Harrison Avenue location was no longer suitable for Boston College, the Commonwealth Avenue site was brought into discussion again.

Father Gasson pointed out that the cost might, on investigation, prove too great, but on the credit side was the fact that Archbishop Williams had already given his approval to the proposed change and appeared disposed to grant parish rights to a church at the new location. What to do with the existing buildings—particularly, the Immaculate Conception Church—was a problem; the Fathers had reason to believe that the archbishop would be unwilling to change the church's status from collegiate to parish. Evidently, Father Gasson seemed to doubt that a new college and the old institution could be maintained simultaneously. In any case, the project was destined to remain in the realm of wishful thinking for several months more.

In May of 1907 Father Gasson aroused the enthusiastic interest of the alumni in the project by announcing at the annual alumni dinner that new buildings and a new location for the College were imperative and that a fund of $10 million would be needed.[4] He eloquently described the role of higher education in maintaining the dignity and welfare of the Church, and he pointed out that Boston College could not do its part in achieving this high purpose in its present location and without being separated from the high school. He concluded by saying that funds should also be made available for the hiring of distinguished lay professors and for the establishment of an expanded program in the natural sciences.

One immediate result of this appeal was the creation of a board of advisers for Father Gasson, selected by him from among the prominent businessmen in the group. The function of this board was to suggest ways and means of securing the financial assistance needed.

On July 24, 1907, the question of securing property was again brought up by Father Gasson. He reported to the Provincial that priests and prominent citizens of the city were urging the College authorities to buy at once, warning that soon it would be too late. Father Gasson seemed to think that this action should be taken at this time, even if it meant yielding the hopes of having a parish connected with the new institution.[5]

Meanwhile, the energetic rector had caused the entire school to be renovated. Classrooms and corridors had been painted during the summer months and a broad stairway had been constructed to provide easier access from the street floor to the gymnasium.[6] When school opened that September, there were 140 young men registered at the college level and 360 in the high school—the largest entering classes in the history of the institution up to that time.[7]

The Chestnut Hill Location

On August 30, 1907, Archbishop Williams died and Archbishop William H. O'Connell succeeded to the See of Boston. This change meant, of course, renewing all permissions and approvals granted by Archbishop Williams in connection with the proposed new Boston College. So, on October 24, the Jesuit Provincial, his Socius, and Father Gasson visited Archbishop O'Connell to lay their plans before him. The prelate showed the keen interest of an alumnus, as well as that of head of the diocese, in the proposals, and gave them his full approval, including permission to buy

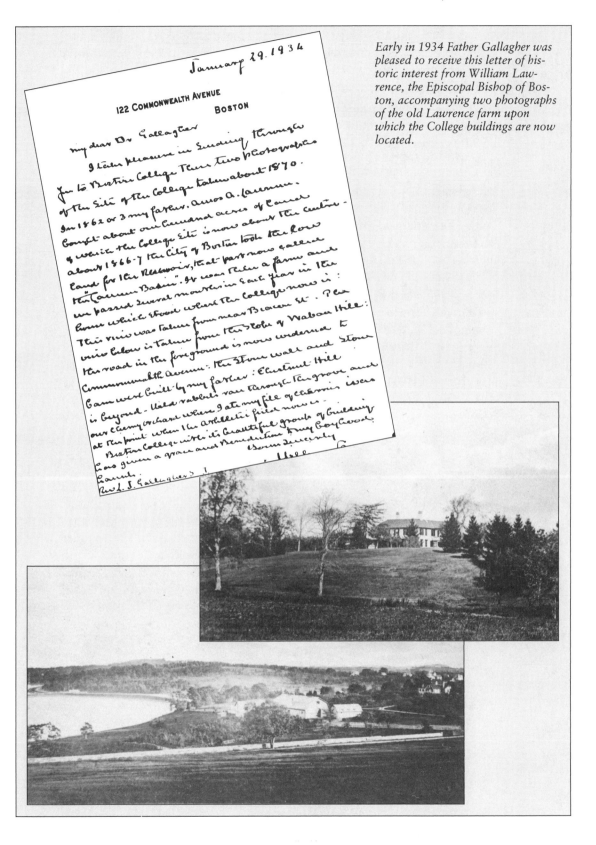

Early in 1934 Father Gallagher was pleased to receive this letter of historic interest from William Lawrence, the Episcopal Bishop of Boston, accompanying two photographs of the old Lawrence farm upon which the College buildings are now located.

property and build.[8] It was still undecided which of three available sites would be more desirable,[9] although the archbishop evidently was strongly in favor of the Chestnut Hill location.[10] As it turned out, the Chestnut Hill land was selected, and on November 11, 1907, a special meeting of the Trustees of Boston College was called. It was voted to purchase two parcels of land: one owned by E. S. Eldridge on Commonwealth Avenue, Newton, and the other, an adjoining parcel, owned by the Provident Institution for Savings.[11] At the same meeting, the president of the College was authorized to petition the legislature for amendments to the charter of the corporation (1) changing its name to the Trustees of Boston College (instead of "*the* Boston College"), (2) for authority to grant medical degrees, and (3) for authority to hold additional real and personal estate.[12]

Two weeks later, on November 25, another special meeting of the trustees was held to authorize the corporation (of the College) to purchase a tract of land owned by Henry S. Shaw and the Mt. Auburn Cemetery Association adjoining the parcels of land voted on previously and fronting on Beacon Street and the driveway. The purchase of the fourth and last section, situated on Beacon, Hammond, and South streets (the latter now College Road) and owned by the Massachusetts Hospital Life Insurance Company, was also approved at this meeting.[13]

Papers were passed on the new property on December 12, bringing to the College a total area of some thirty-one acres[14] with an assessed evaluation of $187,500.[15] Public announcement of the purchase was made in the newspapers of December 18.[16]

The Drive for Funds

Immediately there was enthusiastic talk of erecting buildings—a group that would include dormitories and that would eventually house "the greatest Catholic College in America."[17] A mass meeting was called for Monday night, January 20, 1908, at the College hall,[18] to which the most distinguished alumnus, Archbishop O'Connell, was invited.[19] Eight hundred former students and friends of the College answered the call and heard

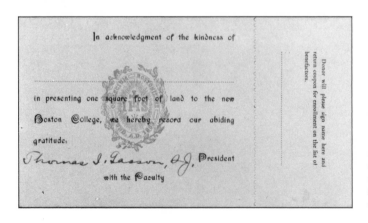

In acknowledgment of the kindness of

in presenting one square foot of land to the new Boston College, we hereby record our abiding gratitude.

Thomas I. Gasson, S.J., President

with the Faculty

Donor will please sign name here and return coupon for enrollment on the list of benefactors.

In the fund drive for the new campus, donors were asked to buy one square foot of the former Lawrence property for the College.

Father Gasson read the archbishop's address, when the latter was prevented by illness from attending. Fifty thousand dollars were pledged by the audience in response to the pleas of the speakers, and thus a beginning was made for the establishment of a new Boston College.[20]

Under the direction of Doctor John F. O'Brien of Charlestown, who had been chairman of the first meeting, a second mass meeting was held on February 17, at which an additional $137,000 was pledged.[21] A week later another impetus was given the drive by the formation of a "Boston College Club," with membership open to those "interested in the extension of Boston College."[22]

On June 20, 1908, the first of the well-remembered lawn parties was held at Chestnut Hill for the benefit of the new institution. The grounds for the campus were dedicated by Father Gasson and named by him "University Heights" upon this occasion. Throughout the day, some 25,000 persons witnessed the exhibits and patronized the many booths, with some 12,000 gathering to hear the Honorable Bourke Cockran deliver the principal address.[23]

Designs and Plans

During the late fall of 1908, Father Gasson devoted some weeks to an inspection of several of the larger colleges and universities east of the Mississippi in order to obtain ideas that might be utilized in the design and equipment. Of the institutions visited, Chicago University impressed Father Gasson most favorably. He felt that this group of buildings showed a unity of idea that was admirable and a flexibility of design that would permit symmetrical growth in the years to come.[24]

On January 25, 1909, a competition to determine the best general plans for the new buildings was announced, and 14 architects were invited to compete.[25] The contest was held in accordance with the regulations governing general professional practice laid down by the American Institute of Architects. The first of the three prizes offered was an award of $1000 for the best general plan of the grounds and positioning of the buildings; the second, $500 for the next best general plan; and the third, a commission to design and supervise the construction of the recitation building, for the best plan of this building. All entries were prepared in a uniform manner, with the only indication of the architect's identity being a code mark placed on each set of plans by a neutral referee to correspond with the marking of a sealed envelope containing the architect's name. The contest closed on March 15, 1909, and the decisions were to be announced on or before April 12.

The committee of judges consisted of the president, Father Gasson; a member of the faculty, Father David W. Hearn, S.J., vice president of Boston College and formerly president of St. Francis Xavier College, New York City; two members of the Board of Trustees, Father J. Havens Richards, S.J., formerly president of Georgetown University, and Father

Several fairs, drawing as many as 25,000 people, were held on the new Chestnut Hill property to raise funds for the new buildings.

Joseph T. Keating, S.J., treasurer of Boston College; an architect, William D. Austin; a builder, Charles W. Logue; and a landscape architect, Arthur A. Shurtleff.

On Saturday, April 10, 1909, after meeting several times to discuss the entries, the judges finally agreed on the plans to be given first prize, but the name of the winning architect was not made known until the following Monday, when it was announced that the Boston firm of Maginnis and Walsh had won first and third prizes and that Edward T. P. Graham of Cambridge, Massachusetts, had won second prize.[26]

According to the prize-winning general plan, provisions were made for a group of about 15 buildings, with large sports fields and a landscaped campus. The architectural style adopted for the group was English Collegiate Gothic, which appealed to the architects as most suitable because of the natural characteristics of the site—uneven topography and lack of parallelism in bounding streets—and because of the appropriate sentiment of this architectural tradition in relation to collegiate life.[27]

According to the architects, the plan was intended roughly to suggest that of a cathedral, the buildings being disposed " . . . so as to form longitudinal and transverse courts, at the junction of which is placed the recitation building. . . . This building, surmounted by a massive Gothic tower, will be the dominating centre of the group."[28] The plan envisioned separate buildings for faculty, library, chapel, philosophy, biology, physics, chemistry, a gymnasium, and a dining hall, and it provided a great quadrangle framed with trees. Friends of Boston College who regret the loss of open space and greenery as building has followed building in the latter twentieth century would have had little space or meadows to mourn had the College been in a position financially to carry out the ambitious Maginnis and Walsh plans, all sited on the present central campus.

At the time these plans were drawn up, it was expected that work would commence on the recitation building during the summer of 1909 and be ready for the first influx of students by September 1910, permitting the class of 1911 to have the honor of being the first to graduate from the new College.[29] As will be seen, these hopes proved too optimistic.

Meanwhile, steps were being taken to raise funds for the building program. The Young Men's Catholic Association omitted its annual "College Ball," a tradition of 30 years, to sponsor a gigantic musical festival at

The architects' conception of the entire campus (the present central campus). Note that their large central building, now Gasson Hall, dominates the design, as it still does.

Mechanics Building in Boston on April 19, 1909, featuring a chorus of 400 voices. For this function, the association achieved the almost unbelievable advance sale of 10,000 tickets at one dollar each.[30]

By the beginning of June 1909, the plans for the recitation building had been submitted to and approved by the Jesuit Provincial and General.[31] At the same time, it was tentatively decided to rebuild the stone barn which was located on the Chestnut Hill property as a temporary faculty residence, pending the erection of the faculty building, in preference to repairing the lodge house on the property or renting a dwelling house in the vicinity. As it turned out, none of these plans was put into effect; the faculty, as will be seen, was obliged to commute each day from Harrison Avenue throughout the College's first three years at Chestnut Hill.

On June 19 a second garden party was held on the grounds at University Heights under the direction of the alumni association president, Dr. Eugene A. McCarthy, of Cambridge. This function was even more successful than the party of the previous year had been, drawing an attendance of over 30,000 persons. The feature of the afternoon was the turning of the first sod for the recitation building, which took place in the presence of a distinguished gathering. Father Gasson spoke the words:

> In the name of the August Trinity, the Father, Son and Holy Ghost, in the name of Jesus Christ, Saviour of the world, and who has given us the only civilization by which a nation can endure, in the name of all that is high and noble, we perform the first act of this series of tremendous acts which are to result in this great blessing for the people of the Commonwealth of Massachusetts.[32]

Then, with a silver spade, he formally turned the first sod.

Father Gasson breaking ground for the first building.

Cast of Macbeth, 1913.

The Irish Hall of Fame

The very month of the ground-breaking for the first building on the Chestnut Hill campus, another project was announced in the Boston papers: the "Daniel O'Connell Memorial Building and Irish Hall of Fame." Had the project succeeded, it might have been America's first hall of fame![33] An energetic Jesuit attached to the Immaculate Conception Church, Father James Maguire, S.J., secured the support of all the Irish-American clubs in Boston for the plan. The scheme called for a gigantic building with a large circular hall with high Gothic arches and massive stone piers surrounded by 32 alcoves, each serving as a museum for one of the counties of Ireland. It was proposed to locate the building on the site where Bapst now stands.

One cannot believe Father Gasson welcomed this competitive fund-raising effort at a time when his own drive for funds was faltering. When the sponsors of the O'Connell Memorial project realized that financial considerations would postpone their scheme indefinitely, they turned over to Father Gasson the money they had collected; it later funded the stately Irish assembly hall in the building later appropriately named Gasson Hall.[34]

*   *   *

Father Gasson had an incredibly bold dream for a new Boston College. Credit must be given to his Jesuit colleagues, especially his superiors, who backed his dream. But on Father Gasson himself fell the burden of translating the dream to reality.

ENDNOTES

1. These paragraphs on the life of Father Gasson are based on William J. Conway, S.J., "Father Thomas I. Gasson, S.J.," *Woodstock Letters,* 60(1931):76–86, and *The Pilot* (January 12, 1907).

2. Thomas I. Gasson, S.J., to Joseph Hanselman, S.J., March 13, 1907, Maryland Provincial S.J. Archives, Georgetown University Library.

3. Letter preserved in the Boston College Archives.

4. *The Pilot* (June 1, 1907).

5. Thomas I. Gasson, S.J., to Joseph Hanselman, S.J., July 24, 1907, Maryland Provincial S.J. Archives, Georgetown University Library.

6. *The Pilot* (September 14, 1907).

7. *Ibid.* (September 21, 1907).

8. Thomas I. Gasson, S.J., to Joseph Hanselman, S.J., October 26, 1907, Maryland Provincial S.J. Archives, Georgetown University Library.

9. *Ibid.*

10. Monsignor Jeremiah F. Minihan to Rev. Robert H. Lord, June 14, 1941, Diocesan Archives, Boston. After consulting with His Eminence, Cardinal O'Connell, in answer to Father Lord's inquiry, Monsignor Minihan reported, "Father Gasson inspected and bought the Lawrence Estate on the advice and suggestion of His Eminence."

11. "Records of the Trustees of Boston College," under date November 11, 1907, Boston College Archives.

12. *Ibid.*

13. *Ibid.,* under date November 25, 1907.

14. Thomas I. Gasson, S.J., to Joseph Hanselman, S.J., December 9, 1907, Maryland Provincial S.J. Archives, Georgetown University Library.

15. *The Pilot* (December 28, 1907).

16. *The Boston Herald* (December 18, 1907).

17. *The Pilot* (December 28, 1907).

18. *Ibid.* (January 11, 1908).

19. *The Boston Herald* (January 12, 1908).

20. *The Boston Globe* (January 21, 1908).

21. *The Boston Herald* (February 15, 1908); and *The Pilot* (February 22, 1908).

22. *The Boston Herald* (February 25, 1908); and *The Pilot* (February 29, 1908).

23. *The Pilot* (June 27, 1908).

24. *The Boston Post* (December 24, 1908).

25. This account of the competition is based on the official announcement and statement of conditions of the contest, and correspondence concerning it, preserved in the Boston College Archives. Charles D. Maginnis of Boston, a member of the firm which won the competition, supplied additional details.

26. *The Boston Herald* (April 13, 1909).

27. *Ibid.*

28. *Ibid.;* also *The Boston Evening Transcript* (May 4, 1909).

29. *The Boston Herald* (April 13, 1909).

30. *The Pilot* (April 24, 1909), and *The Boston American* (January 31, 1909).

31. Thomas I. Gasson, S.J., to Joseph Hanselman, S.J., June 5, 1909, Maryland Provincial S.J. Archives, Georgetown University Library.

32. *The Pilot* (June 26, 1909).

33. *The Boston Globe* (June 27, 1909).

34. Father Dunigan was indebted to Father James I. Maguire, S.J., of St. Joseph's Church in Philadelphia for his kindness and to Charles D. Maginnis of Boston for details concerning the Irish Hall of Fame movement.

CHAPTER 13

The Towers on the Heights

Excavation of the foundation area for the Tower Building began in the fall of 1909.[1] Since the foundations had to be blasted out of solid rock, the work was necessarily slow, but the stone which was removed provided material for the walls, thereby reducing expenses. The laying of masonry began in the spring of 1910,[2] after the Board of Trustees authorized Father Gasson to contract for the building operations.[3] By the following October, a roof was already over two wings of the structure.[4]

That month the grounds were visited by Cardinal Vannutelli, the Papal Legate, who was passing through Boston on his way to attend the Eucharistic Congress in Canada. The cardinal expressed his enthusiastic admiration for the plans of the College and seemed most impressed by the fact that such admirable style was achieved without resort to elaborate and expensive ornamentation.[5]

Sacrifices, Delays, Disappointments

No large donations to the building fund were received, and the many parties and functions held during these years to benefit the College did not realize enough to meet even a sizable fraction of the building costs. The income from the Immaculate Conception Church at this period was devoted almost exclusively to the College fund. Whatever the Jesuit Community could realize through stipends offered for religious retreats, sermons, lectures, and other activities was put aside for the new building.[6] The self-denial and hardships undergone by the Community in their efforts to save every available penny for the fund has never been sufficiently appreciated. But despite these gallant attempts on the part of so many friends of Boston College, both lay and religious, to meet the expenses of the new undertaking, the burden of debt mounted so swiftly that it soon threatened to put an end to the whole project. Father William J. Conway, S.J., administrative assistant to Father Gasson at the time, afterward wrote, "Father Gasson saw all too clearly that unless the unforeseen happened, the building would never reach completion. The winter of 1910 saw him face-to-face with failure."[7] The same authority claims that at one point in the construction of the building, the delay due to shortage of funds threatened to be so lengthy that some kind of temporary covering was rigged over the work which had already been completed.[8]

To meet this financial crisis, Father Gasson obtained permission from the Jesuit authorities in Rome in 1910 to sell the tract of land on Massachusetts Avenue in Boston purchased by the College as an athletic field 12 years before. On March 6, 1911, the trustees authorized the sale of the land to a public utilities company at a favorable price, thereby enabling the rector to continue the construction.[9]

In May 1911, when work was resumed, the tower part of the building had been built up to the level of the roof, and some of the roof tiling had been done.[10] During the summer, the tower was completed, and by October practically all the heavy masonry work had been finished and the heating and ventilating systems, as well as the steel stairways, had been installed. It had even been thought that the laying of the cornerstone might take place during the fall, but the date was postponed until the following May or June, with no one foreseeing that further delays would push the date back for another full year.[11]

One consolation in this period of trial was the phenomenal growth of the high school and college enrollments at James Street. The combined registration in September 1911 exceeded the thousand mark—a growth of 100 per cent in five years! The Boston College enrollment was the largest, next to that of Holy Cross College, of any purely prescribed and classical college in America. Boston College High School, at the same time, had the distinction of being the country's largest classical high school for boys.[12] To provide for this growth, two rooms in the faculty residence on Harrison Avenue had to be converted into classrooms.[13]

Father Gasson found comfort, also, in the reflection that during the year he had had the opportunity of refusing "an enormous and magnificent sum—a sum which would erect a number of our proposed buildings—if I would part with a portion of our grounds. But I concluded that if our site was so good and fitting for other institutions, it was worthy of Boston

College."[14] Oral tradition has it that this offer was made by the authorities of a local university.

Throughout the following winter (1911–1912) work on the new building was pushed forward. From the exterior, the building presented an almost-finished appearance. The windows were in place except those in the assembly hall and in the tower, where it was hoped that stained glass might be used. Electrical wiring and the last of the heating apparatus were being installed, but the task of proper grading and landscaping of the grounds remained.[15] Nevertheless, it was still felt that the building might be dedicated in the spring and classes held on the Heights in September.[16] But again, the unforeseen delays, which were now becoming so familiar, and the length of time required to put the grounds in proper order[17] operated against the scheduled opening. By October (1912) it was hoped that, if all went well, classes would be transferred to University Heights the following Easter.[18]

An Adult Education Program

The winter of 1912–1913 witnessed an attempt to initiate a night school of graduate caliber for adults.[19] In response to a request from a group of prominent Catholic laymen, Father Gasson had delivered a series of lectures on the philosophy of history during 1912. At the close of the course, when another series was demanded, Father Matthew L. Fortier, S.J., of the College staff, was appointed to conduct further series in Catholic philosophy. Father Fortier felt that something more could be achieved than mere casual attendance at these talks, if several courses of lectures were offered simultaneously and if academic credit were granted in connection with them.

Father Gasson approved of the plan, and by December 1912 a postgraduate department was in operation, with the modest schedule of two series of lectures on the philosophy of literature, by Father Gasson, and on professional ethics, by Father Fortier. The postgraduate course was open only to those already having an A.B. degree and whose applications were acted on favorably by the faculty board of admissions. To obtain a degree, candidates were obliged to attend at least two of the prescribed courses and to pass satisfactory examinations in the matter of the courses. Also, they had to have a thesis accepted, said thesis to be an original study of some subject related to the matter of the course and equivalent in length to 100 pages of print. A familiarity with Catholic philosophy was assumed, and for those not acquainted with the subject sufficiently there were prerequisite courses offered by the Young Men's Catholic Association. Twenty-five students enrolled the first year.

This new department granted the master's degree to 19 candidates in 1913, to 42 in 1914, and to 22 in 1915. In addition, several A.B. degrees were granted to adults who had never had the opportunity to finish their college course in the day division.[20] The difficulties involved in providing adequate faculty and library facilities for this postgraduate work and the possible conflict with the regular College department in the matter of degrees led several members of the College staff to petition Father Lyons, shortly after his accession to the presidency, to discontinue the courses. In May 1914 it was decided that new students would not be admitted to postgraduate courses in the night school when classes reconvened in September.[21] The question of graduate classes was not taken up again until after World War I.

The Day Approaches

Through the winter and spring of 1913, construction on the new building consisted largely of finishing work. The plasterers had completed their work by December, and four months were allowed for drying of the plaster before the work of mural decoration was to commence. Father Gasson had secured for this latter task the services of Brother Francis C. Schroen, S.J., who had been a professional decorator before entering the Society of Jesus and who had recently won wide praise for his artistic decoration of Gaston Hall and the Philodemic Debating Society room at Georgetown University. Jesuit churches and other institutions throughout the country bore on their walls paintings that were a glorious testimony to this famous lay brother's skill and genius, so it was with pleasurable excitement that his coming was awaited.[22] In March Father Gasson announced the painter's arrival, and the work was begun which would take until late that year to finish.

The newspapers early in March carried the long-awaited news that the recitation building at Boston College would open for classes later that month.[23] It was decided at this time that the entire student body would not be transferred to the new quarters because of limited laboratory facilities and lack of suitable living accommodations for the faculty, but the seniors, forming the golden anniversary class of the College, would have the honor of finishing the scholastic year at the Heights. Speculation arose as to which professors would be assigned to the new building, but it was soon announced that one, at least, had been settled upon. This was to be the Reverend William P. Brett, S.J., professor of ethics, who was a member of the first class ever graduated from Boston College and who now was to have the distinction of being the first Jesuit to teach a class in the new surroundings. Father Fortier also taught seniors, but since he also had a junior class which was scheduled to remain at James Street, it was thought better to have Father Gasson take over the lectures in psychology at Chestnut Hill.[24]

Open for Class

On Friday morning, March 28, 1913, groups of young men wearing derby hats and carrying "Boston bags" crowded streetcars for the long trip to

*The class of 1913 entering the campus for the dedication of the Tower
building on March 28, 1913.*

Lake Street. Those who had been foresighted enough to purchase newspapers read the tragic news of the Dayton flood and perhaps skimmed the advertisements of the now-defunct Henry Seigal and Company and the Shephard-Norwell Stores. On the amusement page, they read that Maclyn Arbuckle was still playing in "The Round-up" at the Boston and Otis Skinner in "Kismet" at the Hollis. Somewhere on the inside pages they would come upon a brief notice that the new Boston College was opening that day. These lads, 71 in number, left the cars at the end of the line and, with the enthusiasm of a new adventure, began the long trudge up Commonwealth Avenue to the campus.

At about half-past nine, the students assembled at the South Street (College Road) entrance to the grounds, where they were met by Father Gasson and some members of the faculty, in the presence of a number of newspaper photographers who recorded the scene for posterity.[25] The group formed a procession and entered the building through the west porch, coming to a halt in the rotunda. There the students gathered informally about Father Gasson, who turned to them and spoke these simple words of dedication:

> Gentlemen of the Class of 1913; this is an historic moment. We now, in an informal manner, take possession of this noble building, which has been erected for the greater glory of God, for the spread of the true faith, for the cultivation of solid knowledge, for the development of genuine science, and for the constant study of those ideals which make for the loftiest civic probity and for the most exalted personal integrity. May this edifice ever have upon it the special blessing of the Most High, may it ever be a source of strength to the Church and her rulers, a source of joy to the Catholics of Boston and its vicinity, a strong bulwark of strength for our Country and a stout defence for the illustrious State of which we are justly proud.[26]

Following the dedication, the group left the rotunda and began a tour of inspection throughout the building from the basement to the turrets. The seniors were permitted to select their own classroom, and they chose a large, sunny room in the southeast wing.[27] The mural decorations in the president's office (now the office of the dean of Arts and Sciences), in the office of the prefect of studies, and in the senior assembly hall, which were in the process of being painted at the time by Brother Schroen, drew the appreciative attention of the visitors.[28] The building's main art piece, the statue of St. Michael, had not yet been moved from James Street to its destined position in the rotunda.[29]

The building was opened for inspection by the public on the occasion of a party to aid the building fund, on May 17.[30] At this time it was understood that the graduation exercises in June would be held in the hall on James Street, since the new building would not as yet be formally opened,[31] but the date for the dedication of the building was later advanced, permitting the graduation to be held at University Heights.[32]

The ceremony of laying the cornerstone took place on the afternoon of Sunday, June 15, 1913, before a crowd of 15,000 people. In the absence of Cardinal O'Connell, who was in Rome, the Right Reverend Joseph G. Anderson, Auxiliary Bishop of Boston and member of the class of 1887, performed the ceremony, assisted by Father Gasson and by the Very Reverend Anthony J. Maas, S.J., Provincial of the Maryland–New York Province of the Society of Jesus. Six Monsignori, 100 priests, Mayor John F. Fitzgerald of Boston, and state and civic leaders were among the audience which heard the Reverend Walter Drum, S.J., deliver the dedicatory sermon and E. A. McLaughlin give the principal address. That afternoon the friends of Boston College applauded the news that the Golden Jubilee Fund had passed the $30,000 mark.[33]

Three days later, at the commencement exercises celebrating the golden anniversary of the founding of the College, degrees were conferred in the presence of Bishop Anderson upon 79 candidates, including students in the evening division. The Honorable Joseph C. Pelletier, of the class of 1891, was awarded an honorary doctor of laws degree on this occasion, and he delivered the address to the graduates.[34]

On September 17, 1913, the first complete collegiate year in the new building began with a record enrollment of almost 400 freshman students alone.[35] At the same time, the high school, with 430 freshmen, making a total of 1100 students, outgrew in one registration the additional room made available in the James Street building by the departure of the college sections.[36]

One Task Completed, Another Begun

During the fall, the interior of the new building was graced by the erection of five marble statues in the hall beneath the rotunda.[37] The smaller of these

The inspiring rotunda of Gasson Hall.

statues represented Saints Aloysius, Stanislaus, John Berchmans, and Thomas Aquinas; the group in the center of the rotunda depicted St. Michael overthrowing Lucifer. The latter was completed in 1868 at Rome by M. le Chevalier Scipione Tadolini, on the commission of Gardner Brewer of Boston. It took three years to model the allegorical figure and the elaborate pedestal and to reproduce them in marble. On the completion of the work, the statue was placed on exhibition for a period in Rome, where it was received with praise by the critics. Among the many distinguished persons who viewed the figure was Pope Pius IX, who smilingly commented, "The devil is not as black as he has been painted!"[38]

On February 11, 1913, Father Gasson contracted to have the Tower bells, which have since become so closely associated with Boston College by thousands of students and visitors, manufactured and installed in May by Meneely and Company of Watervliet, New York. The four bells are *do* (F), the largest, christened Ignatius of Loyola; *fa* (B♭), Franciscus Xavierius; *sol* (C), Aloysius Gonzaga; and *la* (D), Joannes Berchmans. When this clock chime was ordered, Father Gasson evidently considered enlarging it ultimately to a tune-playing chime, for the frame was made of sufficient

At long last, an athletic field of their own.

Official Score Card

Boston College

vs.

Holy Cross

Dedication of Athletic Field
at
University Heights

CHESTNUT HILL, NEWTON

Beacon, Hammond and
South Streets

Saturday, Oct. 30, 1915

at 2 P. M.

J. Frank Facey, Printer, 36 Prospect St. Cambridge.

strength and size to carry the six or seven additional bells required. As late as 1936 the possibility of such a change was contemplated by the then-president, Father Louis J. Gallagher.[39]

The Fulton Room, a small amphitheater equipped and decorated for the use of the Fulton Debating Society as a gift of the Boston College Club of Cambridge, was formally opened on November 19.[40] The seating arrangements of the room were changed years later to make it a conventional lecture hall, but in the renovation of Gasson Hall in the 1970s, the original amphitheater arrangement of the room was restored and the mural decorations of Brother Schroen retouched.

In the latter part of November 1913, Boston College alumni were reminded, on the occasion of a bazaar held at the high school under the direction of St. Catherine's Guild for the benefit of the Faculty Building Fund, that the need for accommodations for the Jesuit staff at the Heights was acute.[41] As early as August of 1912, Father Gasson had recognized the great inconvenience that would be caused the professors by their daily journeys to and from the city, and he had petitioned the Jesuit provincial authorities for permission to have preliminary plans drawn for a faculty residence. The permission was granted and the slow work of consultation and drawing up trial sketches was begun.[42] But he himself was not to see the completion of this work, for on January 11, 1914, his term of office as president of the College came to an end and he was succeeded by the Reverend Charles W. Lyons, S.J.

*   *   *

During his six-year term as president, Father Gasson was able to complete only one of the projected buildings, the centerpiece, Gasson Hall. But he left a plan to which his successors were faithful through two wars and a depression.

ENDNOTES

1. William J. Conway, S.J., "Obituary: Father Thomas I. Gasson, S.J." *Woodstock Letters*, 60(1931):84.
2. *Woodstock Letters,* 39(1910):109.
3. Records of the Trustees of Boston College, under date January 5, 1910.
4. *The Stylus,* 24(October 1910):1:28.
5. *Ibid.,* 24(November 1910):2:25.
6. James T. McCormick, S.J., to James M. Kilroy, S.J., "A Proposal for Financial Adjustment" (date uncertain: 1926[?]), BCA.
7. William J. Conway, S.J., "Obituary: Father Thomas I. Gasson, S.J.," *Woodstock Letters*, 60(1931):84.
8. *Ibid.,* p. 85.
9. Records of the Trustees of Boston College, under date March 6, 1911, BCA.
10. *The Stylus,* 24(January 1911):29; and 24(May 1911):33.
11. *Ibid.,* 25(October 1911):24.
12. *Ibid.,* and *The Boston Sunday Post* (December 8, 1912), p. "A."
13. *The Stylus,* 25(November 1911):2, p. 34.

14. *Ibid.,* 24(June 1911):9, p. 27.
15. *The Boston Sunday Globe* (November 5, 1911); also *The Stylus,* 25(January 1912):4, p. 36.
16. *The Stylus,* 25(November 1911):2, p. 34.
17. *Ibid.,* 26(October 1912):1, p. 24.
18. *Ibid.*
19. *The Stylus,* 26(December 1912):3, pp. 43–44; and *Woodstock Letters,* 64(1935):446–447.
20. From records preserved in the office of the Boston College Graduate School. Cf. also *The Boston Post* (June 19, 1913).
21. Charles Lyons, S.J., to Anthony Maas, S.J., Provincial, May 28, 1914, Maryland Provincial S.J. Archives, Georgetown University Library.
22. *The Stylus,* 26(December 1912):3, pp. 44–45; and 26(March 1913):6, p. 225.
23. *The Boston Sunday Post* (March 9, 1913).
24. *Ibid.* (March 23, 1913), p. "C."
25. *Woodstock Letters,* 42(1913):246–247; *The Boston Post* (March 29, 1913), p. 6. The *Post* article carries a photograph showing Fathers Gasson, Goeghan, Brett, and Conway with a group of students.
26. *Woodstock Letters,* 42(1913):246–247; *The Stylus,* 26(April 1913):7, pp. 274–275; *Sub Turri,* 1(1913):28–29.
27. *The Stylus,* 42(1913):246–247.
28. *Ibid.,* 26(May 1913):8, p. 335; *The Boston Sunday Post* (March 23, 1913), p. "C."
29. *The Stylus,* 26(April 1913):7, pp. 274–275.
30. *The Boston Sunday Post, loc. cit.*
31. *The Stylus,* 26(June 1913):9, p. 388.
32. *The Boston Post* (June 19, 1913).
33. *Ibid.,* June 16, 1913, pp. 1 and 4; *The Pilot* (June 13 and 21, 1913); (New York) *World* (June 29, 1913). "In the box placed within the stone were a yearbook *(Sub Turri)* of 1913; envelope containing pious articles; envelope containing coins of the United States; history of the building; list of names of ecclesiastical and civic authorities; copies of the *Boston Sunday Globe, Sunday Post, Sunday Herald, Sunday American,* and a *Boston Transcript* of March 26, 1913; catalogue of Boston College High School; catalogue of Boston College; book of spiritual exercises, Roman breviary, Roman missal; list of officers of the Boston College Alumni Association; programme of the exercises of the day, and programme of music by the Young Men's Catholic Association" (*Boston Post,* June 16, 1913).
34. *The Boston Post* (June 19, 1913).
35. *The Stylus,* 27(October 1913):1, p. 42.
36. *Ibid.,* p. 60.
37. *Ibid.,* 27(November 1913):2, p. 116.
38. *Prose e Poesie Intorno al Celerre Gruppo Rappresentante San Michele* (Roma: Tipografia di G. Aurelj, 1869), p. 10. Preserved in the Boston College Archives. Cf. also article by F. Franzoni in *Osservatore Romano,* March, 1869, the main portion of which was translated and published by Joseph E. Kelly, "A Great Art Gift to Boston College," *The Stylus,* 23(April 1909):27–30.
39. F. P. Latz to Rev. Thomas I. Gasson, S.J., February 11, 1913; and Andrew E. Meneely to Rev. Louis J. Gallagher, S.J., August 12, 1936. (Letters preserved in the Boston College Archives.)
40. *The Stylus,* 27(December 1913):169.
41. *Ibid.*
42. Thomas I. Gasson, S.J., to Joseph Hanselman, S.J., Provincial, August 2, 1912, Maryland Provincial S.J. Archives, Georgetown University Library.

CHAPTER 14

The Pre-World-War I Era

It was agreed by all that Father Charles W. Lyons was a fortunate choice to succeed Father Gasson at this critical period in the history of Boston College. He was already experienced both as an administrator and as a builder. His most recent concern before coming to Boston had been the erection of a faculty residence for St. Joseph's College, along much the same lines as the one planned for Boston. He was familiar with the problems connected with such an enterprise, and he brought to his new task a wealth of ideas and suggestions and a sound knowledge of what was practical for such an edifice.

Progress on the Faculty House

Father Lyons devoted himself at once to the business of pushing forward the preparations for the new residence. Maginnis and Walsh, the architects of the first building, had been selected to design the new hall, and they were able in March 1914 to provide Father Lyons with complete plans to show to Jesuit provincial authorities in New York.[1] As envisioned by Father Gasson, the building would rise no more than three stories above the ground, and the community chapel in the building would be no larger than

REV. CHARLES W. LYONS, S.J.
Fourteenth President

Father Lyons was born in Boston on January 31, 1869. He attended the public schools of Boston and graduated from the English High School. He entered the Society of Jesus August 14, 1890, and was ordained a priest in 1904. He taught metaphysics at St. Francis Xavier College in New York and at Boston College. When he assumed the presidency of Boston College, he was already a seasoned administrator, having previously been president of Gonzaga College in Washington, D.C., and of St. Joseph's College in Philadelphia.

necessary to accommodate the Jesuit Community at common prayers. Father Lyons, however, was of the opinion that the building should provide more rooms to accommodate the future growth of the faculty; consequently, he had the architects add another entire floor to its height. Moreover, he caused the plans for the chapel to be altered to accommodate 250 people.

In June 1914 the Alumni Association presented Father Lyons with a check for almost $40,000 to be added to the building fund,[2] and in the fall faculty and alumni had the pleasure of seeing ground broken for the new residence hall. On September 8, exactly as the College chimes were sounding the noon hour, Father Lyons, surrounded by several members of the faculty, blessed the ground where the new building would be erected.

Each fall had witnessed an increased enrollment in the College, and 1914 was no exception. Registration at the opening of classes reached a new high of 432.[3]

The Philomatheia Club

The year 1915 witnessed the formation of an auxiliary organization which was to enjoy extraordinary social prestige, while at the same time providing unfailing assistance to numberless College projects. The new group was the

Philomatheia Club, which united a number of prominent Catholic women from Greater Boston for the purpose of forwarding the general interests of the College.

The idea of such an organization was conceived by James Carney, chairman of the Boston College Athletic Board. In March 1915 he arranged the attendance of 16 representative Catholic women at a meeting sponsored by the Boston College Athletic Board at the Boston Art Club to discuss the feasibility of such a project. Charles D. Maginnis, the architect, was host on this occasion. As originally outlined, the purpose of the proposed club was to provide moral and financial support for the athletic program at Boston College. Although the idea was well received, nothing further was done to carry it into action until the early fall of 1915, when a larger group of women and the Athletic Board met with Father Lyons and reopened the question.

At this meeting, James Carney achieved wider interest for the proposed society by broadening its purpose to include not only the promotion and fostering of the athletic affairs of the College but its scholastic and social interests as well. It was thereupon agreed to organize such a club, and at the election which ensued Mrs. Edwin A. Shuman was named president. Mr. George McFadden, S.J., faculty director of athletics, acted as the College representative during the club's formative period, and upon its final approval, Father Michael Jessup, S.J., became the organization's first spiritual director. The name "Philomatheia," or "Devotion to Learning," was chosen for the club.

Elected third president of the Philomatheia Club in 1919 was one of the great friends and benefactors of Boston College, Mrs. Vincent P. Roberts. For over half a century she retained that office and led the club in a rich

Mrs. Vincent P. Roberts, for over a half century president of the Philomatheia Club.

The first library at Chestnut Hill, on the south side of the rotunda.

array of benefactions to the College. These included gifts such as the flagstaff and flag for the original Alumni Field, equipment for science laboratories, and gold prizes for various student achievements, as well as such major contributions as promoting the building fund drive of 1921 and purchasing the gracious Norwegian chalet on Commonwealth Avenue. (This building was razed in 1988 for a new residence hall.) The club donated one of the stained glass windows in Bapst library as well as one of the library's prizes, a letter of St. Francis Xavier. In addition many a needy Boston College student received partial tuition support from the Philomatheia Club.

A Junior Philomatheia Club was begun in 1931. The two organizations gave significant moral and material support to the College in the decades when an institutional development program was nonexistent or in embryo form.

Maroon Goal Posts

In the fall of 1915, the hopes of 25 years were realized with the formal opening of the College's own athletic field.[4] The gridiron, track, and surrounding campus had been laid out by the Boston landscape architects Pray, Hubbard, and White, and in its setting, the new field won the enthusiastic admiration of all. One of the students writing in *The Stylus* found particular delight in the vision of "maroon goal-posts . . . on a field of green."[5] Before the formal dedication of this portion of the campus, the alumni—at the instance of Messrs. Francis R. Mullin ('00) and Thomas D. Lavelle ('01)—raised $1600 in the space of four days for the erection of a semipermanent grandstand to accommodate 2200 persons.[6]

Shortly after one o'clock on the afternoon of October 30, 1915, a procession including distinguished civic guests, members of the faculty, and alumni formed in the rotunda of the recitation building and marched down to the field to the strains of a military band. There were speeches for the occasion, and in one of them Father Lyons bestowed upon the new facility the title "Alumni Field," as a memorial to "the boys that were."[7] The new grandstand was filled that day and the sidelines were crowded. The weather was fine, too. Only one detail marred the almost-perfect dedication ceremony: Holy Cross won the afternoon's football game in the last six minutes of play, 9 to 0.[8]

That evening, the *Boston Saturday Evening Transcript* appeared with one of the most sympathetic and appreciative articles on the new institution that had yet appeared in the secular press. It described Boston College as "Chestnut Hill's Touch of Oxford" and "one of the sights of Boston," and it sought to correct the misapprehension that the institution was a theological seminary. The tone as well as the content of this article, occurring in what many considered the "official organ" of Yankee Boston, attracted favorable attention from Catholics and non-Catholics alike.[9]

St. Mary's Hall

Shortly before New Year's Day 1917, it was announced that St. Mary's Hall would be opened after the holidays. On the evening of January 4, the last day before the cloister restriction was put on St. Mary's Hall, a small gathering of friends, including Mayor Curley, Mr. Maginnis, the architect, Mr. Logue, the builder, J. B. Fitzpatrick, and others interested in the

A bucolic scene: the view from the road circling the smaller reservoir.

College, sat down to a supper served in the assembly hall of the recitation building by members of the Philomatheia Club under the direction of Mrs. Edwin A. Shuman. In the course of the evening, Father Lyons was pleasantly surprised to receive from the Philomatheia president a purse of $2500 toward the furnishing of the new building. Later, the guests made a tour of inspection of the new edifice, with Mr. Maginnis acting as guide.[10]

The new building, he explained, was modified Gothic, in conformity with the organic architectural scheme of the assemblage. Its massive gray walls were relieved by elaborate Gothic traceries, carved plaques, and the graceful arches of the Gothic windows which encircled the lower floor. At that time the building contained 64 rooms, of which 50 were living quarters, including a bishop's suite on the second floor. A unique feature of the structure was the large, tiled recreation area on the roof, extending almost the entire length and breadth of the building and completely concealed from the ground below. From this vantage point, guests enjoyed a magnificent panorama of Arlington, Watertown, Cambridge, Boston, and Brookline.

The Jesuit faculty took informal possession of the new building on the following evening, January 5, 1917, by a simple ceremony of filing into the long oak-paneled refectory for their evening meal. All stood in their places silently as Father Lyons offered a special prayer of thanksgiving and a plea for God's blessing on the new residence. The following morning, the Feast of the Epiphany, Father Lyons celebrated the first Mass in St. Mary's Chapel at six-thirty, and a short time later other priests of the faculty began their Masses at the eight side altars.[11] Their new home was open.

*   *   *

As the year 1917 began, there was a mood of joy at Boston College as the Jesuits occupied their majestic residence. That mood was short-lived. Four months later international events cast a pall of gloom over the world.

ENDNOTES

1. Charles W. Lyons, S.J., to Anthony Maas, S.J., Provincial, March 11, 1914, Maryland Provincial S.J. Archives, Georgetown University Library.
2. *The Stylus,* 28(October 1914):1, p. 53.
3. *Ibid.,* p. 53.
4. *Boston Sunday Post* (October 17, 1915), p. "A."
5. *The Stylus,* 29(October 1915):1, p. 38.
6. *Ibid.,* p. 39.
7. *Ibid.,* 29(November 1915):2, pp. 82–83.
8. *Ibid.,* p. 96.
9. Rollin Lynde Hartt, "Chestnut Hill's Touch of Oxford," *Boston Saturday Evening Transcript* (October 30, 1915). The article was reprinted in *Woodstock Letters,* 45(1916):131–134; and in *The Stylus,* 29(November 1915):2, pp. 88–90.
10. *The Stylus,* 30(January 1917):4, p. 201.
11. *The Boston Journal* (January 6, 1917); *The Evening Record* (Boston) (January 5, 1917); *The Stylus,* 30(January 1917), p. 201.

CHAPTER 15

Two Months in Khaki

On April 16, 1917, the United States entered World War I against Germany. One of the early government programs to prepare American troops for the war effort was the establishment of an officer training camp at Plattsburg, New York, which was destined to draw heavily upon the colleges in New England and New York. There was no lack of patriotic response among the students at Boston College: As soon as the first camp at Plattsburg was announced in May, a hundred students volunteered. To their dismay, however, only one was accepted. A vigorous protest by the Boston College men eventually found its way to Washington, and a better representation of volunteers from the Heights were enrolled in the August class.[1]

Because of conscription and voluntary enlistment, the enrollment at Boston College, which had stood at 671 in October 1916, dropped to 125 in October 1918—a loss of 81 percent.[2]

First, the SATC

In August 1918, under an amendment to the Selective Service Act, the Students' Army Training Corps (SATC) was authorized,[3] and Boston College was one of the 565 institutions selected to provide training for men needed as officers, engineers, scientists, and administrators. A quota of 750

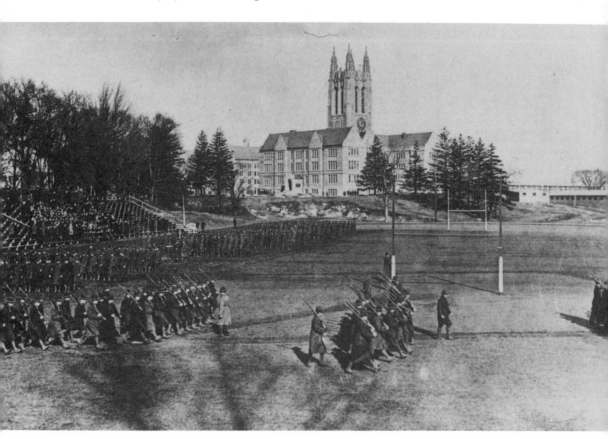

Students' Army Training Corps parade on Alumni Field. Barracks may be seen, east of Gasson Hall.

soldiers were assigned to Boston College. Toward the end of the summer four sleeping barracks and a large mess hall were erected at a cost of $90,000 in the areas now occupied by Devlin and Campion halls. The regular arts curriculum was suspended and a new curriculum drawn up stressing scientific and military subjects.[4] Fifteen hundred young men applied for admission to the Boston College SATC program, but only half could be accepted. The devastating influenza epidemic that swept the country forced the postponement of the start of the program until October 15, 1918, less than a month before the armistice was signed.[5]

The Boston College SATC enrollment, comprised entirely of local youths, was divided into four companies. They were reviewed on November 27 by Major General Clarence R. Edwards and Governor Samuel McCall.[6] The following day the College authorities were notified that all units of the SATC had been directed to demobilize the men, commencing the week of December 1.[7] By December 12 the last elements of the Boston College unit had been disbanded.

To assist colleges adjust to the dislocations encountered with the cessation of SATC programs, the government re-established the Reserve Officers'

Training Corps, which had been suspended during the war. Boston College was one of over 300 institutions applying for the establishment of ROTC units.[8]

Early in January 1919, Father Lyons wrote the Provincial of his satisfaction at learning that Colonel J. S. Parke, the former commandant, and Captain Andrew B. Kelly, the former adjutant of the Boston College SATC, were available to organize and direct a ROTC unit at the college.[9]

Then, ROTC

The inception of the program was announced in "General Orders, Number 1," published from the headquarters of the ROTC at Boston College on February 27, 1919,[10] and the actual training began in the first week of March. It was decided after some discussion that the membership was to be voluntary for all those who, upon examination, could qualify as officer material, and some 137 students enrolled.[11]

The ROTC demanded only two hours weekly of drill, and only one hour a week of class in military science, yet the program apparently became irksome to many of the student soldiers after it was started. Perhaps the students shared the widespread reaction of distaste in the postwar period for everything connected with the military; in any case, disturbing numbers applied for release from the corps during the spring months of 1919, and this undoubtedly motivated the College authorities to discontinue the program the following September.[12]

During World War I, Boston College sent more than 540 students and alumni to the armed forces, of whom 263 were commissioned officers; it also trained 761 SATC soldiers. Her honor roll includes the names of 15 dead, 17 wounded, and 23 cited or decorated by the United States or foreign governments.[13]

If these numbers seem small in contrast to the College's service figures for World War II, it must be recalled that the United States' armed forces in 1918 were less than half the size of the American forces in World War II and that Boston College at the outset of World War I had only 761 students compared with a student body of some 1800 in 1941. Moreover, because the College had but recently increased its enrollment from that of a little over one hundred, her alumni were not relatively numerous.

The history of Boston College in World War I is a proud record of service, "not only for the men whose names are written therein, but also for those who in future ages will bear their names."[14]

* * *

With the war over, the Boston College construction program was resumed. In the 1920s two presidents would surmount daunting obstacles to add to the campus the third and fourth Gothic buildings.

ENDNOTES

1. *The Stylus,* 30(May 1917), p. 370; 31(October 1917), p. 23.
2. *Woodstock Letters,* 45(1916):467; 47(1918): Supplement, "Students in Our Colleges in the United States. . . ."
3. War Department, Committee on Education and Special Training, Circular Aa–1, 1918.
4. Records of the SATC at Boston College, Boston College Archives. A transcript of the more important War Department circulars concerning the SATC and a listing of authorized units will be found in Parke Rexford Kolbe, *The Colleges in War Time and After* (New York: D. Appleton and Co., 1919), Appendix III.
5. *Boston College in the World War, 1917–1918,* p. 304.
6. *Ibid.,* p. 305.
7. *School and Society,* 8:206(December 7, 1918):675–676.
8. *School and Society,* 8:209(December 28, 1918):765–766.
9. Charles W. Lyons, S.J., to Joseph Rockwell, S.J., Provincial, January 7, 1919, New York Province Archives, S.J.
10. *The Stylus,* 32(March 1919), 359–360.
11. Records of the ROTC at Boston College, Boston College Archives. A complete roster of officers and men in the B.C. ROTC will be found in *The Stylus,* 32(April 1919), 425–426.
12. Applications for dismissal on file in ROTC records, Boston College Archives; and discontinuance noted in letter of William Devlin, S.J., to Joseph Rockwell, S.J., Provincial, September 3, 1919, New York Province Archives, S.J.
13. *Boston College in the World War, 1917–1918,* pp. 351–352.
14. *Ibid.,* p. 12.

CHAPTER 16

Boston College
Will Be Big Enough . . .

As we have seen, a physical separation of college and high school faculties took place early in 1917 with the removal of the professors to the new faculty building at the Heights. The separation was not perfect, however, for Father Lyons, the rector of Boston College, was also rector of Boston College High School; the treasurer of the College, Father James F. Mellyn, S.J., was also treasurer of the high school; and both lived on Harrison Avenue. The prefect of studies at the College, Father Michael Jessup, S.J., was acting superior at the new building, and the prefect of discipline at the College, Mr. William V. Corliss, S.J., was acting treasurer. This was understood, of course, to be only a temporary arrangement to last until such time as the College was thought sufficiently well organized to be administered as an independent unit. That time was judged to have come in July 1919, and the change was announced in advance to Cardinal O'Connell by the Provincial in a letter dated July 16.[1] "It is difficult," he wrote, "for one superior to bear the responsibility of two houses as widely separated as the College at Chestnut Hill and the High School on Harrison Avenue." Hence, Father John J. Geoghan was appointed rector of the Immaculate Conception Church and Boston College High School, and Father William J. Devlin succeeded Father Lyons as rector of Boston College, the appointments taking place on July 20, 1919.[2]

REV. WILLIAM J. DEVLIN, S.J.
Fifteenth President

Father Devlin was born in New York City December 15, 1875, but spent most of his youth abroad, attending schools in England or traveling in Europe and spending the summer vacations with his family in Ireland. While he was a student at Stonyhurst, the distinguished Jesuit school in England, he was accepted into the English province of the Society of Jesus. Before he entered, however, his father died in New York and young Devlin returned to America. Shortly thereafter he decided to seek admission to the Maryland province, where he was accepted on September 24, 1893. Before his ordination he taught at Boston College for four years. After his ordination in 1908, Father Devlin was on the faculty of Boston College from 1910 to 1913. In 1914 he became dean, the position he held when named to the presidency.[3]

Postwar Milestones

One of Father Devlin's first tasks in office, shortly after the opening of school in 1919, was arranging a reception at Boston College for Cardinal Mercier, the heroic prelate of Belgium who was visiting America at the time. An enthusiastic assembly of faculty, students, and alumni greeted the Belgian patriot and Cardinal O'Connell in the College hall on October 6.[4]

A few weeks later a Boston College football team came into national prominence for the first time by defeating a favored Yale team 5 to 3 on an historic 47-yard field goal made by "Jimmie" Fitzpatrick. The team, the first coached by the now-legendary "Iron Major," Frank Cavanaugh, was hailed upon its return from New Haven with a welcome which verged on hysteria.[5] The following year, the victory was repeated, 21 to 13.[6]

The first issue of *The Alumni Bulletin*, published in October 1919, announced the creation of a new office, that of alumni secretary, to which Frank Cronin was appointed by action of the executive committee of the association on September 11, 1919.[7] The *Bulletin* unfortunately experienced a rather hectic career during its first years, with change of title and suspended publication of frequent occurrence.

Within a month, another publication was inaugurated, an undergraduate weekly called *The Heights,* which printed Volume I, Number 1, on November 19, 1919, under the editorship of John D. Ring ('20). The first issues of the paper were only six by nine inches in size, giving it the distinction of being the smallest college newspaper in the country, but on April 16, 1920, the format was changed to approximately what it is at present. The twenty-fifth and final edition issued that season was an ambitious 12-page pictorial presenting a review of the persons and incidents that had made Boston College news during the year.

Incidentally, it was in an early issue of *The Heights* that the eagle was suggested as mascot and symbol of the Boston College athletic teams.[8] The sponsor concealed his identity under a pseudonym, but tradition identifies him as the Reverend Edward J. McLaughlin ('14).

An Appeal to the Alumni

Shortly after the turn of the year in 1920, Father Devlin devoted his attention to finding ways and means to erect another building. The need for room was pressing, particularly in the form of laboratory space for the

Pledge card used in Father Devlin's building fund drive. The drawing on the certificate is from the Maginnis and Walsh projection of the campus. It shows that the architects meant the east entrance of the first building to be the main entrance. A plaza such as they envisioned is now in place.

rapidly growing science courses. Two science classes had to be transferred to St. Mary's Hall to secure room, and there was no hall on the campus large enough to accommodate even a representative portion of the student body at one time.[9] Two sections of the third corridor had been cut off to make temporary laboratories for the physics department. Equipment, too, was in demand. The proceeds from the Philomatheia Ball that year had been spent on much needed apparatus for the physics laboratory, and an additional thousand dollars was expended for microscopes and other instruments for biology.[10]

In February 1920, with the Provincial's approval, Father Devlin sent a letter to all Boston College graduates outlining the need for a science building and asking for financial support.[11] Once again the firm of Maginnis and Walsh was engaged to draw up plans for the proposed building. This initial appeal to the alumni had disappointing results, with less than $100,000 realized in cash and pledges.[12] It was decided that an appeal had to be made to a wider public.

The Campaign of '21

Father Devlin courageously determined that this new effort should be a large-scale drive, not only to finance construction of a science building, but to meet the needs of a rapidly growing student body by providing three additional new buildings—a chapel, a gymnasium, and a library—at one bold stroke.[13] His first step was to engage professional direction for the proposed drive, and by the first week in October a rough plan of action had already been blocked out.[14] The campaign, which would have as its objective the raising of $2 million, would begin October 8 in its organizational aspects and run for 30 weeks, ending May 31, 1921. The actual public "drive," as such, was to occupy 10 days, from May 3 to May 12.

Father Devlin met the editors and publishers of the Boston newspapers at a dinner at the City Club on November 10. He outlined the purposes of the campaign and appealed for the friendly cooperation of the Boston press. The following morning the newspapers of the city featured announcements of the new drive and descriptions of the pressing needs experienced at the Heights.

As the time for the intensive collection period approached, the press devoted more and more space to accounts of the campaign and to feature stories concerning the College. A slogan contest during the spring contributed a motto: "Boston College will be big enough if your heart is!" and it soon appeared on numberless billboards, telephone posts, streetcar ads, shop windows, and doorstep flyers.

On the eve of the drive, a large reproduction of the Gothic Tower on the Heights was unveiled on Boston Common near the corner of Tremont and Park Streets, and smaller replicas were placed at South Station, Upham's Corner (Dorchester), Lynn, Lowell, Waltham, and Brockton. On these

A 1922 invitation to a Philomatheia Ball.

Campaign flag at downtown headquarters.

Volunteers with B.C. hats prepare to
motor for the cause.

The crane beside the Tower Building shows the science building under construction.

Work has begun on the library site at the right and young lindens line the road in 1924.

The football teams were in the national spotlight in 1919 and 1920 with victories over Yale.

College Crowd Record Broken 30,000 · Braves Field
B.C. - H.C. Ball Game . . June 18th 1923 ·
Score · B.C. · 4 · H.C · 1.

Photo © F.A. George Boston Arena.

BOSTON COLLEGE BASEBALL SCHEDULE
OLAF HENRICKSEN, Coach

Won 30 Lost 3

	APRIL	B.C.	OPP.		MAY	B.C.	OPP.	
W	Tues. 3 Villanova at Villanova, Pa.	10	9		Tues. 15 Norwich	RAIN		
W	Wed. 4 West Point at New York	5	3	W	Wed. 16 Tufts	8	4	W
	Thur. 5 New York University at N.Y.	RAIN			Thur. 17 Lafayette	22	9	W
	Frid. 6 Syracuse at Syracuse	RAIN			Sat. 19 Colby	Cancelled		
W	Sat. 7 Lafayette at Easton, Pa.	13	9		Wed. 23 Lowell Textile	11	0	W
W	Wed. 11 Rhode Island State	10	5		Frid. 25 University of Pennsylvania	10	0	W
W	Sat. 14 Northeastern	15	1		Sat. 26 University of Vermont	4	1	W
	Mon. 16 Boston Braves at Allston	RAIN			at Burlington, Vermont			
W	Thur. 19 Boston University	17	2		Mon. 28 St. Michaels	19	8	W
W	Sat. 21 University of Vermont	9	8		Wed. 30 Holy Cross at Worcester	2	5	L
W	Wed. 25 Providence	3	0		JUNE			
W	Frid. 27 Rensselaer Polytechnic Inst.	11	4		Frid. 1 Georgetown	5	10	L
	Sat. 28 Syracuse University	RAIN			Sat. 2 Springfield	14	0	W
	MAY				Wed. 6 Springfield at Springfield	3	0	W
W	Tues. 1 Villanova	9	2		Thur. 7 Princeton University			
W	Thur. 3 Middlebury	11	5		at Princeton, N.J.	11	4	W
W	Sat. 5 Seton Hall	13	1		Frid. 8 Lehigh at South Bethlehem, Pa.	5	3	W
W	Thur. 10 Yale University at New Haven	13	4		Sat. 9 Tufts at Tuft's Oval, Medford	4	2	W
W	Frid. 11 Providence at Rhode Island	7	2		Wed. 13 United States Submarine Base	Cancelled		
W	Sat. 12 Crescent A.C. at Brooklyn	7	3		Thu. 14 University of Washington	3	4	W
W	Sun. 13 Crescent A.C. at Brooklyn	4	0		Sat. 16 Pending ALUMNI	19	3	W
					Mon. 18 Holy Cross	4	1	W

ALL GAMES AT UNIVERSITY HEIGHTS UNLESS OTHERWISE STATED

Sat 2nd Holy Cross | 0 | 2 | L

"towers" were conspicuous campaign clocks to indicate the daily progress of the drive.

When May 3 finally arrived, Cardinal O'Connell opened the drive with a gift of $10,000 (which he doubled a few days later), and a legion of volunteer workers set out on the heroic task of approaching every person in Greater Boston to solicit from each a donation for the new Boston College. Meanwhile, the volume of newspaper publicity multiplied until the drive became the topic of greatest interest in the city. A gigantic benefit concert, starring the great Victor Herbert and including Fritzi Scheff and many other artists, was staged in the Boston Arena to signal the drive's halfway mark on Sunday, May 8.

The collectors and their leaders who had labored untiringly for 10 days were cheered at the close of the campaign by the headlined news that the drive had gone over the top. A careful check completed several days later, however, revealed that of the $2 million sought, only $1,746,069 had been paid or pledged, and of this amount only $710,756 had been realized in cash. Later, complete records show that of the outstanding pledges amounting to $1,035,313, only $575,000 was ever redeemed. Expenses connected with the 1920–1921 campaign ran to $158,070. When it was decided in 1929 that no further redemptions would be made, the net cash return from the drive was calculated at $1,127,712.

*   *   *

Hopes for four new buildings thus vanished, for the cost of the science building and library alone would exceed by several hundred thousands the total receipts of the drive. But a beginning had been made, and the great amount of favorable publicity received by the College during the drive was to prove of incalculable value. Boston College was now definitely *known,* and within two decades its student body was to double and treble.

ENDNOTES

1. Joseph H. Rockwell, S.J., to Most Rev. William H. O'Connell, July 16, 1919, Boston Diocesan Archives.
2. *Catalogus Provinciae Marylandiae–Neo Eboracensis S.J., ineunte anno 1920.*
3. *Woodstock Letters,* 67(1938):293–298.
4. W. Devlin, S.J., to the Alumni of Boston College (circular letter), October 4, 1919, Boston Diocesan Archives. Also, *The Stylus,* 33(October 1919):40–41.
5. *The Stylus,* 33(November 1919):106–107 and 118–122.
6. *Ibid.,* 34(October 1920):51–62.
7. A copy of the first issue of the *Alumni Bulletin* is preserved in the Boston Diocesan Archives. In May 1924 a fresh attempt to publish the *Alumni Bulletin* was made under the editorship of John R. Taylor, to appear "from time to time" (p. 2). The introductory editorial gives the impression that Taylor considered this to be the initial effort at a *Bulletin* (pp. 1–2). In 1933 the *Bulletin* was begun once more as a "new publication" under the title, *Boston College Alumnus.*
8. *The Heights* (May 14, 1920).

9. William Devlin, S.J., to Joseph Rockwell, S.J., January 27, 1920, New York S.J. Provincial Archives; and William Devlin, S.J., to the Boston College Alumni (circular letter), February 6, 1920, Boston Diocesan Archives.

10. William Devlin, S.J., to His Eminence, William Cardinal O'Connell, February 9, 1920, Boston Diocesan Archives.

11. William Devlin, S.J., to the Alumni (circular letter), February 6, 1920, Boston Diocesan Archives.

12. The Official Report of the Treasurer, the Reverend Michael J. Doody, preserved in the Treasurer's Office files, Boston College.

13. William Devlin, S.J., and William D. Nugent to the Alumni of Boston College (circular letter), December 8, 1920, Boston College Archives.

14. The following account is based on the official records of the drive which have been bound and preserved in the Boston College Archives.

CHAPTER 17

Gothic Newcomers

At the commencement exercises on June 22, 1921, Cardinal O'Connell broke ground for the science building, the first of the structures to be erected with the funds realized in the recent drive.[1] The excavation for the basement required blasting of rock, so concrete could not be poured for the first section of the foundation until March 16 of the following year.[2] The cornerstone for the science building was laid in the presence of Cardinal O'Connell at the graduation in June 1922,[3] and ground was broken for the library by Mayor Childs of Newton in the following October.[4]

The prospect of increased library facilities encouraged Father Stinson, the librarian, to appeal to friends of the College to donate books for the new library during a drive which opened November 10, 1922, and continued for several months. The Carnegie Foundation in Washington, D.C., congratulated the College on its efforts to secure a representative library and offered to send all the yearbooks and other sets of publications issued by the foundation. Harvard University likewise responded with a generous offer of books and duplicate sets.[5]

In the fall of 1923 the status of the College chapel, which had hitherto been private, was changed by Cardinal O'Connell to permit the faithful of the locality to fulfill their obligation to hear Mass on Sundays and holy days.[6]

The science building won for its architects the J. Harleston Parker medal as the most beautiful new structure in the Greater Boston area during a three-year period.

After the conferring of degrees on commencement day, June 19, 1924, Cardinal O'Connell, accompanied by the faculty and student body, proceeded to the site of the new library building opposite St. Mary's Hall. There with simple ceremony he laid the cornerstone, after placing within it a copper box containing records, coins, and newspapers of the day.[7]

New Quarters for the Sciences

When classes reconvened in September of 1924, the new science building, although not entirely ready, was used for the first time. The workmen who were engaged in finishing the interior of the building did not complete their task until almost Christmas, but in the meantime the science departments, which had occupied the basement of the Tower Building, were able to transfer their equipment to the new structure. This change freed the former chemistry lecture hall for history classes and permitted the former laboratories to be converted into much-needed dressing rooms for the athletic teams. The road near the science building was finished that fall and a beginning made on the extensive landscaping required in the vicinity. The new edifice itself had become the pride of the campus.

The original plan of the architects and College authorities had called for separate buildings for chemistry, physics, and biology, but restricted resources obliged them, at least for the time being, to house all of these sciences within one building. The location of the science building on the campus had also undergone change; as late as the drive of 1921 it was spoken of as occupying the position now held by Bapst, opposite St. Mary's Hall.

The arrangement of laboratories and lecture halls was drawn up after an inspection of the facilities at Massachusetts Institute of Technology, Harvard, Yale, and other leading institutions and after conferences with science instructors from several Jesuit colleges and other universities. The result was the erection of a science building which represented the highest efficiency in design at the time it was built and which won for the architects the J. Harleston Parker Medal, awarded triennially by the Boston Society of Architects for the most beautiful new structure in Greater Boston.[8]

The basement was divided into storage rooms, locker rooms to serve 1000 students, an electric generator room, and machine shops. When the building was planned it was hoped that a seismograph station might be located in the basement.[9] By October 1925, however, it had been determined that the ledge upon which the building rested extended under Commonwealth Avenue and that recording by the instruments would be affected by the traffic.[10] Hence, the seismograph apparatus was installed in Weston on property owned by the New England Province of the Society of Jesus.

Construction of the Library

The library foundations were completely laid by September 1924,[11] and work on the walls of the superstructure was begun on October 20 in the hope of continuing until the basement and first floor were completed.[12] By the following March, the cutstone border of the first floor and the base of the main stairway had been laid,[13] and in May Father Devlin could report to the alumni that the structure was "nearing the second floor."[14] He found

The library under construction in 1925. Note that there is no wing on St. Mary's Hall toward the reservoir. The wing was added in 1931.

REV. JAMES H. DOLAN, S.J.
Sixteenth President

Father Dolan was born in Roxbury on June 4, 1885. After attending St. Joseph's school and Boston College High School, he became a student at Boston College, but after his freshman year he entered the Society of Jesus on August 14, 1905. During his studies preparatory for the priesthood, he spent a five-year period teaching at Georgetown University. He was ordained in 1920 by the great James Cardinal Gibbons shortly before the prelate's death. Father Dolan was a professor of psychology at Holy Cross at the time he was summoned to the presidency of Boston College.[15]

it necessary, however, to plead for financial assistance from them in order that the first floor might be finished, thereby supplying at least an assembly hall, which was much needed on the campus.

A newspaper account in the summer of 1925 stated that the assembly hall and some library facilities in the new building would be ready for the opening of school, but further work on the structure was halted and a temporary roofing erected at the second-floor level due to shortage of funds.[16] This was the situation when Father James H. Dolan, S.J., was announced to succeed Father Devlin as president of Boston College on August 23, 1925.

During Father Dolan's first few months in office, the roofed-over library auditorium was placed in use,[17] and the stacks and circulation desk of the library were put in operation in the library basement. The latter arrangement was effected by screening off a portion of what is now the stack space for book storage and by placing at the entrance of this "cage" a desk where books might be charged out. A large open area in front of the desk was used by the students as a supplement to the regular library reading room in the Tower Building.

As early as October 1925 the auditorium was sufficiently finished to warrant the cardinal's permission to have Sunday Masses said there for the faithful who had been attending Masses in the small domestic chapel in St. Mary's Hall.[18]

During the next month, the first of a series of benefactions was made which permitted Father Dolan to make plans for the finishing of the library. This first gift was made by Mrs. Helen Gargan of Washington, who donated the main reading hall of the library in memory of her husband, the late Thomas J. Gargan, prominent Boston lawyer, philanthropist, and member of the Boston Transit Commission.[19]

In September 1926 Father Dolan was in a position not only to resume building but to contract for the entire remaining work.[20] By Christmas of that year, steel shelves were ready in the stack rooms to accommodate 100,000 books.[21] The rest of the structural work went forward so rapidly that within two years the entire building was completed except for some furnishings and the stained-glass windows. The long-awaited dedication was announced for commencement day in 1928.[22]

The ceremonies which took place on June 13 opened with Benediction of the Blessed Sacrament in the domestic chapel in St. Mary's Hall, after which the faculty and guests proceeded to the new library where they were welcomed in the assembly hall by Father Dolan in the name of Boston College. Charles D. Maginnis, of the architectural firm which had designed the building, gave an interesting explanation of the various features of the building, then made a symbolic transfer of the library to Boston College by a formal presentation of the keys to Father Dolan. The blessing of the

For lack of funds, the new library structure was roofed over in 1925 above the auditorium, but the building was used for library and parish liturgical purposes. The building was completed in 1928.

building was performed by the rector. Following this, the dedicatory address was delivered by His Excellency, the Honorable Alvan T. Fuller, Governor of Massachusetts, whose personal generosity had aided in bringing the library to successful completion.[23]

The auditorium, on the level below Gargan Hall, originally had a seating capacity of 1200. But the demand for classrooms soon forced an alteration whereby the length of the hall was reduced in order to provide space for two additional classrooms facing Commonwealth Avenue. The seating capacity of the auditorium was thereby reduced to 720. When St. Ignatius Church opened in 1951, the auditorium was no longer used for parish Masses. It nonetheless remained the principal place for academic and religious assemblies until 1970, when stacks for books were installed which remained on that level until the grand renovation of Bapst Library after the opening of O'Neill Library.

When the library was opened, only a section of the steel stack shelving was in position. Later, in the presidency of Father William J. McGarry, S.J., the entire steel stack structure—comprising two basement levels—was completed, making room for 300,000 books.

*   *   *

With the completion of adequate quarters, the library service, the intellectual heart of the institution, could function unimpeded, and the establishment of university departments could now be looked forward to as the next step in the achievement of Father McElroy's dream.

ENDNOTES

1. *The Boston Post* (June 23, 1921).
2. William Devlin, S.J., to the Alumni of Boston College (undated circular letter), *Boston College Alumni Bulletin,* I:2–3, May 1924.
3. *The Boston Post* (June 22, 1922); *The Pilot* (June 24, 1922).
4. *The Boston Post* (November 1, 1922); *The Boston Traveler* (November 1, 1922); *The Heights* (November 9, 1922); *The Boston Sunday Post* (November 12, 1922).
5. *The Boston Globe* (November 13, 1922); *The Pilot* (December 2, 1922).
6. *Litterae Annuae Collegii Bostoniensis,* November 1923.
7. *The Boston Post* (June 20, 1924).
8. *The Heights* (May 4, 1926).
9. *The Boston Herald* (July 23, 1925).
10. *The Heights* (October 6, 1925).
11. *The Heights* (September 30, 1924).
12. *Ibid.* (October 14, 1924).
13. *Ibid.* (March 3, 1925).
14. William Devlin, S.J., to members of the Alumni (circular letter), May 1925, Boston College Archives.
15. *The Boston Globe* (August 24, 1925, and August 30, 1925).
16. *The Boston American* (July 18, 1925).
17. *The Heights* (March 16, 1926).

18. *Litterae Annuae Collegii Bostoniensis,* October 1925. The auditorium and the college chapel in St. Mary's Hall were together designated as the temporary "church" of a newly created St. Ignatius Parish by the cardinal in October 1926. The parish was to be served by Fathers connected with the college, and when circumstances permitted, it would have a church of its own (*Litterae Annuae Collegii Bostoniensis,* October 1926; *The Boston Globe,* November 11, 1926).

19. *Litterae Annuae Collegii Bostoniensis,* November 1925; *The Pilot* (August 8, 1908; October 24, 1908; October 31, 1908); *The Boston Evening Transcript* (June 13, 1928).

20. *Litterae Annuae Collegii Bostoniensis,* September 1926.

21. *Ibid.* (December 1926).

22. *The Boston Post* (November 19, 1927, and June 14, 1928); *The Boston Herald* (June 14, 1928); *The Boston Globe* (June 14, 1928); *The Boston Evening Transcript* (June 13, 1928); and invitations preserved in the Boston College Archives.

23. *The Boston Evening Transcript* (June 13, 1928); *The Boston Herald* (June 14, 1928); and programs preserved in the Boston College Archives.

CHAPTER 18

The Many-Rooted Tree

Although the charter granted to Boston College is a university charter, the privileges conferred by it were not fully utilized until the institution was in its sixth decade. The problems connected with organizing and operating the preparatory and undergraduate branches during the College's early years so occupied the attention of the staff that little if any heed was paid to the still more venturesome task of commencing classes for graduate students.

A Master's Program for Boston

At the close of World War I, however, circumstances arose which changed this situation and led Father Devlin to announce the inauguration of the School of Education in the fall of 1919. This project had grown out of negotiations begun during the previous year by the former president, Father Lyons, and Jeremiah E. Burke, superintendent of schools for the City of Boston.[1] The purpose of the new school was to alleviate Boston's postwar dearth of male teachers, especially in the high schools, because at the time, the city's normal school was not yet qualified to grant degrees.

By a plan mutually agreed on, candidacy for the master's degree with a major in education would be offered young men who had previously completed a full undergraduate course of four years at a recognized college

161

Margaret Ursula Magrath was the first woman to earn a degree at Boston College. She was awarded a master of arts degree on June 16, 1926.

and who had successfully taken the entrance examinations conducted by the Boston Normal School. A one-year course for the degree was outlined, in which the first semester was to be devoted to practical training in the elementary, intermediate, and high schools of Boston under the direction of the Department of Practice and Training of the City of Boston Public Schools. Those students satisfactorily completing the assignments of this period would enter upon a second semester of related academic work at either the new School of Education at Boston College or at Boston University. When the first examination conducted by the board of superintendents was held on September 12, 1919, eight young men qualified for the period of training, and all elected to attend Boston College.[2]

Soon after the school year began, Father Mellyn asked the City of Boston School Committee to accept the master's degree in education earned at Boston College as equivalent to two years' experience in teaching for candidates for the high school certificate and for the intermediate certificate. Early in October 1919 the board examined the outline of the course as given at the College and granted the request.[3] This act was not only a gratifying commendation for the quality of work planned at Boston College but offered an advantage which attracted many aspiring teachers to the new school on the Heights.

At the opening of the fall term in 1922, Father Mellyn received the approval of the trustees of Boston College for the following requirements for the degree of master of education, which was being offered for the first time:[4]

1. The degree of A.B. or B.S. from an approved college.
2. Ten half-courses (i.e., 30-hour courses), with appropriate examinations.
3. A master's thesis of 5000 words on some pedagogical subject originally treated, the thesis to count as one of the ten required half-courses.

In January 1923 the Boston School Committee gave formal approval to the new program and voted to give Boston College's degree of master of education full credit on the committee's rating plan.[5]

During the first few years, the tuition for the academic semester under the School Committee's plan was paid by the City of Boston. In May 1922, however, Father Mellyn was notified that commencing with the next entering class, the plan would be modified to require each student to pay his own tuition.[6]

Meanwhile, the Normal School of the City of Boston had been undergoing a metamorphosis. For the academic year 1924–1925 the title was changed to "The Teachers' College of the City of Boston,"[7] and this new institution conferred the bachelor's degree for the first time upon members of the class of 1925.[8] The next step, presentation of courses leading to the master's degree, soon followed; consequently, the city-sponsored training course for college graduates at Boston College and Boston University was considered no longer necessary, and in April 1926 the School Committee gave notice to Father Mellyn that the plan would be discontinued at the close of the current school year.[9]

The Number of Advanced Degrees Awarded by Boston College During the Years 1920–1927[10]			
Year	M.A.	M.S.	M.Ed.
June 1920	9	1	—
June 1921	24	—	—
June 1922	21	3	—
June 1923	1	1	18
June 1924	9	—	—
June 1925	27	1	—
June 1926	39	1	3
June 1927	25	—	2

Higher Education for Religious Teachers

When the plan for the School of Education at Boston College was first announced in the fall of 1919, Father Augustine F. Hickey, the diocesan supervisor of schools, immediately saw in it a means for improving the

SONGS
OF
BOSTON COLLEGE

Compiled and Arranged
by
JAMES A. ECKER
Director Boston College Music Clubs
1926 to 1936

Published for The Boston College Music Clubs
BY
McLAUGHLIN & REILLY CO.
100 BOYLSTON STREET, BOSTON, MASS.

Made in U. S. A.

Jesuit poet Leonard Feeney wrote the words for a dramatic song on the University's colors. It appeared in Songs of Boston College, *published in 1938 and dedicated "to the Ladies of the Philomatheia Club."*

training of the teaching Sisters of the archdiocese. On October 9 he wrote to the cardinal to present certain propositions for the betterment of the parish school system, among which was the following:

> To arrange a course of twenty lectures to be given on Saturday mornings after January 1st, 1920, in the Cathedral School Hall by Reverend James F. Mellyn, S.J., Dean of the new School of Education at Boston College. In January 1920 Boston College is to offer courses in Education to college graduates training for positions in the Boston Public School system. These courses are to be accredited by the Boston School Committee. Father Mellyn is very willing to give to our teaching Sisters a share in the work done at the new School of Education. This could be done most effectively in the form of an extension course on Saturday mornings in Cathedral School Hall.[11]

His Eminence replied at once, giving permission to carry out the plan as outlined. Thereupon, Father Hickey called a conference of all the superiors of the parish schools for October 18, at which he announced the course, with the opening date as the second Saturday in January 1920.[12] The response exceeded all expectations, with some 700 Sisters following the courses,[13] despite their already heavy schedules and, as Father Hickey

To the Colors

observed, the unusual inclemency of the weather during the latter part of that winter.[14]

During the following years, the educational courses were extended throughout the entire school year, and special courses were given at the cathedral hall during the summer.[15] Other extension schools were set up under the joint direction of Fathers Hickey and Mellyn for the Sisters at centers on the North Shore and elsewhere.[16] In addition to Father Mellyn and Fathers of the Boston College faculty, lay professors were engaged for several of these series of lectures,[17] and in 1923 college credit was given in connection with the courses to qualifying Sisters. (Heretofore, only a certificate of attendance at the classes had been issued to them.[18])

Father Mellyn's desire to have the School of Education classes on the Heights open to women students as well as men required a change of Jesuit regulations for the conduct of their colleges. When he sought permission for this innovation in 1920, however, provincial superiors felt that the situation at the time did not justify the change.[19]

But at the Teachers' Institute in August 1922, Cardinal O'Connell voiced the hope that a formal summer school for religious teachers would soon be organized,[20] and the following February he instructed Father Hickey to ascertain if Boston College would be in a position to provide such training leading to advanced degrees.[21] In the light of this expressed interest of His Eminence in the summer school, the case was reopened, and permission for the attendance of women at these classes at the Heights was granted by the Jesuit authorities in Rome on April 7, 1923.[22] Difficulties connected with assembling a teaching staff prevented the inauguration of the school that summer,[23] but on June 30, 1924, the first classes on the Boston College campus admitting women were opened with the Mass of the Holy Ghost offered by the president, Father Devlin. An enrollment of 230 religious was recorded, and the cardinal told the new students during the dedicatory address that the occasion marked an epoch in Catholic education.[24]

The school was in session for five weeks, with six school days each week. Courses of college grade in English, foreign languages, sciences, mathematics, history, philosophy, and education were conducted by regular members of the Boston College faculty under Father Mellyn as director of the school. That fall and winter (1923–1924) a 30-hour extension course was offered as usual at the cathedral center by the Boston College School of Education; it was attended by 600 of the teaching Sisters. During this period, 145 theses prepared in connection with the course were accepted as worthy of college credit.[25]

In the school year 1923–1924, lay women were admitted for the first time to the series of lectures offered in the evening school of the Young Men's Catholic Association and were given credit toward degrees by the Boston College School of Education. Classes were held in the Boston College High School building on James Street, and the low fee of $5 was charged for an entire course. Five hundred students registered for Father Charles Lyons' course in the history of philosophy, and other classes similarly well attended were the psychology of thought, given by Father F. W. Boehm, and the history of education, given by Father Mellyn.[26]

Reorganization of the Graduate Division

At the opening of the school year 1925–1926, the term "Graduate School" was employed for the first time on an official basis.[27] According to the announcement, this school was situated on the campus and was restricted to male students, and it was under the direction of Father Mellyn as dean. In other words, it was a continuation of the previous School of Education arrangement as far as that pertained to the public school teachers' courses at Chestnut Hill.

On September 15, 1926, however, an important reorganization of all graduate and extension classes was announced, to take place on October 1. Under the new system, the Graduate School would be open to men and women, and would hold classes in the afternoon and evening at Boston College High School on James Street rather than at the Heights. The new dean in charge of the program was Father John B. Creeden, S.J., formerly president of Georgetown University.[28]

The reorganized Graduate School would supersede the School of Education on the campus for male public school teachers, the cathedral center for religious teachers of the archdiocese, and the advanced courses at the evening classes of the Young Men's Catholic Association for the general public. But the new project was broader in scope than all of these combined. Now, not only education but many of the fields of concentration usually available to graduate students at a university were provided for. In addition, approved undergraduates were admitted to certain classes for credit toward the bachelor's degree.

The establishment of this school was to prove of service to the religious teachers in the vicinity, who now had the opportunity of pursuing a full schedule of higher studies during the school year. The enrollment of such students during the first scholastic year (1926–1927) numbered 157 Sisters and 5 Brothers. The following commencement day at Boston College on June 16, 1927, was a memorable one in the history of Catholic education in the archdiocese, for on that occasion 14 master's degrees and one bachelor's degree were conferred upon Sisters by Cardinal O'Connell.[29] The interest of the teaching religious in the new Graduate School was further reflected in the summer session by an enrollment of 321 Sisters and 20 Brothers, an increase of 75 over the previous year.[30]

The year 1927 witnessed further growth in the university organization by the affiliation of the novitiate and house of studies of the New England Province of the Society of Jesus at Lenox, Massachusetts, and the large

Philomatheia Club.

Jesuit seminary at Weston, Massachusetts, with Boston College under the titles of the Normal School, the School of Philosophy and Sciences, and the School of Divinity. Thus, with the permission and approval of the Commonwealth of Massachusetts, the courses in these institutions were recognized as accreditable for degrees, and the Jesuit seminarians received their degrees from Boston College. (This arrangement ceased in 1974.)

The Law School Inaugurated

On April 29, 1929, Father Dolan published his plans for the opening of a school of law connected with Boston College the following September.[31] The staff of the new school would be headed by Father Creeden, hitherto director of the graduate school, as regent, and Dennis A. Dooley as dean.

The announcement of the new venture at once received praise from the public press for the high standards which had been established for it.[32] Only those students who had completed at least two years of collegiate academic work at an approved institution were to be admitted, and undergraduates were advised to complete their collegiate training before matriculating in the Law School, because preference would be given to applicants with degrees.[33]

Both day and evening courses were instituted, the first leading to the degree of bachelor of laws in three years and the second requiring four years. Day students were required to attend lectures and conferences for 14 hours a week, while the evening students were obliged to schedule 10 hours. Members of one section were not permitted to take courses in the other section for credit.[34] Only first-year students were received during the opening year, but the very gratifying enrollment of 102 students in both day and evening divisions was recorded. This figure rose to 122 the following year, to 202 the third year, to 230 in 1933, and to 258 in 1934.[35]

Formal instruction was begun September 26, 1929, and the first class graduated on June 15, 1932. With the graduation of this first class, the school was officially approved by the American Bar Association through its section on Legal Education and Admission to the Bar, and in 1937 the school became a member of the Association of American Law Schools.

In 1939 the Law School moved from its original Boston site in the Lawyers' Building at 11 Beacon Street to the New England Power Building at 441 Stuart Street, where it remained until it was transferred to the Kimball Building at 18 Tremont Street in the summer of 1945.

Intown Classes

At the same time the Law School was established and at the same location, an undergraduate center was begun which was the joint undertaking of the Law School and the Graduate School. It was directly under the supervision of the Law School regent, Father Creeden, and it was designed to provide

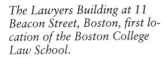

The Lawyers Building at 11 Beacon Street, Boston, first location of the Boston College Law School.

an opportunity for those who had only a high school diploma or one year at college to obtain an equivalent of the two years of college work necessary to enter the Law School. Classes were scheduled for the late afternoon and evening, and they covered in three years' time a special program of studies embracing English, logic, accounting, economics, Latin for lawyers, public speaking, modern languages, apologetics, psychology, ethics, government, and sociology. The response to this plan was immediate, and 60 students enrolled the opening year.[36]

In 1929, when this "Downtown Center" was opened at the Law School, the classes for undergraduates which had been offered afternoons and evenings at James Street in affiliation with the Graduate School were united in a semi-independent organization called "The Extension School," under the direction of the new dean of the Graduate School, Father John F. Doherty, S.J. This school differed from the other extension branch at the Law School by offering the equivalent of a complete four-year college course leading to an A.B. degree and by presenting a variety of major fields of concentration. These extension classes continued to be held at the high school building on James Street.

The Downtown Center, embracing the prelegal extension classes, was accorded a section of the combined Graduate School–Extension School catalog until the 1933–1934 issue, when it became "The Junior College" and issued a separate catalog. Father Patrick J. McHugh, S.J., the dean, was also dean of the Arts College at Chestnut Hill.

The following year, the Graduate School and the Extension School were moved to Chestnut Hill, and the first steps were taken in January 1935 to make them entirely distinct and independent. September 1935 saw the

Extension School separated from the Graduate School and merged with the Junior College in new quarters at 126 Newbury Street under the name "Boston College Intown." Father George A. O'Donnell, S.J., became dean of the reorganized Graduate School at Chestnut Hill, and Father Walter F. Friary, S.J., became dean of the new Boston College Intown.

The Intown College published separate catalogs for the extension courses and for the junior college courses until the entire curriculum was revised and consolidated into progressive divisions, or "stadia," by Father Michael J. Harding, S.J., the new dean, in September 1938. At that time, the terms "extension school" and "junior college" were discontinued, and a single catalog was issued henceforth by the Intown College.

The School of Social Work

Growth was meanwhile noticeable in another direction. Soon after Father Louis J. Gallagher's inauguration as president of Boston College in 1932, he began to encourage Father Walter McGuinn in his investigation of the possibility of starting a school of social work in connection with the College. In preparation for such an undertaking, Father McGuinn engaged in graduate studies in social work at Fordham University in New York, where in 1935 he achieved the unusual distinction of being granted a Ph.D. degree with a major in social work.

Turning his attention to Boston, Father McGuinn was convinced that there was a need for professionally trained social workers taught to view their problems in the light of Catholic social principles. He saw that in this comparatively young field of formal education, there was often lacking a satisfactory synthesis of the principles of Christian philosophy—especially of ethics and psychology—with the various methods and techniques that had been developed in social work. Aid in the solution of these problems, he felt, would be achieved by the institution of social work schools in Catholic universities, from which proper leadership would emanate.

Local and higher Jesuit superiors shared Father McGuinn's view, and in May 1936 permission was granted by the General of the Society of Jesus in Rome to open such a school. On the eighth of the same month, Father McGuinn outlined his plans to Cardinal O'Connell, who at once gave his generous and enthusiastic approval to the project and graciously became honorary patron of the school.

The program of training and studies was drawn up in accordance with the specifications of the American Association of Schools of Social Work. For this task, Father McGuinn engaged the assistance of Dorothy L. Book, who had wide professional training and experience in social work and who became director of field work for the new school. The syllabus was organized to meet all professional requirements, and it provided experience in recognized social agencies under competent supervision. The training period from the beginning required two years to complete, the first devoted

126 Newbury Street, original location of the Graduate School of Social Work, the School of Business Administration, the School of Nursing, and the Intown College (precursor of the Evening School).

to a general foundation in the study of fundamental principles and methods common to all forms of social work, while the second afforded the student opportunities to specialize in some particular phase of social work. The training was of graduate caliber, open only to holders of a baccalaureate degree from an accredited college, and led to the degree of master of science in social work.[37]

A distinguished faculty was recruited from the professional field, and the first classes were held in September 1936 at the school's quarters at 126 Newbury Street. The initial enrollment was 40 students. Two years later the first class, numbering 34, graduated, and the school received its accreditation by the American Association of Schools of Social Work on June 28, 1938.

When war broke out, Father McGuinn was called to serve on the New England regional branch of the War Labor Board, where the exacting nature of his new duties, in addition to the administrative work at the school, gradually took a toll on his health. He developed a serious heart condition in the spring of 1944 and died suddenly on April 1. Upon his death, Miss Book acted as dean until the following September, when she was appointed permanently to that office, with Father James D. Sullivan, S.J., as regent.

The College of Business Administration

The next development at Boston College was the College of Business Administration.[38] For several years previous to the introduction of this school, four courses in accounting had been offered yearly as electives for juniors and seniors in the art course. The classes proved so popular that the question arose in 1938 of providing a fuller curriculum in business subjects. Father William J. McGarry, S.J., president of the college, decided that the situation demanded not additional courses but the institution of a separate school designed to furnish basic training in business at the same time that the necessary cultural subjects were studied. Consequently, early in March 1938 he appointed Father James J. Kelley, S.J., of the College staff, director of the new undertaking and gave him full authority to assemble a faculty and to draw up a four-year undergraduate program leading to the degree of bachelor of science in business administration.

The curriculum embraced the full philosophy course, with much of the literary training and—for Catholic students—the regular religion course (taken in the arts division) in addition to the standard business subjects. In outlining this syllabus, the recommendations of the American Association of Collegiate Business Schools were followed, requiring a distribution of subjects in the following proportions: at least 40 percent business subjects; 40 percent cultural subjects; and up to 20 percent, "border" subjects, which might be common to both business and arts.

At the invitation of Father McGarry, over 30 prominent businessmen and bankers from the Boston and New York areas consented to become members of an advisory committee for the Business School and to assist with their counsel and experience in the efficient direction of the school. The main committee operated through four smaller subcommittees which devoted their attention, respectively, to curriculum, publicity, lectures, and resources. The early success of the school was in no small part due to the generous interest of these business leaders.

At the time the original plans were made, it appeared that the museum building on Hammond Street would serve as quarters for the school, but further investigation showed the structure not suitable for this purpose without extensive alterations. Hence, space was taken in the building on Newbury Street which housed the Intown College and the School of Social Work, and the opening of classes was announced for September 16, 1938.

Over 100 applications arrived at the school offices throughout the spring and summer, and from this number 72 candidates were accepted for the first class. The following year, 75 entered the new freshman class, and this number taxed the available space to the point of serious inconvenience. The third year (1940–1941), the school had to move to the main buildings at

Chestnut Hill to accommodate the incoming class of 100 students, but this location also proved inadequate. In September 1941, the College of Business Administration was finally granted spacious quarters of its own in the newly acquired Cardinal O'Connell Hall, formerly the Liggett Estate, on Hammond Street in Chestnut Hill.

The new school now had a full four-year program in operation for the first time, and it enjoyed a total enrollment of some 330 students. The first graduating class numbered 52 in June 1942; the following February, on a wartime accelerated program, another 54 graduated; and in November of 1943, 40 more took their degrees. The College of Business Administration had come of age, but the demands of war upon the student personnel caused a postponement of further development and made it advisable in the summer of 1943 for the school to transfer its quarters temporarily from O'Connell Hall to the Tower Building on the main campus.

✻   ✻   ✻

Within approximately twenty years, Boston College had grown in a direction and to an extent never anticipated by Father Fulton or even by Father Gasson. The foundation of the Intown College, the Graduate School, the Law School, the Social Work School, and the College of Business Administration had extended immeasurably the educational service Boston College offered to the community. And it pleased the friends of the institution to observe that the development was not merely at the under-graduate level.

ENDNOTES

1. Charles W. Lyons, S.J., to Joseph Rockwell, S.J., February 14, 1919, Province Records, Maryland Provincial S.J. Archives, Georgetown University Library.
2. *Woodstock Letters*, 48(1919):402.
3. Thornton D. Apollonio, Secretary to the Committee, to Reverend James F. Mellyn, S.J., October 6, 1919, Boston College Graduate School files.
4. Notice dated January 27, 1923, signed by Father Mellyn, Graduate School files. A student's account of the course is given in *The Heights* (April 1, 1924).
5. Arthur L. Gould, assistant superintendent, to Reverend James F. Mellyn, S.J., January 13, 1923, Graduate School files.
6. J. E. Burke, Superintendent of Public Schools, to Reverend James F. Mellyn, S.J., May 17, 1922, Graduate School files.
7. *Annual Report of the Superintendent, October, 1925*, School Document No. 9, 1925, Boston Public Schools, pp. 22–23.
8. *Ibid.*, p. 37.
9. Ellen M. Cronin, Secretary to the School Committee, to Reverend James F. Mellyn, S.J., April 23, 1926, Graduate School files.
10. Compiled from records in the office of the Boston College Graduate School.
11. Augustine F. Hickey to the Reverend James F. Mellyn, S.J., October 11, 1919, Graduate School files.
12. *Ibid.*, and Father Hickey to Father Mellyn, October 14, 1919.
13. *Boston College Catalogue*, 1920, p. 74.

14. Father Hickey to Father Mellyn, March 20, 1920.

15. *Ibid.,* April 26, 1921; September 13, 1921.

16. *Ibid.,* February 2, 1922.

17. *Ibid.,* September 13, 1921; February 2, 1922; January 30, 1926.

18. *Ibid.,* April 26, 1921, and April 18, 1923, Boston College Graduate School files.

19. William Devlin, S.J., to Joseph Rockwell, S.J., June 9, 1920; Joseph Rockwell, S.J., to William Devlin, S.J., June 13, 1920, New York Province Archives, S.J.

20. *The Pilot,* September 13, 1924.

21. William Devlin, S.J., to Joseph Rockwell, S.J., March 8, 1923, Maryland Provincial S.J. Archives, Georgetown University Library.

22. William Devlin, S.J., to Joseph Rockwell, S.J., April 11, 1924, New York Province Archives, S.J.

23. William Devlin, S.J., to Joseph Rockwell, S.J., May 23, 1924, New York Province Archives, S.J., supplemented with information supplied to Father Dunigan by the late Father Mellyn in a personal interview, March 2, 1943.

24. *The Pilot* (July 5, 1924 and September 13, 1924).

25. *The Pilot* (September 24, 1924).

26. *Ibid.* (November 3, 1923); and *The Heights* (November 13, 1923).

27. An eight-page brochure issued by the College in connection with the courses being offered at Chestnut Hill for male public school teachers.

28. *The Boston Herald* (September 16, 1926); *The Boston Post* (September 16, 1926); *The Pilot* (September 25, 1926).

29. *The Pilot* (September 24, 1927).

30. *Ibid.*

31. *The Boston Post* (April 29, 1929); *The Boston Globe* (a.m.) (April 29, 1929); *The Boston Transcript* (April 29, 1929).

32. *The Boston Herald* (editorial) (April 30, 1929); *The Boston Transcript* (editorial) (April 29, 1929).

33. *Boston College Bulletin. The Law School. Announcement of the First Session,* 1929–1930, pp. 11–14.

34. *Ibid.*

35. *Boston College Bulletin, The Law School Announcement,* for the respective years.

36. *Boston College Bulletin of the Graduate and Extension Schools,* 1929–1930, pp. 47–49; and *The Heights* (October 1, 1929).

37. This description of the School of Social Work is based upon information supplied Father Dunigan by the Reverend James D. Sullivan, S.J., regent of this school.

38. This description of the College of Business Administration is based upon information supplied Father Dunigan by the Reverend James J. Kelly, S.J., dean of that college.

CHAPTER 19

Depression Decade

The period immediately before World War II was one of continued growth and consolidation, although on the side of physical expansion only one project, the wing on St. Mary's Hall, could be listed as new construction. The rapidly increasing Jesuit faculty had rendered the accommodations of the residence hall inadequate as early as the fall of 1927. At that time a temporary remedy was arranged and finally achieved in January 1928 by transferring the faculty library, which occupied the end of St. Mary's Hall over the chapel, to the new library building and converting the space thus obtained into four living rooms, a bishop's suite, and three private chapels.

Expanding St. Mary's, and the Cohasset Resthouse

The problem of insufficient room was constantly pressing, however, until Father Dolan, late in 1930, decided that St. Mary's Hall should be substantially enlarged. He engaged the architects Maginnis and Walsh to design an addition that would preserve the pleasing proportions and general appearance of the building as well as protect the overall campus pattern which had been agreed on for future development.

Work was actually begun on October 7 of that year and proceeded throughout the following winter and spring. When completed, the L-shaped addition provided 35 more individual living rooms, in addition to 7 rooms on the southeast end of the third floor which were designed as infirmary quarters. Among the changes effected was a new and enlarged refectory, planned to accommodate 104; a recreation room for the Fathers and a faculty reading room, on the first floor of the new section; offices for the president and treasurer, made by remodeling the old refectory; and visitors' parlors created by adaptation of the former offices. The new basement provided area for a large garage, as well as extended facilities for the wardrobe and a number of new rooms for workmen. The new wing was completed in the summer and formally occupied on the feast of St. Ignatius on July 31, 1931.[1]

In May 1932 the trustees announced the purchase of the Brown estate, comprising some eight and a half acres in Cohasset, Massachusetts, and bordering the entrance to Cohasset harbor. The purpose of this acquisition was to provide a resthouse for the Jesuit faculty within easy motoring distance of the College, where some hours each week during the summer could be spent at the shore. This relaxation was considered advisable because teaching schedules, including summer school, were arranged on almost a 52-weeks-a-year basis.

Father Gallagher Becomes Rector

On January 1, 1932, Father Dolan was succeeded in the presidency of Boston College by the Reverend Louis J. Gallagher, S.J., until then Socius to the Provincial and Prefect General of Studies for Jesuit institutions in the New England area.[2] Father Gallagher began his administration at Boston

John O'Loughlin, assistant librarian in Bapst from its early days well into the postwar era.

REV. LOUIS J. GALLAGHER, S.J.
Seventeenth President

Father Gallagher was born in Boston on July 22, 1885. He attended public schools in Dorchester and the Immaculate Conception school in Malden. He entered Boston College High School in 1900, and was attending Boston College in 1905 when he was accepted into the Society of Jesus. During his pre-ordination course he spent five years on the faculty of Fordham University. In 1920, along with the Jesuit he would succeed as president, Father James Dolan, he was ordained by Cardinal Gibbons. He served briefly as principal of Xavier High School in New York and then was assigned to help administer the Vatican Relief Mission to Russia during the famine of 1922. He remained in Russia for two years during the establishment of Communism there. On returning to America he was appointed assistant to the Provincial of the newly established New England Jesuit Province in 1926. At the time of his selection as president of Boston College, he had overall supervision of the educational enterprises of the province.

College when the full impact of the 1929 depression was being felt everywhere. In March 1932 he reported that the depression had forced a policy of financial retrenchment upon the College.[3] The deficit in the payment of tuitions, which had increased with every semester of the previous two years, was particularly large during that term because of conditions prevailing in various banks. Deferred payment and installment paying had affected about 20 percent of the tuitions, and the number of students receiving financial aid from the College had increased 100 per cent over the previous year. He stated that the enforced forfeiture of tuition income did not result in the dropping of any students, partly because some balance was effected by the reduction of expenditures for equipment or developmental projects and by the frugal administration of the community house of the nonsalaried Jesuit faculty. Father Gallagher was also able to report that, up to that time, no reduction had been made in the salary of anyone employed by the College, nor was any contemplated.

Alumni Field Stadium

The depression necessarily obliged him to postpone indefinitely any plans for expansion, but he effected many improvements which were extraordinary in the light of the difficulties under which he labored. Financial restrictions, for instance, had caused the de-emphasis of intercollegiate athletics at Boston College during the last years of Father Dolan's term in office. A steady increase in the seriousness of the depression forced Father Gallagher either to discover a means of reducing in a substantial way the expenditures involved in the athletic program or to suspend the major sports altogether.

In selecting the first alternative, Father Gallagher felt that a transfer of the home football games from the professional park in Boston, which charged 20 percent of the gross receipts of a game for rental, to University Heights would effect a saving which would enable football to continue on a satisfactory scale. Some rather discouraging difficulties, however, lay in the way of such a change. The grandstands on the campus were small, wooden, and, in several sections, of secondhand materials; age had contributed to make them so unsafe that the city authorities finally condemned them. The first step, therefore, in carrying out a program for campus athletics was to provide a suitable set of stands. A large stadium was, of course, out of the question for many reasons, the chief of which was the enormous cost, which had led even heavily endowed universities to discontinue the practice of building them. Further, at Boston College the authorities were unwilling to commit a large portion of the campus which would eventually be needed for college buildings to this distinctly part-time use.

The answer to this problem, announced in May 1932, was the installation of prefabricated steel stands which provided strength at a minimum cost, were easy to erect, and were relatively inconspicuous.[4] The permit to put up the stands was granted by the City of Newton on June 25, 1932, and the work of pouring the concrete foundations and assembling the steel sections was begun shortly after the closing of school.[5] In order to reduce expenses as far as possible and at the same time provide a number of students with employment at a time when work was at a premium, the task of erecting the stands was given to a number of students under the direction of professional steel workers. This arrangement occasioned a protest from one of the labor unions, which objected to the employment of "amateur" help; but the labor officials, after investigating the situation, gave the project their approval.

The completed stands were low-lying and rested in a natural declivity of the land. The field was landscaped in such a manner that the structure not only blended into the general scene but game audiences were protected in some measure from the direct rays of the sun. The capacity of the stands, with both permanent and temporary sections included, was planned to be 20,000; for the convenience of these patrons, parking space for 3000 cars was arranged on the campus. The entire stands were not erected the first

Father Gallagher with three shapers of Boston College athletics: John Curley ('13), long-time athletic director; Jack Ryder, veteran track coach; Joseph McKenney ('27, '83 HON), football captain, 1926, and football coach, 1928–1934.

year, however, and the season—which opened with the dedication of the new "stadium" on October 1 and included games with Fordham and Holy Cross—was played on a field which seated only 15,000. The full complement of portable temporary stands was used during the two following years (1933 and 1934). The largest crowd to gather on Alumni Field was probably the one in attendance at the Diocesan band concert in 1941, estimated at over 25,000.

In the years immediately before the war, the national prominence of the football team, with a consequent large following at its games, caused the transfer of the contests back to Fenway Park and later to Braves' Field, since the installation of facilities to accommodate large crowds properly on the campus would not only entail great expense but could not be effected without defacing the property.

The Thompson Collection

An example of the academic accomplishments that were rivaling nonacademic activities for attention at this period is found in the dramatically successful efforts of Father Terence L. Connolly, S.J., head of the English Department, to gather documentary material for firsthand study of English Catholic poets. In the fall of 1933 Father Connolly arranged for a loan exhibit at Boston College of manuscripts and first editions of the Catholic Victorian poet, Francis Thompson. The exhibition, the first dedicated to that poet in America, was held from October 5 to 8, 1933, through the kindness of the owner of the collection, Seymour Adelman of Chester, Pennsylvania. Loans from the Widener and the Boston Public Library augmented the display, which drew the interest of scholars throughout the East.

Since eight years of devoted labor and great wealth had been employed by Mr. Adelman in assembling the collection, Father Connolly's surprise and pleasure can be understood, when, some four years later, Mr. Adelman offered his treasures to Father Connolly for a sum considerably less than their estimated value, with the understanding that the various items would always be known as belonging to the Seymour Adelman Collection. Within three weeks after Mr. Adelman's offer, loyal friends of the College had raised a fund to buy the manuscripts, and on April 22, 1937, title to the Adelman Collection was transferred to Boston College. The administration readily gave permission for the faculty reading room of the library to be converted into a permanent display center for the Thompsoniana and related items, and the collection was formally opened for public inspection on November 5, 1937.

Bapst auditorium, 1928–1967.

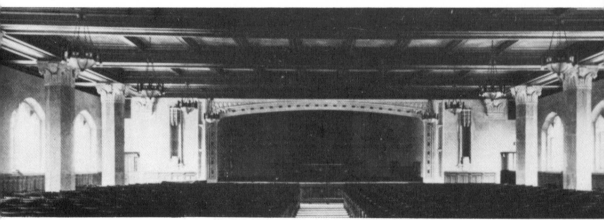

Kresge reading room in Bapst (former auditorium) after the renovation of 1986.

On hearing of Boston College's acquisition of this material, Wilfrid Meynell, the patron and closest friend of the poet, donated to Father Connolly the manuscript of "From the Night of Forebeing." Later, upon the occasion of Father Connolly's visit to Meynell in England during the summer of 1938, he presented to Father Connolly several Thompson notebooks and manuscripts, including the complete manuscript of the *Life of Saint Ignatius*. The story of this meeting and some of the interesting details accompanying the presentation of Wilfrid Meynell's gift can be found in Father Connolly's *Francis Thompson: In His Paths.*[6]

Since that time the Thompson Room has been enriched by additions to the collection through Mr. Meynell's beneficence and by four portraits presented by Mrs. Edward C. Donnelly as a memorial to her late husband. The paintings are: Mr. Wilfrid Meynell, by Sir John Lavery; Alice Meynell, by the Honorable Neville Lytton; Coventry Patmore, by Sir John Lavery; and Francis Thompson, by John Lavalle. The portraits of Patmore and Thompson are hung to face a valuable copy of Raphael's *Madonna del Gran Duca*, symbolizing the dependence of both of these poets upon the Blessed Mother for their inspiration.[7]

Remembrances, Honors, Treasures

The library was enriched in February 1934 by the accession of over 4000 rare volumes which were bequeathed to the College in the will of the late Monsignor Arthur L. Connolly, of the Blessed Sacrament Church in Jamaica Plain, Massachusetts.[8] The collection was particularly strong in Irish literature but also contained other items of great value, among which were St. Bonaventure's *Life of Christ*, printed in 1475, and a *Commentaries on the Gospel*, printed in the same period. In addition to these books, a large number of letters written by English and American literary figures were included in the collection.[9]

In the early summer of 1934, the College assisted in the celebration of Cardinal O'Connell's Golden Jubilee of his ordination to the priesthood, culminating on June 9 with an outdoor Mass celebrated by His Eminence on Alumni Field before a crowd estimated at over 20,000.[10]

Father Joseph J. Williams, S.J., director of the Department of Anthropology at Boston College, was appointed one of the three representatives of the American Anthropological Association and the American Council of Learned Societies to attend the International Congress of Anthropological and Ethnological Sciences in London during the summer of 1934. At the congress, Father Williams presented dissertations before the religious as well as the African sections of ethnology, and was quoted in 65 dailies throughout England and Scotland.[11] Further distinction came to him in his election as a fellow of both the Royal and the American Geographical Societies and also of the Royal Anthropological Institute and the Royal Society of Arts. The previous year Father Williams had established at

Boston College the Nicholas M. Williams Ethnological Collection, consisting of several thousand volumes and with 5000 items in the African section. The collection proved to be the only one of its kind in the United States recognized by the International Institute of African Languages and Cultures.

Along with the varied activities of the depression years that showed the vitality of the institution in trying circumstances, a decision was made regarding the curriculum of the College that some faculty members found sad: the offering of an A.B. degree without Greek. From the day of its opening, Greek as well as Latin had been required by Boston College for the A.B. degree. As fewer and fewer applicants to the College in the 20th century were equipped or interested in taking the classical course, various curricula without Latin and Greek were offered, terminating, however, in a bachelor of science degree. In 1935 Boston College and Holy Cross authorities, working with the Jesuit Provincial Prefect of Studies, Father William J. Murphy, modified the age-old curriculum to include an A.B. degree still requiring Latin but without Greek. This was indeed a major concession, and it earned notice in the Boston press.[12] The reluctance of the College to make this decision was shown in the details of the new A.B. program. Any honors student had to include Greek in his course. Non-honors students were designated either A.B. (Greek) or A.B. (mathematics). It would be another 20 years before Latin would join Greek as an elective instead of a required course for the A.B. degree.

Meanwhile, further interesting developments were occurring outside the curriculum. On May 29, 1935, the Boston College Library acquired an original letter (in Portuguese) of St. Francis Xavier, signed by the saint and addressed to Don John III, King of Portugal. The manuscript is composed of three folio pages and is dated "Cochin, January 31, 1552," the last year of the saint's life, just after his return from Japan and shortly before he sailed to China and his death. It is a confidential report to the king referring to the Portuguese subjects in the Far East, whom the saint recommends for reward and recognition. He also records the work of some of the historical personalities with whom he came into contact in Japan, India, and Malacca, and the missionary work carried on in those countries. Careful study on the part of the Reverend George Shurhammer, S.J., biographer of St. Francis Xavier and greatest living authority on documents pertaining to the Saint, established the Xavier letters as authentic.[13] The letter which is now in the possession of Boston College was dictated, addressed and signed by the saint, but the body of the message is apparently in the handwriting of an amanuensis, very probably Anthony of China, who acted as Xavier's secretary on other known occasions and who was his sole attendant when the saint died on Sancien. The Philomatheia Club of Boston College purchased the letter and presented it to the College as a gift to commemorate the twentieth anniversary of the founding of the club.[14]

Late in 1935 the borders of the campus on Beacon Street were altered to conform with a street-widening program being carried out at the time by the City of Newton. The payment made by the city for the narrow strip of land ceded by the College aided, with private gifts, in defraying the cost of the graceful wrought-iron fence supported by granite pillars which was erected along the entire Beacon Street side of the property. The expanse of fence was broken almost opposite Acacia Street by an ornate gate which was dedicated by Father Gallagher as part of the alumni day activities on June 8, 1936.[15]

His Eminence, Eugenio Cardinal Pacelli, Papal Secretary of State and future Pope Pius XII, paid the College a surprise visit on the morning of October 15, 1936, in the company of the Most Reverend Francis J. Spellman, at that time, Auxiliary Bishop of Boston.[16] The cardinal was greeted at St. Mary's Hall by Father Gallagher and members of the Jesuit faculty, and from there he was escorted to the porch of the library building, from which he briefly addressed the student body gathered on the campus. He then made a presentation to Boston College of a beautifully illuminated fifteenth-century missal as a memento of his visit.

*   *   *

The depression years may have impeded, but they did not thwart, Boston College's academic expansion. The Law School was inaugurated in the year of the stock market crash. The School of Social Work was begun in 1936. Two years later the College would start its first new undergraduate school since 1864.

ENDNOTES

1. *The Boston Globe* (October 11, 1930); *Woodstock Letters*, 60(1931):457–459; *Boston College: Seventy-Fifth Anniversary, 1863–1938*, p. 35.
2. *The Boston Post* (January 2, 1932); *The Boston Herald* (January 2, 1932); *The Boston Sunday Post* (January 10, 1932); *The Boston Sunday Globe* (January 10, 1932).
3. *The Boston Transcript* (March 19, 1932).
4. *The Boston Traveler* (May 5, 1932); *The Boston Post* (May 5, 1932).
5. *The Boston Post* (June 30, 1932).
6. Milwaukee: The Bruce Publishing Co., 1944.
7. Further details on the Thompson Collection will be found in Terence L. Connolly, S.J. (editor), *An Account of Books and Manuscripts of Francis Thompson* (Chestnut Hill, Massachusetts, Boston College, n.d.); Terence L. Connolly, S.J., "Seymour Adelman's Thompsoniana," *America*, 50:16–17 (October 7, 1933).
8. It is heartening that benefactions to the special collections continue. See Chapter 39 for recent acquisitions for Burns library.
9. *The Boston Globe* (February 15, 1934); *The Boston Post* (February 18, 1934).
10. *The Boston Sunday Globe* (June 10, 1934); *The Boston Sunday Advertiser* (June 10, 1934).

11. *The Heights* (October 3, 1934).
12. *The Boston Herald* (March 27, 1935).
13. George Schurhammer, S.J., "Zwei ungedruckte Briefe des hl. Franz Xaver," *Archivum Historicum Societatis Iesu* (Rome), II, 44–45, 1933.
14. *The Boston Globe* (May 29, 1935); *The Boston Traveler* (May 29, 1935).
15. *The Boston Post* (June 9, 1936).
16. *The Heights* (October 16, 1936).

CHAPTER 20

An Expanded Campus

On the evening of July 1, 1937, Father William J. McGarry, S.J., dean of the Jesuit seminary at Weston College, was appointed to succeed Father Gallagher as president of Boston College. It was Father McGarry's intention on taking office to assume a full teaching schedule for himself in both the graduate and undergraduate divisions, but a semester's trial of this work in addition to his administrative duties had such a negative effect upon his health that he was forced to abandon his lecture courses for the balance of the year.

Father McGarry's Short Tenure

Other plans which he sought to put into effect soon after taking office included improvement of the library facilities, which he accomplished not only by completing the steel stackroom accommodations but by launching an extensive purchasing program to strengthen the library holdings in several departments. Father McGarry also took a keen interest in the undergraduate curriculum at the Heights and made several changes to assure continued high standards. The Intown Division also had his attention, with the result that a reorganized educational and administrational structure went into effect in the fall of 1938.

The week of February 20, 1938, was set aside for celebration of the diamond jubilee of the founding of the College.[1] A downtown theater was

185

REV. WILLIAM J. McGARRY, S.J.
Eighteenth President

Father McGarry was born in Hamilton, Massachusetts on March 14, 1894. After attending Hamilton grammar school, he entered Boston College High School, and upon finishing his course there in 1911 he entered the Society of Jesus. During his theological studies he focused on biblical scholarship, pursuing graduate studies at Fordham and being awarded the degree of Doctor of Sacred Theology by Woodstock College. He was ordained in 1925 and later attended the Pontifical Biblical Institute in Rome, where he was awarded the degree of Licentiate in Sacred Scriptures with Honors. He was professor of Sacred Scriptures and dean at Weston College, the New England Province center for theology study, from 1930 to 1936.[2]

engaged for the week and a program of events was arranged for every evening. On Sunday afternoon the opening session was a symposium on Catholic marriage by an intercollegiate Catholic Action unit; that evening the Student and Alumni Musical clubs presented a joint concert. The Philomatheia Club sponsored a public lecture on Monday evening, and on Tuesday Father McGarry met the alumni at their convocation and read to them the Papal Benediction which had been sent to the College from Rome. An intercollegiate debate with Harvard took place on Wednesday evening, and the evenings throughout the balance of the week were occupied with performances of the Dramatic Society's play. On Friday afternoon members of the Spanish, Italian, and German societies enacted scenes from selected masterpieces of the three countries, and the French Academy sponsored the Saturday matinee. A large pictorial and historical brochure on the College and a Boston College song book were published to mark the anniversary. Later, on April 1, a Solemn High Mass commemorating the founding of the College was sung at the Immaculate Conception Church in the presence of His Eminence, Cardinal O'Connell.

Early in March 1938 a departure from the former compulsory entrance examinations for all and the introduction of a new method for admission by certification was announced with the publication of the 1938–1939

Boston College *Bulletin*. Under the new system, candidates might qualify for entrance in any one of three ways: (1) full certification by an approved secondary school, (2) partial certification and passing grades in some of the approved forms of college entrance examinations in all required subjects in which the candidate had not been certified, or (3) passing grades in some one of the approved forms of college entrance examinations in all required subjects. Of course, all who wished to be considered for scholarships were to take the entrance examinations as usual. This arrangement was considered by the College authorities a more equitable method of determining suitable candidates for admission in that it stressed the secondary school record as a better norm of fitness than an isolated examination.[3]

Father McGarry's career as a college president was prematurely brought to a close in the summer of 1939 by the imperative need of an experienced writer and prominent theologian to become the first editor of a new theological review, *Theological Studies*, which was in the process of organization. The creation of this magazine was the result of a meeting in July 1938 of professors of theology representing the five Jesuit houses of theology in the United States. The participants determined to launch the new theological quarterly as the official publication of the American Jesuit provinces. It was unanimously agreed that an urgent request be transmitted to the Jesuit General in Rome that Father McGarry be released from his current duties at Boston College and that he be appointed to the new office of editor. When the Jesuit authorities reluctantly consented to the proposed release, Father William J. Murphy, S.J., was appointed to the presidency of Boston College on the Feast of the Assumption on August 15, 1939.

A New President, a New War

Sixteen days after Father Murphy was installed as rector, the armies of Adolf Hitler marched into Poland and Europe was once more at war. The conflict did not immediately affect life in the United States, particularly life on college campuses. Boston College carried on that year much as usual.

A program for the graduate training of Jesuit scholastics was begun, with 19 of these students living together as a semi-independent community in the brick parish house on Commonwealth Avenue near Lake Street and devoting the time usually allotted to the teaching period (or "regency") to advanced studies in the classics, history, or the sciences.

Another milestone in the College's progress was reached in the summer of 1941, when arrangements were made to purchase the Louis K. Liggett estate to house the rapidly growing College of Business Administration. When the proposed transaction was brought before Cardinal O'Connell for his approval, he not only granted it with enthusiasm but insisted that he be permitted to donate the entire cost of the property. His generous offer was gratefully accepted, and it was determined to name the new building "Cardinal O'Connell Hall." The transfer of the property took place on July 25, 1941, and provided the College with an additional nine

REV. WILLIAM J. MURPHY, S.J.
Nineteenth President

Father Murphy was born in Lawrence, Massachusetts, on October 20, 1895. After completing his sophomore year at Boston College, he entered the Society of Jesus on September 7, 1914. He taught classics at Fordham University and Holy Cross College. He was ordained at Weston College in 1927. He spent two years of advanced study of literature in England and Italy, and in 1932 he became a lecturer in literature at the Boston College Graduate School. In 1934 he was named director of studies of the Jesuit schools in New England, and in 1937 he assumed the added role as assistant to the Provincial.

and a half acres of land in the immediate vicinity of the main campus,[4] bounded by Hammond Street, Beacon Street, and Tudor Road.

When the College took over the property, the rooms in the master section were converted into classrooms for the Business School and those in the servants' quarters into offices for the extracurricular activities of the entire College. The magnificent Reception Hall, rising through two stories in the center of the building, served as the students' foyer, adjoining which were the administrative offices and some of the classrooms. The quadrangle of stables, carriage houses, a garage, and a gardener's lodge, surrounding a court which resembled an old English inn yard, was made over into quarters for the Athletic Association and dressing rooms for the teams. The second floor of this area was taken up with the workshop and scene lofts of the dramatic society.

The College of Business Administration occupied O'Connell Hall from the fall of 1941 until June 1943 when, due to reduced numbers of students as well as to the pressing need of the hall as a Jesuit residence during the use of St. Mary's Hall by the army program, the business classes were transferred to the Tower Building.

On October 4, 1941, the Solemn Votive Mass of the Holy Spirit, known in a tradition which goes back many centuries in Rome, Paris, and London as the "Red Mass," was celebrated for the first time in Massachusetts to mark the opening of the judicial year. The ceremony, which took place in the Immaculate Conception Church, was under the auspices of Cardinal O'Connell and the Boston College Law School.

The function drew the most distinguished legal assemblage ever gathered in the state for a religious service. Governor Leverett Saltonstall and Mayor Maurice J. Tobin led the procession, which formed in the rectory, moved along Harrison Avenue to the main entrance of the church, and then up the center aisle. Among the participants were the chief justice and the full bench of the Massachusetts Supreme Court; the judges of the Massachusetts probate courts and the United States Courts; judges of the land courts, district courts, and Boston municipal courts; the attorney general of the state and his entire staff; the United States attorney and his entire staff; district attorneys and assistant district attorneys; and representatives from all the law schools and law societies in the state. The Mass was said by

1940 football team—national champions.

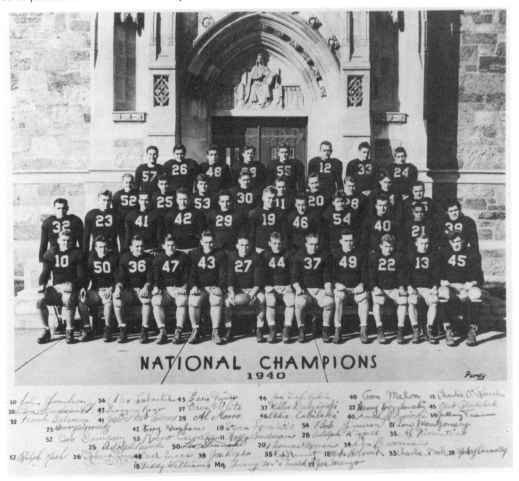

O'Connell Hall.

Father Murphy, president of the College, and the sermon was delivered by the Reverend William J. Kenealy, S.J., dean of the Boston College Law School.

As the months passed during this period, an interest in national defense was gradually taking form, and attractive opportunities in the various military reserves were offered to college men. From time to time students withdrew to begin training for commissions, but their numbers were few enough to draw special mention in the College newspaper. The feature of that era most clearly stamped in the memories of both students and alumni was the meteoric rise to nation-wide prominence of the College's football teams; on three New Year's Days, they participated in national bowl games. Enthusiastic friends hailed this success as the beginning of an epoch, but the hand of war was already lowering the intermission curtain upon sports and on all normal college life.

*   *   *

In a little more than 20 years, Boston College had withstood rather well two external traumas: World War I and the Great Depression. But neither of those events brought the institution so close to the brink as did World War II.

ENDNOTES

1. *The Boston Sunday Post* (February 20, 1938).
2. *The Boston Globe* (July 2, 1937).
3. *The Boston Globe* (March 5, 1938); *The Heights* (March 4, 1938).
4. *Middlesex South District Registry of Deeds,* Book 6520, p. 365.

CHAPTER 21

Soldiers with Schoolbooks

Long before Japanese bombs broke the Sunday morning silence at Pearl Harbor on December 7, 1941, Boston College—like the country at large—had been making readjustments to meet the demands of national defense. As early as 1938 a Boston College unit of the United States Marine Corps Reserve Fleet was inaugurated at the Boston Navy Yard.[1] In 1939 in cooperation with the Civil Aeronautics Administration, the College began a program for civilian pilot training. Flight training was given by instructors of the E. W. Wiggins Airways, under contract to the government, at the Norwood Airport. Seventy-two hours of late afternoon classes in aeronautics were offered on campus. During its three years of operation, the Civilian Pilot Training course graduated 90 qualified pilots, almost all of whom were later commissioned in the Army or Navy air branches. The coordinator of the program, Father John A. Tobin, S.J., chairman of the Physics Department, took the flight training himself and secured a pilot's license.[2]

Boston College was one of six institutions in metropolitan Boston to offer college-level courses to prepare skilled defense workers. The program, subsidized by the government, was known as the "Engineering, Science, and Management Defense Training Course," and it began at Boston

College in October 1941. It was estimated that over a thousand people attended the course at Boston College.[3]

The Draft

The Selective Training and Service Act, constituting the first peacetime conscription in the history of the nation, was passed by Congress on September 14, 1940 and made law by the president's signature two days later. Under this legislation, which made men from 21 to 36 liable for military training, a first registration was ordered for October 16, 1940, and a lottery to determine the order of call, for October 29, 1940. Since only a relatively small percentage of college students were over 21, and since draft boards were inclined, in the period before the war, to grant deferments to students to permit them to finish their course, this act did not at once cause great concern to college administrators.

Various branches of the armed forces continued, meanwhile, to present attractive opportunities leading to commissions for those students who would enlist on a deferred basis. Later, enough requests for advice in matters of draft deferment were received by the Boston College authorities to cause them to establish an organized method of counseling the students. This system was centered about a faculty board composed of Father John A. O'Brien, S.J., Dr. Harry Doyle, and Professor Fred Bryan, who were appointed by Father John J. Long, S.J., dean of the College of Arts and Sciences, early in May 1941 for the purpose of aiding students in preparing statements of information for their local draft boards. At the same time the attention of the students was drawn to the College's Placement Bureau, directed by George Donaldson, which was equipped to give full information on the various officer-training opportunities and which acted as a liaison office between the recruiting services and the student body. Both the Counseling Board and the Placement Bureau had representatives available for student conferences every day of the school week, with the aim of making sure that the individual student would be placed where he would be of greatest service to his country, whether in some particular branch of the armed forces, in a certain position in the ranks of a vital industry, or at his college desk.

Three days after Pearl Harbor, Father Murphy and the deans of the various divisions addressed an assembly of the students on the seriousness of the national situation and cautioned them to remain calm, thoughtful, and prayerful until the situation would clear and they would know best how to serve their country. Five days later, the College celebrated Bill of Rights Day with a solemn blessing of the national colors on Alumni Field. At the same time, it was announced that the curricula and semesters of the entire system would be accelerated to enable those students who were soon to be called to service to finish as much as possible of their course. The

Christmas vacation period would not be altered, but the time usually allotted to the mid-year examinations would be substantially curtailed.

In January 1942, the presidents of Holy Cross and Boston College, Fathers Joseph R. N. Maxwell, S.J., and William J. Murphy, S.J., and the deans of both colleges met with the Jesuit Provincial, Father James H. Dolan, S.J., to discuss the changes in curricula and schedules made necessary by the war. As an outcome of this meeting, an accelerated program affecting the entire college course was approved by the officials of both colleges and went into effect with the opening of the second semester on January 12, 1942.

Enlistments on a deferred basis in the United States Navy Reserve continued briskly through the spring and into the summer of 1942. The College, cooperating with the government, arranged for a Navy indoctrination course to be conducted on the campus for the benefit of the reservists. The lectures were delivered by Navy officers attached to the Causeway Street headquarters.

Meanwhile, the Army took steps to institute a program similar to the Navy's to obtain reserve officer candidates on a deferred basis. On May 18, 1942, the president of Boston College was requested to participate in a program for the pre-induction training of students in the Army Enlisted Reserve Corps and to cooperate in an enlistment campaign for this branch. Father Murphy nominated Father John A. Tobin, S.J., as Army faculty adviser, and this selection was approved in Washington. Shortly after, a quota of 509 students for Boston College was announced and enlistments began. The drive was successful, but on July 8, 1942, the officer-candidate recruiting efforts of all branches of the armed services were combined into a joint procurement program. When this went into effect, Father Stephen A. Mulcahy, S.J., dean of the College of Arts and Sciences, was appointed armed forces representative.

On November 16, 1942, an impressive mass induction of 47 students into the V-1 and V-7 classes of the Navy was held in the auditorium in the presence of College and Navy officials. On December 5, 1942, enlistments in the reserve were closed, and it was announced that henceforth officer-candidate material would be drawn from the enlisted personnel obtained through the ordinary operation of the draft. About three weeks later, on December 24, all members of the Army Enlisted Reserve Corps were notified that they would be called to active duty on the completion of the semester ending after December 31, 1942. In order that the freshman reservists at Boston College might secure the maximum benefit provided by that directive, the opening of their new term was advanced to December 30.

The freshman class entering in February 1943 was admitted on the basis of a new wartime schedule planned to permit a student to finish his entire college course in two years' time, by means of curtailments already in

Proud Refrain

What are you dreaming, Soldier,
What is it you see?

A tall grey Gothic tower,
And a linden tree.

You speak so sadly, Soldier,
Sad and wistfully—

I cannot hear the tower bell
In the swirling sea.

What meaning has it, Soldier,
A tower bell, and tree?

Nothing, nothing—only once
It meant my life to me.

Thomas Heath, '43

Thomas Heath became a priest of the Dominican
Order and is working in Africa.

practice and by omission of the customary vacation periods. This accelerated schedule permitted the seniors in the class of 1943 to finish three months earlier than usual; thus, in the first mid-winter commencement in the institution's history, 247 arts seniors and 50 business seniors were graduated at ceremonies held in the Immaculate Conception Church on Harrison Avenue on Sunday, February 28, 1943.

The Army Proposes a Program

In March 1943 the War Department announced a plan known as the Army Specialized Training Program (A.S.T.P.) whose purpose was to provide technicians and specialists for the Army. Those selected for the program would study, at government expense, at colleges and universities in fields determined largely by their own qualifications. Civilians from 17 to 22 could, in advance of induction, be designated, by success in a special test, for participation in A.S.T.P. They would be soldiers on active duty: in uniform, under military discipline, and on regular Army pay.

Since the Army was to need the facilities of hundreds of colleges throughout the country for this training program, Father Murphy immediately offered to the War Department the staff and physical equipment of Boston College if the government desired it as a training center. Negotiations were opened in the spring and were continued through the early summer. Late in June there was a series of inspections of the College facilities by military groups, and on July 5 the College received the War Department's Letter of Intent. With this official designation of Boston College as one of the institutions selected as a center of training came the appointment of Father Stephen A. Mulcahy, S.J., as local coordinator of the program. On July 7 the newly appointed commandant of the post, Major John R. Canavan, U.S.A., visited the Heights and took lunch with the Jesuit Community.

Under the arrangements agreed on, the Jesuit Fathers would vacate St. Mary's Hall and take up residence in small groups in O'Connell Hall and other properties owned by the College. A central kitchen and dining room for the faculty would be built in the basement of the Tower Building. St. Mary's Hall, meanwhile, would be re-equipped as a barracks to accommodate over 400 soldiers.

On Monday, July 12, 1943, moving of the Jesuit faculty's personal effects was begun. All that week and through part of the next, a number of large moving vans were engaged in distributing the contents of St. Mary's Hall among the outlying houses. As soon as the rooms were cleared, the soldiers' two-tier bunks, plain tables, chairs, and study lamps were brought in, and mess hall equipment was installed. The majority of the individual living rooms were arranged to accommodate four soldiers, with an occasional larger room providing space for six. The faculty dining room and the faculty recreation room were converted into mess halls in which the meals were prepared and served by Howard Johnson, Incorporated, a restaurateur approved by the Army. Since only about 200 men could be accommodated in the mess halls at one time, meals were served at successive intervals.

Marching to Class

The soldiers began arriving on July 25, and the influx continued for several days. Among them were natives of 37 states; they represented Army posts in every part of the country and were drawn from every branch of the service. The two qualifications which these young men had in common were intelligence above the average and a record which indicated that they could profit from academic instruction.

On July 27 the first general assembly of "Army Specialized Training Unit Number 1189" was called by Major Canavan. The soldiers were welcomed by the College authorities and their new duties explained to them. The first activity confronting them was an interview by members of the College's four civilian boards, which would classify them for homogeneous grouping

Drill on Alumni Field.

and assign them to the proper term of work. This processing of the men was carried on until the opening of classes on August 9. In the meantime, refresher courses in the subjects to be studied by the soldiers were opened as a voluntary service of the Boston College faculty to enable men who had been away from books and classrooms for some time to take up their classwork without a feeling of disadvantage.

Although the original quota designated for Boston College was 425 soldiers, 432 were present for the opening of classes. Of these, 132 were in the language and foreign area group, which studied conversational language, geography, and customs of certain countries, and 300 were in basic engineering, which stressed the study of mathematics.

The first 12-week term for the Army Specialized Training Unit was finished on October 30, and the soldiers were granted a one-week furlough before commencing the work of the next semester. During November the unit was visited by Colonel Morton Smith, military director of the program for the First Corps Area, General Perry Miles, commander of the First Corps Area, and Dr. Henry W. Holmes, civilian educational coordinator of the program.

Termination of the Army Program

On February 7, 1944, 22 men were called from the language and foreign area group to active duty, presumably in Italy. This left only 97 men in that section and 206 in basic engineering. Suddenly in March the A.S.T.P. programs around the country were informed that the operation would be terminated by April 1. The decision was not understood at the time even by the military officers in charge of the program. Later, of course, it was clear that the decision was related to the D-Day invasion in June.

The contract between the Army and Boston College ran until June 30, 1944, and the rental for facilities was paid accordingly. One result of this arrangement was that St. Mary's Hall remained vacant until summer before being repainted and reoccupied by the Jesuit Community.

Meanwhile, the civilian students continued to feel the effects of the war in many ways. In June 1943 the sophomore and junior members of the Naval and Marine Reserves were notified that they would be called to active duty on July 1, and freshman members were told that they would be summoned at the end of the semester. Army reservists who had not been previously called (premedical, engineering, and science majors) were also to report for duty on July 1, making a grand total of some 381 Boston College men affected.

An emergency summer schedule was drawn up to provide seniors with 45 hours of each philosophy course and 30 hours of religion in the period from June 28 to July 31, to make sure that they would have had the main portion of their senior matter even if they were called out before graduation in November. In September the wisdom of this plan was demonstrated when 14 senior marine reservists and 40 V-7 naval reservists were activated, in addition to 15 sophomore army reservists.

On November 28 commencement exercises were held at which 73 graduated, of whom 19 V-7 seniors were ordered to report immediately after graduation. The problems confronting the College administration with regard to the civilian student body can be exemplified by an examination of the records for the period following the civilian registration of February 8, 1944. On that day, the Arts and Science course had an enrollment of 306; less than three weeks later, the figure had dropped to 266; and on April 27, it was down to 236—a loss of 70 students in a little over two months.

The War Fund and Adjustments

In the operation of a college there is a threshold, or minimum level, below which expenses cannot be lowered and still have the institution function. When it became evident at Boston College that tuition fees from a greatly reduced student body could no longer meet that minimum level, the trustees decided early in January 1944 to inaugurate a Boston College War Fund Drive among the alumni, friends of the College, and businessmen of New England for the purpose of enabling the College to continue, without abandoning any of its services, through the straitened period of the war. A number of prominent business and professional men volunteered to act as a committee under Jeremiah Mahoney as chairman to secure a fund of $250,000. Cardinal O'Connell began the drive on January 25 with a donation of $5,000, and the appeal progressed so well that the committee was able to announce on September 18 that the goal had been achieved. Although the drive had been formally terminated, contributions continued to be received during the next two months, until the amount reached $277,000.

On April 22, 1944, Boston College's distinguished alumnus, William Cardinal O'Connell, died in his 85th year, and the College shared in the grief and sense of loss experienced by the entire community. After the cardinal's death, another son of Boston College, the Most Reverend Richard J. Cushing, D.D., Coadjutor Bishop of Boston, was elected administrator of the archdiocese. The universal satisfaction felt at this announcement was increased when, on September 28, 1944, he was named as the next archbishop of Boston.

Although the new archbishop did not graduate from Boston College, he entered the College from Boston College High School in September 1913 as a member of the first freshman group to attend class at the Heights, and he remained until the end of his sophomore year, when he entered St. John's Ecclesiastical Seminary in Brighton, Massachusetts, to commence his studies for the priesthood.

The opening of the fall term on August 21, 1944, coincided with the

During the war, Father John Louis Bonn's theatrical summer sessions livened the campus.

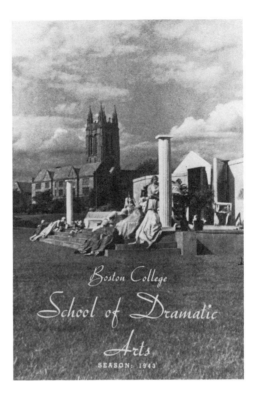

return of the faculty to St. Mary's Hall. The elder members of the Jesuit Community had found the long walks several times a day between their temporary residence and the College buildings a trying experience, and they were grateful when circumstances permitted them to resume living once more in St. Mary's Hall where dining and chapel facilities were centralized and where classrooms were within a few steps.

On September 8 an unprecedented innovation took place on the Heights when 168 Boston College High School seniors took up temporary quarters in one section of the Tower Building. This transfer was caused by a high school enrollment which exceeded the accommodations at James Street and obliged the high school authorities to make some immediate arrangement elsewhere. Since the military call for men of college age had left many of the classrooms at the Heights unused, Father Murphy proffered the high school the loan of needed classroom space for the scholastic year 1944–1945. The high school students were under the direction of their own prefect of studies, Father Joseph E. McGrady, S.J., and were taught by two experienced high school teachers, aided by several of the College instructors whose schedules permitted the additional work. One side of the Tower Building, on the second and third floors, was assigned to the high school classes, and their time schedule was so arranged that there was no conflict with the College students in the use of recreational or lunchroom facilities. The occupancy terminated in June 1945.

Distinctions and Changes

In the summer of 1945 Father Edward J. Keating, S.J., dean of Boston College Intown, announced that a course leading to the degree of bachelor of science in business administration with a major in marketing would be offered at the Intown Division beginning in September of that year. This course was distinct from a similar series of courses offered at the College of Business Administration on the Heights, and it required six years of evening attendance to complete.

Another innovation scheduled by the College at that time was an Institute of Adult Education at the Intown Center, to be opened in September 1945 under the direction of Father James L. Burke, S.J. Three sessions a year were formed during the fall, winter, and spring seasons, each offering a choice of six or more lecture-discussion courses in the fields of religion, philosophy, literature, and public affairs. No academic requirements were established for these programs, nor was academic credit given.

*   *   *

The official announcement of the new undertakings constituted the final major act in Father Murphy's term as president. On August 19, only five days after the abrupt end of the war with Japan, Father Murphy's six-year tenure of office was automatically terminated according to Jesuit custom, and the problem of finding answers to the many questions connected with the College's postwar readjustment devolved on his successor, the Reverend William Lane Keleher, S.J., twentieth president of Boston College.

ENDNOTES

1. *The Heights* (January 21, 1938; March 11, 1938).
2. *The Heights* (October 20, 1939; September 27, 1940; October 10, 1941); *The Boston Globe* (September 22, 1939); *The Boston Herald* (September 23, 1939).
3. This account of the Defense Training Program is based upon records preserved in the Boston College Engineering, Science, and Management War Training Courses Office, Chemistry Department.

Aerial photograph of the central campus, including O'Neill Library, taken at dawn. (Photograph by Dan Dry)

Bapst Library at night. The illumination at the top of Ford Tower is from Alumni Stadium, lit for evening sports. (Photograph by Lee Pellegrini)

The Newton campus, with Trinity Chapel in the foreground. The main Law School building, Stuart Hall, is opposite the chapel, with Kenny-Cottle Library to the right and Barat House in the center. (Photograph by Dan Dry)

Tadolini's 1868 sculpture of St. Michael's triumph over Lucifer dominates a group of religious representations in Gasson Hall's gracious rotunda. (Photograph by Pam Perry, courtesy of the Boston Globe)

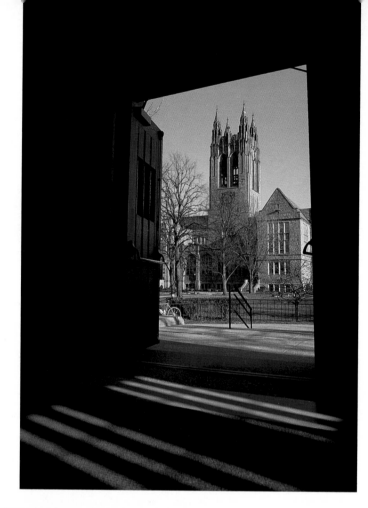

A springtime view from inside the doorway of Bapst Library. (Photograph by Lee Pellegrini)

Rainbow's end: distribution of diplomas on Bapst Library lawn. (Photograph by Dan Dry)

When Bapst Library was renovated, a graceful enclosure for an elevator and air conditioning apparatus was placed inconspicuously behind the northwest corner of the new Burns Library. (Photograph by Lee Pellegrini)

The campus green looking toward Lyons and Fulton halls. (Photograph by Dan Dry.)

A glimpse of fall. (Photograph by Dan Dry.)

An eagle's eye view of the B.C. eagle. (Photograph by Dan Dry.)

The central window of the assembly room in Gasson Hall depicts St. Patrick preaching to King Laoghaire at Tara. (Photograph by Dan Dry.)

CHAPTER 22

Postwar Adjustments

Father Keleher assumed the presidency at a critical moment in national and collegiate history. World War II had come to an end in Europe with the surrender of Germany in May 1945; in the Far East, Japan capitulated three months later in August. Four years of global war, which had involved mobilization of the manpower and vast industrial resources of the United States, had interrupted the normal collegiate programs of thousands of American students. With the cessation of hostilities on all fronts, it was now necessary to restore the orderly rhythm of the campus.

It soon became apparent, however, that the typical American college, whether independent or public, would never be quite the same as it had been before the war. The returning veterans, financially assisted by the Federal Government under the G.I. Bill, brought with them a maturity and earnestness, sometimes lacking in younger students, that would change the character and curriculum of the campus.[1] President Truman, in his letter to members of the President's Commission on Higher Education, summed it up: "As veterans return to college by the hundreds of thousands, the institutions of higher education face a period of trial which is taxing their resources and resourcefulness to the utmost."[2]

On the very day Father Keleher was elected president, the trustees voted to amend a regulation which had previously applied to those *entering* the armed forces. The administration now required that *returning veterans*

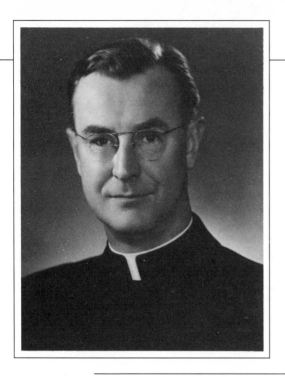

REV. WILLIAM LANE KELEHER, S.J.
Twentieth President

Father Keleher was born January 27, 1906, in Woburn, Massachusetts. After attending Boston College High School, he graduated from the College of the Holy Cross and entered the Society of Jesus in 1926. He was ordained a priest in June 1937. Before his appointment as president he served as assistant to the Jesuit Provincial and as director of Jesuit novices.

who planned to graduate must complete "one semester of senior philosophy and religion in residence at Boston College *or its equivalent.*"[3] "Or its equivalent" was one of several concessions. Two months earlier, on May 23, 1945, it had been agreed that the regulations for the granting of degrees which had applied to students entering the armed forces could now be applied to veterans of the armed forces. The ruling was that, at the time he applied for the degree, the inductee must have acquired 127 credits if a Catholic, or 120 if not; also, the student must show that he had completed one semester of senior philosophy and one of religion in residence at Boston College.[4] War or no war, philosophy was the capstone of a Jesuit education.

The same problem affected all Jesuit colleges. The Jesuit delegates to the 1944 meeting of the Association of American Colleges discussed the question of granting credit to former students for work done at other institutions. The group agreed "that it is acceptable policy during the emergency to grant a degree to a former student who, for military reasons, is in another college and hence cannot complete his work in the Jesuit institution whence he came, provided the student has completed the requirements considered essential to a degree from a Jesuit institution."[5] In responding to a brief questionnaire from the National Secretary of the Jesuit Educational Association, Stephen Mulcahy, dean of the College of Arts and Sciences at Boston College, reported that he had many requests to grant degrees to former students now in other institutions. He insisted that such students must complete a semester of senior year at Boston College and fulfill the other requirements already mentioned.[6]

Return of the Veterans

Under these conditions, veterans began to return to the campus—both former students of Boston College and those from other institutions. In a cordial message to veterans in 1945, Father William Murphy had written, "Boston College sends you this word of welcome and explanation in anticipation of the day you . . . will return to your family and friends." Referring to their wartime experiences in foreign lands, he added, "This is a novel type of college preparation and demands a new set of entrance procedures."[7] In a preamble to the course curricula, the new catalog acknowledged that, in the circumstances, more emphasis must be placed on the study of mathematics and the natural sciences; more, not less, emphasis must be placed on social sciences, "for students must be made aware of their social responsibilities as citizens of America and of the world."[8] Through the exigencies of war, the natives of Dorchester and Jamaica Plain were now familiar with the cultures of Europe, India, and the Far East.

As the eager veterans began to take advantage of the G.I. Bill, the enrollment picture changed immediately and dramatically. To appreciate the contrast, it should be remembered that in April 1944 there were 236 students registered in the College of Arts and Sciences. One hundred freshmen registered in June 1944: 88 in Arts and Sciences and 12 in Business Administration. When the academic year began in September 1945 under Father Keleher's presidency, there was a total undergraduate enrollment of 453 students: 358 in Arts and Sciences and 95 in Business Administration.[9]

The real acceleration began in March 1946 when, restricting consideration to the College of Arts and Sciences, there was a total of 1067 students. Of these, 546 were veterans, 395 were civilians (as they were called), and 126 were in the category of pre-matriculation. In the fall of 1946 *The Heights* had a banner headline: "Enrollment Breaks Record." There were 2811 students in Arts and Sciences and Business Administration, including 894 new veterans. The combined enrollment of Arts and Sciences and Business Administration in September 1947 was 4572. That year, for the first time in the postwar period, ex-servicemen comprised a minority (only 40 percent of the freshmen class). Two years later, in the academic year 1949–1950, in all schools of the University—undergraduate, graduate, and professional—there were 5766 full-time students and 1760 part-time students, making a grand total of 7526.[10] Although the College of Arts and Sciences was probably the largest among the Jesuit colleges in the United States, overall enrollment at Boston College trailed that at Fordham, Saint Louis, Marquette, and Detroit.[11]

The faculty had also been affected by the war effort. Seventeen Jesuits had left the classroom to serve as chaplains in the various branches of the armed services. At least 20 lay members of the undergraduate faculty, most of the Law School faculty, and others had either volunteered or been inducted into the armed forces. With the end of the war and the numerical expansion of the student body, the administration began the recruitment of new faculty and welcomed back those who had served their country.

The Need for Housing

For the administration, the enrollment figure was good news. Among other reasons, income available from tuitions enabled the trustees to allocate funds with more freedom and to secure loans for necessary projects.[12] To provide proper facilities for these new students, however, was a problem. As *The Heights* reported, "With the walls literally bulging at Boston College, it took bewildered freshmen and even the more collected upper classmen the full interclass break to worm their way to the next assignments."[13] There was, in brief, an acute shortage of space. With the exception of O'Connell Hall (acquired in 1941) and the museum on Hammond Street (acquired in 1936), there had been no addition to the Chestnut Hill

Students and other volunteers went from house to house selling "bricks" for the first postwar building, Fulton Hall.

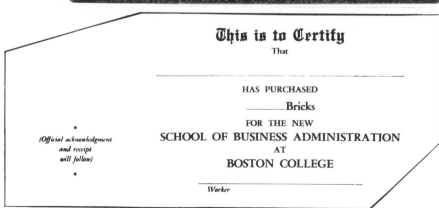

This is to Certify

That

_____

HAS PURCHASED

_____Bricks

FOR THE NEW

SCHOOL OF BUSINESS ADMINISTRATION

AT

BOSTON COLLEGE

(Official acknowledgment and receipt will follow)

_____

Worker

campus since the dedication of the library in 1928. While O'Connell Hall had been renovated for academic purposes, there were, strictly speaking, only two classroom buildings: the Tower Building (Gasson Hall) and Devlin Hall, which housed the science laboratories. Since these were now patently inadequate for the 3000 undergraduates who frequented the Heights every day, the administration searched for immediate relief.

Off-campus facilities were less critical but also needed attention. In May 1946 the trustees approved a new contract for the lease of the building at 126 Newbury Street for the use of the Intown College and the School of Social Work.[14] The Law School, which had a history of peregrinations, was now housed in quarters that were notably inadequate. From its original site in the Lawyers Building at 11 Beacon Street, the school had moved in 1937 to a new home in the New England Power Building at 441 Stuart Street. With a dramatic drop in World War II enrollment, it became financially impossible, even with the help from the College, to provide rent for these relatively commodious quarters.

After an intense search, space was finally acquired in the Kimball Building at 18 Tremont Street in the heart of Scollay Square. Besides the well-known attractions of that area, it was also handy to the courts. In the interest of economy, students assisted in moving the library. The enrollment continued to dwindle and in June 1945 there were only six graduates. In an interview some years later, Professor William J. O'Keefe ("Mr. Chips" of the Law School, who taught there for 30 years) said, "We never knew from one day to the next how long we were going to keep going, but somehow we managed to keep the school alive."[15] And again, when it seemed impossible to find suitable space, he said, "If necessary, we'll meet in my living room, but meet we will!"

The G.I. Bill came to the rescue. By the fall of 1945, five months after the war ended in Europe, 250 students were enrolled and the increase continued every semester thereafter. Father William J. Kenealy, who had just returned from his tour as chaplain in the United States Navy, was appointed dean. With accelerated programs for veterans, the Law School began to overflow its cramped quarters. There would be yet two more moves to take the Law School to its present campus on Centre Street in Newton.

It was at the Heights, however, that the pressure for space was becoming explosive. Fortunately, the presence of veterans who, in the early years after the war, accounted for more than half of the undergraduates, opened the door to the acquisition of surplus government property under legislation passed by the Truman Administration. Congress had appropriated funds whereby the Federal Public Housing Authority (FPHA) had been assigned responsibility for assisting educational institutions to acquire surplus federal structures to be used to house distressed veterans and servicemen and their families. This appropriation also authorized the reimbursement of funds already expended by educational institutions who had acted before the appropriation had been passed. The College took immediate advantage of this federal generosity. In July 1946, after the application had been processed, the Boston Office of the FPHA authorized the relocation from Fort Devens Air Base in Ayer, Massachusetts, to Boston College of three two-story army barracks.[16] Comprising 137 dormitory units, these wooden structures were re-erected on what was known as Freshman Field, the area fronting on Beacon Street and now occupied by Campion Hall. At the same time, the Housing Authority authorized alterations in the basement of the Tower Building to provide dining facilities for the veterans who occupied the dormitories.

These resident halls—although scarcely meriting such an elegant designation—were by law reserved to the veterans. Later on, however, permission was granted by the government to Jesuit scholastics who attended summer school to occupy the Mead-Lantham dormitories, as they were officially known.[17] Still later, permission was extended to nonveterans if space remained after veterans had been accommodated.

Expansion of Classroom Space

While easing the veterans' housing shortage was important, it only exacerbated the need for classroom space, which now became the number one priority. In this crisis, turning again to the government, the Board of Trustees voted to submit an application, under existing legislation, requesting educational facilities "to alleviate an acute shortage of such facilities at Boston College."[18] The plan called for classroom space for 1000 students, 500 in Arts and Sciences and 500 in Business Administration. From the beginning of Father Keleher's tenure there had been talk of a permanent building, but that type of structure would be months in construction and therefore would not solve the immediate problem.

In the spring of 1947 Father Keleher authorized the Bennett-Stewart Company to proceed with the dismantling, transportation, and re-erection of Building No. 26, then standing at the South Boston Navy Yard extension.[19] This building, with extensive alterations and additional safety features made at the College's expense, was erected along Beacon Street where McGuinn Hall now stands. Furnished as a temporary wooden classroom building for undergraduates, veterans, and others, its use was so urgent that the contract called for it to be in place by September 1947.

The third building obtained from government surplus and designed to meet still another emergency was the so-called "Recreation Building," which served as an auditorium and gymnasium. Contractually part of the classroom project and acquired under Public Law 697, this acquisition consisted of "the transfer of government surplus building No. A-14 from Gallups Island, Boston Harbor, to the campus of the College for use for recreation, luncheonette, and laboratory."[20] This multipurpose, three-story structure, completed in September 1947 where Cushing Hall now stands, was used as an auditorium (where several commencements took place), for ROTC drills, and for other functions. In view of its humble origins, the interior was rather lavishly outfitted by John H. Pray and Sons, who laid carpets, rugs, and linoleum.

As the administration discovered, the federal agencies were much more accommodating than the City of Newton. The Garden City, so it seemed to authorities at the Heights, went beyond the call of duty in its insistence upon conformity in these temporary buildings with all the regulations of the city which applied to any structure. Since wooden buildings were under discussion, however, the city was undoubtedly correct in imposing strict standards regarding the boiler room, electric systems, and exits.[21] In any case, conformance was an added expense for the College, which had no choice but to cooperate.

With the army dormitories, classrooms, and recreation center in place, the College managed to survive the accelerated increase in campus enrollments. Father Keleher was understandably delighted with this somewhat unexpected solution to his space problems. While it was meant to be only a temporary and partial solution, he showed himself to be a realist when he remarked to the contractors who had set up the war surplus buildings, "I have a feeling that Boston College will have them on the property for a long, long while."[22] It would be nearly 20 years before the last of these most valued "temporary" buildings was dismantled.

Accommodation with the City

In July 1947 President Truman signed Public Law 239, which terminated certain acts of the Congress connected with postwar emergencies. As a result, educational institutions were instructed to review their contracts for veterans' temporary housing with a view to the removal of those accommodations. Two years were allowed to comply with this legislation. However, there was a proviso by which the use of units that, in the opinion of the institution, were still necessary could be extended for successive periods.[23] The following year, the president signed the McGregor Bill, which "provided for the release of government property to institutions."[24] Boston College, of course, wished to take immediate possession of the temporary units.

In this procedure, however, it was necessary to obtain permission and approval from the City of Newton. The city, as already hinted, was not at all anxious to see these examples of early Army architecture converted into permanent structures along historic Beacon Street. The specific reason given by the aldermen was that the buildings probably did not conform

At a special convocation in October 1947 in Bapst auditorium, Father Keleher conferred an honorary LL.D. degree on Boston's auxiliary bishop (later cardinal) John J. Wright ('31).

with the building code of the City of Newton.[25] Represented by the Boston law firm of Stone, Bosson, Mason and Gannon, the College finally won its case. In order to accomplish a settlement and at the urging of Attorney Gannon, President Keleher wrote a strong letter of intent to the Newton aldermen, two of whom were clearly skeptical of the intentions of the College. In his effort to placate these officials, he said he assumed that they "realized that the College is not at all anxious to have these temporary structures on the property," and that "it is the intention of the College to remove these buildings as soon as the current housing difficulty for veterans can be taken care of." "Moreover," he continued, "it is also the intention of the College to erect as soon as possible a permanent dormitory unit which will take care of out-of-town students and which will meet the requirements of the City of Newton in every respect."[26]

Finally the precious document arrived which "relinquished and transferred, without monetary consideration, to the trustees of Boston College all contractual rights and all property rights, title, and interest of the United States in and with respect to the veterans' temporary housing located in

Newton, Massachusetts, designated as Project No. MASSV–19137."[27] Neither the aldermen nor Father Keleher could envision at the time the number of permanent buildings that would one day line Beacon Street from the old Freshman Field to the corner of Beacon and Hammond streets.

Helping the Veterans' Transition

While the administration was making every effort to supply physical facilities for veterans, the dean and teaching staff were setting up a program to facilitate the resumption of studies by some veterans and the initiation of a collegiate program by others. The 1945–1946 catalog included a notice to veterans at Boston College, each of whom was promised assistance "to continue his education and complete it successfully at the earliest possible time consonant with good scholarship." Every consideration would be given to courses taken in the Army and Navy Schools. More importantly, perhaps, "a special educational advisor has been appointed to care for the individual problems of each veteran." In addition, certain courses were specifically fashioned to give veterans a brief review of material that would be required for advanced courses, "and every effort will be made to prepare them for entrance at the next opening date."[28] Because of accelerated programs, "opening dates" occurred frequently during those years.

Consequently, veterans returning to the campus found a professionally staffed guidance center available to them. The two Jesuits who operated the clinic were particularly well-qualified. Father James F. Moynihan, S.J., was awarded the Ph.D. in Psychology by the Catholic University of America in 1942. A licensed psychologist, he was a senior consultant (1944–1948) at the Veterans Guidance Center at Harvard University, a director of the Rosary Child Guidance Center in Boston, and consultant to state and national committees. Father Moynihan's collaborator at the center was David R. Dunigan, S.J. Awarded a Ph.D. in Education by Fordham University in 1945, he was an active member of the Boston College faculty and a counselor at the U.S. Veterans Guidance Center at Harvard. The guidance clinic was of inestimable value to the returning veterans who, after several years in the regimentation of the service, had to sharpen tools of scholarship which had grown rusty amid the harsh realities of global war. They sought advice in matching their abilities and goals with the degree programs and courses offered at Boston College. Mature in approach, anxious to succeed, and industrious in application, they often needed direction to compete academically with the bright young men who had just received their high school diplomas.

In some cases, to compound the problem, there was also the question of credits. To remedy deficiencies and to assist in orientation, there was a separate program called "Veterans' Matriculation (or Pre-Matriculation) Course." This program was devised and designed by Father Michael G.

Pierce, S.J., dean of freshmen in the College of Arts and Sciences. Father Pierce, who was also the official contact with the government for the purchase of surplus property, had been very active in keeping in touch with the students who were drafted. He was even more concerned with the returning veterans. It would be difficult to exaggerate his contribution to Boston College during the trying years of the war and in the immediate postwar years of adjustment. A key figure in assimilating veterans into the College, Father Pierce's Matriculation Course at one time numbered 160 students.

A Return to Normalcy

As the months went by, the campus gradually returned to normal, both in curricular and extracurricular activities. The Jesuits and their lay colleagues deserve credit for preserving, as far as possible, the traditions of Boston College during the war and effecting a smooth transition from war to peace. Complementing the diplomacy of President Keleher, Father Stephen Mulcahy, S.J., who presided over the College of Arts and Sciences, kept the classical tradition alive when the accent was on physics, engineering, cartography, chemistry, and geography. In point of fact, at this very time, there were those who, in 1945, questioned the validity of the strict classical curriculum. Only seven years earlier in June 1938, the Bachelor of Arts degree at Boston College was conferred for the first time without the Greek requirement.[29] Whether the discussion reflected the exigencies of a wartime curriculum is not clear. However, at meetings held in November 1945 and

"Government surplus" buildings were placed where Cushing and Campion halls now stand. This new building was used for assemblies, theatricals, and basketball, as well as ROTC and student activities; the others were dormitories.

February 1946, the department heads voted 13 to 2 (with 2 abstentions) that Latin should not be required for the Bachelor of Arts degree.[30] After further discussion, it was resolved that "in the Bachelor of Arts curriculum, a substitute for Latin in the original, the classics in translation, be offered, either from a literary or social sciences standpoint." Since the resolution was never submitted to the entire faculty, it was not accepted by Father Keleher. But it was an indication of things to come.

Faculty Remuneration

At the same time, the administration began to take a more professional posture in addressing the needs of the faculty. This development was due to the normal progress of events but more especially to the increase in lay faculty members. In the first place, faculty salaries began to improve. In 1947 Boston College's first salary scale was approved by the trustees and appeared in the minutes of the meeting of April 22.

1947 SALARY SCALE			
Salaries	*Salary Range*	*Term*	*Increment*
Instructor	$2400 to $3200	5 years	$160 per year
Assistant Professor	$3200 to $3800	4 years	$150 per year
Associate Professor	$3800 to $4500	4 years	$175 per year
Professor	$4500 to $6000		On recommendation
N.B. All increments are on merit, not automatic.			

Student tuition, which still reflected the origin and mission of Boston College, was now subject to an annual increase to balance the budget of the institution.[31] A committee on rank and tenure was appointed to stipulate the requirements for promotion. Advancements in rank, and increments within rank, were to be judged solely on merit; these rewards were never to be granted automatically.[32]

Again, in 1947, as further proof of concern, the trustees discussed a retirement plan for full-time faculty, who were eligible to participate after the completion of three years. The plan was tied to the Teachers Insurance and Annuity Association (TIAA). In this plan, which is still in operation at Boston College, teachers would contribute 5 percent of their regular monthly compensation and Boston College would add an equal amount.[33] TIAA was the plan adopted at most universities.

Kudos for the Faculty

At this time the Graduate School of Arts and Sciences was administered by the able and energetic Father George O'Donnell, S.J. Fortified with a Ph.D.

in mathematics from St. Louis University, he adjusted the scientific courses to the Army Specialized Training Program (ASTP), taught a number of those courses himself, and then supervised the transition to a normal schedule. Father James L. Burke, S.J., with a Ph.D. in Government from Harvard University, assisted Father O'Donnell in the administration of the Graduate School and also gave academic leadership to the important History and Government Department. He inaugurated and directed the popular program in adult education. Father John P. Foley, S.J., fresh from his duties as a navy chaplain, resumed his work as freshmen dean, while Father Pierce was reassigned as executive assistant to the president. Father Edward J. Keating, S.J., was dean of the Intown College; Father James J. Kelly, S.J., continued as dean of the College of Business Administration.

An unsung hero who deserves a special accolade was Father John A. Tobin, S.J. Although to some extent a self-made academician, he became an excellent physicist and chaired the Department of Physics for many years. With little notice and a minimum of immediate preparation, he was the key figure in designing the scientific program for the ASTP. A major part of that program concentrated on courses in engineering which, in time, developed into a B.S. in Engineering. Father Tobin had read the signs of the times. In March 1945 he urged the dean to consider continuing the B.S. in Engineering which, he explained, could be expanded into a school like the College of Business Administration. In fact, he had been informed by George Donaldson, director of vocational guidance, that "engineering is still first choice of the returning veterans." Including Father James Devlin, S.J., and Professor John Shork among the immediate stalwarts, he assured Father Mulcahy "of our enthusiastic cooperation in any plan to start this course with a dean of engineering and some small faculty. The need is so great that this should be done at once."[34] The moment was not, however, auspicious for the proposal. The College was being urged to start a school of nursing, and the College of Business Administration (the first professional undergraduate school for men) was still in its infancy. The administration did not warm to the idea of a school of engineering then, nor has it since.

Other Mainstays

There were other sources of the unity and continuity so necessary in the life of a college. *The Heights,* which continued publication during the war, reminded alumni overseas of their collegiate roots. In the spring of 1945, *The Stylus* carried an editorial, "On Post-War Peace," which took a dim view of the peace treaties and the spirit that dictated them. The verdict seems unduly harsh, but the editor felt that "until the United States is the home of a society which instinctively upholds Christian principles, she cannot help but be involved in international injustice."[35] In 1946 *The Stylus* noted that "the veterans have returned from the wars" and the staff was

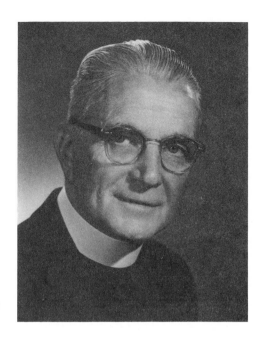

Terence L. Connolly, S.J., director of libraries, 1946–1959.

grateful. In the summer issue, one-third of the articles contained "postscripts to war written by these men, some medal wearers, all battle-scarred in some way or other."[36] One of the articles, by James H. Sullivan, was an account of Padre Pio, the stigmatic priest, whom many of the Boston College students had visited when stationed near Foggia.

The Dramatic Arts Course, which had been offered during summer sessions for two seasons before the war, was reorganized and enlarged into the School of Dramatic and Expressional Arts by Father John L. Bonn, S.J., in the summer of 1947. This new school provided standard dramatic training with stage facilities in the new recreation hall, but in addition it offered related concentrations in literature and criticism, debate and panel discussion, and corporate religious expression.

The football, basketball, and hockey teams, which had resumed their intercollegiate schedules, could now depend upon the band to lift the spirits of the students as they cheered on their local heroes. Under the direction of Walter Mayo ('23), who supervised music in the Watertown schools, the orchestra and glee club provided a cultural resource on campus and shared the stage with local colleges.

Athletics, which had played an important role in the history of Boston College, returned to the campus. After three years of "informal" football, with nostalgia for the glory days of 1941 and 1942, the Eagles took to the field against the Deacons from Wake Forest at Braves Field, the Eagles' new home, on Friday night, September 27, 1946. Boston College, which depended on a few 1942 players and untested freshmen, lost the contest 12–6. But it was no disgrace. With the return of Coach Denny Meyers, who had spent the war years in the Navy, the highly esteemed director of athletics, John Curley, had put together in 1946 the toughest schedule in Boston College history.[37] Although losing to Wake Forest, the Eagles had beaten Michigan State, Georgetown, and Alabama, the Rose Bowl champions. Among the outstanding players coached by Denny Meyers from 1946 to 1948 were Edward J. King (future governor of Massachusetts), Art Donovan, Art Spinney, Ernie Stautner, John Kissell, Butch Songin, and Mario Gianelli.

The Feeney Case

An unhappy episode during the administration of Father Keleher was the so-called "Feeney Case." Father Leonard Feeney, a talented Jesuit poet and engaging personality who had taught at Boston College in the 1930s, headed St. Benedict Center, a Catholic organization that had been started by the priests of St. Paul's parish in Cambridge. Father Feeney preached a very narrow interpretation of the axiom, "Outside the Church, there is no salvation"—an interpretation that did not conform to traditional Catholic teaching. The dynamic priest attracted a number of devoted followers and advocates of his unique view of salvation.

The Feeney case touched Boston College because several faculty members not only became adherents of the St. Benedict doctrine but promoted it in their classes when they were supposed to be teaching nontheological subjects. Fakri Maluf and James Walsh, philosophy teachers, and Charles Ewaskio, a physics teacher, were warned by Dean Mulcahy to restrict themselves to their respective subjects and avoid excursions into theology. Since they would not desist and accused the College of heresy for not agreeing with them, Father Keleher dismissed them. When the newspapers published accounts of the dismissals, Father Keleher submitted an explanation that said, in part, "They [the former faculty members] continued to speak in class and out of class on matters contrary to the traditional teachings of the Catholic Church, ideas leading to bigotry and intolerance."

This episode was unhappy not only for Boston College but for the Society of Jesus and the Boston Church. Father Feeney was not long after dismissed from the Society and excommunicated. Many years later in 1972, through the efforts of Cardinal Medeiros, archbishop of Boston, the excommunication was lifted and Father Feeney was received back into the Church.[38]

*　　*　　*

A glance at the record shows that in the years immediately after the war—a watershed in the life of every U. S. educational institution—Boston College first resumed the tenor of its way, then began a steady growth in student enrollment and a planned expansion of academic and residential facilities. The presence of veterans in fairly large numbers provided an atmosphere of maturity wherein it was easier to propose and to justify innovations. At the same time, there was a renewed effort on the part of the entire academic community to preserve Boston College's heritage as an outstanding Jesuit institution on a plane with other independent institutions in the United States.

ENDNOTES

1. The Omnibus Bill (G.I. Bill), providing benefits for returning service personnel, was signed by the president on June 22, 1944. It was known as Public Law No. 346 (78th Congress) and cited as "Servicemen's Readjustment Act of 1944." Public Law 16 was also available for the vocational rehabilitation of disabled veterans.

2. "Higher Education for American Democracy," *Report of the President's Commission on Higher Education, Vols. I–VI* (New York, 1946).

3. Minutes, Board of Trustees, August 20, 1945. BCA.

4. Minutes, Board of Trustees, May 23, 1945. BCA.

5. Edward B. Rooney, S.J., to Stephen A. Mulcahy, S.J., July 26, 1944. JEA Collection, BCA.

6. *Ibid.* See also Stephen A. Mulcahy, S.J., to Edward B. Rooney, S.J. BCA.

7. *Boston College Bulletin,* 1945.

8. *Ibid.*

9. For these statistics and those that follow, see file, "Enrollment and Faculty Statistics." BCA.

10. See *Enrollment,* Jesuit Colleges and Universities, 1949–50, JEA *Directory* (1950–1951). BCA.

11. *Ibid.*

12. For tuition rates set for each school, see Minutes, Board of Trustees, April 16, 1947. Faculty salaries were also set at this meeting.

13. *The Heights* (September 27, 1946).

14. Minutes, Board of Trustees, May 7, 1946.

15. Todd F. Simon, *Boston College Law School after Fifty Years: An Informal History* (privately printed, 1980), p. 21.

16. Sumner K. Wiley to C. J. Meaney Company, July 2, 1946. Wiley was Director of Region I for FPHA. BCA.

17. Sumner K. Wiley to Stephen A. Shea, S.J., June 21, 1948. So named for the congressional authors of the legislation.

18. Minutes, Board of Trustees, August 26, 1946.

19. William L. Keleher, S.J., to Bennett-Stewart Co., May 2, 1947. BCA.

20. William D. Jones to William L. Keleher, S.J., February 19, 1948. BCA. The date of this letter is accounted for by the fact that the letter summarized the completion of the project. Federal expenses for the classroom building and recreation center totalled $131,564.

21. The federal government was careful to protect itself by insisting on conformity to local regulations and statutes.

22. William L. Keleher, S.J., to Bennett-Stewart Co., May 9, 1948. BCA.

23. Sumner K. Wiley (Director, Housing and Home Finance Agency) to Boston College, June 25, 1947. BCA.

24. See William L. Keleher, S.J., to Thomas L. Gannon, July 6, 1948. BCA.

25. Thomas L. Gannon to William L. Keleher, S.J., September 14, 1948. BCA.

26. William L. Keleher, S.J., to Board of Aldermen, September 27, 1948. BCA.

27. W. P. Seaver, Director, Region II, to William L. Keleher, S.J., November 12, 1948. BCA.

28. *Boston College Catalogue, 1945–1946*, p. 5.

29. See Charles F. Donovan, S.J., *"Boston College's Classical Curriculum,"* Occasional Papers on the History of Boston College, p. 10. BCA.

30. See "Summary of Reports on the Faculty Discussions of the A.B. Requirement." BCA.

31. Minutes, Board of Trustees, March 1, 1946; April 16, 1947. BCA. In 1946 in the Colleges of Arts and Sciences and Business Administration, tuition was $150 per semester; in 1947 it was raised to $175 per semester. On February 11, 1953, the trustees raised the yearly tuition to $500 for the four undergraduate colleges.

32. Minutes, Board of Trustees, April 22, 1947. BCA.

33. Minutes, Board of Trustees, January 10, 1947. BCA. In the 1980s the faculty contribution was 2 percent and the University's 8 percent or 10 percent, depending on length of service.

34. John A. Tobin, S.J., to Stephen A. Mulcahy, S.J., March 27, 1945.

35. *The Stylus* (Spring, 1945), pp. 63–64.

36. See inside cover "Keeping in Stylus," *The Stylus* (Summer, 1946).

37. Jack Falla, *'Til the Echoes Ring Again* (Brattleboro, Vt.: Stephen Greene Press, 1982), p. 25.

38. This brief account is taken from a five-page summary made by Father Keleher at the request of the Father Provincial of the New England Province. BCA.

CHAPTER 23

The College at Mid-Twentieth Century

What sort of curriculum were Boston College students following in the Keleher years after World War II? A short answer is: pretty much the same curriculum, at least for the A.B. degree, that students followed during the presidencies of Fulton (1870–1880 and 1888–1891), Gasson (1907–1914), and Dolan (1925–1932). From their founding, all the American Jesuit colleges had been faithful to the classical-philosophical education that had been the Jesuit tradition for centuries. And while there were some compromises along the way, such as the dropping of Greek for the A.B. in 1938 as mentioned earlier, and some grumblings about the Latin requirement, the old classical curriculum was still prescribed for the prized A.B. degree in the years immediately after the war.

That curriculum was, by today's standards, heavy in hours of classes and courses carried, and it was mostly prescribed. Twenty-four credits, or 18 percent of the curriculum, were devoted to electives. The emphasis in freshman and sophomore years was literary; in junior and senior years, philosophical. Clearly the most honored by Boston College, it was called the A.B. Greek curriculum. The somewhat radical A.B.-without-Greek curriculum was called A.B. Mathematics, wherein courses in history and mathematics were substituted for freshman and sophomore Greek.

College of Arts and Sciences Bachelor of Arts Requirements			
FRESHMAN YEAR	*1st Sem.(hrs.)*	*2nd Sem.(hrs.)*	*Credits*
English 1–2	3	3	6
English 3	1	1	0
Mathematics 1–2	3	3	6
Modern Language 1–2 or 11–12	3	3	6
Theology 1–2	2	2	2
Greek 1–2 or 5–6	3	3	6
Latin 1–2	3	3	6
Fine Arts 1–2	2	2	4
	20	20	36
SOPHOMORE YEAR			
English 21–22	3	3	6
Modern Language 11–12 or 21–22	3	3	6
Theology 21–22	2	2	2
Science (Chem. 11–12 or 21–22 Biology 31–32 or Physics 21–22)	3, 2 lab.	3,2 lab.	8
Latin 21–22	3	3	6
Greek 23–24 or 21–22	3	3	6
	19	19	34
JUNIOR YEAR			
Philosophy 41–42–43–44	6	6	12
Theology 41–42	2	2	2
History 41–42	3	3	6
Electives	6	6	12
	17	17	32
SENIOR YEAR			
Philosophy 101–102–103–104	4	4	8
Philosophy 105–106	4	4	8
Theology 101–102	2	2	2
Electives	6	6	12
	16	16	30

The Bachelor of Science degree, awarded for programs including neither Greek nor Latin, prescribed the same English and philosophy and theology courses as the A.B. curriculum but allowed greater concentration in one of the natural sciences or mathematics, or in history, education, or social science.

A Commitment to the Classics

The commitment to the basic classical education is seen strikingly in the nonbusiness curriculum of the College of Business Administration at this time. Freshman A.B. Greek students were following principles of composition and poetry in Latin and Greek as well as English. The description of English 1–2 in the College of Arts and Sciences catalog reads: "Prose composition. A study of the qualities of style. Narration, description, and essay. Poetry. The nature and types of poetry. Principles of versification; the emotional and intellectual elements of poetry."

In the College of Business Administration, freshman English 1–2 was described in the catalog: "Training in the development of a mature prose style is stressed. Exposition, narration, and description. Frequent theme work in exposition. A play each of the Latin and Greek stage is read in translation. The imaginative, emotional, and intellectual content of poetry, prosody and poetic types. Extensive reading of English and American poetry." Boston College was clearly accommodating its traditional humanistic education to blend with professional courses for its future managers and business people. There was no room for Latin or Greek in the Business Administration curriculum, but Latin and Greek plays in translation were included in the English course.

In the sophomore year A.B. Greek students studied rhetoric in English and the classical languages. English 21–22 was titled "Oratory and Shakespeare" and the course description was: "The theory and practice of oratorical composition. The qualities of oratorical style. Argument, persuasion, analysis, and stylistic study of oratorical masterpieces. Shakespeare. A study of selected tragedies of Shakespeare for their dramatic and oratorical value."

At the same time sophomores in the College of Business Administration were following their version of English 21–22, which was called "English as a Medium of Oral Expression," with this catalog description: "The principles of oratory; their application studied in rhetorical masterpieces, including a speech of Cicero in translation. Six Shakespearean tragedies are read: *Julius Caesar, Hamlet, Macbeth, Othello, King Lear,* and *Antony and Cleopatra*." Again an effort was made to preserve some thread of the ancient classic tradition, and future accountants and bankers were not left unacquainted with Cicero. Back in the nineteenth century the freshman year had been called the "poetry year," while sophomore was the "rhetoric year." That humanistic tradition was still active in the College of Arts and Sciences, while vestiges of the tradition livened the experience of Business School students.

If compromise and some capitulation had taken place as regards the classical languages and literature at Boston College in the fifth decade of the twentieth century, there had been no faltering or retreat on the philosophical front in the junior and senior years. All students, regardless of major, regardless of degree track or professional aspiration, followed the same 10-course, 28-credit sequence in philosophy: logic, epistemology, metaphysics, cosmology, fundamental psychology, empirical psychology, rational psychology, natural theology, general ethics, and special ethics. The purpose of this heavy concentration on philosophy was not to turn the

Fulton Hall opened in 1948.

students into professional philosophers but to give them an acquaintance with and some mastery of a world view that had been developed over a period of many centuries in the Aristotelian-Thomistic philosophy. The method of philosophy classes was largely the lecture, and classes tended to be large. It is significant that when Lyons Hall (opened in 1951) was being planned and when it was first in use, it was called the philosophy building; its basic classrooms accommodated 85 students, while several other rooms provided for well over a hundred students—rooms that were designed primarily with philosophy classes in mind. The talent of the professor, rather than the size of the room or the number in the class, determined the quality of the learning experience in philosophy, as former students of such teachers as Fathers Jones I. Corrigan, Francis Low, or John A. McCarthy can attest.

At midcentury the curriculum at Boston College was far more prescribed than elective. Highly structured, with emphasis on literary and philosophical skill and knowledge, it was geared to produce generalists, not specialists. Its hoped-for product was the gentleman of Newman's ideal. From today's perspective at Boston College and in the wider collegiate scene, the curriculum just described may seem overly structured. It is worth noting, however, that just after the war, in 1945, Harvard's famed curriculum study, *General Education in a Free Society*, appeared, with the purpose of counteracting the unbridled electivism introduced by President Eliot at Harvard. The educational debate between advocates of curricular prescription and electivism raged in the nineteenth century, was alive at the halfway mark of the twentieth, and has not lost relevance today.

The Need for New Buildings

When Father Keleher assumed the presidency of Boston College in August 1945, his concern about the curriculum was not its content but how to administer it for a growing horde of students in only two permanent classroom buildings, Gasson and Devlin. The previous chapter recounted temporary measures that gave immediate patchwork relief to the classroom situation. But even before those measures were effected, plans for permanent building were afoot. Only six months into his presidency in January 1946, Father Keleher requested Archbishop Richard Cushing's approval of an intense, short-duration public drive for funds for three buildings: a classroom building, a gymnasium, and a dormitory.[1]

The classroom building was needed, he explained, because of the large number of returning veterans applying for admission and the growing popularity of the College of Business Administration, whose quarters in O'Connell Hall were inadequate. Interestingly the proposed gymnasium was justified not in terms of the need for student recreation and exercise but because the administration, convinced of the need of an ROTC program at Boston College, had already been informed by Army representatives that the presence of a gymnasium would be a critical item in a decision about awarding an ROTC program. As it turned out, the war surplus "recreation building" was to serve as a gymnasium until the construction of Roberts Center in 1958.

A dormitory was needed, Father Keleher continued, because the number of out-of-town applicants was constantly growing and because the College had never been satisfied with the arrangement whereby such students simply boarded in the neighborhood.

It was an ambitious building program Father Keleher outlined for the

The president's office in St. Mary's Hall from 1932 to 1968.

archbishop, whose support he particularly needed because he envisioned a drive which would largely focus on the parishes of the archdiocese. Indeed the drive, which ultimately took place in the fall of 1947, was the last the College would conduct that had a definitely "parochial" flavor. Perhaps to allay the archbishop's fears that the College, in shaky financial condition after the war, was undertaking too much, Father Keleher wrote as he completed his letter, "I feel that I should add that it is not my intention to build in stone and along Gothic lines. Rather than detract from the present set-up [that is, the collegiate Gothic buildings of the central campus], I would erect these new buildings in brick, but on the Liggett estate" [that is, on the property surrounding O'Connell Hall, bordered by Beacon and Hammond streets and Tudor Road]. Fortunately these frugal plans were not followed. Maginnis and Walsh, architects of the original buildings, were called upon to plan the next two academic buildings, Fulton and Lyons, and the upper campus surrounding O'Connell Hall was preserved and developed exclusively as a residential area.

The new home for the College of Business Administration, which was named eventually for Father Robert Fulton, the first dean and twice president of Boston College, was begun in June 1947.[2] On October 30 there was a laying of the cornerstone, with Father John McEleney, Provincial, and Governor Robert Bradford on hand and Archbishop Richard Cushing officiating and speaking.[3] The building was occupied the following fall. Fulton is perhaps the least successful of the Maginnis and Walsh Gothic buildings, in part because of the squat towers which the architects provided in order not to block the view of Boston College's signature, the

Alumni Hall on Commonwealth Avenue was home to the Alumni Association from 1950 until the move to the Newton campus in 1986.

tower of Gasson Hall, from Beacon Street. In time, of course, Carney and McGuinn blocked that view.

The early occupants of Fulton Hall were proud of the James J. Byrnes Library, which was adequate for a relatively small, entirely undergraduate College of Business Administration. It would be decades before Boston College would have a commodious central library; in the meantime each professional school except Education developed its own library. Another feature of Fulton Hall was an industrial management laboratory in the basement. Though now long abandoned, it was considered innovative in the era of the "efficiency expert" and time-and-motion studies.

Even as work on Fulton Hall was going on, plans for other buildings were being formulated. The boiler room in the basement of Gasson Hall, which had serviced the four original buildings—Gasson, St. Mary's, Devlin, and Bapst—became inadequate. There was also need for accommodations for craftsmen and tradesmen, for storage, and for a garage to house trucks and motorized equipment. A service building was begun in the fall of 1947[4] and completed the following year.

So physical expansion was very much in the air. The minutes of the Board of Trustees for April 9, 1948, show that Father Keleher proposed a new classroom building for the College of Arts and Sciences. Only a few weeks later, on April 26, 1948, the trustees were discussing a building for the Law School at Chestnut Hill. In late April Father Keleher wrote to Maginnis and Walsh[5] about planning the new building for the College of Arts and Sciences, which was to be located on the west side of the campus between the Tower Building and the recently completed College of Business Administration. He said it would consist mainly of classrooms ("the majority of these large enough to accommodate philosophy classes") but with provision also for a number of departmental offices (which were just coming into existence) and secretarial offices. The basement of the building was to be given entirely to a cafeteria large enough to serve 3500 students. The letter mentioned the College's hope of starting a dormitory soon and concluded with a reference to a 1936 plan for a building that might be a good beginning for planning the philosophy building. The significance of that reference is the date. In 1936, two years before the College of Business Administration was begun (in the depth of the depression, during the presidency of Father Louis Gallagher), Boston College and Maginnis and Walsh were pushing ahead with Gasson's dream.

Lyons Hall was under construction from May 1950 to July 1951.[6] The cornerstone laying ceremony was presided over by Archbishop Cushing on November 10, with the architect, Charles D. Maginnis, and contractor, John Volpe, the future governor of Massachusetts, attending. As the building progressed, the students eagerly awaited the availability of genteel eating accommodations. A *Heights* headline proclaimed, "New Philosophy Building Includes Modern Cafeteria (with Seats)." The reference to seats was a wry comment on the cafeteria in Gasson Hall, where eating was

Father Keleher with building contractor (later governor) John Volpe as the cross was about to be set atop the new "philosophy" building (Lyons Hall) in 1951.

accomplished in a standing posture.[7] Another innovation in Lyons was a small faculty dining room in the northwest corner of the first floor. Special presidential concern assured provision for two activities in the new building: facilities for the musical clubs to rehearse and store instruments on the top floor (and incidentally an oversized elevator for the larger musical instruments) and a psychology laboratory.[8] The psychology laboratory, "to accommodate approximately 50 students working at benches rather than at the usual desks," was a facility for the new department of psychology founded by Father James Moynihan, who had recently completed doctoral studies in experimental psychology at Catholic University. Since the traditional philosophy curriculum included courses in philosophical psychology, the title "Modern Psychology" was adopted for the new department. Father Moynihan used to say that after several years—once people became used to the different approach of his department in contrast to that of the philosophy department—he simply took down the sign outside his office, "Modern Psychology," and cut off the adjective. At any rate, for several decades his select and demanding undergraduate major in psychology was one of the most distinguished in the College of Arts and Sciences.

The New School of Nursing

The first totally new postwar academic venture of Boston College was the School of Nursing. Approval for its inauguration was given by Father Vicar General Norbert DeBoyne on December 8, 1945.[9] In seeking the approval, Provincial authorities cited the frequent requests on the matter from Archbishop Richard Cushing. The archbishop's interest was understandable. There were naturally many Catholic nurses in the archdiocese, and advancement in the nursing profession was becoming more dependent on the possession of a bachelor's degree. Archbishop Cushing saw the desirability of a collegiate school of nursing under Catholic auspices, and he made the proposal to his alma mater.

In August 1946 Father Anthony Carroll, a member of the Chemistry Department, was named regent of the Nursing School.[10] Deans of Jesuit colleges had traditionally been members of the Society of Jesus. When laymen first began to be appointed to head Jesuit professional schools, it was not uncommon to appoint a Jesuit with the title of regent, who served as liaison between the president and the dean and faculty of the professional school. This practice remained in effect for only a decade or two, however, and was then abandoned.

With no background in nursing education, Father Carroll proceeded to educate himself. He reviewed the results of a recent survey of 13 representative colleges of nursing throughout the country indicating common practices on such matters as relationship to the university, title of the nursing unit, faculty status, hospital relationships, governance, and finances. From this material he drew up an organizational and operational outline for the new School of Nursing and submitted it to Father Keleher.[11] In late November 1946 Mary Maher, who had served as a faculty member of the Massachusetts General Hospital School, was appointed dean.[12]

The School of Nursing was to serve two classes of students: those who had already earned a diploma from a hospital school and were registered nurses, and high school graduates. The first group of high school graduates entered in September 1947, but the school began functioning in the spring semester of 1947 with a class of 35 graduate nurses.

Mary Maher, who had been the New England regional director of the Children's Bureau and had held leadership positions in the nursing profession, found the regent-dean arrangement awkward and left after a brief tenure. In 1948 Rita P. Kelleher was named dean, and for the next two decades she gave the School of Nursing steady and humane leadership. She held degrees in nursing from Columbia University and Boston University and had been associate director of the Quincy Hospital School of Nursing. A confident Dean Kelleher sought and obtained accreditation for the graduate nurses program only three and a half years after the School began.[13] Similarly in June 1950 the School of Nursing library was approved by the Medical Library Association, which was a tribute to the librarian,

Rita P. Kelleher, dean of the School of Nursing, 1947–1973.

Mary Pekarski, then at the beginning of a distinguished career at Boston College as a librarian of the nursing profession.[14]

The School of Nursing was located at 126 Newbury Street in the early years, sharing the facilities with the Graduate School of Social Work. The only courses the student nurses took on the Chestnut Hill campus were in the sciences. These arrangements lasted until the School of Nursing moved to a new building on the central campus in 1960. The new structure was appropriately dedicated to Cardinal Cushing, inasmuch as he had been the inspirer of the school's beginning as well as the munificent donor of the funds that made the school's new home a reality.

* * *

The School of Nursing broke the long tradition of an all-male undergraduate student body at Boston College. Only five years later the School of Education would extend coeducation. But it would be more than two decades before coeducation would be adopted by the College of Arts and Sciences and the College of Business Administration.

ENDNOTES

1. Father Keleher to Archbishop Richard Cushing, January 16, 1946. BCA.
2. *The Heights* (April 30, 1948).
3. *The Heights* (October 30, 1947).
4. *The Heights* (April 30, 1948).
5. Keleher papers. BCA.

6. *The Heights* (November 3, 1950; March 9, 1951).
7. *The Heights* (October 20, 1950).
8. Father Keleher to Maginnis and Walsh, December 7, 1948. BCA.
9. Father Socius Forrest Donahue to Father General Janssens, December 1, 1946. BCA.
10. Father Keleher to Provincial, August 2, 1946. BCA.
11. Father Anthony Carroll to Father Keleher, September 20, 1946. BCA.
12. Father Keleher to Mary Maher, November 27, 1946; *The Heights* (February 7, 1947). BCA.
13. National Nursing Accrediting Service to Father Keleher, November 20, 1950. BCA.
14. Report of the National Nursing Accrediting Service, p. 22. BCA.

CHAPTER 24

Outline of a University

Under Father Keleher's presidency, Boston College had moved from the shadows of the war years out into the bright sunshine of a surprisingly strong recovery. With enrollments increasing beyond prewar levels, with the addition of a third undergraduate college, and with a campus enlarged by the construction of three new buildings, administration, teachers, students, and alumni could take pride in their educational institution on the Heights. There was an air of optimism in planning for the future. Taking advantage of a solid foundation, the administration, supported by a competent faculty, was prepared to continue a progressive policy of development.

A New Leader for New Times

As was the custom in the Society of Jesus, it was time to choose a new leader. In those days the choice was made in Rome. Appointed rector of the Jesuit Community by Father General John B. Janssens on March 20, 1951, Joseph R. N. Maxwell, S.J., was elected president of Boston College by the Board of Trustees on June 29, 1951.[1] Although only 52 years of age at the time of this appointment, Father Maxwell had had as broad an administrative experience as any Jesuit in the New England Province. In 1935, at age 36, he was appointed dean of the College of Arts and Sciences at Boston

REV. JOSEPH R. N. MAXWELL, S.J.
Twenty-first President

Father Maxwell was born in Taunton, Massachusetts, on November 7, 1899. Educated at Taunton High School, he attended Holy Cross College, entered the Society of Jesus on September 7, 1919, and was ordained to the priesthood in 1932. From 1926–1929 he was an instructor in English at Holy Cross and also taught English to the scholastics at Weston College in 1933–1934. During a year of ascetical studies in Belgium he published *The Happy Ascetic,* the life of a saintly Belgian Jesuit. Awarded a Ph.D. in English at Fordham University, he maintained a life-long interest in the classics and served a term as president of the Classical Association of New England. He authored *Completed Fragments,* a book of verse. He was a member and officer of several regional and national educational associations, including the prestigious Association of American Colleges, of which he was elected the 41st president in 1955. He was awarded four honorary degrees.

College upon the sudden death of a beloved and legendary dean, Father Patrick McHugh. After four years as dean Father Maxwell assumed the presidency of the College of the Holy Cross in Worcester, Massachusetts. After six difficult years (1939–1945), in which he faced the common problems arising from the war, he was appointed rector of the Cranwell Preparatory School in Lenox. Following those serene years in the Berkshires, he moved to the president's office at Chestnut Hill.

The early years of Father Maxwell's tenure were mildly complicated by what the government called a "national emergency." The Korean War, which began in July 1950, had its own effect upon campuses across the country, although minor in comparison with the dislocations of World War II. In August 1950 General Lewis B. Hershey, director of Selective Service, indicated that the September draft quotas were down to the 22-year age group. Students of 21 years or younger were safe for the moment; further, those in school, when called, could postpone induction until they completed the year in good standing. Even so, enrollments were immediately and adversely affected at the undergraduate level by the conflict. For example, in the academic year 1949–1950, there were 3294 students in the College of Arts and Sciences; the following year there were 2599, a difference of almost 700 students.[2] Thus began a precarious existence for both the students and the institution. Although many Boston College students were drafted, there was some compensation in the size of the student body by the expansion of ROTC programs on campus.

Such issues as acceleration, deferment, federal aid, and Selective Service Tests were debated and discussed with educational associations and at various institutions. Papers on the "Pre-Induction Program for Jesuit Students" were presented at the 1951 Annual Meeting of the Jesuit Educational Association.[3] As time went on, the associations and colleges worked for an extension of the G.I. Bill (Public Law 346). Public Law 16, for the rehabilitation of wounded veterans, had already been extended to veterans of the Korean conflict. In passing, it may be helpful to note that on June 19, 1951, President Truman signed the Universal Military Training and Service Act, which became Public Law 51. Finally, after a long congressional debate, veterans' benefits were extended through a new G.I. Bill (Public Law 550), which was signed by the President on July 16, 1952. Although the bill was tied to the number of days a veteran served on active duty, the maximum time allowed for education was 36 months.[4]

It was against this background of the Korean "emergency" that Father Maxwell took up his duties at Boston College. As would be the case with any prudent administrator responsible for the entire enterprise, he was immediately interested in the financial health of the institution. When compared with the university of the 1980s, with its expanded campus and high-rise buildings, Boston College in the postwar years was a relatively small operation. For the fiscal year ended June 30, 1951, total expenses reached the modest sum of $1,961,914; total income from all sources was $2,251,998. This left a net operating income of $290,084 which could be used for salary increments, interest on the debt, renovations, or new projects.[5] (Thirty-eight years later, in fiscal year 1988–1989, the operating budget was over $223 million.) In any case, through good management and increased enrollments in the Keleher years, Boston College remained in sound financial condition. And the growth continued.

The New School of Education

The Heights for October 5, 1951, carried a headline with important news: "Father Maxwell Announces New School of Education to Open Next September." The concept was not brand new. There had been, in previous years, a modest attempt to fulfill this function. Before WW II and after, an undergraduate Department of Education, chaired by Father Dunigan, was developed within the College of Arts and Sciences. It was designed to offer a B.S. in Education and, at the same time, to supply elective subjects for all juniors and seniors interested in teacher preparation.[6] Due to a drop in enrollment in the Department of Education after the war, education courses were offered only to juniors and seniors. In fact, it was more or less assumed that the B.S. in Education would be withdrawn and, in its place, students would be encouraged to take minor elective courses to fulfill the minimum requirements for public school teachers. The proposed courses were psychology of education and methods.

Father Dunigan's successor was Father Charles F. Donovan, S.J., class of '33. He had been awarded a Ph.D. in the Philosophy of Education by Yale University. In 1948 he was appointed chairman of the Department of Education at his alma mater. In addition to rearranging the curriculum and establishing a major in education, he was successful in drawing up a practice teaching program, despite the difficulties in scheduling late afternoon classes in philosophy. This program, incidentally, had to be submitted to the Province Prefect of Studies and the Provincial for approval.[7]

It was becoming more and more evident, however, that a department of education was inadequate. A school of education would be much more satisfactory for several reasons, one of which was the continued elevation of certification requirements for public school teachers in Massachusetts. In this situation, Father Donovan made a strong case for a four-year, coeducational college of education which would confer a B.S. degree in education.[8] Citing an obvious local need and appealing to the success of Jesuit schools in other areas, he concluded that "there is no reason why in so strongly a Catholic center as Boston and Massachusetts, Boston College should not have a good and flourishing school of education, to exercise a beneficial influence on education and educational policies in this part of the country."[9] Father Keleher, who was in the last months of his presidency, sent Father Donovan's proposal to the Provincial with a strong endorsement.[10] Archbishop Richard Cushing, Father Keleher noted, would favor this development, and such a school would also attract the religious sisters of the archdiocese who, up to this time, had to go elsewhere for their training.[11]

The final proposal, which incorporated additional information requested by Father Provincial James Coleran, was submitted by Father Maxwell. This version of the proposal was especially careful to include statistics on the number of women enrolled in schools of education and active in the teaching profession at the elementary and high school levels.[12] Coeducation was still a novelty at Boston College. Apparently, there was no difficulty with or opposition to this part of the plan at any level of authority. Less than three weeks after the proposal had been submitted, "Permission to inaugurate a School of Education as a distinct unit of the College and as a coeducational venture was granted by Very Reverend Father General under date of July 20, 1951."[13]

Suspecting that the Catholic women's colleges in the Boston area would be surprised—and perhaps disappointed—at this new development, Father Maxwell wrote a letter of explanation to the presidents of Emmanuel

College, Regis College, and Newton College of the Sacred Heart. "Since it [the new school] is to be coeducational, I would like to give a word of explanation of our reasons for taking this step, lest our action be inter-preted as an unfeeling entrance into competition with the Catholic women's colleges that are doing such outstanding work in the Greater Boston area." After a brief summary of the reasons, he hoped "that this explanation will prevent any misgivings or misunderstandings on your part. . . ."[14]

The administration appreciated the advantages of publicity within the academic community in preparing for the inauguration of the school. In the late spring, Father Maxwell hosted a luncheon on campus for Boston College alumni engaged in the teaching profession and for superintendents, headmasters, and other officials in the school systems of Boston and other towns. On time, as promised, the School of Education opened its doors to 176 freshmen as the academic year 1952–1953 got under way. As *The Heights* described it, "With the resumation [sic] of classes on the 22nd of September, a new look was seen on the B.C. campus in the person of 110 women who are entering as freshmen in the School of Education."[15] Not only were these students "on the campus," they were in the very heart of the campus, for the offices and classrooms were located in the Tower

Prior to the opening of Campion Hall in 1955, the coeducational School of Education was located in Gasson Hall.

COEDS BOOST REGISTRATION UP TO 3395 GRAND TOTAL

Photo by Paul Ares

FIRST ROW: Left to Right—Mary Lou Sheehan, Kathy Gosselin, Mary Desmond; BACK ROW: Louise Burke, Marianne Peterson, Kathy Donavan. *The Heights,* October 2, 1953.

The office of the Registrar, in a recent announcement, stated that the campus enrollment for this year reached a total of 3395.

Current enrollment in the College of Arts and Sciences is 1404 students, a decrease of 246 from that of last year. This figure is made up of 401 Freshmen, 328 Sophomores, 318 Juniors, and 357 Seniors.

The College of Business Administration discloses that it has 1096 attending, 104 less than last year. Of this number, 280 are Freshmen, 341 Sophomores, 231 Juniors, and 244 Seniors.

This year, there are 292 students enrolled in the School of Education, 122 Frosh, 170 Sophs. The ratio in relation to men and women is 2 to 1 in both classes, in favor of the women.

These figures disclose that the combined campus population of the three undergraduate schools totals 2792 students. The Sophomores rank first with 839. They are followed by the Freshmen, who number 803. The Seniors are 601 strong.

Building.[16] Father Donovan, the dean, was ably assisted by Marie M. Gearan, an experienced administrator, as dean of women. It was an auspicious beginning, and the new school had to wait only four years for its own building. The pioneers of the class of '56 are part of the history of Boston College in that the School of Education was the final step in completing its four-undergraduate-college structure.

Establishing Graduate Programs

With the four undergraduate colleges in operation, the administration turned its attention to graduate programs. No university is truly complete without instruction and research at the highest level. Consequently, in its quest for recognition, the president's academic council in 1952 voted to inaugurate three doctoral programs. To be more accurate, it was a decision to restore or reinstate doctoral departments. This new development had an interesting history of its own.

In a reorganization of graduate and extension courses in 1925 and 1926, a formal Graduate School was established which superseded the Master of Education program which Father James F. Mellyn, S.J., had introduced in 1922. First located at James Street and later moved to the Heights, the Graduate School began to offer fields of concentration in several areas of study. Not only was the master's degree awarded, but a doctorate in philosophy was also offered to those who wished to do some work beyond the master's level. A few years later, however, the doctoral program was severely criticized by the Association of American Universities (AAU), which at that time acted as an unofficial—but influential—accrediting agency for graduate departments.

In 1932 the Committee on the Classification of Universities and Colleges of the AAU undertook a survey of doctoral departments in the United States. In its visitation to the campus, the committee had no serious criticism of the undergraduate departments, and Boston College remained on its approved list. However, in its evaluation of faculty and library resources, "the Committee found it difficult to find any justification for the conferring of the degree of Doctor of Philosophy."[17] After a later and further review at Father Louis Gallagher's insistence, the Committee on Classification of the AAU "was still unsatisfied with your graduate work, particularly that leading to the Ph.D. degree, and we should like to see all work of the Ph.D. degree dropped entirely."[18] Father Gallagher took the advice of the AAU in order to ensure the continued inclusion of Boston College on its approved list. The committee had praised the resources of the library for undergraduate departments.

Aware of the problems of the past, Father Maxwell's advisors were confident that, with the recruitment of qualified faculty and deepening of library holdings, the College of the 1950s was adequately prepared to offer the doctorate in economics, education, and history. This was also the judgment of Father Edward B. Rooney, S.J., president of the Jesuit Educational Association.[19] Father James Burke, who on the death of Father George O'Donnell was appointed acting dean of the Graduate School, accepted the first doctoral candidates in the summer and fall of 1952. Father Paul A. FitzGerald, S.J., with a newly minted Ph.D. in history from Georgetown University, arrived in 1953 to assume the management of the Graduate School for the next seven years. One of his first tasks as dean was to restrict faculty in the doctoral departments to those professors who possessed the Ph.D. degree, in order to eliminate any cause for criticism from an outside agency. Moreover, for the first time, competitive teaching fellowships, graduate assistantships, and research assistantships for sponsored research projects were awarded in order to attract superior students. These assistantships were especially helpful in the science departments, where graduate students supervised laboratory sessions for undergraduates. At the same time, the Graduate School continued to grant a prestigious master's degree in 12 departments.

The First Self-Study

The Graduate School was not the only area that claimed attention at this time. Because professional schools—such as Management, Nursing, and Education at Boston College—are designed for a specific purpose, they are subject to well-defined inspections by the appropriate professional agency. The overall academic health of a university, however, is generally gauged by the strength of the liberal arts college which, in its turn, is evaluated by the regional accrediting association. The College of Arts and Sciences, as the oldest and largest unit at the Heights, is, so to speak, the flagship of the undergraduate schools and preserves the liberal (and Jesuit) tradition.

In 1952 a long-range preparation for the periodic visitation of the accrediting committee of the New England Association coincided with a notice from the Ford Foundation. The Fund for the Advancement of Education announced "a newly established program for college self-studies to be administered by the Committee on College Self-Studies." The program provided "a limited number of grants to liberal arts colleges for the purpose of conducting a self-analysis of the underlying aims of their liberal arts program."[20]

The academic administration grasped this opportunity to conduct an in-depth self-study of the College of Arts and Sciences with, it hoped, the aid of a grant from the foundation. With the assistance of several faculty members and the expert counsel of Sister Josephina Concannon, C.S.J., acting as a resource person, a proposal was submitted to the foundation, together with an application for a grant "to assist us in our evaluation of our liberal arts program at Boston College."[21] The proposal involved three steps: First, enlisting the support and interest of the faculty through papers and discussions which, in fact, had already taken place at the fall faculty

The main campus entrance in the 1950s.

convocation; second, scheduling a year-long series of faculty activities, guided by a special committee, which would evaluate every aspect of the institution from curriculum to athletics; and third, the step for which funding was requested, proposed "a visitation program whose object will be to have a member of each department spend four weeks during the academic year 1954–1955 as an observer in the corresponding department of an outstanding liberal arts college."[22] Boston College requested $21,000 as a reasonable budget for 12 visitors from 11 departments. Worked out in detail, the budget provided compensation for professors whose schedule had been increased to replace those on visitation for transportation, *per diem* expenses, secretarial assistance, and printing.[23]

To implement the second step, the Committee on Self-Study, with Father William V. E. Casey as chairman, was formed to undertake a survey and "to estimate for our advantage the present effectiveness of our college." There was also the possibility that this project "would be associated later with one operating under a Ford Foundation grant and involving several other universities."[24] To accomplish this end, 11 subcommittees were appointed to report on curriculum, faculty, instruction, admissions, guidance, library, campus activities, alumni, public relations, campus services, and athletics. The final reports, done with diligence and objectivity, were submitted to the president in late 1954 and early 1955.[25]

The fact that these efforts were not rewarded with a foundation grant is not important. (In 1955–1956 the Ford Foundation made a grant, in two installments, of $1 million to Boston College.) Similar grants, of varying amounts, were made at that time by the foundation to other colleges to be invested for "increase of faculty salaries or for meeting other pressing academic needs."[26] The real importance of the self-study lies in the fact that for the first time, conscious of its responsibilities, the faculty at Boston College conducted a frank, comprehensive, in-depth appraisal of the strengths and weaknesses of the academic program. It was the first in what has become an impressive series of self-analyses undertaken by the University and its several divisions.

The Law School

In completing the outline of a university, the Boston College Law School was another area of unusual activity in these years of development. The dean, Father William Kenealy, had been successful in recruiting an outstanding faculty, and good students were applying in greater numbers. There was, all admitted, the potential for a distinguished Catholic law school. However, there was agreement also—especially on the part of the American Bar Association—that all efforts would be defeated as long as the Law School continued to occupy the cramped quarters of the Kimball Building. An inspector from the ABA, after listing the factors and facilities that determined the adequacy of a good plant, wrote, "Your quarters at 18 Tremont Street come a long way from meeting these requirements. The atmosphere of the place is that of a trade school which, in spite of the earnest effort of your faculty, cannot be dispelled."[27] He criticized the classrooms, the library space, student lounge, faculty room, and other facilities.

From that time on, using the possible loss of accreditation as leverage, Father Kenealy pressed hard for a new building, first with Father Keleher, then with Father Maxwell—and not only a new building, but a building on the campus. After weighing the advantages and disadvantages, it was the unanimous opinion of the law faculty that, "with a building of our own at the Heights, we can reasonably aspire to the status of a truly great Catholic Law School of national reputation within a few years."[28] Father Kenealy was also persuaded that a prestigious campus law school would enhance the image of Boston College as an emerging Catholic university.

The decision to construct a new Law School building at the Heights was made in the fall of 1952.[29] The original choice of location, where Rubenstein Hall now stands, was later rejected in favor of a site further removed from the undergraduate campus. Although it is not clear how the city was persuaded to sell the property, the trustees empowered the treasurer, Father Edward Whalen, "to acquire from the City of Boston, title to land on Commonwealth Avenue which is to be the site of the Law School."[30] This parcel of land, opposite the MBTA station, was duly purchased for the sum of $28,000, the total amount of which was returned as a gift to Boston College by Mr. and Mrs. Vincent P. Roberts. The new building was constructed in less than a year at a cost of $1,250,000 and formally dedicated by Archbishop Richard Cushing on September 27, 1954.[31] A banquet was held at the Statler Hotel on November 21, 1954, to celebrate

The Law School moved to St. Thomas More Hall in 1955. The scene shows part of the reservoir acquired in 1949 still unfilled.

both the opening of St. Thomas More Hall and the twenty-fifth anniversary of the Law School, at which Professor William O'Keefe was awarded an honorary doctor of laws degree for his 25 years of service.

Secure in its new building, the Law School gradually fulfilled the high expectations of its faculty and the administration. Much of this success was due to Father Robert F. Drinan, S.J. ('42). A graduate of Georgetown University Law School, he was appointed dean in 1956. He approached his task with vision, enthusiasm, and boundless energy. Focusing his immediate attention on the academic quality of the school, he recruited superior students and distinguished faculty members with the assistance of the Presidential Scholarships. He also initiated the annual *Boston College Industrial and Commercial Law Review*. The night school was discontinued, to the disappointment of its alumni, who formed a particularly close circle. But the enhanced standing of the Law School paved the way for the establishment of a chapter of the Order of the Coif in 1964, a tangible award of excellence.

> Local Law School alumni and alumnae have held prominent positions. A few among the many are: Kevin White ('55) was a four-term mayor of Boston; Congresswoman Margaret Heckler ('56) represented Massachusetts' Tenth District from 1967–1982 and later served in the president's cabinet as Secretary of Health and Human Services and as ambassador to Ireland; and Thomas Salmon ('57) was a two-term Governor of Vermont.

A Faculty Manual Evolves

Every well-organized college or university, in addition to a policy-making board of trustees, has a faculty manual or faculty statutes. The statutes give a quasi legal force to regulations governing administrative and faculty responsibilities. The first attempt at such a manual came from the Jesuit Educational Association, which drew up a tentative format for complex Jesuit institutions.[32] Although President Murphy had been anxious to codify regulations at Boston College, pressures of the war years forced him to postpone that project. As a first step with approval of the Board of Trustees, his successor, Father Keleher, issued a general plan covering faculty salaries, rank, and tenure and, at the same time, established a committee on university rank and tenure.[33] This plan was followed by a "Tentative Form of Statutes for Boston College." The language in this attempt was imprecise and descriptive rather than legal, and it was critically reviewed by Father Kenealy, Father George O'Donnell, and other readers. The matter became more complex by reason of Father Provincial's involvement in certain Jesuit appointments and their termination.

The first "University Faculty Manual" was published and circulated in 1953, the second year of Father Maxwell's administration. Father Thomas Fleming, executive assistant to the president, had solicited model statutes from several Jesuit institutions—notably Fordham—as a guide in drafting a manual at Boston College. The result was a concise statement of the administrative plan of the College and the function of its several parts. The manual defined the offices of president, deans, and directors; it also defined departments and the duties of department chairmen. In an area that had been traditionally vague, it was explicit in setting down requirements for advancement in rank that would be enforced and interpreted by a committee on appointments and promotion. The manual also covered faculty salaries, annuity and insurance plans (TIAA), and hospitalization compensation insurance.[34]

The new full-time faculty contracts were also specific in determining faculty obligations and in limiting employment beyond the institution. The administration recognized "that private professional activities of individual faculty members may be desirable from the viewpoint both of the University and the individuals concerned." In general, however, the total amount of time was limited for each individual "in order that no interference with the proper discharge of full-time college duties occurs." Finally, it was forbidden for a full-time faculty member to teach in another institution during the academic year.[35]

All of this meant that, as Boston College expanded, there was a greater professionalism in its governance. Not only that, but the insistence on strict requirements for promotion in rank emphasized the importance of research and fostered publications—normal signs of an active, productive faculty.

The ROTC in Action

After the end of World War II, the War Department made a survey of colleges with a view to an expansion of the Reserve Officers' Training Corps. Boston College expressed an interest in the establishment of an

ROTC unit. After a visit from the Army in January 1947 and a formal application by Father Keleher, the College was informed by the War Department that an ROTC Field Artillery Unit had been approved, to begin the next academic year.

In the 1950s it was a common sight to see uniformed members of the Reserve Officers Training Corps in class and at other campus functions. During the Korean action there was an automatic deferment for those collegians who joined the ROTC and remained in good standing. At Boston College, Colonel Elmer B. Thayer, the commanding officer of the artillery unit, was a strict disciplinarian, and he enforced army regulations and the campus demerit system with rigid impartiality. This rigor was reflected in statistics submitted to the president: In 1951, of a total of 860 ROTC cadets, 400 were freshmen but only 125 survived to graduate as commissioned officers.[36] Reasons for attrition were many. For example, two ROTC cadets who failed to report to the Fort Bragg ROTC camp in 1951 were formally discharged by the commanding general, First Army, and required to reimburse the government for daily subsistence drawn in junior year. The government also requested that they be denied admission to senior year until reimbursement had been made.[37]

In addition to the annual exhibition drill and spring parade, which always drew high-ranking officers to the campus, a military Mass was celebrated in honor of St. Barbara, patron saint of artillerymen. In the early years, a statue of the saint was on loan from Fort Sill for the occasion. Father Maxwell later commissioned an artist at Oberammergau to carve a statue of St. Barbara that would be displayed permanently at Boston College.[38] Moreover, the Boston College ROTC unit had its own distinctive insignia worn as a shoulder loop by cadets and their officers.[39]

In those years the ROTC unit was housed in the old army barracks along Beacon Street, which were beginning to show the ravages of student use. This was one of the reasons later advanced by Father Maxwell in approaching Congressman John W. McCormack for federal assistance in building a new gymnasium which would also provide space for the offices and officers of the ROTC. In the dean's office, however, it was more important to resolve the discussion on academic credit for ROTC courses. In a resolution of this question, Boston College, bowing to pressure from the Army and influenced by the procedure in other colleges, agreed to grant 12 credits for the junior and senior courses in military science. To make up for this substitution, cadets were allowed to take one extra elective.[40] Ultimately, this decision fitted in nicely with the Army's new program which converted all college units into a general military science program for the better distribution of commissioned officers.[41]

Reaching Out

Securely organized from within, the College began to reach out to a larger public beyond the campus. In the early 1950s, with the active encouragement of Mayor John B. Hynes, the politicians and merchants of Boston were beginning to discuss the future development of the city. Boston College provided the forum. Organized by W. Seavey Joyce, S.J., dean of the College of Business Administration (later called School of Management), who was ably assisted by John Collins, S.J., Chairman of the Finance Department, the First Annual Business Conference was held in Bapst Auditorium on May 15, 1954. The program was entitled, "Greater Boston's Business Future." Welcomed to the campus by Father Maxwell, the roster of speakers and guests comprised a list of Who's Who among Boston's merchants, bankers, and developers. They were called "Boston's top thinkers and doers."[42]

The first conference was designed "not to come up with any answers, but merely to get the burning questions that *need* answering out into the open." An immediate outgrowth of the annual conference—and perhaps more important—were the "citizen seminars" at which these questions were discussed. Again, these were organized by the School of Management. The seminars, which met several times a year, discussed urban development, zoning codes, a world trade center, tax protection, and new municipal construction. The first seminar met on October 7, 1954, and Mayor Hynes set the tone with his paper, "Boston—Whither Goest Thou?"

The citizen seminars, hosted by Presidents Maxwell, Walsh, Joyce, and Monan, met regularly on campus for 25 years. They were influential in moving the City of Boston toward the renewal it now enjoys. Carl Gilbert, then president of the Gillette Company and a regular member of the seminar, said, "This University has earned the gratitude of all of Metropolitan Boston, and the whole Commonwealth, for its readiness to open its halls to citizens of every station in life, . . . of every political persuasion so that they might here consider together and debate certain of the pressing questions facing the community."[43] Although the conferences and seminars no longer meet at Boston College, they have continued under a different format in downtown Boston.

Extracurricular Activities

In other ways, too, it was a busy campus. The pages of *The Heights* for these years document the history of those extracurricular activities which began at the end of the last class. In the tradition of Jesuit colleges from the earliest years of the Society, dramatics was an integral part of a liberal education; in the 17th and 18th centuries, Jesuit theater had no equal. For several years in the early fifties, the Boston College Dramatic Society was under the capable direction of Francis Sidlauskas, who continued the polished performances of Father John Louis Bonn. A graduate of Boston College and the Yale School of Drama, Sidlauskas was so well thought of by Elliot Norton, the Boston drama critic, that he secured his appointment as Chairman of the Committee on College and University Theaters of the

New England Conference.[44] He staged a number of memorable performances, one of which was entitled, *All My People Sing.* Written in blank verse by an Arts and Science senior, Leo Hines, this play portrayed the life of St. Francis Xavier from his college days in Paris through his missionary work in the Indies. Again, acknowledging Jesuit roots, he directed an original performance of *Saint in a Hurry,* adapted by the students, which commemorated the 400th anniversary of the death of St. Francis on the island of Sancian.[45] In March 1954 the members of the Dramatic Society travelled to New York. There, for the first time, they participated in the Fordham Jesuit one-act play festival, presenting *Thor, With Angels,* by Christopher Fry.[46]

Sidlauskas was succeeded by Father Joseph Larkin, a graduate in speech and drama from The Catholic University. Father Larkin continued to insist upon a professional approach to dramatic presentations and, at the same time, gave academic respectability to the offerings in speech, communication, and theater. His own choices struck a nice balance between the classics, such as Shakespeare, and modern playwrights. A number of his students went on to fame and fortune on Broadway and in the movies.

In a related area of the performing arts, the Boston College Musical Clubs received their share of local and regional applause. With their trademark, "Songs from the Towers," the Glee Club was immensely popular on campus and at other colleges. In his last concert before joining the Cambridge school system as musical director, Walter Mayo, in a

A late 1950s dance in the auditorium/gymnasium of Campion Hall.

bravura performance at Jordan Hall, rewarded his enthusiastic audience with a program of selections from classical, semi-classical, light opera, and traditional works.[47] He was succeeded by Joseph LoPresti who, in addition to the annual appearance at Jordan Hall, arranged a number of combined concerts with local women's colleges, notably Regis College and Newton College of the Sacred Heart.

Development of the Boston College Character

With the active interest of aspiring young politicians among the student body, Boston College had always provided a platform for state and city candidates for office. As its name became better known in ever-wider circles, candidates for national office came to the Heights to test the waters in an Irish Catholic, academic atmosphere. One memorable visit occurred on March 19, 1954. Adlai Stevenson, Democratic candidate for president in 1952 and titular head of the party, spoke to 1200 students and faculty who had crowded into Bapst Auditorium. Although his address that day was nonpolitical, he was clearly preparing to challenge President Eisenhower for the second time. This "totally civilized man," as he was called, never reached the White House, but in a campus election he defeated Eisenhower by 150 votes, 476–326.[48] Others who were nationally known included the colorful G. Mennen Williams, Governor of Michigan, who also had national aspirations. He spoke to the juniors and seniors of the School of Management on the topic, "The Role of the State Government in the Federal System."

The Candlemas Lectures, founded by William J. Leonard, S.J., and inaugurated on February 2, 1947, continued to attract outstanding speakers—a tribute to the latter's perception of Boston College. The purpose of the lectures is to stimulate interest and scholarly research in the field of Christian letters. The roster of lecturers in the fifties included G. B. Harrison, professor of English literature at the University of Michigan; Bishop John J. Wright ('31), later a cardinal, who was the acknowledged authority on St. Joan of Arc; James Johnson Sweeney, director of the Solomon R. Guggenheim Museum in New York, who spoke on "The Language of Poetry"; and Frank Sheed, Catholic writer, apologist, and publisher.

In later years the Candlemas Lectures became part of the Humanities Series, perhaps the most enduring, popular, and high-quality lecture and artistic series on campus. Sponsored by Boston College, these lectures, readings, and cultural performances are open to the public and free of charge; over the years they have drawn an appreciative and discerning audience from the academic and artistic community in the Boston area. The person most responsible for the success of this series has been Father Francis Sweeney, well known for his own writings and a member of the English Department and faculty moderator of *The Stylus*. Father Sweeney has brought to the campus distinguished figures in every category of art and literature.[49]

The origin of the Humanities Series is usually traced to a lecture given by Robert Frost, who was invited by *The Stylus'* board to introduce a year-long celebration in honor of the diamond jubilee of that literary journal. The premier American poet, four-time winner of the Pulitzer Prize, spoke in the Campion auditorium on April 3, 1957, reading and discussing his own poetry. The Frost lecture, in turn, led to the "Steinman Visiting Poets Series" in 1957–1958. Funded by David Steinman, the internationally acclaimed bridge builder, this series featured Robert Frost, Ogden Nash, T. S. Eliot, and Sister M. Madeleva. The popularity of the Steinman lectures persuaded the administration to fund the Humanities Series. Formally inaugurated in the fall of 1958, the first year of Father Michael Walsh's presidency, this series has proved enormously successful.

Student Societies

The character of Boston College was further enhanced in these years by student societies. In addition to the Sodality of Our Lady, identified with Jesuit colleges since the 16th century, there was the Gold Key Society. Founded to knit a closer bond among the more ambitious students, it organizes campus activities in accordance with its motto, "Service and Sacrifice." The Order of the Cross and Crown, founded in 1939, is reserved to members of the senior class of the College of Arts and Sciences who have achieved distinction during their first three years in studies, extracurricular activities, and school spirit. In recent years, Alpha Sigma Nu, the Jesuit honor society, is recognized as a particularly familial mark of distinction at Boston College. Founded in 1915 at Marquette University, a chapter was established at the Heights in 1939 by Dean Maxwell. Students honored by induction into Alpha Sigma Nu must have distinguished themselves in scholarship, loyalty, and service; by these means, it is expected that they will appreciate and promote the ideals of Jesuit higher education.

Academically more restrictive were the clubs and academies associated with departments or professional schools. Over the years, the Mendel Club of the Chemistry Department has been particularly active in serving the needs of the premedical and predental students. In keeping with the times it has also become involved, through an annual conference, in medical-ethical questions. Many of these organizations, or the schools and departments with which they were associated, supported a magazine or "house" journal by means of which the members were encouraged to write on timely topics. Some were short-lived; others were more enduring and influential. In addition to *The Heights* and *The Stylus,* which represented every constituency, *Caritas* carried its message for the Graduate School of Social Work. *Guidepost,* which had a fairly wide circulation beyond the campus, was staffed by budding executives at the School of Management.

Some excellent articles are found in *Humanities,* which enjoyed a high reputation as the classical journal. The Mathematics Department published the *Ricci Mathematical Journal* and the Chemistry Department edited its own *Bulletin.*

*   *   *

One indication of Boston College's movement from collegiate to authentic university status was the progress of the Graduate School of Arts and Sciences. The history of American graduate schools, it has been said, is the history of the Ph.D. degree. At the 1957 June commencement, Boston College conferred the Ph.D. degree on four candidates and the Ed.D. on one, all of whom did well in their chosen fields. Robert McEwen, S.J., was later chairman of the Economics Department and a national consultant on consumer affairs. With her degree in history, Patricia Goler was subsequently appointed dean of Lowell University and elected a member of the Board of Trustees of Boston College. Sister Josephina Concannon, C.S.J., was an effective superintendent of archdiocesan schools staffed by her congregation, was active in the NCEA, and was a resourceful faculty member at the School of Education. Charles Morgan Sullivan, a college professor and an officer in several economic associations, was the first student in modern times to earn all three degrees at Boston College. Raymond Ahearn became well known in banking circles in addition to his teaching at the Heights.[50]

As Boston College moved toward the 1960s, it was, by ordinary measurements, a healthy institution. It had some problems (there was never enough money), but the programs were sound, the competition for admission made for a more highly selective student body, and the faculty was more highly trained. The future looked bright.

ENDNOTES

1. Minutes, Board of Trustees, June 29, 1951. BCA.
2. Jesuit Education Association Directory, 1950–1951, 1951–1952. BCA.
3. Ralph H. Schenk, S.J., "Pre-Induction Orientation for Jesuit High School Students," *Jesuit Educational Quarterly* (June 1951), pp. 33–44; also Paul O'Connor, S.J., "Pre-Induction Orientation for Jesuit College Students," *ibid.,* pp. 44–48.
4. The amount of allowance for veterans, as full-time students, was as follows: $110 a month with no dependents; $135 with one dependent; $160 with more than one.
5. "Boston College: Analysis of Financial Condition, 1951." BCA. If land, buildings, other immovables, securities, etc. were added, total assets would be $11,387,498. There was also a long list of scholarships, some of which were very small, available for student aid.
6. Annual Report of the Chairman of the Undergraduate Department of Education, March 7, 1946. BCA.
7. Father Keleher to Father Donovan, July 13, 1950. See also Father Donovan to John J. Desmond, Jr., Commissioner of Education, June 1, 1951. BCA.

8. Father Donovan to Father Keleher, February 18, 1951. BCA.
9. *Ibid.*
10. Father Keleher to William E. FitzGerald, S.J., February 20, 1951. BCA.
11. *Ibid.*
12. Joseph R. N. Maxwell to Father FitzGerald, July 3, 1951. BCA.
13. Note signed J.R.N.M., S.J. BCA.
14. Father Maxwell to Sister Margaret Patricia, S.N.D., August 23, 1951. BCA.
15. October 3, 1952.
16. Through the courtesy of the Franciscan Sisters at nearby Mount Alvernia Academy, the School of Education women were allowed the use of the gymnasium for classes in physical education until Campion Hall was built.
17. Adam Leroy Jones, chairman, to Louis J. Gallagher, S.J., October 28, 1933. BCA.
18. Fernandus Payne to Father Gallagher, November 5, 1934. BCA.
19. In a memorandum dated October 8, 1952, Father Maxwell alerted several members of the faculty to a visitation of the campus by Father Rooney "to discuss the proposed restoration of the Ph.D. degree." The president further suggested "that you prepare a complete list of all the teachers in your department, giving their degrees and the sources of their degrees, the number of years they have been teaching, the teaching they have done on the graduate level, whether or not they have had experience in directing research, etc." BCA.
20. John K. Weiss to All University and College Presidents, June 9, 1952. BCA.
21. Father Maxwell to Committee on College Self Studies, October 22, 1953.
22. "Proposal for which Grant is to be Sought from the Fund for the Advancement of Education." BCA.
23. *Ibid.*
24. The Committee on Self-Study to All Members of the Faculty of the College of Arts and Sciences, November 3, 1953. BCA.
25. The list of committee members and their reports are preserved in the Archives.
26. See Minutes, Board of Trustees, September 23, 1955, and July 10, 1956.
27. Will Shafroth to William Kenealy, April 3, 1950. BCA.
28. "General Report on the Condition of the Law School," October 8, 1952. BCA.
29. Minutes, Board of Trustees, January 4, 1952.
30. Minutes, Board of Trustees, May 5, 1953.
31. For a more detailed account of the construction of St. Thomas More Hall and the relocation of the Law School, see Todd F. Simon, *Boston College Law School,* pp. 31–33.
32. Edward B. Rooney, S.J., to William J. Murphy, S.J., April 23, 1941. BCA.
33. William L. Keleher, S.J., to Faculty, April 3, 1947. The regulations were revised in May 1949.
34. Copies of the Faculty Manual are in the Archives.
35. "The Boston College Policy on Private Professional Activities of Full-Time Faculty," Office of the President, December 12, 1956. BCA.
36. E. B. Thayer to Father Maxwell, August 21, 1951. BCA.
37. E. B. Thayer to Father Maxwell, September 6, 1951. BCA.
38. Father Maxwell to Chaplain (Brig. Gen.) James H. O'Neill, November 26, 1951. Also, Hans Heinzeller from Oberammergau to Father Maxwell, July 14, 1952.
39. Father Maxwell to Col. Thayer, December 17, 1951. BCA.
40. Memo to department chairmen and administrators from Dean Francis O. Corcoran, S.J., April 30, 1954.
41. Father Maxwell to Major General Hugh M. Milton, November 12, 1953. BCA.
42. Program, press clippings, and photographs are in the Archives.

43. See "Boston Citizen Seminars 1954–1979: 25 Years of Public Service," p. 2. BCA.
44. *The Heights* (January 16, 1953).
45. *Ibid.*
46. *Ibid.,* March 5, 1954.
47. May 3, 1953. Programs of musical organizations are preserved in the Archives.
48. *The Heights* (March 19, 1954).
49. Humanities Series programs and announcements are preserved in the Archives.
50. See Paul A. FitzGerald, S.J., "To Produce Scholars," *Alumni News* (Spring 1958).

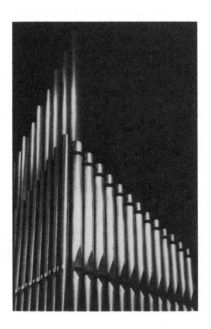

CHAPTER 25

Growth and Change
in the Fifties

The explosion of enrollment after World War II made it necessary to expand the faculty. At the same time, with a new sensitivity to high standards of faculty expertise, the Ph.D. or comparable terminal degree was a prime desideratum. In the years just before and after 1950 the New England Province provided almost a score of Jesuits with newly completed doctorates in a number of disciplines. But many lay faculty had to be recruited also to meet the University's commitments.

A Critical Mass of Faculty

At this time, partly by design, partly by happenstance, a number of Boston College alumni who had opted for a career of scholarship and college teaching completed doctoral studies at distinguished universities and returned to their alma mater to spend their careers. This group created a critical mass of faculty members who knew Jesuit education from personal experience, who were acquainted with and sympathetic to the traditions of Boston College, and who could help ease the transition from the era of a dominantly Jesuit faculty to the time of a largely lay faculty with no Jesuit educational background. This influential band of devoted alumni, along with other alumni and alumnae of the same era who did not pursue the doctoral route, deserve recording in the history of Boston College. The list

John J. McAleer ('47) of the English Department, one of many Boston College graduates who became faculty members at their alma mater.

does not include those receiving the bachelor's degree after 1960, although happily the University has continued to draw to the faculty professionally qualified men and women who completed their undergraduate work at Boston College.

Of course Boston College graduates were a minority among the growing faculty added in the Maxwell years. With the new emphasis on scholarly credentials and commitment, a cadre of talented, ambitious young people came to Boston College. To a large extent they set the standards of future faculty excellence as they recruited colleagues in their several disciplines during the expansion decades that followed.

Construction of Dormitories

It has been noted that as early as 1946 President Keleher had stated the need for a dormitory building. Despite a 30 percent drop in enrollment in the College of Arts and Sciences and the College of Business Administration from 1949 to 1954 (from 4799 students to 3323 according to *Jesuit Educational Quarterly* annual statistics), there was pressure for residential facilities. Campus accommodations in O'Connell Hall and the converted

---

B.C. Undergraduates Who Returned as Faculty

Paul T. Banks, Sr. ('39),
Mathematics
Joseph Bornstein ('46), Chemistry
Joseph Cautela ('49), Psychology
William M. Daly ('42), History
Paul Devlin ('39), Management
Stanley J. Dmohowski ('45),
Management
John J. Donovan ('39), Sociology
Vincent F. Dunfey ('37),
Management
Joyce M. Dwyer ('60), Nursing
Joseph Figurito ('45), Romance
Languages
John J. Fitzgerald ('47), English
Christopher J. Flynn, Jr. ('44),
Management
Albert M. Folkard ('37), English
Arthur L. Glynn ('39),
Management
Walter T. Greaney, Jr. ('43),
Management
Vincent A. Harrington ('51),
Management
William B. Hickey ('34),
Management
Francis J. Kelly ('49), Education
Joseph F. Krebs ('44), Mathematics
Archille J. Laferriere ('45),
Mathematics
Pierre D. Lambert ('49), Education
Robert J. LeBlanc ('45),
Mathematics
John L. Mahoney ('50), English
John J. McAleer ('47), English

Joseph M. McCafferty ('41),
English
Daniel McCue ('40), English
Francis J. McDermott ('39), English
Francis M. McLaughlin ('54),
Economics
Vincent C. Nuccio ('49), Education
Bernard A. O'Brien ('57),
Education
Thomas H. O'Connor ('49),
History
Robert F. O'Malley ('40),
Chemistry
Jean A. O'Neil ('55), Nursing
Thomas J. Owens ('44), Philosophy
Charles L. Regan ('51), English
Irving J. Russell ('43), Chemistry
Pauline R. Sampson ('52), Nursing
Robert L. Sheehan ('49), Romance
Languages
Ernest A. Siciliano ('37), Romance
Languages
Joseph A. Sullivan ('44),
Mathematics
Alfred E. Sutherland ('51),
Management
John F. Travers, Jr. ('50), Education
John E. Van Tassel, Jr. ('50),
Management
John J. Walsh ('49), Education
Norman J. Wells ('50), Philosophy
Donald J. White ('43), Economics
& Dean of Graduate School of
Arts and Sciences
Frederick J. Zappala ('46),
Management

---

museum on Hammond Street (where Roncalli now stands) were makeshift, and too many students were boarding in the neighborhood. Besides, while loyal to its Boston roots and mission, the University felt it was destined to become a national institution and therefore needed residence halls in the tradition of Georgetown and Holy Cross. A student body made up mostly of commuting students would be drawn from a candidate pool that could not contain the talent and potential of a wider geographical pool of applicants. The University's fresh emphasis on quality pointed to a larger residential population. Accordingly, during the academic year 1954–1955 Father Maxwell was busy with plans for the first buildings constructed as residence halls on campus.

The M. A. Dyer Company, architects, produced plans for a three-story half-timbered construction that melded well with the luxury residences on Tudor Road opposite the University property. The building's three units, with accommodations for 260 students, were considered separate although physically one; hence the three designations of Claver, Loyola, and Xavier.

Clearance for the construction of dormitories had to be obtained from the City of Newton. This process entailed negotiations that would be repeated frequently—and sometimes with warmth—over the years. Father Thomas Fleming, executive assistant to the president, made several presentations before the Committee on Claims and Rules of the Board of Aldermen, one of which contained a reference showing that the town fathers anticipated the Jesuit Fathers in concern about the impact of resident students upon the neighborhood. Father Fleming stated, "The dormitory will be operated under the strict rules of a Jesuit university, copies of which have been presented to the committee, and under the supervision of resident members of the Jesuit faculty. Under such rules there is no danger to the neighbors of the area of such type of nuisance as was the intent of the provision of the zoning law prohibiting the erection of dormitories in residential areas."[1] The rules in question reveal the detailed discipline of dormitory life of that era.

A perusal of the semi-monastic rules for the prospective resident students must have satisfied the aldermen, because despite the prescient warning of one of their members that the proposed "building may be the first of a half dozen similar buildings,"[2] the Board of Aldermen unanimously granted permission for the Tudor Road dormitory. Probably no Boston College facility was constructed under such pressure. City approval came in early

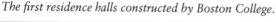

The first residence halls constructed by Boston College.

DORMITORY REGULATIONS

It is the conviction of the college authorities that young men entering college do so with the sincere and earnest purpose of obtaining all the benefits of a college education.

To accomplish this purpose, there must be a well-ordered plan of work, a time for study, and opportunity for relaxation. Whatever rules and regulations are necessary to bring about this desired effect are made with that sole purpose.

Order of Time

Class Day

7:15	Rise
7:45	Mass (optional Mon./Thurs.)
8:25	Breakfast
9:20	Classes
12:00	Lunch
5:00	Dinner
7:30	Study in rooms
9:00	Intermission
9:45	Study in rooms
10:30	End of study
11:00	Retire

Saturday

7:45	Rise (optional)
8:15	Mass (optional)
8:00–9:00	Breakfast
12:00	Lunch
5:00	Dinner
12:45	Freshmen and sophomores retire
1:15	Upper classmen retire

Sunday

7:45	Rise
8:15	Mass
	Breakfast
12:00	Lunch
5:00	Dinner
10:00	Benediction
11:00	Retire

The responsibility for the condition of the dormitories is a corporate one, since it rests with the individuals residing in them. Students are also responsible for the condition of their rooms, and they can be held accountable for damage done therein.

Hence, no one may be invited to occupy your room, or the room of another student who happens to be absent, without the explicit permission of the prefect. Each student upon leaving his room should make certain that the door is locked.

Non-resident students are not to enter any room in the dormitories unless accompanied by the occupant of the room, and they must leave when occupant of room leaves.

Since a student's character is reflected not only in himself but also in his environment, all rooms must be kept neat and presentable. Frequent checks will be made by the prefects to promote this important element of dormitory life.

It is positively forbidden to bring lady visitors, even mothers and sisters, into the dormitories.

The purpose of the college years is to train and prepare the student for life. The chief indication that a college education is attaining this is success in studies. To accomplish this result it is very necessary that each one should manifest the proper consideration due his fellow students. The chief factor militating against this success is unnecessary noise in whatever shape or form it may take.

Hence, during the period of study, students must avoid all unnecessary moving about and remain in their rooms.

Radios may not be used during study hours from Monday to Friday inclusive. When in use at other times, the radios should always be so modulated as not to disturb one's neighbor.

Evidence of intoxication, or the introduction of intoxicating liquor into the college premises, renders the offending party liable to dismissal from college.

Pictures or books of questionable character may not be displayed or retained in private rooms.

Gambling in any shape or form is positively forbidden.

Resident students are generally not allowed the possession or control of automobiles. However in special cases, if the student has written consent from parent or guardian, permission may be granted.

"Out Permission" is a permission to absent oneself from the college premises. "Out Permissions" are granted on:

Friday nights until	12:00 p.m. for freshmen and sophomores
	12:30 a.m. for upper classmen
Saturday nights until	12:30 a.m. for freshmen and sophomores
	1:00 a.m. for upper classmen

On each Sunday night there will be a further permission for the members of the senior class. This permission expires at 10:45 p.m.

Failure in studies or infractions of discipline will incur the loss of "Out Permissions" for a period of time to be decided by the Dean of Men or the prefect.

Permission to visit one's home on the weekend may be granted to those in good standing, provided parents or guardians have signified their consent in a personal letter addressed to the Dean of Men. This permission will begin after classes on Friday and end on Sunday at 9:45 p.m. Slips for weekend permissions are at the Office of the Dean of Men (College of Arts and Sciences). These are filled out by the student on *Thursday* if he plans to spend the weekend at home.

On returning from *all* "Out Permissions," each student must report in person to his prefect.

The dormitories will be closed during the major vacations at Christmas and Easter, and for the entire summer.

April, *The Heights* printed an architect's drawing of the building on April 22, and the new residence halls received students in September, with the formal dedication and blessing of the building occurring on September 27, 1955.

CLX, as the Tudor Road residences are popularly known, were indeed just a beginning of building to accommodate students wishing to live on campus. In November 1956 the University once again petitioned the Newton Board of Aldermen for permission to build dormitories, and on February 4, 1957, they received a favorable reply.[3] Construction went forward once more in haste during the spring and summer, and by opening of classes in September 1957 two residences, Kostka and Gonzaga, welcomed a new group of residents. The buildings bordered Beacon and Hammond streets, and Gonzaga was distinguished by containing a chapel to accommodate 500 students.

Administrative Changes

In 1956 some administrative changes were made in the College of Arts and Sciences that were significant in the development of the University. Father William Van Etten Casey was named dean, Henry McMahon became assistant dean, and Weston Jenks was appointed director of educational guidance. McMahon, a member of the History Department, backed up a succession of deans as assistant and associate dean for nearly 30 years until his death in 1984. Jenks' role grew until he headed all counseling services in the undergraduate schools. Father Casey had been a vigorous and innovative chairman of the Theology Department at a time of considerable ferment in Catholic collegiate circles concerning the teaching of college theology. Under Father Casey's leadership the Boston College theology program had achieved showcase status among Catholic colleges. Father Maxwell now called upon Father Casey to give similar stimulating leadership to the entire college.

Henry J. McMahon ('40), assistant and associate dean of the College of Arts and Sciences, 1956–1984.

Father Casey set about his task with dispatch. In the spring of 1957 he announced a number of changes that in retrospect seem tame but that were, in the context of the traditions of the University, mildly revolutionary. First was a reallocation of the philosophy curriculum. As pointed out earlier, the philosophy curriculum had been for generations the preoccupation of the junior and senior years, a series of courses that earned 28 credits (enough in most colleges for a respectable major). Starting in the fall of 1957 the philosophy curriculum was begun with freshmen and distributed through all four years, with one 3-credit course each semester plus an extra course in senior year on the history of philosophy.

The new distribution of the philosophy curriculum gave upperclassmen more leeway in the pursuit of their majors, but Father Casey stressed other advantages: The four-year distribution of the philosophy curriculum would allow for a more gradual and thorough assimilation of the method and content of the subject. Philosophy's relation to other disciplines would be perceived throughout the collegiate experience. And, since philosophy and theology are twin pillars of the Jesuit liberal arts core, they should be studied side by side through all four years.[4]

Another change had to do with the honors program. For two decades there had been a limited honors program, whose purpose was to entice talented students to the study of Greek, once Greek ceased being a requirement for the A.B. degree in the 1930s. Only select students who chose the Greek curriculum could be members of the honors program, which was called A.B. Greek Honors. Now that system was dropped. The new honors program would touch all parts of the curriculum, the liberal arts core, and especially the academic field of concentration. Honors students were to be freed of some of the academic lockstep of the college experience and encouraged to pursue independent study in addition to special tutorials set up for them.

Other accommodations for gifted students were announced: early admission (the admission of qualified high school students having completed three years) and sophomore standing (the placement of outstanding high school graduates directly into the second year of college). Another new program, "Junior Year in Europe," was begun one year earlier to allow "better students to pursue their studies for a year in one of the great centers of Western culture, to master one or more European languages, and to achieve that cosmopolitan point of view that comes from a prolonged residence in Europe."

Perhaps the most revolutionary prediction that Father Casey made about the curriculum of the College of Arts and Sciences was that in the near future the Latin requirement for the A.B. degree would be dropped.[5] One might have expected an outcry of protest at such a proposed break with hallowed Jesuit tradition. But hardly a murmur was heard. Administrators of Jesuit colleges in the United States had been quietly questioning the viability of the Latin requirement for over a decade. Students at Jesuit

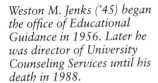

Weston M. Jenks ('45) began the office of Educational Guidance in 1956. Later he was director of University Counseling Services until his death in 1988.

colleges for years had been voting against the Latin curriculum by opting for the B.S. rather than the A.B. degree. In 1955 at Boston College and Holy Cross alone out of the 28 Jesuit colleges, slightly more than 30 per cent of the students earned the A.B. degree with Latin; the national average was under 11 percent.[6] The catalog for the 1958–1959 academic year made no mention of Latin as a requirement for the A.B. degree. So ended a nearly century-old academic tradition at Boston College, and the way was open for the sweeping curriculum changes for the A.B. degree that were to follow in the next decade.

Professional Schools

Boston College's professional schools established a pattern of seeking national recognition through the medium of accreditation by the appropriate organizations as early as feasible. Started in the depression and struggling through the WW II period, the College of Business Administration was not in a position to consider accreditation until the period of Father James Sullivan's deanship (1948–1953). The American Association of Collegiate Schools of Business (AACSB) set as one norm for accreditation a faculty of whom at least 50 percent possessed appropriate terminal degrees. Father Sullivan enlisted members of the Economics Department to help CBA meet that standard. When Father Joyce was named to succeed Father Sullivan in 1953, he retained the chairmanship of the Economics Department, thereby facilitating cooperation between the two units.

The administration of CBA contacted the business schools at three Jesuit universities having recent accreditation experience for guidance: Loyola University in New Orleans, the University of Detroit, and Creighton University in Omaha.[7] In the spring of 1955 Father Joyce engaged a consultant from the Harvard Business School to examine the School of Business Administration and advise about its readiness for an accreditation visit. After some adjustments to meet the consultant's advice, application was made for accreditation by AACSB. At this time, in the fall of 1955, Donald White of the Economics Department was named associate dean for the internal administration of the school because of the heavy external commitments of Father Joyce. And it was Dean White who wired the happy news from the annual AACSB meeting at Berkeley, California, that CBA had been admitted to full membership rather than associate membership in the association. Only one other college in the previous ten years had received full membership on initial application.[8]

After the visit of the AACSB evaluation team, Father Joyce wrote to Father Maxwell with some surprise—and even a little skepticism—that the chairman of the visiting team had commented that the College of Business Administration was already capable of offering an MBA program.[9] In 1956 Dr. Vincent Wright, a former member of the Economics Department then associated with Northeastern University's Evening College of Business, was named by Father Maxwell as dean of the Evening College of Business Administration on campus, with authority to begin a part-time graduate program in business administration. The graduate program was launched in the fall of 1957 with a student enrollment of 150.[10]

Intown College to the Heights

By the mid-fifties there was thought of providing a building for the Nursing School on campus.[11] With the Nursing School would go the library from 126 Newbury Street, along with its capable librarian, Mary Pekarski. Hence there was concern in the Intown College about being isolated at Newbury Street. Father Maxwell's discussion with Vincent Wright at the time of his appointment revealed that the establishment of an Evening College of Business Administration on campus was a deliberate test to see if evening students would come to the Heights. It was feared that a move of the evening operation to Chestnut Hill might result in a drastic drop in enrollment.[12] But the administration's fears were unfounded, because in its first semester of operation the newly established campus Evening College of Business Administration drew a hundred students.[13] This response paved the way for the move of the Intown College to Chestnut Hill a few years later.

During the fifties the Intown College prospered, reaching an enrollment of over a thousand. It should be noted that from its earliest years of degree-granting, the Intown College—or Evening College—was not merely a purveyor of eclectic or unrelated practical or vocational courses for working people. Rather it was a college offering at an alternative time (evening) basically the same collegiate programs that the University offered during the day in the College of Arts and Sciences and the College of Business Administration. The catalogs of the 1950s, for example, reveal that the same Latin requirements for the A.B. degree that existed—and were debated—in the College of Arts and Sciences at the Heights obtained likewise for the Intown College. True, a minority of Intown students opted for the A.B. degree because of the rigid classical language requirement, but that was also becoming true of the campus College at the time.

A New Home for the School of Education

As it prepared for its opening in September 1952, the School of Education was given remarkable latitude by the administration in selecting a faculty. All of the faculty, liberal arts teachers as well as professional faculty members, were chosen by the School of Education, and for the first five years they functioned as a unit. Thus faculty meetings, even dealing with professional education requirements, were attended by professors of English, philosophy, and physics as well as teachers of education subjects. The purpose from the first was to integrate the professional aspects of the school with the liberal arts tradition of Boston College. Indeed, several of the liberal arts disciplines—namely, music, fine arts, and speech—which later blossomed in the College of Arts and Sciences got their foothold at Boston College in the School of Education. In the early years, School of Education students were sometimes teased by Arts and Sciences students for being associated with a "vocational" college, but they were urged by the School of Education administration to retort proudly that they attended a liberal arts college with a purpose.

As has been noted earlier, the School of Education was favored by its initial location in the flagship of the campus, Gasson Hall. The dean's office was in the southwest corner of the first floor on the College Road side of the building. The original library and current honors program room was given to the School of Education, separated into four or five rooms for offices and faculty gatherings.

During the 1950s and until the opening of Carney Hall in 1962, nothing was in shorter supply at the University than adequate faculty office space. In earlier days the mostly Jesuit faculty had their rooms in St. Mary's Hall for study and a series of parlors on the first floor of St. Mary's for consultation with students. The sudden growth of the lay faculty resulted in makeshift office accommodations for most—a desk in a converted classroom with a dozen other teachers, or a cubbyhole at the end of a corridor with a temporary partition closing off corridor traffic (but not noise). The School of Education faculty, which was growing not only because of the need to staff the infant school but also because of the new doctoral program, shared some of the end-of-corridor offices in Gasson. Such four-person offices undoubtedly inhibited scholarly reflection, but surely promoted togetherness.

But it was not the inadequacy of faculty office space or any other academic exigency that determined from the day of its opening that the School of Education must have a new building. The reason was mundane but compelling: plumbing. The existing buildings on campus had been built with an all-male student body in mind and typically each provided one large lavatory in the basement. With a hundred coeds in the freshman class, it was clear that soon as many as 500 female students would grace the School of Education's facilities. Before classes began in September 1952, Father Maxwell was wielding his architect's ruler on a proposed building for the latest (and last) undergraduate unit of the University. When colleagues in teacher education throughout New England learned that Boston College was immediately planning a new building for its new school, they congratulated School of Education personnel on having an administration that gave such high priority to professional education. The expressions of admiration were duly accepted, and no mention made of plumbing.

The School of Education's Campion Hall.

The architect for both the Law School and the School of Education buildings was once again the firm of Maginnis and Walsh. Obviously Father Maxwell told them to proceed with plans for both buildings almost as soon as the School of Education opened its doors, because in May of 1953 Charles Maginnis sent Father Maxwell contracts for the Law School building and the School of Education. Father Maxwell replied that he could not sign the School of Education contract because "we have not as yet submitted to Rome any plans for the School of Education."[14] But without much delay permission was obtained, and nine days after More Hall was dedicated, ground was broken for Campion Hall on October 7, 1954.

Campion Hall was planned as one of the least costly buildings provided by Maginnis and Walsh. The others, even relatively scrimped Fulton Hall, were done in stone, whereas Campion was to use a combination of stone and brick. Even as the building developed in June of 1954, Father Maxwell gave the architect orders to cut back further on the stone.[15] The brick in color and style reflected the nearby service building and was to be matched a few years later in Roberts Center. But the stone-brick combination of Campion Hall was not repeated elsewhere on the middle campus (in McElroy, Carney, Cushing, McGuinn, Higgins, or O'Neill).

Campion Hall was ready for the opening of classes in September 1955, so that the first class in the School of Education spent their senior year in the new building. A dedication ceremony was held on September 22 with Archbishop Richard Cushing presiding.

The School of Nursing

The decade of the fifties brought some important changes to the School of Nursing. The regent at the time, Father James Geary, asked Father Edward Gorman of the Philosophy Department to handle the philosophy course in the School of Nursing and act as counselor for students. The 19-year association of Father Gorman with the School of Nursing proved to be a significant formative influence for the nursing students and faculty of that time. His name is still venerated in Cushing Hall.

In 1954 the office of regent was abolished and Dean Rita Kelleher gained direct access to the president. The original academic curriculum for basic (non-R.N.) students when the school opened called for a five-year program. This was eventually rearranged into a standard four-year program.

The School of Education joined the School of Nursing in starting a program leading to a master of education degree with majors in the clinical areas of medical and surgical nursing, maternal and child nursing, psychiatric nursing and community health nursing. By 1958 the School of Nursing had sufficient faculty with the necessary academic background to consider establishing its own program in the Graduate School of Arts and Sciences. Father Maxwell gave his approval, and a program leading to a master of science degree with a graduate department in the School of Nursing was begun. Marie Andrews was the first head of this program.

The Student Mood

Some hints as to the student mood and intellectual style of the 1950s may be gleaned from the student paper, *The Heights*. It is interesting to note that as early as 1957 *The Heights* reprinted an article from a national Catholic magazine praising Martin Luther King.[16] In the same issue the paper carried an article that addressed the integration of the races as a national, not only a southern, issue: "Integration Our Problem—North and South."

While evincing social enlightenment for a national problem, students also showed some concern about campus issues. In May of 1957 the student paper complained that the recently announced tuition increase of $100, which brought the following year's tuition to $700, had been implemented without a letter to parents on the subject such as had been sent two years earlier for a similar increase. Nevertheless the paper editorialized that the University should plan to raise tuition to $1000 by the year 1962 in order to provide higher salaries for the faculty.[17] The editorialist was a prophet. Five years later the tuition was, in fact, $1000.

A quarter of a century before O'Neill Library opened, there were student complaints about the shortcomings of Bapst. In October 1957 a *Heights* editorial, alleging that Bapst Library was uncomfortable and lacked an adequate book collection, called for the erection of a new library.[18] During the following months *The Heights* carried a series of student interviews about Bapst. Student opinion ran seven to one against the library, complaining mostly about the number of books reported as "NA" (not available) and about the amount of socializing occurring in the library.[19]

Father Casey might have been spearheading an academic revolution in the College of Arts and Sciences, but the students were not revolutionists. In 1956 a *Heights* editorial took a stand against unlimited "cuts." In those days, class attendance was obligatory and the editorial writer believed there should be no change unless, perhaps, some greater liberty might be allowed for students in elective courses or for honors students.[20] This expression of opinion was not followed by a flood of indignant letters to the editor calling for the abolition of required class attendance. The following decade, however, would bring radical contrasts both in college regulations and in student mood.

*   *   *

Father Maxwell was a poet, a bookish man with little interest in sports of any kind. Given his personal leanings, it was natural that he enthusiastically backed the introduction of doctoral programs in the Graduate School of Arts and Sciences and arranged for the start of a graduate program in business administration. But it came as something of a surprise to many in the University community that before the end of his term in office he was seen as a champion of Boston College athletics.

ENDNOTES

1. BCA.
2. *News-Tribune* (April 5, 1955). BCA.
3. Ernest G. Angevine to Father Fleming. BCA.
4. *Alumni News* (Summer 1957).
5. *Ibid.*
6. For an account of the decline and fall of the Latin requirement for the A.B. degree see Charles F. Donovan, "Boston College's Classical Curriculum," Occasional Papers in the History of Boston College. BCA.
7. Raymond F. Keyes, *History of the College of Business Administration and School of Management, 1938–1978,* p. 30. BCA.
8. *Ibid.,* p. 32.
9. Father Joyce to Father Maxwell, December 28, 1955. BCA.
10. Keyes, *op. cit.,* p. 56.
11. Memo of M. A. Dyer Company, August 28, 1956. BCA.
12. Keyes, *History,* p. 55.
13. *Ibid.*
14. Father Maxwell to Charles Maginnis, May 25, 1953. BCA.
15. Father Maxwell to Eugene Kennedy, Jr., June 14, 1954. BCA.
16. *The Heights* (January 11, 1957).
17. *The Heights* (May 3, 1957).
18. *The Heights* (October 18, 1957).
19. *The Heights* (November 22, 1957).
20. *The Heights* (November 9, 1956).

CHAPTER 26

Postwar Athletics

At a press conference at Alumni Hall on March 26, 1957, Father Maxwell had good news for faithful alumni who had begun to think that they were about to witness the end of an era:

> In connection with the return of our football games to our campus and the efforts of our alumni to raise a quarter of a million dollars for the renovation of our stadium, I feel that it is not an exaggeration to say that we are on the threshold of a new era for Boston College athletics.[1]

According to rumors following the 1956 football season, many alumni had feared that Boston College might imitate the drastic decisions taken by Georgetown and Fordham, long-time football powers in the East, to drop football.[2] Quite the opposite. Not only would there be a new stadium, located on the lower campus adjacent to the reservoir parking area, but the master plan included a gymnasium and an ice hockey rink. This bold and imaginative program completely reversed a brief period of indecision.

A Home for the Football Team

Father Maxwell's announcement recalled several pages of sports history at Boston College. The first stadium erected at the Heights in 1915 was called "New Alumni Field." Seating 5000 spectators, the stands—on one side only—ran along College Road, and the playing field occupied what was once referred to as the "dust bowl" and later called the "college green."[3] It was dedicated at mid-season in a game with arch rival Holy Cross, which the Crusaders won 9–0.[4] Built on the same site, the second stadium was dedicated in 1932 during a game with Loyola College, Baltimore, wherein the Eagles were the victors 14–0. This stadium, which pre-empted some of the prime property on the campus, was never envisioned—even by those who built it—as a permanent home for the football team. It was, in reality, an expansion of the first stadium, seating 22,000. Its location, destined for academic construction, was far from ideal, and the parking facilities were totally inadequate even for those days. It was used for home games only from 1932 to 1936; from 1937 through 1939 the football games were played at Fenway Park as often as at Alumni Stadium. Coach Frank Leahy, who was at the Heights for only two seasons (1939–1940), was in favor of moving the games permanently to Fenway Park. After World War II, from 1946 through 1952, games were played at Braves Field. The Eagles returned to Fenway Park in 1953 for their home games through the 1956 season.

After the 1956 season, the owners of Fenway Park served notice that the Eagles' cleats would no longer be allowed to chew up the Red Sox infield. In fact, built for the smaller baseball gate, Fenway Park was judged too small for big-time football, and thought was being given to the installation of additional seats for the football season when the owners made their decision.[5]

This was the situation and the dilemma faced by Father Maxwell. The one who must make a financial decision which affects the future of the institution and its academic programs cannot be too sentimental about past athletic glories. Moreover, at this time Boston College was also embarking on a program of construction of residential facilities to attract students from a larger geographical pool. It was in this context that both alumni and sports writers began to speculate on the dreadful possibility that Boston College would discontinue football. It did not help to recall the recent 7–0 loss to Holy Cross. In fact, as oral history has it, the discussion was short and to the point. "We could drop football," said Father Maxwell to Bill Flynn, alumni secretary and line coach. "Or we could build a stadium," replied Flynn.[6] Responding to alumni pressure and persuasively backed by alumni generosity, on January 23, 1957, Father Maxwell announced a $250,000 Alumni Stadium Fund drive to be organized by alumni secretary, varsity line coach, and soon-to-be athletic director Flynn and to be chaired by 1926 captain and former coach Joe McKenney.[7]

In the meantime, the existing stadium on campus had been dismantled, leaving only a few stands (reminiscent of the 1915 stadium) along College Road.[8] The relocation of the stadium was largely an intramural operation. With alumni and student volunteers supplementing the professional supervision and assistance of an outside crew, it was literally transported from the upper campus to the new site on the Beacon Street end of the small reservoir acquired in 1949. The move included the curved end zone and lower stands on the west side, as well as the flat end zone stands. To these were added 6,000 on the east side, making a total of 25,000 seats.

An Expanded Stadium Plan

The response of alumni—including subway alumni—was so enthusiastic and generous that the stadium plan was expanded to include a gymnasium with a basketball court, connected to a large lobby which would provide for student and faculty lounges, offices for student publications, ROTC, and athletic offices. This part, in turn, would be connected to a third unit which would contain a regulation-size hockey rink with facilities to accommodate 2000 spectators. This three-unit building was eventually abandoned in favor of the original gymnasium, with a seating capacity of 4000 and a separate hockey rink with a seating capacity of 6000.

Completed in September 1957, the stadium was called "an epic in community teamwork." It will always remain a silent memorial to the indefatigable labors of generous workers, including Joseph McKenney (stadium chairman), John Griffin (alumni president), Daniel Driscoll (chairman of the alumni fund), Dr. Christopher Duncan, John Curley (manager of athletics), Father George Kerr (all-American guard), and a host of others. Many colleges in the area contributed to the fund, as did the Boston clubs of other Jesuit institutions.

The new Alumni Stadium was dedicated on September 21, 1957, during a game with Navy. The handsome brochure of 105 pages commemorating the event contained letters of congratulations from, first of all, President Dwight Eisenhower and from local and national personalities, and it also recognized the contribution of those who made the dream possible.[9] Alas, the fortunes of war do not always reward the brave: Boston College bowed to Navy 46–6.

The gymnasium, built at a cost of $1,235,400, was located as originally planned in a triangular area along Beacon Street and the inner reservoir road. To inaugurate the project, Archbishop Cushing turned the first sod on May 3, 1957.[10] Named after Mr. and Mrs. Vincent P. Roberts, outstanding benefactors of the University, the gymnasium was dedicated on October 3, 1958, in an elaborate ceremony which featured Arthur Fiedler and 55 members of the Boston Pops Orchestra. With officers and directors of the Boston College Alumni Association on hand, there were short speeches by Dr. Edmund Flaherty, chairman, Dr. Christopher Duncan, alumni president, and Father Michael Walsh, president.

The New Ice Hockey Rink

The new hockey rink, initially referred to as the Auditorium Arena, was built parallel to the west stands of the stadium and completed the sports complex on the lower campus.[11] In drawing up plans for this facility, which

McHugh Forum, the ice hockey rink completed in 1958, alongside Alumni Stadium, opened a year earlier.

was a new venture for Boston College, Father Maxwell, Bill Flynn, and other interested people visited several New England colleges that had recently constructed ice hockey rinks. These on-site visits were extremely helpful. The authorities of Boston College learned what to exclude and what to include; they also discovered the economic advantages to a college with a major collegiate hockey team.

Built at a cost of $800,000, the rink had a floor space of 195 by 85 feet (the exact dimension of that at Boston Garden), with ten miles of pipe attached to two large Frick refrigeration units. While it was always primarily an athletic facility, with dressing rooms for visiting teams, it could be easily converted into an auditorium for commencement exercises and other large gatherings. It was dedicated on November 14, 1958, to the memory of Father Patrick J. McHugh, S.J., for 13 years the popular and respected dean of the College of Arts and Sciences. In the evening, a capacity crowd was on hand to witness the ice show, headed by world champions Carol Heiss and Alan Hayes Jenkins. After the featured performance, the rink was opened for general public skating.[12]

As Bill Flynn observed in an interview, "This is all rather amazing when you consider that in little more than a year we have moved our varsity sports activities back to the campus and provided improved and expanded facilities for our intramural sports program."[13] The old "temporary" wooden gym was torn down, intramurals took over the former Alumni Field on the upper campus, and the baseball diamond was, in time, moved to the large area known as Commander Shea Field on the Cleveland Circle side of the reservoir. These facilities, plus new student residences, strained the University's finances. In a jocular mood, at the Annual Laetare Sunday Breakfast in March 1957, Father Maxwell suggested a new organization which might be called, "Get Maxie off the Hook Club."[14]

Watching over this athletic enterprise was the imperious eagle. Chosen as the Boston College mascot in the early twenties, a live Texas eagle lived out its natural life in a large cage near the Science Building. In more recent years, however, a gold-leafed bronze eagle, four feet high, with six foot wings, has perched atop a 30-foot granite pedestal in front of the Gasson Tower.[15] This eagle, cast in Japan, adorned U.S. Ambassador Lars Anderson's residence in Tokyo. It was brought to the United States at the turn of the century and rested for many years on the Anderson estate in Brookline. In October 1954, with Father Thomas M. Herlihy, pastor of St. Ignatius Church, acting as an intermediary, it was donated to Boston College and placed on a base in front of Alumni Hall.[16] Two years later, the eagle was moved to its present location on the granite column, which once stood in front of the South Station in Dewey Square.[17]

Leaders of the Program

The successful execution and completion of this ambitious athletics program depended, of course, on people. In his statement to the press on March 26, 1957, Father Maxwell announced the newly created position of director of athletic facilities, which would be filled by John P. Curley. Replacing Curley, William J. Flynn would become director of varsity and intramural sports. These two men were most responsible for implementing the design for a new era in athletics. "Gentleman John" Curley, who provided a bridge linking the past with the future, had graduated from Boston College in 1913. After returning to the Heights in 1929 as graduate manager of athletics, he had impressed his stamp for 28 years upon the Athletic Department while earning the respect of his peers across the country. As Father Maxwell said, he had found the man who from the point of view of experience and ability "is best suited to direct these consolidated facilities."

A schoolboy star at English High School and a 1939 graduate of Boston College, Bill Flynn was captain of the football team in his senior year. Returning to the Heights in 1948, he was a member of the Mathematics Department and an assistant coach; five years later he was appointed alumni secretary. Partly by reason of his long tenure as director of athletics, but mostly because of his talents and personality, Flynn enjoys a national reputation in athletic circles, and he has served two terms as president of the NCAA. Boston College acknowledged his contribution to alma mater by naming the enclosed athletic facility the William J. Flynn Student Recreation Complex.

The faculty moderator of athletics, traditionally a Jesuit, has an important role to play. Father Joseph L. Shea ('40), who had succeeded the legendary Maurice V. Dullea, S.J., in 1957, held this position during these years of expansion. He was also dean of men. As moderator he was, in effect, the Jesuit advisor to the president and the president's liaison with the graduate manager and the coaches. Father Shea, in a job which he enjoyed, had the confidence of the Athletic Department, which was reluctant to see him depart in 1962 for his new post as rector of Boston College High School. He returned to the campus in 1977, where he served once again as the University representative to the Athletic Department until his death in December 1987.

Boston College has been fortunate in attracting the loyal services of men and women who have exercised a positive influence over their colleagues and students. Such a man, for example, was track coach Jack Ryder. Not only did he develop some of the finest track stars in the East (the relay was his special event), but he directed their competitive instincts toward life's goals. In dark tie and business suit, always pictured with a stop watch in his hand, John A. Ryder came to Boston College in 1919. For 33 years he enjoyed the confidence of students, faculty, and administration. With a trackman's explanation, "The legs won't take it any more," he became coach emeritus on September 16, 1952. On the occasion of his retirement at age 76, a large testimonial Communion breakfast was held in Lyons Hall; he died the following year. He was later honored by a bronze plaque

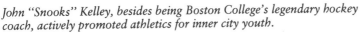

John "Snooks" Kelley, besides being Boston College's legendary hockey coach, actively promoted athletics for inner city youth.

presented to Boston College by the Jack Ryder Track Club on Alumni Day, June 4, 1955, before 1000 alumni, family, and friends.[18] The plaque says it all: "Moulder of men and maker of champions."

There is another who must be mentioned. Anyone who has ever walked along Linden Lane, attended class in Gasson Hall, or watched a football game knows the legendary name of Joseph McKenney of the class of 1927. An outstanding quarterback during his collegiate years, he was appointed head coach the year after graduation. His teams won national acclaim through 1934. Joe McKenney has been the recipient of many honors from his alma mater. Former president of the Alumni Association, he received the McKenney Award and most recently the Bicentennial Râle Medallion; he was awarded an honorary doctor of education degree in 1983. As we have seen, he was a good choice for chairman of the Alumni Stadium drive. But his real distinction has been in his strength of character and his unwavering commitment to the Jesuit enterprise at University Heights.

*   *   *

With the completion of these new facilities, the administration at Boston College renewed its commitment to an expanded intercollegiate program and, in fact, inaugurated a new era. This program brought Boston College, alone among Jesuit colleges in the United States, to the forefront of national competition in all major sports.

ENDNOTES

1. BCA.
2. Georgetown University dropped football in 1951. See Hunter Guthrie, S.J., "No More Football for Us!" *Saturday Evening Post* (October 13, 1951). Fordham dropped football in 1954. In both cases financial deficits were the controlling factor.
3. It is almost impossible to erase labels attached by students. In the construction of Carney and McGuinn Halls, the heavy equipment chewed up the sod of old Alumni Field. It was an eyesore for years and was dubbed the "dust bowl" by a generation of students. As a college green, it is now a gathering place for students and is used for their outdoor activities.
4. *Boston Sunday Globe* (May 26, 1957).
5. In a memo dated June 30, 1955, John P. Curley, Graduate Manager of Athletics, informed Father Maxwell that Boston College would contribute $6000 for the erection of 3000 sideline seats at Fenway Park. BCA.
6. Jack Falla, *'Til The Echoes Ring Again: A Pictorial History of Boston College Sports* (Brattleboro, Vt.: Stephen Greene Press), p. 28.
7. *Ibid.*
8. These stands were used for commencement and other outdoor functions through 1957.
9. This collector's item, preserved in the archives, is a valuable source of information for this entire enterprise.
10. For additional information, see *Alumni News* (Spring 1957), p. 2.
11. See the interesting article, with photographs, *Alumni News* (Winter 1959), pp. 18–20.

12. *The Heights* (November 21, 1958).
13. *Alumni News* (Summer 1957), p. 5.
14. *Boston Globe* (April 1, 1957).
15. *Boston Herald* (December 19, 1958).
16. *The Heights* (October 22, 1954), p. 8.
17. *Ibid.* (October 19, 1962).
18. *Alumni News* (Summer 1955), p. 22; also *Boston Sunday Post* (June 5, 1955).

CHAPTER 27

Approaching the Centenary

Since Father Maxwell had continued as president for several months beyond the usual six-year term for Jesuit rectors, it was rumored that he might remain in office for the foreseeable future. An extension of his administration was made plausible by reason of a policy decision in Rome, where it was decided that in large institutions such as Boston College, Fordham, and Georgetown, a superior of the Jesuit Community should be appointed to ease the burden of the rector. The first to fill this office had been Father Urban W. Manning, who arrived at St. Mary's Hall in February 1954. Due to illness, he was replaced within two years by Father Robert A. Hewitt, a former rector of Weston College, who was appointed superior of the Jesuit Community on May 13, 1956.

Putting an end to speculation, however, Jesuit General John B. Janssens chose the chairman of the Biology Department as the next rector of Boston College.[1] Elected 22nd president by the Board of Trustees, Michael P. Walsh, S.J., took office on February 5, 1958. A popular choice, he was fully prepared to accept his responsibilities. Entirely familiar with the University and its administrative machinery, it was soon clear that he had formed definite ideas as to where he would like to lead his institution. As former chairman of the crucial committee on rank and tenure, he had helped to design the mechanism for promotion. This, in turn, had brought him into contact with professors at every level and convinced him of the

REV. MICHAEL P. WALSH, S.J.
Twenty-second President

Born in South Boston on February 28, 1912, Father Walsh maintained a lifelong loyalty to his home town. In the opinion of some, the cordial relationship that existed during his presidency between Father Walsh and Cardinal Richard Cushing was not unrelated to their both being natives of South Boston. Michael Walsh graduated from Boston College High School in June 1929, entered the Society of Jesus that summer, and was ordained a Jesuit priest at Weston College in 1941. His academic bent was towards science and in 1948 he was awarded a Ph.D. in Biology by Fordham University. During the decade 1948–1958 Father Walsh served as chairman of the Biology Department at Boston College. During this period he was prominent in several professional associations related to his work in biology, especially in cytology and genetics, his areas of research. A satisfying corollary to his academic work was his chaplaincy of the Catholic clubs of the Harvard, Tufts, and Boston University medical schools.

necessity of faculty research and publication. With many years of experience as an advisor to the premedical and predental students, he became familiar with the admissions process and student aid, two areas in which he would later become much involved. Through his work with St. Luke's Guild of Catholic Physicians, he came to know many members of the Alumni Association and other "outside" constituencies of the University. Building on this background, Father Walsh would, in time, become a leading spokesman for Catholic higher education in the United States as he further enhanced the national image of Boston College.

Upon taking office, Father Walsh presided over a burgeoning campus that included four undergraduate colleges and four graduate and professional schools. Boston College was in fact, if not in name, a university offering the doctorate in three departments and the master's degree in fourteen departments; in addition, it offered the LL.B., the MBA, and the MSW. Total enrollment stood at 7877 students, with 600 residential undergraduates. The full-time faculty numbered 345; full- and part-time combined totaled 557. Of this number, 135 were Jesuits.

In an interview held shortly after he moved into his office, the new president indicated his areas of concern. Competitive salaries would receive serious consideration; of equal importance to the faculty were office facilities, opportunities for individual research, and added fringe benefits that would facilitate publication. Again focusing on research in his response to an interviewer's question, Father Walsh briefly described some of the research projects at Boston College, several of which were sponsored by governmental agencies, and revealed that he planned to establish "a central office of research to coordinate and develop the work of our present research bureaus." Commenting on the nursing programs and noting the inadequate facilities at 126 Newbury Street, he expressed the hope of bringing the School of Nursing out to the campus as soon as possible. As for a medical school, which was provided for by the charter, he did not see that as a viable possibility in the foreseeable future. Father Walsh was especially interested in expanding campus residences in order to accommodate bright students who were applying for admission; he also envisioned the expansion and modernization of the Bapst Library. As their former advisor, he was proud of the record of science majors and the acceptance of premedical students into recognized medical schools.[2]

A Change of Name?

Since a university is an ongoing enterprise, a new president inherits the projects initiated or undertaken by his predecessor. During his term of office, Father Maxwell had begun to think about the advantages, and disadvantages, of changing the name of Boston College to include the word *university,* which would more accurately describe the true status of the institution. The question first surfaced in 1953 at a meeting of the Board of Trustees. A motion was duly made and seconded "to empower the president to negotiate a change of the name to Boston Catholic University, reserving the name of Boston College to the College of Arts and Sciences."[3] Again in 1956 there was a discussion at a board meeting "about the change of the name Boston College to some title with *university,* such as Botolph University, but it was voted to postpone action to another meeting."[4]

Father Maxwell then decided to open the discussion to Jesuits, administrators, faculty, and alumni. The agenda for a University Council Meeting in February 1957 included an item, "Change in Title to Include University." Father W. Seavey Joyce, dean of the College of Business Administration and a member of the Council, took the occasion to pen a thoughtful five-page letter to the president on this subject. Citing the more glaring problems with the present name, confusion with Boston University, the connotation of a single-unit institution, the not uncommon European application of *college* to secondary schools, the redundancies such as "Boston College

Brendan Connolly, S.J., director of libraries, 1960–1974.

Graduate School," he came down hard in favor of a change. Eliminating other possibilities and dismissing the mystical allegiance to the second and third letters of the alphabet, he strongly urged "Jesuit University of Boston" which, he explained, could be accomplished in several stages.[5]

The question of the name began to generate a great deal of interest among the alumni, who took sides for and against a change. Henry G. Beauregard ('36) addressed an open letter to Father Maxwell with historical arguments for a change. While "*college* may have been adequate in 1863 and 1911," he argued, "it has become a complete misnomer of what, in fact, is a large and expanding university."[6] Like others, he claimed that the change would have been made years ago if it had been a mere matter of substituting *university* for *college*. But that was not possible in Boston. Beauregard opted for "Bellarmine University" in honor of the Jesuit Cardinal and Doctor of the Church. He also provided for the retention of "Boston College" for an undergraduate school.[7]

Using similar arguments, William F. Joy ('40) suggested St. Robert Bellarmine, St. Thomas More University, and Boston Catholic University. "Above all," he wrote, "we must be objective—not sentimental, emotional, or, worse, provincial." Traditional college songs and cheers should not be a determining factor.[8] But Charles W. O'Brien ('33) would have none of it. The former Fulton Prize Debater, employing the rhetorical devices he had learned in his sophomore year, made an impassioned defense of the current name of his alma mater. Examining the word *university,* he wrote, "What magic, then, attached to this mystic word that men desire it?"[9] "It is high time," he continued, "that we junked the inferiority complex that has so long beset us and begin in all humility to take ourselves for granted as a great *university* and 'Boston College' is its name."[10] O'Brien's juxtaposition unwittingly served to clarify the *status questionis*.

Six months into his presidency, Father Walsh appointed a Change of Name Committee, because, as he wrote, "There is a pressing need to seriously consider our present name of Boston College and to change it in the not too distant future."[11] The committee, chaired by Paul FitzGerald, S.J., dean of the Graduate School, held its first meeting in September 1958; the meetings continued through November.[12] It was agreed that, in addition to the confusion with Boston University of which there were many examples, the name penalized the graduate and professional schools. In response to a letter from the chairman, the president of the Jesuit Educational Association wrote, "I do not know on how many occasions I, myself, have had to stop to explain to foreigners . . . that Boston College is not merely a college but a university."[13] He had also encountered problems in proposing Boston College for membership in the International Association of Universities.

The problems were real enough, but the committee realized that there were formidable constituencies that would oppose a change. The greatest opposition would, understandably, come from the alumni whose diplomas have been certified by the Trustees of Boston College. The Development Office, which was planning a fund-raising drive, feared that potential benefactors would be confused. Enrolled undergraduate students were generally satisfied with the name, but there were exceptions. In a thoughtful and somewhat humorous piece in *The Heights,* Brian McNiff clearly voted for the inclusion of University in the name. "We have been an authorized university since 1863, and it is time that we officially recognized the fact in the title of the school."[14] The whole question was further complicated by the work of two other committees, the Planning Committee and the Centenary Committee, whose members wanted to know what suggestions the Name Committee was going to make.

While there was unanimity within the committee on the advantages of changing the name, it was difficult to find a consensus on a new name. In the first place some members preferred to identify *university* with a place, others with the name of a person. But there were problems with both preferences. "University of New England," for example, had a number of votes. However, it was discovered that there existed, in Henniker, New Hampshire, a small school known as New England University. "Newman University" was seriously considered. But, as one member explained, graduates of non-Catholic universities who had belonged to Newman Clubs often referred to themselves as Newman alumni. There was unanimous opposition to Boston College University, Boston Catholic University, Catholic University of Boston, and Jesuit University of Boston.[15] At the same time, there was complete agreement that the name Boston College should be preserved for one of the undergraduate schools.

In the end, the committee made several recommendations to the president. Reasons for and against were attached to the recommendations. For identification with Boston and the Commonwealth of Massachusetts there were: Commonwealth University, Chestnut Hill University, Botolph University, and Tremont University. Other suggestions were: Cheverus U., after the first Bishop of Boston; Campion U., after the Jesuit martyr and man of letters; and Fenwick U. However, since Bishop Fenwick, a Jesuit and the second Bishop of Boston, had founded Holy Cross, there was less enthusiasm for that name. Commonwealth University, one of the preferred titles, was a high-sounding name, identified with the state and situated on Commonwealth Avenue. Boston College would still be used for the name of the undergraduate College of Arts and Sciences, and there were a number of examples of this academic arrangement.[16]

For reasons of his own, the president did not act on the report of the Name Committee. Opposition among the alumni had increased. The fund-raising campaign, organized around the name and achievements of Boston College, may also have been an important factor. Moreover, after the centenary, which had been a target date for the committee, interest waned. There was one last reference in *The Heights*. In a 1963 editorial, which appeared to reflect student opinion, the campus newspaper opposed a change of name. With a rather tortuous and, to some extent, specious, argument, the editorial explained that *university* was derived from *universality*. Since Boston College, in its academic programs, did not embrace every field of learning, it did not deserve to be called a "university."[17] Since then the question has not been revived for serious discussion or resolution.

A New Agenda

The new president lost no time in mapping a course for the future. Throughout his presidency he was a firm believer in the efficacy of committees. In May 1958 he appointed a University Planning Committee, which was charged to develop a 10-year projection in the growth of Boston College. This committee, which was chaired by Father W. Seavey Joyce, plotted its work in two stages: from 1958 to the centenary in 1963; and from 1964 to 1968.[18]

In a memorandum to the administration and faculty, Father Joyce explained that "the objective of the UPC is *to work out a plan for the directed growth of Boston College*." He further stated that "most of the elements involved in the growth of a university may be grouped under four headings: *faculty, students, educational environment,* and *buildings*."[19] It was also hoped that an orderly growth would provide a basis for a financial appeal. To accomplish all this, subcommittees were appointed to interview faculty, key personnel, and other segments of the University. During the first year, 95 persons were interviewed (some in groups), while others submitted written recommendations.

Meeting weekly and guided by materials from the president's office, federal agencies, and private foundations, the committee calculated future enrollments and their effect on faculty recruitment and construction. Father George R. Fuir, director of housing, recommended the immediate addition of 300 rooms for residential students and an increase in dining facilities to accommodate 1000 students.[20] Professor Paul Devlin submitted a new and complex organizational chart for the governance of the University.[21] In an effort to solve a perennial problem, Dean of Students Father Joseph L. Shea presented a plan for a circumferential campus roadway, with innovative traffic and parking patterns, that would reserve the center of the campus for pedestrian use. The location of future buildings also came within the purview of the committee.

In the first year of its existence, the UPC submitted two lengthy reports to the president.[22] The ideas contained in these early reports were expanded and refined in the following years. The committee considered the advisability and extent of an increased student enrollment, an expanded program in scholarship aid, the recruitment of a distinguished faculty (including professorial chairs), the renovation of existing buildings, new construction, boarding facilities, and alumni relations. For new construction, the committee recommended an art center and a new library, both of which were added in later years. With remarkable prescience and anticipating future situations, the committee suggested that a faculty committee, "to serve at least in an advisory capacity, would be a good adjunct to the athletic program."[23] The committee also emphasized the importance of the newly

Martin P. Harney, S.J., of the History Department, whose work from 1936 to 1976 laid the foundation for the current Irish Studies program.

established Office of University Development, which should be considered a continuing and regular part of the life of the University.

In his final report for 1959, Father Joyce "respectfully suggested" that the UPC be continued in the form of a standing committee with a rotating membership. The president accepted this recommendation and the committee, with Father Joyce as permanent chairman, continued beyond the centenary. While the committee had generally focused on the physical growth of the campus, the 1963–1964 report placed a distinct emphasis on fostering the spiritual and religious development of the students. Among other things, it strongly urged the restoration of the annual retreat for all students. Incidentally, this report echoed the resolutions of the 1962 Jesuit workshop on philosophy and theology as academic disciplines and their role in the moral, religious, and spiritual life of the Jesuit college student.[24]

In receiving each report, Father Walsh was effusive in his appreciation of the genuine contribution of the committee, although he did not always agree with its recommendations. A good example of disagreement would be the location of Cushing Hall. The committee urged that the nursing building be placed along Beacon Street facing Campion Hall. Father Walsh decided upon its present location because, among other reasons, he could not afford at that time to raze the temporary wooden structure on Beacon Street which provided essential space for offices and classrooms.

Appointed at the same time as the UPC was the Centenary Committee. Its mandate, as expressed by the president, was to plan "an academic program of a very high calibre to be conducted at an appropriate time near the 100th anniversary of the issuance of a charter to Boston College by the Commonwealth of Massachusetts on April 1, 1863."[25] The committee was given five years to construct a program that would document "the miracle of Chestnut Hill." With an added word of caution, the committee was asked not to collide with the development or public relations offices.

In the early meetings the committee, which was chaired by Father Robert F. Drinan, quickly agreed upon three major areas of concentration that would enhance the University's image.[26] First, it was decided to invite learned societies and other academic groups to schedule their meetings on the campus during the centennial year. Secondly, the committee, by whatever means possible, would endeavor to stimulate the faculty of the various schools in two areas of research: to trace in a professional way, with adequate documentation, the history of Boston College as it evolved in the several undergraduate and graduate programs and, also, to illustrate in an appropriate way the scholarship of the University as reflected in faculty publications. Finally, the committee laid plans for "an impressive academic function lasting for some days, dedicated to top-level discussion of an important theme, to culminate in a convocation at which every major university would be represented." The theme that was eventually chosen, and around which the celebration was planned, was "Strength in Excellence." This theme carried forward the motto of Boston College: "Ever to

Excel." The committee's long-range preparations, under the dynamic leadership of the chairman, insured a successful centennial celebration which will be described in its proper place.[27]

A More Complex Governance

During Father Walsh's tenure, the governance of the University evolved from a relatively simple design to a more complex mechanism which, the experts said, would bring more efficiency to the whole enterprise. In 1957 Boston College was administered by a small staff which included the president, his executive assistant, a treasurer, a director of admissions, academic deans, and department chairmen. Ten years later, in addition to the Board of Trustees, there were the Board of Regents, five vice presidents, the secretary of the University, and several directors of key areas.[28]

In view of their impact on the academic life of the University, two of the more important faculty committees were the University Committee on Promotion and the Faculty Committee on Research. The promotion committee, operating within the 1960 revised university statutes, applied with impartiality the prescriptions for advancement in rank and tenure. Chaired by Father Robert McEwen, chairman of the Economics Department, the committee included several professors who had rendered yeoman service to Boston College. P. Albert Duhamel, a graduate of Holy Cross with a Ph.D. from Wisconsin and a Shakespeare scholar, came to Boston College in 1949 and served the University in many capacities. In 1956 he delivered the Candlemas lecture, choosing as his subject, "The Mind and Art of Thomas More." For several years he was book editor for the *Boston Herald* under the byline, "I've Been Reading." Cornelius Moynihan, another member of the committee, was a respected Law School faculty member, former dean (1936–1937), and later a judge. Trained at Princeton and Columbia, John R. Betts of the History Department was familiar with the strict standards of scholarship applied in the best universities across the country. These men were anxious to advance the academic standing of the University.

Academically linked to the Committee on Promotion was the extremely important Faculty Committee on Research, which was chaired by Russell G. Davis, a member of the School of Education faculty. Successful in obtaining research grants, he was familiar with the design and composition of research applications that would attract the attention of foundations and government agencies. Father William D. Sullivan, another member of the committee, was also instrumental in raising the level of research in the Department of Biology. In the fall of 1959 the president reported that, in the past year, national foundations and federal agencies had provided grants and assistance in the amount of $1,370,000. The National Science Foundation and the Federal Public Health Service had funded research programs in physics, mathematics, chemistry, and nursing.[29]

These grants were not large when compared with the research funding in

Colleagues in the English Department, P. Albert Duhamel and Richard E. Hughes. Duhamel was director of the Arts and Sciences honors program in its formative years. In 1956 he was appointed Philomatheia Professor of English. Hughes was dean of Arts and Sciences 1969–1972.

other universities at the time, but it was a start. Each year the grants became larger, reflecting the increased professional activity of the faculty.[30] In addition, the grants enabled the University to acquire the more sophisticated instrumentation necessary for advanced research in nuclear physics, electrochemistry, and the disease of cancer.[31] And, for the first time, serious thought was given to the construction of a second science building to relieve the cramped laboratory space in Devlin Hall.

Well-equipped buildings are obviously important, even though major discoveries have been made in dimly lit rooms in basement quarters. But the faculty is even more important. A university faculty has a double responsibility: In the search for truth, a committed faculty member seeks to expand and enlarge our knowledge of the world in which we live. In a related capacity, the teacher must pass on to students the accumulated wisdom of the past in order to prepare them for the future. This latter function, which is concerned with the intellectual development of the student, is generally associated with and applied to the undergraduate programs. In the "civilization of intelligence," the Catholic university may be more aware than others of the interrelation of the sacral and secular sciences. In this endeavor, the deans and faculty members at Boston College proposed creative innovations "to lead men to knowledge," as Cardinal Newman would have it.

An Enhanced Honors Program

Mention was made earlier that soon after his appointment as dean in 1958, Father William Casey started a radically new honors program. Since at age 34 the Boston College honors program is nearly a venerable institution as curricular experiments go, some detail should be given of its development and influence. An early "Working Paper for a Definition of an Honors Program" defined its goal in terms of the Parable of the Talents: "It should be the goal of an honors program to make sure that no student buries his talents," and "every student blessed by heredity or early training with more talents than the average should be provided with every motive and opportunity for developing those talents to the utmost."[32] As in other collegiate honors programs, there were certain common notes. The most common characteristic was the provision for freedom in the selection and pursuit of courses—freedom, however, modified by intensification. Another characteristic was the effort to broaden the student's knowledge through a better integration of courses. As a capstone, the honors program seeks to develop the academic and social poise of a student.

A further refinement of the honors program, again initiated by Father Casey, was the "Scholar of the College Program." Few in number, those admitted to this elite rank were the intellectual stars of their class. Identified in second semester of junior year, they were students "who have demonstrated the highest level of academic ability, have intellectual maturity, and (have) demonstrated scholarly accomplishments."[33]

William Van Etten Casey, S.J., academic vice president and dean of the College of Arts and Sciences, with Sir Alec Guinness.

Appointed as Scholars of the College in April 1958 by the dean in consultation with department chairmen and faculty were Carney E. Gavin, an outstanding student from Boston Latin School who later became a priest of the Archdiocese of Boston and associate director of Harvard's Semitic Museum, and Daniel J. Geagan, who had attended La Salle Academy in Providence, Rhode Island. In consultation with his director, each scholar during his senior year had complete freedom to select a program of studies; he was also free to attend classes (which were optional) in any department. Finally, he must submit an honors thesis, and he was expected to graduate *Summa Cum Laude*, which was the case with the first four scholars. In essence, it was an effort to duplicate the English system, with an emphasis on tutorials.[34]

These efforts to improve the academic climate of the campus did not go unrewarded. In March 1958 Father Casey and Professor P. Albert Duhamel collaborated on a proposal which was submitted to the Carnegie Corporation of New York for a grant to fund the honors program. In his covering letter, the dean wrote that the application was submitted in order "to help us in our attempt to improve the quality of education in the Boston area." He continued:

> My interest, and the interest of the newly appointed President of the University, in this particular program is a reflection of our determination to devote the next six years, terminating in our hundredth anniversary, to the development of sound academic policy and the improvement of the quality of education both on and off the campus.[35]

Father Walsh fully supported this endeavor, as he explained in a letter to John Honey, executive associate of the Carnegie Corporation. "In my first interview with the press," he wrote, "I emphasized that one of the central concerns of my administration would be the establishment and development of programs designed to advance quality as the key factor in education."[36] As correspondence, telephone calls, and visits continued, the president, the dean, and Professor Duhamel developed a cordial relationship with Mr. Honey and the Corporation.

In its proposal, Boston College had asked for $79,700 to be paid over a three-year period in four installments. These funds were to cover the salaries for the contracted services of a director, faculty seminar leaders, secretarial staff, and other items. In June 1958 the Carnegie Corporation awarded Boston College a grant of $84,700 to be paid in four installments, "toward development of its honors program." Boston College was free to announce the grant at any time and in any suitable manner.[37]

With this grant, the honors program came under the academic supervision of Professor Duhamel, who was appointed director of the Office of Special Programs. He was assisted by the Honors Advisory Committee. In describing the program in its own publication, the Corporation acknowledged that "some Catholic educators have expressed concern that Catholic

*Father Frederick Adelmann,
chairman of the Philosophy
Department, 1956–1965.*

education has not made a large enough contribution to the preparation of
scientists, research men, and college teachers." (The editor added paren-
thetically, "They might be relieved to know that their colleagues in secular
colleges feel the same way about their own institutions.") But the members
of the Corporation were also convinced that "Boston College is determined
to provide superior programs for talented students and challenge them to
think in terms of excellence."[38]

Women in Arts and Sciences

In concluding its account, and implying that the Carnegie Corporation had
some part in it, the *Quarterly* gratuitously noted that, after 96 years,
women were to be admitted to the College of Arts and Sciences. Although
not quite accurate, this comment introduces an interesting story, even in its
briefest form. It is also rather complicated. After the announcement of the
honors program, which was described in a special flyer, college advisors
and student counselors in high schools informed the Office of Special
Programs that a number of their gifted female students had expressed an
interest in the program. Somewhat familiar with the policies at Boston
College, these advisors wrote to ask if the honors program was open to
women as well as men.[39] These inquiries forced the president, the deans,
and the director to search for an answer that would be acceptable to all
concerned.

On the one hand, the director of special programs did not want to turn away gifted female students who were planning a career in research, medicine, or law. These students were not interested in a career in elementary or secondary school teaching. On the other hand, women had never been admitted to the undergraduate College of Arts and Sciences, and permission to do so would require an affirmative response from the Jesuit General and the New England Provincial. It was finally decided to admit women to the Arts and Sciences courses. To observe the existing policy of admission, however, they were required to register in the School of Education, which was already coeducational. But this arrangement, in turn, caused jurisdictional and administrative problems.

The Arts and Sciences dean wanted a clarification. "Does Father Donovan, dean of the School of Education, clearly understand," he asked the president, "that academically talented women who do not want education courses or practice teaching will be under the jurisdiction of the College of Arts and Sciences in special programs once they have been admitted?"[40] Initially, Father Donovan had misgivings. Pointing out that inaccurate statements had been made in *The Heights* and elsewhere and left uncorrected, he preferred to disassociate the School of Education from the program for women that was being formed in A&S.[41] Two weeks later he relented and spelled out his and Albert Duhamel's understanding of the arrangement: "Women in the A&S program will be registered in the School of Education but will have no further academic connection with it. They will be fully admitted to the A&S Honors Program (under Professor Duhamel's direction), will take all courses in the College of Arts and Sciences, and will get an A.B. degree."[42]

That is exactly what happened to six female students who registered in the School of Education in the fall of 1959. They were immediately enrolled in the honors program and, during four years, were gradually assimilated into the College of Arts and Sciences and graduated with an A.B. honors degree in June 1963. As some had predicted, however, there were repercussions beyond the campus. The Jesuit Provincial of New England, while allowing the six students to continue, reminded Father Walsh that permission would have to be obtained from Rome before additional female students were admitted to Arts and Sciences. In retrospect, it was clear that these women had paved the way for a fully integrated coeducational College of Arts and Sciences when that permission was granted in 1969.

Funding from Outside

The School of Education did not lag far behind the College of Arts and Sciences in designing its own honors program. With the encouragement of Father Donovan, Professor Russell Davis was the chief architect of the new program which, although tailored to the professional curriculum of the School of Education, manifested the characteristics of this type of program.

Stanley Bezuszka, S.J., long-time chairman of the Mathematics Department and director of the Mathematics Institute. He introduced an early form of computer to the campus in the late fifties.

Thus, according to Professor Davis, "Schools must provide programs which *will stretch students* toward the limit of their intellectual capacity."[43] This was the rationale, of course, of all such programs.

A proposal was submitted to the Ford Foundation (Fund for the Advancement of Education) for funding. The initial request, for a four-year cycle, was for $56,815. After officials of the foundation explained to Father Walsh that this sum was in excess of what the foundation might be prepared to do, the proposal was scaled down to a more acceptable amount.[44] The revised proposal was submitted, and in December 1958 Father Walsh was notified that the Ford Foundation would fund the honors program with a grant of $25,000.[45] Father William E. FitzGerald, former Provincial Superior of the New England Province, was appointed director of the honors program in the School of Education.

There were other signs that the faculty and programs at Boston College were making a favorable impression beyond the campus. In October 1958 the National Science Foundation made a grant of $200,000 to the Boston College Institute of Modern Mathematics. The institute, with a grant of $10,000, had been founded by Father Stanley Bezuszka, S.J., who had gained widespread recognition for his fresh approach to the teaching of mathematics. With advanced degrees from Brown University, Father Bezuszka became a nationally recognized leader in the preparation of teachers of mathematics, and he has been a frequent participant in national and international conferences on teacher preparation.[46]

The preparation of secondary school teachers was not confined to mathematics. For three consecutive summers, beginning in 1959, the Coe Foundation in New York City funded an Institute in American Studies with an annual grant of $10,000 under the sponsorship of the Department of History and Government of the Graduate School.[47] Each summer the institute awarded 25 fellowships to outstanding high school teachers in history, social studies, and American literature. The fund also provided a stipend for two visiting professors for the Summer Institute, which was under the direction of John R. Betts, professor of American history. During the year 1958–1959 another grant from the Coe Foundation underwrote a series, the Coe Lectures in American Civilization, which brought to the campus such well-known figures as Allan Nevins, Clinton Rossiter, Charles Callan Tansill, and Oscar Handlin.[48]

There was also cause for satisfaction at the graduate level. Although the doctoral programs in economics, education, and history were still in their infancy, federal agencies were willing to support them. With the passage of the National Defense Education Act in 1958, in the wake of Sputnik, federal programs were funded which aimed at producing college and university teachers from institutions of wide geographical distribution. Five of these fellowships were made available to doctoral students at Boston College. The stipends, beginning with $2000 the first year and gradually increasing, were for three years. In a three-year period, Boston College Graduate School received about $70,000. These awards, which also provided stipends for dependents, enabled several students in the Graduate School to plan a career in teaching.[49]

A Changing Student Body

In September 1959, while the president, his deans, and faculty were organizing an improved sequence of courses, Boston College welcomed the largest class in its history. Selected from 4300 applicants, 1350 freshmen arrived on campus for the start of the academic year. The total number of resident students—also a record—was 670: 300 freshmen, 200 sophomores, and 170 juniors. With a director of housing, Jesuit prefects in the dormitories, and expanded dining facilities in Lyons Hall, students from New York, New Jersey, Ohio, and Pennsylvania were introduced to the famous Boston accent. Irish surnames still outnumbered others on the class rosters, but an increased representation from other ethnic backgrounds brought a cosmopolitan atmosphere to the campus—a good development in every way.

That same class (September 1959), which would graduate in the centennial year, was by ordinary academic indexes the best prepared scholastically to accept the intellectual challenge at Boston College. It was generally agreed by the admission officers that the influx of superior students was due at least in part to the announcement of the honors program. It was, indeed, one of the fruits of a program which encourages advanced standing. It was also due to the president's aggressive recruitment of national merit scholars and the dramatic increase in student aid which began to match the offers of other schools. On-site visits by Boston College faculty members encouraged a better articulation between high schools and the University.

Not only were the students challenged in the classrooms, but their horizons were broadened by the appearance on campus of some of the most exciting personalities in the United States and abroad. Sir Alec Guinness, the distinguished British actor of stage and screen, charmed the audience with his readings of Christian verse and prose. The medical missionary, Dr. Thomas Dooley, who had shocked the conscience of the world by his charitable work in Laos, moved the students with stories of the sick and starving people of Southeast Asia. James "Scottie" Reston, the Washington bureau chief of the *New York Times*, introduced students to the precarious and controversial world of the political pundit. And the presence of the distinguished British economist, Lady Barbara Ward Jackson, attested to the quality of the Tobin Lecture Series and provided an ideal role model for the women on campus who were struggling with ambitions of their own.

*   *   *

As the years went by and Boston College approached its one hundredth birthday, the Tower Building was no longer the solitary sentinel erected by Father Gasson. In the early 1960s, it had become the centerpiece of an attractive campus that boasted 30 buildings—some constructed, some purchased. With the relocation to Chestnut Hill of the Intown College and the School of Nursing, it was easier to coordinate the academic programs in the various schools now clustered on a single campus. It also made for a more judicious and equitable assignment of University faculty members.

But, in common with other institutions, there were also problems. There was never enough money to do all the things that the administration wanted to do. The very small, almost nonexistent endowment yielded very little income to fund selected projects; the absolute necessity of an increase in student aid limited other initiatives. The faculty worked in cramped office space. With a faculty that had been traditionally teaching-oriented, research and publication were only now beginning to receive the attention that professional standing demanded. Although proud of its history, Boston College had launched an effort to change its image from that of a local college to a broader image that would more accurately reflect its changing student population.

But the problems were not insuperable, nor did they bring discouragement. They only increased the determination to excel.

ENDNOTES

1. As he left Boston College, Father Maxwell accepted an invitation to act as a consultant and advisor to the president of the Pontifical Catholic University of Rio de Janeiro, Brazil, for a period of six months to direct the reorganization of that Jesuit institution. He later had an influential career as a missionary pastor in Jamaica.
2. *Alumni News* (Spring 1958), pp. 5–7.
3. Minutes, Board of Trustees, November 3, 1953. BCA.
4. Minutes, Board of Trustees, November 29, 1956. BCA.
5. W. Seavey Joyce, S.J., to Father Maxwell, February 20, 1956. BCA.
6. May 28, 1956. See *Alumni News* (Commencement issue, 1956), p. 18.
7. *Ibid.*
8. *Alumni News* (Fall 1956), p. 2.
9. *Ibid.*
10. *Ibid.*
11. Father Walsh to Donald J. White, August 7, 1958. BCA.
12. The other members of the committee were Charles Donovan, S.J., Robert Drinan, S.J., Donald J. White, John Donovan, John Walsh, and William Daly.
13. Edward B. Rooney, S.J., to Paul A. FitzGerald, S.J., November 21, 1958. BCA.
14. October 24, 1958, p. 5.
15. Although these names were not favored by the committee, there were others within the University and beyond who were strongly in favor of one of them. These names were revived (along with Kennedy University) several years later, at the time of the centenary. At that time, Father Charles Donovan, academic vice president, surveyed 30 presidents and academic vice presidents of substantial private universities nationwide on the wisdom of changing the name. Several urged that no change be made.
16. Committee minutes and associated materials are preserved in the archives.
17. October 25, 1963, p. 8.
18. The other members of the initial UPC were Paul A. Devlin, J. J. Collins, S.J., Paul T. Heffron, William G. Guindon, S.J., John E. Murphy, S.J., John E. Van Tassel, and Vincent P. Wright.
19. "Some Notes on Planning." BCA.
20. Minutes, UPC, August 5, 1959.
21. *Ibid.*
22. One is entitled "Preliminary Report of the UPC," February 1959. The second is entitled "University Planning Committee: Final Report," July 1959.
23. "Preliminary Report," p. 30.
24. This workshop was sponsored by the Jesuit Educational Association and held at Loyola University, Los Angeles. It is found in the JEA Collection, BCA.
25. "Preliminary Report of the Committee on the Centenary of Boston College." BCA.
26. The other members of the committee were Russell G. Davis, James O. Dunn, Walter J. Fimian, Richard W. Rousseau, S.J., and Francis W. Sweeney, S.J.
27. Assisting the Centennial Committee were John Larner, Director of Public Relations, and John Tevnan, Office of Development. A complete account of the work of the Centennial Committee is preserved in the archives.
28. Established in 1960, the Board of Regents was comprised mainly of prominent businessmen who acted as advisors to the president. The origin and function of the regents will be treated in a later chapter.
29. "Report from Father Rector," *Alumni News* (Fall 1959), pp. 5–6.
30. In 1984 total grants from federal agencies and other sources totaled $6,788,000.

31. "Research the Key to the Unknown," *Alumni News* (Fall 1961), pp. 4–11.
32. BCA.
33. *The Heights* (April 25, 1958).
34. See *The Pilot* (May 24, 1958); also an excellent article in the B.C.–B.U. Football Program, November 15, 1958.
35. Father Casey to John C. Honey, March 18, 1958. BCA.
36. May 5, 1958. BCA.
37. Florence Anderson to Father Walsh, June 19, 1958. BCA.
38. *Quarterly* (Carnegie Corporation of N.Y.), vol. VII, No. 3 (July 1959).
39. See, for example, Frederic T. Hawes, College Advisor at Stamford High School, to Office of Special Programs, October 27, 1958. BCA.
40. Father Casey to Father Walsh, October 30, 1958. BCA.
41. Father Donovan to Father Walsh, March 28, 1959. BCA.
42. Father Donovan to Father Walsh, with copies to Father Casey and P. Albert Duhamel, April 11, 1959. BCA.
43. "Proposal: An Honors Program for Undergraduates in Education." BCA.
44. Father Walsh to Dr. Clarence H. Faust, October 29, 1958. BCA.
45. Stanley W. Gregory to Father Walsh, December 5, 1958. BCA.
46. Correspondence and proposals in archives. See *The Heights* (October 24, 1958).
47. William Robertson Coe, born in England but a naturalized American citizen, amassed a fortune in the insurance industry. Among his best-known benefactions are the Coe Collection in Western Americana and the Coe Chair in American Studies at Yale University.
48. BCA. See also *The Heights* (December 4, 1959), p. 1.
49. *The Heights* (January 15, 1960).

CHAPTER 28

The University
at Age One Hundred

The rapid growth of the University in the postwar decades made every president a builder whether he was attracted to that role or not. Father Maxwell was an enthusiastic builder who drew floor plans of buildings at his desk in St. Mary's Hall. In contrast, Father Michael Walsh protested his inexperience where building was concerned, claiming that his only preparation had been building boxes for the biology greenhouse and cages for the laboratories.[1] Yet there were very few months during Father Walsh's 10-year tenure that a new building was not under construction.

A Time of Building

The first academic building in the Walsh era was a facility for the School of Nursing. Since Cardinal Cushing had been influential in the founding of this school, it was fitting that the funds for its building came from his impressive fund-raising talent. The cardinal contributed nearly a million dollars.

Father William Guindon, chairman of the Physics Department, headed a planning committee for Cushing Hall and acted as advisor to the president on the project. A ground-breaking ceremony was held on February 20, 1959, and 13 months later the faculty and students of the School of

Cushing Hall.

Nursing moved from Newbury Street to the new building at Chestnut Hill. Cardinal Cushing presided at dedication ceremonies on March 25, 1960.

Three months before Cushing Hall was completed, in December 1959, ground was broken for three more residences on Tudor Road and Hammond Street. These were eventually given the last names of the first three bishops of Boston: Jean Louis de Cheverus, Benedict Fenwick, and John B. Fitzpatrick. They were planned to accommodate 378 students and 19 resident prefects.[2] Under construction for nine months, the dormitories were ready for the opening of classes in the fall and were dedicated, with Cardinal Cushing once more presiding, on September 15, 1960.

With the resident student population growing, the need for adequate dining facilities had become truly desperate, a need that Father Walsh began to address as soon as he became president. But there were many other needs—almost as urgent—for offices and meeting rooms for student clubs, for recreational space, and for an enlarged bookstore, to name only a few. The administration's preliminary thinking about how to meet these varied needs was expressed by some of the president's top aides in a 34-page document that appeared in July 1959 entitled, "The University Center." The document's diffuse focus and assorted recommendations showed how "underbuilt" the University was despite the ambitious building program that had been under way for more than a decade.

The first page of "The University Center" paper contained this statement: "Although a physically large proportion of the Center will be dining rooms for boarding students, this preponderance must not overshadow the main purpose of providing a cultural home for all members of the University family . . . stimulation of the cultural life of Boston College should issue from every aspect of the Center."[3] These were noble aspirations, but practical necessity won out, and the finished building emphasized dining far more than culture. Indeed, the authors of "The University Center" proposed that the building house an interesting melange of noncultural facilities: an infirmary, a post office, a university store, the placement bureau, a bowling alley, a billiard room, and rooms for crafts and hobbies. On the cultural side it was proposed that the center have music listening rooms, accommodations for musical clubs, an art salon, speaking rooms, and a theater. The last suggestion would seem to have been very difficult to carry out simply in terms of space requirements, but a year later Father Walsh wrote to the architects about a theater.[4]

At the time construction began, Father Walsh referred to the new building as the student-faculty center.[5] The groundbreaking ceremony was held after the Mass of the Holy Spirit for the start of the academic year on September 21, 1960. Begun just after Cheverus, Fenwick, and Fitzpatrick were completed, the building—eventually named McElroy, for the University's founder—was under construction for 15 months and was dedicated on November 9, 1961.

The array of needs that planners of McElroy Commons hoped the building would fill proved how facility-poor Boston College was at the time Father Walsh assumed the presidency. Yet McElroy offered no solution to a perhaps more pressing problem from a collegiate viewpoint: lack of suitable office space for the faculty. The professional schools on campus—Law, Business, Education, and Nursing—had been provided with new buildings, and while these structures were not exactly generous in their provision of space for offices, they were light years ahead of what was available for the Arts and Sciences faculty. The ends of corridors in Gasson were blocked off with temporary partitions, converting the space into offices for as many as four faculty members. A few classrooms were converted into "offices" by introducing 10 desks for faculty. In short, the high-quality faculty the University had attracted, and was attempting to attract, needed better accommodations for scholarly work and interaction with students. Carney Hall was to be the answer to this need.

In writing to Father James Coleran, S.J., the Provincial, about his plans for a faculty building, Father Walsh made some revealing comments:

> The first of the buildings that I would like to construct from the funds we are receiving for our Development Program is the Graduate Center. This is a building that will give us some more classroom space, seminar rooms, and primarily office space for faculty.
>
> At present we are cramped for suitable space for our Jesuit and lay faculty. Our Jesuits are generally forced to use the parlors in St. Mary's Hall for consultation and guidance of our students. Many of the lay faculty are in offices with anywhere from six to ten other individuals.
>
> It is my hope through this new building to give each of our faculty an individual office or cubicle. In this way I think we can achieve greater results in research, publication, counseling, and teaching from our faculty. As you

perhaps know, our faculty have been very satisfied with the salaries and fringe benefits they have attained in recent years. The only drawback at times is adequate faculty office space.

I have been calling this building a graduate center, but for the most part it will be a faculty office building. . . .[6]

Almost a year after Father Walsh's letter to the Provincial, ground was broken for the faculty office building on April 16, 1963, right in the midst of Boston College's centennial celebrations. The building was under construction for nearly a year and a half. Carney was dedicated on September 18, 1964, named for the earliest major benefactor of Boston College, Andrew Carney.

While Carney was still under construction in the spring of 1964, the final three residence halls of the upper campus—Welch, Williams, and Roncalli—were begun. To make room for the new buildings, the former Stimson home on Hammond Street, purchased for the University by the Philomatheia Club in 1936, was razed. Welch and Williams were ready for occupancy in September, but Roncalli's completion was delayed until December because of the need to move a house from that site to a location on Beacon Street. Roncalli was occupied by students in September 1965.[7]

As a scientist who had been promoted from the chairmanship of the Biology Department to the presidency, Father Walsh was well aware of Boston College's inadequate science facilities as the institution's centennial approached. Opened in 1924, Devlin Hall had been planned primarily for undergraduate science courses. With the new emphasis on graduate education and, indeed, with the impending start of doctoral programs in chemistry (1960), physics (1961), and biology (1963), new and more sophisticated facilities were needed. The science departments were encouraged to plan for expansion. As early as January 1960 the Physics Department prepared a 22-page document entitled, "A Study of the Space Needs of the Physics Department, 1960–1975."[8] Two months later the Biology Department submitted a proposal for a biology building.[9] To make the planning more comprehensive and coordinated, Father Walsh appointed a faculty committee, with Father James Devlin of the Physics Department as chairman, to make recommendations for a new science building. The committee submitted a report in August 1961.[10] Another committee, referred to as the 1961–1962 Science Building Committee, submitted a preliminary report in February 1962 which recommended that Devlin Hall be renovated and modernized for the Chemistry Department.

Father Walsh's own thinking about the proposed science facility was developing along different lines from those of the departments and the committees. As late as August 1962 he said that he had considered having all undergraduate science remain in Devlin, with a new science building serving as a research and graduate center for two or three sciences.[11] But not long after that Father Walsh settled on the plan for separate new and complete facilities for physics and biology, explaining that each science would be in its own wing—the equivalent of separate buildings.[12] Chemistry would remain in Devlin.

Ground was broken for the new science building on March 29, 1965. Assisting Father Walsh in the ceremony were Stephen P. Mugar, president and director of Star Markets, who contributed over half a million dollars for the building, and John P. Higgins of Arlington, a long-time personal and professional friend of Mugar's, for whom Mugar wanted the new science facility named. The cost of Higgins Hall was $5,500,000 with $1,600,000 in federal grants aiding the project. The 136,000 square foot V-shaped building, with one wing devoted to biology and the other to physics as planned, was equipped with laboratory facilities and equipment that provided the two sciences it served with the most up-to-date resources for advanced research as well as basic collegiate science courses.[13]

Higgins Hall was dedicated with elaborate two-day ceremonies on the 11th and 12th of November 1966. Scientific papers were read and discussed on the first day and representatives of 135 universities attended a convocation in Roberts Center the following day. Honorary degrees were awarded to Dr. George Beadle, president of the University of Chicago and 1958 Nobel laureate in medicine and physiology; Dr. William B. Castle, of the

In the spring of the centennial year, ground was broken for a building whose major function was to provide long-awaited faculty offices. Assisting Cardinal Cushing and Father Walsh was distinguished classics professor Joseph P. Maguire. The building was named for early benefactor Andrew Carney.

Harvard Medical School and Boston City Hospital; Dr. James Van Allen, pioneer in space physics, of the University of Iowa; and Dr. Donald F. Hornig, special advisor on science to President Johnson.[14] In his welcoming remarks Father Walsh used the science setting to stress a theme familiar at Boston College—namely, the danger of slighting the humanities. He said, "I sometimes wonder if there might be a danger of overemphasis on science research, due primarily to the availability of grants from government agencies and foundations. As a biologist myself, I think I might be absolved of any charge of minimizing the importance of research, but as an educator I sometimes wonder if the comparative neglect of some areas of the humanities might indicate a danger of neglecting the training of the scientist as a man."

Even as preparations were under way for the dedication of the new science building, the fall issue of the *Alumni News* announced the imminent start of a building dedicated to the social sciences. Father Walsh was aware that the full range of social sciences was late in developing at Boston College and needed special attention and encouragement. As a sign of commitment to the social sciences, Father Walsh invested considerable personal effort and University funds in setting up a research center that came to be called the Institute of Human Sciences. It was expected that the institute would attract major research grants concerning social problems that a university with Boston College's ideals would want to address. Father Walsh's ambitious hopes for the institute were not fully realized, although it attracted talented social scientists, some of whom have remained at the University and made significant contributions within their several disciplines. Though the Institute of Human Sciences disappointed expectations, it may have indirectly benefited the basic social science departments; certainly those departments are far stronger than they were in 1968.

A member of the Board of Regents, Sidney Rabb, along with a colleague, Alfred L. Morse, headed a drive among the Jewish community of Greater Boston for funds for the social sciences building. Significantly the group established to assist Rabb and Morse was called the Institute of Human Sciences Fiscal Committee. It was fitting that when ground was broken for the proposed building in the spring of 1967, Sidney Rabb and Alfred Morse joined Father Walsh and Cardinal Cushing for the ceremony.[15]

One of the principal purposes of the social sciences building was to provide a campus home for the Graduate School of Social Work, which until then had been located at 126 Newbury Street. Appropriately the building was named for the founder and first dean of the Graduate School of Social Work, Father Walter McGuinn, and his brother, Father Albert McGuinn, who served many years as chairman of the Chemistry Department. McGuinn Hall opened in September 1968.

The Board of Regents

In carrying out the ambitious building program he had undertaken, Father Walsh relied heavily on the prudent advice and support of the Board of Regents. This distinguished group, distinct from the Jesuit Board of Trustees, was an innovation in the governance of the University. The board was organized in 1959. At that time, working with Thomas J. Cudmore, an alumnus of the Graduate School of Social Work and then director of the Office of Development, the president's office assembled a list of names—including alumni and non-alumni—of people who had achieved outstanding success in their fields of endeavor. In moving toward such an advisory body, Father Walsh had the example of a number of Jesuit universities that had established similar boards. Although the title varied from institution to institution, the purpose of the boards was generally similar: to meet periodically, usually between meetings of the Board of Trustees, to assist in long-range planning, to evaluate current problems, and to advise the president on such matters as capital development and deficit financing. The board members, as prominent men in the local community, were especially helpful in promoting public understanding of and support for the institution. In response to Father Walsh's invitation to join the board, these men were remarkably enthusiastic in offering their services to Boston College. Henry M. Leen, Esquire, class of 1929, became chairman of the board. Christopher Duncan, who was chairman of the Centennial Development Program, was also on the board. The names of other members appear at the end of the chapter.[16]

The Board of Regents met for the first time on September 27, 1960. In his remarks that afternoon, Father Walsh said, "It is a source of real satisfaction and consolation to have men of your calibre on whom we can rely and on whose judgment and recommendations we can depend."[17] He was confident that "you can assist not only on some of the financial and business problems of the University but also in the field of public relations and in many other areas that I will touch upon toward the end of this meeting."[18] After drawing a detailed picture of the University at that time—enrollments, faculty, assets, operational expenses, and budget—the president outlined his plans for the future and touched upon some of the problems. His immediate concern was the successful outcome of the Centennial Fund Campaign, on which he enlisted their advice and assistance. From 1960 to 1968, when the Board of Regents was replaced by the Board of Directors, these men, generous with their time and money, were of inestimable value to the president. In launching the University on its second century, they provided a needed cushion of security.

A Self-Appraisal by Arts and Sciences

With all the building that was going on during his presidency, one might conclude that Father Walsh was totally preoccupied with construction. Far

*Robert Frost was a star attraction of
the Humanities Series for years.
With him are Father Francis Sweeney and Wayne A. Budd ('63), now
U.S. Attorney for Massachusetts.*

from it. He was primarily an educator, and no project during his regime
had more of his interest than the self-study of the College of Arts and
Sciences. At the convocation in 1962 the president announced that there
would be a far-reaching self-appraisal of the College of Arts and Sciences
the following academic year, 1963–1964. The self-study was launched by
Father Walsh in a letter to the Arts and Sciences faculty in April 1963.

The executive committee of the self-study consisted of the academic vice
president, Father Charles Donovan, chairman, Father John McCarthy (the
College dean), Robert Carovillano (physics), John Mahoney (English),
Donald White (economics), and the president, *ex-officio*. Mahoney served
as executive director of the self-study. President Victor Butterfield of
Wesleyan University agreed to be adviser to the project. A prominent
spokesman for liberal education, Butterfield brought a wise and sympathetic outsider's view to the faculty's deliberations. He gave the keynote
address at the fall faculty convocation in 1963, met with several of the
committees in subsequent months, and after reading the final reports
submitted a wise and paternal critique. A faculty advisory council, consisting of two members from each of the academic divisions (humanities,
physical sciences, and social sciences) was elected to serve as liaison
between the faculty and the executive committee. The departmental membership of the advisory council was Joseph Chen (chemistry), William Daly
(history), Malcolm McLoud (classics), Paul Michaud (history), David
O'Donnell (chemistry), and Maurice Quinlan (English). Father Walsh's
original vision for the self-study was a department-by-department exami-

nation and updating of curriculum not only in the core area but especially in the majors.[19]

It was decided that while the departments were working on their self-appraisals, some committees should be attacking a few broad issues of concern to the entire college. At the fall convocation the faculty chose six areas for special study and established committees on total curriculum, intellectual climate, library, research activities, the honors program, and guidance.[20] These committees and topics became quite influential in the eventual outcomes of the self-study. It is somewhat ironic that what was envisioned as primarily a departmental undertaking had mild results at the departmental level, whereas many sweeping changes emerged from the college committees. In his final letter of advice after reading the self-study reports, President Butterfield gently warned against excessive emphasis on departmental autonomy at Boston College. It is significant that the major changes of the self-study came not from departmental but from collective deliberation.

The most far-reaching and lasting ideas came out of the Committee on the Total Curriculum, chaired by Father James Skehan. Generations of Boston College students had carried a heavy course load: six courses a semester, for a total of 48 courses for graduation. The curriculum committee recommended a decrease of 12 courses for the bachelor's degree. The Executive Committee ultimately modified this recommendation to a 10-course reduction (for a total of 38 in four years), with five courses per semester for each of the first three years and four courses per semester (with an optional fifth course) in senior year. This distribution of courses is in effect at the present time.

As the total curriculum, so the core curriculum was reduced. The final recommendation was that half of the courses (19) be devoted to the common core, to be distributed as follows:

Theology	5 courses
Philosophy	4 courses
English	2 courses
History	2 courses
Natural Science	2 courses
Mathematics	2 courses
Languages	2 courses

In the years immediately following the self-study, under the influence of the Second Vatican Council and other forces at work in the Church, the Theology and Philosophy departments voluntarily reduced their participation in the core curriculum. Otherwise, the recommended core curriculum was eventually adopted and was in effect until further revisions in 1971.

The rationale for a slimmed-down course load can probably best be gleaned from correspondence of Father Walsh with the Provincial, Father

John V. O'Connor, in the following year when he was seeking approval for the proposed new curriculum. In his first letter, Father Walsh explained:

> In an effort to provide a more scholarly and reflective setting for the college experience, it is our hope to cut the present 48-course schedule to 38 courses, with five in each of the first three years and four in the senior year (per semester). Within this less course-burdened schedule, there has also been an attempt to provide for the freedom to take advanced electives in the traditional humanistic areas such as English, languages, and history, while at the same time giving adequate but not overbalanced attention to the student's major area of study and to preparation for graduate study.[21]

In reply, Father O'Connor said that he felt he had to get approval from Rome, because the suggested changes departed so sharply from the curriculum last approved by Father General in 1959. To help him make the most suasive case in favor of Boston College's request, the Provincial posed a series of probing questions.[22] The nub of Father Walsh's reply is found in the following paragraph.

> As a preface let me say, since several of your questions focus on our requested reduction of courses required in the core curriculum, that we are keenly concerned to preserve the integrity and spirit of the Jesuit liberal arts tradition as far as this can possibly be done within a reduced course load. The key factor here, as is obvious, is our conviction—a conviction not unique to us among Jesuit colleges—that our students are carrying a course load that is too heavy. With some of the finest colleges turning to a schedule that limits each student's courses to three per term and many more colleges not permitting their students to carry more than four courses per term, it has become evident that to have our students carry six courses per term makes it difficult to achieve some of the best goals of contemporary education in terms of more reflective study and writing, more independent work, and greater opportunity for the enjoyment of genuine scholarly leisure. It is, therefore, not by any means for the purpose of lessening the effectiveness or contribution of the liberal arts that the suggested reductions are made, but in order to provide what we sincerely feel is a schedule of studies better fitted to the talents and previous education of our current students, more consonant with the present trend in higher education to place more responsibility upon the individual student for self-direction in his education, and better adapted to the realistic needs of today's undergraduates as regards preparation for graduate education.[23]

Father Walsh's thinking on the reasons for the proposed curriculum change clearly reflected a consensus that had been established among the faculty at Boston College. Approval eventually came, and the new program of studies was put in place in September 1965.

In the letter just cited, Father Walsh's reference to a three-course load per term was significant because that became the cause championed by the Committee on the Total Curriculum. In reviewing alternative scheduling programs, the committee became familiar with the Dartmouth College plan of three courses a semester spread over a trimester that included an occasional summer. Not a great deal of enthusiasm for the Dartmouth plan was generated among the faculty at large, but the Total Curriculum Committee made a heavy commitment to it. Indeed, the committee's strong recommendation of the so-called three-three program was undoubtedly the most radical proposal to come out of the self-study. But the community did not warm to the suggestion.

At the conclusion of the self-study the academic vice president drew up for Father Walsh a list of 30 recommendations adopted and transmitted by the Executive Committee calling for action by the University administration.[24] A sample, including some challenging and some routine recommendations, follows:

- Establish an educational policy committee.
- Move toward the election of department chairmen.
- Establish a system of sabbatical leaves to replace the somewhat restricted faculty fellowships.
- Expand secretarial service for faculty.
- Increase funds for graduate assistantships.
- Give high priority to the building of a new library.
- Increase the funds available for book purchases.
- Increase the library staff.
- Expand the admissions office.
- Add a full-time clinical psychologist to the guidance office.
- Appoint a director of foreign students.
- Review the system of spiritual retreats for Catholic students.

Of these recommendations, the one concerning the library was slowest in being fulfilled. Higgins, McGuinn, the theater, and lower-campus residences preceded O'Neill Library. This delay, in hindsight, was fortuitous. It is highly unlikely that in the mid-sixties the University would have undertaken a project as massive or successful as O'Neill.

The great majority of the recommendations of the self-study were put into effect—if not immediately, then within a year or two. The self-study should not, however, be given total credit for all that followed, for a number of changes were already under active consideration before it was undertaken. For example, academic administrators at Boston College and other Jesuit colleges had long been aware of the heavy course load carried by the students. But the self-study involved the academic community and gave the blessings of collegial consensus to changes toward which the institution had been moving.

Butterfield's Recommendations

In his response to the reports and recommendations of the self-study, President Butterfield of Wesleyan was generous in his praise and sage in his admonitions, several of which deserve recording here. Butterfield felt there was danger of the University moving too far toward a graduate school orientation, with primary emphasis on specialization in a discipline rather than on breadth of culture. He saw departments, in growing strength and self-absorption, as potential villains. He wrote:

> It seems to me that the heavy emphasis on departmentalization symbolizes and encourages a kind of specialization that we don't want. It tends to exclude or discourage cultural breadth and range and intellectual variety and versatility in scholars and teachers, and puts them in the false position of insisting on such qualities in their students while they don't have them themselves. It also limits the possibilities for a genuine community of scholars, and tends to weaken rather than strengthen the kind of intellectual climate or atmosphere that is so vital in the life of scholars and the education of students.

Related to his reservations about heavy departmental orientation was Butterfield's second warning, on the subject of research:

> Research is now a loaded word with faculty members, and to be at all critical is apt to put you in the position of seeming to be against the whole idea. I wish there were a better word for it, and that we could conceive of our faculty members as being constant "learners" as well as teachers. Perhaps the word "research" has this connotation for some, but I doubt for many since it has become a kind of fetish, and its essence is symbolized in both academic and popular mind by scientific research.

President Butterfield believed in institutional—not merely departmental—involvement in faculty recruitment. As president he was active in the process of appointments to the faculty. Indeed the author first met him on a plane when he was traveling to visit the campus of a prospective member of the Wesleyan faculty. His third admonition reflected his philosophy of faculty recruitment:

> Most faculty members should be good with the average undergraduate, though it is important to recognize those teachers who are especially good with majors or with graduate students. Some faculty people have to be good administrators and like it. Some are especially good to carry the educational adventure to the extramural world, and this is important too. A faculty must, in fact, in the right balance reflect collectively the various functions of the institution, and I think we have to stay aware of this and be careful not to apply the same formula to all faculty appointments although of course the dominant type should be the broad, cultivated scholar-teacher who is thoroughly competent in a special field.[25]

President Butterfield had a richly articulated philosophy of liberal education. He served Boston College well as adviser in the 1963–1964 self-study. The College of Arts and Sciences might serve its own interests well by reconsidering, after several decades, the advice Butterfield gave.

Honor Societies: The Long Road to Omicron

The accreditation of colleges and universities—their several schools, departments, and programs—by regional and professional associations attests to the fact that degrees from an accredited institution will be recognized by the academic world. But accreditation, of and by itself, does not measure the level of quality. The approval of national honor societies, however, has always carried with it the mark of academic distinction. As indicated earlier, Alpha Sigma Nu, the National Jesuit Honor Society, had been installed in 1939; Gamma Pi Epsilon was later merged with ASN. Students in the School of Management had been honored by Beta Gamma Sigma, the honor society in the field of commerce and business, which is recognized by the American Association of Collegiate Schools of Business. A Sigma Xi Club (the first step) was installed at Boston College on May 2, 1957. A petition for elevation to a chapter of Sigma Xi, the national honor society for the promotion of scientific research, was made in 1964; a chapter was installed on May 24, 1966.

Chapters of Phi Beta Kappa, the most prestigious of the honor societies, had already been established at two Catholic institutions.[26] At Boston College in the late fifties, there was a feeling that the academic program in the College of Arts and Sciences and the governance of the University generally had reached a level of achievement that would justify an application for a campus chapter. The initial overtures, it may be said in advance, were not auspicious. In 1958 a faculty committee of Phi Beta Kappa key holders, chaired by Professor Joseph Sheerin of the Classics Department, filed an application for a chapter at Boston College. Since the University administration was not involved in the petition (which is the proper procedure), negotiations were carried on between the secretary of Phi Beta Kappa and the faculty committee. Things appeared to go well.[27] After completing and submitting answers to a lengthy questionnaire, the chairman was informed that the Committee on Qualifications, after screening a large number of applications, had selected 11 colleges for further examination. Boston College was one of the eleven. With this encouragement, the committee began to prepare the general report and schedule on-site visits.[28]

In the meantime, Father William Casey, who had been kept informed of the progress of negotiations, had occasion to visit a leading Catholic institution that had submitted the required documentation, including the general report, in its petition for a chapter in the previous triennium. That petition was rejected. When the Phi Beta Kappa committee at that institution allowed Father Casey to see the confidential file, he discovered that the application had been rejected because of their policy on financial assistance to athletes.[29] Of the total scholarship aid, more than half went to athletes, some of whom had grade point averages of less than 2.00. In a further consultation with Dr. Helen C. White, a Phi Beta Kappa senator to whom

Boston College had recently given an honorary degree, Father Casey learned that an institution's policy on athletics is of crucial importance in the decision to grant a local chapter of Phi Beta Kappa.[30]

After making a survey of financial assistance to athletes at Boston College, Father Casey concluded that "the College of Arts and Sciences would have no hope of winning final approval for a local chapter of Phi Beta Kappa."[31] He then instructed Professor Sheerin to withdraw the application; the latter did so with the lament that practices "in one or two of (our) undergraduate schools are such as seriously to prejudice our chances for final approval of a chapter of Phi Beta Kappa in the College of Arts and Sciences."[32] In his reply, the secretary of the United Chapters, while appreciating how difficult and distressing the decision was, felt that it was a wise one. Assuming that the weaknesses would be corrected, he reminded Professor Sheerin of the next triennium when the committee members might renew their application if they decided that the time was ripe.[33]

The Phi Beta Kappa members of the faculty did, in fact, feel that the time was ripe in 1962, the next triennium. A new committee was formed, chaired by Professor Frederick White of the Physics Department, and on October 15, 1962, an application was filed with the National Office. Boston College was again selected for further examination. On-site visits were arranged and the general report was presented in October 1962 for consideration by the Committee on Qualifications. The report, 110 pages long and eight months in preparation, covered a wide range of the University's operations.[34]

Economist Lady Barbara Ward Jackson speaking with students after her Centennial Lecture, just before the anniversary convocation.

Alas, the petition was rejected. In his letter to Professor White, the secretary cited three reasons for turning down the committee's application for a chapter. First, the Committee on Qualifications felt that the faculty should have a greater voice in the governance of the University, in administrative appointments, and in institutional policy. Secondly, "the committee was unfavorably impressed by the fact that nearly one half of the present faculty are Boston College alumni," even though "most, if not all, have advanced degrees earned elsewhere." Such a recruitment policy, the committee felt, could lead to provincialism and inbreeding. Finally, the committee was critical of the "heavy curricular requirement in philosophy." The 27-hour requirement—highest among Jesuit colleges—plus 16 hours of theology "leaves students very little room for electives over and above the major."[35]

While the letter necessarily gave first attention to considerations that led to rejection, Phi Beta Kappa was impressed with several aspects of Boston College. Except for the too-heavy requirement in philosophy, "the Committee had only favorable things to say about the content and quality of the undergraduate program."[36] The committee commended the admissions policy, the plant, and especially the library collections. In summary, the committee "would encourage the Phi Beta Kappa members of the faculty to continue working toward the establishment of a chapter."[37]

In his reply to Carl Billman's letter, Professor White pointed out the steps that had been taken and were being taken, in conjunction with the self-study project, to correct what Phi Beta Kappa perceived to be negative aspects of the University's administration and curriculum. In reference to alumni on the faculty, White pointed out that a high of 58 percent in 1958 had been reduced to 44 percent in the academic year 1963–1964. Moreover, the relatively high number of alumni on the faculty could be explained by the fact that almost all of the Jesuits, of whom there were many, had taken their undergraduate degrees at Boston College.[38] In concluding, White hoped that "you will consider a new application and recommend the establishment of a Phi Beta Kappa Chapter at Boston College to the next triennial meeting."[39]

These two applications for Phi Beta Kappa were by no means futile or unproductive. The administration addressed these weaker areas honestly and responsibly. In every instance there was improvement, and the self-study project itself benefited from the recommendations that came from sources beyond the campus. Although it anticipates somewhat the progression of events, it should be mentioned that improvements brought success. Chaired by Professor Robert Carovillano of the Physics Department, a third Phi Beta Kappa faculty committee was formed and an application was submitted in 1968.[40] This application was approved and, with an appropriate ceremony, the Omicron Chapter of Massachusetts was installed at Boston College on April 6, 1971. Boston College was the 105th institution to be invested with a chapter, and the 10th Catholic college.

The American Association of University Women

While the American Association of University Women (AAUW) is not an honor society, Boston College's relation to AAUW may well be mentioned in the context of the Phi Beta Kappa story. The AAUW is an association of women graduates of colleges and universities on the association's approved list. Established to further the interests and professional status of educated American women, the AAUW is a women's network lobbying in Washington and active in major academic bodies, offering fellowships for advanced graduate studies for women and promoting the presence and influence of women in the academic world. Mary Kinnane, who became dean of women in the School of Education in 1955, applied for and received membership in AAUW on the basis of holding a degree from the University of Kansas, an approved AAUW institution. She set in motion an inquiry about AAUW membership for Boston College on behalf of women graduates of the School of Education, the School of Nursing, and the Graduate School of Arts and Sciences. AAUW's 1958 statement of membership eligibility standards included five points: regional accreditation, provision for basic liberal education, adequate provision for women students, professional opportunities for women in faculty and administration, and maintenance of academic freedom. It was feared that the absence of women from the central liberal arts division, the College of Arts and Sciences, might be a bar to approval for Boston College. But as a result of a series of exchanges between Father Walsh and the AAUW, Boston College was placed on the approved AAUW list in December 1963 and became a corporate member of AAUW with Dean Kinnane as liaison.[41]

The achievement of AAUW approval is a reminder that women's interests were actively promoted before full coeducation in all undergraduate divisions was instituted and before there was a Women's Resource Center. Other examples of breakthroughs in the 1960s for and by women were the winning of the first Woodrow Wilson fellowship by a School of Education woman, despite a somewhat reluctant A&S Woodrow Wilson committee; acceptance of women students in the junior year abroad program; admission of women in the previously all-male University Chorale; and acceptance of women cheerleaders—an issue that provoked prolonged discussion among the undergraduate deans.

The Centennial Celebration

When Father Michael Walsh became president of Boston College in February 1958, he had no way of knowing that his term would run a whole decade. As long as the presidents of Boston College served a dual role, president of the University and rector of the Jesuit Community, it was unusual for a president's term to exceed six years. That is because, according to canon law, the term of a religious superior (rector) is normally three years, renewable once. This rule accounts for the large number of presidents in Boston College's relatively short history. It was not until Father Monan's presidency that the rectorship of the Jesuit Community was held by a person other than the University president.

When Father Walsh assumed the presidency in 1958, expecting to serve six years, he knew that he was fated to orchestrate the centennial celebration of 1963. He lost little time in setting in motion planning for the centennial. As mentioned in the last chapter, in August 1958 he set up a Centenary Committee chaired by Law School dean Father Robert Drinan. In July 1961 John Tevnan of the Development Office was appointed executive director of the centennial program. Since the Boston College charter was granted on April 1, 1863, it was decided that major centennial events would be scheduled for the spring of 1963.

Bearing a publication date of 1962 was a commemorative book, *The Crowned Hilltop: Boston College in Its Hundredth Year.* Commissioned by Cardinal Cushing as a centennial gift to his alma mater, *The Crowned Hilltop* contained 55 pencil sketches of Boston College buildings, settings, and leaders by the New England illustrator, Jack Frost. Father Francis Sweeney, whose pen has so often beautifully served Boston College, provided a text outlining the University's history as companion to the Frost sketches.

The first formal centennial event was the annual Candlemas Lecture on March 21, 1963. Rev. Hans Küng of the University of Tubingen, later a controversial theologian, addressed a gathering of 3500 at Roberts Center on the topic, "The Church and Freedom." In the audience were Richard Cardinal Cushing and Metropolitan Athenagaros of Montreal.

Five days after the Küng lecture, a formal academic convocation was held in Roberts Center for conferring an honorary degree upon Augustin Cardinal Bea, who served the Vatican as president of the Secretariat for Christian Unity. Revered in the Christian world for his ecumenical leadership, Bea was that ecclesiastical rarity, a Jesuit who was made a cardinal. For years after the event, the Jesuit Community at St. Mary's Hall remembered Cardinal Bea's visit as a joyous benediction.

The liturgical celebration of the centennial took place on Saturday, March 30, at the Holy Cross Cathedral, with a Pontifical Mass of Thanksgiving. Cardinal Cushing preached and the University Chorale, assisted by an orchestra, presented *Missa Domini,* a Mass written for the occasion by the chorale's director, C. Alexander Peloquin. In the afternoon a luncheon on campus was attended by church dignitaries and alumni and addressed by the bishop of Pittsburgh, John J. Wright of the class of 1931.

On Monday and Tuesday, April 15 and 16, 1963, a centennial theological conference was held on "The Church and Tradition." It presented such

President John F. Kennedy addressing the Centennial Convocation on April 20,
1963. To his left is Father Walsh and, at the edge of the photo, the president's
brother, Edward. Behind the president, to his right, is academic vice president
Father Charles Donovan.

speakers as Jaroslav Pelikan of Yale, Father Hans Küng, Father Walter
Burghardt of Woodstock College, Father Jean Danielou of the Institut
Catholique in Paris, George H. Williams of Harvard, and Robert McAfee
Brown of Stanford. The concluding paper, delivered by Cardinal Cushing,
was entitled, "A Bridge Between East and West," on the desired dialogue
between the Latin and Greek churches. Of the Cushing address Hans Küng
wrote later, "The cardinal's extraordinarily well-documented, realistic, and
constructive address matches the best I have ever heard a European bishop
deliver on ecumenical problems."[42]

During the next three days of Easter week some sixty scholars representing the humanities, the physical sciences, and the social sciences gathered
for a colloquium on "The Knowledge Explosion—Liberation and Limitation." Several years later the principal papers of the colloquium were
published in book form under the title, *The Knowledge Explosion*, with a
deft introduction by Father Francis Sweeney, as a permanent record of

what Hans Küng called Boston College's "brilliant centennial celebration."[43]

The climactic and most public event of the centennial year was the academic convocation in Alumni Stadium on the afternoon of Saturday, April 20, graced by the presence of President John F. Kennedy. Honorary degrees were conferred on the president of America's oldest university, Nathan Marsh Pusey of Harvard; on the president of the country's first Catholic university, Father Edward B. Bunn, S.J., of Georgetown; and on Lady Barbara Ward Jackson, who had given a Centennial Lecture the preceding Wednesday evening on the subject, "The Units of the Free World." In his address President Kennedy won the hearts and laughter of the assembly by saying at the outset how good it was to be back in a city where his accent was considered normal and where they pronounce words the way they are spelled. By a coincidence, the talks of both Lady Jackson and the president leaned heavily on the recent encyclical of Pope John XXIII, *Pacem in Terris*. Kennedy remarked of the encyclical, "As a Catholic, I am proud of it; as an American, I have learned from it."

President Pusey brought the felicitations of the higher education community and graciously expressed the reasons why Boston College was heartily celebrating its hundredth anniversary:

> We welcome the advent of strong Catholic colleges and universities of which surely this is one of the chief, into the advance ranks of our institutions of higher learning. Together these institutions have already done much to build value into our common life and on them our hopes for a worthy future in large measure must surely now depend. The colleges and universities, and among them I should like to say personally Harvard, congratulate Boston College on the accomplishments of her first century. We salute her on this happy day for her achievement. We would speak of our pride in our association with her and we wish for her long life and a continuation of that strong forward surge with which she now so clearly and so creatively is moving ahead.

The centennial celebrations wound down with emphasis on theater. On April 22 and 23 the Dramatic Society, under the direction of Father Joseph Larkin, presented an English version of the famous Jesuit morality play, *Cenodoxus: Doctor of Paris,* written by the distinguished seventeenth century Jesuit dramatist, Jakob Bidermann. On Sunday, May 5, students of the Classics Department presented the *Rhesus* of Euripides on the library lawn.

On May 11 to 14 there were five performances of a play written for the centennial by the Scottish playwright James Forsythe, *Seven Scenes for Yeni*. The director was the well-known Broadway artist Eddie Dowling. The cast consisted of professional actors in the main roles, with some support from student actors. The play was held in McHugh Forum. Prior to the premiere of *Yeni*, there was a two-day seminar, "One Hundred Years

---

SETTING FOR THE CONVOCATION (*Sub Turri,* 1963)

For weeks the campus had been alive with activity. Now army helicopters hovered over the campus and Secret Service men patrolled the buildings. April 20 dawned bright and clear, but still foul-weather preparations went on in McHugh Forum and Roberts Center, where over one hundred closed circuit television sets were being installed. The face of the campus had undergone a startling transformation. The colors of the nation and of the university billowed out in swaths of bunting along the President's route and great quantities of flowers covered the speakers' platform at the reservoir end of Alumni Stadium. At eleven o'clock a violent rainstorm swept the campus. By one o'clock only a high wind and a fine mist buffeted the Chestnut Hill area. By two o'clock over twenty thousand people had swarmed into the stadium. The chairs and seats were wet and a handsome brochure became a valued sponge. At 2:15 a great procession began to wind its way down from Roberts Center to the stadium. As the band struck up its martial music, the weather began to clear and soon the only sign of rain was the glistening lawn of the field. A great cry of welcome rose from the stands as representatives of over three hundred colleges and universities began to file into the stadium. The delegates of fifty learned societies and the faculty of Boston College, over six hundred strong, made their entrance in a stream of gold, crimson, blue, and maroon robes and hoods. They were followed by the distinguished guests, officers of the university, and Church and state officials. In the place of honor strode John F. Kennedy, President of the United States, wearing the honorary Boston College degree he received in 1956. The band struck up "Hail to the Chief" and an enthusiastic audience thundered its welcome to the President.

---

of the American Theater," during which some thirty playwrights, actors, and critics analyzed and honored the evolution of American drama.

*   *   *

It was a proud centennial year. Somehow the University managed to go about its ordinary business despite the heady and joyous celebrations of the anniversary.

ENDNOTES

1. Father Walsh to Richard Cardinal Cushing, May 19, 1958. BCA.
2. Father Walsh to Father Socius, Peter McKone, October 21, 1959. BCA.
3. "The University Center," an intriguing document, is in the archives.
4. Father Walsh to Frederick Dyer Co., June 21, 1960. BCA.
5. Announcement of ground-breaking. BCA.
6. Father Walsh to Father Coleran, May 25, 1962. BCA.
7. Letter from Father Edward Hanrahan, former Dean of Students, to Father Donovan, February 5, 1985. BCA.
8. BCA.
9. BCA.
10. BCA.

11. Father Walsh to Father Guindon, August 1, 1962. BCA.
12. Father Walsh to Rene Marcou, November 9, 1962. BCA.
13. *Alumni News* (Winter 1966).
14. Programs, clippings and other materials related to the dedication are preserved in the archives.
15. *Alumni News* (Spring 1967).
16. Sidney R. Rabb, Chairman of the Board, Stop & Shop, Inc.; Adrian O'Keeffe, President, First National Stores, Inc.; Ralph Lowell, Chairman of the Board, Boston Safe Deposit & Trust Co.; Ernest Henderson, President, Sheraton Corporation of America; Thomas J. McHugh, President, Atlantic Lumber Co.; Roger C. Damon, President, First National Bank of Boston; Edward F. Williams, Business Consultant; Thomas M. Joyce, Esq., Trial Attorney; Carl J. Gilbert, Chairman of the Board, The Gillette Co.; John B. Atkinson, President, Atkinson Shoe Co.; Wallace E. Carroll, President, American Gage & Machine Co.; Peter Fuller, President, Cadillac-Oldsmobile Co. of Boston; and Augustus C. Long, Chairman of the Board, Texaco, Inc.
17. "Address: Board of Regents Meeting, September 27, 1960." BCA.
18. *Ibid.*
19. Father Walsh to Father Donovan, August 5, 1963. BCA.
20. The membership of the committees on six general areas of concern are given here:

    Committee on the Total Curriculum: J. Frank Devine, S.J., P. Albert Duhamel, Paul T. Heffron, Lawrence G. Jones, John J. Long, S.J., H. Michael Mann, Robert F. O'Malley, John P. Rock, S.J., and James W. Skehan, S.J., chairman.

    Intellectual Climate Committee: Raymond F. Bogucki, Joseph Bornstein, Gary P. Brazier, James J. Casey, S.J., Brendan Connolly, S.J., chairman, Albert M. Folkard, Donald A. Gallagher, and Raymond McNally.

    Library Committee: John R. Betts, Gerald C. Bilodeau, John H. Kinnier, S.J., Donald B. Sands, and Norman J. Wells, chairman.

    Committee on Research Activities: Robert Becker, chairman, Joseph Criscenti, Joseph A. Devenny, S.J., Walter Driscoll, Erich Von Richthofen, Joseph McKenna, William Pare, and Chai Hyun Yoon.

    Honors Program Committee: Edward L. Hirsh, chairman, Edward V. Jezak, Louis O. Kattsoff, Edgar Litt, David Loschky, and John J. Walsh, S.J.

    Committee on Guidance: Robert Cahill, Leonard R. Casper, Joseph R. Cautela, chairman, George L. Drury, S.J., Robert T. Ferrick, S.J., John F. Norton, and John vonFelsinger.
21. Father Walsh to Father Provincial John V. O'Connor, May 22, 1964. BCA.
22. Father O'Connor to Father Walsh, June 3, 1964. BCA.
23. Father Walsh to Father O'Connor, June 12, 1964. BCA.
24. Father Donovan to Father Walsh, August 27, 1964. BCA.
25. President Butterfield's lengthy memorandum is attached to the final report of the Executive Committee of the Arts and Sciences Self-Study of 1963–1964. BCA.
26. The Catholic University of America and the College of St. Catherine in Minnesota.
27. Carl Billman to Joseph E. Sheerin, October 16, 1958. BCA.
28. Billman to Sheerin, December 19, 1958. BCA.
29. William V. E. Casey to Father Walsh, June 25, 1959. BCA.
30. *Ibid.*
31. *Ibid.*

32. Joseph Sheerin to Carl Billman, June 3, 1959. BCA.
33. Billman to Sheerin, June 9, 1959. BCA.
34. Copies of the report are in the archives.
35. Carl Billman to Frederick White, December 11, 1963. BCA.
36. *Ibid.*
37. *Ibid.* This correspondence was printed in *The Heights* (February 7, 1964).
38. Frederick White to Carl Billman, n.d.
39. *Ibid.*
40. The general report is dated October 1, 1969. BCA.
41. BCA.
42. *America* (June 8, 1963), p. 829.
43. *Ibid.*

CHAPTER 29

Years of Accomplishment

In September 1967 Father Walsh began his last year as president of Boston College. A decade at that level of administration, with ultimate responsibility for the academic and financial health of an institution, can seem a long time to be the incumbent. The pressures of fund-raising, campus expansion, public relations, and competing on-campus constituencies pose daily tests of leadership and diplomacy. Although successful in meeting his responsibilities, Father Walsh decided that ten years as rector-president had given him sufficient opportunity to reach his immediate goals and to point the way to future distinction for the University.

He could take satisfaction in what had been accomplished, although he did not deny that there were clouds on the horizon. The University was, in fact, flourishing. Enrollments continued to climb, with 8125 full-time and 1604 part-time students, for a total of almost 10,000. The class of 1971 was the most highly qualified and most highly subsidized ever admitted to Boston College. In addition to unusually high SAT's, 5 percent were former class presidents, others had been involved in social and welfare projects, and many had been high school newspaper editors. To teach these promising students and those in the graduate and professional schools there were 540 faculty members, supported by lecturers, graduate fellows, and assistants.[1] While total assets, including investments and property, had reached $58,000,000, the operating budget had increased to $31,000,000.[2] The growth, though not spectacular, had been steady and substantial.

Father John A. McCarthy, long-time professor of philosophy and dean of the College of Arts and Sciences from 1960 to 1964.

In assessing the growth of institutions, university histories tend to be written from the perspective of the president's office. But the president does not work in isolation. For the academic enterprise, the next most important offices are those of academic deans. Hence a picture of the Walsh administration depends for completeness on recognition of the supporting deans.

Contributions by the Academic Deans

When Father Walsh assumed the presidency in 1958, the dean of the College of Arts and Sciences was William V. E. Casey, S.J., appointed in 1956. One of the first decisions of the new president was to elevate Father Casey to the newly created post of academic vice president. (Father Casey retained the deanship of the College of Arts and Sciences.)[3] In 1960 Father Casey moved to Holy Cross College and was replaced as dean by Father John A. McCarthy of the Philosophy Department, who was the first to be given the student government's teacher-of-the-year award. The gentle and scholarly Father McCarthy, however, who was dean during the critical period of the A&S Self-Study and the centennial, was not temperamentally inclined to administration, and in 1964 he was permitted to return to his beloved classroom. He was succeeded by Father John R. Willis of the History Department. A graduate of Amherst College and educated for the Protestant ministry with a Ph.D. from Yale, Father Willis was a convert to Catholicism. He brought intellectual sophistication and broad cultural interests to the office.

One of the dynamic forces in the Walsh administration was Law School dean, Father Robert F. Drinan. Like Father Casey, he took over the top post in his school in 1956, succeeding another activist, Father William J. Kenealy. Drinan brought the Law School national prestige and attention and remained dean until 1971, when he resigned and ran successfully for Congress.

A rock-steady influence during the Walsh years was Dean Rita P. Kelleher of the School of Nursing, whose administration spanned more than two decades. She steered the school to accreditation and oversaw the move from Newbury Street to Cushing Hall in 1960.

Succeeding Father James D. Sullivan as dean of the College of Business Administration in 1953, the talented W. Seavey Joyce, S.J., led the CBA until his appointment by Father Walsh as vice president for community relations in 1966. Because Father Joyce devoted so much of his time to external projects such as the citizen seminars and a television series on the city, he was supported by a succession of associate deans: Donald J. White of the Economics Department (1955–1961), Father William C. McInnes (1961–1964), and Father Alfred J. Jolson (1964–1968). Father Jolson was acting dean of the College of Business Administration in 1966–1967.

In Father Walsh's last year in office (1967–1968), he appointed the first lay dean for the Business School, Albert J. Kelley. Kelley was an unusual choice, not only because he was the first lay dean of CBA, but because of

Albert J. Kelley, first lay dean of the College of Business Administration. He changed the name to School of Management.

his unique background of experience and education. A native of Boston, Kelley graduated from the United States Naval Academy. While still in the service, he earned an engineering degree at MIT, later returning to earn a Ph.D. in systems engineering. During the Korean War he served as a test pilot. In 1960 he joined the NASA program, where he gained experience at high management levels. It was not the expected background for dean of a school of management, but Kelley's forceful personality and managerial skill gave unhesitating and positive forward impetus to the school.

In 1961 Father Walsh appointed the dean of the School of Education, Father Charles F. Donovan, to the post of academic vice president, which had been vacant for a year after Father Casey's departure from Boston College. Father Donovan continued to act as Education dean until 1966, when he began to devote full time to the vice presidency. William C. Cottle, who came from the University of Kansas to head the Boston College counselor education program, was acting dean in 1966–1967, with John Travers as acting associate dean. In 1967 Donald T. Donley was named dean.

Father John V. Driscoll, an alumnus of Boston College and of the School of Social Work, became dean of the School of Social Work in 1958 when Father Walsh assumed the presidency.[4] Father Driscoll added to the prestige of the school by overseeing a thorough curriculum revision and by increasing the number of faculty members with doctoral degrees. He also worked with Father Walsh in preparing the move of the school to McGuinn Hall.

When Father Walsh took office, the dean of the Graduate School of Arts and Sciences was Father Paul A. FitzGerald of the History Department, who succeeded another historian in that office, Father James L. Burke, in 1953. When Father FitzGerald joined the administrative office of the national Jesuit Education Association in New York in 1960, Father Joseph A. Devenny became dean and served through the 1965–1966 academic year. When Father Devenny became dean of the Weston School of Theology in Cambridge, Father Walter J. Feeney of the Mathematics Department was named dean of the Graduate School.

What was known as the Intown College became the Evening College early in Father Walsh's presidency, when the school was moved to the Chestnut Hill campus. The dean, Father Charles Toomey, was succeeded by Father Charles W. Crowley in 1960. Father Crowley served until the last year of the Walsh administration, when the present energetic dean, Father James A. Woods, became dean.

There were other appointments that reflected a growing concern for the administration of student life on campus. In 1967 a new position was created for Father Edward J. Hanrahan. Formerly director of resident students, he was appointed dean of students. Father Hanrahan, a former officer in the U.S. Army, was to earn the respect of the students through a fair and impartial enforcement of the regulations for 18 years. (The students were convinced that he had eyes in the back of his head!) To

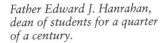

Father Edward J. Hanrahan, dean of students for a quarter of a century.

provide further help for the growing number of female students, Ann Flynn was appointed assistant dean of women. Brian J. Counihan became assistant dean of students.

The 1967–1968 academic year began with problems that were new to Boston College. On Monday morning, September 18, 1967, the maintenance workers (custodians, painters, carpenters, electricians, truck drivers, maids, and ground crew) picketed the gates to the campus. It was the first strike at Boston College. The workers wanted recognition as a bargaining union and a new contract. Although initially opposed to arbitration by the Labor Relations Board, the administration finally agreed to LRB jurisdiction; but at that point the union declined the board's mediation. The five-day strike ended on September 25, when the administration recognized Local 254 as their official bargaining agent (which was, in turn, certified by the LRB). Over 90 percent of Boston College maintenance workers had signed union cards.[5]

A Commitment to Academic Progress

Father Walsh's presidency was a period of determined commitment to academic progress. The president's determination was reflected in the agendas of deans and faculty and echoed by a number of the students. At the graduate level, this was an era of building faculty strength and academic resources for the inauguration of doctoral programs. The first three years of the 1960s saw doctoral programs begun in three sciences: chemistry (1960), physics (1961), and biology (1963). In 1966 the Philosophy Department started its doctorate, and the following year doctoral programs in modern languages and psychology were begun. As the decade ended five more Ph.D. programs were launched: Germanic studies (1969), English and sociology (1970), and political science and theology (1971). Because of a change in personnel, the Ph.D. in Germanic studies was discontinued in 1977.

While the inauguration of these later doctoral programs belonged to the Joyce era, the foundation for them was firmly laid in earlier years. The growth of faculty strength at this time is seen in the number of new faculty members added in successive years: 1962–1963, 14; 1963–1964, 37; 1964–1965, 54; 1965–1966, 46; 1966–1967, 83; 1967–1968, 75; 1968–1969, 101. It was a period of heady and optimistic expansion. Nevertheless, the expansion was done with prudent planning and with appropriate checkpoints. Proposals for doctoral programs had to survive stiff departmental skepticism, then scrutiny by the Educational Policy Committee of the Graduate School, and finally review by the central administration and trustees. Also at this point in the University's governance, each doctoral program had to receive approval from the Provincial of the New England Province of the Jesuits and, more significantly, from Father General in Rome. Rome was already wary of what was perceived as a tendency of American Jesuit colleges and universities to overexpand, so approvals were not given lightly. Indeed, each approval was a vote of confidence in the institution.

At the undergraduate level, especially in the College of Arts and Sciences, there was an almost competitive intellectualism. Father Walsh, aggressively abetted by his strong-minded dean of A&S, Father William Van Etten Casey, considered the College of Arts and Sciences the flagship of the institution, and he was determined to achieve dramatic academic advances there. Reflecting such ideals, as early as 1958 *The Heights* was calling for more "eggheads" at Boston College and lamenting that only 193 Boston College alumni had earned the Ph.D. degree in 21 years.[6] There was great concern about the winning of national fellowships such as Woodrow Wilson, Marshall, NSF, and Danforth fellowships by Boston College seniors, and the University's success was compared with that of other institutions. Departments announced with pride the number of their majors opting for graduate study, especially in Ph.D. areas. In 1963 *The Heights* trumpeted that 60 percent of the senior class was committed to graduate study the next year.[7] The 1960s was probably the most self-consciously intellectual period in Boston College's history.

The 1960s saw a number of academic beginnings—sometimes fledgling beginnings—of programs that have burgeoned in subsequent decades. John Eichorn came to Boston College from the University of Indiana to head the special education program, which has won substantial federal funding. William Cottle, at about the same time, joined the School of Education faculty from the University of Kansas to lead the robust counseling psychology program.

The College of Business Administration began to attract faculty members with strong quantitative backgrounds—a development that led to establishment of the influential Quantitative Management and Computer Science Department. Indeed, CBA at this time (1963) offered the first computer science course at Boston College. The first computer for academic use was obtained by the Mathematics Department under Father Stanley Bezuszka's direction. At about the same time the registrar, Father John Fitzgerald, introduced a computer for administrative uses.

In an effort to bring the Theology and Philosophy departments into harmony with major thrusts of the Second Vatican Council, sweeping curricular changes were initiated in 1966. In place of the rather limited fixed set of courses that had been prescribed for decades, broad new programs of electives—as many as 64 in philosophy—were introduced.[8] In keeping with the ecumenical emphasis of the recently concluded Council, Boston College was active in promoting the concept, and then the reality, of the Boston Theological Institute, a consortium of prime theological schools in the Boston area for cross-registration in courses and sharing of library and other facilities.[9]

Toward the end of 1967 Dean Rita Kelleher announced her resignation. She had been with the School of Nursing since its inception and had given it masterful leadership. In recognition of her unique contributions, the trustees voted to confer on her an honorary degree at the June 1968 Commencement.

Dean Kelleher's successor was Margaret Foley, who had earned a doctorate at St. Louis University and for 20 years had served as executive secretary of the Conference of Catholic Schools of Nursing. Unfortunately her term was a brief one due to ill health. Rita Kelleher returned as acting head of the school while Dean Foley was hospitalized. When Dean Foley died in September 1970 a new president, Father Joyce, presided at her funeral mass.

Student Protest: Civil Rights

In the 1960s and early 1970s many American colleges, reflecting or perhaps even exaggerating the mood of American society, were in turmoil, particularly regarding issues of civil rights and the Vietnam war. *Turmoil* is probably too strong a word to describe the student protest that developed at Boston College. Student protest of the disruptive sort did not become a phenomenon of campus life at Boston College until the presidency of Father W. Seavey Joyce (1968–1972). Still, it is worth reviewing student reaction to the protest issues during the earlier 1960s. One can get an impression of how these issues influenced the Boston College community by scanning the pages of *The Heights*.

In April 1960 a *Heights* article charged that the Boston College campus was apathetic about the constitutional rights of Southern blacks.[10] The next month there were scoldings because the University was not yet represented in a proposed Greater Boston collegiate rally against segregation.[11]

During the 1960s Father Robert Drinan, Law School dean, was Boston College's leading spokesman on civil rights matters, and the *The Heights* faithfully recorded his opinions. Early in the controversy about ethnic separation in the Boston schools, Father Drinan condemned what he called the *de facto* segregation of the public schools in Boston.[12] Father Drinan openly challenged Boston College students to become involved in the racial issue by associating themselves with the programs of CORE and NAACP.[13] In a Red Mass sermon for jurists and lawyers in Jamaica, New York, the Law School dean criticized Catholics for racial apathy, and this was reported to the campus community.[14]

In late 1965 the University proudly announced the inauguration in the following summer of the "Upward Bound" program to help prepare minority children for college entrance. Upward Bound was to continue for 10 years.

In 1967 the Boston College community's attention was called to a document from the Superior General of the Society of Jesus in Rome, addressed to all American Jesuits, concerning racial justice. Father Pedro Arrupe noted the identification of American Jesuits with the middle class and their lagging behind in promoting the interests of blacks. He said, ". . . the Society of Jesus has not committed its manpower and other resources to the interracial apostolate in any degree commensurate with the need [of blacks] to share in our services." He urged Jesuit schools and colleges to encourage blacks to apply for admission and to offer them scholarships and other financial assistance.[15]

A December 1967 issue of *The Heights* carried a story that showed positive action on the racial issue by one academic department. The Speech Department, under the leadership of its dynamic chairman, John Lawton, launched a program in which Boston College students travelled to parish and Catholic school audiences to inform them of the church's stand on racial justice. The program cited not Father General Arrupe's exhortation but rather the admonition in the Papal Encyclical, "On Progress of Peoples," which deplored discrimination against blacks. The question addressed by Dr. Lawton's speakers was, "To what extent have American Catholics implemented the papal teaching on interracial justice?" The principal topics covered were the education, employment, and housing of blacks. The Speech Department program was one of the University's most constructive responses to the race issue. It became an apostolic project of the chairman of the Speech Department, who even raised funds from friends to subsidize the travel of his student speakers.[16]

In the spring of his last year in office, Father Walsh announced the establishment of a $100,000 scholarship fund to attract black students to Boston College.[17] This fund was to grow dramatically as a subsidy to what came to be called the "Black Talent Program" under Father Joyce. This program will be treated in detail in the next chapter.

Student Protest: The Vietnam War

A second protest issue on campuses during the 1960s was the Vietnam War and the concomitant draft. For many the memory of the war in Southeast Asia remains both fresh and bitter. United States involvement, begun under President Dwight Eisenhower, continued to grow under President Lyndon Johnson. After the Tonkin Gulf Resolution of 1964, the president increased U.S. troop strength to 200,000; General William Westmoreland requested that 540,000 troops be made available by 1967. As the casualties climbed and the draft came closer to the collegiate population, the potential for student reaction increased.

During Father Walsh's regime, reaction on campus to the Vietnam war was somewhat restrained and balanced—that is, two-sided. For example, the first reference in *The Heights* to the Vietnam war was in October 1965 when the paper published two articles presenting pro and con arguments concerning the war.[18] A week later *The Heights* had two articles justifying U.S. intervention in Vietnam.[19] In November *The Heights* carried a report of a debate on the war between a Boston University professor *(pro)* and Professor Raymond McNally of Boston College *(con)*. In December there was an account of a *New York Times* ad signed by 190 faculty members from 17 New England colleges, including 19 from Boston College, supporting the United States position in Vietnam.[20] A January 1966 issue reported that a number of Boston College students attended a downtown rally in support of the Vietnam war.[21] The following month *The Heights* editors again presented contrasting pro and con views of the war.[22] In March the Catholic Peace Fellowship of Boston ran an ad in *The Heights* signed by nine faculty members and some students calling for an end of the Vietnam hostilities.[23]

The following fall *The Heights* noted the pope's plea for a month of prayer to bring about a peaceful settlement of the Vietnamese conflict. The same issue outlined the special Masses and services that the University would conduct in responding to the Holy Father's request. One was to be a campus demonstration for peace, and the University religious director, Father John Gallagher, was quoted as saying, "This is not a pacifist demonstration, but a demonstration of concern for peace. Of course, pacifists are welcome, as are all people who are opposed to war and violence."[24]

A big event of the fall of 1966 was the visit to the campus of Vice President Hubert Humphrey. Various antiwar groups planned to picket Humphrey's talk in Roberts Center, and they distributed flyers around town and on the campus. A small group of Boston College students objected to their activity on campus and succeeded in having them withdraw; *The Heights* condemned the actions of these students.[25] On the day of the address, as 3500 people awaited Humphrey's arrival in Roberts, a group of picketers including a handful of Boston College students marched on the sidewalk along Beacon Street. A crowd of Boston College students (estimated by *The Heights* at 500) shouted at the pickets, "Get off our campus." *The Heights,* in condemning the counterdemonstrators, attributed their actions not to support for the war but to concern for the "image" of Boston College that would be projected by the picketing of the vice president.[26]

In the spring of 1967 *The Heights* reported plans for a Vietnam week, with some activities sponsored by the Catholic Peace Fellowship and counteractivities under the aegis of Young Americans for Freedom. The same issue carried an editorial calling for an end to the Vietnam War and urging support for the upcoming antiwar marches in New York and San Francisco.[27]

By the fall of 1967 *The Heights'* editorial policy was clearly aimed at opposing the war effort. The paper called attention to a massive antiwar demonstration to be held in Washington.[28] But the following week there was an account of a rally on Bapst lawn in support of our men in Vietnam sponsored by YAF (Young Americans for Freedom).[29] In November a *Heights* article reported conflict at the Law School, with some faculty and students protesting the presence of recruiters from Dow Chemical, manufacturer of napalm. In the same issue there was a full-page ad signed by faculty members at local colleges, including 31 from Boston College, protesting the war in Vietnam and U.S. use of napalm.[30] A later issue in the same month noted that the national AAUP had condemned student protest blocking recruiters or speakers as an interference with academic freedom.[31]

In December 1967 *The Heights* reported that a Boston College faculty antiwar committee had been established, with 30 present at the organizational meeting. The group planned to counsel draft resisters and support them if arrested.[32] Two weeks later 102 faculty members had a full-page ad condemning "the government's" war in Vietnam.[33] But still the campus was neither radicalized nor radically split. In February the Campus Council, in an attempt to "break the relative silence in the Vietnam war debate on the B.C. campus," planned a "Vietnam Week" to present and explore all sides of the issue.[34]

Perhaps unconsciously presaging things to come, in the final semester of Father Walsh's presidency a policy on student demonstrations was published. Any proposed protest must be registered with the Office of the Dean of Students. The policy stated in part, "Violence in every form and peaceful intimidation which incites violent reactions are repugnant and intolerable in any expression of assent or dissent."[35]

From 1960 to 1968 the Boston College campus was definitely aware of the issues of race and war that were troubling American society and leading to violent confrontations at some universities. But the atmosphere at the University was restrained and polite compared with what it would become a few years later.

Matching Societal Changes: New Regulations

The 1960s were a period of student unrest and agitation. Many of the relaxations of collegiate rules that occurred during that decade at Boston College, however, were not initiated by the students but were part of a societal movement toward decreased regimentation. For example, when student residences were opened after World War II, the administration simply adopted dormitory customs that had been in effect for a century at established Jesuit boarding colleges such as Holy Cross and Georgetown, including obligatory attendance at daily Mass. In the academic year 1959–1960 that rule was reduced to attendance at Mass twice a week, and during the following decade the Mass attendance requirement was removed entirely.

Another standard feature of student life at Boston College and other Jesuit colleges during the nineteenth century and the first half of the twentieth century was the annual religious retreat—two or three days completely dedicated to spiritual talks by priests, frequently distinguished Jesuits who made a career of such apostolic activity. In 1964 it was decided that instead of an annual retreat, each student would be bound to make two retreats during his four years at college. The following year—the year, incidentally, of the conclusion of the Second Vatican Council—the requirement concerning retreats was abolished.

In the strictly academic realm, class attendance had been obligatory since the founding of the University. To take care of sickness or other emergency absences, a "cut" system was in effect in the 1940s and 1950s whereby a student might, without adverse administrative action, be absent from a number of classes in a course equal to twice the credits assigned to the course. Since most semester courses carried three credits, six unexplained absences were tolerated. In the 1960s there began to be discussion of a more relaxed regulation. In 1961 a policy was adopted making class attendance voluntary for Dean's List students. In 1965 the voluntary class attendance policy was extended to all students in all courses.

In the early post-WW II period the student handbook set forth definite dress standards for the all-male student population. Coats and ties were to be worn in class. As time went by there was a gradual relaxation in the College of Arts and Sciences, so that sweaters and other informal dress became acceptable. However, under the stern eye of its indomitable dean of men, Father Francis McManus, the College of Business Administration (as it was then known) held fast to the coat and tie requirement until 1966, when a relaxation of the CBA dress requirements merited notice in *The Heights*.[36]

As noted above, the changes during the 1960s described here did not occur as a form of yielding to student pressure or organized protests. In fact, in some instances—especially the issue of voluntary class attendance—

there was some initial doubt or resistance on the part of some students. One area where students did actively lobby for change, however, was participation in academic policy-making bodies. Shortly after the Educational Policy Committee was established in the College of Arts and Sciences in 1964, students petitioned the EPC for student representation on that body; the request was denied. But in the spring of 1968 the A&S student senate celebrated victory; the Educational Policy Committee made provision for two student representatives, later increased to four.

Participation in University Governance

During his last year in office, Father Walsh established a committee to draw up a blueprint for the University Academic Senate. Uppermost in his mind was the involvement of the faculty more intimately in the decision-making process for University affairs.[37] The planning committee agreed upon a 3:2 ratio of faculty to administrative members on UAS. This having been settled, the question was raised as to whether there should be any student representation. Some felt that since faculty were just gaining a common deliberative forum with the administration, this advance might be somewhat diminished by the inclusion of student representatives. Others suggested that students would not be given any kind of proportionate representation but would have a few slots to insure the presence of the student viewpoint. Ultimately it was agreed to include two student members on the UAS. The planning committee felt that it had taken a liberal and progressive stand in granting two places to students, but they soon learned that many

Helen Landreth, first curator of the Irish Collection.

students were incensed by such limited representation, which was condemned as tokenism.[38] The proposed charter for the University Academic
Senate went to the full faculty for ratification in March 1968. There was a
good faculty response: 62 percent of the entire faculty voted, and 51
percent of the entire faculty approved the charter. Of those voting, 82
percent approved the charter with two slots for students.[39] The UAS was
not organized until the following fall, when Father W. Seavey Joyce was
president, and he was to find that student unhappiness with the structure
of the University Academic Senate would lead to the first student demonstration in his regime.

While the Undergraduate Government of Boston College (UGBC) became a reality the year after Father Walsh left the presidency, the planning
for and authorization of UGBC took place in 1967–1968; accordingly, this
is an appropriate place to consider the gradual evolution of student
government at Boston College. Over a period of three decades, student
organization went from an exclusive emphasis on class (senior, junior,
sophomore, freshman) activities to a senate organization in each undergraduate school topped by a coordinating council, to the present UGBC
structure embracing the entire undergraduate student body as a single
political entity.

The student handbooks of the 1950s explained that each class would
have five officers: president, vice president, secretary, treasurer, and Athletic
Association representative. That the focus of the government was mainly
social was shown by the provision that in the junior class an additional
officer would be elected to run the junior prom and the junior week tea
dance. In the days of the more or less prescribed curriculum, students were
assigned to fixed divisions or sections, groups of students who took most
of their classes together. This rather domestic arrangement was reflected in
the advisory councils for each class president, composed of the class officers
and one representative of each division or section in the year. Each year
also had a moderator, usually a Jesuit assigned by the president.

In 1959, possibly because at last the School of Nursing was at the
Chestnut Hill campus and the entire undergraduate student body could act
in consort, a new form of student government was inaugurated. Each of
the undergraduate colleges had its own senate to care for internal matters.
The activities and concerns of the four classes were entrusted to four
interclass councils. Campus-wide issues and interests came under the
jurisdiction of the Campus Council, composed of a few senators from each
of the student senates. The Campus Council's constitution, published
annually in the Boston College Handbook, noted that it would be in effect
when approved by the student senates and the deans of the respective
colleges and by the president of the University. The constitution also
provided for a moderator, appointed by the president, who would attend
all meetings. The moderator had power to suspend or veto council action;

in the event of a suspension or veto, the council, upon a two-thirds vote, could appeal to the Council of the Deans. It is therefore clear that in 1959, when the Campus Council's constitution was published, there was still considerable dependence by the students on the authority and guidance of the administration, as demonstrated by their seeking the approval of deans and the president to establish the legitimacy of their government and by the strong role assigned to the faculty moderator.

The Campus Council, with its concomitant governmental bodies, was operative from 1959 to 1968. The last time the Campus Council's constitution appeared in the student handbook, the title of the moderator was changed to advisor, which reflects the less directive spirit of the late 1960s; but the definition of the role and authority of the advisor remained the same as that of the original moderator.

As the student body grew larger and more residential in the 1960s, scheduling of events by classes and organizations became more complex. The Campus Council addressed this problem and, after appropriate consultation and approval, established the Social Commission. An eight-page charter for the Social Commission appeared in the handbook for 1967–1968, the last year of the Campus Council's existence. The need for a Social Commission underscored the need for a stronger coordinating organization for student government, and during the academic year 1967–1968 a constitutional convention was held for the purpose of chartering an entirely new vehicle of student government. The work of the convention proceeded calmly and in a nonadversarial atmosphere during a period of student activism, and there emerged a radically different structure, a much stronger central government for the entire undergraduate student body, whose validity derived from its own constitution rather than from a relationship with the senates of the four schools. The description of student government in the 1970–1971 University Student Guide points out that the constitutional convention and the resultant UGBC were a byproduct of the University Committee on Student Life in 1967, headed by the then new vice president for student affairs, Father George Drury. So the development of a stronger and more independent student government was achieved under the guidance of the administration. The new UGBC constitution provided for ratification by the student body, with no reference to approval by deans or the president. No provision was made for a faculty or other advisor.

At least two factors contributed to the success of UGBC. The first was financial clout. The administration acquiesced in the arrangement called for by the UGBC constitution whereby the funds resulting from the student activities fee were controlled and managed by UGBC. This gave student government extraordinary fiscal responsibility and leverage. The second factor enhancing the prestige of UGBC was its continuation and enlargement of the role of the Campus Council's Social Commission, acting as arbiter and in many respects controller of the extra-class calendar of the students. However, UGBC has been the student government structure of the 1970s and 1980s, so its growth and achievement will be noted elsewhere.

The Connection with Weston College

An account of these years in the development of the University would be incomplete without a brief description of the relationship between Boston College and Weston College. At Weston College, which had a pontifical charter, the young Jesuits of the New England Province pursued their philosophical and theological studies for civil and ecclesiastical degrees in preparation for their priestly apostolate. Boston College played an important role in the academic formation of New England Jesuits.

Located in the nearby suburb of Weston, the School of Philosophy at Weston College had for many years been a constituent college within the University, and was so designated in the official catalog. The bachelor's and master's degrees were granted by Boston College, but the two schools were financially and academically distinct and geographically separated. The School of Philosophy had its own dean and faculty; at the undergraduate level, the courses, examinations and papers were given, graded, and directed by the Jesuit faculty.[40] This working arrangement, while academically justified, was a little unusual and, to some extent, casual. As might be predicted, there was friction from time to time over the lines of jurisdiction.

With this in mind, and wishing to improve the procedures, "A Statement of the Relationship of the School of Philosophy to Boston College" was drawn up and signed on December 9, 1959, by John V. O'Connor, S.J., rector of Weston College, and Michael P. Walsh, S.J.[41] It reaffirmed the fact that the School of Philosophy was a constituent college in the University structure and subject to the broad policies of the University. In certain matters, those especially that pertained to the A.B. and B.S. degrees, the dean of the School of Philosophy was responsible to the president of Boston College; in matters that concerned the master's degree, he was responsible to the dean of the Graduate School. Even the new procedures did not entirely eliminate friction, but these problems were usually resolved in a fraternal way. The point is, however, that as time went on academic administrators and religious superiors were persuaded that it would be advantageous to both the young Jesuits and the University to cement even closer ties. Progressive Jesuit fathers at Weston were convinced that the academic isolation of the scholastics was not a good thing.

So, in September 1965 the campus on the Heights had a new look. The Provincial Superior and his counselors agreed, with the approval of the trustees of Boston College, that the Jesuit scholastics should take their philosophy courses and upper division electives at the Heights. Consequently, there was an unaccustomed influx of young men in cassocks and birettas taking their places in the classrooms with the Boston College undergraduates. The mixture was something of a novelty for both groups, and it added another dimension to the campus. Certainly the Jesuit character of the University was further enhanced. The Jesuit faculty at Weston, of course, contributed their services to this new enterprise.

Three years later, the dean of the School of Philosophy, Oliva Blanchette, S.J., proposed a "Program for Jesuit studies at Boston College."[42] The program was designed to be a replacement for the School of Liberal Arts at Shadowbrook, where young Jesuits completed their classical studies, and the School of Philosophy. It was to be administered by a Jesuit (Father Blanchette was later appointed to this task) with the title of Associate Dean of Jesuit Studies. He was assisted by an academic committee for overall supervision of the program and by a subcommittee. The special subcommittee, with five of its members chosen from the Department of Philosophy, was responsible for implementing a specific program in systematic philosophy and had to be approved by the Jesuit Provincial. Basically, it was a new effort to prepare Jesuit scholastics, who were now eligible for the honors program, for their undergraduate degree and also to ensure a proper foundation in philosophy for their future studies in theology.

The administration of the program was admittedly complicated, inasmuch as it involved the academic vice president, the chairman of the Philosophy Department, and the Jesuit dean. The New England Provincial, who had ultimate responsibility of his scholastics, was necessarily involved in its operation. Boston College, in addition to its academic contribution, gave full scholarship aid to each Jesuit scholastic. As is clear from this brief description, the University had become a key component in the academic formation of the New England Jesuits.

The School of Theology at Weston College was also listed in the Boston College catalog as a constituent school of the University, and the names of those who received theological degrees were printed in the commencement program. However, the connection between Boston College and the School of Theology had never been properly defined. The academic association between the two schools was vague enough when the School of Theology was located at Weston; it was even more tenuous after the school moved its operation to Cambridge in 1968. The reasons for the move to Cambridge, in view of the educational advantages it offered in consort with other divinity schools, were compelling.[43] However, the decision to change the degree offered caused further confusion.

The School of Theology, with pontifical approval, offered a Licentiate in Sacred Theology (STL) to those who qualified after four years of theology. This was an ecclesiastical degree. After the move to Cambridge, the school offered a Bachelor of Divinity (B.D.) and an advanced Master of Divinity degree (M.Div.)—both considered civil degrees. In anticipation of the move to Cambridge, the dean at Weston began to discuss some of these questions with Father Donovan, the academic vice president at Boston College. The latter referred the questions to the president, who wrote, "I am not too sure, either, what arrangement we have with the School of Theology at Weston. There is actually no legal tie-in with them. It is sort of a handshake agreement."[44] Father Walsh's main concern was with the M.Div. as a terminal degree for hiring and promotion purposes. His advice to the dean at Weston, Father J. A. Devenny, was that he should do as he wished but refrain from "raising these technical difficulties."[45]

After the Weston theologate moved to Cambridge, the confusion continued. In 1971, when Robert White, S.J., president of Weston College, informed the president of Boston College that he was appointing a new dean, Father W. Seavey Joyce, S.J., did not conceal his annoyance in a letter to his academic vice president. Since Father White was informing him of this change, Father Joyce assumed there was some connection between the two schools. If there was a connection, he wanted an answer to certain questions:

> If Weston College and/or its School of Theology form a constituent school of our University, why must they have a separate President besides a separate Dean? I am aware, of course, that Weston has always been financially separate from Boston College. This is a considerable difference. On the other hand, according to our Statutes, the President of Boston College appoints our deans, and these appointments require the concurrence of the Directors.[46]

In his opinion, the whole situation was "very messy." He suggested that "we face up to the fact that Weston College is, in fact, not a constituent school of Boston College."[47]

In the ensuing years, Weston College at Cambridge and Boston College have indeed become two completely distinct and separate institutions. Weston College which, in addition to the Jesuits, enrolls laymen and laywomen as well as religious men and women, confers its own civil degrees, which have state and regional approval. As Jesuit institutions in the New England Province, they share a fraternal bond and the theological faculties enjoy a cordial academic relationship.

While many Jesuits associate Weston College with their philosophical and theological studies, other scholars—locally, nationally, and internationally—associate the name with the physical sciences. Over the years, the Weston Observatory, founded in 1928 by Edward P. Tivnan, S.J., has brought to Boston College both prestige and, indeed, financial emoluments through government contracts. Henry M. Brock, S.J., a graduate of MIT, was appointed the first director of the observatory. Through his contacts, Francis Tondorf, S.J., an eminent seismologist at Georgetown University, donated a 25-kilogram Bosch-Omori seismograph, the first major piece of equipment acquired by the observatory. This was augmented in 1934 when Father Francis J. Dolan, S.J., president of the College of the Holy Cross, donated a Wiechert (80 kg) seismograph to Weston. As a result of personal gifts to him, Father Michael J. Ahern, S.J., one of the best-known Jesuits in New England and director of the observatory from 1940–1950, purchased a 3-component Benioff in 1936.[48] The observatory was in business.

From 1930 to 1949, these delicate instruments were located in the "Mansion," the original building on the grounds, and the observatory was supported by the New England Province. The construction of a new, modern seismological observatory, built adjacent to the "Mansion," was completed in 1949, and the instruments were transferred to the new facility at that time.

In a true sense, Father Daniel Linehan, S.J., an internationally recognized seismologist, is the father of the Weston Observatory of Boston College. Director of the observatory from 1950 to 1972, he founded the Department of Geophysics in 1949, which was located at the observatory but affiliated with Boston College. Father James Skehan, S.J., with a Ph.D. from Harvard, established the Department of Geology at Boston College in 1956. In 1968 these two departments were merged to become the Department of Geology and Geophysics at the undergraduate and graduate levels. The Weston Observatory itself, where many of the classes are held in proximity to the specialized library, became financially and academically a constituent part of Boston College in 1946. The seismic unit has, perhaps, garnered the lion's share of publicity as part of a world-wide network that reports on earthquakes and other natural phenomena.

The Downtown Club

A promising, but short-lived, project of the 1960s deserves mention. A group of young alumni drew up plans for "The Boston College Downtown Club." In proposing this new venture, the "founding fathers" explained that it would bring the alumni closer together by providing social and recreational facilities; it would also deepen Boston College's interest in and commitment to the City of Boston. It would, in the words of Vice President W. Seavey Joyce, S.J., "give a new visibility, a new evidence of Boston College in the heart of the city."[49]

At the Founders Day Dinner in April 1967 at the Sheraton-Plaza Hotel, Father Walsh declared that "The Boston College Downtown Club is a milestone in the history of Boston College." The 600 alumni who were present on that occasion vowed, "It can be done."[50] These same alumni, with $35.00 each, acquired charter membership; and 30 alumni each gave $1000 for life membership. The club had been incorporated in October 1966 as a nonprofit organization with a charter. A building had been selected and a bank was committed to the mortgage. The proposed structure was a four-story brick building on Hawkins Street near the newly developed Government Center. The building had to be purchased from the Boston Redevelopment Authority and renovated for approximately $360,000; another $40,000 would be spent on furnishings.[51]

The president of the club, John E. Joyce ('61), explained to his constituency that the immediate goal was 900 regular members. With 800 annual members and 70 life members, the club could count on $100,000. When the club reached that mark, the president explained, the Charlestown Savings Bank would provide a mortgage of $300,000.

The original plan, as events turned out, was too ambitious and had to be drastically amended. In October 1970 the Boston College Downtown Club opened its new home at 280 Devonshire Street, site of the much-loved and well-remembered Warmuth's Restaurant. The club was available for luncheons, parties, and social events; it was used by the alumni to meet business acquaintances and associates. But complications developed. The club had occupied Warmuth's with the understanding that it could remain for two years, giving the president and directors an opportunity to explore other possibilities. However, Blue Cross–Blue Shield, which had an option on the building, moved in more quickly than had been anticipated. The president and board of directors then made the difficult decision to terminate the club in order to avoid a future debt. The club closed down officially in May 1971.[52]

The Alumni Association

The Downtown Club episode calls attention to the Alumni Association itself. The Alumni Association at Boston College has always been close-knit, generous (according to individual means), fraternal, and enthusiastic. The first issue of the *Alumni Bulletin,* published in October 1919, announced the appointment of the first alumni secretary. The *Bulletin,* like many new ventures, had its ups and downs, with frequent lapses in publication. In October 1933, however, volume 1, number 1 of *Alumnus* appeared. This journal, which was designed to "disseminate news concerning Alma Mater" and act as a channel for alumni activities, has gone through several formats. But publication has been continuous, consistent, and interesting as *Alumni News, Bridge* and, presently, *Boston College Magazine*—the last justly praised for its design and content.

Even a casual perusal of alumni publications reveals the intense loyalty and genuine pride of Boston College graduates. The formal association itself, with outstanding officers, has been energized and motivated by such popular directors as William Flynn ('39), the late Walter Boudreau ('43), football and hockey star, and the present incumbent, John Wissler ('57), who was appointed to this office in 1967. For 36 years the attractive chalet that used to stand at 76 Commonwealth Avenue was the Alumni Association headquarters and scene of innumerable alumni gatherings, class reunions, dances, banquets, and football game celebrations. When the chalet, along with the former Philomatheia Club building, was razed to make room for attractive new dormitories, the Alumni Association found a new home in Putnam House on the Centre Street campus, one of the two original mansions with which Newton College of the Sacred Heart was begun. The new headquarters provide a gracious and efficient setting for Alumni Association business and functions.

Several alumni groups celebrate and support varsity athletics. The annual Varsity Club dinner is one of the highlights of the year. One such memorable dinner was held at the new Sheraton-Boston on January 6, 1966, with 1700 in attendance, including members of the 1940 Bowl Team.[53] The Blue Chips, an organization for the specific support of the hockey team, was founded in 1969 by Alfred Branca, M.D. ('39), who had been president of the Alumni Association in 1967–1968. The Hall of Fame was inaugurated in 1970.

Athletics in the Sixties

To comment briefly on athletics in the 1960s, the football team did not enjoy national ranking at that time, although there were bright spots. The 1967 season, for example, was disappointing, ending with a 4–6 record. Army, Syracuse, Penn State, and Villanova were worthy opponents, but the other teams on the schedule were not considered formidable. The loss through graduation of all-American Bob Hyland, who was a first-draft choice for the NFL, was probably the difference. Gary Andrachik from St. Ignatius High School in Cleveland, an outside linebacker, gave promise but suffered injuries in his senior year. Barry Gallup, a wide receiver on the 1967 team, was nationally recognized and later became an outstanding coach at Boston College.

The incomparable Robert Cousy, formerly a member of the world champion Boston Celtics, came to Boston College as head basketball coach in 1962. During his five years on the Heights, Boston College became one of the top 10 teams in the country. In 1967 Coach Cousy's team won 17 and lost 7. His teams went twice to the NIT and once to the Eastern NCAA. It was a dramatic improvement over previous years in this sport.

For more than a generation, John "Snooks" Kelley and hockey were practically synonymous at Boston College. A graduate of the class of 1928, "Snooks" became head coach in 1936; as he began his 30th year in 1966, he had won 400 games. Dean of American collegiate hockey coaches, he retired in 1972 after joining that exclusive group of coaches whose teams had won over 500 games. In those years Boston College won the NCAA national championship in 1949; went twice to the NCAA finals (1956 and 1965); and won the Boston Bean Pot trophy several times. He was succeeded by one of his former players, Leonard Ceglarski.[54]

The "great American game" has had a long tradition at the Heights. In the 1920s and 1930s the fierce rivalry between Boston College and Holy Cross drew literally thousands of spectators. In the 1960s, however, collegiate baseball seemed to be losing its attraction on every campus. In 1967 the Boston College baseball team, under Coach Eddie Pellagrini, did

Robert Cousy, basketball coach,
1962–1967.

not get off to a fast start, although it boasted some long-ball hitters. There was no home field and, due to poor weather, no home games. Nevertheless, Boston College managed to slip into the NCAA regionals, much to the dismay of Harvard, which had had a good season. In a crucial game of a three-game series, Boston College managed to beat the University of Massachusetts 7–6 in 12 innings in the rubber game. The Eagles then went on to the final in Omaha, where they won their first game over Ryder College 3–1. The bubble burst two days later when they lost to Houston, 3–2.[55]

Track and field was another major intercollegiate sport at this time. Coach William Gilligan succeeded the legendary Jack Ryder in 1952. Where Coach Ryder had concentrated on the sprints and the relay, Gilligan concentrated on the weights and developed some outstanding performers in the hammer throw, the discus, and the shotput. George "Dizzy" Desnoyers and John Fiore were accorded all-American honors in the hammer throw; they also threw the discus. Many remember that Harold Connolly ('53), who began under Ryder, was developed by Gilligan and won the

Gold Medal in the 1956 Olympics. Coach Gilligan retired after 29 years and was succeeded by Coach Jack McDonald in 1981.

Any reference to athletics at Boston College in these "middle years" would be incomplete without a bow to Eddie Miller ('57, MBA '68, Ed.D. '90). Popular with the alumni, coaches, and press, he was for a number of years the director of sports publicity at Boston College. His friendly contacts with the Boston sports writers assured coverage of every event, and his winning personality made him a friend of every writer. His contribution to the sports program was large, indeed. He was later appointed director of public relations for the University, but many were convinced that his heart remained in sports publicity.

Debating the Status of the Jesuit Community

Late in Father Walsh's administration, a question emerged that would engage the attention of Jesuits at Boston College—and, indeed, on every Jesuit campus—for the next several years. Basically, the discussions revolved around the legalities and advantages of restructuring the Board of Trustees and separating the Jesuit Community from the University. The resolution of these problems would, in time, drastically affect both parties. This question will be taken up in greater detail later on in the narrative, but, chronologically, it surfaced at this time.[56]

The Heights of October 6, 1967, carried the headline: "Walsh Consulting Jesuits in Community Restructure." The writer went on to explain that the Jesuits wanted more time to explore the implications of such a separation, but even those who were opposed admitted that the trustees would ultimately make the decision. *The Heights* expanded on this question in an editorial comment in the same issue. The editor went further on November 17 when, after a conversation with Father Walsh, he implied that an announcement was imminent. Such was not the case.

From other sources, it is clear that Father Walsh was convinced that the legal separation of the Jesuit Community and the University was desirable and inevitable.[57] In this whole matter, he was influenced by his presidential comrade-in-arms, Paul C. Reinert, S.J., of Saint Louis University. Father Reinert, in fact, had already restructured his board of trustees and separated the community and university into two distinct legal corporations, all of this with the tacit approval of the Superior General in Rome.[58]

These discussions were very important, but the wheels turned slowly. Although it would be several years before the "new order" was in place, it was Father Walsh, a leader in the movement, who set the machinery in motion at Boston College.

The End of the Walsh Era

Father Walsh submitted his resignation to the Board of Trustees on January 25, 1968, effective June 30, 1968. The narrative makes it abundantly clear that he was a talented and effective administrator who substantially advanced the growth and influence of the University.[59] As the director of public relations observed, "Study the reports, tote up the accomplishments, count the buildings in the physical expansion, measure the University's increased prestige, compute the academic achievements, gauge the performance—all of it is an open book."[60]

Father Walsh's experience was utilized in the Jesuit Educational Association, the National Catholic Educational Association, and the national organizations of independent colleges and universities.[61] Within the JEA he led the movement for the large, complex Jesuit university at a time when other members of his order favored the small, liberal arts college.[62] He argued that, in higher education, Catholics should not yield graduate and professional education exclusively to public and nonsectarian universities. In this "in house" controversy, as history testifies, he was successful.

As a spokesman for the NCEA, he was often called upon as an officer and representative to articulate the philosophy of education that motivates and guides Catholic higher education. Although he was the author of many articles on this subject, his basic thesis is contained in an article that appeared in *Alumni News* the year before his retirement entitled, "Why a Catholic University?" Father Walsh held that the Catholic university is "the place where the Church does its thinking."[63] The Catholic University is the borderline, as Father John Courtney Murray had first observed, where the Church meets the world and the world meets the Church."[64] For this reason, among others, Father Walsh considered it a blessing "to have on our own faculty [at Boston College] scholars who are not of the Catholic faith, whose insights and perspectives illumine our task and make possible within the University family the kind of open discussion that helps the Catholic university be the center of living thought that serves the intellectual mission of the Church."[65]

A testimonial dinner was tendered Father Walsh on May 5, 1968, at the Sheraton-Boston. It was a gathering of notable Bostonians from church and state and from the world of academia. Business leaders, who had

---

As a permanent monument to his achievements, Walsh Hall, a high-rise student residence, was dedicated to the memory of Father Walsh on October 2, 1982. In the program notes for that occasion is the following encomium:

No sooner had Father Walsh stepped away from the leadership of Boston College than the Trustees at Fordham University prevailed upon him to assume its presidency. Four years later, Father Walsh tendered his resignation to a grateful and reluctant Board and returned to Boston. The conclusion of fourteen years in a Presidency did not bring any form of retirement for Father Walsh. During the last ten years of his life, he was perhaps the most respected Trustee, and certainly the most cherished and relied-upon counselor in Catholic education.[66]

admired Father Walsh's financial acumen, were also present. Eulogies were given by Governor John A. Volpe, Richard Cardinal Cushing, and Dr. Abram Sachar, president of Brandeis. Father Leo P. O'Keefe, S.J., represented the Jesuits at Boston College. Cardinal Cushing summed it up when he said, "Father [Walsh] is that rare and wonderful sort of person who seems too good to be true, but he is in fact both good and true. . . . He has never tried to be spectacular or dramatic, but simply by being himself he has achieved universal success."[67]

*   *   *

Father Walsh may have been fortunate in the timing of his leaving the presidency of Boston College. The unsettled events of the following years would have stretched his administrative skills to the limit. It fell to the lot of an equally talented man, Father W. Seavey Joyce, to meet the challenge ahead.

ENDNOTES

1. There were 437 lay members of the faculty, and 103 Jesuit administrators and faculty members.
2. During these years the Jesuits continued the practice of "contributed services." The salaries paid to Jesuit faculty members and administrators were deposited in the Loyola Fund and, after taking what was necessary for the support of the Jesuit Community, were returned to the University for development.
3. After the long tenure as dean of the beloved Patrick J. McHugh (1921–1935), the College of Arts and Sciences had a series of relatively short-term deans: Father Joseph R.N. Maxwell (1935–1939), Father John J. Long (1939–1941), Father Stephen A. Mulcahy (1941–1948), Father Ernest B. Foley (1948–1951), Father Francis O. Corcoran (1951–1954), and Father John W. Ryan (1954–1956).
4. Father Driscoll's predecessor, Father Richard P. Burke, served as dean for three years 1955–1958, having succeeded the cofounder and distinguished second dean, Dorothy L. Book. In his rather brief administration, Father Burke skillfully adapted the School of Social Work to a radically changed set of accreditation standards.
5. *The Heights* (September 22 and 29, 1967).
6. *Ibid.* (October 10, 1958).
7. *Ibid.* (September 27, 1963).
8. *Ibid.* (December 3, 1965).
9. The Boston Theological Institute, formally incorporated in 1968, involves the following institutions: Andover Newton Theological School, Boston College Department of Theology, Boston University School of Theology, Episcopal Divinity School, Gordon-Conwell Divinity School, Harvard Divinity School, Holy Cross Greek Orthodox School of Theology, Saint John's Seminary, and Weston School of Theology.
10. *The Heights* (April 29, 1960).
11. *Ibid.* (May 6, 1960; May 13, 1960).
12. *Ibid.* (October 4, 1963).
13. *Ibid.* (November 8, 1963).
14. *Ibid.* (October 1, 1965).

15. *Ibid.* (November 13, 1967).
16. *Ibid.* (December 15, 1967).
17. *Ibid.* (March 5, 1968).
18. *Ibid.* (October 22, 1965).
19. *Ibid.* (October 29, 1965).
20. *Ibid.* (December 17, 1965).
21. *Ibid.* (January 14, 1966).
22. *Ibid.* (February 11, 1966).
23. *Ibid.* (March 4, 1966).
24. *Ibid.* (September 30, 1966).
25. *Ibid.* (October 14, 1966).
26. *Ibid.* (October 21, 1966).
27. *Ibid.* (April 7, 1967).
28. *Ibid.* (October 6, 1967).
29. *Ibid.* (October 13, 1967).
30. *Ibid.* (November 3, 1967).
31. *Ibid.* (November 13, 1967).
32. *Ibid.* (December 1, 1967).
33. *Ibid.* (December 15, 1967).
34. *Ibid.* (February 2, 1968).
35. *Ibid.* (January 2, 1968).
36. *Ibid.* (April 1, 1966).
37. Since the University Academic Senate (UAS) was to be so prominent in campus life during the next few years, the composition of the drafting committee should be noted: Father Charles Donovan, Academic Vice President; Father Robert Drinan, Dean of the Law School; Paula Fellows, School of Nursing; Walter Greaney, School of Management; John Mahoney, Department of English; John Schmitt, School of Education; Father Robert White, Weston College; Father John Willis, Dean of Arts and Sciences.
38. *The Heights* (February 9, 1968).
39. *Ibid.* (March 19, 1968).
40. The qualifications of the Weston faculty, most of whom had advanced degrees, were never an issue.
41. BCA.
42. BCA.
43. See James A. Donohoe, J.C.D., "Seminary Reform," *Alumni News* (Winter 1967).
44. Father Walsh to Father Donovan, November 15, 1967. BCA.
45. *Ibid.*
46. Father Joyce to Father Donovan, November 23, 1971.
47. *Ibid.*
48. For most of this information, see Annual Report: Weston Observatory, Boston College, 1973–1974. BCA.
49. "Eagles in the City," *Alumni News* (Fall 1967).
50. *Alumni News* (Fall 1967).
51. *Ibid.* According to an item in *Bridge* (November 1970), the initiation fee was $100 and annual membership $100.
52. This explanation for termination is based upon information supplied by John E. Joyce in a telephone conversation with Paul A. FitzGerald, S.J. on October 1, 1985. In 1987 some alumni were talking about trying a Boston College center in the city again.
53. See *Alumni News* (Spring 1966).
54. See "Snooks," *Bridge* (January 1972).

55. In 1987 Coach Pellagrini announced that the 1988 baseball season would be his last as coach.
56. See below, Chapter 34.
57. See Paul A. FitzGerald, S.J., *The Governance of Jesuit Colleges in the United States* (University of Notre Dame Press, 1984), p. 206.
58. See Paul C. Reinert, S.J., "First Meeting of a Board," *Jesuit Educational Quarterly* (October 1967), pp. 112–117.
59. See *A Ten-Year Report: 1958–1968.* BCA.
60. John Larner, *Alumni News* (Spring 1968).
61. See P. A. FitzGerald, S.J., *Governance,* pp. 161–67. Also Robert Harvanek, S.J., "The Objectives of the American Jesuit University: A Dilemma," *JEQ* (October 1961).
62. After retiring as president of Boston College and Fordham University, Father Walsh was advisor to Dr. Robert Wood, president of the University of Massachusetts.
63. *Alumni News* (Winter 1967).
64. *Ibid.*
65. *Ibid.*
66. Father Walsh died in the Jesuit Community residence at Boston College High School on April 23, 1982. The funeral Mass was held at St. Ignatius Church, Chestnut Hill. The large representation of Jesuit college presidents attested to the esteem in which he was held in the Society of Jesus.
67. BCA.

CHAPTER 30

A Restless Campus

It was apparent to those reading the signs of the times that Father Walsh's successor would inherit a restless campus. And, indeed, student activists of the 1960s won a place for themselves in American history. The final assessment has not yet been made, but the general pattern of events is fairly clear. Some background will be helpful in understanding what happened on the American campus—and more specifically at the Heights.

The National Context

It really began in 1954, when the Supreme Court's landmark decision, "Brown versus Board of Education," protected the equality of all Americans, including blacks. Thus was the way opened for a massive civil rights movement, which extended from the nonviolent marches of Martin Luther King to riots in the ghettos.

But campus unrest focused much more on antiwar and antidraft protests than on civil rights issues. The University of California at Berkeley was called the Bastille of the student revolution.[1] The movement began there in 1964 under the leadership of Mario Savio when the administration and regents tried to restrain student activists. The Free Speech Movement of Savio spread to Columbia University, where Mark Rudd and his student cohorts forced the resignation of President Grayson Kirk. Between January 1 and June 16, 1968, the National Student Association counted 221 major demonstrations at 101 colleges and universities involving nearly 40,000 students.[2]

In the beginning, at least, most student protests were nonviolent and their goals were reasonable. In fact, student activists in the mid-1960s confined themselves to doing good works locally. They contributed substantially to the national peace movement in 1965, and many of their demands were met. As it turned out, the Limited Test Ban Treaty of 1963, which outlawed atmospheric testing of nuclear weapons, had weakened the peace movement, but the war in Vietnam brought it back to life. That war, which strained the patriotism of so many Americans, affected a large segment of the collegiate population in a way no other war had ever done. In another curious departure, women on campus were as vocal as men in denouncing the draft, recruitment, and service. The coeds also shouted, "Hell no, we won't go!"[3] All of this activity would reach its peak in 1970 and 1971, but when the administration changed at Boston College in 1968, the campus was deceptively quiet.

New Directions from a New President

For the first time in the history of Boston College, faculty members—mostly laypersons, but with some Jesuit associates—engaged in a discussion of the qualities the new president should have and the kinds of policies he should promote and the challenges he would meet. Such discussion may have found its way indirectly into the selection process, but at that time there was no direct participation in it since the Superior General of the Society of Jesus, in consultation with the New England Provincial and his consultors, made the choice. On May 15, 1968, the Very Reverend Pedro Arrupe announced that Father W. Seavey Joyce would succeed Father Walsh as rector of the Jesuit community and president of Boston College. Father Joyce was the last president of Boston College to be named by the administration of the Society of Jesus. It was later decided that the new president would assume office on July 1.[4]

On Sunday, October 20, 1968, Father Joyce was inaugurated as the twenty-third president of Boston College. It was the first such ceremony in the history of the institution. A procession of faculty, representatives of other universities, and guests went from Gargan Hall in Bapst Library to a gathering of some 3700 people in McHugh Forum. Greetings were extended to the new president by Massachusetts Governor John A. Volpe, Boston Mayor Kevin White, faculty representative Thomas O'Connor, and James Stanton, president of the Boston College Alumni Association. President Nathan Pusey of Harvard welcomed Father Joyce to the university community of Boston. The Honorable Henry M. Leen ('29), chairman of the Board of Directors, presented the president with a medallion designed by Allison Macomber, artist-in-residence, to be handed down to future presidents.[5]

REV. W. SEAVEY JOYCE, S.J.
Twenty-third President

Born September 3, 1913, Father Joyce graduated from Boston College High School in
June 1931, entered the Jesuits that summer,
and in due course was ordained to the
priesthood at Weston College in 1943. He
earned a master's degree in economics
from Georgetown University and a doctorate from Harvard in the same discipline. He
joined the Boston College faculty in 1949 as chairman of the Economics Department and, while retaining that role, became dean of the College of Business
Administration in 1952, a position he held for 14 years. For the last two years
before his election as president, Father Joyce was vice president for community
affairs. In the 1950s he initiated the Boston citizen seminars, served as president
of the Metropolitan Planning Council, and was featured on a weekly television
program on metropolitan planning.

A few weeks before his inauguration, Father Joyce sent a message to the
students in which he indicated some of the items on the administration's
agenda. McGuinn Hall, the new social science center, would open; the
Graduate School of Social Work, housed at 126 Newbury Street, would
move into the new facility. He had high hopes that by the second semester
Devlin Hall would be substantially reconstructed, and plans were in
progress to convert the Bapst auditorium to library use, as was the original
intent of the architect. He mentioned an art center and new dormitories
which would include, for the first time, accommodations for women.[6]

There were ambitious plans for new and expanded academic programs.
The faculty, it was envisioned, would increase by 122 members, although
it was calculated that only 30 would soon retire or leave. In part this
increase was necessary to meet the challenge of the largest freshman class
in the history of the University. The University Academic Senate, organized
in 1967, would play a larger role, and the channel between the undergraduate government and the president would be widened. Beyond the faculty,
there would be changes in administration. Most immediately, for example,
the academic vice president became the senior vice president and dean of

faculties, and the vice presidents, with the academic deans, formed the president's cabinet.

One of Father Joyce's most important announcements, with far-reaching consequences, concerned the Board of Trustees. Father Walsh had established the Board of Regents in 1959 as an advisory body. This group, with the addition of newly appointed Jesuits, would now become the Board of Directors. The 10 Jesuit trustees would also be members of the new board, which would be responsible for the normal "direction and conduct of business and affairs of the University as of October 8, 1968."[7] The trustees reserved to themselves several critical prerogatives, such as amending the University's statutes and electing the president.

Although not intended as such at the time, the trustees/directors arrangement proved to be temporary (four years) and transitional—a bridge between exclusive Jesuit control and the present form of the trustees. A further discussion on the matter is found in Chapter 34. Several academicians were added to the Board of Directors: Robert F. Byrnes, chairman of the History Department at Indiana University, and Joseph G. Brennan ('33), chairman of the Philosophy Department at Barnard College. These men brought to the board particular concern for faculty interests. While Father Joyce remained *ex officio* a member of the Board of Trustees, he was no longer chairman; Father Joseph L. Shea, S.J., was elected to that position. These boards functioned in parallel until the fall of 1972, when both were consolidated into one Board of Trustees. The new board, with Jesuit and lay members, was a startling innovation which, as a catalyst, hastened the separate incorporation of the Jesuit Community.[8]

In bringing to a close his message to the students, the new president expressed the hope that we "may live and work and pray and play together, bound by the profound unity of our character and aspirations."[9] Fortunately for his own peace of mind, he could not foresee that his administration would be buffeted by the storms that blew across all American campuses; nor could he predict that his relations with a sizable segment of the student body would be less than pleasant. In the end he could not help but be disappointed in the truncated realization of his dreams and the frustrations that plagued his administration.

New Appointments

In addition to the Board of Directors, which obviously affected the administration of the University, Father Joyce made several new appointments that reflected his priorities and his philosophy of governance. In the process the traditional Jesuit influence in academics and campus policy was reduced and, conversely, the role of the layman was enhanced. As his executive assistant he chose Richard J. Olsen, 34 years old and a 1955 graduate of the University. With an MBA from Babson Institute, he had been a senior research associate in the Boston College Bureau of Public Affairs. In

December 1968, a few months into his term, he selected Francis X. Shea, S.J., as his executive vice president—the first to hold that office at Boston College. Involved in most of the crucial decisions of this administration, Shea was an enthusiastic innovator with an abundance of ideas. He entered the Jesuits in 1943, was ordained in 1956, and later earned a Ph.D. in English at the University of Minnesota. As a member of the faculty he had been involved in many initiatives, such as the Boston Theological Institute, the civil rights struggle (he had marched with Martin Luther King from Selma to Montgomery), Upward Bound, and other programs. Popular with the students, he was *Heights'* "Man of the Year" in 1968. As time went on, many thought that his recommendations were not sufficiently researched and that his effectiveness was limited by his lack of administrative experience, yet he was an important part of the Joyce administration.

Some other appointments were interpreted as the implementation of suggestions made by Father Joyce during his term as chairman of the Planning Committee under Father Walsh. James McIntyre was named vice president for student affairs, one of the first laymen to move to that level of administration. McIntyre ('57) has served the University in several capacities and is at present senior vice president. George Drury, S.J., moved from student affairs to become vice president for community affairs, a sensitive position in which he had to reconcile the interests of the University with the legitimate concerns of the surrounding community. Another distinguished layman, Paul Devlin ('39), whose academic career had flourished in the School of Management, became a vice president of the University and continued as assistant treasurer.[10]

There were other changes that, in time, would affect the University. On July 1, 1968, Francis J. Nicholson, S.J., was appointed superior of the Jesuit Community. A graduate of Boston College, class of '42, he had earned his LL.B. degree at Georgetown and a doctorate at Harvard Law

James McIntyre ('57), named vice president for student affairs in 1968.

School. At this time he was a professor of international law in the Boston College Law School. In 1971 he was elevated to rector (a title previously held by Father Joyce) and negotiated the separate incorporation of the Jesuit Community. His was an important role in the transition which will be explained later in detail in its proper context.

Naturally the president wanted his own team as he began his first academic year, and there were new faces among the deans. Samuel Aronoff (formerly of Iowa State), who had come to the campus as vice president for research, succeeded Father Walter Feeney as dean of the Graduate School of Arts and Sciences in 1969. The growth of the University and the professional competence of lay colleagues led to lay administrators and faculty filling positions that in earlier years had been reserved to Jesuits. Mary T. Kinnane was dean of the Summer School; Albert J. Kelley was dean of the School of Management, and Christopher Flynn was his associate dean; Donald J. Donley was dean of the School of Education; and Margaret Foley was dean of the School of Nursing.

A similar pattern which shifted administrative responsibilities from Jesuit to lay faculty was discernible in the various academic departments. While laymen and laywomen normally administered the professional schools and their departments, the trend to lay preponderance was most noticeable in the College of Arts and Sciences. In 1969–1970, only 6 out of 19 departments in the college were administered by Jesuits, while 13 were managed by laymen or laywomen.

The Theology Requirement: An Issue

As the 1968–1969 academic year opened, two problems that had been simmering reached the boiling point. One had to do with theology requirements and the other with student representation on campus committees. A petition composed by an ad hoc student committee was circulated in September demanding (1) that all theology requirements in the four undergraduate colleges be abolished; (2) that there be a 50 percent student membership on the educational policy committees of the four undergraduate colleges; and (3) that there be a 50 percent student membership on the University Academic Senate.[11]

The Boston College curriculum required students to take four semesters of theology to graduate—that is, 12 semester hours. While a few extremists called for the abolition of this requirement, most students and faculty recommended a reduction in credits. To some extent the problem had been exacerbated by Vatican Council II, which had revised the thrust of traditional courses: Everything had to be relevant. As time went on and votes were taken, 75 percent of the students and most of the faculty were in favor of a reduction in credits, but not abolition of the requirements. Oddly enough, the Arts and Sciences EPC seemed to be moving in the direction of a drastic reduction from 12 hours to 6. Father William Leonard, chairman of Theology, tried to persuade the EPC to accept 9 hours and also to make theology obligatory for all, irrespective of creedal adherence. In addition to valid academic reasons for endorsing 9 hours, faculty members were understandably anxious to continue their course offerings.

In the meantime, however, a sharp controversy broke out between the University Academic Senate, which attempted to legislate for the four undergraduate schools, and the EPCs who guarded their own prerogatives. In essence it was a jurisdictional question. The Arts and Sciences EPC maintained that where a department of the University administers courses in more than one undergraduate college, change should be determined by the separate colleges. In point of fact, since the Department of Theology was located in A&S (and serviced the other colleges), A&S assumed responsibility for any change that might be made.[12] But the jurisdictional conflict persisted through several meetings of the UAS, which held for 9 hours.

Finally, in a joint meeting of the executive committee of the University Academic Senate and the A&S Educational Policy Committee, there was an attempt to resolve the two questions of jurisdiction and credit hours. For practical purposes—but without yielding on the principle—A&S agreed to register for 9 hours of theology for 1969–1970. The A&S EPC did not wish to put pressure on the other schools to reduce their curriculum to 6 hours, nor did the committee wish to change registration or catalogs without sufficient notice.[13]

The controversy continued under the chairmanship of Father O'Malley, who had replaced Father Leonard. The Theology subcommittee, chaired by Professor Brian Cudahy, recommended that the requirement remain at 9 hours for 1970–1971; the requirement would then be reduced to 6 hours commencing in September 1971. Due to the ecumenical choice of courses, it was also decided that theology would be required of all students. It is worth noting that although a few faculty and many students had proposed dropping theology as a curriculum requirement in the course of this discussion, a majority felt that Boston College, as a Jesuit institution, should include the "queen of the sciences" which has been defined as *fides querens intellectum*. As of March 5, 1970, theology remained safely within the proposed basic, liberal core curriculum at Boston College.

The Students' Desire for a Greater Role

Theology was not the only area where students, becoming more aggressive every year, were putting pressure on the administration. They were determined to have a greater voice in forming campus policy. Although they had enjoyed a modicum of success in gaining access to the Educational Policy Committees, they quickly realized that the University Academic Senate would be a more important power base because it could affect every corner of the campus. The UAS (formed in 1967) as originally constituted included

Father Joyce moved the president's office from St. Mary's Hall to Botolph House on Mayflower Road. He was to find the new location easier for students to picket and occupy.

14 administrators, 28 faculty members, and 2 students. Opening with a strong bid, the students demanded 50 percent representation on the basis of its larger constituency.[14] This was, as they knew, an unrealistic demand, and they gradually scaled down their request, but they refused to settle for tokenism.

Accordingly, the Congress of the Undergraduate Government at Boston College presented a resolution, unanimously approved by its members, directing the president of UGBC "not to accept an increment of less than 12."[15] The Committee on Student Affairs of the UAS, after a series of heated meetings, endorsed the student resolution and sent its recommendations on to the full senate. In November 1968 the senate approved the increase of students to 14, which was approximately 25 percent of the membership, and at its December meeting the Board of Directors approved the addition of 12 students (5 graduate students and 9 undergraduates).[16] As *The Heights* noted, 25 percent gave the students "more power in making academic policy than they have at any other Catholic university."[17]

By early March 1969 the undergraduate and graduate student governments had presented their selections to the senate, which formally welcomed them as members. Not even *The Heights* editorial staff, which enjoyed its adversarial role, could quarrel with the sympathetic response of administrators, faculty, and directors to student demands. For their part, the student senators made a significant and responsible contribution in the areas of prime concern to them: resident life, food services, recreational facilities, and student organizations.

While the students were privy to many campus initiatives, the budget—strictly guarded by the Board of Directors and financial vice president—was beyond their purview. In September 1968 the president announced a tuition increase of $400, which would raise the total to $2000, effective

September 1969.[18] The budget for 1967–1968 was $23,155,500; the projection for 1968–1969 was $24,147,800. The figures would continue to climb with the growth of the University, and income and expenses had to balance as in any other enterprise. The reasons for the increase were (1) additional faculty members, (2) current inflation, and (3) the anticipated elimination of the Loyola fund (which amounted to $850,000 in 1968) through separate incorporation of the Jesuit Community.

Predictably, students protested the tuition increment and recommended guidelines for future increases. A tuition hike, they insisted, should affect only those enrolled after the effective date; students should be immune from further liability during their student years—for example, a hike in freshman year would not be repeated for those students in sophomore, junior, or senior year. The most recent increase, they argued, should affect only those who enrolled in September 1969.

To comply with such demands would have been irresponsible on the part of the administration and, indeed, a design for fiscal disaster. But student protest became an automatic reaction to a tuition increment, which was the initial pretext for a student strike in 1970.

The Mary Daly Controversy

It was, to some extent, ironic that the students, some of whom had favored the abolition of the theology requirement and others a reduction in credits, should have so vociferously protested the administration's decision to terminate the contractual services of a theology professor. *The Heights,* always prepared with editorial comment, carried a banner headline on May 11, 1969: "Professor Mary Daly Fired: No Promotion or Extension." Although the subject of the ensuing controversy was a junior faculty member at that time, the case became a *cause célèbre.*

Mary Daly, an assistant professor with two doctorates (a pontifical S.T.D. and a Ph.D.) and the author of two books and several articles, had been at Boston College for three years. She herself had initiated the process of promotion to associate with tenure. With customary confidentiality, the application moved from the department committee to the dean's committee, through the University committee to the president. According to the statutes, he made the final decision—and it was negative. Approached by the students, who proved to be a forceful lobby, he refused to change his mind; nor would he reveal his reasons.[19]

As the students continued their protest in earnest, a number of faculty members joined the crusade in support of Professor Daly, and petitions with 4000 signatures were presented to Father Joyce. UGBC condemned the dismissal. Members of the faculty argued that the basic question was one of academic freedom, since Daly's ideas and opinions were not endorsed by everyone; she was known to have critics within her own department and in a wider circle. The Arts and Sciences Senate passed a resolution indicating that Daly's dismissal would jeopardize the reputation of Boston College in the academic world. The Undergraduate Government Congress recommended that seniors withhold their contribution to the University and that the senior gift committee cease its activities.

At a meeting in late March 1969, the UAS voted to make Boston College completely coeducational and to cut theology to nine credits, but it voted against a reconsideration of what had become known as "the Daly case." But pressure continued as 1500 students marched in protest and picketed Botolph House, the president's residence. The effect of the protest on the administration resulted in the appointment by the president of a special committee, chaired by Professor Edward Hirsh, for a tenure review. The committee was charged to recommend a decision to the president based on a view "of the total situation." On the recommendation of the committee, the president reversed his decision and Daly was promoted to associate professor with tenure. It was, as the press pointed out, an unusual move in academic circles, but Professor Daly felt that her reinstatement was "a significant victory for Boston College."[20] The resolution of this case clearly demonstrated that the administration was no longer immune to pressure from faculty and students—a development which would have come as a surprise to an earlier generation at the Heights.

A New Dean for Arts and Sciences

Father Joyce's first year in office must have seemed endless. While the Arts and Sciences faculty was searching for a solution to the controversy on the theology requirement, the president was presented with yet another problem for which the administration itself was at least partially responsible. Early in 1969 it was decided at the highest level that a new dean was needed for the College of Arts and Sciences. The executive vice president wanted a dean of Arts and Sciences who would be attuned to his own style of administration and who at the same time would be sympathetic to the growing activism of the students. He persuaded Father Joyce that a change of administration in the College of Arts and Sciences should be made. His choice for the office was a respected member of the English Department, Richard E. Hughes, one of the most productive scholars on the faculty.

In March 1969, after Dean Willis had been informed of the administration's intention, Father Shea asked Professor Hughes to accept appointment as acting dean of the College of Arts and Sciences. When Hughes declined that designation, he was offered the deanship without qualification. After the fact, the administration decided that faculty consultation was needed. However a series of unforeseen events forced the administration to go to the Board of Directors for confirmation before advising the chairmen of this decision.

The faculty, while admitting the statutory right of the president to appoint a dean, vehemently protested the procedure. At a special, late afternoon faculty meeting in the Bapst auditorium, Academic Vice President Donovan first apologized for the manner in which dean-elect Hughes had been appointed, then called upon the faculty to affirm the appointment by acclamation. The faculty refused the vice president's request and insisted upon participation in the process.[21] At the same time, faculty leaders made it quite clear that their objections were not directed at Professor Hughes, who was personally acceptable. A special committee of the A&S EPC was formed to investigate the chain of events and to recommend a response. After the investigation, which received the complete cooperation of the administration, the committee recommended that the faculty refuse to endorse the appointment and suggested instead a selection committee for nominations.[22]

At this point, in late May, the appointment had gone beyond the possibility of revision and the administration wished to save the dean-elect further embarrassment. In commenting on the faculty recommendations, which he considered advisory, the president declined to accept their advice. As he wrote to the dean of Arts and Sciences, "I have requested Prof. Hughes to accept the deanship; he has received the concurring approval of the Directors. . . . Prof. Hughes is, therefore, the dean designate as of July 1st."[23] Professor Hughes agreed and so informed the faculty, observing, "I'm damned if I do and damned if I don't accept the appointment." In the circumstances, he decided "to go with the affirmators, who seem to have the edge."[24] Dean Hughes held office during the period of student unrest and confrontation. He was, in fact, and was perceived by students to be sensitive to student concerns and viewpoints.

The End of ROTC

There was never a dull moment at University Heights during these times. When the administration put out one fire, another started. Repercussions from the Vietnam war ran wide and deep, and national legislation brought the war closer to the campus. The Selective Service Act of 1967 deferred undergraduates in most instances, but it abolished deferments for students applying to and accepted at graduate schools. In any case, Vietnam was the prism through which students looked at the military and its pervasive presence. One of the casualties of the war on many American campuses was the Reserve Officers Training Corps (ROTC). Ivy League schools (Harvard, Yale, and Darmouth) were among the first to attack these programs, and Boston College was not far behind. The academic arguments against ROTC at the Heights were about the same as at other universities: (1) ROTC courses should not be granted academic credit; (2) ROTC instructors should not be granted professorial status, because they are affiliated with and controlled by an outside agency; (3) ROTC should not exist through the Military Science Department, nor should free space be allocated to this group.[25]

The Student Coordinating Committee (SCC), a subcommittee of Students for a Democratic Society (SDS), took the larger view and adopted the classic arguments of campus liberals against ROTC. The program, they insisted, was an important implementation of American foreign policy whose object was to advance the cause of American imperialism. Imperialism, in turn, provided an umbrella for American multinational corporations. And in all of this, the Defense Department (really the Army) controlled policy on campus. Consequently, the SCC believed that arguments favoring the retention of ROTC on the Boston College campus were invalid. Members of the committee consequently committed themselves "to work for the complete removal of ROTC from this University."[26]

The question was first introduced to the UAS by George O'Toole, an undergraduate senator, who, on February 19, 1969, filed a motion which was sent to the Committee on Curriculum and Educational Policy. O'Toole recommended that Boston College effect a complete and immediate severence of all its relations with the U.S. Army ROTC Program. This included the abolition of the Department of Military Science and the withdrawal of University facilities.[27] Like it or not, the UAS was handed an explosive issue and the question was debated in that forum during the next year and a half.

At the upper echelon of authority, the executive vice president, who was expected by the students to support the SDS, stated that the University "considered [ROTC] a valid option for students, and, since some of them find it desirable, they should have it."[28] The administration, explained Father Shea, had made several concessions. Arts and Sciences had dropped the credit it once gave for certain courses; only CBA gave these credits for a course to juniors and seniors, and the administration had urged CBA to drop even those credits. No credit was given for ROTC courses in the

Peace in the world, but not on campus.

School of Education. So it was not an honest academic question. Facilities, it was true, were allocated "rent free," but that was the case with other extracurricular activities. The latest contract with the Army was signed on March 23, 1965, and could be terminated by either party with one year's notice.

Acting on the motion submitted by George O'Toole, the Curriculum Policy Committee of the UAS issued its report on December 3, 1969. The committee was of the opinion that the existence of the ROTC program at Boston College should be considered on the basis of objective criteria, not whether it is good or bad for students on campus. Following this line, and as a result of its investigation, the committee recommended that the program be maintained but also insisted that changes should be made in its relationship to the University.[29]

Basically, the committee thought it undesirable for the United States to have the military academies supply the entire officer corps of the armed services. There was a need and a place for officers broadly educated in the liberal arts who would add another dimension to planning and policy within the military complex. At the same time, the committee cautioned that the contract with the Department of Defense should be carefully worded so as to preserve the complete independence of the University in the decision process. Autonomous control should not be relinquished even to the Department of Military Science.

The UAS, however, rejected the recommendation of the subcommittee. Instead, at the UAS meeting on May 6, 1970, Senator Michael Malec from the Sociology Department introduced a resolution strongly urging the University "to immediately take whatever actions are necessary to sever all ties with the Reserve Officers Training Corps." This was subsequently amended "in the light of the recent direction of U.S. foreign policy in Southeast Asia," and the UAS instructed the subcommittee to re-examine the "role and propriety" of ROTC at Boston College.[30] The subcommittee was given until the fall to report back.

But events now moved rapidly toward a denouement. On June 1 the UAS overwhelmingly endorsed a proposal to end all ties with the government program. Since this position apparently reflected his own opinion, Father Joyce, on June 14, brought the UAS proposal to the Board of Directors. On the following day, a reluctant and pensive board declined to approve the UAS resolution of May and tabled the motion. The board decided, instead, to ask its own subcommittee on academic affairs to discuss the motion with the UAS. This orderly process broke down when, in early September, about 350 students marched on Roberts Center where the ROTC offices were located. Ten or fifteen broke into the offices and smashed furniture, scattered records, and damaged military property.[31]

Although the board was reluctant to yield to pressure tactics, the directors felt that, in the interest of campus peace, it would be unwise to continue to oppose the president, the UAS, many of the faculty, and a large segment of the student body. Though several options were open, one of which was off-campus programs, the board decided upon a clean break. On October 5, 1970, Colonel Schofield, the ranking officer of Army ROTC, received notification from President Joyce that the ROTC contract would not be renewed. He requested the Army to vacate the premises by June 1, 1971, the expiration of the academic year.[32] This decision was denounced in certain quarters, notably among the alumni, and was characterized as a corporate capitulation to a noisy pressure group which did not represent the traditional values of the University. Never entirely dormant, interest in ROTC was revived in the eighties when the campus enjoyed a more favorable climate of opinion.

Extending a Hand to Blacks

With the rise of the civil rights movement and the new emphasis on minorities and women, it was inevitable that colleges and universities would be called upon to advance the intellectual and academic opportunities of black students and black professionals. Boston College, like other area colleges, felt the pressure to develop black studies programs. As a Jesuit institution, Boston College was additionally obligated to respond to Father General Arrupe's 1968 letter on the "Inter-Racial Apostolate."[33] In October 1967 Father Michael Walsh was approached by Melvin King and Bryant Rollins, leaders of the black community in Roxbury, to discuss what Boston College should be doing about black students. The meeting turned on such points as recruitment and admission. Accordingly, a "Black Talent Search" was created in February 1968 to seek out members of the black community who were capable of completing four years at Boston College but who had not had the opportunity of applying or being considered.[34] In seeking out and identifying these prospects, Vice President for Student Affairs McIntyre decided to employ criteria which "were not culturally biased" and which went beyond the traditional methods employed by Boston College. To cite one of the innovations, two members of the selection committee were from the Roxbury community.

The Black Talent Search yielded 47 new black freshmen in September 1968. These were screened from an applicant pool of 130. Each student received at least $1000 in aid from a $100,000 special scholarship fund established in February by Father Walsh just before he left office.[35] It was originally intended that 25 students would be accepted the first year and $25,000 assigned for scholarships. This quota was not adhered to, and from the beginning more money was used than originally assigned. Administrative expenses for director, tutors, and secretarial staff were also assumed by the University. The class of '72, therefore, was not only the largest to date and the most qualified, but it was the most culturally diverse. McIntyre had correctly anticipated that these cultural initiatives would cause tensions, and the Black Forum had its share of growing pains on the Chestnut Hill campus.

*Melvin King, community pro-
poser of a program for black
students at Boston College.*

In February 1969 Boston College staged its first Black History and Culture Week. Black students took this opportunity to comment on their reception at the Heights, and most were critical. As one student put it, "I found just what any other black student would have found walking on a white, Irish Catholic campus."[36] There were pockets of sympathy. The black community on campus had a powerful advocate in Father Robert Drinan, dean of the Law School and chairman of the Advisory Committee of Massachusetts to the National Commission for Civil Rights. He agreed that Boston College, as a Catholic institution, had for too long been indifferent to the academic needs of the black students.[37] This expression of support led to a series of demands by the Black Forum which revolved around the issue of black studies. The Forum wanted a survey of offerings in Boston area colleges, recruitment of black faculty members, cross registration with other schools, an increase in course offerings, and 50 black students for September 1969. In general the demands pointed to the creation of a genuine black studies program.[38]

Yet another demand stipulated that all personnel hired for the black studies program would have to be approved by the Black Forum. This peremptory claim to competence cost the Forum sympathy and votes, and not even *The Heights* would support such an extraordinary prerogative.

Basically, the Forum wanted the establishment of a black studies department and the right to control that department regarding offerings and faculty. To implement this plan, the Forum asked for a full time black administrator to supervise the program and a minimum of two black faculty members to teach core courses. And, finally, they expected the administration to develop plans for an endowed Black Chair.

In voicing his reaction at a March meeting of the University Committee on Black Students and Studies, Father Joyce said that he was generally favorable to the demands of the Black Forum. He suggested, however, that the Forum should first begin to move its demands through the UGBC and the UAS. With regard to the demand that new hires be subject to Forum approval, Father Joyce explained that new faculty would have to go through normal channels for final approval by the academic vice president.[39]

New programs are normally subject to "hitches and glitches." So it was not surprising—although it was unfortunate—that from the beginning of the Black Talent Program there were several controversies.[40] In general terms, there were three problems, all of which revolved in one way another around jurisdictional privileges and prerogatives. The first controversy concerned the question of committees: Should there be one for admissions and another to supervise the students after their admission? Connected with this problem—and probably more serious—was the question of who would have ultimate authority in admissions. And the third controversy—which also generated heated exchanges between administrators—concerned the relaxed standards of admission for Black Talent students and the adjusted standards for those with deficiencies in required courses.

In August 1968 Father Joyce appointed the Reverend Theodore L. Lockhart the first director of the program; he was also given the title of assistant dean. However, he resigned in May 1969. His place as director was taken by A. Robert Phillips, a member of the Urban League of Greater Boston. The projected two committees (admissions and supervision) were reduced to one, and Professor Theodore Howe of the School of Social Work became the supervisor of the program in its day-to-day operation. Although administrators were in place, authority over admissions became the sticking point. Who would make the final decision? As time went on, it was more or less agreed—though many remained unhappy with it—that the Black Talent Program would be, for admissions purposes, distinct from the regular Office of Admissions. Father Edmond Walsh, S.J., dean of admissions, was never reconciled to this solution. Several times he pointed out that no other college in the Boston area allowed a separate admissions policy and procedure.[41]

After one year in operation, the Black Talent Program began to take shape. By January 1970, with three semesters completed, there emerged three distinctive divisions or components which made up the whole: (1) the Black Talent Program, which assumed responsibility for recruitment and admissions; (2) the Black Studies Program, which designed the academic curriculum; and (3) the Black Forum, composed entirely of black students, which had a good deal of authority and—in some areas—autonomy in the administration of the program. The entire program, in all its parts, was under the overall supervision of the Committee of Black Students and Studies. These administrative complexities made the operation of the program cumbersome and irritated key personalities.

The cost of the program to the University quickly escalated beyond the administration's expectations and intentions. As initially planned, Father Walsh's commitment of $100,000 exclusively for 25 black scholarships was to be disbursed in increments of $25,000 per annum over a four-year period until the full level was reached. This quota was never adhered to, and from the beginning more money was used than originally assigned. In a letter dated February 12, 1970, Father F. X. Shea wrote to Carl Lewis, President of the Black Student Forum, to make these points:

> The University is now prepared to make a commitment of five times the original amount: that is, increments of $125,000 each year until the four years of the fully operating program are complete and the $500,000 is reached. This is a commitment of Boston College funds, in addition to Federal funds.[42]

The Board of Directors confirmed this commitment and also agreed that 10 percent minority student enrollment would be an ideal goal, although funds for that were not readily available.

February 1970 was a critical month. There were 157 full-time and 29 part-time black students, a total of 186 on campus, and problems began to accumulate. Although the Board of Directors had agreed on 10 percent minority students, the University had to operate under fiscal restraints. The designation of an all-black dormitory was under legal study; the decision on a black coed residence had to wait on further consideration. The black students, so it seemed, wanted more of everything, while the white students criticized what they saw as "excessive" funding for them. Even the faculty was critical of the mixed signals and confused statements coming from the administration. Resentment spilled over and, on March 19, 1970, black students took over Gasson Hall.[43] White students, in retaliation, sealed off the building and would allow no food to be passed to those inside. The occupants left the building at 5:00 p.m.

Shortly after this incident, the University Committee on Black Students and Studies was dissolved, and the EPCs and UAS tried to pick up the pieces. In January 1971 Phillips resigned as director of the Black Talent Program, alluding—in an otherwise cordial letter—to the difficulties he had encountered from the "Western Man."[44] In restructuring the program, Father Joyce established the Black Talent and Coordinating Committee, with Professor Albert Folkard as chairman. In a series of confrontations in the summer of 1971, the black students again insisted on autonomy in processing applications to the Black Talent Program, in the appointment of a black lecturer, and in a "tuition freeze" at $2000, although it had been raised to $2600 for all others.

At this point the administration, in a break with the past policy of concessions and with the academic vice president now in control, rejected these demands. After this action there remained only one last major controversy, which revolved around the title of the administrator of the program. While the black students strenuously lobbied for the title of dean and wrote the job description, the administration favored assistant or associate dean. The search for a highly qualified black administrator continued through the fall of 1973. In February 1974 Father J. Donald Monan, the new president, appointed John L. Harrison associate dean in the College of Arts and Sciences with responsibility for the Black Talent Program. And in 1975 fiscal control of the program was transferred to the office of Francis Campanella, executive vice president. A later chapter will recount how, after this rather shaky start, the program for black and other minority students has matured as an important and enriching part of the University.

Other Public Issues

There were other signs that continued to remind the administration that campus activists were alive and well. Their efforts for public exposure reflected a national student compulsion to make headlines in local or campus papers. This tendency seemed to combine with a desire to test the limits of toleration on a Catholic campus. For example, a good deal of publicity was focused on Boston College when William Baird was invited to speak at the Heights. Because of his calculated efforts to circumvent the law in Massachusetts, which at that time forbade the public display or sale of contraceptive devices, he found himself in the toils of the law in 1967 after an appearance at Boston University. The administration at Boston College made a strong effort to discourage any overtures to him from student organizations at University Heights.

In late March 1969, however, *The Heights* editorial staff interviewed Baird in the paper's office and published a full account with obvious embellishments. A month later, against the expressed wishes of the administration, Baird spoke to an audience in Fulton Hall. As reported by *The Heights*, "He addressed himself to the inadequacy of Massachusetts birth control laws, the inhumanity of illegal abortions, and the hypocrisy of 'Humanae Vitae.' "[45] In particular, he challenged state officials to explain why it was illegal for him to distribute birth control information when the archbishop of Boston was free to distribute pamphlets on the rhythm method. Apart from the merits of the arguments, the student activists had succeeded in embarrassing the University.

In addition to the Baird affair there were incidents of crude language, offensive pictures, and journalistic bias in *The Heights*. The matter came to a head in February 1970 with an article about and a purported interview with Paul Krassner, one of the founders of the Yippie movement. An alumnus who was a Boston journalist and former member of *The Heights* staff called the article "the lowest form of journalism he ever saw in his life."[46] The article, extremely offensive in its obscene, descriptive language, was, according to legal counsel, open to criminal libel—that is, the trustees, as official publishers of the paper, would be liable in any lawsuit. The administration took action. In implementing the recommendation of the University Communication Board, the editorial staff was notified that the newspaper would be legally and fiscally separated from the University, because the latter "could no longer support patent irresponsibility."[47] Although use of the name was initially prohibited, the newspaper was later allowed to use "The Heights" on its masthead with the qualification, "Boston College's Independent Student Weekly." It was also given office space in McElroy.

*   *   *

And so Boston College came through the restless years relatively un-scathed. But quiet would not yet return, for the worst was yet to come.

ENDNOTES

1. William L. O'Neill, *Coming Apart: An Informal History of America in the 60's* (Chicago: Quadrangle Books, 1971), p. 279.
2. *Ibid.*, p. 289. See also Allen J. Matusow, *Unravelling of America: A History of Liberalism in the 1960's* (New York: Harper & Row, 1984).
3. An editorial in *The Heights* (September 24, 1968) urged the removal of the American flag and the flagpole from the College green.
4. *The Heights* (June 20, 1968) contained an excellent brief biography of Father Joyce.
5. BCA. Some students picketed the academic procession from Bapst Library to McHugh Forum with signs saying that the money for the elaborate inauguration should have been given to the poor.
6. *The Heights* (October 2, 1968).
7. *Ibid.*
8. See below, Chapter 34.
9. *The Heights* (October 2, 1968).
10. In 1985 Bernard Cardinal Law, Archbishop of Boston, appointed Paul Devlin chancellor of the archdiocese, the first layman to hold that post.
11. At this time there were no student representatives on SOM and SON EPCs. A&S had 2 students and 14 faculty members; SOE had 2 students and 9 faculty members. *The Heights* (October 2, 1968).
12. Minutes, A&S EPC, October 2, 1969. BCA.
13. Minutes, A&S EPC, *passim,* 1969. BCA.
14. *The Heights* (October 2, 1968).
15. BCA.
16. BCA.
17. *The Heights* (December 10, 1968).
18. *The Heights* (September 24, 1968).

19. The AAUP does not require reasons for the termination of non-tenured faculty.
20. *The Heights* (July 11, 1969).
21. Minutes, A&S Faculty Meeting, May 6, 1969. BCA.
22. Report to the Faculty of the College of Arts and Sciences by the EPC, May 20, 1969. BCA.
23. W. Seavey Joyce to John R. Willis, May 22, 1969. BCA.
24. Richard E. Hughes to Ladies and Gentlemen of the Faculty, June 3, 1969. BCA. Since he had been a presidential appointment, Richard Hughes resigned when Father Joyce left office in 1972.
25. See *The Heights* (February 25, 1969).
26. *Ibid.*
27. *Ibid.*
28. *The Heights* (March 11, 1969).
29. Minutes, UAS Meeting, May 6, 1970. BCA.
30. *Ibid.*
31. *The Heights* (September 15, 1990).
32. This arrangement allowed juniors to finish the program. See *The Heights* (October 20, 1970).
33. The *Boston Globe* (April 27, 1968) reported that of a student body of 6289 at Boston College, only 13 were blacks.
34. *The Heights* (August 2, 1968).
35. The *Boston Globe* (March 28, 1968) carried a feature article on the new program.
36. *The Heights* (February 11, 1969).
37. *Ibid.* (February 18, 1969).
38. *Ibid.* (March 4, 1969).
39. *Ibid.* (March 18, 1969).
40. "Black Talent and Black Studies Program: A Summary." Hereinafter this item will be referred to as "A Summary."
41. "A Summary," p. 7.
42. *Ibid.*, p. 8.
43. *Ibid.* See *The Heights* (April 29, 1970).
44. "A Summary," p. 10.
45. *The Heights* (April 29, 1969).
46. *The Heights* (February 24, 1970; March 18, 1970).
47. *Ibid.*

CHAPTER 31

"The Strike" and Other Protests

While, as previously noted, there were several student protests and building or office occupations during the troubled years of Father Joyce's presidency, none of them substantially interrupted the daily routine of the University as did "the strike" in the spring of 1970. While the tactic employed may have been suggested by student reaction elsewhere to national and international issues, the trigger for the strike was purely local and economic: a proposed tuition increase of $500. Although nonviolent and, indeed, almost gentlemanly in comparison with the student protests and takeovers on some other campuses, this strike nevertheless was a trauma of major proportions for a normally peaceful and rational community. As such, it deserves attention in some detail in this history.

The Tuition Trauma

During the 1950s and 1960s tuition increases had usually taken place every other year. Thus, a freshman arriving in September 1961 found a tuition of $1000. In this student's junior year, there was a $200 increase to $1200, where the tuition remained during the final two years. A student entering the University in 1965 paid a tuition of $1400, which rose to $1600 in the junior and senior years. In Father Walsh's final year, 1967–1968, the tuition for the following year was not raised, so that when Father Joyce assumed the presidency the tuition was still $1600. During his first year, a tuition increase of $400 was adopted for 1969–1970. There was, as the last chapter showed, some protest at the size of the increase, but no demonstration or other outbreak occurred.

Since finances were the most serious, if not the most visible, problem that Father Joyce encountered, a brief explanation of the origin of the fiscal crisis is presented here. For nearly 90 years Boston College's budget had included no salaries for Jesuits. Jesuit services were contributed as a "living endowment" to the institution. In the 1950s it was decided to assign salaries to Jesuits comparable to those paid to laymen for similar service. These Jesuit salaries were paid back in one check to the rector of the Community. Each year the Jesuits tallied their accounts and calculated the excess. They contributed this excess to Boston College. The College set the gift aside as the Loyola fund, intended for building expansion. In the mid-1960s the University began to have an annual operating deficit, but the auditors offset the losses by transferring portions of the Loyola fund to balance the books. This method of balancing operating results had obscured the need for tuition increases, but when Father Joyce took office, the Loyola fund was running out and the reality of an operating deficit faced him. It took extraordinary measures, including substantial tuition increases, to move toward a balanced budget.

In view of the operating deficit disclosed in the early part of the Joyce presidency, it was clear that during the 1950s and 1960s tuition increments had been too modest. Nevertheless it is understandable in the light of past practice that students who had absorbed a $400 raise in tuition in 1969–1970 would be shocked at the prospect of an additional $500 increase for 1970–1971. The manner of announcing the increase may also have contributed to student activism. The president's office issued a release stating that, at its March 20 meeting, the Board of Directors had authorized and recommended a $500 increase in tuition, but added, "The final determination will be made during the week of April 6 after University officers meet with representatives of the undergraduate government." Thus the students, instead of being faced with an administrative decision, could conclude that the tuition issue was a matter of negotiation. The president's release explained that the University's financial report for the fiscal year 1969–1970 showed that operating expenses were expected to exceed income by an estimated $4.2 million. To pay current bills Boston College would have to borrow up to $2 million; were the tuition increase not established, borrowing at the end of the following fiscal year would reach about $5 million. Even though the Budget Committee had effected cuts of more than a million dollars for 1970–1971, the $500 tuition increase was needed to stem the University's mounting indebtedness.

On the Wednesday after the Easter break, Father Joyce addressed some

4000 students in Roberts Center, explaining the University's financial crisis and the meaning of a $500, $400, or $300 tuition increase in relation to the deficit. As the session ended there was stamping of feet and cries of "Strike!" were heard.

The following day the undergraduate government cabinet met with Father Joyce and agreed to a tuition increase of $300 for 1970–1971, with a strong likelihood that there would be another increase in 1971–1972 and that this increase could be in excess of $300. It was agreed that any further increase would involve student participation in the Budget Committee and other bodies determining the amount of increase. The undergraduate congress, however, rejected this agreement. On Sunday the student government announced a strike, and on Monday, April 13, it began.

The vast majority of students were passive participants in the strike. Most commuting students did not come to campus. Resident students remained in their quarters or wandered the campus. Throughout the strike some classes were held quietly, particularly in the School of Management. A small number of activists manned the entrance to the campus, turning away most cars seeking entrance. Entrances to classroom and office buildings were also picketed. As the strike became protracted, some resident students went home.

Nevertheless, at first it seemed as though the strike might be short-lived. On Wednesday, April 15, the administration and student negotiators agreed upon a 19-point package, which included a tuition increase of $240. The student representatives stipulated that the proposed agreement must

Making banners for the first student strike in Boston College history.

be submitted to a student referendum, which they insisted could not be held until the following Tuesday, April 21. Obviously they expected a favorable vote, but an activist group lobbied for rejection and the student poll rejected the agreement by a vote of 3395 to 1203. A stalemate had been reached.

The faculty found themselves in the awkward position of onlookers as the administration and students negotiated. They were sympathetic with the financial plight of the students but deplored the disruption of classes. As a further round of administration-student negotiations was imminent, on April 22 the faculty voted to establish a four-member "committee of accountability" to monitor the discussions. John Mahoney of the College of Arts and Sciences, James Bowditch of the School of Management, Mary Griffin of the School of Education, and Dorothy Walker of the School of Nursing were chosen to constitute this committee. Many faculty meetings were held during the strike, as well as several emergency meetings of the University Academic Senate. Later in the decade the UAS came to seem an ineffectual organization, with diminished faculty and student support, but during the strike it was a valuable instrument for bringing all elements of the University together to wrestle with the crisis. At a meeting on April 22 the senate resolved that while negotiations continued, the time would be a reading period, professors and students would be free to meet with one another, and final examinations would be held on material covered before the strike began on April 13.

Some more radical students concluded that the protest was lagging, so on April 23rd they occupied the president's office in Botolph House. They remained there eight days, with the administrative activities shifted to other locations. At this time an article appeared in the *Boston Globe* under the headline, "Restraint Key to BC Strike." The article began:

> The tuition strike that has all but closed Boston College is unique among campus protests. The boycott of classes will go into its third week tomorrow, and the watchword is restraint. The strike has produced no violence, vandalism, or any other of the elements associated with campus unrest. Strike leaders have gone out of their way, in fact, to condemn a building takeover by a small but peaceful group of dissidents who do not have the general support of the 6000 undergraduates.
>
> None of this is surprising to anyone familiar with the academic climate at the Heights. The surprising thing is that the strike occurred at all on a campus that had long been exempt from the tensions that generate student uprisings.[1]

But an editorial cartoon appeared in another Boston daily depicting a large eagle perched atop Gasson Hall; a huge teardrop hung from the eagle's eye. The sadness and shock of that cartoon surely expressed the sentiments of many loyal alumni and friends of the University who were unhappy that the administration had allowed students to bring everything to a standstill.

One outcome of the tuition struggle was Father Joyce's formation of the Coalition for Aid to Private Higher Education. In this effort he had the

Strikers manning the "battlements" of Gasson Hall. Note the strike banner on the tower.

eager support of students. Twenty-four colleges in New England joined the coalition, and on April 30 a group of college administrators (including Father Joyce) and students went to Washington, where they made presentations to congressmen and congressional committees.

Continued negotiation between the administration and student representatives resulted in agreement on 16 points, most of which had been proposed in the earlier agreement. No student would be forced to leave for financial reasons because of the tuition increase, and the administration guaranteed significant student participation in recruiting and admission policy, a student-faculty-administration committee to pursue federal and state funding, and severe curtailment of University spending. There were two points on which agreement was not reached: The students agreed to a tuition increase of $240 for 1970–1971 but wanted a promise of no increase for the following year—a promise the administration was unwilling to give. The administration accepted the students' suggestion that two students be full voting members of the Budget Committee, but rejected the further demand that any two members of the committee could have veto power on any item under discussion.

A student referendum on the agreed and non-agreed points was scheduled for May 5. At this point, on April 30, an influential faculty member, vice-chairman of the University Academic Senate and chairman of the History Department, Thomas O'Connor, sent a letter to the student body that expressed the issues and the gravity of the situation as viewed by the faculty. An astute and statesmanlike assessment of the University's anguish, it stated in part:

> Here in brief is a faculty comment and account of what has happened: When the $500 tuition increase was first announced, the faculty overwhelmingly sympathized with the students' reaction of anger and surprise. Many, or even most, of the faculty were clearly in sympathy with the notion of a nonviolent tuition boycott of classes. While we understood the serious financial problems which Fr. Joyce had to face, we also understood the desire of the students to make absolutely clear to the Administration how burdensome such an increase would be to them, and to insist that the Administration not settle on such a large tuition increase without a determined attempt to solve the immediate fiscal problems of B.C. in other ways, if at all possible. On this issue, students and faculty stood together.
>
> After the first negotiated settlement was rejected in the referendum, and the newspapers carried stories that all classes were cancelled for the remainder of the term, students began to drift away from the campus. Then began a sequence of developments frequently observed in campus controversies elsewhere. The direction of the strike and of the negotiations came more and more under the influence of political activists. In particular, one faction gained power in and over the UGBC, the strike tactics committee, and the student negotiating team—power far out of proportion to their number and influence in the student body as a whole. Botolph House was occupied. Then broad *political* demands were introduced into the controversy, demands which were not part of the original tuition protest. The key demand, which became central to negotiations, concerns the University Budget Committee.

Concerned alumnus and faculty member Thomas H. O'Connor addressed a helpful letter to the student body urging an end to the strike.

All parties agreed that there should be student members on this committee for the purpose of information and assurance of good faith. But now the issue has escalated into a demand for an absolute veto over the committee's decisions, a demand which the Administration, the Faculty, and many students as well, agree is unreasonable and unworkable.

As a result the second phase of negotiations has been brought to an absolute deadlock over these political issues. There is no chance whatever that the strike can be resolved at the bargaining table. Our only hope, as I see it, is to accept those points on which both students and administration are agreed, and leave the long-range issues for future resolution. I can assure you that this will *not* mean allowing the Administration simply to "file and forget" these questions. The Faculty will stand firmly with you to see that this does not happen.

On to the Next Issue: Vietnam

The student referendum was to be held on May 5. But events external to the University suddenly thrust themselves into the midst of campus decisions. The Vietnam war was escalated by the United States move into Cambodia, and on May 4 at Kent State, protesting students were killed by National Guardsmen. Across America, college campuses exploded and the National Students' Association called for a nation-wide strike. Boston College students' reaction to the proposed nation-wide strike was added to the May 5 referendum. By a narrow margin, 1464 to 1282, the students rejected the administration position against a tuition cap for 1971–1972 and a student veto on the budget committee. But continuation of the strike as an instrument to get the students' view accepted was overwhelmingly rejected. However, by a vote of 1669 to 900, what came to be called the "strike against Cambodia" was endorsed. So on the very same day, the tuition strike ended and an antiwar strike began. That same day Father

---

EXCERPTS FROM JOYCE LETTER TO PARENTS CONCERNING COURSE AND EXAMINATION REQUIREMENTS

1. Any day undergraduate who, for good reason, wishes to postpone the completion of his work for the semester, including examinations, may do so providing that he makes suitable arrangements with the professor(s) involved to complete all such requirements and in fact does complete such requirements on or before October 1, 1970.
2. Any student presently enrolled in any course may withdraw from that course without prejudice prior to May 15, 1970.
3. All students may elect to be graded on a pass–fail basis in their present work.
4. Any student may take finals if he so desires.
5. Study projects and papers assigned before April 13 must be completed, or agreements made with individual professors for the completion of course requirements.

Joyce issued an eloquent condemnation of the war in Southeast Asia and urged other universities along with Boston College to support the nation-wide strike. The following day the faculty adopted Father Joyce's statement as its own. The University Academic Senate adopted flexible plans to enable students to satisfy course and examination requirements.

The turbulent year ended with an uneventful commencement on June 8. Sixteen years later a participant in the strike negotiation, Professor John Mahoney of the English Department, gave an address to a group of alumni priests. Reminiscing about the strike period, he said:

> Vietnam was a trauma. We knew what a strike was; we knew what dissent was; we knew what argument was; we knew what student protests were; and yet somehow or other we came through that phenomenon with a degree of what one might call soberness and a kind of wisdom. It seemed to me we learned from the trauma of Vietnam. We learned something about how a university can be resilient and strong, about how a university can continue its activity as a university while not isolating itself from the world. So many of the young men and women of that time seem so very different from the people sitting in my classes today, especially at the undergraduate level. They seemed so much more troubled, so much more angry, so much more disturbed. There also was a very special dimension, an enthusiasm, intellectual curiosity, a kind of idealism, a kind of interest in putting one's talents to use, a kind of need to build a better world. With all the negative things, and heaven knows there were enough of those, disruptions, disorder, a challenge to authority, there was a sense of growing, a sense of somehow or other becoming a part of the new world.[2]

There was indeed, as Professor Mahoney remembers, a kind of relief when classes resumed quietly in September 1970. Perhaps there was, as he put it, a soberness and wisdom on campus. But while there was no repetition of any campus-wide disruption during the final two years of Father Joyce's presidency, there were occasional limited disturbances.

In December representatives of the Air Force came to recruit civilian personnel for their Electronic Systems Division. The Placement Office scheduled the interviews in the old Alumni Hall building on Common-wealth Avenue. A group of 12 protesting students entered the interview room and disrupted proceedings by shouting, chanting, and banging on the table. The students were warned four times by University officers of their breach of regulations. Finally in late afternoon a temporary restraining order was issued in Middlesex Superior Court. A week later the injunction was broadened to restrain Boston College students from preventing applicants and employers from conducting placement interviews on campus.

Coeducation and Women's Issues

The academic year 1970–1971 was the first year of campus-wide under-graduate coeducation, and women students were not slow to employ the

In occasionally turbulent sessions of the University Academic Senate and in meetings during the strike, Law School dean Richard G. Huber was a respected advocate of reason.

demonstration methods common on American campuses to press their interests. No doubt, through inertia and inexperience rather than disinterest, the institution was slow to make all the provisions necessary to adjust to the advent of a large female population. The women's protest was sparked by the announcement that the position of dean of women, then held by Ann Flynn, would be abolished in June. A Women's Action Coalition was formed, in part to petition the retention of Dean Flynn but also to demand improved and equal treatment in a number of areas, including admissions, financial aid, counseling, health services, placement service, courses, security, and athletic facilities. A petition on these matters was submitted to Father Joyce. Dissatisfied with the president's written response, on March 19 some 30 members of WAC and supporters occupied the offices of Vice President for Student Affairs McIntyre and Dean of Students Father Hanrahan. The students refused to leave when requested, so another temporary restraining order was obtained from Middlesex Superior Court specifically against the occupation of administrative offices. The protest ended and the order was dissolved on April 2.

Military Recruitment

There was more intense opposition to military recruitment in 1971–1972. It is true that a poll by the undergraduate government in November revealed that on the issue of the acceptability of military recruiting on campus, 1338 students voted in favor, with 1192 opposed. But a small group, appealing sometimes to religious principles and obtaining the support of several Jesuits, were more adamantly than ever opposed to what they saw as cooperation in the war effort. Two disruptions of military recruiting sessions, one in October and one in December, led to disciplinary hearings before the University Conduct Board; to the chagrin of the administration, in both instances the student protesters were exonerated. Their defense pointed to the University's commitment in the student guide to high principles of Christian humanism and contended that the protests were precisely in support of such ideals. The conduct board was convinced and found the students not guilty. The tensions on this issue at Boston College might have been an early presage of the debate in the Catholic Church a decade and a half later, when the American bishops addressed themselves to issues of nuclear armaments.

When the protesters were turned away from the building where military recruiting was taking place in December, about 30 people (not all of them Boston College students) occupied Hopkins House, then the offices of the senior vice president and dean of faculties. During the night, Boston College officers urged them to leave so that outside authorities would not have to be involved. At 5:45 in the morning they were informed that if they did not leave in 15 minutes Newton police would be called. Fifteen persons remained, eight of them Boston College students, and at 6:30 a.m. they were arrested and charged with criminal trespass. Later in the month they were found guilty and put on probation.

The announcement of Father Joyce's resignation in January 1972, to be effective in June, may well have had a tempering effect on protest in the second semester. In April there was widespread escalation of antiwar activity on many American campuses because of the escalation of the air war over Vietnam, and locally there was some violence and arrests at Harvard and Boston University. A call for an academic strike at Boston College was rejected by a student referendum, but a large majority (1997 to 181) felt that the University should continue to be involved in antiwar activities.

Intrusion by *The Heights*

Father Joyce ruefully learned, as did many of his fellow presidents, that the 1968 to 1972 period was not a time of ease or tranquility on college campuses. Besides the various protests recorded here, the student paper, *The Heights,* was a particular irritant for the administration, as indicated in the previous chapter. Representatives of *The Heights* also planted a listening device in a trustees' meeting in the president's office on February 19, 1971. On March 2 *The Heights* ran the full text of the meeting, along with some derisive editorial comments.

Most of the faculty queried by the staff found *The Heights* conduct a shocking invasion of privacy.[3] Father Joyce issued a statement apologizing to the trustees and indicating that the University was undertaking a serious investigation of the matter. After assembling evidence with the help of a private investigator, the University turned the matter over to the Attorney General's office, which studied the case for six weeks. Then on May 20 two former editors of *The Heights* were arrested and charged with conspiring to obtain information illegally and to use the information thus obtained. The trial was deferred until September, when the Attorney General's office and the judge accepted a plea of *nolo contendere*. The former editors were assessed small court costs, ending an unhappy episode in the University's history. Relations between *The Heights* and the administration remained strained for the remaining months of Father Joyce's presidency.

It should be recorded that after the few years that saw the strike, the several protests and occupations of buildings, and the disruption of the customary campus routine—with occasional examples of incivility—the University soon returned to its accustomed academic serenity. There were changes, but by no means were all of them aftereffects of the protest movement.

Back to Normal

Many observers thought that students now became more relaxed, more casual, more comfortable in their university surroundings. While it is true that the old dress code (ties and jackets prescribed for an all-male student body) had passed away, a new mode of conduct came into being. Gradually the extreme forms of "hippie" dress—long hair, beards, shells, sandals, and the like—began to disappear. Men did not return to shirts and ties, tending instead to dress in a relaxed and casual style. Sweaters, jerseys, slacks, and occasionally Levi's and jeans (although these, too, began to disappear) indicated that the future process of learning would take place in a much less rigid atmosphere. Relations between students and faculty became more relaxed and informal, and there was more interaction; students freely talked with teachers (including Jesuits) and vice versa.

Jesuits, too, showed signs of change, presumably not motivated by the protest movement. Younger Jesuits, especially, began to wear civilian garb (shirts, ties, tweed jackets, and slacks) rather than black suits with clerical collar or the black habit of earlier days, and some even called themselves and had others call them by their first names rather than "Father." On campus, at least, these changes in clerical attire and style were taken in stride. The faculty in general seemed more responsive to the needs and desires of the students, offering new courses, experimental seminars, and lively interactive tutorials that were far different from the formal type of lecture that had formerly been prevalent.

Another factor that quietly but profoundly influenced the campus was the extension of coeducation to all four undergraduate schools in 1970.

School of Nursing students had been on campus for 10 years and School of Education women for 18 years when coeducation was made universal, so the presence of women undergraduates was not an abrupt phenomenon. But an immediate result of universal coeducation was the doubling of an applicant pool for what remained a relatively steady undergraduate enrollment after the mid-1970s, and this meant a more highly selected student body. In addition to this academic impact of coeducation, there is little doubt that the influx of a large number of women students in the 1970s and thereafter had a benign effect on the life and spirit of the campus. To give one example: The happy burgeoning of musical and artistic activity on campus in recent years might have happened without universal coeducation, but it probably would not have blossomed as soon or with such vigor.

Another development simultaneous with full coeducation was the explosion of on-campus housing for students. When Father Walsh left office in 1968, the upper campus dormitories he and Father Maxwell had built housed 1500 students. The next two decades would see provision for three times that number in campus residences. The combination of these two factors—increased numbers of women students and more students residing in dormitories—posed a new problem for University authorities in the 1970s: the question of coeducational housing and parietal rules. It was clear that Boston College had left behind its simple and uncomplicated origins and had moved into the complex context of modern university life.

*   *   *

The less pleasant aspects of Father Joyce's administration have been recorded in this chapter. Fortunately there were positive developments and achievements that call for other chapters.

ENDNOTES

1. *Boston Globe* (April 26, 1970).
2. Tape of address in the University historian's office.
3. *The Heights* (March 9, 1971).

CHAPTER 32

Academic and Social Innovations

On April 11, 1969, President Joyce addressed the Boston College faculty on "the contemporary university."[1] The traditional university, "thought of primarily as a reservoir of accumulated knowledge and a haven for wise and reflective men," was mirrored in the "shaped lindens and Gothic structures" of the campus which recalled a "day that valued both elegance and detachment and wished to provide for the faculty and students . . . a setting that fostered such qualities of mind."[2] But today, he said, "all this is changed." He argued that new expectations call for hard, pragmatic action; that students call for relevance and immediacy; that there will be new knowledge, new forms that will respond to the needs of the day. In summary, "the new university is summoned to play a role in social change."[3]

In the course of his remarks, Father Joyce had referred to the objectives and hopes of a Catholic and Jesuit university which recognized the mystery of a transcendent God.[4] Lest there be any misunderstanding, however, a faculty member wanted to set the record straight. While not openly disagreeing with Father Joyce's comments in the context of a Catholic university and its value system, Professor Severyn T. Bruyn, Department of Sociology, subscribed to the thesis that a university has its own set of values expressed in the development of civilized society: "The premise that education must be independent of both church and state in its aims, in its rhetoric, in the pursuit of values and knowledge is fundamental to the future of the university."[5] Expressed in various, though substantially similar, formulae, this thesis has been expounded by many educators on Catholic campuses in recent years. It has always been the theme of those who profess to believe that a Catholic university is a "contradiction in terms." But Father Joyce, while he had no intention "of abandoning our Catholic identity, much less our Catholic heritage and tradition," was not going "to accept the narrowly apologetic and catechetic role in which some have cast the Catholic university."[6] The faculty prepared itself for innovations.

The Committee on Liberal Education

In the light of these thoughts on the new goals for the American and Catholic university, Father Joyce then reviewed with the faculty the programs and proposals that were under discussion in his office and elsewhere on campus. Among others, the University Academic Senate Committee on Curriculum and Education had, in the spring of 1969, commissioned a blue ribbon committee on undergraduate education. With Professor Rich-

The crown jewel of the campus, Bapst library.

ard Hughes as chairman, it was entitled University Committee on Liberal Education, which yielded the avuncular acronym U.N.C.L.E. (With reference to a popular television program of the day, Professor Hughes became "the Man from U.N.C.L.E.")

Shortly after he was asked to coordinate U.N.C.L.E., Hughes was appointed dean of Arts and Sciences amid the controversy described in a previous chapter. On becoming dean, he sent an open letter to students and faculty which was a frank assessment of the situation as he saw it. He wrote in part:

> I hope I can say this without sounding stuffy: There's no reason why we shouldn't be creating a superb educational experience in the college. Almost all the ingredients are here—a high-level student body, a superior faculty as our best resources—but somehow we're bedeviled by Aristotelian *harmatia*, we're just missing the mark. There are some grand things going on . . . but it's not hanging together very well. We've got dynamic enclaves but no community. And unless we can create a community here, we're not going to move very far or very fast.[7]

In a sense, this was the challenge to the U.N.C.L.E. committee, at least as interpreted by its chairman. This committee, composed of 10 faculty members and students from the four undergraduate schools, went about its work in a businesslike way. There was a fact-finding subcommittee and another for inspecting programs at other universities. U.N.C.L.E. began its meetings in early September 1969 with a discussion of several key questions such as the integrity, influence, and reaction of academic departments, the future effects of substantive changes on the undergraduate colleges, and perceived faculty apprehension about a slide toward "a general college."[8]

The crucial question was: What is a liberal education? Is it aristocratic or democratic? Is it objective or subjective? Since this question has never been satisfactorily resolved, though perennially posed, there was no reason to believe that U.N.C.L.E. would have the final answer. But the committee did make a valiant effort by proposing, discussing, and refining in order to make suggestions tailored to existing structures at Boston College. The most significant contribution of the committee was its proposal that there should be a "core curriculum," however that was defined and designed.

U.N.C.L.E. submitted an interim report on April 27, 1970.[9] Working on a tight schedule, the committee was anxious to hear the reaction of departments and faculty in order to produce a final report in the fall. A basic premise for the committee was that "all students entering the University, regardless of school or major, will participate in the liberal education program, and sections will be established without regard to school affiliation."[10] Moreover, the program could be satisfied "either through a university core or alternative programs," both of which had provisions for honors candidacy.[11] Although a revised list might be proposed for the final report, the interim report contained a core program with the following alternatives: To fulfill the core, students would take 2 courses in history, English, theology, and philosophy; 3 courses in the humanities (any approved courses from the above disciplines or from the classics, modern languages, fine arts, and speech); and 2 courses in the natural sciences (with a choice from mathematics, physics, chemistry, biology, and geology).[12]

The interim report noted that the distribution of these courses could be satisfied throughout the regular four years and would not affect departmental requirements for the major. The committee was extremely generous in permitting alternate programs, called "counter programs," and experimental programs which, some thought, only served to dilute the core requirements.

At the end of the semester, the EPC of Arts and Sciences appointed a subcommittee to seek opinions from the members of the College and the University on the interim report throughout the summer and into the fall.[13] One of the most interesting critiques came from the School of Management. Although it may have gone beyond the complaints of the School of Nursing and the School of Education, the School of Management faculty probably represented the general reaction of the professional schools to the interim report. Sympathetic to U.N.C.L.E.'s desire to provide liberal education programs that are "dynamic, viable, and relevant," the School of Management felt that it could best do this by continuing to offer an "intensive four-year *integrated* program to students having a strong professional orientation."[14] The School of Management also reminded U.N.C.L.E. of requirements for accreditation by the Association of Colleges of Business.

But that was not the real problem. The basic issue—which was not new—was that the deans and faculties of the professional schools continued to resent "the inequality of the education offered to students from the different colleges."[15] Repeating an old grievance, the School of Management maintained that objectives of fairness, equality, and quality could be quickly obtained, "if that is what is wanted," by addressing directly the undergraduate admission policy, cross registration, and assignment of faculty. "In brief," commented the SOM representatives with candor, "we reject forthrightly the notion that *where* a course is taught in the University determines whether it is liberal or not."[16] This was an undisguised challenge to Arts and Sciences' claim as the guardian of liberal arts in the University. Finally, for good measure, the School of Management also hinted that Professor Hughes, as both dean of Arts and Sciences and chairman of U.N.C.L.E., could be involved in a subtle conflict of interest.[17]

U.N.C.L.E.'s Report

In drafting the final report, U.N.C.L.E. kept in mind two principles accepted by the EPCs (and always encouraged by the AAUP), namely that students should be permitted to arrange their schedules as freely as possible and that "the determination of the curriculum is the province of the faculty."[18] Making an honest effort to incorporate suggestions, the commit-

In the era before the opening of O'Neill Library there were few vacant chairs in Bapst's Gargan hall.

tee submitted its report in October 1970. With this report and recommendations, U.N.C.L.E. considered that it had fulfilled the charge given to it by the Curriculum and Educational Policy Committee of the UAS in March 1969.[19]

Actually, this final report did not differ significantly from the first draft. A philosophical preamble had been added and minor changes were made in recommendations. Once again it stressed choice among viable alternatives and recommended a standing committee in each college to supervise alternatives. Certain core courses would be designated "honors" courses, and a student would have to include 10 such courses to be considered for honors. Mathematics and modern language were not required but—like sociology, political science, and psychology—could be taken as alternatives.

The Arts and Sciences EPC showed no deference to the committee chairman (and dean) in its review of the U.N.C.L.E. report. It pointed out that U.N.C.L.E. provided no reasons for its choices; that there was nothing to show that U.N.C.L.E.'s core was better than the one in place;[20] that improved advisement and more classroom space would have to be found; and that faculty adjustments might be difficult. The academic vice president, however, in a strong plea for core, underlined the argument that with 4000 undergraduates enrolled in professional schools, there must be a liberal core to their education.

The last hurdle was U.N.C.L.E.'s recommendation that the UAS establish, by election, a university core curriculum committee. This proposal immediately became controversial and revived the earlier dispute between the UAS and the individual EPCs. The EPCs feared that the UAS or one of its committees would preempt responsibility for the core and, by implication, for liberal education at Boston College. As an example of faculty support, Professor Louis Kattsoff of the Mathematics and Philosophy departments wrote a long letter to the academic community to make a strong case for the UCCC. If it is to be a "University Core," he wrote, it should have a University committee to oversee it.[21]

The New Core Curriculum

Tying together comments and reports of the past two years, the UAS Standing Committee on Curriculum and Educational Policy submitted its own report on February 17, 1971.[22] An excellent history of the case, it was especially clear on the constitution and purpose of the UCCC versus the authority and responsibility of the individual EPCs. Elected members of the UCCC would include two faculty members from each of the three divisions of Arts and Sciences, one faculty member from each of the professional schools, and three members of the student body. The dean of faculties would chair the committee. The purpose of the UCCC, constituted by the UAS, would be to request and approve courses in the core, to provide direction for programs, and to set controls over experiments or alternatives.

This important question, so long debated, was finally settled in May 1971. At that time the UAS adopted a new core curriculum in which the required courses were reduced from 17 (as in the old core) to 12. But options were increased. As approved there were two courses in philosophy, theology, social sciences, mathematics/natural sciences, history, and humanities. Since the underlying premise was that the "core" was a *University* program, the UAS insisted on cross-registration so that all courses would be open to all students, regardless of undergraduate affiliation. This would eliminate past inequities. There was provision for extensive advisement to assist students in choices.[23]

Opposition to a core curriculum, past or present, came from UGBC. It preferred the system adopted by Holy Cross, which eliminated all core requirements in favor of electives. Timothy Anderson, who had been elected president of UGBC in February 1971, ran on a platform which promised an end to the core curriculum.[24] Incidentally, Anderson assumed an important leadership role in the protests and strike which hit the campus in that spring semester.

To insure that the core curriculum would indeed provide a true framework of liberal learning, the UAS created a permanent Council of Liberal Education (a variation on UCCC), which was charged with approving courses to be included in the *minimum* liberal education core. This council is still operative.

The Board of Directors, which had discussed the question at its April meeting, made its decision in May. After listening to an explanation by the academic vice president, the board unanimously approved "the Liberal Education Core Curriculum approved by the University Academic Senate."[25] In a second resolution, including a Solomon-like compromise, the board further decreed that *minimum* core requirements would come under the jurisdiction of the UAS; "otherwise the curriculum of each college remains in the jurisdiction of each college."[26] In other words, the individual EPCs might add to the core, but could not delete courses from it.

Over the years, despite occasional criticism, the University Academic Planning Committee has several times reaffirmed "a belief in the wisdom and educational value of a soundly conceived, well-taught, and skilfully administered core that reflects the distinctive goals of Boston College."[27] Other models were offered, but always within the parameters drawn by the Board of Directors and the UAS. In 1986 there was a discussion of the core at a faculty day program. "Boston College has a good core curriculum, but there is still room for improvement," was the general consensus of those present at the annual meeting.[28] That same year the seniors thought it pertinent to explain in their yearbook why and how the core courses "were intended to provide the cultural background, intellectual training, and structures of basic principles by which students could comprehend a complex world and cope with rapid changes as they occurred."[29] Mention will be made later of another study of the core curriculum, ongoing in 1990.

Participating in Societal Change: Pulse

Father Joyce insisted that, in addition to the academic programs, Boston College should play a role in shaping social change. The University had long been involved with urban problems and inner-city issues, but these had been addressed by faculty and administrators. He thought it time to involve the students. In October 1969 the Social Action Committee of the UGBC was formed and charged with responsibility for establishing a social action agency. The Social Action Committee, now known as "Pulse," came from the initiative of former UGBC president Joseph Fitzpatrick and a group of concerned students. Two consultants were hired, a budget was set up, and assistance was supplied by supervisors in a work-study program.

In October 1970 the Pulse program directorship was placed in the University table of organization under Weston M. Jenks, University Director of Counseling.[30]

Pulse gained instant recognition and success. The committee immediately identified as spheres of interest the Jamaica Plain Youth Center, a project concerned with drugs, delinquency, and unemployment; housing development and public housing ownership; and a cerebral palsy Montessori class, a pilot pre-school class in cooperation with the Massachusetts Department of Public Health. Several other projects of a similar nature followed.

The two unique features of the program as it developed—and not duplicated at other area institutions—were (1) the academic accreditation given to social action projects and (2) the substantial financial commitment of the University. The support given to Pulse by the administration and faculty was clear proof of Boston College's intention to become involved with society beyond the campus gates. This endorsement was, in fact, envied by students at other institutions in the Boston area.

Over the years Pulse has made an enormous contribution to social programs in Massachusetts, beyond the state, and even overseas. It is an enriching program for students, and those fortunate enough to be involved consider it one of the great experiences of their collegiate years. At the faculty level, one of the driving forces behind the program has been Joseph Flanagan, S.J., chairman of the Philosophy Department.[31] There will be

Father Joseph Flanagan, chairman of the Philosophy Department since 1965, was a major force behind the Pulse program and the Perspectives on Western Culture curriculum.

occasion to mention his contribution in subsequent pages. For the past several years the director has been Richard Keeley who, with the Pulse Council, edits the program's paper and publishes the annual report.

Another example—one of several that could be cited—of the social conscience of the students was, as the director put it, "an adventure in service and learning." In February 1970, 46 seniors and 2 graduate students from the School of Education went to work as reading tutors with children in South Boston.[32] Under the direction of Professor John Savage, these students, in lieu of a class session each week, spent one hour every Monday afternoon tutoring children with reading disabilities. Although all had completed student teaching, few had ever worked in an intensive clinical or tutorial program in the inner city. According to Professor Savage, "For the children and youth service workers in South Boston, it was novel to be 'invaded' by such a large group at one time for this purpose."[33]

The program was set up with the cooperation of the South Boston Action Center and consisted in tutoring disadvantaged children in the so-called "D Street Project," a low-income city housing development located in South Boston. The Boston College students worked in four adjoining apartments with 74 children from grades 1 through 6 who were selected by Action Center personnel from public and parochial schools in the area.

This was the beginning of a number of such programs in the undergraduate colleges that reflected the growing awareness on the part of students and faculty alike of the potential for social action that resided within the academic community. Some programs were not unique to Boston College. However, as the projects—which ranged from reading programs to building houses—moved from Boston to Appalachia to Jamaica, they took on the added dimension of a ministry or apostolate traditionally associated with a Jesuit institution. More will be said of this aspect in a later chapter.

The Academic Calendar Revised

A revision of the academic calendar had been under discussion for some time at various levels. (Experimentation had also been going on at other institutions.) With the appointment of a university registrar, the adoption of new registration procedures, and a change in the format of the University catalog, it seemed an appropriate time to review the semester schedule. Consequently, the UAS Curriculum and Educational Policy Committee, chaired by Louis Kattsoff, took a new look at the calendar at its meeting in October 1971. The UAS also appointed a subcommittee on semester division, with Robert O'Malley of the Chemistry Department as chairman.

A change in the term calendar, which might appear to be a simple adjustment, immediately provoked reactions from a number of interest groups, including student body, faculty, administration, advisement-orientation, food services, athletics, and plant services. Even the weather, storm cycles, excessive heat or cold, family vacations, and summer jobs were proposed as factors to be taken into account. Although there was talk of quarters and trimesters (year-round facilities for a 3-term 3-course schedule), the semester was still the most popular format at Boston College and other area institutions. The real question was whether the first term should extend beyond Christmas—that is, one or two weeks of class or, alternatively, readings, followed by examinations. In November Professor O'Malley reported that, a result of researching calendar changes, two possibilities had emerged: first, there could be early semester beginnings and endings, or, second, there could be two 4-month semesters with a month off between them.[34]

Criticism of the plan for ending the first semester before Christmas holidays usually centered on insufficient time for examinations. Moreover, there was no unanimity on the number of required class days in a semester. Harvard and MIT held to 70, Boston University and Tufts to somewhat fewer. The academic vice president's office supplied data for the past decade which, although there were fluctuations, showed a median of 68 days a semester at Boston College.[35] It was agreed by all that examinations before Christmas would necessitate classes beginning immediately after Labor Day, which would bring students and faculty back to campus in late August.[36]

After Professor O'Malley's explanatory article had appeared in the February 10, 1972, *Thursday Reporter* (an administration publication later called *Biweekly*), people began to take sides. Though some faculty expressed opposition to the early termination of the first semester, most favored it or were indifferent. Students expected a change and, for the most part, did not see the question as a big issue. In fact some felt that, in the traditional schedule, the time between Labor Day and the beginning of class was wasted.[37] The subcommittee's proposal, therefore, was: first semester—15 weeks (66 days of class, 5 examination days, and 4 days for

---

1972–1973 CALENDAR

Fall Term: September 5—classes begin
                December 18–22—examinations
                December 23–January 7—recess
Spring Term: January 8—classes begin
                May 14–25—examinations
                June 4—commencement

1973–1974 CALENDAR

Fall Term: September 4—classes begin
                December 17–22—examinations
                December 23–January 13—recess
Spring Term: January 14—classes begin
                May 2–10—examinations
                May 27—commencement

Since 1970 the Campus School, founded by John Eichorn (pictured here), has served some 60 multihandicapped pupils between the ages of 6 and 25.

registration); second semester—15.2 weeks (68 days of class, 5 examination days, and 3 days for registration).

Opposition to the proposed new calendar was directed mainly at the decision to implement the change in September 1972. This was particularly true of the University Orientation Committee, which needed more time to reorganize the freshmen assistance program. The director of athletics was, perhaps, the most outspoken critic, since winter and spring sports events had been scheduled for the next several years. While the Council for Counseling Services favored experimenting with a new calendar, it felt the adjustment could not be made for September 1972.[38] Despite this opposition, the experiment began in September for the 1972–1973 academic year.

Expanding the Doctoral Program

Social programs and social involvement must, indeed, be a concern to the modern educational institution in the United States. But many maintain that the classic university, in its historical origins and setting, is still measured largely by its scholarly contribution to knowledge in the arts and sciences. At American universities, given their German heritage, this is usually done at the highest academic level—that is, at the doctoral level, where research and publication are normal products of a professor's efforts.

Over the years, the Boston College Graduate School had offered a widely recognized and rigorously defined master's degree in the arts, sciences, and education. That degree entitled recipients to apply to prestigious universities for the pursuit of higher studies. During Father Walsh's tenure, the major emphasis was on the attraction of outstanding undergraduate students and the improvement of undergraduate programs. But the graduate offerings were not neglected. From 1960 to 1968, biology, chemistry, philosophy, and physics were added to the three existing doctoral programs (economics, education, and history) that had been inaugurated in 1952. In the late sixties and early seventies, chairmen from other departments, with pressure from vocal faculty members, felt that the time had come when Boston College should not only preserve the wisdom of the past but should add to it. This was one reason to expand doctoral programs, but the emphasis in proposals was on the responsibility of training future Ph.D.s for college and university faculties. The administration took this obligation seriously, and there was a dramatic expansion of such programs.

It is not necessary to describe each program in detail here, for the basic format for doctoral studies follows a prescribed design, and the reasons adduced for initiating a program therefore are quite similar. That department growth and stability are critical to the success of this kind of academic venture, however, is proved by an example. The first doctoral program inaugurated in the Joyce presidency had to be canceled. The Department of Germanic Studies had two internationally recognized scholars, Professor Heinz Bluhm, who had formerly held a chair at Yale, and Professor Joseph Szöverffy, an acknowledged authority in German philology. With a good supporting staff, the department was quite adequate to offer the Ph.D.—a program that had a bright future, inasmuch as its only competitor was Harvard. However, the sudden resignation of Professor Szöverffy, who was politically unhappy at Boston College, forced the department to turn away doctoral applicants, of whom there were many. One senior professor (as opposed to two at Harvard) was not sufficient to carry the program.[39] (In addition, the Priorities Committee had recommended that the doctoral program in Germanic Studies be discontinued.)

Located for nearly two decades in Roberts Center, the Campus School now occupies quarters built for it in 1989 in the former auditorium-gymnasium of Campion Hall.

The English Department's proposal for a doctoral program is an example of a mature, responsible, honest, and highly academic approach to this critical decision. In one sense, this department—considering its faculty strength—was perhaps the best prepared to offer the Ph.D., yet it was the most cautious in electing to do so. As the chairman wrote to the president, "Having, I think, established ourselves as an effective graduate department, we're anxious to expand but not to endanger our reputation."[40] The department discussed the proposed Ph.D. in 1957 and 1958, taking an inventory of library holdings, faculty, publications, and present and future course offerings. It was immediately recognized that there were deficiencies in library resources, the most serious gaps being in reference, English history, medieval Latin literature, Germanic language, and—most serious of all for the Ph.D.—in the periodical collection.[41]

Ten years later, after much discussion, the chairman submitted a progress report on the Ph.D. program. This report concentrated on a review of the market for Ph.D.s. Noting that "the American universities produce only a fraction of what the field ideally requires" (with most of these granted by a small number of high-yield institutions), the report, with facts and figures, explained "the unique contribution smaller universities might make to the academic community."[42] In discussing the competition for students and faculty, the department felt that Boston College's philosophy of education, which affected the thrust of the program, was an advantage. Moreover, given the newness and smallness of the program, there was ample opportunity to try new approaches to a research degree with added emphasis on insight, creativity, and discovery.[43] The course requirements were necessarily traditional. The report also added an impressive list of faculty publications.

The department was so confident of success that, in the fall of 1968 (although the program had not been formally approved), an attractive brochure describing the chief features of the program was distributed. Confidence was based in good part on the extremely favorable evaluations of faculty members from distinguished universities. For the administration, the last hurdle was financial. In order to attract superior doctoral applicants, the chairman strongly recommended generous subsidies for their support—subsidies that exceeded those of other doctoral departments. But this was a negotiable component, and patience was its own reward.

Early in the second semester (1968–1969), the president communicated to the chairman "the good news that that Board of Directors has unanimously endorsed the application of your department for permission to begin a program of studies leading to the Ph.D. degree."[44] Father Joyce congratulated Professor Hughes for his part in "steer[ing] the proposal through to a successful conclusion, and your colleagues for an excellently structured doctoral program."[45] The first students were accepted for the fall term of 1969–1970. Over the years, as it was meant to do, the program has enhanced the academic reputation of Boston College.

Other Investments in Reputation

Although some were beginning to have second thoughts on the implications of the financial burden, other doctoral programs came into existence in quick succession at about this time. The Modern Language Department, which submitted its application in 1966, was an interesting case because its appeal to the administration was based almost entirely on the job opportunity market. A regional study for the years 1960–1964 revealed that only 111 doctoral degrees in modern languages were granted by all New England institutions combined, with 58 of those coming from Yale. Harvard had granted 17 in romance languages and 17 in German. In addition to the academic and commercial markets, the federal government, as exemplified by the establishment of the NDEA doctoral scholarships, was anxious to increase the pool of language experts for sensitive government posts and for the advantages language fluency brought to international business transactions. The Modern Language Department began its doctoral program in the late sixties. Professor Normand Cartier, Father Joseph D. Gauthier, Professor Maria Simonelli, and others made it an attractive undertaking.

The departments of Sociology, Political Science, and Theology (which participates in a joint program with Andover-Newton Theological School) launched their doctoral programs in 1970–1971.[46] All of these programs were thoroughly researched, cogently presented, and academically solid. The Board of Directors accepted the academic rationale of the departments.

Departments offering the doctorate—as every dean knows—exercise a strong attraction for senior faculty who are oriented toward research and publication. A graduate school with many doctoral departments, however, is a very expensive investment. Once the decision is made, there is a ripple effect: Science laboratories and instrumentation must be adequate, library holdings must be increased in certain fields, salaries may be higher for those whose schedules are reduced, and graduate assistants and fellows must be subsidized. But the rewards are beyond a mere price tag in terms of prestige and influence. Those former students who earned their Ph.D.s and Ed.D.s at Boston College are now senior faculty members in institutions across the country, superintendents of school systems, and research scientists. These scholars have carried the name of Boston College to the highest levels.[47]

The University Chaplain's Team

The Joyce years saw a change in an important aspect of student life. At a Jesuit college or university, the spiritual formation of students has a high priority. In the late sixties and early seventies the team approach to campus ministry was gaining advocates at Catholic schools across the country. Boston College was an early convert to this practice.

The whole concept of a university chaplain was fairly new. For many years, as the four undergraduate colleges grew and developed their own identities, a chaplain was assigned to each one. He was responsible for the spiritual and personal counseling of his students and, indeed, was frequently an academic advisor as well. The system had certain advantages, one of which was the frequency of personal contacts. But there was no University policy, no collaboration, no coordination, no one person in charge. This situation began to change in the 1967–1968 year when Father "Jack" Gallagher was appointed University chaplain, although chaplains were still assigned to particular schools.

Stability, and a new approach and new style, came with the appointment of Father Leo "Chet" McDonough in 1971. He, with the other Jesuits assigned to that mission, had been expelled from Iraq in 1968. A typical missionary, he was energetic, personable, enthusiastic, available to students, and totally committed to his apostolate. He was ably assisted by Fathers James Larkin, "Jack" Seery, Frank Lazetta, and James Halpin, all of whom had formerly been assigned to a particular school. Father Halpin, who was director of the Program for the Study of Peace, led a liturgy every day for the students at the Chestnut Hill Avenue apartments where he lived. These four members of the team were unofficially—but generously—assisted by Fathers David Gill of the Classics Department and Frederick Adelmann of Philosophy.

As Father Halpin explained, "The chaplain has to create his office and make his presence felt on campus."[48] It was in this sense that Father McDonough made a special difference. The students of those days will always remember the coffee and donut hour after the Saturday night liturgy at St. Joseph's chapel. Father McDonough said, "I am laughed at a lot for

Father Leo "Chet" Mc-Donough, head of a team of chaplains in the early 1970s.

this, but we still manage to get 600 people to come together."[49] For him, that was the point. The entire student body mourned the loss of a good friend when, in August 1975, Father Chet McDonough died from a persistent heart condition.

Other Changes and Notes of Interest

In the second semester of the 1971–1972 academic year—the last six months of the Joyce administration—there was movement on several fronts. Although computers had been in use for years in banks and other business operations, universities were just beginning to realize their potential for record keeping. At Boston College, the computer center—tucked away in the basement of Gasson—was fast becoming the nerve center of the campus. Financial, registration, and grade records, no longer filed in steel cabinets in deans' offices, were now stored in an IBM 370/145. (Of course, the equipment became more sophisticated as the years went by.) Father Joseph Pomeroy, S.J., a computer expert, commuted daily from Holy Cross to supervise the center. Bernard Gleason, a senior analyst at the center, spent much of his time training staff in the proper methods to retrieve information, and was also occupied in devising defenses against the theft of confidential information—a problem that has continued to plague the industry.[50]

Computer keyboards and screens, printers, and optical scanners have, in recent years, become the tools of publication, as the typewriter has become a museum piece. To coordinate this vast endeavor for both established professors and those looking for recognition, Charles Flaherty ('60) was appointed director of research administration. A man of wide commitments, Flaherty is a state representative from Cambridge who has also served as state Democratic party chairman. In his work as director, he identifies sources for funding research projects, assists faculty members in preparing their proposals for foundations or federal agencies, and, when necessary, negotiates with a possible sponsor. As a representative in the Massachusetts legislature, he has often been helpful in explaining and interpreting for the administration education bills that have been introduced to the General Court. At the same time, of course, he is careful to avoid a conflict of interest in discussing issues that might affect his position at Boston College. While not always successful with proposals in Washington, Boston College did receive over $5 million in federal grants for research in 1971, and better than $5.5 million from all sources—state, local, private.[51]

Other people were also bringing credit to Boston College. Two members of the alumni added episcopal purple to their maroon and gold. In February 1972 Lawrence J. Riley ('36) and Joseph F. Maguire ('41) were appointed auxiliary bishops of Boston by Pope Paul VI. Bishop Riley had been active

Albert M. Folkard ('37) of the English Department was director of the honors program in the College of Arts and Sciences, 1964–1981. In 1980 the University declared Folkard a Doctor of Humane Letters, honoris causa.

in the Fulton Debating Society; later on he became an eloquent spokesman for the Church. Bishop Maguire is now the Ordinary in Springfield.

As the semester came to a close, a search was under way for a new dean of Arts and Sciences. Controversial in his appointment, Dean Hughes was again in the news as he left office. The dean's tenure was tied to President Joyce's administration; when the president resigned, Hughes rightly concluded that his mandate had ended. Professor Thomas Owens of the Philosophy Department chaired the search committee. Since the search was on for a new president, the committee decided to recommend an acting dean in the person of Father James Skehan, chairman of Geology and Geophysics.[52]

For some reason or other, the professional schools always seemed to escape the internal controversies that were so easily generated within Arts and Sciences. In April, when the campus grounds were beginning to recover from the winter snows, the School of Nursing celebrated its 25th anniversary with a day-long conference. Many of those present remembered the early days in 1947 when the school occupied cramped quarters at 126 Newbury Street. Despite the austerities of those years before the move to Cushing Hall, the school had earned almost instant recognition for the quality of its programs and the dedication of its faculty. Rita Kelleher, in particular, who as dean had nurtured the school in its infancy, could take pride in the achievements of its graduates.[53]

*   *   *

Referring to the 1972 commencement, the *Thursday Reporter* summarized "Four Years of Change":

> The men and women, who this weekend will end their careers as undergraduate students at Boston College, have lived through four years unlike any others in the history of the University. They arrived at the tail-end of the rapid growth which transformed the campus from a small, commuter-oriented college to a university teeming with residents, and at the beginning of years of social unrest and financial strain which still have not run their entire course.
>
> They witnessed the inauguration of a new president, W. Seavey Joyce, S.J., and saw the last year of his term, experiencing with him all of the traumas and growing pains of an institution which was only just learning how to manage its new size.[54]

These same students now return to the campus with fond memories, like those who went before them and those who followed. There is, however, a difference. They have more to talk about.

ENDNOTES

1. This address was later published in pamphlet form under the title, "Notes Toward the Idea of a Catholic University." BCA.
2. *Ibid.*, p. 1.
3. *Ibid.*, p. 6.
4. *Ibid.*, p. 11.
5. *The Heights* (April 22, 1969) carried excerpts from Professor Bruyn's comments.
6. "Notes," p. 11.
7. *The Heights* (May 6, 1969).
8. *The Heights* in almost every weekly issue in 1969–1970 reported the progress of U.N.C.L.E.
9. BCA.
10. See Interim Report, p. 5.
11. *Ibid.*
12. *Ibid.*
13. EPC, College of Arts and Sciences, Annual Report, 1969–1970, p. 5. BCA.
14. Report of Curriculum Committee of SOM to U.N.C.L.E. Report of April 27, 1970 and June 10, 1970. BCA.
15. *Ibid.*
16. *Ibid.*
17. *Ibid.*
18. Minutes, EPC meeting, A&S, May 12, 1969.
19. The report is found in the archives.
20. It should be remembered that Boston College already had a "core," but not as well defined as the one that replaced it.
21. BCA.
22. BCA.

23. For an excellent account of the UAS action, see *Bridge* (Summer 1971).
24. *Ibid.* (March 1971).
25. Minutes, Board of Directors Meeting, April 23 and 24, 1971; also, June 18 and 19, 1971. Botolph House file.
26. *Ibid.*, June 18 and 19, 1971.
27. Memo from John L. Mahoney to All Members of UAPC. Subject: Core Curriculum, September 11, 1974. BCA.
28. See *Biweekly* (May 1986).
29. *Sub Turri* (1986), p. 268.
30. For the early history of Pulse see "First Annual Report," November 2, 1970. BCA.
31. See "Joseph Flanagan, S.J., Attracts National Notice for His Teaching." *Biweekly* (April 24, 1986). The article draws attention to Father Flanagan's work in Perspectives and Pulse.
32. "An Informal Report on the Boston College–South Boston Tutoring Project," by John Savage. BCA.
33. *Ibid.*
34. Minutes, UAS Committee on Curriculum and Educational Policy, November 18, 1971.
35. Father Donovan to R. O'Malley, December 29, 1971.
36. Memo from R. O'Malley to Curriculum and Educational Policy Committee, January 13, 1972.
37. Memo from R. O'Malley to Curriculum and Educational Policy Committee, February 22, 1972.
38. Weston M. Jenks to Father Donovan, March 21, 1972.
39. Heinz Bluhm to W. Seavey Joyce, June 14, 1971. Annual Report. BCA.
40. R. E. Hughes to Michael P. Walsh, November 7, 1961. BCA.
41. "Discussion of Proposed Ph.D. Program, 1957–1958." BCA.
42. "The Ph.D. in English." A Report, May 1969. BCA.
43. *Ibid.*
44. Father Joyce to R. E. Hughes, February 4, 1969. BCA.
45. *Ibid.*
46. For a good description of the political science doctoral program see *Bridge* (Summer 1971).
47. As further recognition of Boston College's contribution to higher education, Graduate School Dean Donald J. White has served as chairman of the Council of Graduate Schools in the United States. Significant doctoral programs mounted by the Graduate School of Social Work, the School of Nursing, and the Graduate School of Management will be mentioned later.
48. See "Campus Ministry: The Team Approach," *Bridge* (February 1972). There was also provision for ministry for non-Catholics and Jews.
49. *Ibid.*
50. *Thursday Reporter* (February 10, 1972).
51. "The Three Lives of Charlie Flaherty," *Bridge* (April 1972).
52. See *Thursday Reporter* (February 3, 1972; April 20, 1972).
53. *Bridge* (June 1972); *Thursday Reporter* (April 20, 1972).
54. June 2, 1972.

CHAPTER 33

An Overview of the Joyce Era

Although the Joyce administration was beset by daunting financial problems, a surprising amount of construction planning, renovation, and building took place. Several projects carried over from the previous administration. The finishing touches were being put on McGuinn Hall in the summer of 1968, and the building opened in the fall. Higgins Hall had been completed in 1966 and became home to the Biology and Physics departments, which moved from Devlin.

Renovation and Conversion

Devlin Hall, the original science building, was in need of major renovation to give enlarged facilities to the Chemistry Department and the Geology and Geophysics Department and to accommodate a science library. Plans were drawn and the cost estimated at about $2.4 million. Before a contract was signed, Father Joyce's appointment to succeed Father Walsh was announced. When Father Joyce was consulted, he agreed that the project should go forward.[1] The renovation and modernization of Devlin Hall—a massive undertaking—was completed in the summer of 1969.

Other significant renovations took place as well. In the spirit of Vatican Council II, St. Joseph's chapel in Gonzaga Hall was redone to create a more intimate arrangement of altar and benches to reflect the closer relationship of congregation and priest in celebrating the eucharistic liturgy. At the same time, however, there was a change in the time-honored tradition of no class on holy days of obligation. In 1970 only the civil holidays were recognized as legitimate interruptions of the academic program—which prompted some to ask if the University was becoming too secular.

The Bapst auditorium, which had been the scene of so many liturgical and academic functions, was converted into stack space. Even a superficial survey of Bapst, which had been dedicated in 1928, revealed the inadequacies of this building. Designed for a student body of 1200, at this time it was expected to serve 8000. Among other deficiencies, there was no space for further book acquisitions.

The decision for conversion to stack space was made final in September 1969, and the contract was given to John Bowen Building Contractors. The second floor (auditorium) was refashioned into a double stack section with a mezzanine (a second deck) similar to the first floor. This new facility provided shelving for 190,000 volumes and 70 new carrels along the walls for individual study. Done at a cost of $170,000, the conversion was completed for use in January 1970.[2]

Provision of housing for resident students seems to have been a perennial problem for Boston College in the decades after World War II, but in the Joyce era the phrase "housing crisis" expressed a pressing emergency. In 1966 Father Walsh had the architectural firm of Sasaki Associates do a development and feasibility study of the lower campus, with emphasis on dormitories.[3] On Laetare Sunday 1969, Father Joyce announced to the alumni that ground would soon be broken for twin towers, Boston College's first venture in high-rise residences, on the former reservoir behind Alumni Hall.[4] But a month later it was announced that plans for the 22-story dormitory had to be scrapped because of engineering and financial problems (the interest rates for construction loans were too high).

An interim solution to the housing problem was the purchase of a number of apartment properties on South Street which provided 344 beds. Extensive renovation was involved. The cost of the property and improvements was $1.4 million. These apartments, with the exception of the Greycliff dormitory, were sold in 1981.[5]

Other Remedies for the Housing Crisis

The 1969–1970 academic year was notable for a desperate remedy for the housing crisis. The large Jesuit house of studies in Weston had been partially vacated when the Jesuit theologate was moved to Cambridge. Arrangements were made to house 99 freshman men and four prefects in one wing of the great building in Weston. The students were transported to and from

Weston by bus. The frisky freshmen, however, were not compatible neighbors for the Jesuit fathers resident at Weston, some of whom were infirm. A number of pranks caused tensions, but the final straw was a fire set in a former science laboratory in the basement early in December. The best solution seemed to be to evacuate the students at once and send them home for Christmas vacation, with examinations postponed. During the vacation makeshift accommodations for second semester were found in upper campus residences—in prefects' rooms, study halls, lounges, kitchens, and chapels.[6]

In the spring of 1970 overtures were made for the purchase of the Somerset Hotel in Kenmore Square. According to a press release (April 16, 1970), the University was prepared to make payments to the City of Boston in lieu of taxes. An attractive feature of the hotel, according to the release, was the 350-car garage that would provide parking for the resident students and supervisory staff. It was thought that junior and senior students would be assigned to the Kenmore Square residence. However, the city objected to the proposed purchase and the project was abandoned.

In subsequent months a much more promising housing acquisition was pursued: The Towne Estates in Brighton were for sale. Acquisition of these apartments so close to the campus would have been a giant step toward solving the University's housing problems. The purchase price of $8 million was a pleasant contrast to the estimated $25 million for the abandoned plan for twin towers.[7] Boston Mayor Kevin White led opposition to the

The popular modular apartments, known as the "mods," were erected in the summer and fall of 1970.

Boston College plan. On July 21 in a City Hall hearing room, the Board of Appeals received opinions on the Boston College proposal. Father Joyce made a lengthy and eloquent presentation of the University's housing needs, stating that Boston College's survival as a major educational institution depended upon the Board's approval. Through the manager of the Allston-Brighton Little City Hall, however, Mayor White urged the board to reject the Boston College plan. Not unexpectedly, the mayor prevailed.

While these negotiations were in progress, the University had engaged the architectural firm of Hugh Stubbins and Associates to draw plans to accommodate 500 students in mobile homes on the "Lawrence Basin" (the land made by filling the small reservoir).[8] But the architect found that there was not enough space for a sufficient number of mobile units, so the best alternative seemed to be a two-story, duplex-type modular construction. The proposed construction was in the City of Boston, and this time it proceeded with the mayor's blessing. The "mods," as the residences came to be known, were shipped in halves on flatbed trucks by the manufacturer, Arbor Homes, Inc., from Waterbury, Connecticut. Ground was broken on August 25, 1970. Forty-three modular apartments were erected to house 516 students. The project proceeded through the first semester.[9] This construction was financed initially by a bank loan of $2.4 million. In 1974 the loan balance was refinanced on more favorable terms with the Massachusetts Health and Educational Facilities Authority.[10]

In September 1970 some 500 students were placed temporarily in apartments in Brighton and motels scattered from Brighton to the Route 128 Holiday Inn. They were moved to campus on a weekly basis as the new modular apartments became available, with full occupancy of the new campus facilities by Christmas. Another 200 students started the academic year living in the Howard Johnson's Motel at Newton Corner. Also starting in September 1970 and continuing for two years, the University leased 25 apartments in Byron Village on Lagrange Street in Newton, which accommodated 84 students.

Growth of the resident student population on the upper campus created the need for some kind of commons for entertainment and social activities. Although O'Connell Hall seemed ideal for this purpose, it was housing 82 students. Plans therefore were made to construct small townhouses near Tudor Road to accommodate the students from O'Connell. Known originally as the Townhouses and later as Medeiros Townhouses, these buildings were designed by architect Hugh Stubbins. The cost of construction was $948,000, financed partly with a HUD loan at 3 percent for $710,000 and partly from internal University resources. The new facilities, completed in 1971, provided 98 beds.[11]

A more permanent solution to the housing problem was undertaken in what turned out to be Father Joyce's last year as president. At its December 1971 meeting, the Board of Directors authorized the Flatley Construction

The Medeiros townhouses were completed in 1971 on the upper campus.

Corporation to build four mid-rise dormitories behind St. Mary's Hall, with an eventual capacity for 724 students.[12] Approval for this project was given by the City of Newton in March 1972.

First Steps Toward a Recreation Complex

The only nonresidential construction during the Joyce presidency was the first phase of the recreation complex. For years the students had lacked facilities for games and exercise. Indeed it is a tribute to the forbearance of the resident students that, especially during the 1950s and 1960s, there were not outbursts of animal spirits due to the absence of an outlet for physical activity. The closest the students came to mounting a protest was an announcement in an April Fool issue of *The Heights* in 1969, wherein they had Father Joyce proclaiming a $4 million athletic complex.

But the following fall William Flynn, director of athletics, proposed a multipurpose athletic facility and field house that would be a bubble construction.[13] Flynn was told there were no University funds for such an undertaking. He proposed to the undergraduate students that they make an annual $25 contribution toward an athletic facility. The issue was put to the student body at the time of student elections in early 1971. Close to 80 percent of the students voting approved the special fee.

Flynn discovered that Daniel Tully could provide a structure in the shape of a hyperbolic paraboloid which would give more style and permanence than the proposed double bubble. Tully designed and engineered the building, and it was constructed by Creative Building Systems of Melrose, Massachusetts, at a cost of $1.6 million. The initial part of the ultimately much-expanded complex was dedicated in March of 1972.[14]

Two Opinion Polls

Father Joyce authorized two professional studies of opinion about Boston College known as the Becker Report and the John Price Jones Report. The Becker Research Corporation of Cambridge did an in-depth interview of 343 alumni in December 1969 and January 1970. Of this group 294 were from a representative sample of all Boston College alumni and 49 were from a group of influential alumni considered close to the University.[15] The Becker Report was published in April 1970. It should be noted that the interviews on which the report was based took place some months before the student strike of 1970. The most significant conclusion of the researchers was that, to a considerable extent, the alumni constituted at that time a benign but uninformed and largely unexploited potential, and that much improved communication with the alumni was needed.[16]

Some individual findings were that the majority (92 percent) had positive feelings about Boston College. They rated its academic excellence as high, and they had enjoyed their undergraduate experience (especially the older

William J. Flynn ('39), director of athletics since 1957, has actively promoted athletics for young people.

graduates). Consistently, the better-informed alumni tended to be more favorable. Open hostility was marginal and sprang mainly from older alumni who were alienated by the disappearance of cherished traditions of discipline, Jesuit influence, and Catholic orientation and by the perceived indulgence of radical youth.[17] Noteworthy minority—and, in some cases, majority—opposition was registered against such things as free class attendance, tolerance of hippie dress and hair style and liquor in rooms, and a campus office for Students for a Democratic Society (SDS). The strongest opposition (68 percent) was to unlimited freedom of the press; even 4 in 10 among most-recent graduates opposed this.[18]

The alumni wanted the University to do even more to build quality education,[19] but at the same time they insisted that more should be done for the average student.[20] While placing top priority on the need for a new library, respondents had other funding interests in addition to further capital construction—namely, endowments for scholarships, faculty salaries, and fellowships.[21] The alumni as a whole did not place a very high priority on unbeaten football seasons and bowl games. Less than a third felt that the University should put great emphasis on varsity football.[22]

In November 1971 the John Price Jones Company of New York submitted to the Board of Directors a study of the development potentials of Boston College which had been prepared over the preceding six months.[23] Preparation for the report had included interviews with trustees, directors, administrators, faculty, students, alumni, parents, foundation and corporate executives, members of the President's Council, educators, government officials, and churchmen. The "bottom line," as the saying goes, was positive: "All of the information acquired in this study has convinced us that Boston College has a latent, 'dammed up' potential which is more than adequate for its future needs. . . ."[24] Much sound development advice was given in the report, most of which has been put into operation in subsequent years. One last piece of advice may be taken as a general summary of the thrust of the report. "Boston College stands on a temporary plateau from which it can go up or down. The re-establishment of credibility in its Christian and fiscal integrity will provide an upward thrust which will place it in the forefront of American Universities."[25]

Presidential leadership was assessed in the report. Father Joyce's credentials were presented most favorably:

> Father W. Seavey Joyce, the 23rd President of Boston College, brought a wealth of experience to the post. He is one of the few Jesuit administrators in the country who includes both a distinguished academic record and key leadership in the surrounding community as parts of his credentials. The College of Business Administration flourished under his leadership, and he is well-known to all major Boston executives for his role in the Citizen Seminars.[26]

But, perhaps inevitably, many who were dissatisfied with the way things

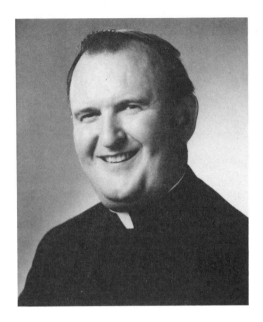

James A. Woods, S.J., dean of the Evening College since 1968 and dean of the Summer Session since 1983.

were going at the University tended to lay much of the blame upon the president. As the report puts it:

> There was universal appreciation that the times, economic and social, are turbulent and that Father Joyce may have inherited more problems than is generally recognized.
>
> However, among alumni, faculty, administration, and the Jesuit Community, there was almost universal disapproval of the manner in which University problems have been handled. The financial situation, "administrative permissiveness," the decline of Catholicity and "the Jesuit presence"—all were mentioned repeatedly in the interviews.[27]

The perception that vocal minorities were unduly influencing University decisions was expressed by faculty who claimed that the majority mood of both students and faculty did not require the decision to remove the ROTC unit from the campus.[28]

Administrative Changes

As can be seen from the Becker and John Price Jones reports, there was some vocal opposition to the administration, and at times Father Joyce suffered unnerving manifestations of it. In the fall of 1970 rumors surfaced to the effect that the Joyce presidency was in peril with the trustees.[29] The matter was serious enough that after the trustees' meeting of December 20, a press conference was held the next day at which the chairman of the board, Father Joseph Shea, announced that the trustees had recommended certain changes in the structure of the administrative office of the president to strengthen it, particularly in the areas of development, finance, and communication.[30] It was perhaps unfortunate that at this press conference it was also announced that as of January 1, 1971, Father Francis Nicholson would succeed Father Joyce as rector of the Jesuit Community. Although Father Shea made it clear that a number of other Jesuit presidents were being relieved of the duties of rector and that this change at Boston College had been in the making for some time, the timing of the change was misread by some as a reflection on the president's leadership.

One of the changes in the structure of the president's office had to do with the executive vice president, Father Francis X. Shea. Father Shea had been a controversial administrator. While no announcement was made about the elimination of his position, rumors arose to the effect that he had been asked to resign.[31] The actual situation was stated by Father Joyce in writing letters of recommendation for Father Shea for several college presidencies: "Since many of the functions which he originally performed [as executive vice-president] have been essentially phased out by the Board of Directors, Father Shea is very much interested in applying his academic ideas and programs at the highest administrative levels at other universities which offer challenging opportunities."[32] Father Shea had no administrative function in the spring semester of 1971. He submitted his resignation as executive vice president on July 8, the day after his appointment as president of St. Scholastica College in Duluth.[33]

Francis J. Nicholson, S.J. ('42), of the Law School faculty, first rector of Boston College Jesuits after separation of the offices of rector and president.

Genesis of the Priorities Committee

There was some supportive student reaction to rumors of Father Joyce's departure. The *Boston Herald* account of the press conference mentioned above noted that Mark Shanahan, a senior "who identified himself as a leader of campus leftists," said that he had organized a movement in support of Father Joyce and that 500 students had signed the endorsement.[34] In an interview with *The Heights* concerning the same press conference, it was significant that Father Joyce said, "I think the faculty are worried about the academic priorities."[35] The significance was that shortly thereafter, Father Joyce established a Committee on University Priorities that came to be known simply as the Priorities Committee. A small body with a wide-ranging commission, membership included Robert Anzenberger ('72), Paul August ('73), Professor P. Albert Duhamel of the English Department, Rev. Charles Donovan, S.J., dean of faculties (chairman), Rev. Donald MacLean, S.J., of the Chemistry Department (who replaced Professor Robert O'Malley of the Chemistry Department in June when the latter became ill), Professor Richard Maffei of the School of Management, Rev. Thomas O'Malley, S.J., of the Classics Department, and Professor Donald White of the Economics Department. An indication of how seriously the work of the Priorities Committee was taken is that when Professor White was named dean of the Graduate School of Arts and Sciences to replace Samuel Aronoff, who resigned at the end of the 1970–1971 academic year, the effective date of Professor White's assumption of office was *after* the submission of the Priorities Committee report, with Father Walter Feeney in the role of acting dean until that time.

The Priorities Committee consulted widely and met often. As things turned out, however, its effectiveness was probably more a matter of sustaining community morale during its deliberations than in the impact of its report, which Father Joyce had published in full (23 pages) in the February 17, 1971, issue of the *Thursday Reporter*. Since Father Joyce had submitted his resignation the month before, it was clear that a new administration would be addressing the issues raised by the Priorities Committee. The Priorities Committee report became a springboard for two important committees, one on finance and one on academics, that Father Monan established in the early months of his presidency.

A few of the concrete recommendations of the Priorities Committee were implemented at once—for example, closing of the Institute of Human Sciences, phasing out of doctoral programs in Italian and German studies, and centralization of registration functions. In some respects the Priorities Committee was understandably reacting to the traumas of the strike era—for instance, in its emphasis on judicial systems and the building of community. The Priorities Committee was the first nonfinance body to study University finances. It did so in depth, and this may have been one of its major contributions inasmuch as committee member Dean Donald

John R. Smith, financial vice president and treasurer.

White was drafted by Father J. Donald Monan to head his first major committee, on financial planning, shortly after assuming the presidency in 1972.

Addressing the Fiscal Situation

Several of Father Joyce's key appointments were made with an eye to turning around the fiscal situation of the University. During his second year in office he persuaded the dean of the Law School, Father Robert Drinan, to assume the new office of vice president and provost, which had as its responsibility leadership in development, public relations, and alumni relations. It was felt that Father Drinan's national visibility and personal dynamism would energize a new development movement. How this arrangement would have prospered was never known, for Father Drinan left Boston College to run for, and win, a seat in Congress. His replacement as dean of the Law School was Richard Huber, who had been a member of the Law School faculty since 1957. During his 15 years as dean, Huber was to bring the Law School to maturity. During the early and sometimes turbulent days of the University Academic Senate (UAS), Huber's was an influential voice of reason.

A significant recruit to the Joyce administration was John R. Smith, who became financial vice president in December 1970. Smith had held top budgeting and management positions with the Raytheon Company and Bendix Aviation Corporation. With support from the Board of Directors, he was able to effect a positive turnaround of the financial situation of the University in a relatively short period. The financial vice president was chairman of the University Budget Committee, which in the aftermath of the strike included two faculty and two student members, along with leading administrators. With a happy combination of openness and humor, Smith has led the Budget Committee through its annual struggles and developed it into an important instrument in promoting University policy.

THREE APPOINTMENTS TO DEAN

Upon the retirement of Dean Donald Donley of the School of Education, Lester Przewlocki was appointed successor in 1970. Dean Przewlocki was one of several School of Education faculty to have earned a doctorate at the University of Chicago. He had served as a public school administrator in the Chicago area before moving to Chestnut Hill. When Father John V. Driscoll chose to move to other professional work in 1971, the deanship of the Graduate School of Social Work was assumed by Edmund Burke, a graduate of the Graduate School of Social Work in 1956, who had joined the faculty in 1967. After the death of Dean Margaret Foley in 1970, Eleanor Voorhies of the School of Nursing faculty served as acting dean until the appointment of Mary Dineen in 1972. Coming from a prestigious career with the National League for Nursing, Dean Dineen was to give the School of Nursing 14 years of assured professional leadership.

Mary Dineen, dean of the School of Nursing, 1972–1986.

The Joyce Administration Draws to a Close

The first semester of the 1971–1972 academic year seemed somewhat upbeat for the Joyce administration. While protests of military recruiting were still threatened and relations with *The Heights* remained strained, the financial posture of the University was much improved. The completion of the modular apartments had alleviated the most pressing residential crisis, a glamorous recreational facility was under construction, a new core curriculum was in place, and the work of the Priorities Committee was coming to a conclusion. Perhaps with these positive developments in mind the president addressed an optimistic letter to the *Students of Boston College* in September. Characterizing the academic year 1970–1971 as "a very difficult one," he noted their intense involvement in University affairs and their "moral outrage at the evils of society," which "were replaced by a sense of frustration and a year of student apathy." But, he wrote cheerfully, "all that is behind us now."[36] However, Father Joyce was more optimistic than the times or circumstances warranted. *The Heights* staff had just been evicted from their campus office in McElroy and the editorials were bitter; Timothy Anderson, UGBC president, was calling for the abolition of the core program, the abolition of tenure, the reinstatement of *The Heights*, and the adoption of a new judicial code for campus offenses.[37] Unfortunately, the president was never able, even in his last year, to capture the high ground; in fact, a September 1971 issue of *The Heights* featured an article that had appeared in *Boston After Dark* which predicted the president's ouster. The prediction, though at the time a mere speculation, was correct as regarded the length of Father Joyce's term in office. On January 7, 1972, Father Joyce submitted his resignation, effective at the end of the academic year or upon the naming of a successor.

The esteem in which Father Joyce was held in the Greater Boston Community was reflected in the page one editorial that appeared in the *Boston Globe* on January 24, 1972, entitled "Father Joyce Steps Down." The thirteen paragraphs of the editorial enumerated the major problems Father Joyce had faced—finances, the Daly case, the tuition strike, and conflict with the student newspaper. Its effort to put these in perspective is quoted in part:

> The role of the college president in recent years has been much like that of a bullfighter—exciting, certainly, and perhaps even ennobling at times, but fraught with possibilities for conscious pain and suffering.
>
> This, plainly has been the case with the Very Rev. W. Seavey Joyce, S.J., a modest, earnest scholar whose presidency of Jesuit-run Boston College will close when his resignation becomes effective at the end of the current academic year.
>
> An economic historian, Father Joyce was inaugurated in October 1968. He brought to his new tasks a distinguished background in urban affairs, both academic and actual.

*   *   *

He became president of B.C. at a time when campus turmoil was at or near its peak around the nation, and almost from the start faced a crossfire of claims and pressures from students, faculty, alumni, and the virtually all-powerful trustees, the latter being a self-perpetuating body of ten Jesuits.

*   *   *

But amid all the *Sturm und Drang,* there has been significant progress, for which Fr. Joyce deserves immense credit. The financial situation, desperate two years ago, has been turned around. A broadening of the base of university control is planned, with laymen sharing authority with the Jesuits. Doctoral programs have been established in a number of areas.

As Father Joyce departs, bearing the scars of his struggles, the good wishes of all ought to accompany him. It is fair to say that he has faced up to the tasks assigned him with great patience, strength, and dedication. No more could be asked of any man.

A President Not a Rector

For the first time in Boston College's history, a president was to be appointed who was not rector of the Jesuit Community. The trustees announced (*Bridge*, February 1972) that an 11-member search committee would be established, comprised of two trustees, two directors, one alumnus, one administrator, three faculty members, and two students. The faculty and student members were to be chosen by the respective UAS caucuses. The mandate of the committee was to submit five candidates to the trustees.[38] Father James Devlin of the Boston College staff and Father William O'Halloran, rector of the Jesuits at Holy Cross College, represented the trustees, with Father Devlin serving as chairman of the search committee. The chairman of the Board of Directors, Joseph Loscocco, and David Nelson, Massachusetts Assistant Attorney General for Consumer Affairs, represented the directors. Richard Schoenfeld of the class of 1943, past president of the Alumni Association, was the alumnus member. The administrator of the committee was Dean Lester Przewlocki of the School of Education. The faculty members were Professor Alice Bourneuf of Economics, Professor P. Albert Duhamel of English, and Professor Mary Griffin of Education. The student members were Thomas Flynn, president of UGBC, and Richard Hogan, a student in the Graduate School of Business Administration. There never had been a Boston College committee so constructed, cutting across all elements of the University community, nor had any committee ever had so weighty a mandate. It fulfilled its charge energetically and with happy results.

*   *   *

Most American college presidents between 1968 and 1972 had problems similar to those Father Joyce faced. For reasons that need not be repeated, the times were troublesome in society, in academe, and in the Church. Yet through all the contentious episodes of his administration Father Joyce was self-possessed and uncomplaining. He served as president in an era that was often frustrating for the chief executive, and he served with dignity and grace.

ENDNOTES

1. James Devlin, S.J., former director of campus planning, to Charles Donovan, S.J., January 21, 1986. BCA.
2. A good description of this project is found in *The Heights* (September 16, 1969).
3. BCA.
4. *Alumni News* (April 1969).
5. Francis Mills, Director of Financial Resources, to Father Donovan, March 26, 1986. BCA.
6. Edward J. Hanrahan, S.J., former dean of students, to Father Donovan, April 10, 1986. BCA.
7. *Alumni News* (July-August 1970).
8. See Budget Committee file, BCA.
9. *Alumni News* (September-October 1970).
10. Francis Mills to Father Donovan, 1986.
11. *Ibid.*
12. *Bridge* (February 1972).
13. *The Heights* (October 14, 1969).
14. Letter of William J. Flynn, December 30, 1985. BCA.
15. Becker Report, p. 1. BCA.
16. *Ibid.*, p. v., p. viii.
17. *Ibid.*, p. vi.
18. *Ibid.*, p. xv.
19. *Ibid.*, p. xix.
20. *Ibid.*, p. xx.
21. *Ibid.*, p. xxii.
22. *Ibid.*, p. xvii.
23. John Price Jones, A Study of the Development Potential of Boston College. BCA.
24. *Ibid.*, p. viii.
25. *Ibid.*, p. 328.
26. *Ibid.*, pp. 176–177.
27. *Ibid.*, p. 34.
28. *Ibid.*, p. 60.
29. *The Heights* (December 15, 1970).
30. Press conference transcript, December 21, 1970. BCA.
31. *The Heights* (February 8, 1971).
32. BCA.
33. *Thursday Reporter* (September 23, 1971).
34. *Boston Herald* (December 22, 1970).
35. *The Heights* (January 14, 1971).
36. September 1971. BCA.
37. *The Heights* (September 20, 1971).
38. *Bridge* (February 1972).

CHAPTER 34

The Man from New York

J. Donald Monan, S.J., assumed the presidency of Boston College on September 5, 1972. A man of many talents, he was at home in the library, the classroom, and the board room, as well as on the hockey rink and the golf course. A philosopher by training and temperament, he was the co-author of *The Philosophy of Human Knowing: A Prelude to Metaphysics* and author of *Moral Knowledge and Its Methodology in Aristotle*. These learned publications entitled him to join the select circle of Aristotelian scholars who meet periodically to discuss a common interest.

Father Monan was born in Blasdell, New York on December 31, 1924. He attended Canisius High School in Buffalo and at age 18 entered the New York Province of the Society of Jesus at St. Andrew-on-Hudson. At the conclusion of his philosophical studies, he taught at St. Peter's College in Jersey City. Following study of theology at Woodstock College, he was ordained to the priesthood in 1955. After earning his Ph.D. in Philosophy at the University of Louvain, he continued his postdoctoral research at Oxford, the University of Paris, and the University of Munich. In 1960 he joined the Philosophy Department of LeMoyne College in Syracuse, New York, and the next year became chairman of the department.

In 1968 Father Monan became academic dean and vice president of LeMoyne, serving as director of the long-range academic and fiscal planning committee. At this time he also observed and influenced the operation of a complex major Jesuit university as a trustee of Fordham University. With this preparation and these credentials, Father Monan was ready to meet the challenge of being the twenty-fourth president of Boston College.

The New England Province of the Society of Jesus was established in 1926, separating the region from the Maryland-New York Province. Since 1926 eight presidents of Boston College (Fathers Dolan through Joyce) were New Englanders. By the year of Father Monan's appointment, province lines were no longer barriers in the assignment of Jesuits. Individual Jesuits could engage in apostolic work in another province with their Provincial's approval. Similarly, Jesuit institutions in a given province could recruit Jesuits from other provinces. Thus Father William McInnes, formerly associate dean of the School of Management, served as president of the University of San Francisco, and Father Donald MacLean, formerly of the Boston College Chemistry Department, was president of St. Joseph's College in Philadelphia and Spring Hill College in Alabama. It was this policy of flexibility in recruitment of Jesuits nationally that enabled Boston College to secure the services of a Jesuit of the New York Province as its twenty-fourth president.

Father Monan was subjected to the ritual interviews of new presidents by the Boston press, the Boston College community, and students. He was restrained, circumspect, and prudent in his responses—virtues which would characterize his administration. Although reporters—especially on campus—tried to draw him into controversial statements on Catholic education, student involvement, faculty appointments, ROTC, and academic goals, his responses were designed to preserve his freedom of action.[1] In the years ahead, he would lead the University to new heights in academic enrichment, in renovation and construction of the physical plant, in alumni relations, and in fiscal solvency. He would also be sympathetic to the expansion of athletic programs for men and women.

Changes in Governance

Upon his arrival the new president was faced with a revision of the governance of the University which had been evolving under his two predecessors. At a meeting in 1967, Father Walsh had requested the Board of Trustees to take formal action on a proposed change in the corporate structure of Boston College.[2] The trustees unanimously agreed that, on amendment of the by-laws, two boards would be established: The first, called the Board of Trustees, would all be Jesuits; the second, called the Board of Directors, would number not more than 25 Jesuits, laymen, and women.[3] At a subsequent meeting, the Board of Trustees, in refining plans for the governance of the University, began to anticipate the separate incorporation of the Jesuit Community at Boston College.[4]

Rev. J. Donald Monan, S.J., twenty-fourth president.

The 1967 revision of the by-laws preserved "the paramount legal authority and responsibility of the Board of Trustees" but reserved to the Board of Directors "all necessary and convenient powers to direct and manage the business and affairs of the corporation, hereinafter referred to as the University."[5] These powers included the right to adopt all major changes in educational policies and programs, to approve the granting of degrees (in course and honorary), to enact and amend statutes of the University, to act on tenure and promotion, to establish new schools or institutes, to review the budget, to authorize sale of land, and to purchase property.

At a special meeting of the trustees on September 6, 1968, Father Joyce stated that when he met with the Board of Regents on October 8, he would announce the implementation of the new Board of Trustees and the new Board of Directors, as approved during the year.[6] At the same time, letters were sent to the regents inviting them to accept appointment to the new board.[7] The newly constituted Board of Directors met for the first time on October 8, 1968. The principal business of the meeting was the election of officers (Henry Leen became chairman), the appointment of an executive committee, and determination of the terms of office for board members.

Since, in the revised by-laws, the president of Boston College was no longer chairman of the Board of Trustees, the trustees turned their attention to the election of a chairman. After considering Jesuit candidates from inside and outside the New England Province, the trustees, voting by written ballot, authorized the president to approach Father Joseph L. Shea, at that time rector of Cheverus High School in Portland, Maine. Father Shea accepted the invitation to serve and was duly appointed a trustee of Boston College.[8] Consequently, by the fall of 1968, in accordance with the revised by-laws, two University boards were in place and functioning. There remained only one further legal alteration to complete the new order of governance.

Separate Incorporation of the Jesuit Community

There was a movement at this time within the Jesuit Educational Association to separate the office of rector from that of president in Jesuit colleges and universities in the United States.[9] A leader in this movement was Father Paul C. Reinert, president of St. Louis University and also of the Jesuit Educational Association. He had convinced several administrators, including Father Michael Walsh, that the separate incorporation of the Jesuit communities would be in the best interest of all.[10] There would be several advantages to this approach. It would make the Board of Trustees and its actions better reflect the University's several constituencies; it would capitalize on the emergence of the laity after Vatican II in highly responsible positions; and it would separate policy making from internal administration in keeping with modern university practice. At a meeting of the board on January 25, 1968, Father Walsh urged the members to study documents which he provided on the separate incorporation of the Jesuit Community at St. Louis University.

The creation of a separate corporation was, of course, the responsibility of the Jesuits at Boston College and the superiors of the New England Province of the Society. The Provincial at this time was Father William G. Guindon, who had served as chairman of the Boston College Physics Department from 1953 to 1963. He was familiar with the process because he had recently been involved in the separate incorporation of the Holy Cross community. The Jesuit Community at Chestnut Hill was fortunate to have as its agent in these negotiations Father Francis J. Nicholson who, as a professor at the Boston College Law School, had an appreciation of the legal issues involved in forming a separate corporation. He had been appointed superior of the Jesuit Community on July 1, 1968; and, when the offices of rector and president had been separated, he became rector on January 1, 1971.

Shortly after Father Nicholson's appointment as rector, and confirming his status as official agent for the Community and the Province, the Provincial briefly outlined the issues that should receive particular attention: residence and property; pension benefits; an estimate of annual revenues and expenses; hiring and retirement of Jesuits; and the continuing interest of the Jesuits in Boston College as an apostolate.[11]

Father Nicholson, now rector, accompanied by Father Ernest Foley, his advisor on pensions, Daniel Holland, Esq., counsel to the corporation, and Paul Devlin, financial advisor, made his first presentation to the board on June 18, 1971.[12] The rector explained that the Community had all but completed the legal process of incorporation. (In fact, the corporation, under the name of the Jesuit Community of Boston College, with all the powers, rights, and privileges of a corporation in Massachusetts, was approved on July 20, 1971, by John F. X. Davoren, Secretary of the Commonwealth.)[13] Father Nicholson then went on to review the proposed agreement with Boston College, which covered the following points: a pension plan for retired Jesuits, provision for housing arrangements for Jesuits in St. Mary's Hall and Bellarmine House in Cohasset, and provision for an annual contribution by the Jesuit Community to the University.[14] In brief, the basic purpose of separate incorporation was to clarify the legal and financial relationship of the Community to the University.

S. Joseph Loscocco, Joseph F. Cotter, and John Lowell formed the subcommittee of the Board of Directors to work out an agreement with Father Nicholson and his advisors, Fathers Ernest Foley and John Trzaska. The sympathetic attitude of this committee can be measured from its comments:

> We strongly believe that a Boston College without Jesuits is no Boston College, and we wish to do everything in our power to encourage a greater Jesuit apostolic mission at Boston College. . . . We also believe that the entire

past service credit to Boston College be actuarially computed and recognized in a legal way as an obligation of Boston College to the Jesuit Community.[15]

In this atmosphere of mutual cooperation, an agreement was signed on June 22, 1972.

MAJOR PROVISIONS OF THE JESUIT-B.C. AGREEMENT

The University agreed:
1. To transfer to the Jesuit Community fee simple title to St. Mary's Hall and the Cohasset property.
2. To remunerate Jesuit members of the faculty and staff at the same level as their non-Jesuit colleagues.
3. To provide an annual pension of $2900 to retired Jesuits. (Since, in 1971, living costs per Jesuit per annum were set at $6500, the New England Province agreed to pay $3600 as a pension to the same Jesuits. The University also agreed to pay a lump sum to fund pensions for those already retired in compensation for contributed services over the years.)
4. To perform certain services for the Community, such as accounting and repairing.

The Jesuit Community agreed:
1. To recompense the University for resident use of University property.
2. To supply personnel for academic, administrative, and religious needs of the University.
3. To make financial contributions to the University in such amounts and for such purposes as may be determined by the Board of Directors of the Jesuit Corporation.[16] (In fact, as a pledge of future gifts, in early December 1972 Rector Father Nicholson presented a check from the Community for $400,000 to President J. Donald Monan for scholarships to Boston College students.)[17]

At the time, many interpreted the legal incorporation of the Jesuit Community as a sign that the Jesuits intended to disassociate themselves from the University. Actually, in the years following signing of the agreement, the relationship between the two corporations has been marked by mutual respect and cooperation. Although a few critics still register opposition to the separate incorporation of the Jesuit Community, this new form of governance has added a professionalism that was sometimes lacking when a more fraternal form of administration was the order of the day. By reason of an exception written into the by-laws (since no one actively involved with the University is eligible as a board member), the rector of the Jesuit Community sits on the Board of Trustees and represents the interests of the Community in those deliberations. The advantages of dual incorporation will become clearer as the story unfolds.

A Reconstituted Board

As the months went by, however, it became more difficult to determine the proper forum for particular University policy decisions. Clearly, having two independent boards (trustees and directors) did not solve all the problems of governance at Boston College. There was duplication and, indeed, ambiguity, in dealing with the owners of the corporation as distinct from those who managed its affairs. Accordingly, on September 3, 1972, Father Devlin (secretary) notified the Board of Trustees of a special meeting to be held on October 13 at which the main topic for discussion would be the establishment of a single board with an expanded membership. On November 19 the trustees voted unanimously to merge both boards into one, with an initial membership of 35.[18]

With the elimination of the Board of Directors, the reconstructed Board of Trustees met on December 8, 1972. Father Joseph Shea, chairman, commented on the historical significance of the first meeting of the enlarged board. Father Monan then introduced the new members. (Many of the former directors had accepted an invitation to join the expanded board.) The first piece of business was the election of officers: Cornelius Owens ('36), executive vice president of AT&T, was elected chairman; Thomas Galligan ('41), chairman of the board of Boston Edison Co., was elected vice chairman; William J. O'Halloran, S.J., rector of the Jesuit Community at Holy Cross, was elected secretary.[19] With Chairman Owens presiding over a highly qualified and enthusiastic board, Boston College began a new era of growth, vitality, and institutional influence.

David S. Nelson ('57, J.D. '60). Judge Nelson was a member of the Board of Directors under Father Joyce, became a member of the Board of Trustees in 1972, and has served as chairman of the board.

The Commuter Center

The 1972–1973 academic year was just getting under way when Father Monan moved into Botolph House. According to John Maquire, dean of admissions, 2555 freshmen had been admitted to the class of 1976. For many who had been promised campus housing, there was no room at the inn. As had happened on previous occasions, off-campus housing had to be found until the Hillside apartments were completed. In a temporary arrangement, 200 students lived in relative luxury from September 1972 to March 1973 at the Howard Johnson Motel in Newton Corner. The theme of student housing in the Monan years will be taken up in the next chapter when building construction is considered.

Resident students were not the only concern. The University was making a new effort to accommodate commuters who, though only a few short years ago the mainstay of the University, were now a minority. Indeed, they were beginning to feel like the proverbial poor relations. They sometimes spoke of seceding from UGBC—which, they thought, had not done enough for them—and forming their own organization. Just as hundreds of students before them in the 1930s, 1940s, and 1950s, these commuters plodded up the hill from the Green Line in the morning and returned in the afternoon. Many came in cars, it is true, and thereby caused a parking problem. But it was nine to three, just like high school, and they felt left out. James Scannell, who later became director of admissions, said, "I was a sophomore before I knew where the infirmary was and a senior before I knew there were handball courts, let alone that I could use them."[20] According to Father James Halpin, who became their advocate, the plight of the commuter surfaced at every student meeting: Parking was insufficient; facilities were inadequate; campus functions, especially if scheduled in the evening, were difficult to attend. They were, they said, second-class citizens.[21]

Finally, as a result of discussions between the commuters' council and the administration, and with a big assist from Father Halpin and the cooperation of James McIntyre, vice president for student affairs, a commuter center was established at Murray House on Hammond Street. (This facility was named in honor of John Courtney Murray, S.J., well-known American theologian of the Second Vatican Council.) UGBC gave an initial funding of $6000, and a board of governors for the center was formed. A series of events was scheduled, including seminars, lectures, films; there was also a dining room and a large kitchen which made it possible to serve lunches and dinners. From the beginning, the Board of Governors insisted that the center was not to be used as a hangout. Although it was primarily for the commuters, it was open to the University at large, since it would defeat its purpose if it further isolated the commuters from the rest of the campus. So, while the center gave the commuters an identity, with a facility of their own, it also provided a place for resident students and faculty to meet the commuter population outside the formal classroom environment.

*Francis B. Campanella, named exec-
utive vice president in July 1973.*

It was agreed by everyone with a sense of history that if Boston College lost its commuter population, it would lose an important link with the past—with its history, origins, traditions, and mission. Having a significant commuter population was also one way to avoid the charge of elitism—a word that was never found in the vocabulary of the founding fathers. In Jesuit terms, all the students were indeed *selecti quidem*; but not elite as society generally understands that word today.

The Boston College Women's Center

In contrast to the commuter center, which had its origins in antiquity, another center evolved from the modern character of the University. On March 8, 1973, International Women's Day, the Boston College Women's Center was opened in McElroy 123. On that day, 200 members of the Boston College community dropped by to borrow books, sip coffee, chat, or just to satisfy their curiosity. This event took place eight months after Alice Jeghelian, director of affirmative action, and Ginger McCourt of the Placement Office, with an assist from Carole Wegman, who presented the budget, submitted a proposal to the Office of Campus Planning.

The center opened under the direction of Elizabeth Wyatt, director of women's affairs, although it came under the larger umbrella of the Women's Action Committee as the organization ultimately responsible for all functioning matters. It was programmed to serve as a multipurpose facility for all women on campus—that is, faculty, staff, and students. Its sponsors spoke of a three-fold purpose: It would provide a sense of identity, through common interests, for Boston College women; it would act as a resource center for information on jobs, medical referrals, and career counseling; and it would gradually build up a specialized library of books by women for women, with an emphasis on career encouragement through illustration of historical accomplishments. The center was open daily in the afternoon from one to six.[22]

A Foothold for the Arts

Another acquired property, on the corner of Hammond and Beacon streets, was Hovey House. Originally destined for a University Art Center, it was given to the Fine Arts Department, which had been looking for a suitable home on campus. Unfortunately, the high expectations of that department were short-lived when the City of Newton imposed crippling restrictions on this structure. Citing zoning laws and fire regulations, city inspectors allowed offices to function but refused permission for classrooms, even on the first floor. The required renovations, which involved electrical work, new fixtures, new exits, and other safety measures, would be extensive and expensive. This sudden reversal of fortune forced the department, at a moment's notice, to find classrooms on campus wherever it could.[23]

In fact, it was an uphill struggle for the arts to gain support from the administration and to find a hospitable climate for growth on the Heights. For too long such a department was looked upon as a luxury, although it was fully compatible with the Latin inscription on the University's seal, *religioni et bonis artibus*. In a certain sense, however, the University has made up for a slow start by its generous support in recent years of the fine arts, applied arts, and performing arts.

NOTABLES IN THE ARTS AT BOSTON COLLEGE

In applied arts, Allison Macomber, artist-in-residence, maintained a studio on the top floor of Lyons, where he attracted a large group of budding painters and sculptors. Alexander Peloquin, well-known composer and conductor, brought his engaging personality, talent, and wit to his classes in the history of music as well as to the University Chorale, which performed in many cities in the United States and Europe. In her lectures on the Renaissance art of Italy, Josephine von Henneberg trained her students, as she insisted, not to practice but to intelligently enjoy art. Olga Stone, never far from her grand piano, is remembered for her survey of western music, her advanced piano instruction, and her eagerly awaited recitals in Barat House. Joseph Larkin, S.J., and J. Paul Marcoux communicated their enthusiasm and professional competence to the students in drama and theater. In another category of the performing arts, Robert Ver Eecke, S.J., introduced interpretive dance to campus liturgical functions such as the always impressive Baccalaureate Mass. And Father Francis Sweeney, director of the Humanities Series, over the years brought to the campus an incredible range of artists—poets, dancers, writers, choristers, and musicians—to inspire Boston College students to profit from their example, to imitate their excellence, and to applaud their accomplishments. Through the efforts of these people, art gained a foothold at Boston College.[24]

Military and CIA Recruitment

Going from sublime to more mundane matters, a brief reference should be made to the difficulties that developed over recruitment efforts by members of the military and the CIA. To the more disciplined ranks of an older generation of alumni, news reports of protest and demonstration were always distressing. The Vietnam syndrome died slowly at the Heights. In October 1972 Navy, Marine, and Air Force recruiters visited the campus. The University Academic Senate had affirmed an open policy on recruitment; UGBC decided not to interfere, since there were so many more important things to do. Moreover, learning from past experience, they considered it "hopelessly frustrating to block recruiters from entering buildings."[25] But a small group of students promised that there would be demonstrations.

In the fourth week of October some 30 students picketed Alumni Hall and blocked the entrance for about 45 minutes. Dr. James McIntyre told the students that the court injunction, which Boston College had requested in 1971 when 20 students were arrested, was still in effect. On his arrival at the scene, Philip Burling, University attorney, informed the protestors that they were "now in contempt of court." Faced with the prospect of arrest, the students left the scene, and recruiters entered Alumni Hall.[26] The students tried to have the last word by showing films and providing information on the horrors of war, suggesting by implication the contribution of those who succumbed to the persuasion of recruiters. In this connection the confrontation continues to the present day over the restoration of ROTC.[27]

The New Team

Every chief executive picks his own staff—at least, those who will be his top advisors. Indeed, it has been said that the character of a university reflects to some degree the personalities of its chief officers. In an early interview with *The Heights*, Father Monan was asked if he had any present or future plans to appoint an executive vice president. He replied, "Not at the present, no. As far as the creation of new vice presidential positions or the changing of any other vice president, I don't contemplate it."[28]

However, new appointments were being made at the beginning of the second semester. In February 1973 Margaret A. Dwyer, assistant academic dean at Le Moyne College, was named executive assistant to the president. A native of Syracuse and a graduate of Le Moyne College, she had earned her master's degree in counseling at Boston College in 1956. Returning to Le Moyne, Dwyer held a number of administrative positions, including registrar and dean of women, which brought her into contact with students and faculty.[29] In subsequent years, she was a key figure in negotiations which led to the consolidation of Boston College and Newton College, and was promoted to a vice presidency.

Margaret A. Dwyer (M.Ed. '56), vice president.

After careful deliberation and an extensive search, the president made a key appointment in July 1973. At that time Francis B. Campanella, an associate professor in the School of Management, was offered the position of executive vice president. His educational credentials and management background eminently fitted him for this post. A 1958 graduate of Rensselaer Polytechnic Institute with a B.S. degree in management engineering, he earned an MBA at Babson Institute and a doctorate in business administration at Harvard in 1970. A nationally recognized management consultant, Campanella was charged by Father Monan to introduce up-to-date management practices in the University, which, in some areas, were sorely needed. His two top priorities were to develop an information system for the vice presidents and middle administrators and to establish management standards. Over the years he has worked very closely with John Smith, financial vice president, in shaping the University budget. While open to dialogue with all campus constituencies, he is well known for having the courage of his convictions in facing student protests over tuition increases. By assuming responsibility for the internal management of the University, the executive vice president has allowed the president to concentrate on academic programs, development, alumni, and the many demands of professional organizations in which he is an officer.

A good development program was a necessity at Boston College, where academic programs were becoming more expensive, where new construction was in progress, and where renovations could not be postponed. The hard work of James A. Hayden, Jr., director of development, was reflected in the increase in annual giving from $359,000 in 1972 to $500,000 in 1973. Hayden worked closely with Robert J. Desmond, who had been appointed vice president of university resources in the summer of 1973.[30] With an MBA from Syracuse University, he had experience in fund raising at St. Louis University, the University of Dallas, and Le Moyne College. He directed his attention and energies to foundation relations, the deferred giving program (with particular emphasis on the University's endowment), and favorable press coverage.[31]

To complete the team, Thomas P. O'Malley, S.J., was appointed dean of Arts and Sciences. He succeeded James Skehan, S.J., who had been acting dean from January 1972 to July 1973. Father O'Malley, a 1951 Boston College graduate with an M.A. from Fordham and a doctorate from the University of Nijemegen, Netherlands, was an administrator of proven experience. Former chairman of the Classics and Theology departments and a member of the Priorities Committee, he had a broad knowledge of the campus and its academic programs. He would try, he said in an interview, to give job coherence to his own office and to influence the

Thomas P. O'Malley, S.J. ('51), dean of the College of Arts and Sciences, 1973–1980. Father O'Malley left Boston College to assume the presidency of John Carroll University in Cleveland.

quality of life at Boston College. As a personal contribution, he was for many years an enthusiastic member of the University Chorale. He had a good voice and, while a graduate student at Fordham, sang in the chorus with the Metropolitan Opera Company in New York. An accomplished and witty speaker, he brought a flamboyant style to his office which was a delight to those who attended his meetings. He was later elected president of John Carroll University in Cleveland.[32]

In a continuing effort to establish closer and better rapport with the University's neighbors, Neil P. O'Keefe, S.J., was appointed director of community relations. A 1953 Boston College graduate, Father O'Keefe served as a naval officer in the post-Korean War period, then entered the Society of Jesus. After his ordination, he earned a Ph.D. in Political Science at the University of Pennsylvania. There was a growing awareness that local constituencies had a legitimate claim on certain University services. Coordinating the community service activities for all campus departments and agencies, he encouraged people to think about community problems. Many of his days were spent at Newton City Hall working out joint endeavors for Boston College and Newton.[33]

It should be emphasized that Boston College did not have to apologize for its service to the City of Newton and surrounding towns; the concern has always been there. In a sense Father O'Keefe was continuing the earlier work of Fathers Seavey Joyce and George Drury, who were vice presidents for community affairs.[34]

Addressing Fiscal Matters

It is generally conceded that the two most important areas in collegiate management are the fiscal and academic needs of the institution. Father Monan inherited a financial situation at Boston College that was at best precarious, at worst dangerous. In fact, if the financial officers and trustees had not combined to make the hard decisions, it could have been disastrous. When fiscal year 1971–1972 came to an end on June 30, Boston College had a balanced budget, reversing a deficit trend and also representing a 25 percent reduction in the University's short-term debt. This was accomplished, according to the financial vice president, through a $100 increase in tuition, a 1971–1972 freeze on faculty and administrative salaries, and fiscal frugality across the board.[35] However, a long-term liability of several million dollars still had to be retired.

Father Monan was determined to improve the financial health of the institution which, in his set of priorities, was the first step in "developing an over-all academic and fiscal plan."[36] His immediate remedy was creation of a long-range fiscal planning committee that would, in addition to balancing the budget, project both revenues and expenditures for the next five years. Part of his plan was to absorb the deficit with which the school was saddled. In November 1972 the president sent out letters of appoint-

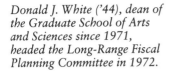

Donald J. White ('44), dean of the Graduate School of Arts and Sciences since 1971, headed the Long-Range Fiscal Planning Committee in 1972.

ment to the Long-Range Fiscal Planning Committee. Donald J. White, dean of the Graduate School, was named chairman. Other members of the committee included vice presidents and deans; also, John Bolan, director of institutional research, Professor Evan Collins of the School of Education, Professor Mary Ann Glendon of the Law School, and two students. The committee held its first meeting on November 27, 1972.[37]

The point made by the president to the committee was that sound fiscal planning was a necessary prerequisite for commitment to quality academic goals and auxiliary programs. He made the same point to a general gathering of faculty on March 8, 1973, when he said, "My first financial priority will be to maintain and improve the academic distinction of the University."[38] Fiscal planning and academic planning were, he said, two sides of the same coin. He also mentioned at that time that faculty increases would again be lower than they should be, but would increase the following year. He then informed the faculty that there were 8000 applications for the undergraduate colleges, with 50 percent from the top 20 percent of their high school class. Finally, he confided to the faculty that Boston College would have to find new sources of revenue to subsidize the advanced academic and professional programs.[39]

In his charge to the Fiscal Planning Committee, Father Monan set May

1, 1973, as a deadline for submitting its five-year plan for University finances. Observing the deadline, the committee turned in its report to the Board of Trustees and projected balanced budgets for the next five years. A comfortable amount of growth was built into this report, about $14 million dollars in additional income and expenditures by academic year 1978–1979, and a modest surplus was expected if the U.S. economy was sufficiently stable. At the same time, the University had to reduce costs and build revenues on new sources of support. The basic goals of the fiscal plan included: (1) reduction of the University's short-term debt, (2) building a reserve fund for emergency needs, (3) funding physical renovation of the campus, and (4) an increase in the University's endowment, which was embarrassingly small.[40]

The report also called for a 2 percent increase in enrollment and an annual tuition increase of about 5 percent. As a result of these measures, the report projected income from tuition and fees at $37,178,000 by the academic year 1978–1979—more than $10 million over current income. In addition, the report seriously recommended that auxiliary enterprises—housing, food services, and athletics—which for some time had been a

A scene (Act II, Scene IV) from Henry IV, directed in 1973 by Father Joseph Larkin in the challenging confines of Campion auditorium. From left to right are Peter J. Brash ('76) as Francis, Jay Korejko (ex-B.C.) as Bardolph, Karola Hillenbrand ('74) as Mistress Quickly, Gary Trabolsi ('74) as Falstaff, and Paul Lambert ('75) as Prince Hal.

drain on the operating budget, be made self-supporting as soon as possible. It was anticipated that University expenses would increase by 5 percent a year for supplies and 6 percent for personnel. This was an added reason for more effective use of present and future resources.[41]

To begin to implement these recommendations, the Board of Trustees approved a $1.5 million spending cut for 1973–1974. Cuts were made from each category across the board, with a precise saving of $1,444,000. There was also a modest tuition increase of $50 which, of course, was protested by the UGBC.[42] However, the Board of Trustees had, at their meeting on December 8, 1972, frozen room and board fees for 1973–1974. With the increase in tuition, budget cuts, and revenue from the recreational complex and football, John Smith, financial vice president, predicted a breakeven budget for 1973–1974 and a zero-based budget for 1974–1975. The picture was looking a little brighter.

As an integral part of this consolidated long-range plan, there was an accelerated effort to broaden and deepen other sources of income. For example, the Development Office alerted alumni who worked with firms with matching gift programs that a personal gift would be doubled in value by the company's contribution. In 1972–1973 this program amounted to $32,595. In the same year, corporations sympathetic to the philosophy of education at Boston College contributed gifts in the amount of $72,275, while foundation support continued to increase. The annual telethon carried on by devoted alumni and the Estate Planning Council also made substantial contributions.

In the long term, perhaps the most important innovation has been the Fides banquet and its derivative receptions. As originally organized, those alumni who contributed $1000 during the year were given membership in the Fides organization. The first annual Fides banquet, a formal dinner, was held in the Oval Room of the Copley Plaza Hotel on the Sunday night before commencement in May 1973. In recent years, the format has changed and the banquet, now the President's Circle dinner, has been moved to McElroy Commons. Since the growth in numbers and the increase in contributions have been spectacular, there are now several categories within the original organization, and dinners and receptions are held for each group. For many members the most interesting feature of the banquet before commencement is the presence of the honorary degree candidates of that year, who make a few remarks.

A review of figures from the late sixties into the early seventies indicates the steady growth of annual giving by alumni. In 1967–1968 there were 1915 alumni donors who contributed $66,199; in 1970–1971, 3916 donors contributed $237,845; and in 1972–1973, 6125 donors contributed $500,166. It was encouraging for the administration to note that, in just four years, the annual giving fund had grown from less than $100,000 to over half a million dollars.[43] The steady growth would continue. In

1988–1989, with 28,729 donors, the annual giving fund reached $5,686,050.[44]

*   *   *

With a solid financial plan which promised positive results, the president was prepared to examine the academic programs already in place, the changes or substitutions that might be made, and the possibility of new programs that would enlarge the reputation of the University. At the end of his first year in office, Father Monan had the confidence of the faculty and had given sound leadership to the administration. With the cooperation of all segments of the campus community, slowly but surely he was moving Boston College into a new era.

ENDNOTES

1. See *The Heights* (September 19, 1972).
2. Minutes, Board of Trustees, December 14, 1967. BCA.
3. *Ibid.*
4. Minutes, Board of Trustees, January 10, 1968.
5. Trustees of Boston College, By-Laws, 1960–1972. BCA.
6. Minutes, Board of Trustees, September 6, 1968. BCA.
7. *Ibid.*
8. Minutes, Board of Trustees, November 8 and 23, 1968. BCA.
9. See P. A. FitzGerald, S.J., *Governance,* passim. It was customary for Father General to appoint the rector of a given college; that person was then elected president by the trustees.
10. See Paul C. Reinert, S.J., "First Meeting of the Board," *Jesuit Educational Quarterly* (January 1968).
11. William G. Guindon, S.J., to Francis J. Nicholson, S.J., January 11, 1971. BCA.
12. Minutes, Board of Directors, June 18, 1971. BCA.
13. BCA.
14. Minutes, Board of Directors, June 18, 1971. BCA.
15. S. Joseph Loscocco to Francis J. Nicholson, S.J., October 17, 1971. JEA file, BCA.
16. Francis J. Nicholson, S.J., "Jesuits Incorporate," *Bridge* (February 1973).
17. *Ibid.,* "A Scholarship Gift."
18. See Minutes, Boards of Trustees, 1960–1972. BCA. On November 9, 1971, by an act of the Massachusetts Legislature, the original limitation of 10 members of the Board of Trustees was removed. In the composition of the new board, there were 33 men and 2 women; 22 laypeople and 13 Jesuits; 33 white people and 2 blacks.
19. Minutes, Board of Trustees, December 8, 1972. BCA.
20. "Boston College Rediscovers the Commuter," *Thursday Reporter* (September 28, 1972).
21. See *Bridge* (December 1972); also *The Heights* (October 10, 1972).
22. *Thursday Reporter* (March 8, 1973); also *The Heights* (March 6, 1973).
23. *The Heights* (October 17 and 31, 1972).
24. For a good summary see Marylou Buckley, "The Arts at Boston College," *Bridge* (February 1973).
25. *The Heights* (October 17, 1972).

26. *Ibid.* (October 31, 1972).
27. For a fuller account of these confrontations, see the papers of Edward J. Hanrahan, S.J., dean of students at the time. BCA.
28. *The Heights* (September 19, 1972).
29. *Bridge* (May–June 1973).
30. Annual giving has increased every year, and by the mid-eighties it was well over $5 million.
31. *Bridge* (October–November 1973).
32. *Ibid.* Father Charles Donovan, John Smith, and James McIntyre remained in their respective offices.
33. The more recently established Office of Community Affairs, with Jean McKeigue as director and with ambitious outreach initiatives, continues the work of the men mentioned here.
34. *Thursday Reporter* (September 28, 1972).
35. *The Heights* (December 5, 1972).
36. *Thursday Reporter* (November 30, 1972).
37. *Ibid.* (March 15, 1973).
38. *Ibid.*
39. *Bridge* (October–November 1973).
40. *Ibid.*
41. *The Heights* (December 5, 1972)
42. See Annual Fund comparison chart, *Bridge* (October–November 1973).
43. Figures from the office of University Development.
44. See A Report on the Boston College Development Year 1988–1989.

CHAPTER 35

Spectacular Progress

In September 1973 Father Monan proceeded to the next phase of planning with the appointment of the University Academic Planning Council (UAPC). The president himself became titular chairman of the council and attended all meetings during the many months of its deliberations. The director of the routine operation of the council and chair of its meetings was Dean of Faculties Father Donovan. The council had 26 members: 4 administrators; 12 faculty members (one from each professional school and seven from the College of Arts and Sciences); and 10 students (seven undergraduates and three students from the Graduate School of Arts and Sciences).[1]

Two important subcommittees were established: one on University goals, headed by John Mahoney, and one on resources for financing academic plans, headed by Frank Campanella. A first draft of a goals statement was submitted to the community for reaction in December. At the same time the UAPC issued a planning document to each instructional unit—that is, each school and department—asking for a five-year plan including not only school or department goals but also a projection of the unit's contribution to the University goals. While the schools and departments were preparing their reports, the UAPC developed position papers on six broad topics: faculty development, quality of instruction and advisement, research, instructional workloads, the core curriculum, and undergraduate admissions policy.

Unless an institution decides to depart radically from its current mission, goals statements can sound like an assertion of the obvious. To some extent that was true of the UAPC goals statement, since it was an unswerving reaffirmation of the traditional commitments of Boston College. In view of the turbulent times higher education, including Boston College, had recently been through, however, the UAPC felt its reaffirmation of the University's historic goals necessary and significant. While many ideals were proposed in the nine-page goals statement, three mandates were fundamental for the entire document: (1) reaffirmation of the religious tradition and commitment of Boston College, calling especially for a strong and influential Theology Department, an assertive and effective chaplaincy, and a continuation of the Jesuit presence at existing levels; (2) a continuing commitment to quality undergraduate liberal education, with renewed emphasis on effective teaching; and (3) a continuing commitment to University status, evidenced by support for professional education, quality graduate programs, and emphasis on scholarship and research.

As the story of Boston College in the 20th century unfolds, attention focuses on the relative numbers of Jesuit and lay faculty members. When the institution was exclusively a liberal arts college for under 1500, it was not difficult to staff it mostly with Jesuits, since the number of classes was not great and the disciplines were those Jesuits usually pursued. Once the University decided to add professional schools in law, social work, nursing, management, and education—subjects pursued by very few Jesuits—it was inevitable that the proportion of lay faculty would grow dramatically.

The table below shows the gradual rise and then decline of Jesuit faculty as well as the steady growth of lay faculty:

	Jesuit Faculty	Lay Faculty
1920	28	3
1930	45	30
1940	71	41
1960	100	246
1980	63	495
1990	32	538

The above figures represent full-time Jesuit teachers. They do not show the much larger Jesuit presence at the University in other roles. For example in 1989–1990, in addition to the 32 full-time teachers, there are 17 university administrators who are Jesuits, 15 Jesuits who teach part-time in retirement, 26 Jesuits from many parts of the world who are students, and 36 Jesuits who have ministries outside the University, administer the Jesuit Community, or are in retirement. The Boston College community of 132 Jesuits is among the largest in the world.

"Jesuit Education at Boston College"

An interesting byproduct of the UAPC planning process was a document produced by members of the Jesuit Community, "Jesuit Education at Boston College." The document was the product of a grassroots discussion group including Jesuits varying widely in age, experience at Boston College, and academic background. It was a splendid overview of the mission of education in Jesuit history and the postwar change at Boston College from a highly structured philosophical-literary education to what the document called the "hegemony of the departments."

While sharing with non-Jesuit colleagues the motivation and vision of Jesuit education, the document was also a thinking through for the Jesuits' own consideration of whether the Boston College of the 1970s was an appropriate setting for Jesuits in an educational apostolate. After carefully weighing pros and cons, "Jesuit Education at Boston College" concluded optimistically that Boston College was an attractive setting not only for New England Jesuits but for national and international Jesuits as well. Since Jesuits at other Jesuit colleges were wrestling with similar problems and options at that time, this document was widely circulated, and it became something of a blueprint for the American Jesuit mission in higher education. Shaped principally by Father Joseph Appleyard, it was published in pamphlet form, enhanced by engaging illustrations by Professor Thomas O'Connor, whose talented pen has graced so many Boston College publications. The document was reprinted in *The Heights* in October 1974 and in *Boston College Focus* in December of that year.

The UAPC Report

In February 1975 the UAPC report was completed and published. Some of its highlights were a strong reaffirmation of the importance of a good core curriculum with a guaranteed distribution of liberal arts courses for every undergraduate, including courses in philosophy and theology. Particular

Thomas F. Flynn ('74) and Stephen E. Fix ('74) were student members of the University Academic Planning Council. That service may have presaged things to come, for both are now college deans: Flynn at Mt. St. Mary's College in Maryland and Fix at Williams College.

attention was paid to the kind of teaching needed for core courses and suggested mechanisms, such as a continuing seminar on core curriculum teaching, to keep faculty attention focused on the special nature and needs of core instruction. The report stressed University-mindedness and collegiality, a note established in the goals statement and echoed throughout the report. The College of Arts and Sciences specifically was urged to develop comprehensive institutional goals and esprit to counteract department insularity—the same exhortation President Butterfield of Wesleyan had addressed to the A&S faculty in 1963.

Among the report's specific responses to school and departmental plans was the suggestion that the Philosophy Department develop strength in areas traditional in Jesuit education—namely, classical and medieval philosophy—and the department was discouraged from the use of many teaching fellows for core courses. Two undergraduate programs, economics and psychology, were warned about being too pre-professional; and two doctoral programs, psychology and sociology, were asked to review their programs and resources with outside help. The report suggested that the School of Management consider streamlining its administrative structure and warned the School of Education about an apparent lessening of emphasis on the liberal arts component of the curriculum.

The trustees reviewed the UAPC report and asked the president to inform them in a year on progress in implementation of its recommendations. One of the suggestions of the UAPC report was that a successor planning committee be established. In September 1975 Father Monan set up a University Planning Council composed of 15 members (8 faculty members, 4 administrators, and 3 students).[2] The principal charge the president gave to the UPC was to prepare the University's report preliminary to the spring re-evaluation visit of the New England Association of Schools and Colleges. Much of the work of the committee was stimulation and coordination, because each academic unit had to prepare a statement about its own programs. The final report, finished by February, contained only 147 pages, but they were pages packed with data and tables, giving a remarkably comprehensive picture of the University in 1975–1976. Particularly impressive were the concise statements from the several departments and professional schools—forthright and rather low-key expressions of achievement and aspiration. The New England Association's visiting team, headed by University of New Hampshire president Eugene S. Mills, filed a favorable report, and re-accreditation was granted.

The impressive reports of the Arts and Sciences departments for the re-evaluation document once again reminded the administration of an ongoing worry that had been voiced by President Butterfield in 1963 and repeated by the UAPC report in 1975: that self-centered disciplinary strength in the departments might inhibit a general vision of liberal education. One strategy the University adopted to minimize faculty fragmentation and promote interdisciplinary dialogue was a series of faculty weekends at the Andover Inn on the campus of Andover Academy. The first was held in October 1974, and by January 1990 a total of 103 such faculty gatherings had been held. Sponsored by the University Council on Teaching, the Andover workshops have gathered twenty or so faculty at a time, from varied disciplines and professions and at diverse stages of academic and Boston College experience, to discuss in a relaxed and relatively unstructured way the challenges and opportunities of the teaching profession. In recent years new members of the faculty have been invited to fall weekends. On a few occasions faculty groups have gone to Andover to focus on a special issue such as the core curriculum, but the principal purpose of these meetings has been an exchange of faculty views on teaching. Organizer and hostess for all of these faculty retreats has been Katharine Hastings, assistant to four academic vice presidents.

The Consolidation with Newton College

In late 1973 Father Monan and the trustees were unexpectedly faced with a decision that may rank in importance with Father Gasson's 1907 decision to move Boston College from the South End to Chestnut Hill. Newton College of the Sacred Heart, tragically unable to survive as an independent private college because of unmanageable debt, approached Boston College to see if the Newton College traditions and educational commitments could survive consolidation with Boston College.

The Newton College of the Sacred Heart was begun by the Society of the Sacred Heart in 1946 at the generous and insistent invitation of then Archbishop Richard Cushing. In 1944 Archbishop Cushing contacted Sister Eleanor Kenny, R.S.C.J., superior of the Country Day School of the Sacred Heart on Centre Street in Newton, to inform her that the Schrafft estate (now Barat House) was available. If the adjoining Harriman estate (now Putnam House) were purchased, the Sisters would have one of the most attractive sites on the East Coast for a women's college. He promised financial help in acquiring the properties.[3] In a short time, the estates were acquired, and in September 1946 a total of 41 students (11 commuters and 30 boarders) became freshmen in the new college.

Because of the outstanding reputation of the Religious of the Sacred Heart as educators and through contact with their own preparatory schools around the world, Newton College prospered and very soon had an enrollment quite satisfactory for a small college for women: nearly 400 in 1957, over 600 in 1961, and over 800 by the late sixties. In only its eighth year of existence the college was accredited by the New England Association of Schools and Colleges. After several intermediate accreditation reviews, in 1964 the college received accreditation for a 10-year period, the normal approval for a mature and well-functioning institution of higher education.

With faith, energy, and courage the leaders of the young college embarked on a remarkable schedule of building. Architects were Maginnis

A dramatic setting for a liturgy, beneath the St. Patrick window in Gasson assembly hall.

and Walsh, the firm that had beautified the Boston College campus. The buildings were not lavish or extravagant, but they were of high quality and impeccable taste. The unusual vitality of this educational enterprise is revealed in an impressive statistic: Between 1948 and 1969 Newton College erected 12 buildings that comprised a complete and gracious campus.

Few educators in the robust 1950s foresaw—or even dreamed of—the changes that would shake higher education in the 1960s. One thing not predicted was the variety of social forces that would suddenly make the small college for women an endangered species. One statistic that authorities at Newton College could ruefully report to their constituencies when their own plight became evident was that of 300 liberal arts colleges for women in existence in 1960, only 146 remained in 1973. In 1969 James Whalen became the first lay president of Newton College.[4] By 1972 President Whalen was beginning to inform the faculty and friends of the college that the institution's huge debt would have to be retired if the college was to survive.[5] In 1973 a major fund drive was undertaken, with a goal of $6 million. But, gifts and pledges did not meet a third of the goal, and catastrophe faced the gallant institution.

PRESIDENT WHALEN'S STATEMENT IN THE ALUMNAE MAGAZINE

In the last month of 1973, we were beset by very serious problems. Our lending institutions, which had pledged financing through 1976, reviewed the results of the capital campaign and indicated that they were no longer able to extend unsecured credit to the college. This reduced our "survival time" by eighteen months and certainly created a more immediate problem. It was clear to them we were not getting sufficient support and would not be able to retire the debt. Without a successful campaign the college was in serious financial condition. In addition, applications for admission were quite inadequate in terms of our budgetary needs. Applications to Newton had been dwindling over the past ten years in spite of a really fine effort on the part of our admissions staff. This decline, which would ultimately result in operating deficits, coupled with the huge debt, dictated the necessity to determine an alternative course of action. We began, at that time, to examine the possibilities for affiliation with another college.[6]

In some respects it was natural for Newton College to turn to Boston College at this juncture. The Society of the Sacred Heart and the Society of Jesus had been allied in many parts of the world in educational and spiritual matters for more than a century and a half. Locally, two Boston College Jesuits, Father Thomas Fleming, long-time treasurer, and Father W. Seavey Joyce before his presidency, had been chaplains to the religious community at Newton College from the day it opened through the early years of growth. Before the erection of the Barry Science building, Newton College students took some of their science classes at Boston College. But besides such ties there was the more basic reality that the two institutions shared a common religious impulse and ideal. Of course, the proximity of the two campuses was a positive factor in the consideration of a possible union.

Discussions and negotiations between the two boards of trustees and the two presidents proceeded during January and February 1974.[7] Father Monan called upon Professor Evan Collins of the School of Education, who had been a college president himself, and Professor John Neuhauser of the School of Management to help work out some of the details of the consolidation. At a meeting on February 28 the Newton College trustees, and on March 1 the Boston College trustees, approved a cooperative agreement leading to consolidation of Newton College into Boston College. It was agreed that the two presidents would speak to their respective constituencies at noon on Monday, March 11, and that a press conference making public the consolidation would take place at Newton College at 2:00 p.m. the same day.

Essential elements of the agreement were that Boston College would assume the liabilities of Newton College, which were approximately $5 million. Boston College would also assume Newton's assets, which had a book value of approximately $11.5 million and an estimated replacement value of $25 million. Newton College agreed to transfer to Boston College its land and buildings and certain equipment and furnishings, effective June 30, 1974. Newton College would continue to function as normally as possible under its board of trustees through the academic year 1974–1975. As of June 30, 1975, Newton College was to cease to exist as an undergraduate college except for the purpose of conferring degrees. With the commencement of the class of 1976, this function would cease also.

In 1976 Mary Kinnane (Ph.D. '63), professor of speech and higher education, was named an honorary Fultonian by the debating society. Congratulating her with Father Monan are John Lawton, chairman of the Speech Department, and James Unger ('64), one of the stars in Fulton's history.

Under the terms of the consolidation agreement, Newton College students in the classes of 1974 and 1975 were to receive Newton College academic degrees. Students of the class of 1976, who were sophomores at the time of the agreement, could qualify, at their option, for either a Boston College or a Newton College degree. Students of the class of 1977, who were freshmen, would receive Boston College degrees. Newton College would not accept a class of 1978, though Boston College would consider all applicants to the class of 1978 at Newton. Former Newton College students wishing to complete their degrees could apply to Boston College as transfer students, and their admittance would be automatic if they left Newton in good standing.

To strengthen the consolidation and provide continuity, T. Vincent Learson, chairman of the Board of Trustees of Newton College, and Sister Jean Ford, Provincial of the Washington Province of the Society of the Sacred Heart and also a Newton College board member, accepted membership on the Boston College Board of Trustees.[8]

The Implementation Task Force

In announcing the consolidation to its several publics, the University listed pertinent facts about Newton College. The campus consisted of some 40 acres containing 15 major buildings. There was residence hall capacity for 735 students. There were 55 classrooms and seminar rooms, with an additional 32 locations equipped for laboratory or specialized use. Particular features noted were a fully air-conditioned library with a 200,000-volume capacity and a seating capacity of 531; a fully air-conditioned chapel seating 800, with a basement function room seating 750; an air-conditioned faculty wing and student center; and a new air-conditioned science building with laboratories, rooftop greenhouse, and a 330-seat auditorium.

Father Monan set up a task force to recommend possible uses of the Newton facilities as well as new uses for Chestnut Hill facilities freed by movement across town. Director of Admissions John Maguire was named chairman of this important body.[9] In his charge to the task force in his letter of invitation, Father Monan prescribed that recommended uses of the Newton Campus be such as to provide a sense of full citizenship in the University on the part of students and faculty in the two locations; to guarantee utilization of the distinctive characteristics of Newton facilities to their maximum advantage; and to fulfill already identified needs and improve the status of existing University programs.[10] Father Monan asked that recommendations be submitted to him by January 15, 1975.

The task force proved to be an extraordinarily active body. Thirty plenary sessions were held in addition to the meetings of important subcommittees that were set up. The experience of other universities with several campuses was studied, and four such centers were visited in New

Jersey, West Virginia, and Ohio. Community opinions were sought in meetings with Newton College alumnae, the Newton Neighborhood Association, the Chestnut Hill Association, Boston College women administrators, the University Academic Planning Council, the Jesuit Community, the Newton Planning Department, the Newton Board of Aldermen, and the mayor of Newton.

One of the task force's early decisions was the unanimous rejection of a proposal to maintain Newton as an all-women's college. It was felt that the problems Newton College had been experiencing in attracting students might persist under Boston College's aegis, and that such a solution would leave unaddressed the pressing problems of women at the Chestnut Hill campus.

One of the aims of the task force was to identify programs that might preserve the Newton College tradition. One of these was studio art, and Professor Robert Carovillano headed a subcommittee on this program. After studying the matter with the advice of the chairman of the Fine Arts Department at Amherst College, Professor Carovillano's committee recommended that the Boston College Fine Arts Department expand to embrace the studio art program that had been a strong feature of the Newton College curriculum—a proposal embraced by the task force. A second Newton emphasis was continuing education for women; it was decided that this program should be adopted by Boston College. The current Boston College program for women in politics and government, located at Newton and headed by Betty Taymor, is a result of that commitment.

Decision: What to Newton?

The School of Education, the School of Management, and the School of Nursing were all considered for location at Newton. These suggestions were vetoed principally because of the interdependence of these undergraduate professional schools with Arts and Sciences. The School of Management studied the proposed move in a position paper, but a poll of faculty and students showed that well over 80 percent of the SOM community opposed relocation. But the Law School, which had been raising funds for an addition to More Hall, expressed interest in the ample facilities of the Newton site.

After considering a number of alternative options, the task force recommended four possible uses for the Newton campus:

1. Location at Newton of both the Boston College Law School and, as a coordinate emphasis, a series of distinctive undergraduate programs under a common umbrella such as a center for innovative instruction. Student population at Newton would be 1200 to 1500, including some 735 dormitory residents.

In 1979 the Office of Student Affairs on College Road was named Donaldson House in honor of George Donaldson ('29), the founder and director of the Office of Career Planning and Placement. Kevin Duffy, vice president for student affairs, joined Father Monan in honoring Donaldson and his wife, Genevieve.

2. A combination of distinctive undergraduate programs at Newton, with the Graduate School of Social Work as a smaller co-tenant. About 1100 to 1300 students would study on the campus under this plan.

3. Use of the Newton facilities entirely for undergraduate residence and instruction. Estimated enrollment would be 1000 to 1200.

4. Undergraduate utilization of the Newton campus as a "busing satellite," with dormitory residents transported to the Chestnut Hill campus for virtually all classes, and one or more professional schools such as the Graduate School of Social Work and the Law School located at Newton.

Of these four plans, the task force strongly favored the first, believing the others to be feasible but progressively less desirable.[11] In the event that the task force's first option was adopted by the University, including the move of the Law School from More Hall, the task force recommended that More Hall become a comprehensive arts center for both art history and studio art, as well as an academic student union—a concept that may have been borrowed from the UAPC, whose deliberations overlapped those of the task force.

Father Monan discussed the Newton task force recommendations with the trustees. At a press conference in Barat House on March 3, 1975, he announced that the Newton task force's first option, the Law School and distinctive undergraduate programs, would be lodged at Newton. The hope was to have the Law School in operation at Newton by September and the undergraduate program or programs by the following January.[12] The president's next move was to set up a committee to plan distinguished undergraduate programs. Professor Paul Doherty of the English Department chaired the committee, which had a representative from each Arts and Sciences department plus four students. The brunt of the work in shaping the committee's proposals was done by a subcommittee also headed by Paul Doherty, joined by Professors Michael Connolly, John Donovan, Robert O'Malley, and Paul Thie, plus a student, Marc Thibadeau.[13]

Interdisciplinary Programs

The committee suggested 10 interdisciplinary core programs, most of which would involve two or three departments. It was not the committee's role to implement the proposals; that was up to interested faculty members in the various departments. (It must be noted that none of the suggested new programs came into being.) The committee included in its recommendations two interdisciplinary programs that already existed, Pulse and Perspectives, which were originally sponsored by Father Joseph Flanagan, chairman of the Philosophy Department.

It is interesting that although the University Academic Planning Council had extended an invitation to departments to create alternatives to the core curriculum, none was forthcoming. Similarly no new curricular experiment followed the report of the Newton Undergraduate Programs Committee. This lack of action may have been due to departmental inertia or perhaps to faculty skepticism about the viability or value of interdisciplinary courses, an attitude the Doherty committee noted in its report: "We are cognizant of the fact that, to some, interdisciplinary courses are, almost by definition, courses which lack the rigor and accountability of normal departmental offerings; that in seeking accommodation, two disciplines will find a least-common denominator of agreement."[14] At any rate Perspectives, which was indeed scheduled on the Newton campus starting in 1975–1976, has undoubtedly been the most popular and longest-lived interdisciplinary program at Boston College. It started in 1973 under the sponsorship of the Philosophy and Theology departments. The original course, which is still being offered, was Perspectives on Western Culture, planned for incoming freshmen and granting six credits of the philosophy-theology core requirements. In 1975–1976 there were 10 sections of Perspectives on Western Culture, with 25 students in each section.[15]

Father Flanagan and his associates who started Perspectives were rewarded by substantial and continuing grants from the National Endowment for the Humanities, which supported summer developmental planning and enabled Perspectives faculty to bring outstanding scholars from other campuses to share in the planning process. Perspectives on Western Culture was developed into a two-year sequence for a possible 12 credits.

Marianne Martin came to Boston College in 1977 to chair the expanded Fine Arts Department on the Newton campus. She was later director of the new gallery in Devlin Hall until her sudden death in 1989.

Year-long Perspectives sequences have also been fashioned for the fields of humanities, science, and social science.

So the Law School moved to Newton along with Perspectives. But in the end it was the newly expanded Fine Arts Department that, with Music, became the principal undergraduate presence on the Newton campus. The former Barry Science Pavilion became the Barry Fine Arts Pavilion, with laboratories transformed into studios and a gallery. Putnam, the former home of studio arts at Newton College, became a conference center until the Alumni Association took it over in 1986. Thus the Newton task force's recommendation to locate Fine Arts in More Hall was not followed. At the time it was appropriate to unify studio art and art history at Newton, since studio art had been a strong feature of the Newton College experience. Under the chairmanship of Marianne Martin, a distinguished art historian, the newly structured department attracted outstanding faculty and enthusiastic students. Exhibits of faculty and student work as well as exhibits of contemporary artists have given the department well-earned recognition. Ten years later the gallery has been given a more central location in Devlin Hall, and plans are afoot for a fine arts building to be constructed near Robsham Theater.

Monan the Builder

Like his immediate predecessors, Father Monan found that—whatever his inclinations—he was to be a builder. When his term began, the Hillside dormitories were already under construction. Even after the notice of resignation by Father Joyce and long before a successor was named, on February 11, 1972, the Board of Directors approved the construction of a series of student residences behind St. Mary's Hall. It had been hoped that over 800 students could be accommodated in the new buildings, but certain compromises had to be made with the City of Newton after some protests about the proposed size of the structures. Approval was granted by the Board of Aldermen in April for four buildings.[16] Construction was begun in the spring by the Fahey (later the Flatley) Construction Co. of Braintree. The architectural firm was Design Alliance.

When Father Monan arrived on campus he found under construction two five-story and two six-story buildings to contain 110 3-bedroom apartments and 22 2-bedroom apartments, with all bedrooms scheduled to accommodate two students. The 1972–1973 academic year began with about 200 students lodged in the Howard Johnson's Motel in Newton Corner. It was expected that one building of the new residence complex would be completed in the fall so that the students could be moved from the motel, but construction went more slowly than anticipated. Then, in the winter of 1973, the Newton town fathers were reluctant to approve occupancy of one unit when the others were in what was called a "hard hat" status. Finally on March 28 and 29, 187 students were moved into Building A of the Hillside dormitories.[17] The remaining buildings were finished later and occupied in September of that year. The Hillside residences were built and furnished at a cost of $4,765,854, financed through the Massachusetts Health and Educational Facilities Authority (HEFA).[18]

Even while the Hillside dormitories were under construction, plans went forward for what were originally called the Reservoir dormitories, later named Edmond's Hall in honor of long-time admissions administrator, Father Edmond Walsh. In September 1974, 874 students were housed in dormitories on South Street, in apartments in the Cleveland Circle area,

Walsh and Edmond's halls, student residences.

and in the Chestnut Hill Motel; the aim of the added campus facilities was to give these students Boston College housing.[19] Brian Massey of Design Alliance was architect and the Peabody Construction Co. of Braintree the general contractor for the Reservoir dormitories.

Ground was broken on February 28, 1974. The nine-story building was to contain 208 apartments to house 808 students. The cost of the building was $6,326,500 and of the equipment, $400,000. A HUD interest subsidy grant assisted in the financing of Edmond's Hall.[20] The new dormitory was occupied in the fall of 1975 and dedicated on September 19.[21]

While new buildings were being planned and constructed, old buildings needed repair and renovation. The most ambitious and costly renovation involved the flagship structure of the campus, Gasson Hall. The external renovation of Gasson began in the spring of 1974. Appropriately the architects, Kennedy, Kennedy, Keefe and Carney, were the direct successors to the original architects of Gasson Hall, Maginnis and Walsh, and the contractor, Walsh Bros., had been the builders of St. Mary's Hall and Devlin. Gasson's masonry was pointed, eroded stones were replaced, and the roof was repaired. The tower pinnacles and the east and west porches were restored. Leaded Gothic windows were repaired and new thermal-pane wooden sash windows installed.

The interior renovation of Gasson was more dramatic. Graduates of classes before the mid-1970s will recall the four interior staircases off the rotunda. Fire regulations required the elimination of these staircases and the installation of stairways close to the building's exits. Two elevators took the place of former stairways. Central heating and air conditioning replaced the sputtering and banging radiators that had been a cold weather

In November 1977 renovated Gasson Hall was rededicated. The elegant assembly hall, which had served as the treasurer's office for many years, was returned to its original beauty and function. Admiring a replica of the building is Boston College's oldest alumnus, Monsignor Charles Finn ('99). On Monsignor Finn's right is Father Paul FitzGerald, university archivist, and on his left, Father Francis McManus, long dean of men in SOM, secretary of the university, and alumni chaplain.

The renovated Fulton room in Gasson Hall.

feature of Gasson. Renovated classrooms in the upper floors made Gasson one of the largest teaching centers of the campus. Painstaking restoration of the original Irish Room, the assembly hall, the honors program library, and the Fulton room on the third floor recaptured the pristine elegance of those facilities.[22] Gasson Hall was rededicated on November 6, 1977. The dean, Father O'Malley, read Father Gasson's words at the original dedication of the building.[23] Roy Heffernan of the class of 1916 spoke for the alumni. The cost of the extensive renovations of Gasson Hall was nearly $3.5 million, financed through Massachusetts HEFA bonds.[24]

The popular modular apartments assembled in 1970 needed major attention by 1974. The roofs were not sufficiently sloped for effective drainage, so more sharply sloped roofs were added and new red cedar shingles applied to the sides of each unit at a cost of $300,000. These renovations were accomplished in the spring and summer of 1974.[25]

In February 1974 the Board of Trustees authorized an addition to the Recreation Complex. The $1,366,000 expansion was funded by raising the student fee from $25 to $32. Among the new facilities in the RecPlex were 4 tennis courts, 3 handball courts, 2 squash courts, and a large wooden floor for judo and dancing. The extension provided flexibility in the rapidly developing sports activities for women.[26] The dedication of the completed complex was held on February 28, 1976.

In 1976 the Cutler home at 300 Hammond Street was acquired by the

University. The University Academic Planning Committee had suggested several years earlier the desirability of a faculty center. Father Monan designated the new property for that purpose, and the building was named Connolly House in honor of two former University librarians, Fathers Terence Connolly and Brendan Connolly. A subcommittee of the University Council on Teaching composed of Michael Connolly, Mary Griffin, Richard Huber, Vera Lee, and Richard Stevens, along with Father Thomas Fitzpatrick (who became coordinator of scheduling) and Katharine Hastings (who represented the dean of faculty's office), with much assistance from Frank Campanella, guided the renovation and decoration of the elegant facility that opened in the spring of 1976.[27]

Before the addition of the Newton campus, plans were afoot for an extension to More Hall to accommodate growth of the Law School, and a fund drive had been launched for this project. When the decision was made to move the Law School to the Newton campus, over a million dollars was needed to renovate Stuart House for Law School purposes. Large pitched classrooms, an elaborate moot courtroom, lounges, and other facilities gave the Law School a fresh and commodious home.

At the same time, the former science facilities of Newton College were converted into studios and a gallery was created to transform Barry Science Pavilion into the Barry Fine Arts Pavilion. Parking lots and new roads were added to the Newton campus. By September 1976 over $1,370,000 had been expended in converting Newton College to Boston College uses.[28]

The elegant apartments of Edmond's Hall were occupied in September 1975. It had been hoped that, with the addition of these living accommodations for over 800 students, the University would be able to divest itself

Connolly House, the faculty house on Hammond Street, was named for two librarians, Fathers Terence and Brendan Connolly.

of properties on South Street. But demand for housing increased each year, so that in the spring of 1978 the trustees authorized another high-rise residence hall to be built between Edmond's and St. Ignatius Church.

The new structure was planned mostly for sophomore students. It provided a living style transitional between that of the upper campus and Newton campus dormitories and the complete apartment living of Hillside, Edmond's, and the modulars. The eight-person suites contained all the amenities of Edmond's, with the exception of cooking facilities. Walsh Hall provided dining accommodations for 650, as well as laundries, lounges, and common areas. The building consisted of three wings of eight, six, and four stories as it moved northward from the height of Edmond's towers to the lower levels of More Hall and St. Ignatius Church. Design Alliance was architect for Walsh Hall and Perini, the contractor. The cost of the building was $9,166,000, with an added $1,744,000 for equipment.[29] With the completion of Walsh, Boston College was finally able to divest itself of eight three-story brick buildings on South Street, which since 1969 had housed 200 students.[30]

The new building was being completed when Father Michael P. Walsh died on April 23, 1982. The trustees decided to name the building for him, and a dedicatory ceremony was held with his brothers, sisters, and friends present on October 7, 1982.

While residential facilities were being pushed forward, another badly needed facility was undertaken: a parking garage. It was decided to locate it to the east of McHugh Forum and the stadium in a position where it could be expanded alongside the stadium. Sasaki Associates drew the plans and Richard White and Sons did the construction. The garage provided spaces for 429 cars. Its cost was $2,422,000, financed through Massachusetts HEFA bonds.[31]

The New Library

In the 1970s the University's greatest building challenge since the move to Chestnut Hill was the need for a new library. Beautiful Bapst Library was built for an undergraduate student body of approximately a thousand students. Even with the addition of satellite libraries in the professional schools, the library facilities of the University were inadequate. For twenty years faculty planning committees, students, accrediting agencies, and the administration had acknowledged and bemoaned the library crisis. Early in his administration Father Monan made a new library a building and fundraising priority. With the appointment of Thomas O'Connell as University librarian in 1975, Boston College had a professional who had recently directed major library construction at York University in Canada. O'Connell knew that it fell to him to carry out and enlarge upon the plans of his predecessor, Father Brendan Connolly.

A library building program committee and a library design committee were established. By spring 1978 The Architects Collaborative, with Royston T. Daley as principal architect, had been commissioned to design the library. The site chosen for the new building was the one named by Father Brendan Connolly some years earlier. But its proximity to the original Gothic structure posed a problem: how to achieve the mass needed for the library without clashing with Gasson Hall, the architectural centerpiece of the campus. From beginning to end, the architects' sensitivity to the primacy of the original Maginnis and Walsh buildings was edifying. The hillside site had advantages. It permitted a low-profile facade of three stories facing Gasson, Devlin, and St. Mary's, with five stories on the downhill side. The problem of strong western sun on the Gasson side was handled by minimizing windows and introducing a deep loggia two stories high. The windowless wall above the loggia provides a serene background for the ornate Gothic buildings and at the same time sets a frame for the spacious plaza that replaced the old parking lot.

Groundbreaking in that parking lot took place on October 18, 1981, with Smith College president Jill Conway as principal speaker. She said of the new library, "This will be a great and much needed addition to the scholarly resources of this great city of libraries . . . a unique contribution, one which . . . only this institution can make." Father Monan noted the significance of the occasion in his remarks:

> After fifty years of Boston College's existence in the South End, in 1909 Father Gasson stood only a few feet from where we are assembled and placed a spade in the earth to convert it from fertile farm land into this magnificent University campus. Seventy-two years later, I have the privilege of welcoming each of you as we reenact Father Gasson's beginning—and, indeed, begin anew.[32]

Construction so close to St. Mary's Hall gave the Jesuits ringside seats during the 30 months of mechanical wizardry. Considerable blasting was needed to prepare the site, and it was not until mid-March 1982 that *The Heights* could report that this activity was 90 percent completed.[33] As the building progressed during the cold weather, huge yellow tarpaulins covered the ends of the operation, allowing work to continue. Observers became so used to this color configuration that the ultimate removal of the tarpaulins made the finished wall of the building seem almost bland. The general community had a say in the choice of the stone cladding for the library. Five stone mockups of different coloring and texture were set up outside Devlin Hall and people were asked to express a preference. A warm Rockville granite from Minnesota was chosen. Cut in large pieces, it at times spans floor to floor. The exception to the granite cladding is the loggia, which presents plain concrete. The architect sought a cloistral effect in the loggia that would echo the ecclesiastical roots of the University.[34] Construction manager of the library building was Richard White Sons of

Auburndale, Edmond White ('51), president. Project manager was Kevin Hines ('70).

When completed, the $28 million structure, with a capacity of a million books, embraced the holdings of the Bapst, Management, Science, and Nursing libraries. The long-familiar card catalogues from Bapst are in the new library—but in storage. They were replaced by the Geac Library Computer System, which was available to library patrons through video display terminals throughout the library. (In 1989 the Geac system had already been outgrown and was replaced by a more sophisticated system dubbed Quest, which runs on the University's IBM mainframe.) The system also facilitates management of the circulation and acquistions functions of the library. Facilities not hitherto available in the University's libraries are a media services department, a library photocopy center, and a vision resources room to aid blind or limited-vision patrons. The south end of the building houses the University Computer Center, a student terminal area with 150 terminals, 9 classrooms, faculty research space, and the University Telecommunications Center.

Complementing the generous services of the library is its attractive interior, with mauve wall-to-wall carpeting, natural oak furniture and woodwork, royal-blue shelving, cozy alcoves, and spectacular views of the Boston skyline.

Long before the building's completion, the trustees had decided that it should bear the name of an illustrious alumnus, Thomas P. O'Neill, Jr. ('36), Speaker of the United States House of Representatives. October 14, 1984, was chosen as the day for dedicating the library and honoring the man whose name it bears. Despite a chilling wind, the event was, both intellectually and artistically, one of the most sparkling in the University's history. Guests were seated in the plaza facing the library. The faculty marched from Gasson in academic gowns, and the platform participants approached a temporary stage from the new building. The invocation was given by a classmate of Speaker O'Neill's, Lawrence Riley, auxiliary bishop of Boston. Chairman of the trustees, Judge David Nelson, welcomed the gathering and, speaking for the faculty, Professor P. Albert Duhamel gave a bookman's delighted response to the occasion. The principal address was given by Ernest L. Boyer, president of the Carnegie Foundation for the Advancement of Teaching.

There followed an interlude of music and dance. Alexander Peloquin led the University Chorale in a rendition of "God My Glory," which he had composed for the occasion. The text of "God My Glory" is a poetic interpretation of Psalm 19 by Father Francis Sullivan of the Theology Department, written for the ceremony as a piece to be performed outdoors and choreographed. Jesuit artist-in-residence Father Robert VerEecke was choreographer and led the Boston College dance group in a dramatic interpretation.

In his dedicatory remarks Father Monan stressed the practical outcomes

Thomas F. O'Connell ('50), university librarian from 1976 to 1986, stands before the O'Neill Library, which he planned and saw to completion.

expected from Jesuit education as exemplified in the enlightened public service of Speaker O'Neill. He said, "Throughout the history of Western culture, human knowledge and understanding have been recognized as good within their own right, worth pursuing for their own sake. But in the entire history of Jesuit education since the founding of our first lay college at Messina in 1548, learning has never been regarded as a good only for itself—but as the critical ingredient of leadership for effective service to others."[35]

In his response Speaker O'Neill said, "The soul of a Catholic University is its chapel. Its heart is its library. . . . I have declined many offers to name buildings after me. Quite honestly, I do not believe in naming them after public officials who are still in office. But this time I made an exception because this college has meant so much to me, to my family, and to my community."

Master of ceremonies for the occasion was University Librarian Thomas O'Connell, who reflected the long-delayed satisfaction of many when he observed, "This library is not the work of any single person or group. Some of its roots, intellectual and physical, are buried in antiquity, and some of its attributes contain computer technology that is incorporated in no other library on this continent. Truly the many who have been involved in this building must have received in full measure the grace to see, as William Butler Yeats has said, 'In all poor foolish things that live a day, Eternal Beauty wandering on her way.' "

Renovation of Bapst

Even while O'Neill was under construction, the exterior of Bapst Library underwent thorough rehabilitation similar to that given to Gasson a few years earlier. When that was completed, and just after the dedication of O'Neill, an elaborate interior renovation of Bapst was begun. The Architects Collaborative, with Royston Daley as co-principal, were responsible for design, and the construction management team of Richard White Sons, with Kevin Hines as project manager, oversaw construction.

The original floor in the basement of Bapst was removed and the ground further excavated to provide ceiling room in the floors above for utility purposes. A heavier floor slab was installed suitable for the expected increased weight of the compact shelving needed to double the capacity of the Burns stacks. For months jackhammers cut holes through the granite beneath all the windows of Gargan Hall and the floor below (now Kresge Hall) to provide vents for the heating and airing of Bapst.

The most magical transformation in Bapst was what was done to the area that for many years had been an auditorium and, in later years, the upper stacks. The border paintings on the original ceiling, barely discernible in the years when stacks obscured them, were meticulously redone. Quiet carrels and an ingenious mezzanine provide one of the choicest study spaces on campus.

The most dramatic renovations of Maginnis and Walsh's masterpiece were in the north end facing Commonwealth Avenue, where state-of-the-art and exquisitely beautiful quarters have been provided for the Burns Library, dedicated to the memory of Judge John J. Burns ('21). Burns Library houses the University's rare books and special collections, as well as the University archives. The magnificent Ford Tower, dark and mostly unused for better than half a century, has been brought into central use; its stone walls were cleaned and brightened, with one wall becoming backdrop for an imposing tapestry. Burns is, of course, air-conditioned and climate-controlled and is equipped with a Halon fire-suppressant system. To accommodate air-conditioning, the stained glass windows on the top level had to be sealed with thermal-panes; these the architects placed on the inside and, in one of their most impressive accomplishments, managed to make the thermal-pane glass practically unnoticeable.

The architects were faced with one external challenge: providing the elevator that had to be an appendage to the building. Many shuddered at the prospect of an ugly protuberance marring Bapst's fine exterior lines. Fortunately Maginnis and Walsh had provided a tiny wing, making the north end of the building slightly wider than the body of the library. Behind that wing, tucked into the northwest corner along College Road, a tower was erected for the elevator and for air-conditioning machinery for Burns Library. Thought was given to using pudding stone for the tower to match that in the original building, but such stone is no longer available. So it was decided to use limestone that matches the trim of Bapst. The elevator tower is a masterpiece, which, only a few months after its completion, seemed to have always been part of the building.

When built in the 1920s, Bapst Library cost $800,000; the renovation cost $6.2 million. The Kresge Foundation, which in 1979 had contributed $250,000 toward Robsham Theater, donated half a million dollars for the Bapst renovation.[36]

Bapst Library was rededicated and Burns Library dedicated in ceremonies in Gargan Hall on April 22, 1986, with members of the Burns family in attendance. The invited speaker for the occasion was Yale historian Jonathan Spence, who related the treasures of the Burns Library to one of his scholarly interests, the cultural legacy left by the sixteenth- and seventeenth-century Jesuit missionaries to China. University Librarian Thomas O'Connell was awarded the Joseph Coolidge Shaw medal, which had been struck to honor the completion of O'Neill Library. Thus O'Connell wound down his very productive 10 years of service as shaper of the University's libraries. (Some months earlier he had announced his retirement.) He was succeeded in September by Mary J. Cronin, who had been director of university libraries at Loyola University in Chicago. With a doctorate in German literature as well as a degree in library science and having experience with the Boston Public Library and the Marquette University libraries as well as that at Loyola, Dr. Cronin brought a rich background to the task of managing the enhanced facilities of the University's libraries.

*   *   *

Mary J. Cronin, university librarian.

This account of the construction that has taken place in the first decade and a half of Father Monan's presidency has brought us well into the 1980s. It is necessary in the next chapter to return to other important developments of the 1970s.

ENDNOTES

1. The administrators were Father Monan, Father Donovan, Frank Campanella, and Donald White. The faculty members were James L. Bowditch, SOM; Laurel A. Eisenhauer, Nursing; Joseph F. Flanagan, S.J., Philosophy; Ernest L. Fortin, A.A., Theology; Jocelyn N. Hillgarth, History; James L. Houghteling, Law; John L. Mahoney, English; Michael Malec, Sociology; Francis M. McLaughlin, Economics; Edward J. Power, Education; Irving J. Russell, Chemistry; and Carolyn Thomas, Social Work. The students were Joseph J. David, A&S '75; Cynthia L. Feldman, SOM '75; Stephen E. Fix, A&S '74; Thomas F. Flynn, A&S '74; John F. McDonough, A&S '75; Howard A. McLendon, SOM '75; Josephine L. Ursini, SOM '74; and Robert W. McNutt, Robert J. Santoro, and Marilyn J. Terry of Graduate A&S.

2. The faculty members were Geraldine Conner, Social Work; Marjorie Gordon, Nursing; Francis Kelly, Education; Cynthia Lichtenstein, Law; Thomas Owens, Philosophy; Harold Petersen, Economics; Donald Plocke, S.J., Biology; and David Twomey, Management. The students were Linda Bucci and Mary Mac-Vean, '76, and Carl Ostermann, a graduate student. The administrators were Frank Campanella, Executive Vice President; Father Charles Donovan, Dean of Faculties (who served as chairman); Kevin Duffy, Director of Housing; and John Maguire, Dean of Admissions, Records, and Financial Aid.

3. See Sister Eleanor Kenny, ed., "Early Days at Newton College." Newton College archives, BCA.

4. Sister Eleanor Kenny was president from 1946 to 1956; Sister Gabrielle Husson was president from 1956 to 1969.

5. *Newton Newsnotes* (August–September 1974), p. 8. BCA.

6. *Ibid.*

7. The chairman of the Boston College Board of Trustees at the time was Cornelius W. Owens, '36, LL.B. '73, Executive Vice President of AT&T. The Newton College Board Chairman was T. Vincent Learson, retired chairman of the board of IBM.

8. "Fact Sheet on the Consolidation of Newton College into Boston College," issued by Father Monan's office on March 10, 1974. BCA.

9. In addition to John Maguire the task force included three administrators: Father Robert Braunreuther of the Housing Office; Kevin Duffy, Director of Housing; and Father Thomas O'Malley, Dean of A&S; plus nine Boston College faculty members and two members of the Newton College faculty. The Boston College faculty members were Robert Carovillano, Evan Collins, P. Albert Duhamel, Anne Ferry, Mary Griffin, John Lewis, Harold Petersen, Helen Manock Saxe, and Richard Stevens. The Newton College faculty representatives were Frances Fergusson and Marie Mullin McHugh. Student members of the task force were, from Boston College, John Brennan, Matthew Fissinger, James Moran, and Joan Quinlan; from Newton College, Kathy Joyce and Jacqueline Regan.

10. Father Monan to members of the University Task Force on Newton College, March 27, 1974. BCA.

11. Newton Task Force Final Report. BCA.

12. *The Heights* (March 10, 1975).

13. Paul Doherty to Father Charles Donovan, August 20, 1986. BCA.
14. Report of the Newton Committee, p. 5. BCA.
15. *Ibid.*, p. 3.
16. *The Heights* (April 25, 1972).
17. *The Heights* (April 3, 1973).
18. BCA.
19. Director of Housing Kevin Duffy, *The Heights* (September 23, 1974).
20. BCA.
21. *Focus* (October 1975).
22. *Ibid.* (September 1974); *Bridge* (Winter 1978).
23. See p. 129.
24. BCA.
25. *The Heights* (March 25, 1974; September 16, 1974).
26. *The Heights* (September 22, 1975).
27. *Focus* (May 1976).
28. BCA.
29. BCA.
30. *Biweekly* (January 29, 1981).
31. BCA.
32. "A Celebration of Heritage and Promise."
33. *The Heights* (March 18, 1982).
34. "A Celebration of Heritage and Promise."
35. *Ibid.*
36. *Biweekly* (September 26, 1985).

CHAPTER 36

A Mission Redefined

Classes, library research, office consultations, academic meetings, student activities, staff assignments, and administrative decisions make up the daily routine of a campus community. To the uninitiated, these undertakings may seem isolated and unrelated, and it may be difficult to connect one to another. In reality, however, the people involved combine their efforts to implement what is generally called the "mission" of the university—that is, fulfilling the fundamental reason for the founding of the institution and its continued existence. This mission, in turn, is accomplished through stated goals, some of which are immediate and others long-term.

Boston College, in common with all universities, must search for truth. But it also embraces a particular value system rooted in the Judeo-Christian tradition which is basic to the Jesuit method of education. Since institutions of learning are located in a particular time and place, from time to time the mission has to be tested, measured, reappraised, and reaffirmed. Coming as it did after the rebellious sixties, Father Monan's administration presented a good opportunity for reappraisal.

At the end of Father Monan's fifth year as president, the University published *A Report: Boston College 1972–1977*. With an introductory message from the president, the report was an excellent summary of plans, projects, and achievements, and it clearly indicated the direction in which the University was moving. During those five years, the president, as already

447

mentioned, commissioned several University-wide planning efforts which would bear fruit in the late 1970s and early 1980s. The report in fact not only reviewed the past but set the tone for the future. But "mission" was at the heart of the enterprise; the president was clear on that point:

> During the years covered by this report, our nation . . . faced history's recurring lesson that intellectual dexterity and public power by themselves are shallow grounds in which to fix personal or national pride. The moral dilemma of Vietnam, the unraveling of Watergate, . . . the reversal not merely of legal protection but of society's reverence for the human unborn, posed for all colleges a fundamental question of mission. If colleges had confined their educational interests in the past to the values of truth and aesthetics, did not the public good require that they now assume responsibility to assist students with other values as well?
>
> This is not a new question for Boston College. Indeed it voiced a presupposition about the integrality of the person to be educated, to which the tradition of Jesuit education had addressed itself since its beginnings. The currency of the question throughout American society, however, provided one of the first signs in a quarter of a century that the college whose mission embraces values of specific religious and ethical tradition will be newly prized for its distinctive contribution to the society's larger welfare.[1]

A Vision of Purpose

In February 1975 Boston College issued a newly defined statement of purpose that affirmed once again its humanistic and professional goals and clearly carried forward the religious aspirations that were enunciated at its founding in 1863. The University Academic Planning Council, described

Kevin P. Duffy became vice president for student affairs in 1977.

and analyzed in the preceding chapter, emphasized this aspect of the total program. Boston College, the council noted, "subscribes to a fundamentally religious vision, not narrow or restrictive, but generous and open."[2] The University reaffirmed a belief in God as Creator and Redeemer "whose life and teachings proclaimed a higher goal of thought and action."[3] Moreover, as part of a contemporary institution of learning with this ideal, administrators, faculty, staff, and students were encouraged to share in this common vision and in this common purpose.

The fulfillment of this religious dimension obviously involved the Jesuits in a special way, since they were particularly concerned with the moral and religious dimension of the whole enterprise. The mission of Boston College is closely tied to the Jesuit Community and influenced by the Society's history and ideals. In an address to the presidents of Jesuit universities throughout the world, the General of the Society of Jesus had this to say:

> On this point, the Jesuit community at the university ought to exercise—not its power, but its authority: that is to say, it should be the "author" of the task to be accomplished by all the members of the educational community. Its role is that of guaranteeing, with and for all of the members of the educational community, the transmission of Gospel values and the discovery of an evangelical life orientation, which is the distinctive mark of the Catholic university.[4]

The so-called Jesuit Statement, referred to in Chapter 35, elaborates at length on this characteristic of Boston College. Noting that "the society we live in is deeply influenced by values which we do not share as Jesuits, . . . the purely academic ideals of the secular university tradition in America are not reliable enough guides for our purposes."[5] If Boston College reflected that tradition exclusively, "then we need a very searching examination of academic conscience."[6] But the Jesuits who designed this statement were confident that faculty and students chose Boston College because of the values they expect to find here, educationally, morally, and religiously.[7] The Jesuits, many of them trained to the doctoral level at secular universities, did not in any way intend thereby to dismiss or dilute the academic thrust of the institution. As Father General Kolvenbach said to the presidents, "Ignatius was well aware of the fact that a school is a school; a university is a university. It has its own finality; it is not simply an opportunity for evangelization or the defense of the faith."[8]

Boston College alumni and alumnae are living proof of the principles that permeate a Jesuit education. They are the extension of the University in the world of politics, medicine, law, teaching, business, the home, or other occupations. As Father Monan has often said, "the true value of a Boston College education is to be found in the lives of the alumni and in the quality of the decisions they make."[9] In this instance, numbers can make a difference, especially when Boston College graduates are combined with those of other Jesuit colleges and universities in the United States.

June Gary Hopps became dean of the Graduate School of Social Work in 1977.

Many Jesuit graduates in the military, government agencies, and other associations have expressed the existence of a fraternal bond which came from their common educational experience.

Financial Support of Alma Mater

In 1964 there were roughly 34,000 alumni. By 1977 there were 67,000, and in 1990 the number stood at about 100,000. In addition to the credit they bring to their alma mater by their personal lives, alumni have become more and more active in various aspects of the University's life. Nowhere has this been more apparent than in their increased financial support, which testifies to their faith in its future. In 1976 the Alumni Association received the United States Steel Foundation Award from the Council for the Advancement and Support of Education, in recognition of the continued success of the annual giving program. Alumni also gave of their time in soliciting other alumni and sympathetic donors who did not matriculate at Boston College. In particular, hundreds of alumni volunteered their time manning telephones in the Annual Fund Telethon, which in 1976–1977 raised nearly $450,000. This effort represented 3500 hours spent by 600 alumni, faculty, and students calling "For Boston."

Beginning in 1973, the second year of Father Monan's administration, there was a noticeable increase in philanthropic support from corporations, foundations, and friendly admirers which, as far as the administration is concerned, demonstrated renewed trust in the mission and management of the University. With this encouragement, the president began to feel that the time was right to consider a capital funds drive. In April 1976 the New Heights Advancement Campaign was launched with a dinner at the Copley Plaza Hotel. Its objective was to raise $21 million over five years. The national chairman, James P. O'Neill ('42), senior vice president at Xerox, put the campaign in perspective: "Our goal is to provide present and future Boston College students with the best educational, spiritual, and social dimensions of a college experience. . . . For, unless we respond with enthusiasm and generosity, how shall Boston College continue to challenge students to do *their* best?"[10]

A capital funds drive had become a necessity. In 1976 the operating budget was in excess of $53 million. The sources of the University's budget were tuition and fees (65 percent), sponsored programs and sponsored research (18 percent), auxiliary services such as dormitories, food service, and the bookstore (14 percent), and annual gifts and endowment income (3 percent). This picture clearly showed that tuition was bearing the brunt of operating costs and that the direct costs of education accounted for more than 75 percent of expenditures.[11]

The attractive campaign brochure contained a clear exposition of needs. The University's priorities were grouped under four headings: new construction (library, theater, recreation complex, and Law School), $10.5 million; endowment (professional chairs, faculty enrichment, and scholarships), $3 million; University renovation and modernization (Gasson Hall, Newton College, classrooms, studio art, and health facility), $2.25 million; and University support programs (scholarships, library acquisitions, and salaries), $5.3 million.

These priorities, it should be stressed, were needs, not luxuries, and, in turn, all were realized. By June 30, 1977, more than $8.2 million had been given or pledged to New Heights; by 1979 an additional $10 million had been donated or pledged. Finally, as reported by Chairman O'Neill, by 1981 the New Heights Advancement Campaign had raised more than $25 million.[12] The success of the campaign was further proof that Boston College was moving forward with substantial support from several sources. It was an encouraging sign.

Financial Objectives

When he accepted the presidency of Boston College, Father Monan staked out three objectives in the financial area: first, to eliminate the accumulated deficit; second, to create a system for keeping the operating budget in balance; and third, to reduce the high interest cost of long-term debt through refinancing. By the end of 1976 the president informed the trustees that all three objectives had been met. While initiative and direction may come from the top, Father Monan was quick to give credit to the Long-Range Fiscal Planning Committee, which operated under the overall direction of the executive vice president.[13] Their long-range plan was built on

At commencement in May 1980, the University further emphasized its commitment to the Universal Church. In conferring an honorary doctor of laws degree on Joseph Cardinal Malulu, archbishop of Kinshasa, Zaire, Boston College greeted the good shepherd of 6 million Catholics and the recognized leader of the Christian churches in Africa. At the conclusion of the exercises, Cardinal Medeiros, who presided, and Cardinal Malulu simultaneously blessed the students and their families.

two assumptions which involved the heart of the enterprise—namely, student-faculty ratio. The committee stated, "With minor exceptions, Boston College plans to maintain enrollments at current levels for the existing mix of academic programs."[14] This meant in practice that the undergraduate enrollment would remain at 8500, with necessary fluctuations in the Graduate School, the Law School, the MBA program, and the Graduate School of Social Work. Since the most significant expenditures were those for salaries and wages, there was an absolute commitment at Boston College not to increase numbers of personnel over the next five years.[15] With no enrollment growth and a freeze on faculty "slots," the current student-faculty ratios could be maintained without detriment to the academic programs. The freeze on positions also affected administrative

Mary D. Griffin, who had served for seven years as associate dean of the School of Education, became dean in 1979 and held that position until 1986.

officers, as well as secretarial, clerical, security, and custodial hiring. The hard-working committee concluded with this summary:

> This is a plan which results in balanced operating budgets under conditions where no growth is foreseen in the student body, in faculty or staff, or in physical facilities. It anticipates a time for consolidation after decades of continuous growth. During this period (1976–1981) we must continue to upgrade our academic programs, to develop our management personnel at all levels, and to improve our administrative practices.[16]

Endowed Academic Chairs

The New Heights Advancement Campaign gave a much-needed impetus to the funding of endowed academic chairs at Boston College. The first was the Thomas I. Gasson, S.J., Chair, named in honor of the 13th president of the University. Endowed by the Jesuit Community at Boston College, it is reserved to a Jesuit scholar. The first holder of the Gasson Chair, in 1980–1981, was William B. Neenan, S.J., a member of the Missouri Province of the Society and, at the time of his appointment, professor of economics at the University of Michigan. Upon completion of one year, Father Neenan was named dean of the College of Arts and Sciences when Father Thomas O'Malley moved to John Carroll University as president.

The second holder of the chair in 1981–1982 was Avery Dulles, S.J., called "one of the finest minds on the American university scene." The son of the late Secretary of State John Foster Dulles and a convert to Catholicism, he taught a graduate seminar on the uses of Scripture in theology and

Father William B. Neenan was the first Gasson professor in 1980–1981. The next year he became dean of the College of Arts and Sciences, and he succeeded Father Joseph Fahey as academic vice president and dean of faculties in 1987.

led a seminar on the phenomenon of knowledge. After a vacancy in 1982–1983, the next occupant of the chair in 1983–1985 was F. Paul Prucha, S.J., a historian from Marquette University considered the country's leading authority on the relationship of the American Indians to the United States Government. Author of 15 books, he won several national awards for his most recent publication, *The Great Father* (2 vols.). His public lectures in Gasson 100 were always well attended.

He was followed in 1985–1986 by Robert Barth, S.J., a literary scholar at the University of Missouri specializing in the English romantic poets. His further interest in the relationship between literature and religion is reflected in his publications, such as *Coleridge and Christian Doctrine* (Harvard, 1969). Happily, in 1988 Father Barth accepted the University's invitation to become dean of the College of Arts and Sciences. The next occupant of the Gasson Chair was Gerald Cavanaugh, S.J., in 1986–1987. Professor of Management at the University of Detroit, he researches, writes, and lectures on the ethics of business and the corporation. In September 1987 Joseph A. Fitzmyer, S.J., internationally renowned Scripture scholar and ecumenist, began a two-year occupancy of the Gasson Chair. During his tenure as Gasson professor, he guided through to publication *The New Jerome Biblical Commentary,* which has been hailed as a monumental achievement of American Catholic biblical scholarship. Father Fitzmyer was succeeded by a mathematician, Paul A. Schweitzer, S.J., a New England Jesuit who is a professor at the Pontifical Catholic University of Rio de Janeiro.

The second endowed chair was named in honor of the Speaker of the U.S. House of Representatives, a graduate of the class of 1936. Ranking high among the University's celebrations, a gala dinner was held in Washington on December 9, 1979, to honor Thomas "Tip" O'Neill, Jr., on his 67th birthday. More than 1000 friends of the Speaker and his alma mater, including President Jimmy Carter, attended the affair and contributed over $1.3 million to endow a chair in political science in his name. The O'Neill Chair was inaugurated on January 30–31, 1980, by a symposium, "The United States Congress," sponsored by the Political Science Department and attended by 500 political scientists, journalists, and members of the Boston College community.[17]

Samuel Beer, Eaton Professor of Government at Harvard, was the first occupant of the O'Neill Chair. His appointment was effective January 1982, upon his retirement from Harvard, and his public lectures in Gasson Hall were well attended and well received. Beer was succeeded by Congressman Richard Bolling, Democrat from Missouri. Retiring from the House in the fall of 1982, Bolling accepted an appointment for January 1983. He was a popular choice who, according to the *Congressional Record,* had "influenced the House more than any member of his generation." His fascinating book, *House Out of Order,* was required reading for House members.

Bolling was followed in the O'Neill Chair by Jody Powell, press secretary in the Carter administration. His lectures on the use and misuse of the press—especially in official Washington—were always lively, enlightening, and amusing. Next, for the academic year 1986–1987, was Herbert Kaufman, an acknowledged authority on bureaucracy, bureaucrats, and American federal agencies.[18] In 1987–1988 the chair was held by Francis E. Rourke of the Johns Hopkins University, an authority on the presidential bureaucracy. In the spring and fall of 1989 the O'Neill Chair occupant was a professor of law at Georgetown University, Eleanor Holmes Norton, who had chaired the Equal Employment Opportunity Commission in the Carter administration. She was succeeded for the 1990–1991 academic year by William Schneider, political analyst and journalist, and a former senior resident fellow at the Hoover Institute.

A third endowed chair is located in the Accounting Department of the Carroll School of Management. Joseph L. Sweeney (class of 1923), retired chairman of the board of Barclay, Brown and Jones, made a substantial gift to the University for this purpose. Following Mr. Sweeney's wish, expressed in his will, President Monan appointed Professor Stanley Dmohowski, School of Management, as first occupant of the Sweeney Chair. The

Samuel H. Beer was the first occupant of the Thomas P. O'Neill Chair in political science. With Professor Beer and Father Monan is Gary Brazier of the Political Science Department.

appointment, effective September 1, 1984, will continue as long as he is a member of the Boston College faculty. Another chair in the Carroll School of Management is the Peter F. Drucker Chair in Management Science, established in 1987 by John A. McNeice ('54), CEO of Colonial Management Association. The first Drucker Professor, Frank Morris, former president of the Boston Federal Reserve Bank, joined the Boston College faculty in September 1989.

A gift in 1989 from Chairman of the Board of Trustees Thomas A. Vanderslice ('53) established the first endowed professorship in the physical sciences, the Margaret A. and Thomas A. Vanderslice Chair in Chemistry. Professor T. Ross Kelly, a 20-year veteran of the Chemistry Department, was named to fill the Vanderslice Chair. Kelly, an organic chemist, was a former National Institutes of Health Career Development Award Winner.

Alumni in the medical profession funded the Michael P. Walsh, S.J., Chair in Bioethics. Named to honor the former Boston College president who had been so devoted to premedical students and alumni doctors, the chair is to be occupied for the first time in September 1990 by Father John J. Paris, S.J. ('59). Father Paris is professor of social ethics at the College of the Holy Cross and adjunct professor of medicine at the University of Massachusetts Medical School. He has served as visiting scholar and visiting professor at the University of Chicago, Yale Law School, Georgetown University, Princeton University, and the University of Minnesota.

Among other chairs endowed in the current development campaign are two in the School of Education. The Boisi Professorship in Education and Public Policy has been endowed by Geoffrey T. Boisi ('69) and Norine Isacco Boisi ('69). George F. Madaus of the School of Education faculty has been named the first Boisi Professor. John V. Brennan established the Anita L. Brennan Professorship in Education in honor of his wife.

Trustee Thomas J. Flatley established the John J. and Margaret O'Brien Flatley Endowment, part of which funds the Margaret O'Brien Flatley Chair in Catholic Theology for the scholarly preservation of the Roman Catholic tradition of Christianity.

Patrick G. Carney of the class of 1970 has established the Frederick J. Adelmann, S.J., Chair in honor of the long-time professor and former chairman of the Philosophy Department.

James F. Cleary ('50), co-chair of the Campaign for Boston College, and Barbara Coliton Cleary have endowed the James F. Cleary Chair in Finance. The John J. L. Collins, S.J., Chair in Finance honors a former member of the Finance Department. Corporate gifts by Merrill Lynch and Chase Manhattan and individual gifts from former students of Father Collins funded the chair.

The Boston Edison Foundation and other donors established the Thomas J. Galligan, Jr., Chair in Strategic Management. Mr. Galligan ('41, Hon. '75) is former chairman and chief executive officer of Boston Edison and has served as chairman of the Boston College Board of Trustees.

Staff meeting in the Francis Thompson room of Burns Library. Burns librarian Robert O'Neill is at the end of the table at the right. Next to him with her back to the window is university librarian Mary Cronin. (Photograph by Dan Dry)

The beauty of Burns Library illumined at night by its interior lights, by spotlights on Ford Tower, and by the mellow glow of street lamps on Linden Lane. (Photograph by Lee Pellegrini)

The gracious dormitories on Commonwealth Avenue blend well with their Gothic neighbors. The dormitory nearer Linden Lane is Vouté Hall. (Photograph by Lee Pellegrini)

In 1988 the campus entrance at Linden Lane was beautified with a landscaped circle and an iron fence with granite pillars, echoing the style of the
first Chestnut Hill buildings. The upper photograph was taken at dawn.
(Photographs by Lee Pellegrini)

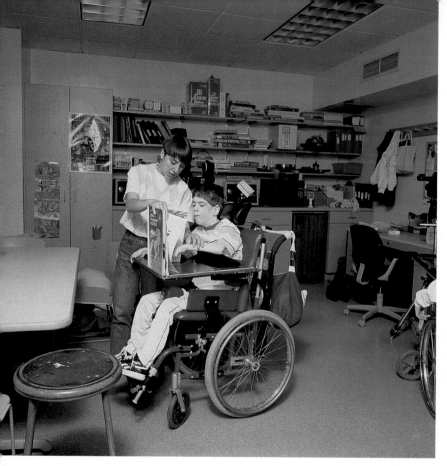

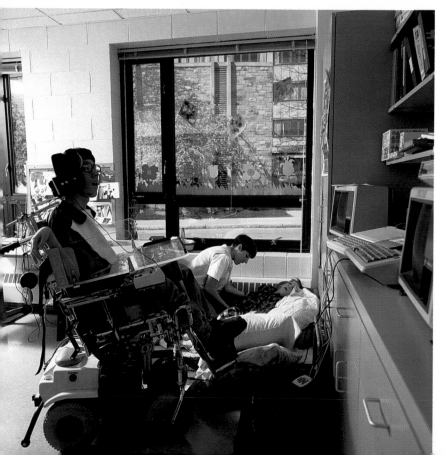

Class activities in the Campus School's magical new quarters in Campion Hall. The photograph at the top shows a teacher, Maria Braz, working with student Eric Nolan, who, through eye movements, is communicating with the help of a picture board. In the other photograph, using a DEC talk computer activated by a barely visible head switch, student Neil Bowen is scanning words that he is to deliver in a play. Artie DePietro is being positioned by Maria Braz so that he can see his lines for the play on the pink sheet behind his head. (Photographs by Lee Pellegrini)

The opening game in renovated Alumni Stadium, September 1, 1988, against Southern California. (Photograph by Dan Dry)

Entrance to Conte Forum, facing Beacon Street. (Photograph by Lee Pellegrini)

1984 Heisman Trophy winner, Doug Flutie. (Photograph by Dan Dry)

Conte Forum provides spacious and state-of-the-art facilities for basketball and hockey as well as a long-needed setting for Baccalaureate Mass and other major assemblies. (Photograph by Lee Pellegrini)

The Burns Foundation, established by the family of John J. Burns ('21) for whom Burns Library is named, has established a Burns Library Visiting Scholar in Irish Studies Chair beginning in the 1991–1992 academic year. Distinguished contributors to and scholars of Irish literature and culture will serve for a semester or year, using the resources of the Irish collection in their classes and research.

In April 1974 the Boston College community was saddened by the death of Director of Libraries, Father Brendan Connolly. The first American Jesuit to earn a doctorate in library science, Father Connolly had succeeded Father Terence Connolly as head of the Boston College library system in 1959. His intelligence and wit made him a popular figure on campus, as well as a forceful—though frustrated—advocate of a new library building. Upon Father Connolly's death Father Monan commented in a campus publication, "The heart of Boston College skipped a beat at the loss of Father Brendan Connolly. If there is truth in the saying that a university is its library, it is truer still that the library reflects the librarian. Father Brendan Connolly was a university librarian of broadest vision and discriminating judgment. He was a student's librarian who opened the full range of library treasures to the student body. He was a librarian's librarian in foreseeing unerringly the directions the science would assume."[19]

New Appointments

For over a year after the death of librarian Father Brendan Connolly, Bapst librarian Jeanne Aber served as interim director of libraries while a search committee headed by Philip McNiff (class of '33), Director of the Boston Public Library, sought a replacement for Father Connolly. Eventually an alumnus, Thomas O'Connell ('50), was chosen as university librarian. O'Connell, with experience at Harvard's Widener and Lamont libraries, had served as director of libraries at York University in Toronto, where he supervised the construction of new library facilities and a dramatic expansion of the university's collection. In a decade of service to his alma mater, O'Connell was to move the Boston College libraries from the nineteenth century to the twenty-first.

Father Monan made two other important academic appointments in the 1970s: new deans for the School of Management and the School of Education. After 11 years of creative leadership, Albert Kelley resigned as SOM dean to accept a vice presidency with Arthur D. Little, Inc., and John Neuhauser of the Computer Science Department was named acting dean while a national search was undertaken. When the interviews were over, the search committee and faculty recommended that Neuhauser become permanent dean. Neuhauser had joined the SOM faculty in 1969, after earning a doctorate at Rensselaer Polytechnic Institute. Assuming charge of a prospering, self-confident School of Management, he was to give it humane and cheerful leadership into even more prosperous days.

Alice E. Bourneuf joined the Economics Department in 1959 as a tenured full professor, the first woman faculty member of the College of Arts and Sciences with that rank. The University conferred on her an honorary Doctor of Science degree in 1977, the year of her retirement. In October 1979 the office of the academic vice president and dean of faculties was named Bourneuf House.

A change of guard in the School of Education followed a similar path. When Lester Przewlocki decided to devote his energies to the classroom, associate dean Mary Griffin was acting dean in the year 1979–1980, then received appointment as permanent dean. Like Przewlocki, Mary Griffin's doctoral studies were done at the University of Chicago, and she had held varied teaching and administrative posts before joining the School of Education faculty in 1965. She had served for seven years as associate dean. Dean Griffin was to give eight years of buoyant and imaginative leadership during difficult times for schools of education.

Celebrating the Bicentennial

As the two-hundredth anniversary of American independence approached, Father Monan announced that from April 1975 to July 1976 Boston College would celebrate the bicentennial with a variety of events and awards. Mary Kinnane, professor of higher education, headed the Presidential Bicentennial Committee that orchestrated a lively and varied series of events throughout the year. The first event in the busy schedule was a specially arranged football engagement with Notre Dame at Schaeffer (now Foxboro) Stadium on September 15th that featured a spectacular patriotic halftime performance by the Boston College band. Several weeks later on September 28th, the academic highlight of the bicentennial program occurred, a convocation in the Recreation Complex at which the attorney general of the United States, Hon. Edward H. Levi, was the speaker. Jazz pianist Mary Lou Williams played the "Gloria" from her *Mass.* Levi, Williams, and four others were awarded honorary degrees. Alexander Peloquin led the chorale in a performance of his own composition, "A Prayer for Us." Dean Donald White of the Graduate School chaired the committee that planned the convocation.

A feature of the bicentennial celebration that involved a broad spectrum of the University was the creation of 200 Good Citizen Awards. For those awards the artist-in-residence Allison Macomber created the Râle Medallion, which showed the figure of Sebastian Râle, S.J., a scholar and missionary to the Abnaki Indians of Maine in the late seventeenth and eighteenth centuries who spent 30 years compiling a dictionary of the Abnaki language. The reverse of the medallion showed the bell tower of Gasson Hall, beloved symbol of the University.

Dean Richard Huber of the Law School chaired the committee that distributed the medals to departments, schools, officers, and organizations throughout the University for conferral upon locally designated medal recipients. The medalists formed a rich and varied company. The Undergraduate Government of Boston College conferred a medal upon the beloved and recently deceased University chaplain, Father Leo "Chet" McDonough, *in memoriam*. Similarly memorialized was Richard Leonard ('50), who had been controller for 14 years before his death in 1976. Other medal recipients were Helen Landreth, curator of the Irish Collection in Bapst Library for 30 years; John Cardinal Wright ('31), head of the Congregation for Religious at the Vatican; Philip J. McNiff ('33), director of the Boston Public Library; Theodore Marier ('34), director of the Archdiocesan Choir School; Cornelius Moynihan ('26), retired associate justice of the Massachusetts Superior Court and a former professor of the Law School; John L. "Jack" Foley ('56), associate director of audio-visual

Vice President George Bush received an honorary degree and was the speaker at commencement in 1982.

services for many years; and Samuel E. Carter, S.J., (GSSW '58), bishop of Jamaica.[20] The distribution of the medals provided wide community involvement in the bicentennial celebration at the same time that it honored 200 distinguished friends of Boston College.

The Alumni Awards of Excellence that have become a feature of the University's calendar each spring were awarded for the first time in 1976 as part of the bicentennial commemoration. Library exhibits, musical and dramatic programs, and special course offerings were other facets of the University's hearty salute to America's bicentennial.

A Home for the Performing Arts

For decades a major cultural need on campus had been a proper home for the performing arts. With architectural plans for a theater finally complete, America's premier entertainer accepted an invitation to visit the campus on behalf of this cause. On the evening of May 19, 1978, Bob Hope gave a benefit performance to launch a fund-raising campaign for the new University theater, which would cost $5,032,244. Governor Hugh Carey of New York, who appeared on stage with Father Monan and Hope, attended the show with his daughter Marianne, class of 1978. It was a classy but jovial affair (Father Monan presented Hope with a B.C. jacket), with tickets at ringside going for $1000. John and Gloria Cataldo worked long and hard

In May 1978 Bob Hope starred in a fund-raiser in Roberts Center for the proposed theater.

Robsham Theater opened in 1981.

to create a proper environment at Roberts Center and especially in Mc-
Elroy Commons, where florists and chefs freely contributed their services
to prepare a magnificent setting for the supper at which Bob Hope and his
wife, Dolores, made a brief post-performance appearance.[21] The event
raised well over a quarter of a million dollars.

The main theater seats 600 and there are smaller stage rooms and several
classrooms. It opened to a black tie audience on October 30, 1981, with a
production of *Camelot*. Speaking on that occasion, Father Monan said,
"At last we have a superb instrument for teaching and learning in the
performing arts, whose values Jesuits have integrated into their curricula
for more than 400 years and for the last 116 here at Boston College."[22]
The theater, it should be noted, was the first to be opened in the Boston
area in 50 years.

On the evening of October 25, 1985, in an emotional ceremony, this
facility was named the E. Paul Robsham, Jr., Theater Arts Center, in honor
of a young man who died in a tragic automobile accident in the summer of
1983. His parents unveiled the plaque in the presence of many friends from
the campus and beyond. Paul was in the class of 1986.[23]

The Irish Connection

It is interesting that during the nineteenth and early twentieth centuries,
when Boston College's Irish heritage was a daily reality in its students and

most of its faculty, there was nothing about Ireland or Irish culture in the curriculum. Father John E. Murphy introduced Gaelic literature in Irish and English in the 1930s, but the program waned after the war. Father Martin Harney of the History Department founded an extracurricular club in the 1950s named after Blessed (now Saint) Oliver Plunkett, whose purpose was to celebrate and perpetuate Irish culture.

But it was not until the late twentieth century (after the advent of much greater curricular flexibility) that Irish studies became available to Boston College students as an organized academic program. Adele Dalsimer of the English Department and Kevin O'Neill of the History Department are directors of this lively undertaking. An organization, Friends of Irish Studies, supports the program with gifts that facilitate its scholarly and artistic activities. One course in the program, "Field Study in Ireland: Early Christian Ireland," is concerned with the religious and artistic effects of Irish monasticism. It includes a two-week study tour visiting major monastic sites. A related development is a junior year abroad at University College in Cork. Margaret Dever of the English Department leads an annual five-week Summer Theatre Workshop at Dublin's Abbey Theatre for Boston College students. The Maeve Finley Scholarship, established by a member of Friends of Irish studies, enables a Boston College graduate to pursue Irish studies in the Emerald Isle. The University is proud that a respected international journal, *The Irish Literary Supplement*, is now publishing in association with the Irish Studies Program at Boston College.

Adele M. Dalsimer of the English Department, co-director of the Irish Studies program. In the spring of 1990 approval was given for an M.A. in Irish Studies.

In 1989 the Carroll School's Management Center established a program to help business men and women from Ireland to develop entrepreneurial skills. Named "Development of Entrepreneurs in Boston for Ireland" (DEBI), the program, headed by Boston College's John McKiernan, aims to assist the economy of Ireland. To date participants have come both from the Republic of Ireland and from Northern Ireland.

Thus, in some ways the ties between Boston College and Ireland are stronger today than they were in the days of the redoubtable Irish founder, Father John McElroy.

One cannot discuss Irish studies at Boston College without mention of the grand lady who presided for years over the Irish Collection. Helen Landreth, known to decades of students and faculty, came to the Bapst Library in 1946 at the invitation of Father Terence Connolly. Her publications, scholarship, and encyclopedic knowledge of all things Irish commanded the respect of scholars on both sides of the Atlantic Ocean. Her close friendship with such legendary figures of Ireland as Eamon DeValera, Sean McBride, Maude Gonne, and Mrs. Erskin Childers gave authenticity and authority to her talks and writings.[24]

Helen Landreth wore with pride the Golden Medal of the Eire Society, just as she cherished the Bicentennial Medallion from Boston College. She was, indeed, the ideal curator of the Irish Collection in Bapst. Only age and infirmities could force her to retire, and she died, mourned by all, on November 8, 1981.

J. Paul Marcoux, faculty director of drama, coaching Paul O'Brien ('66) for the opening presentation in Robsham Theater, Camelot.

The Pope's Visit, and Anniversaries

Boston and Boston College welcomed the Holy Father at the beginning of his first visit to the United States. Pope John Paul II's plane touched down at Logan International Airport on Monday afternoon, October 1, 1979, where he was met by Humberto Cardinal Medeiros and Mrs. Jimmy Carter, the president's wife.

To share in the Pope's visit, the Office of Student Ministry sponsored a walk, beginning at five o'clock in the morning, from the Snake and Apple to the Common. There were not enough tickets to accommodate the enthusiastic response. Several students fluent in French, Spanish, Italian, or German were asked to lend their assistance at the media center. Laetitia Blain, director of the University Chorale at St. Ignatius Church, sang the responsorial psalm at the papal Mass. And 30 Boston College choristers joined the 275-voice choir under the direction of Father Francis Strahan.

Later in the evening, Father Monan and the Boston College band met His Holiness at the entrance to the cardinal's residence on Commonwealth Avenue. The band played "Highlander, you won't mind leaving your country," which was played at Warsaw when Karol Wojtyla was elected Pope. His message on the Common, as elsewhere, was, "I want to repeat what I keep telling youth. You are the future of the world, and the day of tomorrow belongs to you."[25]

In 1980 Boston celebrated the 350th anniversary of its founding. Boston College deemed it appropriate to present a doctor of laws degree, *honoris causa*, to Kevin Hagan White, who had presided as mayor for 16 years over the affairs of the "City on a Hill." A 1955 graduate of Boston College Law School, Mayor White, as the citation read, "blended . . . a feeling for tradition with courage for innovation." On the same platform was the Governor of the Commonwealth, the Honorable Edward J. King ('48). The first graduate to win the governorship, he was cited for bringing to his high position a "leadership that [was] energetic, unselfish, and straightforward." Alma Mater was pleased to confer on him a doctor of public administration degree, *honoris causa*.[26] The other recipients of degrees on that occasion were Germaine Bree, authority on French literature who was the commencement speaker; Bernard O'Keefe, master of business enterprises; and Albert M. Folkard, for many years director of the honors program at Boston College.

Two important anniversaries were commemorated in 1979. On October 25, a special Boston College Citizens Seminar was held at Faneuil Hall to commemorate the 25th year of the program. Governor Edward King, the principal speaker, reviewed the highlights of the program from the point of view of one who had been involved in the growth of the city and the state. An honored guest was Father W. Seavey Joyce, S.J., former president of Boston College who, as dean of the then College of Business Administration, was largely responsible for the institution of the seminars in 1954.

Thomas J. Flatley, a trustee of Boston College and patron of Irish programs at the University, with Kevin O'Neill of the History Department, co-director of the Irish Studies program.

In 1979 the Law School celebrated its fiftieth anniversary with a convocation in the RecPlex. Senator Edward M. Kennedy (LL.D. '66) was principal speaker. At the time he was an unannounced candidate for the presidency, and former Law School dean Father Robert Drinan ('42, LL.M. '49), at the podium, made capital of the situation. On the platform, from the left, are Hon. Joseph P. Warner ('58, LL.B. '61), Alumni Association president; Law School dean Richard G. Huber; Chief Justice Edward F. Hennessey of the Massachusetts Supreme Judicial Court; Senator Kennedy; Father Monan; Father Drinan; James M. Langan ('30, J.D. '34), president of the Fellows of the Boston College Law School; and Father Francis J. Nicholson ('42), Law School faculty member.

The determined gleam in Father Joseph Larkin's eye may reflect relief that, after his 25 years of directing plays in less-than-ideal settings, Robsham is a reality.

The seminars have been a continuing forum for local and national business leaders.

The following day, October 26, an elaborate convocation commemorated the 50th anniversary of the founding of Boston College Law School. Held in the recently dedicated William J. Flynn Student Recreation Complex, the ceremony attracted 2000 attendees—students, faculty, alumni, friends, and leaders of the legal profession in Boston. Undoubtedly, the most excitement was created by Senator Edward M. Kennedy, the main speaker, who was widely known to have presidential ambitions. In fact, he was accompanied by a Secret Service detail which insisted upon a sweep of the complex before the public was allowed to enter. In his address, the senator said:

> For fifty years, you have educated students to adapt the law's great purposes to public and private use. And, for fifty years Boston College's lawyers, judges, professors, and public servants have provided distinguished service to our Boston community, our Commonwealth, and our nation as a whole.[27]

On October 14th, a cold, blustery afternoon, 1400 people from the Boston College community gathered to witness the dedication of the William J. Flynn Student Recreation Complex. On the platform outside the "RecPlex," as it was called, were Daniel Tully, architect; Daniel Cotter, president of UGBC; Governor Edward King, former varsity football player; William J. Flynn; Judge John J. Irwin, president of the Alumni Association; and J. Donald Monan, S.J.

To those who offered congratulations, Bill Flynn insisted, "It's the

Student Recreation Complex, and always will be." One of the most popular facilities on campus—and the most used—it was brought to completion largely through the efforts and inspiration of Flynn. In addition, the occasion afforded an opportunity to honor this man for his 33 years of service to Boston College as teacher, coach, alumni director, and director of athletics. Father Monan observed that "Bill Flynn has set standards of excellence for all of us." A black tie testimonial dinner followed the dedication, at which many national and local sports figures spoke.[28]

New Opportunities and More Appointments

An important change in the administration took place at the end of the 1978–1979 academic year. Father Charles Donovan, who had planned to retire as academic vice president in 1978, agreed to remain at his post for another year to give the search committee more time to choose his successor. The committee at length extended an invitation to J. Allan Panuska, S.J., who accepted and was confirmed by the president and trustees. His appointment as AVP was effective July 1, 1979.

Father Panuska came with impressive credentials. A member of the Maryland Province of the Society, he had earned his Ph.D. in Biology at St. Louis University and was a teacher-researcher for several years at Georgetown. As former rector of the Jesuit Community at Georgetown and Provincial of the Maryland Province, he was an experienced administrator.

Father J. Alan Panuska, academic vice president and dean of faculties, 1979–1982. Father Panuska left Boston College to become president of Scranton University.

He possessed in abundance those qualities necessary for the chief academic officer of the University: leadership ability, high academic standards, and familiarity with the goals and mission of the institution. Father Panuska's warm and engaging personality endeared him to students and faculty alike during his three busy years in office. He left Boston College in 1982 to become president of the University of Scranton.[29]

Father Donovan's retirement as AVP was the occasion of several campus receptions, culminating in the presentation of a Festschrift, *Inscape*, published in his honor. His retirement was short-lived however, as he immediately accepted the position of University historian.[30] One result of that appointment is the present volume, co-authored with an able historian, University archivist Father Paul A. FitzGerald, S.J.

Shortly after Father Panuska's arrival, the College of Arts and Sciences received good news about a proposal for a grant made two years earlier. In May 1977 the Andrew W. Mellon Foundation had contacted the president's office to indicate that it would be open to a proposal in the faculty development area. With that encouragement, Father Donovan, Dean White, Father O'Malley, Father Panuska (on visits to the campus), Richard Landau, and several faculty members drew up a proposal.[31] In response to the proposal from Arts and Sciences, the Mellon Foundation awarded Boston College $360,000 in October 1979 "for use during a period of approximately four years in support of a program for faculty and curricula development."[32] In communicating this good news to the faculty of Arts and Sciences, Dean O'Malley wrote:

> The grant is, clearly, a reflection of the high regard in which the Mellon Foundation holds the faculty in the College of Arts and Sciences. It will provide much-needed support services for research and related activities, and will afford people who develop proposals the opportunity to do some quite interesting things which otherwise would be impossible for them and for the College.[33]

A Mellon Committee of nine members, with Professor Michael Mann of Economics as chairman, was installed, and procedures were set up for faculty applications. Although the proposal was aimed primarily at tenured faculty members, in practice junior faculty could also apply for grants to develop their careers. The principal criteria used in evaluating proposals were the quality of the work proposed and the degree to which the project would contribute to a faculty member's scholarly productivity. Some faculty grants were very generous and were funded up to $8000. Smaller grants, however, were more often the case.

Over time the Mellon Grant was an important component in encouraging faculty to complete projects that had been languishing for one reason or another. It also expanded the possibility of summer grants to faculty hard pressed during the year. The new AVP, as Father O'Malley noted, was very much interested in the idea of faculty career development.[34] The

On April 30, 1984, a welcoming reception was held in McElroy Commons for Boston's new archbishop, Bernard (now cardinal) Law. Dean Mary Griffin of the School of Education is shown with the archbishop and Father Monan.

Mellon Grant also motivated other schools of the University to look for ways and means to encourage their faculties to be more productive.

Two More Controversies

While the faculty members in Arts and Sciences were savoring their good fortune, students were involved in a divisive campus controversy revolving around MassPIRG (Massachusetts Public Interest Group) and its funding. PIRG, which came to the campus in 1972, provides an opportunity for students to join in concerted action on problems that concern them, such as environmental protection, consumer misrepresentation, corporate abuses, and racial restrictions. At this time PIRG was a popular student organization active on many campuses in the Boston and New England area.

But to be successful, it had to be adequately funded. At Boston College, it was agreed that if a majority of the students (as actually happened) voted to fund PIRG, the administration would allow four dollars to be added to each student's tuition as a means of collecting contributions. At the same time, there was a guaranteed refund provision for those students who did not wish to support PIRG. These provisions brought about a confrontation between two groups: PIRG, abetted by UGBC, lobbied for the four dollars while others, notably the Young Americans for Freedom (YAF), opposed the method of collection. YAF, in fact, mounted an aggressive campaign to convince students to ask for a refund. This active campus group was quite successful, and long lines formed at the Murray conference room seeking refunds. In November 1979, 35 percent of the students collected refunds, which drastically reduced the effectiveness of the PIRG operation. Support for PIRG has continued to be a controversial issue.

Another item of ongoing campus discussion, which concerned faculty and students alike, was the much-debated question of "grade inflation." Unknown to students of an earlier age, this new phenomenon, which conferred academic honors on almost everyone, was not confined to Boston College. Nation-wide in scope, it supposedly had its origin in the Vietnam War, when good grades insured exemption from the draft through entrance to graduate or professional school. At that time faculty members felt that assigning even a formerly respectable grade such as "C" reductively made them agents sending students to war; hence the scale of grades became largely limited to "A" and "B." After the war this grading aberration continued as a settled pattern, so that even indifferent students resented a grade of "B–". Father Joseph Fahey, successor as academic vice president to Father Panuska, made the issue of inflated grades a major focus of his administration.

*   *   *

As the decade of the 1980s began, Boston College had achieved a position of academic prominence nationally. As the decade unfolded, the University's athletic teams, both male and female, would also attract national attention.

ENDNOTES

1. *A Report: Boston College 1972–1977*, p. 3.
2. Report of the University Academic Planning Council, 1975, p. 2. BCA.
3. *Ibid.*
4. Peter-Hans Kolvenbach, S.J., "The Jesuit University Today" (Frascati, Italy, November 5, 1985). JEA Collection. BCA.
5. *Jesuit Education at Boston College* (October 1974), p. 8. BCA.
6. *Ibid.*
7. *Ibid.*, p. 9.
8. Kolvenbach, "Jesuit University," 1985.
9. *A Report, 1972–1977*, p. 13.
10. See brochure, "Boston College New Heights Campaign." BCA.
11. *Ibid.*
12. See *Annual Reports* for 1977–1980 and 1980–1981. BCA.
13. *The Boston College Long-Range Financial Plan, April 1976.* Foreword. BCA.
14. *Ibid.* p. 20.
15. *Long-Range Fiscal Plan*, p. 12.
16. The committee was speaking of the operating budget. Physical facilities and renovations were planned and carried forward under the capital funds drive.
17. *A Report of Boston College, 1977–1980*, p. 6.
18. See *Biweekly* (November 6, 1986), p. 4.
19. *Bridge* (June 1974), p. 14.
20. *Focus* (May 1976) listed all the medalists.
21. At a later ceremony, Dolores Hope was awarded Boston College's Ignatius Medal, its most prestigious honor.
22. *Boston College Magazine* (Winter 1982).
23. The dedication was followed by a production of "Amadeus" by the Dramatic Society.

24. *Boston College Magazine* (November 1978).

25. See *The Heights* (October 8, 1979); *Colleague* (October 1979).

26. Though Governor King was the first graduate to hold that office, he was not the first alumnus. The Hon. Charles F. Hurley (ex '16) was Governor of the Commonwealth from 1937–1939.

27. *Boston College Magazine* (November 1979), p. 8.

28. *Ibid.,* pp. 5–6; *The Heights* (October 15, 1979).

29. *Boston College Magazine* (June 1979).

30. See *ibid.* for an interview with Father Donovan on his 18 years as AVP.

31. See "Proposal to Mellon Foundation," August 2, 1979. BCA.

32. John E. Sawyer to J. Donald Monan, S.J., New York, October 4, 1979. BCA.

33. T.P. O'Malley, S.J., and Donald J. White to All Faculty Members, College of Arts and Sciences, October 12, 1979. BCA.

34. O'Malley and White to Board of Chairmen, November 1, 1979. BCA.

CHAPTER 37

Progress in Athletics

Boston College had an athletic program long before the turn of the century. Intramural track and baseball began in the 1870s. In 1891 a group of students received permission—but no money—to form a football team.[1] Two years later an officially sponsored team took the field and thus inaugurated a varsity sports tradition that would eventually bring Boston College to the forefront of collegiate athletics in New England. There have been glory days and less than glorious days, but in good times and bad the administration has taken the position that athletics is an integral part of the total collegiate experience and an asset to the institution.[2] A brief survey of the years from 1978 to 1990 will document the peaks and valleys that frame the victories and defeats on the playing field, on the hockey rink, in the gymnasium, and on the basketball court.[3] Like the ancient Greeks, the men and women who directed these programs were dedicated to the proposition that competition is a necessary ingredient for growth.

Background

Because football has a way of dominating athletic programs and is the current popular measure of success or failure, the 1978 season was a depressing experience for students and alumni. A new coach had arrived to replace Joe Yukica, who had departed for Dartmouth. Success did not follow Edward Chlebek from Eastern Michigan to Boston College, which played a demanding schedule that included Pittsburgh, Texas A&M, and Syracuse. The 1978 season opened on September 16th against the Air Force Academy. Boston College lost this game and every one thereafter, with the last being the hardest for the Eagle fans to accept: a 29–30 loss to arch-rival Holy Cross, which brought to an end the worst season (0–11) in the proud history of football at the Heights.[4] The 1979 season was somewhat better at 5–6, and Coach Chlebek had a winning season in 1980 at 7–4; but the pressure for change prevailed.

Coach Jack Bicknell came to the Heights in the spring of 1981. An assistant coach at Boston College under Joe Yukica (1968–1975), he had been head coach at the University of Maine for five years. Known as "Cowboy Jack" because of his love of country music, big boots, and horses, he had developed a philosophy of sports that fitted well with the philosophy of education at a Jesuit institution. He was also known as a clever offensive strategist. The future looked good.

When Coach Bicknell moved into his office at Roberts Center, an intramural discussion was going on about the proposed formation of a new nine-team conference that would be known as the Eastern Football Conference. It would include Boston College, Penn State, Pittsburgh, Rutgers, Temple, Syracuse, West Virginia, and possibly Army and Navy. It was an attractive proposal that seemed to be beneficial to Boston College football, but there was a problem. If Boston College and Syracuse joined the new football league, they would probably have to withdraw from the Big East Conference, which was working so well for all concerned in basketball. Athletic director Flynn finally voted against it, to the disappointment of Penn State coach Joe Paterno, who had sought to make the new conference a reality.[5] In essence, Paterno was attempting to use the football league as a lever to create an all-sports conference, which would improve Penn State's failing basketball program. Located in remote State College, Pennsylvania, the Nittany Lions constantly had problems attracting both opponents and recruits to visit their rural area. Boston College and Syracuse tried to interest Paterno in a football league only, but to no avail.

By way of parenthesis, the Big East Conference—an idea that originated with athletic director Dave Gavitt of Providence College—was formed in 1979. The original members were Boston College, Connecticut, Georgetown, Providence, St. Johns, Seton Hall, and Syracuse; they were later joined by Villanova and Pittsburgh. The Big East brashly challenged basketball powerhouses in the Southeast, Midwest, and the Pacific Coast—and more than held its own. In the first season, 1979–1980, Syracuse and St. John's were in the top ten in the country. Georgetown shortly emerged as a national contender; Boston College was not far behind and would, as we shall see, move rapidly up the ladder of national recognition. The conference lived up to its potential when, in the 1981–1982 season, four of its teams (including Boston College) went to the NCAA tournament.[6]

The Big East Conference is best known for its great basketball competition, but the league also offers other sports for men and women. The men's sports are cross-country, indoor and outdoor track, baseball, swimming, soccer, golf, and tennis. Women compete in cross-country, indoor and outdoor track, tennis, swimming, and volleyball.

Increasing Women's Participation in Sports

Sports programs at Boston College—especially women's sports—were greatly influenced by certain federal legislation. In 1972 Congress passed the Education Amendments Act, which included Title IX. This law prohibited the exclusion of anyone on the basis of sex from participating in intercollegiate athletics. Violations of the act would result in the denial of benefits to any education program or activity receiving federal assistance. Boston College of course wanted to comply with this legislation, but as originally written, Title IX was vague and difficult to enforce.

Finally, in December 1979, Secretary of Health, Education, and Welfare Patricia Harris issued the long-awaited interpretation of Title IX. Colleges and universities receiving federal funds for any of their educational programs must provide scholarships for women's and men's athletics in proportion to their participation in sports programs. The ruling also included "equivalent" benefits and opportunities.

Coincidentally, the Recreation Complex opened in 1972, the same year that Title IX was passed. According to Mary Carson, associate director of the Athletic Association, the opening of the RecPlex had as much to do with the growth of women's sports as Title IX—and perhaps more.[7] In any case, both developments combined to establish a women's varsity program at Boston College. In 1972 there were only 4 women's teams on the varsity level: basketball, swimming, tennis, and volleyball. In 1978 there were 8 varsity teams, and in 1980 there were 13. And by 1985 there were 15 men's varsity sports and 15 women's.

Because the NCAA did not sponsor women's intercollegiate championships in 1971, Boston College joined the Eastern Association of Intercollegiate Athletics for Women (EAIAW); and in 1973 it joined the Association of Intercollegiate Athletics for Women (AIAW). The women's swimming and diving team, coached by Tom Groden, won immediate recognition; success by track, lacrosse, and tennis teams followed. The basketball team was beginning to attract national attention.

Football in the Flutie Era

A brief account of the major sports during the 1980s will illustrate the accelerated interest in and support of athletics at the Heights. Triumphs and trophies became frequent, but of course there were disappointments, too.

The track, with the press box high above the field, in the pre-Conte Forum era.

To begin with football,[8] Coach Bicknell's first year—with an admittedly tough schedule—was a 5–6 season. He did, however, discover a quarterback: Down 38–0 at the end of the third quarter against Penn State, he decided to go with a fourth-string freshman quarterback who had been belatedly recruited from Natick High School. Boston College lost the game (38–7), but in the final quarter Doug Flutie had passed for 135 yards and a touchdown. As Coach Bicknell later put it, "It was like somebody hit a switch and the tempo picked up."[9] It was the beginning of the Flutie era.

For the next three seasons, Doug Flutie led his team to national recognition and three bowls. There were a few losses, but the overall record established Boston College as a major team that often played before a television audience. The financial reward to the University was significant. Flutie, of course, did not do this by himself. In addition to head coach Bicknell and his staff, there were outstanding players such as Mike Ruth, Steve DeOssie, Gerard Phelan, Brian Brennan, Troy Stratford, Steve Strachan, Tony Thurman, Kelvin Martin, and Ken Bell. Several members of the 1984–1985 squad were named to the first and second All-American teams, while others received honorable mention.

At the end of the 1981–1982 season, Boston College was invited to the Tangerine Bowl in Orlando, Florida, where the Eagles played Auburn on

December 18th. To the disappointment of the large Boston College contingent on hand, the Eagles lost (33–26). The following year, the Eagles played in the Liberty Bowl against the University of Notre Dame on December 24, 1983. Although the score was close, Notre Dame prevailed (19–18).

But Boston College would have its day. After an excellent season in 1984, which saw victories over Alabama, Temple, Rutgers, Syracuse, and Miami (which featured the "miracle pass" from Flutie to Phelan), Boston College was invited to meet Houston in the Cotton Bowl at Dallas on January 1, 1985. It was vintage Flutie, but it also showed off the strong Eagle defense and running attack. Boston College won (45–28)—the first victory bowl since Frank Leahy's national champions beat Tennessee (19–13) in the Sugar Bowl on January 1, 1941.[10]

In a fitting climax to his extraordinary collegiate career, Doug Flutie was selected as winner of the Heisman Trophy for 1984 and was thus identified as the outstanding college football player in the country. Flutie became a household name across the nation, and Boston College, as a result, enjoyed unprecedented publicity.[11] In 1986 the football team peaked again in a 9–3 season which culminated with the defeat of Georgia in the Hall of Fame Bowl. The following three seasons brought diminished scoreboard success but much stirring play. A highlight was the defeat of a bowl-bound Army team in the first collegiate football game to be played in Dublin, Ireland, in November 1988. The 1989 season tested the composure of Boston College fans because of an incredible series of near misses—last-minute defeats by powerhouses Penn State and Ohio State as well as by Rutgers and West Virginia. The quality of the Boston College teams in this era is indicated by players drafted by the National Football League, such as Troy Stratford, Darren Flutie, Tom Waddle, Bill Romanowski, Doug Widell, and Jim Bell. The last three were starters in the 1990 Super Bowl.

Men's Ice Hockey

Hockey comes naturally to boys from Boston and its suburbs. In the recruitment of players at Boston College, a long tradition has favored Americans, with a preference for local talent. Boston College was a latecomer to a varsity game that had long been dominated by the Ivy League. But the Eagles were able to catch on quickly, and there were moments of glory. At the end of the 1922–1923 season, the Eagles laid claim to the mythical national championship. With a win over Dartmouth in the NCAA finals, the 1948–1949 team was the undisputed national champion. All-American Bernie Burke ('50), a member of the B.C. Hall of Fame, was probably the hero of that game, with several crucial saves.[12] He has since coached the goalies for many years.

The modern period began with the arrival of the legendary John "Snooks" Kelley as head coach in 1932. With four years out for war duty, he coached the Eagles for 36 years (1932–1972) and posted his 500th win with a victory over Boston University in the 1971–1972 season. His total record was impressive: 501–243–15.[13]

Len Ceglarski ('51), a member of the national championship team of 1949, succeeded Snooks Kelley as head coach in 1972.[14] As coach at Clarkson he had achieved an enviable record, and he was the first choice to replace his mentor. He continued the tradition of recruiting local talent, boys who had learned to skate on ponds and later honed their skills in suburban high schools. The record clearly shows that they were able to hold their own with the best in the country.

Annually, Boston hockey fans look forward to the first two Mondays in February when the Beanpot Tournament takes place before a packed house at Boston Garden. Inaugurated in 1952, the tournament is a round-robin in which the four area NCAA Division I hockey teams—Boston College, Harvard, Boston University, and Northeastern—vie for possession of the prized Beanpot. Coach Kelley's teams won eight Beanpots. In more recent years, Boston College won the Beanpot in 1976 and 1983. Under Coach Ceglarski, the Eagles have played in the NCAA championships seven times. The calibre of talent the hockey program has been attracting in the 1980s may be judged by the success in the National Hockey League of such

Bernie Burke ('50), goalie of a national championship hockey team, Boston College Hall of Fame member, and for many years coach of B.C. goalies. In spanking new Conte Forum rink he reflects on the 255,000 fans drawn to the Forum in 1989–1990: 118,000 for hockey, 116,000 for men's basketball, and 21,000 for women's basketball.

alumni as Joe Mullen, Bob Sweeney, Bill O'Dwyer, Doug Brown, Scott Harlow, Kevin Stevens, Brian Leetch, and Craig Janney.

Men's Basketball

Boston College has sponsored an intercollegiate basketball team for many years, but only in recent times has it gained national respect. The change began with the arrival of Bob Cousy as head coach in 1963. He had just retired from the Celtics, ending a remarkable career, and his prominence in the sport gave an immediate psychological lift to the program. His first year was one of rebuilding; then the team found success. During Cousy's five seasons, there were invitations to NIT and NCAA tournaments. Coach Cousy was the first to recruit "scientifically" with the scholarships he had to offer.

The next few years under coaches Chuck Daly and Bob Zuffolato were fairly lean. Then basketball at Boston College earned a national reputation. Tom Davis, a Ph.D. in sports history and 38 years old, took over as head coach in the spring of 1977, coming from a successful career at Lafayette College. In his five seasons at Boston College, the Eagles were champions of the Big East in 1981, with a victory over Seton Hall, and received four

Big East basketball in Roberts Center.

post-season bids. In 1981 Boston College was one of the 16 finalists in the NCAA tournament, ultimately losing to St. Joseph's in the final eight. As one sportswriter put it, "The Eagles flew as high as only they knew they could, to the top of the Big East and the NCAAs."[15] Much of the publicity focused on John Bagley and Michael Adams—and with good reason—but Jay Murphy, Martin Clark, Rich Schrigley, and others were extraordinarily competitive team players.

In 1982 Davis accepted an invitation from Stanford University, and Gary Williams, a graduate of the University of Maryland and an assistant to Davis at Lafayette and Boston College, took over the head coaching job. In Williams' first season (1982–1983), the Eagles were 25–7 overall and 12–4 in the Big East. It was a good start, especially with a team that had to be rebuilt. In the words of a sports writer:

> Williams took over a team that lost three starters from 1982 and was picked to finish fifth in the highly competitive Big East Conference. Instead, he piloted the young and exciting Eagles to a 25–7 record (setting the school record for most wins in one season), the Big East regular season championship and No. 1 seed in the Conference playoffs, and the school's first-ever top-tier seed in the NCAA Tournament.[16]

Williams' second season, 1983–1984, was slightly less successful, with an 18–12 record overall and 8–8 in the Big East. Beginning in the 1984–1985 season, with a 20–11 record, the coach began to experience recruiting problems. He alleged that lack of big-time facilities hampered these efforts, and it was true that some of the high school superstars in the Boston area had gotten away. Williams' last season was 1985–1986, after which he accepted an invitation to coach the Buckeyes at Ohio State University.

Former assistant coach Kevin Mackey (now head coach at Cleveland State) was primarily responsible for recruiting a number of highly talented players, such as Michael Adams, John Garris, Stu Primus, Dominic Pressley, and Tim O'Shea. As a result of the graduation of these players and very little recruiting by Williams, however, there was little talent left for new head coach Jim O'Brien ('71), who arrived in 1986. In his second season O'Brien brought his team to the National Invitational Tournament (NIT) where, after two victories, it lost to Connecticut. Michael Adams, John Bagley, and Dana Barros are recent players who graduated into the National Basketball Association.

Other Men's Varsity Sports

With the possible exception of the University of Maine (which has an indoor practice facility), collegiate baseball in New England—at least in the north—seems to be on the decline. A new academic calendar that calls for final examinations to start early in May leaves only the month of April for outdoor baseball competition. New England winters and cold springs are a hazard, and talented players now prefer to go south. Moreover, at Boston College, where baseball scholarships are not available, it is difficult to attract local high school stars. Attendance has fallen off drastically, and at some games only the players' families are there to applaud a double play or a home run. One can only think nostalgically of the 30,000 spectators who crowded Braves Field to watch the Boston College–Holy Cross baseball game in 1923.

But there have been some good years. Eddie Pellagrini, who had played with four major league clubs, became head coach in 1958. In 1987 he announced that his thirtieth year as coach would be his last, ending with the 1988 team. Beginning in 1960, there were eleven consecutive winning seasons, with a trip to the NCAA finals in Omaha in 1967. From 1972–1984, however, it was a different story, with only four winning seasons—the last in 1978.[17] Coach Pellagrini said, "I know we don't have the big stadium, or the fifty-game schedule, or the scholarship money, or even the sunny weather, but we have kids who put out and know they have to hustle for everything they get."[18] Those whose memory goes back a few years will remember Bill O'Brien and Bill Ruane (pitchers), Dan Zailskas, Tom Sarkisian, Ned Yetten, Rod Luongo, George Ravanis, Greg Stewart, and Tim Dachos, catcher. Pellagrini was succeeded as coach by one of his former players, Richard Maloney ('60).

A brief account of track and field, even for recent years, presents a problem. In view of the variety of events and the number of participants—men and women—it is impossible to compress a readable summary into a few paragraphs. It may be of interest to note, however, that there have been only three track and field coaches in the modern history of Boston College: the legendary Jack Ryder; his protégé, Bill Gilligan, who succeeded Ryder in 1952; and his protégé, Jack McDonald, who, on Gilligan's retirement, became track coach in 1981.[19]

Coach Ryder concentrated on the sprints and the relays. Coach Gilligan developed outstanding athletes in the field events, including Harold Connolly, who won the Olympic gold medal for the hammer throw in Melbourne, Australia in 1956. All three coaches, as the records testify, developed outstanding athletes who have participated in local and national meets, in special games such as the Millrose, and now in the Big East Conference. Many have set records in their specialty.[20] Other men's varsity sports programs do not always receive the publicity they deserve. These would certainly include cross-country, which has proved to be one of the best programs in the East; soccer, which—after tentative beginnings—by 1982 earned the respect of competitors in the Big East and a NCAA bid (Coach Ed Kelly was named Big East coach of the year in 1989); and tennis, which has brought Boston College nine Big East championships in the last decade. Swimming and diving, skiing, golf, sailing, and lacrosse are other programs supported by enthusiastic and competitive Boston College teams.

The RecPlex and the middle campus before the construction of O'Neill Library.

Women's Varsity Sports

The rise of women's varsity sports at Boston College, as already noted, was assisted by the opening of the RecPlex. Women's interest in sports was not sparked by the novelty of the new climate or by temporary enthusiasm. Rather, it represented a serious effort on the part of women athletes to test their skills against their peers in other colleges, some of whom had the advantage of established programs. In the process and under good coaching, the women have won their share of honors.

The women's teams with the most visibility and recognition are swimming, tennis, basketball, soccer, field hockey, and track. The improvement in these sports has been dramatic. For example, in the 1981–1982 basketball season, the Lady Eagles finished with an 11–15 losing record in Division II. A year later, after moving to Division I, they completed a winning 17–9 season and achieved national ranking.[21] In 1985–1986 they finished fifth in the tough Big East Conference and defeated fourth seed St. John's in the conference championships before ending a 16–13 season. The basketball team has remained competitive, and as the decade of the nineties begins, its prospects are even brighter.

Women's tennis has also enjoyed success. Ranked 13th in 1982 in the Eastern Regional Championships in Division II, the Lady Eagles have now moved to Division I. The 1985–1986 team went 10–3 on the year, won the 1986 Hilton Head Island Springfest Tourney, and finished fourth in the ECAC championship tourney.[22] Since then the women's tennis team has won four ECAC and Big East championships.

The women's swimming and diving team has firmly established itself as one of the leading women's athletic programs within the University, as well as in the East.[23] In the 1985–1986 season, the team finished first at the ECAC Women's Swimming and Diving Championships in Springfield, Massachusetts, second at the Big East Championships in Pittsburgh, and ninth in the NCAA Division II National Championship Meets in Orlando, with seven swimmers named to the All-America Team. Women swimmers won the New England championship in 1989. A similar story could be told of the women's track and field team, which has provided fierce competition in New England meets. And the women's ski team won the regional championship in the 1985–1986 season and again in 1989.

Looking at the records, a picture of consistently improved standings emerges for women's field hockey, soccer, volleyball, lacrosse, softball, and golf. Talented women athletes are coming to Boston College, which is the ultimate indication of the program's success. And women have brought their share of trophies to the Athletic Department's showcases.

Perspectives on Athletics

There are basically three points of view among the members of the Boston College community who have expressed their opinions on "big-time" athletics at the Heights. Some have always supported the sports program with enthusiasm and season tickets; others have shown indifference; and a

Viewing football from the president's box in the renovated stadium.

third group have seen a conflict between academic standards and athletic scholarships. A challenge to the academic standards associated with the athletic programs occurred in 1984. In March of that year Martin Clark, tri-captain and star of the basketball team, suddenly quit the team and cited "serious problems" with the program.[24] The situation was further exacerbated when it became known that a basketball player had twice flunked out of the College of Arts and Sciences but was allowed to retain his eligibility through enrollment in the Evening College.[25] Academic officials of the University were then put in a defensive position by the intervention of faculty members who now questioned the academic integrity of the athletic program. One professor was quoted as saying, "The University's image is under a very heavy cloud. It will take a long time to clarify matters and remove the tarnish."[26] This dispute precipitated an unfortunate explosion of adverse publicity in the Boston press and on television.

In order to put matters in perspective, the president clarified his position in a five-page letter addressed to "The Faculty and Other Members of the Boston College Community."[27] Father Monan justified the policies that had been in force through 1984, whereby athletes were eligible under NCAA rules if they were enrolled in a full-time program and making due progress. Rejecting as inappropriate the setting of policy for eligibility by educational policy committees, Father Monan asked the vice presidents for advice in dealing with the relationship between extracurricular and academic spheres. As a result of that consultation, the president appointed a committee in the fall of 1984, chaired by the academic vice president, "to determine whether there should be a single standard of 'academic good standing' applicable to all students across the University and whether good standing . . . should become a condition for participation. . . ."[28] An athletic advisory board was also appointed, as well as a faculty advisor to athletes. These steps have helped, and the problems based on the academic performance of some athletes in the past seem to have been solved. The establishment of the Office of Learning Resources for Student Athletes, with Kevin Lyons as director and Ferna Phillips as assistant director (both full-time positions), produced unmistakably positive results in assisting student athletes to meet the academic requirements of the University.

Of course, the problems at Boston College were not unique. For some years, accusations had been leveled at various institutions regarding recruitment, admission standards, and private gifts to athletes. A number of presidents felt that the situation was getting out of hand and that they themselves should play a more active role in controlling abuses. The American Council on Education appointed an *ad hoc* committee of 20 college and university presidents in 1982 to draft proposed changes toughening initial eligibility and academic progress rules for student athletes. Father Monan was a member of that committee.[29]

At the annual NCAA convention in January 1983, the presidents proposed to the NCAA that, for initial eligibility, the student athlete should combine a minimum grade point average in a high school core course with minimum standardized test scores. To remain eligible, the athlete would have to make progress toward a degree and remain in good academic standing.[30]

At the 1984 NCAA Convention, the membership adopted a proposal to establish a 44-member NCAA presidents' commission. Father Monan, representing the National Association of Independent Colleges and Universities, was asked to serve on the 13-member nominating committee to choose 31 of the 44 members of the commission.[31] As a result of that process, Father Monan was himself elected to serve on the first NCAA presidents' commission for Division I-A.[32] When his term expired in January 1985, he was elected to a second term. It would appear that this choice signified the confidence of the other presidents in Father Monan and also reflected national recognition of the Boston College varsity program in Division I-A.

Personal Notes

Although his name has already appeared in this narrative, one final reference must be made to the man who has worked closely with the president on matters relating to athletics and given integrity to the athletic program. The influence of athletic director William J. Flynn has extended far beyond Chestnut Hill. On January 10, 1979, 750 voting members elected him president of the NCAA—only the second athletic director to be chosen for that post. In June 1982 the NACDA honored Flynn by naming him winner of the James J. Corbett Award, symbolic of outstanding achievements and contributions to athletic administration.

One of his closest collaborators was Father Joseph L. Shea, S.J., special assistant to the director of development and University representative for athletics. Unobtrusive but effective, he was the confidant of coaches, administrators, and athletes. On November 14, 1986, he was inducted into the Boston College Hall of Fame, a distinction he richly deserved.[33] When Father Shea died in December 1987, St. Ignatius Church was crowded to the doors at his funeral Mass. Among the mourners were many present and former athletes.

Indeed, Boston College has always been singularly grateful to those who have contributed to its character and growth. In June 1985 the whole community—but especially the Athletic Department—was saddened by the death of Frank Power ('42). Admired by all, he had been associated with the basketball team for 33 years as assistant coach and, for the 1962–1963 season, as head coach. With an analytical approach, he was an acknowledged student of the game, and he co-authored a book with Bob Cousy.[34]

As the Boston College athletic program grew in size and national importance, it became more and more apparent that the sports facilities were inadequate. In fact, there were complaints from both the Big East Conference and the television media, who found it impossible to work in

Sarah Behn ('93), basketball standout and Big East Rookie of the Year in 1990.

the crowded corners. Consequently, the Board of Trustees approved the construction of a new sports center. A few days after the last hockey game in 1986, a wrecking crew began to dismantle McHugh Forum. On the site of McHugh Forum and surrounding land a new state-of-the-art athletic facility, providing for both basketball and ice hockey, was erected. Named for a 30-year veteran congressman, Silvio O. Conte ('49), Conte Forum houses all athletic offices, a modern weight room, band room, basketball practice court, and function room. The hockey rink has been named for former coach John Kelley, the auxiliary basketball facility for former coach Frank Power, and the function room for Father Joseph Shea. The forum seats 8500 for basketball, 7600 for hockey.[35]

On February 18, 1989 Congressman Conte was honored at a dedication ceremony for the new athletic facility that featured videotaped greetings from President George Bush, Senator Edward M. Kennedy, and major league baseball commissioner and former Yale president, A. Bartlett Giamatti. The video presence of these distinguished well-wishers looming large on the giant screen above the arena made a statement about the high-tech style of Conte Forum.

*   *   *

In the last decade of the 20th century the scope of competitive programs for men and women athletes and the spacious new athletic facility matched the maturity the University had achieved on many other more directly academic fronts.

ENDNOTES

1. Falla, *'Til the Echoes Ring Again*, p. 6.
2. Nathanial Hasenfus, *Athletics at Boston College: Football and Hockey* (1943), pp. 1–3.

3. For a general account of sports in the 1970s see "A Decade in Review," *The Heights* (February 1980).

4. Boston College also lost to Temple, 24–28, in the Mirage Bowl, Tokyo, on December 10, 1978.

5. *The Heights* (August 31, 1981), p. 11

6. For a full explanation and history, see Falla, *Echoes*, p. 101; also *The Heights* (November 19, 1979).

7. *The Heights* (November 20, 1978), p. 7.

8. In 1981 Boston College and Holy Cross were the only two Jesuit institutions in the country to field varsity football teams. In February 1987 notice was served, on the initiative of Holy Cross, that the Boston College–Holy Cross football rivalry was terminated. This ancient series, with an enthusiastic following from both schools, began in 1896. The decision was not unexpected. Two years earlier Holy Cross had joined the Colonial League which, in effect, placed its football team in Division IAA in the NCAA. Boston College remains in Division IA.

9. Ian Thomsen, *Flutie: The Story of Boston College Quarterback Doug Flutie, Winner of the 1984 Heisman Trophy* (The Globe Pequot Press, 1985), p. 32.

10. On December 23, 1986, B.C. posted a victory (27–24) over the University of Georgia in the Hall of Fame Bowl at Tampa, Florida. It was the fourth bowl in five years. Shawn Halloran, in a last-minute effort, was the winning quarterback.

11. Mike Ruth was winner of the Outland Trophy as top lineman of the country in 1985.

12. See Hasenfus, *Athletics at Boston College*, for an account of the early years; also Falla, *Echoes*, chapter 3.

13. See "The Passing of a Legend—John (Snooks) Kelley," *Boston College Magazine* (Spring 1986), pp. 34–5. Coach Kelley died on April 10, 1986.

14. On February 9, 1987, in the consolation Beanpot game, Ceglarski became the winningest coach in college hockey with 556 career victories, with a win over Harvard.

15. *Boston College Magazine* (Spring 1981), p. 22.

16. *Boston College Basketball: 1983–84 Media Guide*, p. 8.

17. For yearly statistics see *1989 Boston College Baseball*. BCA.

18. Falla, *Echoes*, pp. 142–43.

19. See *Boston College Magazine* (Winter 1982), p. 31.

20. Falla, *Echoes*, chapter 5, probably has the best account of track and field in recent years.

21. *The Heights* (March 14, 1983).

22. *Boston College: Intercollegiate Athletics, 1986–87 Media Guide*, p. 9.

23. *Ibid.*, p. 18.

24. *The Heights* (March 19, 1984), p. 1.

25. *The Heights* (March 26, 1984), p. 1.

26. *Ibid.*, p. 22.

27. This letter is reprinted in full in *The Heights* (April 9, 1984), p. 18.

28. *Ibid.* During his tenure as academic vice president, Father J. Allan Panuska had issued two reports on athletics and studies. In 1981 he reported that scholarship athletes had met NCAA admissions standards and that 75 percent of scholarship athletes graduated, compared with 79 to 80 percent for non-athletes (*The Heights*, January 19, 1981). In March of 1982 he emphasized two areas of concern: the transfer of athletes from one school to another, and the number and timing of course withdrawals.

29. "Higher Education and National Affairs," v. 31, no. 26 (October 1982), p. 4.

30. *Ibid.*

31. John L. Toner to J. Donald Monan, S.J., Mission, Kansas, January 27, 1984. Botolph House File.

32. John L. Toner to Members of the NCAA President's Commission, Mission, Kansas, March 21, 1984. Botolph House File.

33. In 1978 another Jesuit, Maurice V. Dullea, S.J. ('17), captain of the 1916 football team and former director of athletics, was inducted into the Hall of Fame.

34. See obituary, *Boston Globe* (June 5, 1985); also *Boston College Basketball, 1983–1984*, p. 9.

35. See *Big East 1985–1986 Basketball Yearbook*, p. 47.

CHAPTER 38

A Mature University

As the 1981–1982 academic year wound down, Father Monan was completing his tenth year as president. It is natural to evaluate performance at the end of a decade, and by internal standards the president's report card showed high grades. Throughout the University there was evidence of faculty achievement. Each year increasing numbers of applicants sought admission to Boston College. Fiscal and academic planning never lagged. Fund-raising for the new library proceeded apace, and the long-awaited building was under construction. From the perspective of those within the Boston College community, it had, indeed, been a decade of healthy progress and sure-footed leadership.

Kudos for Monan

But what grade would those in the academic community outside Boston College add to that report card? Such evaluation normally comes to universities from various accrediting agencies, whose judgments are private rather than public. But Father Monan's accomplishments at Boston College received a dramatic public grade of *A* from Harvard University, which invited him to accept an honorary doctor of laws degree at its 331st commencement on June 10, 1982.

Harvard has raised to an art form the pithy one-sentence salutation to its honorary degree recipients at the commencement ceremony, relegating appropriate biographical data to the accompanying program. Father Monan's citation was a gem of gracious collegiality: "With the philosopher's dedication to truth and goodness, he has given fresh strength to the mission of an admirable neighbor." Of course Father Monan's scholarly forte is philosophy, so the reference to philosophy was appropriate. But he is also a Jesuit priest, so the emphasis on truth and goodness may have been meant as a double bow. The citation implies no lack of esteem for Father Monan's predecessors; he is praised for bringing not strength but *fresh* strength to Boston College. And he is saluted not for adding buildings or benefactors but for strengthening the mission of Boston College. One may, of course, parse the sentence too subtly. Every university has essential academic commitments. But Boston College, as a Catholic university, has special religious concerns, and the word "mission" may have been used to embrace those. Finally there was the gracious tribute to Boston College as Harvard's "admirable neighbor," making it clear that Harvard was honoring Boston College in honoring its president.

It was a historic occasion, a far cry from the time eight decades earlier when a president of Harvard and a recently retired president of Boston College contested in print the merits of a Jesuit education and the elective system.[1] Much had changed, and as he sat in Harvard Yard, resplendent in his new doctor's hood, Father Monan may well have reflected on the 82

At Harvard's commencement on June 10, 1982, Father Monan was awarded an honorary degree. The photograph shows a fellow honorary degree recipient, Mother Teresa of Calcutta (far left), with Father Monan and Harvard president Derek Bok.

members of his faculty at that time (lay and Jesuit) who had earned degrees at Harvard.

The following day the *Boston Globe* ran an editorial with the heading, "Crimson, maroon, gold." After mentioning that among the other honorary degree recipients were Tennessee Williams, Virgil Thomson, and Mother Teresa, it focused on the degree to Father Monan. "In the cultural life of New England, fresh winds stirred when Harvard conferred an honorary doctorate of laws on Rev. J. Donald Monan, S.J., president of Boston College. This symbolic event officially ends generations of rivalry—some good natured, and some not—between two groups of alumni and two sociopolitical strains. It confirms an era of mutual respect between two major universities that began long ago." The editorial praised the citation for Father Monan, remarking, "Whoever writes Harvard's honorary degree citations deserves one for conciseness and accuracy." Then, after printing the citation, the writer commented, "Father Monan, a metaphysician by training, is also a priestly man whose gentleness and good humor have won friends for Boston College in the 10 years he has been its president."

In October the Board of Trustees and past presidents of the Alumni Association sponsored a sparkling dinner attended by 1000 alumni and friends to honor Father Monan upon the completion of a decade in the presidency. Held in McElroy Commons dining hall, it was in all respects a gala event that resulted in a substantial contribution to the new library. The *New York Times* of October 12th, under the heading, "Boston's Convocation of Catholic Elite," carried the following account of the dinner:

> When 1,000 of Boston College's alumni and friends came home to the school's Great Hall for a banquet Sunday night, it looked like a convocation of power brokers: a demonstration of the Irish and Italian Roman Catholic communities' ascension to the heights of Massachusetts and Washington.
>
> There, at the table of honor, was the great silver head of Thomas P. O'Neill, Jr., Speaker of the United States House of Representatives, class of '36. There, in the audience, was his son, Lieut. Gov. Thomas P. O'Neill 3d, graduate of the law school, '68. Others were Representative Edward J. Markey, class of '68, law school, '72; the president of the Massachusetts Senate, William M. Bulger, class of '58, law school, '61; the Jesuit and former Congressman Robert F. Drinan, class of '42; and John Kerry, the Democratic candidate for lieutenant governor, law school class of '76. . . .
>
> "We who were the college-bound Irish and Italian Catholics, we were the feeders for this school," Mr. Markey said, as the crowd moved into the $100-a-plate dinner to honor the 10th anniversary of the school's president, the Rev. J. Donald Monan. "We were encouraged and coerced in very subtle ways to go to Boston College to build a Catholic intelligentsia to serve its community."
>
> The children of that community, and their children, came back Sunday night to a 119-year-old Jesuit college that has matured and broadened through the decades. . . . a fact for which Father Monan is given considerable credit.

A light-hearted salute was given to Father Monan a few months later by the Jesuits at St. Mary's Hall. The genial and gifted administrator of St. Mary's Hall at that time was Father John Christopher Sullivan, who enjoyed celebrations and liked to compose proclamations in verse or prose, and in a variety of languages, for special occasions. He feted Father Monan at dinner one evening and posted appropriate Latin verses on the dining room bulletin board. *Biweekly* of March 17, 1983, gave this account of the event:

JESUITS PAY TRIBUTE TO FATHER MONAN

On Monday evenings, members of the Jesuit community gather to honor one of their own for significant accomplishments.

Such an occasion was held on Feb. 7th, as the community recognized President J. Donald Monan, S.J., for his recent elections to the chairmanships of both the National Association of Independent Colleges and Universities (NAICU) and the Association of Jesuit Colleges and Universities (AJCU).

To pay tribute to Fr. Monan, Fr. Christopher Sullivan, S.J., composed the following poem:

> *Gaudeamus, quoniam*
> *Don honorat Bostoniam.*
> *NAICU praesul et solus princeps*
> *AJCU—nunc fit anceps*
> *Honores summos retulit*
> *Honores summos retulit.*
> *Gaudeamus igitur*
> *Jesuitae nam sumus.*
> *Donald praeses, nos respice*
> *Fratres tuos, te auspice*
> *Vocantes te supra "super" ter!*
> *Vocantes te supra "superman!"*

For those whose Latin is a bit rusty, University Secretary Leo McGovern, S.J., provides the following "loose" translation:

> *Let's all rejoice for this good reason:*
> *The honors Don's done us, this season,*
> *In the city whose patron's St. Patrick,*
> *Prexy thrice is a cool hat trick.*
> *Pres BC, NAICU and AJCU,*
> *These high honors honor us, too!*
> *Therefore, let's rejoice,*
> *For we are his fellow Jesuits.*
> *Pray, Don our pres, do us behold,*
> *Your brothers in your care and fold,*
> *As we hail you tops and super thrice,*
> *As we hail you our Superman!*

Note: According to the poem's author, "Fr. McGovern opined candidly that the translation was terribly loose and needed to be tightened up—considerably. Alas, so it goes in academe."

*   *   *

The history of an institution as complex as Boston College in a period of explosive development must necessarily record details of land acquisition, construction of buildings, and appointment of principal administrators. But, of course, everything else exists for academics. As we approach the end of the present update of Boston College's history, it therefore is appropriate to give an account of the academic status of the University. This will be done in the form of a school-by-school review.

The School of Nursing

The School of Nursing celebrated its fortieth anniversary in 1987, and faced the future with hope and confidence. Despite a decline in undergraduate enrollment that had affected schools of nursing nationally, the Boston College School of Nursing enjoyed several signs of recognition and success. Upon the retirement of Dean Mary Dineen in 1986, after 14 years of constructive leadership, the School attracted as her successor Mary Sue Infante. Dean Infante, a product of Catholic University and Columbia University and an author and editor, had been a professor at the University of Connecticut School of Nursing. She assumed the leadership of a faculty of 53, of whom 43 percent held the doctoral degree.[2] The faculty had authored over fifty books, two of which had been chosen as Book of the Year by the *American Journal of Nursing*. A 1982 ranking of school of nursing faculties by deans and nurse researchers placed the Boston College School of Nursing in the 33rd spot among some 400 baccalaureate degree programs.[3]

Mary Sue Infante, appointed dean of the School of Nursing in 1986.

Traditional pinning ceremony for School of Nursing seniors on the Saturday before commencement, Dean Dineen presiding.

The school has long been proud of its outstanding library, assembled under the insightful direction of its committed librarian, Mary Pekarski. In 1984 that library was merged with the collections in the new O'Neill facility. Special collections that distinguish the nursing holdings include: the Rita Kelleher Collection of archival, historical, and research materials in nursing; the Guild of St. Luke of Boston Health Ethics Collection, which contains print and audiovisuals on the ethics of medicine and health care; and the National Health Planning Information Center, which is one of 26 U.S. and European depositories for NHPIC noncopyrighted materials in microfiche format. In 1988 the Josephine A. Dolan historical collection was established. It was with great sadness that in 1988 Boston College and the School of Nursing mourned the death of Mary A. Pekarski. Her memory lives on in the library holdings which she so carefully amassed.

The maturing scholarship of the faculty and its unique research resources were acknowledged in September 1986 when the Board of Trustees approved the establishment of a Ph.D. program in nursing, to commence in 1988. The program is research-oriented, because of the need for clinical research and the high demand for clinical researchers. The emphasis of the new doctoral program is on the formation of ethical reasoning, diagnostic/therapeutic judgments, and human response patterns to such judgments.[4]

Ten full-time candidates enrolled in the program in 1988 and another 10 in 1989; a total enrollment of 30 is envisioned in 1990. Through this significant move, the School of Nursing joined a select group of approximately 10 percent of schools of nursing which offer doctoral study.[5]

To underscore the School of Nursing's commitment to the highest level of scholarship in nursing education, the University awarded an honorary degree at the 1983 commencement to a premier exemplar of such commitment, Virginia Henderson, professor emerita of the Yale School of Nursing. Through her teaching and writing, Dr. Henderson helped shape generations of nurses and her bibliographical scholarship opened treasures for research in the nursing profession. Another nurse scholar and historian, Josephine A. Dolan, formerly of the University of Connecticut, received the honorary degree of Doctor of Nursing Science at the 1987 commencement.

At the time of the fortieth anniversary celebration, two important works were published. Associate Professor Mary Ellen Doona contributed *Nursing Commemorative,* a history of the school. Dean Emerita Rita Kelleher printed her rich *Memoirs: Boston College School of Nursing, 1947–1973.*

As the Boston College School of Nursing enters the new decade of the 1990s, it is poised for growth and continued recognition for the quality of its graduates. Curricula and teaching are meeting the challenges of today's youth; research activities of faculty and students are enhancing the pursuit of knowledge; laboratories, classrooms, and office space in Cushing Hall have been upgraded to support research and learning. In 1990, 78 percent of the faculty hold the earned doctorate and student enrollment in all programs compares favorably with that in leading schools of nursing. And graduates are working more closely with the school through the newly established Boston College Nurses' Association.

The Carroll School (and Graduate School) of Management

Since 1978 the deanship of John J. Neuhauser in the Carroll School and Graduate School of Management has seen the continuation and strengthening of two trends begun in the Kelley administration: development of faculty and upgrading of the student body. Earlier deans of undergraduate professional schools had felt somewhat disadvantaged by the heavy emphasis in admissions strategy on the College of Arts and Sciences. But by the end of the 1970s, the situation had changed. With the admission of women to CSOM in 1971 and with a growing emphasis in society on education for business, competition for admission to the school escalated. A place in the freshman class of CSOM became just as prized and as hard to come by as one in the entering class of A&S.

Recent deans' annual reports show a healthy presence of Carroll School of Management faculty in top scholarly journals. CSOM now recruits faculty in competition with the very best schools in the country, and its

John J. Neuhauser, dean of the Carroll School of Management since 1978.

success is indicated by the attempts of Harvard and MIT to lure away junior faculty. But research progress has not meant less attention to teaching. The faculty believe that recent course evaluations by students, as well as syllabi, outlines of term projects, and examinations, show that current courses are intellectual, demanding, stimulating, and up-to-date.[6]

One of the promising developments in recent years has been the establishment of academic programs across school and departmental lines. While this has happened principally at the graduate level, a notable undergraduate example has been the inclusion since 1984 of CSOM honors program students in the A&S honors program's Western cultural tradition courses for freshmen and sophomores. Since only about 7 percent of any Arts and Sciences class is invited to participate in these challenging courses, the inclusion of these CSOM students is a measure of the calibre of students attending CSOM. The Western tradition sequence fulfills the core requirements in theology, philosophy, English, and in some cases social sciences. Among the freshman texts studied are the Bible (Genesis, Exodus, Job, one or more of the Prophets, selections from the Psalms, one synoptic Gospel, John, and Romans), Homer, Greek drama and philosophy, Vergil, Augustine, Aquinas, Dante, and Shakespeare. Among texts studied in sophomore year are Machiavelli, Thomas More, Luther, Milton, Pope, Goethe, Kant, and Darwin. Dean Neuhauser is enthusiastic about this rich liberal arts experience for his future managers and wishes it could be expanded.[7] Currently juniors and seniors in the CSOM honors programs take honors seminars in the College of A&S, and several CSOM faculty teach seminars for the A&S program.

The Carroll Graduate School of Management has a J.D.-M.B.A. program in cooperation with the Law School, a joint M.S.W.-M.B.A. program with the Graduate School of Social Work, and a joint M.B.A.-Ph.D. in sociology with the Department of Sociology. The M.B.A. program was established in 1957 and steered successfully through the rigorous process of accreditation in 1975 under the leadership of Richard Maffei, who served as associate dean from 1969 to 1975, and Raymond Keyes, assistant dean from 1968 to 1978. Maffei's successor, William Torbert, helped establish a new M.B.A. core curriculum, of which the school is rightly proud as a program that integrates functional skills, critical analysis, and ethical inquiry. When first established, it was the only program in the country that required first-year M.B.A.s to work with real clients, their grades being affected by the success or failure of such experience.[8] A master's degree in computer science was begun in 1988.

The ultimate vote of confidence by the University in the Carroll Graduate School of Management came in December 1987, when the Board of Trustees approved a new doctoral program—the first for GSOM—with a specialization in the field of finance. The Finance Department had previously conducted a successful master's program in finance, with a large enrollment. The Ph.D. program will admit its first class in September 1990.

The graduate school has been attracting national attention. Among the various measures of a school's effectiveness is beginning salary for its graduates. A national survey of starting salaries of business school graduates in 1986 placed GSOM 23rd out of 50, understandably behind Harvard, Stanford, and Chicago, but ahead of such major institutions as Ohio State, Texas, Notre Dame, and Illinois. That same year Boston College ranked 33rd in number of M.B.A.s granted.[9]

Fulton Hall, home of the School of Management, was undoubtedly the least successful of the Maginnis and Walsh buildings in the Gothic style. As the first postwar building, its construction budget was very spare. (It will be remembered that students went from door to door selling "Bricks for Boston College" at one dollar apiece.) In recent years the University has wisely and continually upgraded the interior facilities of Fulton, and the removal of the business library to O'Neill made available large spaces that have become gracious and comfortable rooms. In 1990 there are plans to add a floor to Fulton Hall and to enclose the rear courtyard. Raising the height of the building seems achievable with no embarrassment to the Gothic quadrangle, since at present only two stories of Fulton border the quadrangle.

During the school's golden jubilee in 1988, an honorary doctorate was awarded to a graduate, Richard F. Syron ('66), president of the Federal Reserve Bank of Boston. As mentioned earlier, the fiftieth year also saw the first endowed professorship in the school, the Peter F. Drucker Chair in Management Sciences, a generous gift of John and Margaret McNeice. In 1989 the school became the Carroll School of Management and the Carroll

Graduate School of Management in honor of a generous alumnus, Wallace E. Carroll ('28).

In the last decade of the twentieth century, alumni of the Carroll School of Management are found at top levels of American business management. The alumni, the diversified faculty, and the coeducational student body have come a long way in five decades from the tentative beginning at Newbury Street and O'Connell Hall under Father James Kelley, a former professor of classics.[10]

The School of Education

During the early days of the School of Education in the 1950s and 1960s, under the entrepreneurial leadership of such faculty members as Marie Gearan and Sister Mary Josephina Concannon, program initiation and outreach became a way of life. Later, John Eichorn (in special education) assumed the mantle of innovation and succeeded in attracting substantial external funding. But the pace in the School of Education during the last decade and a half has been so lively that only a few activities and promising developments can be mentioned here.

As is generally known, the past several decades have not been happy ones for schools of education nationally. With a declining younger population, many state institutions for teacher education have been phased out. Nor has Boston College been immune to the general decline of interest in teaching as a career. The undergraduate enrollment reached a peak of 1344 in 1973, but then a decline set in: below a thousand in 1977 and a low of 623 in 1984. A small increase then began into the 700s. The current levels of enrollment (larger, incidentally, than the enrollment in the 1960s, when it was agreed that SOE was a fine, robust school) are a tribute to the ingenuity and adaptability of the faculty and to the leadership of recently retired Dean Mary Griffin.

One of the programs that makes the Boston College undergraduate School of Education unique in America—and no doubt in the world—is the out-of-state/overseas final teaching practicum. Joan Jones, director of the semester-long teaching practicum of the seniors, decided to try something different in 1973. Instead of limiting student teaching to local school systems, she sent several students to England and others to Indian reservations in New Mexico and South Dakota. Since then 20 percent of each senior class has done student teaching either out of state or in a foreign country. Students have had their final teaching practicum in Arizona, Hawaii, California, Puerto Rico, and Colorado, as well as in several of the New England states besides Massachusetts. Overseas sites in addition to England have been Scotland, Ireland, Wales, Austria, Spain, Switzerland, Sweden, Venezuela, Germany, France, and Australia. Whether out-of-state or overseas, the students are visited by Dr. Jones or one of several faculty members. Naturally such an unusual—even daring—experience impresses employing superintendents when reviewing dossiers.

In the early 1980s both the School of Education and its graduate department began to include computer components in all courses. Technology was permeating the entire curriculum, and computer literacy became a requirement. Since then, all students master word processing, communications, computer-assisted instruction, data analysis, and programming. A few nonrequired courses make available advanced competencies in such areas as artificial intelligence, robotics, and speech synthesis and recognition. These beginnings led to the establishment in 1984 of a master's program in educational technology.

In the early 1980s, Catholic school superintendents in New England approached the faculty in educational administration with the idea of a program to prepare Catholic laypeople for administrative positions. In 1982 the Catholic School Leadership Program was begun under the direction of Sister Clare Fitzgerald. Already hundreds have taken advantage of this important *ad hoc* training for the Catholic school systems.

In 1983 the Division of Counseling Psychology of the Department of Education in the Graduate School achieved national status when its doctoral program was accredited by the American Psychological Association. The division became one of 35 APA-accredited doctoral programs in counseling psychology in the country, and one of two in New England.

A good example of significant service to the community by the School of

Joan C. Jones, creator of School of Education out-of-state and overseas student teaching placements.

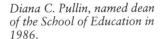

Diana C. Pullin, named dean of the School of Education in 1986.

Education is what came to be known as the District B–Boston College Collaborative. This effort stemmed from the May 1975 desegregation court order of Judge W. Arthur Garrity, Jr., for the Boston public schools. District B., with which Boston College was paired, covered parts of West Roxbury, Roslindale, Dorchester, and Mattapan and included one high school, three middle schools, and 13 elementary schools. The partnership lasted 10 years, from 1976 to 1986, and was funded annually by the State Department of Education with grants usually exceeding $100,000. George Ladd orchestrated and managed the diverse and lively collaboration. Activities varied from year to year but included such things as a newsletter for parents under the direction of a parent editor; computer literacy workshops; a public speaking program to increase student leadership and self-confidence; workshops for teachers of gifted pupils; workshops for individual school racial ethnic parent councils; and assistance in furthering development of student governments and other student activities within each school. The contribution of the School of Education has been judged effective in facilitating the process of desegregation in a major area of the City of Boston.

The leadership of the School of Education passed to a new dean in September 1987. Diana Pullin, possessing both a doctorate in education and a law degree from the University of Iowa, had served as associate dean for graduate studies at Michigan State's College of Education. No stranger to Boston College, she had taught here as an adjunct professor in 1982–

1983 while associated with the Center for Law and Education in Cambridge. Her own record in administration and scholarship prepared her well for her leadership responsibilities in practice and research.

The Graduate School of Social Work

The 12-year deanship of Father John V. Driscoll ended in 1970 after he had brought the Graduate School of Social Work from its original home on Newbury Street to its splendid quarters in the building named for the school's founder, McGuinn Hall. When Father Driscoll left Boston College for other professional endeavors, he was succeeded by a faculty member, Edmund Burke, an alumnus of the School of Social Work who had earned his doctorate at the University of Pittsburgh. Dean Burke led the school for six years, then opted to return to his faculty post. Later, he assumed his current position as director of the Center for Corporate and Community Relations.

In September 1976 the deanship was assumed by June Gary Hopps, who was to win national recognition for the Graduate School of Social Work and for herself. Having earned a doctorate at Brandeis University, she was associated with Ohio State University before coming to Chestnut Hill. Dean Hopps became the second woman and the University's first black administrator at that level of responsibility.

The two most prestigious honors to come to Dean Hopps during the first

Edmund R. Burke, dean of the Graduate School of Social Work, 1971–1977; currently director of the Center for Corporate Community Relations.

10 years of her administration were her four-year appointment by the National Association of Social Workers as editor of the association's journal, *Social Work*, in 1985, and her election in 1986 as president of the National Conference of Deans and Directors of Graduate Schools of Social Work. *Social Work*, with more than 30,000 subscribers, is the most influential periodic publication in social work and public policy. In 1979 the Massachusetts Chapter of the National Association of Social Workers named Dean Hopps "Social Work Educator of the Year."

Since June Hopps assumed office there have been a number of significant developments in the School of Social Work. A new course, "Comparative Social Policy Analysis and Field Experience," has given students an opportunity to study and observe welfare policy and service systems in nonmarket or socialist countries. Classes have visited Cuba, Greece, Yugoslavia, and the People's Republic of China, and visits are planned to Scandinavia and Eastern Europe. The course has attracted students from other local universities and colleges, including Harvard, MIT, Brandeis, Simmons, and Boston University.

In 1979 an A.B.–M.S.W. program was established in cooperation with the Arts and Sciences Psychology and Sociology departments. Carefully selected students, limited to 10 a year, can complete the double degree program in five years. The program has proved to be a good tool for recruiting talented undergraduates to the field of social work and a valuable acceleration for undergraduates prepared to make an early commitment to the profession.

The most important academic development in the Hopps era was the establishment in 1979 of a doctorate in social work. As was true of the School of Nursing a decade later, the University made a public declaration of confidence in the school when the carefully crafted doctoral proposal of the GSSW was approved. In the program's first eight years, 64 students enrolled for the doctorate; 10 had graduated by 1987, with 5 D.S.W. degrees awarded that spring and 16 more candidates reaching the dissertation stage. Some of the graduates have assumed faculty positions at other distinguished schools of social work.

Three joint professional degree programs were established in the 1980s: an M.S.W./M.B.A., with the Carroll School of Management; an M.S.W./J.D., with the Law School; and the M.S.W./M.A., with the Institute for Religious Education and Pastoral Ministry. In an effort to embrace human services and professional educational opportunities in outlying communities and, in particular, in response to requests from the Worcester and Portland (Maine) Diocesan Catholic Charities, the school arranged for four off-campus sites to offer many of the first-year foundation courses. While part-time students matriculate at Chestnut Hill for the final full-time academic year, field work can be arranged in the students' own locale. To date, sites have been established in the Plymouth, Worcester, Springfield, and Portland areas.

In 1979 the school established the Bureau of Continuing Education to coordinate many of the research and nondegree educational activities of GSSW. The bureau conducts training programs for public and private human service providers through workshops, seminars, and short-term courses. In 1985 the state of Massachusetts established licensing for social workers, and the bureau set up courses for alumni and other M.S.W.s in the Greater Boston area to help them update knowledge in special areas and to enable them to obtain their required continuing education credits. In 1986 a full-time director was appointed for the program.

In 1986 two faculty members were honored by the Massachusetts chapter of the National Association of Social Workers: Carolyn Thomas, for distinguished contributions to social work practice, and Robert Castagnola as social worker of the year. The University's continued recognition of the school's goals and the contributions of its graduates was symbolized by the 1979 honorary doctorate awarded to GSSW alumna Dorothy Baker ('46) for her work in India preparing professionals to bring social services to the poorest of the poor.

The College of Arts and Sciences

In professional schools, progress is sometimes measurable by new initiatives and projects generated by the administration and faculty to adapt to changing societal needs. The account elsewhere in this chapter of recent developments in the School of Education is a good example. A college of liberal arts in the traditional Jesuit view, on the other hand, represents considerable curricular and programmatic stability, so that innovations and experimental enterprises are of secondary importance compared with the ongoing main business of the college. The College of Arts and Sciences fits this pattern. It has never become addicted to the academically peripheral; rather it has been resoundingly loyal to the basic liberal studies, the disciplines represented by the A&S departments. As we have seen, when the A&S faculty was invited to consider new configurations of studies and cross-disciplinary programs for the Newton campus when it was acquired in 1974, there was no response except from the Perspectives Program, which was already in operation and externally funded. This lack of faculty reaction was seen not as a reflection of inertia or indifference but as a reassertion of commitment to the parent disciplines.

In the 1950s the College of Arts and Sciences (and Graduate A&S) began to organize enthusiastically and ambitiously along departmental lines. Each departmental faculty renewed itself and increased its numbers by rigorous selection of candidates with prestigious academic pedigrees. When Victor Butterfield of Wesleyan University warned against excessive departmental emphasis in A&S early in the 1960s, little attention was paid that advice. In the last decade of this century the A&S faculty may be more fragmented than Butterfield would think desirable, but the departmental faculties are a

Father Joseph Fahey, academic vice president and dean of faculties, 1982–1987.

credit to their respective professions as well as to the University, and they have developed serious and challenging curricula. Dean Robert Barth has initiated an ongoing program of external review of all departments, which will lead to a long-range plan for each.

Given its basic stability, the College of Arts and Sciences has, nevertheless, introduced new programs in recent years. It is hardly surprising that a major in computer science was approved by the Educational Policy Committee in 1980. This program takes advantage of computer courses in the School of Management, which was the first campus unit to introduce this specialization, plus appropriate courses in the A&S Mathematics Department.

In 1985 a major in biochemistry was begun. A response to the strides being made in the investigation of life processes, it focuses on new discoveries and techniques in genetics, such as genetic cloning, genetic slicing, and DNA research. The biochemistry major is jointly administered by the Biology and Chemistry departments.

The Department of Geology and Geophysics has responded to current social and student concerns by establishing a major in environmental geosciences, whose purpose is to provide students with a knowledge of the delicate balance of nature and methods of preserving it.

For some time language majors have been able to live together in

Greycliff, the "modern language house." More recently the "Immersion Program" enables qualified students to take some required or elective courses entirely in the French or the Spanish languages in the departments of History, Philosophy, and Fine Arts and in the School of Social Work.

In 1980 the Educational Policy Committee of Arts and Sciences approved a major in classical studies. This major reflected increased enrollment in Latin and Greek courses and a more aggressive stance by the department. A concession from the practice of earlier years allowed students a choice of reading classical works in the original language or in translation. The chairman, Eugene Bushala, Father David Gill (who was also director of the honors program), and Professor Dia M. Philippides were largely responsible for this progress. Father Carl Thayer, of course, always kept the candle burning.

In 1988 the college established the Music Department, followed in 1989 by a music major. This effort has happily resulted in a burst of musical activity on campus.

In order to enable students to make connections between disciplines and integrate their academic programs, the college has established a number of interdisciplinary minors "designed to provide a coherent grouping of courses drawn from various disciplines and focused around a specific theme."[11] There are currently 19 such minors, which range from black studies through women's studies. The most recent addition is the minor in "faith, peace and justice." The latter program has a dual purpose: to utilize the curriculum so that students may focus on faith, peace and justice study and to sponsor and organize related campus-wide activities. So the College of Arts and Sciences, long devoted to carrying on and keeping up to date the major liberal arts disciplines, has not been timid about trying new academic paths.

To help students chart their course through the maze of majors and electives available to them, a reinvigorated and elaborate faculty advising program was established in 1980. A system of class deans has been instituted. The freshman dean is responsible for administering the advising program and keeping up to date the 130-page "Faculty Advisor Handbook" developed by former Assistant Dean Patricia De Leeuw. The handbook facilitates—even for new faculty members—the sometimes daunting role of helping students make enlightened academic decisions.

The Graduate School of Arts and Sciences

What has been said above about the steady strengthening of Arts and Sciences departments obviously is pertinent to the Graduate School of Arts and Sciences which, since 1972, has been guided by Dean Donald J. White. Liberal arts faculty recruiting committees tend to assume that faculty candidates from first-rate universities are competent in undergraduate teaching, and they focus more particularly on scholarly expertise and interests that will strengthen graduate programs.

The major development for the Graduate School of Arts and Sciences in the past decade was the review of its role and direction stimulated by the Graduate Educational Policy Committee in the spring of 1983. Academic Vice President Father Joseph Fahey responded positively to the EPC's intention of exploring the identity and future of the school by organizing a weekend retreat on the subject for 37 faculty members and administrators from the full spectrum of graduate programs. This exploration was followed in June 1984 by a meeting with Father Monan, in which he enthusiastically endorsed an 18-month planning effort.

At the faculty convocation in September 1984, Father Monan announced the planning program for the graduate school and his serious commitment to it. After reminding the faculty that the Graduate School of Arts and Sciences administratively embraces graduate programs in education and nursing as well as in arts and sciences disciplines, the president stated:

> . . . It will be important for each of the faculties involved with graduate education . . . to conduct a realistic assessment of the present status and prospects of the individual program. But the purpose of this study will be to express a vision of graduate education at Boston College that will be realistic, will be a stimulus to progress and a guarantee to the fulness of our stature as a university. Obviously, the world of graduate education has been changing in recent years—if anything, at a faster rate than at the undergraduate level, as financial pressures and job markets and career preferences continue to shift. Yet, I would want you to know from the outset that the inspiration of this study is not any cost-cutting imperative or preference for contraction. This study will proceed not from any suspicion of weakness but with the sincere necessity to define our own ambitions and clarify the distinctive role

Father Leo J. McGovern, secretary of the University, 1982–1985.

of graduate education in the identity of the university. The fact of the matter is that our academic planning of the mid-70s laid principal emphasis upon undergraduate education, and it is at that level that our stature is more spontaneously recognized. But in a genuine sense, our repute as a university and our distinctive contribution to scholarship will depend in a particular manner upon our graduate programs. I believe that both the impressive quality of the scholarship of our individual faculty members and the importance of our graduate programs to our stature as a university make it important that we carefully, but ambitiously, search into this aspect of our identity. Once again, ambitions and ideals translate into needs, and I would expect the enumeration of our needs in Graduate Arts and Sciences to feed directly into the university-wide goals for the nineties that I mentioned earlier.

With that comprehensive charter and challenge, the study went forward. The Graduate Educational Policy Committee (GEPC), under the chairmanship of Dean White, was supplemented by two elected faculty members from the School of Education, the academic vice president and dean of faculties, and the dean of the College of Arts and Sciences as voting members for the duration of the study. The first step was the formulation of a "Mission Statement for the Planning Effort," which was sent to the faculty of every department in November 1984. In turn the individual departments prepared mission and target statements and profiles of faculty accomplishments and activities, and submitted them to the GEPC in February 1985.

While these projects were under way, the office of the executive vice president prepared careful analyses of current program costs. The GEPC used the Graduate Program Self-Assessment Service of the Graduate Record Examination Board to survey faculty, students, and alumni concerning program quality. In addition, five areas were selected for external review, since the committee believed that outside consultation about them would be helpful. By late summer 1985, the targets specified by each program were translated into specific resource requirements and an evaluative instrument was devised to insure uniformity in the review of each program. In the fall of 1985 the GEPC reviewed each submitted program and developed individual reports without recommendations. These were submitted to the respective departments for review and comment to insure accuracy and completeness. After receiving responses from the departments, the GEPC held intensive meetings in December to arrive at final recommendations. The committee's report was submitted to Father Monan in February 1986.

The report outlined the mission of the Graduate School of Arts and Sciences. It emphasized the special contribution the school should make to facilitating and reinforcing the University's continuing pursuit of higher levels of academic excellence through the quality of faculty research and the preparation of students to carry on the quest for new discoveries and a deeper understanding of the world and its peoples. It saw this effort as adding an academic quality dimension not only at the graduate level but widely in the University and specifically in undergraduate education. The report envisioned a continued commitment to the University's Jesuit and Catholic traditions, which gave special motivation in the unwavering search for truth and in the application of rigorous methodology to the issues and problems of the scholarly discipline, a concern for the worth and integrity of persons engaged in the pursuit of higher learning, and a desire to be of service to those in need in the world beyond the campus. The report perhaps went beyond any prior planning document in eliciting from the departments statements of aspiration accompanied by resource requirements as explicit as possible. It also presented a set of more general recommendations, including such matters as endowed chairs, improved research and learning facilities, the possibility of a University press, and graduate student housing.

The report assigned programs to one of three categories: high priority (among the first to receive additional resources), priority (eligible for added resources after high-priority needs have been met), and steady state (not recommended for added resources). In the humanities, theology and philosophy were given high priority, and the same ranking was given to political science and psychology in the social sciences and to chemistry and mathematics in the physical sciences and mathematics. In education, high priority was given to counseling psychology and special education, and high priority was also assigned to nursing. Almost at once the University began to respond to the recommendations. Two dramatic examples were the approval of the doctoral program in the School of Nursing and plans for a new chemistry building which, as the 1990s dawned, was being erected on the site formerly occupied by Roberts Center.[12]

The Law School

The year 1985 was an important one in the history of the Law School: Dean Richard Huber's productive 15-year leadership ended and a new dean was named, and an important national legal journal rated the Law School faculty among the elite in the country in terms of scholarly writing. The Law School had been blessed with three outstanding deans: Father William Kenealy, Father Robert Drinan, and Richard Huber, men who led the school to national prominence and professional distinction. The search for a successor scoured the legal world—and found the new dean nearby in the prestigious Boston law firm of Palmer and Dodge. Daniel Coquillette attended Williams College and won a Fulbright Scholarship at Oxford University, where he studied law and legal history. At Harvard Law School Coquillette was editor of the *Harvard Law Review*. Upon graduation, he held one of the most prized clerkships a young lawyer can hold, under Hon. Warren Burger, chief justice of the United States Supreme Court. He served for several years on the faculty of Boston University Law School and was a

Daniel R. Coquillette, dean of the Law School since 1985.

visiting professor at Cornell University and Harvard Law School. His *Lawyers and Moral Responsibility: Problems and Materials* has been used as the basis for an advanced seminar in legal ethics at Harvard Law School. He was the editor of *Law in Colonial Massachusetts, 1630–1800.* In 1988 his *The Civilian Writers and Doctors' Commons, London* was published.

No sooner had Dean Coquillette taken office than good news arrived to give a forward surge to his administration. A major article in the *Journal of Legal Education* of the Association of American Law Schools ranked Boston College Law School among America's foremost research law schools. Forty-four law schools were ranked according to the scholarly productivity of senior faculty. Three "cohorts" were established, and Boston College Law School was ranked thirteenth in Cohort One, along with Chicago, Cornell, Stanford, Harvard, Yale, Virginia, Columbia, and other first-line schools. Analyzing this extraordinary accolade, Dean Coquillette said it was based upon an impressive effort by all ranks of faculty, with a particular emphasis in the areas of comparative law, taxation research, domestic relations law, international law, federal and constitutional law, and legal philosophy.[13] Leading treatises, articles, and casebooks were published by Hugh J. Ault and Paul R. McDaniel, on federal income and comparative tax law; by Charles H. Baron, on the use of applied social research in courts; by Arthur L. Berney, on legal problems of the poor; by Robert C. Berry, on sports and entertainment law; by George D. Brown, on federal courts; by Robert J. Cottrol, on legal history; by Peter Donovan, on trade regulation; by Sanford J. Fox, on modern juvenile justice; by Mary Ann Glendon (now at Harvard), on comparative family law; by Ruth-Arlene W. Howe, on child neglect law; by Sanford N. Katz, on family law; by Zygmunt J. B. Plater, on environmental protection law; and by Frank K. Upham, on Japanese comparative law. And this list is only a sample of recent faculty publications.

Symbolic of the faculty's success was the election in 1987 of Professor Cynthia C. Lichtenstein as president of the North American Division of the International Law Society, the appointment of Dean Daniel Coquillette as Reporter to the Judicial Conference of the United States, and the election in 1987 of the former dean, Professor Richard Huber, to the highest office in American legal education, president of the Association of American Law Schools. Finally, in 1988, John J. Curtin, Jr. ('57), long an adjunct teacher on the faculty, was elected to the ultimate professional honor, President-Elect of the American Bar Association. The faculty's research activity has been bolstered by generous funds established by the alumni: the Florence Fund, the Kane-McGrath Fund, the Lawless Fund, the Moynihan Fund, the Simon Fund, the Perini Fund, the Carney Fund, and the Fellows Fund. A major endowed fund, the Huber Endowed Visitorship (named for the former dean), enables outside scholars to visit the Boston College Law School, and the Simon Fund has provided an endowment for the Law School's championship advocacy teams.

The student body, as well as the faculty, is a matter of pride for the Law School. During a decade of extraordinary decline in law school applicants nationally, Boston College Law School enhanced its position and reputation as a first-rate institution of legal education. It is now among the twenty most selective American law schools, currently receiving more than 6000 applications for 250 spaces in the entering class. For the entering class of September 1989, the median grade point average was 3.46 and the median LSAT score was at the 93rd percentile. In 1987 the average age of the entering student was 24, with only 40 percent entering directly from college. Many first-year students have had 10 years of experience since graduating from college, and 10 percent of entering students have earned a graduate degree. A significant change in the composition of the student body in recent years has been the remarkable increase in the number of women, with the 1987 entering class being 50 percent women. The Law School also has a good record of attracting and graduating minority students. In 1987 William Mathis, then a second-year student, was elected president of the National Black Law Students Association.

In the past decade the Boston College Law School has confirmed its stature as a national school. Well over 200 undergraduate institutions are represented in its student body, from Hawaii to Florida. The 17 colleges sending the largest numbers of graduates to the Law School are located in the eastern part of the country, but they are also among the nation's most select institutions. The initiation in 1987 of a major loan forgiveness program through alumni gifts and the generosity of a former faculty member, William F. Willier, promises to increase the distinction and diversity of the student body. There are additional funds to aid minority students from the Stevens and Nelson Scholarship Funds, named for distinguished judges who are black alumni of the Law School. In 1987, Richard P. Campbell ('74) and his firm made a major gift of endowment to assist minority students in obtaining excellent legal placement.

The faculty has been active in the past decade in modifying the traditional curriculum by the introduction of teaching methodologies drawn from faculty and student experience with the off-campus, hands-on clinical education courses the school developed for some students in the 1960s and 1970s. The most innovative changes have been made in the past several years in the first-year curriculum to give students broad perspectives early in their legal studies in areas such as ethics and jurisprudence. A new course, "Introduction to Lawyering and Professional Responsibility," introduces the adversary system and tensions in the lawyer's role through a simulated lawsuit, from initial interview to litigation and settlement. Students are videotaped and critiqued by faculty members, 8 of whom teach sections of only 32 students (compared with the traditional first-year

In 1984 Maya Angelou's performance in Roberts Center drew one of the largest audiences in the long history of the Humanities Series.

class of over 100 students). Ethical issues are intertwined with the simulation, giving students realistic exposure to common professional responsibility and ethical problems.

In its sixty-first year of service in 1990, the Law School holds an honored position in American legal education in terms of its faculty, student body, and curriculum.

The Evening College

As was mentioned earlier, studies at the Evening College are not for dilettantes. Substantially the same as those of the undergraduate day colleges, they demand students of talent. Because evening courses are superimposed upon full-time employment, successful students have an unusual level of commitment and drive. A document submitted by the Evening College in 1985 to the "Goals of the Nineties" planning project revealed that recent students are older and more experienced academically than was true of similar students several decades ago. Over 53 percent of beginning students in the Evening College are over 24 years of age. Ninety-six percent have had some post-secondary education or academic experience prior to admission, and—perhaps most surprisingly—nearly 30 percent have already earned a bachelor's degree. The students tend to be mature adults and young professionals, serious about the academic enterprise and demanding of themselves and of the college.

On the occasion of the fiftieth anniversary of the Evening College in 1979, a survey of alumni was conducted. Asked about their motivation in attending the Evening College, the largest number of respondents gave personal satisfaction in earning a bachelor's degree as the primary motivation. The second most frequent reason was the desire to understand and improve one's skills and to establish personal interests. And the third reason was the need for a bachelor's degree for career advancement. That the Evening College is attracting academically ambitious individuals is confirmed by the survey, which revealed that of those receiving a degree from the college, almost 70 percent pursued some graduate education and 42 percent earned a graduate degree. Furthermore, the experience at the Evening College seems to stimulate a desire for further education: 51 percent of those alumni who, on entering, stated that they had no intention of going beyond the bachelor's degree did, in fact, engage in graduate study, and of these an impressive 54 percent earned a master's degree.

In addition to the leadership of Father James Woods, dean since 1967, a continuing strength of the Evening College is its faculty, drawn mainly from the full-time undergraduate and graduate faculty of Boston College and supplemented by highly qualified and long-term teachers. The previously mentioned report, "Goals for the Nineties," made the point that of 225 courses presented in the 1984–1985 academic year, only three had instructors teaching in the college for the first time. It is fortunate for the

Evening College and its students that faculty get special satisfaction from teaching the dedicated people attending college classes "after hours."

Excellence in Publications

One measure of faculty achievement is quality of publication, especially in books. To acknowledge and encourage the publication of books by the faculties of the 28 American Jesuit universities and colleges, the Association of Jesuit Colleges and Universities (AJCU) began in 1980 to award annual prizes of $1000 for the books judged best of those submitted in the areas of humanities and physical science. In the first year of the awards, called Alpha Sigma Nu awards after the Jesuit honor society, both prizes were won by Boston College faculty members. The award in the humanities went to Samuel Miller of the History Department for *Portugal and Rome c. 1740–1830: An Aspect of the Catholic Enlightenment*. James Gips of SOM (computer science) received the science award for *Algorithmic Aesthetics*.

A few years later AJCU added a third book prize, for the social sciences, and in 1984 Gasson chair incumbent Father F. Paul Prucha, S.J., won that award for *The Great Father: The United States Government and the American Indian*. That same year, honorable mentions were given to John McAleer of the English Department for *Ralph Waldo Emerson: Days of Encounter* and to Thomas O'Connor of the History Department for his biography of the bishop who helped Father McElroy found Boston College, *Fitzpatrick's Boston, 1846–1866*. Also in 1984, AJCU gave a special

Donald Brown, director of AHANA student programs.

The Voices of Imani is a choir whose performances celebrate the beauty of religious and concert music, with a predominant focus on people of color.

citation to honor Father Paul FitzGerald, university archivist, for his book, *The Governance of Jesuit Colleges in the United States, 1920–1970*. It was when he had finished the manuscript for that impressive book that Father FitzGerald undertook co-authorship of the present history of Boston College, a project that benefited from his scholarship and judgment until his sudden death in April 1987.

The Black Community at Boston College

Chapter 30 gave an account of the earnest but troubled initial efforts at Boston College to increase the enrollment of black students and to make them an integral part of the Boston College experience. We may now record the maturation and progress of that program. In 1978 Donald Brown became the director of minority programs, with an office located in Gasson Hall; several years later the office was moved to 72 College Road. Because other houses on College Road are the headquarters of such important University offices as the dean of faculties, the vice president for student affairs, the senior vice president, and the Office of Communications, the College Road location gave visibility and prestige to minority programs. The name was changed to the acronym AHANA, standing for African-American, Hispanic, Asian, and Native American. As the acronym indicates, black students were merged with other minorities as beneficiaries of the special concern and encouragement of AHANA student programs, yet the black students maintained an identity and have developed a black cultural and social agenda that livens each academic year. Black parent weekends have been held. Starting in 1981 special events have marked Martin Luther King Day. Lectures and musicals featuring nationally prominent personalities and artists have been used as fund-raisers for the Martin Luther King scholarship. In 1981 the scholarship award was $500; by the end of the decade, a scholarship of $5000 was awarded each year to a junior.

The black community at Boston College has actively participated in the annual "Blacks in Boston" conferences that have been held in recent years, as well as in the rich offering of Black History Month, and UGBC has cosponsored cultural lectures with AHANA. Among prominent black Americans who have been featured in these campus events are Alex Haley, Angela Davis, Julian Bond, Coretta Scott King, Jesse Jackson, Mary Berry, and Martin Luther King III. In 1984 the Humanities Series presented "An Evening with Maya Angelou" at Roberts Center. It drew one of the largest audiences in the history of the series, comparable to the crowds that packed the basketball court and stands to hear T. S. Eliot and Robert Frost in the sixties. At commencement in 1989 the University awarded an honorary degree to one of America's outstanding black Catholic leaders, Sister Thea Bowman, a member of the Franciscan Sisters of Perpetual Adoration. The following October Sister Bowman stirred an audience in the Gasson assembly room as she responded in song and speech to Father Monan's naming AHANA house on College Road the Thea Bowman Center. Boston College's success in attracting, supporting, and retaining minority students (in recent years the graduation rate of minority students has equalled or surpassed that of nonminority students) has been recognized by several major grants to strengthen AHANA. In 1988 the L. G. Balfour Foundation gave the University a million dollars as an endowment for AHANA scholarships and activities. In 1990 the General Electric Foundation, expressing a desire to be a partner in the University's AHANA program of outreach and retention of minority students, gave a grant of $150,000 to Boston College.[14] Donald Brown, Amanda Houston (director of black studies), and Richard Jefferson and Barbara Marshall (past and present directors of affirmative action) must be credited with much of the progress of the black presence at Boston College, but the principal credit goes to the black students themselves. The 1985 edition of *The Black Student's Guide to Colleges* gave a positive assessment of Boston College as an academic environment for black students.[15]

Emphasis here has been principally upon the undergraduate schools, but the graduate schools have also been active in recruiting minorities and sponsoring minority programs. The Graduate School of Social Work has an exemplary record in this regard, and the Law School enjoys the reputation of being hospitable to minority students, with a 20 percent presence of minority representatives among the student body (compared with a national average of 8 percent). Following a recommendation of the recent

Sister Thea Bowman, for whom the AHANA house on College Road was named in October 1989. Sister Bowman died in March 1990. A moving memorial service was held for her in St. Joseph's Chapel on April 18.

report of the Graduate A&S Educational Policy Committee, in 1987 the University established four minority fellowships with full tuition remission and stipends up to $8000. Master's stipends may be renewed once and doctoral fellowships may be held for four years. Each succeeding year, four additional fellowships will be given until a total of 16 is reached in 1990. So, although blacks are still underrepresented among the student population and on the faculty, progress has been made.

A wise counselor, encourager, and role model for two decades, Judge David Nelson ('57 B.S., '60 J.D.) was a member of the Boston College Board of Directors when the Black Talent Program started. Later he served as a trustee and as vice chairman and chairman of the Board of Trustees until his retirement in 1987. Judge Nelson was a gentle but persuasive advocate for the black programs. In an interview in 1987, on the occasion of his stepping down as chairman of the trustees, he remembered that as an undergraduate he was the sole black in the school.[16] He is impatient that progress has been so slow, but he is a major reason for the progress that has been achieved and for the good health of current minority programs.

ENDNOTES

1. Pp. 108–109.
2. Letter of Dean Infante to School of Nursing Alumnae, December 23, 1986.
3. *Nursing Outlook* (September/October 1984), p. 238.
4. *Biweekly* (September 25, 1986).
5. *Biweekly* (December 4, 1986).

6. Letter of Jerry A. Viscione to Dean Neuhauser, March 12, 1987.
7. Letter to C. F. Donovan, April 28, 1987.
8. *Boston College Magazine* (Spring 1985), p. 17.
9. *MBA: The Magazine for Business Professionals* (January 1987).
10. For the school's fiftieth anniversary, Professor Raymond Keyes prepared a detailed account of the first four decades: 1938–1978.
11. *Boston College Bulletin* (1985–1986), p. 19.
12. The account of the Graduate School of Arts and Sciences planning process, 1983–1986, is based on a communication to the author from the dean's office on August 7, 1987, and on the *Biweekly* article on it on March 13, 1986. Dean Donald J. White was chairman of the planning committee. Other members of the committee were Ali Banuazizi, Associate Professor of Psychology; Paul Breines, Associate Professor of History; Stephen Brown, Professor of Theology; Robert (Duff) Collins, master's candidate in geology; Russell Eckel, doctoral candidate in sociology; Rev. Joseph R. Fahey, S.J., Academic Vice President and Dean of Faculties; Marjory Gordon, Professor of Nursing; Irving Hurwitz, Associate Professor of Education; William Keane, Associate Professor of Mathematics; T. Ross Kelly, Professor of Chemistry; George Ladd, Professor of Education; Spencer MacDonald, Director of Admissions and Financial Aid, GSAS (ex officio); John L. Mahoney, Professor of English; Rev. William B. Neenan, S.J., Dean of the College of Arts and Sciences; James M. O'Neill, Assistant Dean, GSAS (ex officio); Alec F. Peck, Associate Dean for Graduate Studies, School of Education; Kenneth Wegner, Associate Professor of Education; and Lisa J. Day, recording secretary.
13. Communication to the author, January 26, 1988.
14. *Biweekly* (February 1, 1990), p. 5.
15. *Biweekly* (March 28, 1985), p. 2.
16. *Biweekly* (November 5, 1987), p. 3.

CHAPTER 39

Pointing to the Twenty-First Century

As we come to the final chapter of this history of Boston College, there is a troubling awareness—perhaps on the reader's part, certainly on the historian's part—that a somewhat shadowy and incomplete image of Boston College as a community of scholars and learners has been presented. Buildings and budgets, committees, planning groups, administrative appointments and activities—topics that, without disrespect, may be called important incidentals of a university—have received far more space than the pioneering scholarship, prestigious publications, and innovative teaching that have become common in all schools and departments of the University. But a single writer in a single volume cannot do justice to the scholarly contributions of faculty members in 40 or more diverse disciplines. In this regard, it is significant that in his three-volume tercentenary history of Harvard, Samuel Eliot Morison covered the first two and a half centuries himself with broad strokes in the first two volumes. When he came to the last fifty years, a period that saw Harvard emerge as a true research center with doctoral programs in most disciplines, Morison turned to representatives of each school and department for an insider's exposition of the development of each faculty. That is to say, for the third volume Morison was editor, not author.

At Boston College, the Law School is fortunate in having a good brief history of its first 50 years. For the fiftieth anniversary of the Carroll School of Management, Raymond Keyes wrote an excellent account of the first four decades, and Mary Ellen Doona did the same for the School of Nursing for its fortieth anniversary in 1987. The other professional schools, and especially the individual departments of the College and Graduate School of Arts and Sciences, need detailed intimate accounts of their coming of age written by faculty members who witnessed and abetted the maturing. But those must await another publication.

Three Profiles in Excellence

To give the reader a glimpse—albeit tantalizingly brief—of the quality of the Boston College faculty at the end of the twentieth century, profiles of three faculty members are given here. These outstanding teachers are Pheme Perkins, professor of theology; T. Ross Kelly, professor of chemistry; and Father William Meissner, S.J., university professor of psychoanalysis. Many other professors have records of similar distinction; these three are presented as an indication of current faculty excellence and—perhaps more important—as examples of the ideals of excellence promoted by the University in the recruitment and advancement of faculty members. Equally impressive profiles of faculty members from each of the professional schools could be presented. But, because the quality of teaching and research at the doctoral level is the most challenging measure of a university, selections were made from arts and sciences disciplines.

Professor Pheme Perkins did her undergraduate work at St. John's College (Annapolis, Md.) and earned a doctorate at Harvard in New Testament and Christian Origins. She joined the Theology Department at Boston College in 1970. Among the dozen books she has published as a Boston College faculty member are *Reading the New Testament: An Introduction, The Gnostic Dialogue: The Early Church and the Crisis of Gnosticism,* and *Resurrection: The Early Christian Witness and Contemporary Reflection.* Her latest contribution is her introductions and commentaries for St. John's Gospel and the letters of St. John in the *New Jerome Biblical Commentary.* This monumental work, called a triumph of American Catholic biblical scholarship, was published in 1990. (One of its three editors was Father Joseph Fitzmyer, S.J., recently Gasson professor at the University.) Among a half dozen books Professor Perkins has in progress are *Peter in the New Testament and Early Christianity* and *Gnosticism and the New Testament.* There have also been some 80 articles on biblical subjects in journals or in books edited by others.

Professor Perkins has had the distinction of being the first woman elected president of the Catholic Biblical Association of America (1986–1987). She is current editor of the Society of Biblical Literature Dissertation Series, has served (1982–1985) as associate editor of *Harper's Biblical Dictionary,* is on the executive committee of the Society of Biblical Literature, and is

me Perkins   *Father William W. Meissner*   *T. Ross Kelly*

treasurer of the American Theological Society. In 1978–1979 Professor Perkins had a research fellowship from the National Endowment for the Humanities, and in 1989–1990 she served as Kaneb Visiting Professor in Catholic Studies at Cornell University.

Among courses Professor Perkins has taught at Boston College are Parables of Jesus, New Testament Ethics, Pauline Letters and Theology, and New Testament Christology.

Father William Meissner received his bachelor's degree from St. Louis University. Ordained to the priesthood in 1961 as a member of the New York Province of the Society of Jesus, he attended Harvard Medical School and received the M.D. degree in 1967. After training at the Boston Psychoanalytic Institute and a residency in psychiatry at the Massachusetts Mental Health Center, Father Meissner joined the faculty of Harvard Medical School, becoming clinical professor of psychiatry in 1981. In 1987 he joined the faculty of Boston College as university professor of psychoanalysis. From 1975 to 1977 Father Meissner was chairman of faculty at the Boston Psychoanalytic Institute.

Father Meissner has authored or co-authored 12 books, among them *The Paranoid Process, The Borderline Spectrum: Differential Diagnosis and Developmental Issues, Psychoanalysis and Religious Experience,* and *Treatment of Patients in the Borderline Spectrum.* An important monograph is *Internalization in Psychoanalysis.* Besides contributing chapters to 36 books, Father Meissner's frequent articles have appeared in such diverse periodicals as *Journal of Religion and Health, Journal of Existentialism, Theological Studies, Journal of the American Psychoanalytic Association, International Journal of Psychoanalytic Psychotherapy,* and *Psychoanalytic*

Inquiry. He is currently editor, associate editor, consulting editor, or editorial board member of a dozen journals in the field of psychoanalysis.

Among honors conferred on Father Meissner are the Felix and Helene Deutsch Prize from the Boston Psychoanalytic Institute in 1969 and the Osker Pfister Award by the American Psychiatric Association in 1989.

Among courses Father Meissner has given are Psychoanalysis and Method, for the Philosophy Department; Psychoanalysis and Ethics, for the Theology Department; and Treatment of Borderline Personality, for the Graduate School of Social Work. Each year he arranges and presents a series of psychoanalytic lectures by leading members of the profession.

Professor T. Ross Kelly, a graduate of Holy Cross College, earned his doctorate in chemistry at the University of California, Berkeley. After a year at Brandeis University on a National Institutes of Health postdoctoral fellowship in 1968–1969, he joined the Boston College Chemistry Department.

Professor Kelly's research focuses on the application of organic synthesis to the preparation of molecules for biomedical research, including drugs for the treatment of cancer and other diseases. In recent years he has done pioneering research into the design and synthesis of artificial enzymes.

Of Professor Kelly's numerous research publications, three that have brought him wide recognition are T. R. Kelly, J. Vaya, and L. Ananthasubramanian, "A Short Regiospecific Synthesis of ($\pm$)-Daunomycinone," *Journal of the American Chemical Society, 102,* 5983 (1980); T. R. Kelly, N. Ohashi, R. J. Armstrong-Chong, and S. H. Bell, "Synthesis of ($\pm$)-Fredericamycin A," *Journal of the American Chemical Society, 108,* 7100 (1986); and T. R. Kelly, C. Zhao, and G. K. Bridger, "A Bisubstrate Reaction Template," *Journal of the American Chemical Society, 111,* 3744 (1989). Kelly's research has been supported by 18 competitive grants, mostly from the National Institutes of Health, totalling nearly $3 million. He received an NIH Research Career Development Award in 1975 and sits on several study sections for the evaluation and ranking of proposals in NIH grants.

Besides graduate courses in his areas of specialization, Professor Kelly is described as spectacular in his general chemistry course for freshmen. Extending his scientific influence into the community, he volunteers on Sunday afternoons at the Boston Museum of Science. In September 1989 Professor Kelly was named to the Margaret A. and Thomas A. Vanderslice Chair in Chemistry, founded by the chairman of the Board of Trustees, Thomas Vanderslice ('53), a graduate of the Chemistry Department.

An Encouraging Survey

In the spring of 1989 a study was circulated that reflected considerable credit upon the faculty of Boston College, present and past.[1] The study, which involved doctoral-granting private institutions, focused on the baccalaureate origins of doctorate recipients from 1920 to 1986. The report ranked 76 universities according to the number of baccalaureate graduates of these institutions earning doctorates (at their alma mater or elsewhere) in 20 disciplines. The data were presented in two lists, giving the number of doctorates earned in each discipline from 1920 to 1986 and also from 1976 to 1986. The purpose of the second list was undoubtedly to identify institutions that only recently have begun to encourage or stimulate undergraduates to pursue doctoral degrees. A surprising result for Boston College was how well the institution fared in the total 1920–1986 period, where it ranked 29th in all disciplines. The University ranked 24th in the shorter 1976–1986 period. When one considers that these lists include the Ivy League institutions plus Chicago, Stanford, Duke, MIT, Carnegie-Mellon, Caltech, and similar universities, ranking in the top third overall is creditable, indeed. Boston College's special strengths may be seen in the table below listing discipline areas.

	1920–1986	1976–1986
Total Non-Sciences	21	17
Mathematics	24	19
Economics	17	12
History	22	20
English Literature	17	16
Health Sciences	10	7
Education	16	7
Professional Fields	27	17

Louise M. Lonabocker, university registrar.

The study did not give definitions of categories such as health sciences, professional fields, and education, which leaves some doubt as to what the categories include, but in any case to be ranked 16th behind Columbia University in English, 12th behind Harvard in Economics, and 7th behind the University of Pennsylvania in Health Sciences is reason for institutional satisfaction. Undergraduates are motivated to doctoral-level study by the example of stirring, enthusiastic scholar-teachers. Boston College's impressive record of alumni with doctorate degrees is a tribute to the faculty of the University over the past half century.

A Night to Remember

A stellar night in Boston College history was the St. Patrick's Day dinner in 1986 in Washington, D.C., honoring Speaker Thomas P. "Tip" O'Neill as he approached retirement. Generous alumnus that he is, the Speaker turned a celebration of his years of honorable public service into a fundraiser for his alma mater. Friends and colleagues from all over the country and from overseas, 2300-strong, gathered at the Washington Hilton to salute the guest of honor and, incidentally, to raise $2 million for O'Neill scholarships to Boston College for poor and working-class youth of the Boston area. Among the speakers at the dinner were former president Gerald Ford, O'Neill's golfing partner and generous friend of Boston College, Bob Hope, and President Ronald Reagan, whose witty one-liners matched Hope's.

A Presidential Appointment

Reference to President Reagan calls to mind the important appointment of a Boston College faculty member in 1985. Professor Thomas H. O'Connor of the History Department was one of 23 distinguished Americans named by President Reagan to serve on the Commission on the Bicentennial of the United States Constitution, under the chairmanship of Warren Burger, then chief justice of the United States Supreme Court. The commission's aim was educational as well as celebratory, and it involved Professor O'Connor in significant presentations and meetings nationally. In 1988 Professor O'Connor accompanied Warren Burger to England and Ireland, where they lectured on the U.S. Constitution to legal scholars and jurists at Oxford and University College, Dublin.

Continuity and Change in the Administration

As long as the president of Boston College was also rector of the Jesuit Community, he served for a term of six years or less, according to church law for religious superiors. Exceptions were made for two president-rectors, Father Fulton in the nineteenth century and Father Michael Walsh in the twentieth, each of whom had terms of 10 years. Since Father Monan was the first president who, when appointed, did not have the burden and

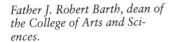

Father J. Robert Barth, dean of the College of Arts and Sciences.

limitation of the office of rector, fortunately the University has enjoyed his continuing leadership well into a second decade. Stability at the presidential level has not only allowed the development and execution of long-term programs but also assured a steady ship when key administrative changes took place.

In late 1986 the academic vice president and dean of faculties, Father Joseph Fahey, announced that he would resign from that position at the end of June 1987. (When he accepted the vice presidency, he had committed himself to a five-year term. Father Fahey, an alumnus of Boston College High School as well as of Boston College, assumed the presidency of B.C. High.) Although a national search was conducted to determine Father Fahey's successor, the vice presidential mantle fell upon a Jesuit ensconced in Gasson Hall, Father William B. Neenan, dean of the College of Arts and Sciences since 1980. In commenting on the opportunity facing him, Father Neenan observed, "We are a national university now. We weren't before, and this rapid advance has brought its share of problems and challenges." He added, "The collective internal perception of the University seems to lag behind the reality; we haven't internalized our quality status."[2]

Father Neenan's appointment left a vacancy in the deanship of the College of Arts and Sciences. Associate Dean Marie McHugh stepped into the breach as acting dean for the 1987–1988 academic year, while a formal search for a permanent dean was initiated by a committee headed by Graduate School dean Donald White. The search led to the University of Missouri, to Father J. Robert Barth, who had been Gasson Professor in the English Department in 1985–1986. Father Barth, who earned his doctorate at Harvard, is a distinguished literary critic who had been at the University of Missouri since 1974. The Jesuit-sponsored Gasson Chair thus has yielded rewards beyond the presence of outstanding Jesuit visiting scholars, for two Gasson professors—Fathers Neenan and Barth—have become key academic administrators.

After 10 years as vice president for university relations, James McIntyre assumed the newly created position of senior vice president. The new role allows him to concentrate on special aspects of major giving. Succeeding McIntyre as vice president of university relations was Paul H. LeComte, who had most recently been senior vice president for development and alumni relations at Brandeis University. LeComte joined the University as it began the most ambitious fund drive in its history.

An era ended when Father Edward Hanrahan, long-time dean of students, resigned in 1986 to join the Development Office. Robert A. Sherwood succeeded Father Hanrahan in a restructured and retitled office, as dean for student development. Sherwood came to Boston College from MIT, where he had been associate dean of student affairs and dean of residence and campus activities.

In September 1987 Robert K. O'Neill was appointed director of the recently named Burns Library of Rare Books and Special Collections. O'Neill had been director of the Indiana Historical Society's library in Indianapolis. A highlight of his first year at Burns Library was the publication by the Yale University Press of a biography of Francis Thompson by a scholar from Bath, England, Brigid Boardman, whose work was based principally on the Burns' Thompson collection. The appearance of Boardman's book, *Between Heaven and Charing Cross,* under the sponsorship of a distinguished university press, is the most notable fruit to date of the enlightened collecting begun 50 years ago by a former University librarian, Father Terence Connolly.

Two other important administrative appointments were made in the fall of 1987. As the University grew more complex in financial structure and needed services, the trustees concluded that the office of financial vice president and treasurer covered too many departments, so a new vice presidency was created: vice president for administration, to oversee the major services that support the academic mission of the University, including physical plant, campus security, bookstores, and dining services. A seasoned and respected administrator, John T. Driscoll, Boston College class of 1949, was named to the new post. Driscoll had long served as chairman of the Massachusetts Turnpike Authority, and earlier he had been treasurer and receiver-general of the Commonwealth of Massachusetts and a state representative. An active alumnus, Driscoll was president of the Alumni Association in 1980–1981.

Another Bostonian experienced in public service joined the administration when Jean Sullivan McKeigue became director of the Office of Community Affairs. An alumna of Newton College of the Sacred Heart, with

John T. Driscoll ('49), named vice president for administration in 1987.

master's degrees from Columbia University and MIT's Sloan School of Management, McKeigue had earlier in the decade served for four years on the Boston School Committee, including terms as vice president in 1981 and president in 1982.

In 1988 Robert S. Lay, who had prior experience at Boston College as director of enrollment management, returned as director of the offices of financial aid, university registrar, and enrollment management research. Also in 1988 Douglas Whiting ('78), who had been on the staff of the Office of Communications, was named director of that office. There was also a change in command at St. Mary's Hall: Father Joseph Duffy's term

Father Joseph P. Duffy, after a six-year term as rector of the Jesuit Community at Boston College, was named university secretary in 1988.

as rector ended and he was replaced by Father William A. Barry, a clinical psychologist and prolific author in the field of spirituality and pastoral counseling. Father Duffy was named by the trustees to the office of Secretary of the University, vacant since the untimely death of Father Leo McGovern in 1986. Still in the spiritual realm, the University chaplain, Father John Dineen, announced that at the completion of his tenth year in that office he would resign. In the fall of 1989 he joined the Office of Development. He was succeeded in the University chaplaincy by Father Richard T. Cleary, who had served as Provincial of New England Jesuits and was a member of the Boston College trustees. A final administrative change in the fall of 1989 was the elevation of Leo V. Sullivan, long-time director of the Office of Human Resources, to a vice presidency in that office.

Library Awards and Advances

In January 1988 *Interiors,* a respected journal in architectural circles, named the Bapst Library renovation the winner of its ninth annual Interiors Award. The competition was nation-wide and included the acclaimed renovation of New York's Carnegie Hall. *Interiors* praised the conversion of "old classrooms into exquisitely detailed new library space that echoes the original grandness" of the building.

A few months later Albert M. Folkard donated to Boston College his personal library of 1800 carefully chosen books, mostly in the field of English letters. The gift was made to honor the Jesuits of Boston College, past and present. Folkard, a veteran of the English Department, had a long tenure as director of the A&S honors program. At the 1980 Commencement, in recognition of his valued service for 35 years, the University most aptly named Albert Folkard Doctor of Humane Letters, *honoris causa.*

The libraries' humanities holdings and influence were further enhanced in 1989 by a $700,000 challenge grant from the National Endowment for the Humanities. The grant challenged the University to generate four dollars for each NEH dollar—$2,800,000 over four years. By 1990 the University had raised more than half of its goal. The purpose of the endowment is to strengthen collections and programs in the humanities. University librarian Mary Cronin said that besides broadening the libraries' scope of coverage in collecting, the endowment will support a scholar-in-residence who will use the Irish materials of Burns library. In 1990 Burns library was the recipient of a significant collection of rare books by and about William Butler Yeats. Named for its donors, the gift will be known as the Brian and Jane Leeming Collection of Irish Literature.

Professor of the Year

The humanities received further stimulus in the fall of 1989 when the Council for the Advancement and Support of Education named John L.

The name of John L. Mahoney ('50) of the English Department has appeared often in these pages. In 1989 he was named Massachusetts Professor of the Year.

Mahoney of the English Department Massachusetts Professor of the Year. This was a fitting tribute to one who gave enlightened leadership to the department in several stints as chairman and whose teaching for close to 40 years was accurately described by a *Biweekly* writer as passionate and erudite. Complementing Mahoney's spirited teaching have been his books on Coleridge and Keats, Hazlitt, the English Romantics, and the Enlightenment. His generous service to the University, decade after decade, on major University committees and boards is recorded in these pages.

Father Kolvenbach Helps Celebrate an Anniversary

The year 1988 marked the University's 125th anniversary, and a year-long series of celebrations were held under the leadership of Senior Vice President James McIntyre. The climax of the year was the visit to the campus on October 5 and 7 of the Superior General of the Society of Jesus, Peter-Hans Kolvenbach, S.J. He brought messages of congratulations and inspiration first to a large gathering of alumni of Boston College and Boston College High School in Conte Forum and to a more intimate and informal group of students and faculty in Gasson Hall. A month later the anniversary was brought to a solemn conclusion with the first liturgy held in Conte Forum.

The homilist was the New England Jesuit Provincial, Robert E. Manning, S.J. He told the large gathering that the University had prospered so exuberantly that it had grown beyond the capacity of any group of Jesuits to staff and maintain it, and that the Jesuits must now depend on the collaboration of lay colleagues to carry on the mission of the once small institution. Some 60 alumni and faculty priests joined Father Monan in the concelebration. Presiding at the Mass was the Most Rev. Roberto O. Gonzalez, O.F.M., auxiliary bishop of Boston.

Significant Presidential Missions

Father Monan was one of 18 Americans invited to a conference on education in Rome on April 18–25, 1989. Preliminary to issuing a document on Catholic colleges and universities around the world, Pope John Paul II had a draft document developed by Vatican aides. This was circulated world-wide for commentary and suggested revision. After a revised draft was circulated, the congress at the Vatican was held, attended by 175 representatives. At the Faculty Day meeting on May 2, Father Monan spoke of the open and democratic spirit of the Vatican sessions and expressed confidence that a forthcoming document will address the interests and concerns expressed by the delegates.

The world at large, but especially the network of Jesuit campuses around the globe, was stunned and saddened by the assassination of six Jesuit priests and scholars at the Jesuit university in San Salvador on November 16, 1989. Three days later, St. Ignatius Church was thronged with mourners at a somber, stirring Mass. In attendance were students, alumni, and

Father Francis J. Murphy of the History Department is one of several priests of the Boston archdiocese who are valued faculty members.

neighbors, with 40 concelebrating priests and two bishops assisting. Joining Father Monan at the altar were the Provincial, Father Robert Manning, and the rector of Boston College Jesuits, Father William Barry. Father David Gill of the Classics Department, an acquaintance of several of the martyred Jesuits, was homilist.

American Jesuit universities kept the assassination in the public eye and significantly influenced the investigation into it. In February 1990 Father Monan was one of six representatives of American Jesuit higher education who spent four days in El Salvador to express solidarity with the Jesuits at the Central American university and to heighten pressure on the investigation process. The visit included meetings with President Alfredo Cristiani, the president of the Salvadoran Supreme Court, the chief of staff of the militia of El Salvador, and the United States Ambassador, as well as the archbishop of San Salvador and the Jesuit Provincial. Upon his return Father Monan was of the opinion that the mission advanced both of its goals—namely, sympathy and support for the Jesuits, and a spotlight on the judicial process. One of Father Monan's companions on the El Salvador mission, Father Paul S. Tipton, president of the Association of Jesuit Colleges and Universities, reported on the Jesuits' visit in his Laetare Sunday address to the alumni.

Plans for the Future

Planning has become a major preoccupation of the University's administration, and an account is given here of recent and current planning which, it is hoped, will provide vision, direction, and resources as the University enters a new century. Boston College's initial self-study of 1954, though modest by later standards, struck the participants as a massive and once-in-a-lifetime undertaking. In the next decade the A&S self-study of 1963—though somewhat more extensive—seemed perhaps by its association with the University's centenary to be a unique and not repeatable project. In those simpler times the faculty and administration did not foresee that in the 1970s and 1980s self-study and University-wide and school planning would be ongoing—an uninterrupted feature of the University's life.

In the mid-1980s, so much diversified planning and self-assessment was going on that when the time came for another 10-year accreditation review by the New England Association of Schools and Colleges, the University asked that a review of four planning programs be substituted for the usual examination of academic programs. The association agreed, and the visiting team spent most of its time scrutinizing the following: (1) an ambitious forward look that Father Monan set in motion in 1984 to establish goals for the nineties; (2) the study of the Graduate School of Arts and Sciences; (3) a document on computing and communications strategic planning; and (4) a lower campus facilities plan. All of these studies had been completed by early 1986 and were incorporated into a volume for the New England Association, which, after review, renewed accreditation.

Father William A. Barry became rector of the Boston College Jesuit Community in 1988.

"Goals for the Nineties" was a landmark document. It stated aspirations for Boston College in the year 2000, outlined a distinctive academic excellence to be aimed at, reaffirmed and redefined the Catholic and Jesuit identity of the institution, and proposed an enriching intellectual and moral environment for the University. Position papers were developed and given in summary in the final report on six topics: academic excellence, core curriculum, Catholic and Jesuit identity, enrollment challenges, academic goals and residential life, and financing the future. Critical to the significance of the report were goals statements by the several schools and colleges of the University, with ideals translated into proposals concerning space, facilities, and personnel. For the first time in the University's planning history, the individual college goals statements were followed by a practical section called "resource implications," which listed and priced stated needs such as a new chemistry building, an additional wing for Campion Hall, a doctoral program and more offices for the School of Nursing, a building for Fine Arts, renovation of McElroy Commons, and a new doctorate in the School of Management. An important result that should bolster the morale of future planning bodies was the immediate response of the trustees and administration to major recommendations. The financial implications of "Goals for the Nineties" have been translated into a daring capital fund campaign to underwrite many of the targets of the planning document.[3]

The lower campus facilities plan summarized elements to be replaced or renovated and elements under design or construction. They are listed here, with action taken by 1990 in parenthesis to indicate the massive activity that has occurred since 1986:

Elements to be replaced or renovated:

McHugh Forum—demolition (completed).

Modular Apartments—demolition to be coordinated with construction of lower campus housing.

Alumni Hall and Philomatheia Hall—demolition (completed).

66 Commonwealth Avenue (former Baptist Home)—renovation (completed).

Flynn Recreation Complex—to be demolished by 2000.

Roberts Center—reprogramming/renovation (later decision to demolish to make room for chemistry building).

Elements under design or construction:

Stadium Parking Facility Phase II (completed).

Sports Center (completed).

Commonwealth Avenue Housing, Buildings A and B (completed).

In 1989 Leo V. Sullivan (M.Ed. '80) was promoted from director to vice president of Human Resources.

The new student residences on Commonwealth Avenue deserve more than the above terse reference. They are by all measures the most stylish of any dormitories, externally and inside, and their architecture blends well with the Gothic buildings above them. What began life with the plain name "Building B" became William J. and Mary Jane Vouté Hall, in honor of University trustee William J. Vouté, in November 1989. The approach to Linden Lane was further beautified by the construction in the summer of 1989 of an elaborate gateway entrance that echoes the Gothic style of the surrounding buildings. Another piece of construction not planned in 1986 was the adaptation of the gymnasium/auditorium of Campion Hall for the Campus School, which had formerly been located in Roberts Center. When it was decided to raze Roberts to make space for a chemistry building, the gymnasium wing of Campion Hall was completely remodeled and a second story added, with many small classrooms and other facilities for the handicapped children who attend the Campus School.

In "Goals for the Nineties" the Fine Arts Department suggested a new building on the central campus. While this project remains only a hope at present, in 1988 an excellent art gallery was created in Devlin Hall in space occupied by the science library before O'Neill Library opened. Since the

Father Richard T. Cleary became university chaplain in 1989.

Chemistry Department will be moving from Devlin to the building under construction on Beacon Street, the moving of the Fine Arts Department to Devlin is one of the options being considered.

In June 1989 the Board of Trustees authorized the engagement of an architect to develop plans for a campus center for improved dining and bookstore facilities, offices for student activities, and improved accommodations for several other University services. In September 1989 the trustees also approved preliminary planning for a residence for graduate students. The spring of 1990 saw satisfactory progress on the chemistry building and the start of work on the extension of Campion Hall.

Computer Progress

If action has outrun planning in building, it has so outstripped planning in the computer area that a summary of the 1986 strategic plan for communications and computing is not the best way to represent the computing situation as this chapter is being written.[4] In February 1990 Rodney Feak, director of the computer center, sent the author an account of the development of computing at Boston College, taking 1981 as the baseline. Feak reported an astonishing upgrading of computer hardware, year by year. For each change of equipment, he gave two measures of power: the number of instructions per second the machines are capable of and the on-line

GROWTH OF COMPUTER FACILITIES, 1980–1990		
	1980	*1990*
Computer workstations in administrative offices	133	1080
Computer workstations in faculty offices	5	439
Computer workstations in laboratories	50	400
Computer workstations in the library	2	200
Micro computers purchased by students annually	0	1200

storage capacity of the computer. These quantitative measures chart a dizzying trajectory of growth from 1981, when the computers were capable of executing 1.2 million instructions per second and had an on-line storage capacity of about 8 billion characters, to 1990, when computing capacity reached 25 million instructions per second and there was on-line storage of 55 billion characters. Faculty and student research, as well as administrative operations, have benefited from this extraordinary growth in computing power.

The Council on Catholic and Jesuit Identity, and the Jesuit Institute

A direct outgrowth of "Goals for the Nineties" was the establishment by Father Monan of the Standing Council on the Catholic and Jesuit Identity

In the spring of 1989 the University Chorale had a memorable trip to Rome. After performing at the Vatican, members had a papal audience on March 1. With Pope John Paul II is C. Alexander Peloquin, director of the chorale. In the front row are officers of the chorale, from the left: Philip Rectra ('90), men's secretary; Christopher Downing ('89), president; Joseph Gesmundo ('89), vice president; Terry Bonello ('89), social director; Linda Wilenski ('90), women's secretary; Katherine Soriano ('89), publicity director; and Mariflor Maulit ('90), librarian. On April 20, 1990, the chorale celebrated 35 years of Peloquin's musical leadership with a concert at Boston Symphony Hall.

at Boston College in December 1987. In his initial letter to council members, Father Monan set three purposes for the group: to redevelop and express a philosophy of Catholic and Jesuit higher education; to communicate the key elements of the Jesuit educational tradition to the larger University community; and to offer recommendations on operational ways Boston College might strengthen its Catholic and Jesuit identity.[5]

The council was established as a permanent body, like the University Council on Teaching and the Council on Liberal Education, with members serving two-year terms. In his invitational letter Father Monan set down the challenge to the council: "In all cases, it will need breadth of vision to conceptualize and reinforce the Jesuit and Catholic character of the institution, not as a limit or barrier to our full responsibility as a University, but as a source of distinctive cultural enrichment both for the University and for the larger community we serve."[6]

Before the year 1987 was out, there were exhilarating developments not directly due to council action, but surely compatible with its hopes, that proved how strongly the University was committed to its religious roots. For several years, under the leadership of their rector, Father Joseph Duffy, and abetted especially by Fathers Joseph Appleyard and Joseph Flanagan, the Jesuits at Boston College had been inviting lay colleagues to weekends at their Cohasset house to discuss ways in which lay and Jesuit faculty and administrators could cooperate to maintain and promote the Jesuit ethos of the University. As a result of these meetings and through ongoing apostolic planning by the Jesuits concerning possible new structures for fulfilling their mission at the University, the Jesuit Community pledged $1.5 million for a Jesuit Institute whose purpose would be to promote research on the religious and Jesuit traditions of the institution, especially on their relatedness to the universe of scholarship and learning. Father Monan, who had been part of the planning process for the institute, warmly embraced the Jesuit Community's proposal and funding, and agreed to match the Community's gift. Thus the new body reached a formative stage of existence with a substantial endowment. Father Robert Daly, who had chaired

Father Robert J. Daly of the Theology Department, director of the Boston College Jesuit Institute. In the spring of 1990 he was named editor of the prestigious national Jesuit journal, Theological Studies.

the Theology Department for 15 years, was named director, and a 12-member administrative board was appointed to assist him in giving shape and life to the Institute.[7]

The Jesuit Institute was launched publicly with a two-day academic symposium and celebration in Conte Forum on April 21 and 22, 1989. The keynote address was given by noted historian and director of the Institute of Jesuit Sources, Father John W. Padberg. He called Boston College's new institute a forum of science and scholarship, sympathy and respect, where heritage and imagination will be together welcome and nurtured.[8] It already funds an annual research scholar and confers research grants. The 1990 Institute Research Scholar is a Jesuit from Loyola University in Chicago, Father Philip J. Chmielewski, who will write about a German Jesuit, Oswald von Nell-Breuning, one of the 20th century's seminal influences on Catholic social thought. Supported by a 1990 institute research grant, Randy Kafka, a research fellow in psychology at Harvard's Graduate School of Education, will analyze the psychological and faith development of students participating in the Boston College Pulse program.

Core Curriculum

The most elaborate planning effort under way as this account of Boston College's history nears its end has to do with the core curriculum, the designated liberal arts courses from which all students in all of the undergraudate schools must choose a fixed number. The regulation in effect since 1981 assigned to the core curriculum 14 of the 38 courses needed for graduation. In the spring of 1989 Academic Vice President William B. Neenan, S.J. appointed 20 faculty members, administrators, and students to a task force to examine the core curriculum, with special attention to its philosophy as well as to procedures for the inclusion of courses in the core and general oversight of the core curriculum. Since 99 percent of core courses are offered by A&S departments, previous review committees have been staffed mostly by A&S faculty. But the core curriculum involves students in the professional schools as well as A&S, and this involvement is reflected in the composition of the present task force, which includes two professional school deans along with the six faculty members and one student from professional schools.[9]

The task force followed a busy schedule in 1989. After study and discussion sessions in May, June, and September, it held five fall meetings with departmental and professional school representatives. A presentation on the core curriculum was made at the February 1990 meeting of the Board of Trustees. Six winter meetings were scheduled, starting with an evening session with Father Monan and including further meetings with departmental chairpersons, student affairs officers, black studies faculty, and interested faculty and students. The task force is to give a report to the faculty at the 1990 May Faculty Day.

The magnolias in bloom proclaim this a spring scene on the "dustbowl,"
more properly called the college green.

The "Campaign for Boston College"

To support the ambitious programs and projects that have emerged from
the several recent planning efforts, the University launched a fund-raising
drive equally ambitious: a goal of $125 million. Called the "Campaign for
Boston College," the first phase (1986–1988) sought major individual gifts
for progress toward the ultimate goal. The public aspect of the campaign
began in the fall of 1988. The trustees set a mighty target for themselves:
one-fifth of the campaign's goal, or $25 million. By 1990, $25.6 million
had been pledged by trustees, and the drive had reached the $94.5 million
mark.

Since Boston College has until recently had a history of low endowment,
the campaign aims to provide $73,000,000 for endowment funds. But the
University has made dramatic progress in endowment in the past decade.
The February 21, 1990, issue of *The Chronicle of Higher Education*

published a list of the value of 330 endowments of universities as of the previous June, compiled by the National Association of College and University Business Officers. Boston College placed 50th on this list of institutions with endowments of over $2 million. The University's endowment was given as $250,005,000. The endowment status will obviously be improved by the success of the Campaign for Boston College. Other goals of the fund drive are $17 million for new construction and renovation of facilities and $35 million for general support of academic activities.

Co-chairing the Campaign for Boston College are two trustees, James F. Cleary ('50), managing director of Paine Webber of Boston, and John M. Connors, Jr. ('63), president of New England's largest advertising agency, Hill, Holliday, Connors and Cosmopoulos. Joining the co-chairmen to form the campaign's national committee are four members of the Board of Trustees and an associate member who had served on the board for more than 20 years and as chairman from 1981 to 1984, William F. Connell ('59), chairman and chief executive officer of the Connell Limited Partnership. The other members of the committee are Thomas J. Flatley, president and chief executive officer of the Flatley Company; Samuel J. Gerson ('63), president and chief executive officer of Filene's Basement Stores, Inc.; John A. McNeice, Jr. ('54), chairman of the Colonial Group, Inc. in Boston; and E. Paul Robsham (M.Ed '83), president of Robsham Industries, Inc.

With this powerful group energizing the drive and with the growing national prestige of the University attracting interest and support, the prospects for success are promising. An article in the October 12, 1982, issue of *The New York Times* observed that the allegiance of the University's graduates to their alma mater "has earned Boston College a place with Dartmouth and Notre Dame as having the most fiercely loyal alumni of the nation's private schools."[10] That level of enthusiastic commitment to the future of Boston College on the part of its alumni and friends all but guarantees the success of the critical effort to broaden the University's financial base.

*   *   *

At the beginning of the last decade of the 20th century, the University is in a position of strength. Applications for admission to the undergraduate schools and to the graduate and professional schools continue at a volume that guarantees selective student bodies. Applications for faculty and major administrative positions are of a quality and number that underscore the University's reputation and attractiveness. The support systems of the University—in administrative operations, in student affairs and housing, in libraries and computer facilities, in student activities, and in the influence of music and art on the campus—are at an all-time high. Finances are sound and a major fund drive is moving toward a successful conclusion. Such is the state of the University as it approaches the twenty-first century.

This, then, is a good point in the recorded history of Boston College to set aside the pen and reflect in admiration on the vision, the courage, the faith, the sacrifices, the adversities overcome, and the determined progress that have led to the Boston College of 1990.

ENDNOTES

1. "Baccalaureate Origins of Doctorate Recipients, 1920 to 1986. A Ranking by Discipline of Doctoral-Granting, Private Universities," Offices of Planning and Institutional Research, Georgetown University and Franklin & Marshall College. April 1989.
2. *Biweekly* (April 9, 1987) pp. 1 and 4.
3. Members of the Goals for the Nineties Planning Council: J. Donald Monan, S.J., President (titular chairman); Robert R. Newton, Associate Dean of Faculties (chairman); Richard S. Bolan, Social Work (1984–1985 only); Mary C. Boys, S.N.J.M., Theology; Donald Brown, Director, AHANA; Patricia A. Casey, Development (1984–1985 only); Michael T. Callnan, Budget Director; Geraldine L. Conner, Social Work (1985–1986 only); Louis S. Corsini, Accounting; Robert S. Daly, S.J., Theology; John A. Dineen, S.J., University Chaplain; Laurel A. Eisenhauer, Nursing; Theresa M. Fitzpatrick, A&S ('86); John M. Flackett, Associate Dean, Law; Philip W. Jennings, A&S ('86); Jeong-long Lin, Chemistry; Marilyn J. Matelski, Speech; Thomas J. Owens, Philosophy; Joseph F. Quinn, Economics; John F. Savage, Education; and David J. Smith, Associate Director, Counseling Services.
4. The members of the 1986 Committee for Strategic Planning for Communications and Computing were the following: Frank B. Campanella, Executive Vice President (chair); Christopher F. Baum, Economics; Michael T. Callnan, Budget Director; Rhoda K. Channing, Assistant University Librarian; Rodney J. Feak, Director, Computer Center; Eileen M. Gaffney, Financial Analyst; Bernard W. Gleason, Director, Information Technology; William Griffith, Computer Science (CSOM); Louise M. Lonabocker, University registrar; Donald F. Mikes, Director, Audiovisual Services; John J. Neuhauser, Dean, Carroll School of Management; Robert R. Newton, Associate Dean of Faculties; C. Peter Olivieri, Computer Science (CSOM); Leo F. Power, Director, Space Data Analysis Laboratory; Christine Rinaldi, Senior Development Officer; and Donald S. Zitter, Computer Science (CSOM).
5. *Biweekly* (January 15, 1987), p. 1.
6. *Ibid.* A&S Dean William B. Neenan, S.J., was named chairman of the Standing Council on the Catholic and Jesuit Identity of Boston College. Other council members were: James L. Bowditch, Associate Dean, CSOM; Robert F. Capalbo, University Housing Director; Robert J. Daly, S.J., Theology; Joseph P. Duffy, S.J., Rector of the Jesuit Community; Scott T. Fitzgibbon, Law School; George J. Goldsmith, Physics; Marjory Gordon, SON; June Gary Hopps, Dean, GSSW; Louise Lonabocker, University Registrar; Michael C. McFarland, S.J., CSOM; Marie McHugh, A&S Associate Dean; James A. O'Donohoe, Theology; Harold A. Petersen, Economics; Virginia Reinburg, History; and Judith Wilt, English.
7. Members of the administrative board were: Anthony T. Annunziato, Biology; Joseph A. Appleyard, S.J., Honors Program Director; William A. Barry, S.J., Rector, Jesuit Community; James W. Bernauer, S.J., Philosophy; James L. Bowditch, Associate Dean, CSOM; Mary J. Brabeck, SOE; Lisa Cahill, Theology; Scott T. Fitzgibbon, Law; June Gary Hopps, Dean, GSSW; Mary Sue Infante, Dean, SON; John L. Mahoney, English; Robert J. McEwen, S.J., Economics; William W. Meissner, S.J., University Professor of Psychoanalysis; William B.

Neenan, S.J., Academic Vice President and Dean of Faculties; and Paul G. Schervish, Sociology.

8. *Biweekly* (April 27, 1989), p. 1.

9. The members of the Core Curriculum Task Force were: William B. Neenan, S.J., Academic Vice President (Chairman); Joseph A. Appleyard, S.J., A&S Honors Program; George Aragon, CSOM; Robert J. Barth, S.J., Dean, A&S; Lisa Cahill, Theology; Jeffrey R. Cohen, CSOM; Rose Mary Harvey, SON; Katharine Hastings, Assistant to the Academic Vice President; June Gary Hopps, Dean, GSSW; John L. Mahoney, English; Martha McAtee, CSOM ('91); John J. Neuhauser, Dean, CSOM; Robert R. Newton, Associate Dean of Faculties; Rita J. Olivieri, SON; Edward J. Power, SOE; Joseph F. Quinn, Economics; Clarence Redd, A&S ('91); Frances Restuccia, English; David C. Roy, Geology; Paul G. Spagnoli, History; and John F. Travers, Jr., SOE.

10. Cited in *Biweekly* (February 3, 1983), p. 6.

On June 23, 1990, in Frederick, Maryland, Father Monan, as president of Boston College, participated in the dedication of a memorial for Father John McElroy, commemorating his role as founder of Boston College and his 23 years as pastor of Frederick's St. John's Church.

Epilogue

The preceding chapters record the history of Boston College to 1990. What of the future? The last chapter is practically an administrative blueprint for the future, with its long-range planning projects and subsequent initiatives. While the University cannot determine its future precisely, it is clear where and how the trustees and administration intend to guide it.

As far as the authors are concerned, their business as historians is with the past. As persons, as Jesuits committed to Boston College, their action regarding the future is not prediction but hope—hope that may be expressed as a prayer. Presuming to speak for the two co-authors who are deceased, our simple prayer is this:

> Father Ignatius, we pray that this Jesuit university may, for centuries to come, be true to your apostolic vision and uncompromisingly committed to scholarly excellence. We ask this for Boston College through Him whose name you, bold Inigo, gave to your Company, *ad majorem Dei gloriam*. Amen.

THE EVOLUTION OF
FATHER GASSON'S DREAM
An Aerial Photographic Essay

St. Mary's Hall, completed in 1917. This picture was taken before construction of Bapst Library began in 1924.

The serene beauty of University Heights between 1928, when Bapst Library was completed, and 1947, when Fulton Hall was begun.

545

A closer view of the campus as it was for two decades after the completion of Bapst Library. Behind Devlin was the "freshman field." The photograph was taken before the elaborate fence was erected along Beacon Street in the mid-thirties.

"Annex A," an indispensable classroom and office building near the tennis courts. The College survived the sudden increase in enrollment after WW II by building Fulton Hall (1948) and also by using government surplus structures. The large structure across from Fulton was the "recreation building," site of theatricals, assemblies, basketball games, and ROTC.

The campus between 1951, when Lyons Hall was completed, and 1957, when the stadium opened.

The upper campus between 1958, when Gonzaga was completed, and 1960, when Fitzpatrick, Cheverus, Fenwick, and McElroy opened. Behind the original Tudor Road dormitories, the carriage house of O'Connell Hall was still standing.

The scene before Carney Hall was built in 1962, showing added buildings: St. Thomas More and Campion (1955), McHugh Forum and Roberts Center (1958), Cushing and McElroy (1960). The "temporary" classroom building still stood behind Fulton.

The campus after 1966, when Higgins Hall was completed, and before 1968, when McGuinn was built. "Annex A" has been removed to make way for McGuinn. The partially filled reservoir is seen beyond the playing fields.

Completed McGuinn (1968), as well as the latest of the upper campus dormitories: Roncalli, Welch, and Williams (1965). But the "mods" had not yet been introduced; they were built in 1970.

The central campus, including University properties across Beacon Street. At the left, opposite McElroy, is Hovey House, where some History Department faculty are located. Next along Hammond Street is Murray House, the commuter center. Beside Murray is the faculty center, Connolly House. Next is Haley House, an administration building. The University owns four other properties in this triangle.

The Newton campus. At the bottom is the gracious home of the Alumni Association, Alumni House, with student residences nearby. The top cluster of buildings includes Trinity Chapel, Stuart, the central building of the Law School, Barry Pavilion to the left, and Kenny-Cottle Library to the right. (Photograph by Alex S. Maclean.)

A 1987 photograph showing the development of the lower campus that took place in the 1970s and 1980s: the modular apartments (1970); Hillside dormitories (1973); Edmond's (1975); RecPlex extension (1976); Walsh (1980); Robsham Theater (1981); Vouté Hall and its companion residence and Conte Forum under construction (completed in 1988). Roberts Center still stood in 1987, but was razed to make way for the new Chemistry building. (Photograph by Alex S. Maclean.)

APPENDICES

Founder of Boston College

Rev. John McElroy, S.J.

Presidents of Boston College

1.	John Bapst, S.J.	1863 – 1869
2.	Robert W. Brady, S.J.	1869 – 1870
3.	Robert Fulton, S.J.	1870 – 1880
4.	Jeremiah O'Connor, S.J.	1880 – 1884
5.	Edward V. Boursaud, S.J.	1884 – 1887
6.	Thomas H. Stack, S.J.	1887
7.	Nicholas Russo, S.J.	1887 – 1888
8.	Robert Fulton, S.J.	1888 – 1891
9.	Edward I. Devitt, S.J.	1891 – 1894
10.	Timothy Brosnahan, S.J.	1894 – 1898
11.	W. G. Read Mullan, S.J.	1898 – 1903
12.	William F. Gannon, S.J.	1903 – 1907
13.	Thomas I. Gasson, S.J.	1907 – 1914
14.	Charles W. Lyons, S.J.	1914 – 1919
15.	William Devlin, S.J.	1919 – 1925
16.	James H. Dolan, S.J.	1925 – 1932
17.	Louis J. Gallagher, S.J.	1932 – 1937
18.	William J. McGarry, S.J.	1937 – 1939
19.	William J. Murphy, S.J.	1939 – 1945
20.	William L. Keleher, S.J.	1945 – 1951
21.	Joseph R. N. Maxwell, S.J.	1951 – 1958
22.	Michael P. Walsh, S.J.	1958 – 1968
23.	W. Seavey Joyce, S.J.	1968 – 1972
24.	J. Donald Monan, S.J.	1972 –

Trustees of Boston College
December 1972 through September 1990

Honorary Degrees Awarded
by Boston College 1952–1990

1952
Gregory Peter XV Cardinal Agagianian,
  LL.D.
  (January 14, 1952)
James B. Connolly, Litt.D.
James M. O'Neill, LL.D.
Most Rev. Thomas F. Markham,
  LL.D.*
Rt. Rev. Thomas J. Riley, LL.D.
James J. Ronan, LL.D.

1953
Dorothy L. Book, LL.D.
Most Rev. James L. Connolly, LL.D.
Clifford J. Laube, LL.D.
Francis J. O'Halloran, A.M.
Most Rev. Leonard J. Raymond, LL.D.*
Alex Ross, A.M.
John C. H. Wu, LL.D.

1954
Edward H. Chamberlin, LL.D.
John J. Hearne, LL.D.*
James W. Manary, Sc.D.
Thomas A. Printon, LL.D.
Ven. Bro. William Sheehan, C.F.X.,
  LL.D.
Most Rev. Christopher J. Weldon,
  LL.D.
Louis de Wohl, Litt.D.
William J. O'Keefe, LL.D.
  (November 21, 1954)

1955
Fred J. Driscoll, LL.D.
Christian A. Herter, LL.D.
Edward A. Hogan, Jr., LL.D.*
Rear Adm. Bartholomew W. Hogan,
  Sc.D.
John B. Hynes, LL.D.
His Beatitude Maximos IV, LL.D.
  (August 23, 1955)
Valerian Cardinal Gracias, LL.D.
Russell Kirk, Litt.D., Nov. 1, 1955
Edward A. Sullivan, LL.D., Nov. 1,
  1955

1956
Bartholomew A. Brickley, LL.D.
Peter J. W. Debye, Sc.D.
Most Rev. Frederick A. Donaghy, LL.D.
John F. Kennedy, LL.D.*
John W. King, LL.D.
Charles Munch, D.Mus.
Edward F. Williams, LL.D.

1957
Wallace E. Carroll, LL.D.
Arthur J. Kelly, LL.D.
Augustus C. Long, LL.D.*
Adrian O'Keeffe, LL.D.
Very Rev. Msgr. Patrick W. Skehan,
  LL.D.
Nils Y. Wessell, LL.D.

1958
Most Rev. Amleto G. Cicognani, LL.D.
  (April 21, 1958)
Carl J. Gilbert, LL.D.
Paul Horgan, Litt.D.
Barnaby C. Keeney, LL.D.*
Henry M. Leen, LL.D.
Jacques Maritain, LL.D.
Raissa Maritain, LL.D.
Harold Marston Morse, D.Sc.
Rev. John B. Sheerin, C.S.P., LL.D.
Francis Cardinal Spellman, LL.D.
  (December 8, 1958)

1959
His Excellency Sean T. O'Kelly, LL.D.
  (March 22, 1959)
Ernest Henderson, LL.D.
Rev. John LaFarge, S.J., LL.D.
Henry Cabot Lodge, LL.D.
George Meany, LL.D.
Carlos P. Romulo, LL.D.*
Helen C. White, Litt.D.

1960
Marian Anderson, D.Mus.
J. Peter Grace, LL.D.
Caryl P. Haskins, LL.D.

---

*Commencement Speakers

1960 (Continued)
Robert F. Kennedy, LL.D.
Charles Malik, LL.D.*
Most Rev. Russell J. McVinney, LL.D.
Samuel Eliot Morison, LL.D.
Rt. Rev. Matthew P. Stapleton, LL.D.
Rev. Henry M. Brock, S.J., D.Sc.
   (October 12, 1960)

1961
Allen W. Dulles, LL.D.
Anthony Julian, LL.D.
Robert D. Murphy, LL.D.*
Louis R. Perini, LL.D.
Abraham Ribicoff, LL.D.
Rt. Rev. Robert J. Sennott, LL.D.
Edward Teller, LL.D.

1962
Detlev W. Bronk, D.Sc.*
Ralph J. Bunche, LL.D.
Christopher J. Duncan, M.D., LL.D.
Sir Alec Guinness, D.F.A.
Rt. Rev. Francis J. Lally, Litt.D.
Ralph Lowell, LL.D.
Phyllis McGinley, Litt.D.
Perry G. Miller, Litt.D.

1963
Augustin Cardinal Bea, S.J., J.U.D.
   (March 26, 1963)
Rev. Edward B. Bunn, S.J., LL.D.
   (April 20, 1963)
Lady Barbara Ward Jackson, Litt.D.
   (April 20, 1963)
Nathan Marsh Pusey, L.H.D.
   (April 20, 1963)
Bruce Catton, Litt.D.
Anthony Joseph Celebrezze, LL.D.*
Arthur Joseph Goldberg, LL.D.
John Jay McCloy, LL.D.
James Barrett Reston, LL.D.
Rt. Rev. John Joseph Ryan, L.H.D.
Jose Luis Sert, Litt.D.
Joseph Leo Sweeney, LL.D.
Robert Clifton Weaver, LL.D.
James Edwin Webb, D.Sc.

1964
John Coleman Bennett, LL.D.
Henri Maurice Peyre, LL.D.

Most Rev. Ernest John Primeau, LL.D.
Sidney R. Rabb, L.H.D.
Paul Anthony Samuelson, LL.D.
Rev. Joseph L. Shea, S.J., LL.D.
Robert Sargent Shriver, Jr., LL.D.*
Mary Sullivan Stanton, LL.D.

1965
John P. Birmingham, LL.D.
Robert McAffee Brown, LL.D.
J. N. Douglas Bush, Litt.D.
Victor L. Butterfield, L.H.D.
John T. Connor, LL.D.
Edith Green, LL.D.
Rev. John Courtney Murray, S.J.,
   L.H.D.*
Rt. Rev. Lawrence J. Riley, LL.D.
Alan T. Waterman, D.Sc.

1966
Most Rev. John W. Comber, M.M.,
   L.H.D.
Edward F. Gilday, L.H.D.
Edward M. Kennedy, LL.D.
Francis Keppel, LL.D.*
Mother Eleanor M. O'Byrne, R.S.C.J.,
   LL.D.
Stephen P. Mugar, LL.D.
Abram L. Sachar, L.H.D.
Rene Wellek, Litt.D.
George Wells Beadle, D.Sc.
   (November 12, 1966)
William Bosworth Castle, M.D., L.H.D.
   (November 12, 1966)
Donald Frederick Hornig, LL.D.
   (November 12, 1966)
James Alfred Van Allen, D.Sc.
   (November 12, 1966)

1967
Sarah Caldwell, Litt.D.
Richard Palmer Chapman, LL.D.
Very Rev. John Francis Fitzgerald,
   C.S.P., L.H.D.
John Kenneth Galbraith, LL.D.
John William Gardner, LL.D.*
Everett Cherrington Hughes, LL.D.
John Anthony Volpe, LL.D.

1968
Kingman Brewster, Jr., LL.D.*
Rev. Henri de Lubac, S.J., L.H.D.

Erwin N. Griswold, LL.D.
Rita P. Kelleher, D.Sc.
Most Rev. John J. McEleney, S.J., LL.D.
Cornelius W. Owens, LL.D.
James J. Shea, Sr., LL.D.
Roger J. Traynor, LL.D.

1969
R. Buckminster Fuller, D.F.A.*
Katharine Graham, D.Journ.
Philip J. McNiff, L.H.D.
Talcott Parsons, D.S.S.
A. Philip Randolph, LL.D.
Henry Lee Shattuck, D.C.S.
Terence Cardinal Cooke, LL.D.

1970
James Edward Allen, Jr., D.Sc.Ed.
Rt. Rev. John Melville Burgess, LL.D.
Joan Ganz Cooney, D.Sc.Ed.
Sterling Dow, L.H.D.
Hartford Nelson Gunn, Jr., L.H.D.
Rev. Bernard Joseph Francis Lonergan,
    S.J., Hist.Phil.D.
Elliot Norton, L.H.D.
Perry Townsend Rathbone, D.F.A.
Earl Warren, D.Sc.L.*

1971
Walter Jackson Bate, H.D.
Andrew Felton Brimmer, S.S.D.
Rev. Msgr. George William Casey,
    Litt.D.
Mircea Eliade, R.D.
Eli Goldston, LL.D.
Elma Lewis, D.F.A.
Michael Joseph Mansfield, LL.D.*
William James McGill, S.S.D.
Most Rev. Humberto Sousa Medeiros,
    S.T.D.
Walter George Muelder, D.Sc.T.
Leverett Saltonstall, LL.D.

1972
Mary Ingraham Bunting, D.Sc.
Arthur Fiedler, D.Mus.
Northrop Frye, L.H.D.
John James Griffin, D.C.S.
Sir William Arthur Lewis, L.H.D.
Louis Martin Lyons, D.Journ.

Rev. John Anthony McCarthy, S.J.,
    Litt.D.
Hildegarde Elizabeth Peplau, D.N.S.
Adlai Ewing Stevenson, III, LL.D.*
Walter Edward Washington, LL.D.

1973
A. J. Antoon, L.H.D.
Harold Bloom, L.H.D.
Fred J. Borch, D.B.A.
Vernon E. Jordan, Jr., LL.D.
John George Kemeny, D.Sc.*
Rev. Daniel Linehan, S.J., D.Sc.
Thomas Philip O'Neill, Jr., LL.D.

1974
Soia Mentschikoff, LL.D.*
Thomas L. Phillips, D.B.A.
Carl Thomas Rowan, L.H.D.
Thomas Paul Salmon, LL.D.
Sir Ronald Syme, L.H.D.
Henry Bradford Washburn, Jr., L.H.D.

1975
Melnea A. Cass, L.H.D.
Silvio O. Conte, LL.D.
John Thomas Dunlop, LL.D.
Rev. Francis J. Gilday, S.J., L.H.D.
Edward Lewis Hirsh, L.H.D.
Paul Ricoeur, L.H.D.*
Vincent Charles Ziegler, D.B.A.

Bicentennial Convocation
September 28, 1975
Thomas Joseph Galligan, Jr., D.B.A.
Oscar Handlin, L.H.D.
William J. Harrington, M.D., D.Sc.
Edward Hirsh Levi, LL.D.
Rev. Michael Patrick Walsh, S.J.,
    L.H.D.
Mary Lou Williams, D.A.

1976
Abram Thurlow Collier, D.B.A.
John Hope Franklin, L.H.D.
Rev. Martin Patrick Harney, S.J., H.D.
Mildred Fay Jefferson, M.D., D.Sc.
Asa Smallidge Knowles, D.Sc.Ed.
Joseph Francis Maguire, LL.D.
Daniel Patrick Moynihan, LL.D.*

*Commencement Speakers

1977
Rev. Raymond Edward Brown, Litt.D.*
Gerhard D. Bleicken, LL.D.
Alice Bourneuf, D.Sc.
James F. McDonough, M.D., D.Sc.
Maria Tallchief Paschen, D.A.
Michael Joseph Walsh, Litt.D.

1978
Bruno Bettelheim, Litt.D.
Rev. Charles F. Donovan, S.J., L.H.D.
Charles D. Ferris, LL.D.*
Marvin E. Frankel, LL.D.
John William McDevitt, LL.D.
Leo Perlis, D.S.S.

1979
Dorothy Baker, D.S.S.
Edward Patrick Boland, LL.D.
George P. Donaldson, LL.D.
Richard Ellman, L.H.D.
Robben W. Fleming, L.H.D.
Walter F. Mondale, LL.D.*
David S. Nelson, LL.D.*

1980
Germaine Bree, Litt.D.*
Albert M. Folkard, L.H.D.
Edward J. King, D.Pub.Admn.
Joseph Cardinal Malula, LL.D.
Bernard J. O'Keefe, D.E.Sc.
Kevin H. White, LL.D.

1981
Thomas Cardinal Ó Fiaich, Litt.D.
  (October 1981)
Rev. Joseph Delphis Gauthier, S.J.,
  L.H.D.
Margaret M. Heckler, LL.D.
Rose Fitzgerald Kennedy, L.H.D.
Donald F. McHenry, LL.D.
Joseph Harry Silverstein, D.A.
Paul Donovan Sullivan, D.S.S.
Thomas P. O'Neill, Jr., The Ignatius
  Medal*

1982
Rev. Robert I. Burns, S.J., L.H.D.
George Bush, LL.D.*
Robert A. Charpie, D.Sc.
Josephine L. Taylor, D.Sc.Ed.

1983
Maya Angelou, L.H.D.
Virginia A. Henderson, D.N.S.
Joseph McKenney, D.Ed.
Vincent T. O'Keefe, S.J., L.H.D.
  (March 1983)
Bruce J. Ritter, O.F.M., D.S.S.*
An Wang, LL.D.

1984
Leon Higginbotham, LL.D.
Richard Hill, D.B.A.
Most Rev. Bernard F. Law, S.T.D.*
Robert Merrifield, D.Sc.
Muriel Sutherland Snowden, D.S.S.
Otto Phillip Snowden, D.S.S.

1985
Rev. Frederick Joseph Adelmann, S.J.,
  L.H.D.
Lena Frances Edwards, D.Sc.
Rev. J. Bryan Hehir, LL.D.
Agnes Mongan, D.F.A.
Anthony John Francis O'Reilly, D.B.A.
  (March 1985)
Andrew J. Young, LL.D.*
Edward Zigler, L.H.D.

1986
Corazon C. Aquino, The Ignatius
  Medal
  (September 1986)
Guido Calabresi, LL.D.
Jacques d'Amboise, D.F.A.
Annie Dillard, L.H.D.
Lionel B. Richie, Jr., D.Mus.
Francis C. Rooney, Jr., D.B.A.
Jamie Cardinal Sin, S.T.D.*

1987
Josephine A. Dolan, D.N.S.
Garret FitzGerald, LL.D.
Walter E. Massey, D.Sc.
John G. McElwee, LL.D.
Rev. Francis W. Sweeney, S.J., L.H.D.
Vernon A. Walters, LL.D.*

1988
His Grace, Samuel E. Carter, S.J.,
  S.T.D.*
Esmé Valerie Eliot, D.Litt.

---

*Commencement Speakers

Hans-Georg Gadamer, L.H.D.
Robert Francis O'Malley, D.Sc.
Richard Alan Smith, LL.D.
Paul A. Volcker, LL.D.

1989
Thea Bowman, F.S.P.A., R.D.
George E. Doty, The Ignatius Medal
  (April 6, 1989)
Jonathan Kozol, D.S.S.*
Thomas S. Murphy, LL.D.
Kenneth Gilmore Ryder, D.Sc.Ed.

Richard Francis Syron, LL.D.
  (March 18, 1989)
Jerzy Turowicz, L.H.D.

1990
Edward A. Brennan, D.B.A.
Thomas J. Brokaw, L.H.D.*
Raymond G. Chambers, The Ignatius
  Medal
  (April 5, 1990)
Franklyn G. Jenifer, LL.D.
César A. Jerez, S.J., L.H.D.
Eunice Kennedy Shriver, L.H.D.
Robert M. Solow, LL.D.

*Commencement Speakers

Buildings Related to Boston College Operations
Location and Primary Use, Fall 1989

Name	Location	Primary Use	Date Constructed or Acquired
Alumni House	885 Centre Street	Administrative	1974
Alumni Stadium	2601 Beacon Street	Sports	1957
Bapst Library	Middle Campus	Library	1928
Barat House	885 Centre Street	Jesuit Res. & Admin.	1974
Barry Fine Arts Pavilion	885 Centre Street	Academic & Administrative	1974
Bea House[1]	176 Commonwealth Ave.	Jesuit Residence	1965
Botolph House	18 Old Colony Road	Administrative	1967
Bourneuf House	84 College Road	Administrative	1985
Brock House	78 College Road	Administrative	1972
Campion Hall	Middle Campus	Academic & Administrative	1955
Canisius House[1]	67 Lee Road	Jesuit Residence	1966
Carney Hall	Middle Campus	Academic & Administrative	1962
Cheverus Hall	127 Hammond Street	Student Residence	1960
Claver Hall	40 Tudor Road	Student Residence	1955
Commonwealth Avenue Dormitories-Building A	80 Commonwealth Ave.	Student Residence	1988
Connolly Carriage House	300 Hammond Street	Storage	1975
Connolly Faculty Center	300 Hammond Street	Academic	1975
Silvio O. Conte Forum	2609 Beacon Street	Sports & Administrative	1988
Cottage and Garage	885 Centre Street	Residence	1974
Cushing Hall	Middle Campus	Academic & Administrative	1960
Cushing House	885 Centre Street	Student Residence	1974
Daly House[1]	262 Beacon Street	Jesuit Residence	1981
Devlin Hall	Middle Campus	Academic & Administrative	1924
Donaldson House	90 College Road	Administrative	1975
Duchesne East	885 Centre Street	Student Residence	1974
Duchesne West	885 Centre Street	Student Residence	1974
Edmond's Hall	200 St. Thomas More Dr.	Student Residence	1975
Faber House	102 College Road	Academic	1938
Fenwick Hall	46 Tudor Road	Student Residence	1960
Fitzpatrick Hall	137 Hammond Street	Student Residence	1960
William J. Flynn Student Recreation Complex	Lower Campus	Sports & Administration	1972
Fulton Hall	Middle Campus	Academic & Administrative	1948
Gasson Hall	Middle Campus	Academic & Administrative	1913
Gonzaga Hall	149 Hammond Street	Student Residence	1958
Greycliff Hall	2051 Commonwealth Ave.	Student Residence	1969
Gym (Newton)	885 Centre Street	Gymnasium	1974
Haley House	314 Hammond Street	Academic & Administrative	1969
Haley Carriage House	314 Hammond Street	Child Care Center	1969
Hancock House	223 Beacon Street	Academic	1907
Hardey House	885 Centre Street	Student Residence	1974
Higgins Hall	Middle Campus	Academic & Administrative	1966
Hopkins House	116 College Road	Administrative	1968
Hovey House	258 Hammond Street	Academic & Administrative	1971
Ignacio Hall	100 Commonwealth Ave.	Student Residence	1973
Kenny-Cottle Library	885 Centre Street	Library	1974

[1]Rented to Jesuit Community of Boston College.

Name	Location	Primary Use	Date Constructed or Acquired
Keyes North & South	885 Centre Street	Student Residence	1974
Kostka Hall	149 Hammond Street	Student Residence	1957
Lawrence House	122 College Road	Administrative	1968
Loyola Hall	42 Tudor Road	Student Residence	1955
Lyons Hall	Middle Campus	Academic & Administrative	1951
Mary House	885 Centre Street	Academic & Administrative	1974
McElroy Commons[2]	Middle Campus	Student Services & Admin.	1960
McGuinn Hall	Middle Campus	Academic & Administration	1968
Medeiros Townhouses	60 Tudor Road	Student Residence	1971
Mill Street Cottage	29 Mill Street	Residence	1974
Modular Apartments	Lower Campus	Student Residence	1970
Murray House	292 Hammond Street	Commuter Center	1967
Murray Carriage House	292 Hammond Street	Storage	1967
O'Connell House	185 Hammond Street	Student Union	1938
Thomas P. O'Neill, Jr. Library	Middle Campus	Central Research Library	1984
Parking Garage	2599 Beacon Street	General Parking Facility	1979
Rahner House	96 College Road	Administrative	1952
Robsham Theater Arts Center	Lower Campus	Student Services & Academic	1981
Roncalli Hall	182 Hammond Street	Student Residence	1965
Rubenstein Hall/Hillside D	90 Commonwealth Ave.	Student Residence	1973
Service Building	Middle Campus	Trade Shops & Admin.	1948
Shaw House	377 Beacon Street	Student Residence	1962
Commander Shea Field	Lower Campus	Baseball Diamond	1960
Southwell Hall	38 Commonwealth Ave.	Administrative	1937
St. Mary's Hall[3]	Middle Campus	Jesuit Residence	1917
St. Thomas More Hall	St. Thomas More Dr.	Administrative	1955
Stuart House and the James W. Smith Wing	885 Centre Street	Academic & Administrative	1974
Thea Bowman AHANA Center	72 College Road	Administrative	1970
Trinity Chapel (Newton)	885 Centre Street	Chapel	1974
Vouté Hall	110 Commonwealth Ave.	Student Residence	1988
Michael P. Walsh Hall	150 St. Thomas More Dr.	Student Res. & Dining Fac.	1980
Welch Hall	200 Hammond Street	Student Residence	1965
Weston Observatory	Weston, MA	Research & Administrative	1948
Williams Hall	143 Hammond Street	Student Residence	1965
Xavier Hall	44 Tudor Road	Student Residence	1955
—	36 College Road	Administrative	1974
—	66 Commonwealth Ave.	Student Residence	1989
—	31 Lawrence Avenue	Academic	1979
—	55 Lee Road	Residence	1978

[2]Student Services in McElroy Commons include bookstore, dining halls, mail room, and the U.S. Post Office.
[3]Owned by the Jesuit Community of Boston College.
Source: Boston College Fact Book, 1988–1989.

INDEX